WALES AND THE FRENCH REV

General Editors: Mary-Ann Constantine and Dafydd Johnston

Welsh Ballads of the French Revolution 1793–1815

FFION MAIR JONES

UNIVERSITY OF WALES PRESS
CARDIFF
2012

www.uwp.co.uk

British Library Cataloguing-in-Publication Data
A catalogue record for this book is available from the British Library.

ISBN 978-0-7083-2461-5
e-ISBN 978-0-7083-2462-2

Typeset in Wales by Eira Fenn Gaunt, Cardiff
Printed by CPI Antony Rowe, Chippenham, Wiltshire

I Heledd Haf

WALES AND THE FRENCH REVOLUTION

The French Revolution of 1789 was perhaps the defining event of the Romantic period in Europe. It unsettled not only the ordering of society but language and thought itself: its effects were profoundly cultural, and they were long-lasting. The last twenty years have radically altered our understanding of the impact of the Revolution and its aftermath on British culture. In literature, as critical attention has shifted from a handful of major poets to the non-canonical edges, we can now see how the works of women writers, self-educated authors, radical pamphleteers, prophets and loyalist propagandists both shaped and were shaped by the language and ideas of the period. Yet surprising gaps remain, and even recent studies of the 'British' reaction to the Revolution remain poorly informed about responses from the regions. In literary and historical discussions of the so-called 'four nations' of Britain, Wales has been virtually invisible; many researchers working in this period are unaware of the kinds of sources available for comparative study.

The Wales and the French Revolution Series is the product of a four-year project funded by the AHRC and the University of Wales at the Centre for Advanced Welsh and Celtic Studies. It makes available a wide range of Welsh material from the decades spanning the Revolution and the subsequent wars with France. Each volume, edited by an expert in the field, presents a collection of texts (including, where relevant, translations) from a particular genre with a critical essay situating the material in its historical and literary context. A great deal of material is published here for the first time, and all kinds of genres are explored. From ballads and pamphlets to personal letters and prize-winning poems, essays, journals, sermons, songs and satires, the range of texts covered by this series is a stimulating reflection of the political and cultural complexity of the time. We hope these volumes will encourage scholars and students of Welsh history and literature to rediscover this fascinating period, and will offer ample comparative scope for those working further afield.

Mary-Ann Constantine and Dafydd Johnston
General Editors

Contents

1793

Figures

Preface

Welsh Ballads of the French Revolution 1793–1815 forms part of the research into Welsh responses to the Revolution in France and the subsequent wars, carried out by a dedicated team housed at the University of Wales Centre for Advanced Welsh and Celtic Studies (CAWCS) in Aberystwyth. The project, led by Mary-Ann Constantine, began in January 2009, and aims to bring to public view texts from the period produced in Wales, in both Welsh and English, and in a range of different genres. It will also be accompanied by a fully-bilingual website, 'Wales and the French Revolution', *http://frenchrevolution. wales.ac.uk*. The present volume is an anthology of Welsh-language ballads composed between 1793 and the end of the Napoleonic wars in 1815. It draws on collections of printed ballads housed in major collections in Wales (at Bangor University Library, Cardiff City Library and the National Library of Wales in Aberystwyth), many of which have been rendered significantly more accessible since the research on this volume began. The database 'Welsh Ballads Online' includes most of the texts found in Cardiff and Aberystwyth, while a fully searchable database of the titles of eighteenth-century Welsh ballads (including those found in Bangor) is available on the web resource, 'Cronfa Baledi'. In view of this wider degree of accessibility, my task has been to draw out the most engaging and most representative texts from among those available. These highlight the variety that exists in Welsh balladry of the period, in spite of a strain within Welsh scholarship which denigrates the authors as avid Tories, incapable of producing anything of real interest. While their politics (with a few notable exceptions) cannot be described as radical or reformative, this anthology seeks to show the vibrancy of Welsh ballad writers' responses to the huge upheavals of the period in question. By offering translations of the Welsh texts into English, it seeks to reach as wide an audience as possible, demonstrating to the English-speaking world how Welsh people, often side-lined in British scholarship of this period, reacted to events in France. At the same time, it is hoped that the edited Welsh texts will be widely read and enjoyed by Welsh speakers, for whom they form a vital part of their national heritage.

The research carried out builds on the foundations for the study of the Welsh ballad first laid down by J. H. Davies, who meticulously catalogued the vast majority of eighteenth-century Welsh ballads at the beginning of the twentieth century. Besides the major web-based projects mentioned already, work by Tegwyn Jones, Siwan M. Rosser and Ben Bowen Thomas, some of which has been published within the last decade, has been of great help in preparing this anthology. Where relevant, the wider ballad traditions of England and Ireland have also been taken into consideration, with the Bodleian Library Broadside Ballad collection, together with recent research on these other song traditions by Tom Dunne and Mark Philp, among others, proving to be extremely helpful. I have benefited hugely from working within a team of researchers, all with their individual but interconnected points of interest. I am grateful to Mary-Ann Constantine, Cathryn Charnell-White, Elizabeth Edwards, Marion Löffler and Heather Williams for providing me with inspiration and encouragement. The fruit of their individual research will appear in the form of anthologies dedicated to serial literature, Welsh-language poetry, English-language poetry and travel diaries from the period, in addition to further work on the issue of translation. Work produced by Alaw Mai Edwards of CAWCS and A. Cynfael Lake of Swansea University on the earlier eighteenth-century ballad writer, Huw Jones of Llangwm, was generously made available to me prior to its publication, and greatly aided me in setting the ballads of 1793–1815 within their literary context. Dafydd Johnston, the director of CAWCS, made invaluable suggestions on the translations of the ballads, and Mary-Ann Constantine, editor of the series, undertook the task of reading the work in its entirety. I am extremely indebted to them both. My decision to include musical settings of a selection of the texts on the tunes named by the ballad writers has involved research into Welsh traditional music. This was greatly facilitated by the publications of Phyllis Kinney and Cass Meurig, and both Phyllis Kinney and Meredydd Evans enthusiastically helped me to locate any missing tunes. In setting the ballads to the music I have been greatly assisted by Dylan N. Jones of Gwasg Nereus, Bala, to whom I am very grateful.

Further thanks are due to Dafydd Glyn Jones for his generosity and his unflagging interest in my work; to Branwen Ioan, Wendy Morgan and Scott Waby of the 'Welsh Ballads Online' project at the National Library of Wales; to Huw Walters of the same library for helping me locate ballad texts; to members of staff at Cardiff Central Library, Cardiff University Salisbury Library and the National Library of Wales; and to members of the 'Wales and the French Revolution' project advisory panel. In preparing the work for the press, I have relied heavily on Gwen Gruffudd of CAWCS, together with Sarah Lewis, Siân Chapman and Dafydd Jones of the University of Wales Press. My thanks to them all. Lastly, I take this opportunity to thank family and friends for their support and interest in my work, most especially my parents, my husband, Dylan, and my daughter, Heledd, to whom (on her own special request) I dedicate this volume.

February 2012   Ffion Mair Jones

Acknowledgements

Digital Landscapes / Jon Isherwood and Marion Löffler: Fig. 1

The National Library of Wales: Figs. 2, 3, 4

Abbreviations

Bangor	Cerddi Bangor (collection of printed ballads at Bangor University Library)
BBCS	*Bulletin of the Board of Celtic Studies*
BC	Baledi a Cherddi (collection of printed ballads at the National Library of Wales)
BLBB	Bodleian Library Broadside Ballads: The *allegro* Catalogue of Ballads at *http://www.bodley.ox.ac.uk/ballads/ballads.htm*
BWB	J. H. Davies, *A Bibliography of Welsh Ballads printed in the Eighteenth Century* (London, 1911)
CGPLE	Casgliad o Gerddi Prydyddion Llŷn ac Eifionydd (collection of printed ballads at the National Library of Wales)
Cronfa Baledi	Database of eighteenth-century Welsh ballads at *http://www.e-gymraeg.org/cronfabaledi*
DWB	*The Dictionary of Welsh Biography down to 1940* (London, 1959)
EHR	*English Historical Review*
ELH	*English Literary History*
GPC	*Geiriadur Prifysgol Cymru* (4 vols., Caerdydd, 1950–2002)
JDL	J. D. Lewis, Casgliad o Faledi (collection of printed ballads at the National Library of Wales)
JHD	Number given to eighteenth-century Welsh ballads in *BWB* and by later cataloguers (see, for example, Cronfa Baledi)
JWBS	*Journal of the Welsh Bibliographical Society*
LW	Eiluned Rees, *Libri Walliae: A Catalogue of Welsh Books and Books printed in Wales 1546–1820* (2 vols., Aberystwyth, 1987)
NLW	National Library of Wales
NLWJ	*National Library of Wales Journal*

ODNB	*Oxford Dictionary of National Biography* at *http://www.oxforddnb.com*
OED	*Oxford English Dictionary* at *http://www.oed.com*
TCHB	*Trafodion Cymdeithas Hanes y Bedyddwyr*
Welsh Ballads Online	Ballad database on the National Library of Wales website at *http://cat.llgc.org.uk/ballads*
WHR	*Welsh History Review*

Introduction

I have written a Ballad for the Blackguards to bawl about the streets, imitated from Newberry's well known Chapter of Kings; written at first to teach Babies the English History, but lately set and sung at Catch Clubs, Bow Meetings, etc.[1]

A confirmed conservative, Hester Lynch Piozzi was quick to see the potential of the ballad to spread an anti-French and anti-radical message among ordinary 'Blackguards'. The song to which she refers in this extract from a letter written in September 1794 warned its audience that, in spite of the bold attempts of the Revolutionaries across the Channel to replace their king with alternative governors ranging from Lafayette to the National Assembly and then 'nothing at all', the result was that 'They all lose their heads in their turn'. Modelling her song on 'A Favorite Historical Song Sung by Mr. Collins in the Evening's Brush', Piozzi deliberately sought an accessible style, contrasting the happy-go-lucky successes of the British monarchs in the original song ('Yet barring all Pother the one and the other, / Were all of them Kings in their Turn') with the inevitability of French failure.[2] Whether the streets in which she intended the song to be 'bawl[ed]' were those of Denbigh in north-east Wales, from where she wrote the letter quoted here, is uncertain.[3] Her words, however, display the elite's increasing interest in the ballad as a genre during the 1790s, as the French Revolution turned bloody and popular radicalism gained ground in Britain. Piozzi was not alone in recognizing the role balladry and song might play in guiding the responses of ordinary people. A correspondent of John Reeves, founder of the Association for Preserving Liberty and Property against Republicans and Levellers, wrote on 4 December 1792 'that any thing written in voice & especially to an Old English tune . . . made a more fixed Impression on the Minds of the Younger and Lower Class of People, than any written in Prose'.[4] 'In [the] struggle for the loyalty of the British public, songs and music played a crucial, but thus far little discussed, role', writes Mark Philp, charting the rise and fall in the fortunes of loyalist and radical songs between 1792 and 1805.[5] Across the Irish Sea, and on the other side of the political divide, the United Irishmen encouraged literacy 'as the first step to emancipation' and engaged in publishing English-language material including ballads and songs to spread their message of hope for a free Ireland.[6]

In England, loyalist ballads outnumber radical ones by some considerable margin, the latter limited in the chronological scope of their appearance by the tightening of repressive laws and, possibly, as some commentators have suggested, because there was not such a broad base for popular radicalism as there was for popular loyalism.[7] The circulation of loyalist propaganda was boosted by the involvement of elite figures such as William Jones of Nayland and, most famously of all, Hannah More. Many broadsides produced in the critical year of 1803, when the scare of a Napoleonic invasion was at its height, had first appeared in reputable journals such as *The Gentleman's Magazine* or *The British Neptune*, which gives an indication of their pedigree.[8] A host of poems and songs relating to the troubled politics of the Revolutionary decade and beyond was copied by Elizabeth Baker, a wealthy Englishwoman resident in Dolgellau in rural Merionethshire, including material taken from *The Sun* and *The True Briton*.[9] It is unclear whether Baker collected this material for herself alone, or whether she was involved in circulating it within the district: an exploration of her papers suggests the latter.[10] Elite interest in and use of ballads and songs were also well-supported by the work of numerous 'minor scribblers', including clergymen and magistrates, who contributed to the production of anti-radical songs.[11] Work on Hannah More demonstrates that, for reasons of evangelical piety and with an eye on reforming manners, the Mendip-based author and social reformer instinctively mistrusted popular culture; indeed, according to one recent study, 'Popular ballads were the major provocation for the Cheap Repository Tracts campaign'.[12] This view seems to be corroborated by a diary entry of More's, detailing 'a Plan for abolishing ballad singing, & trying to substitute religious Papers – Hymns, ~~Communions~~ – happy deaths'.[13] While some scholars have concluded, largely on the basis of the shortage of directly anti-radical ballads and tracts within More's work, that she was concerned 'less [with] an attack on Tom Paine than on Simple Simon', others argue that she was responding to a 'twin threat', both 'moral and political'.[14]

More's commentary on popular balladry in ballads and pamphlets which she herself composed typically involved denigration of their 'wickedness' or of their 'vicious' moral influence, an influence which invariably lead those who listened to them into the throes of drunkenness, ribaldry and irresponsibility.[15] She also produced songs addressing issues of social unrest and disorder, using the genre to dissuade the poor from rioting and complaint.[16] These latter songs may be identified with a significant stream of protest poems, indicating tension between social classes, within traditional eighteenth-century

English balladry, which in turn may well have fed into the mistrust of ballads evidenced in the attitudes of More and others.[17] Over the border in Wales, ballad writers in the early to mid-eighteenth century were more likely to be subjected to scorn and derision for the quality of their work than judged for its immorality – understandably so in view of their penchant for producing what the Augustan poet Goronwy Owen described as 'trifling godly songs for young men and women to learn, so as to lighten the burden of the priest' ('mân ddyriau duwiol i hoglangciau a llangcesi i'w dysgu, i ysgafnhau baich yr offeiriad').[18] This changed, however, with the spread of Methodism, which threatened the survival of various aspects of popular culture, reputedly killing off the popular dramatic genre of the 'anterliwt' (notorious for its evocation of sexual licentiousness among other sins) by the early years of the nineteenth century.[19] When anxiety about the possible influence of the French Revolution upon the masses at home hit the elite in Wales in late 1792 and early 1793, it does not appear that ballads were seen either as a particular threat to social stability or as a medicine to correct any unrest. Although, as Hywel Davies has demonstrated, massive effort was put in by the ruling classes at the turn of the 1790s to ensure that loyalist propaganda reached ordinary Welsh people in their own language, ballads were apparently not seen as a potential avenue for distributing the message. Richard Poole, the clerk of the peace for Anglesey, rejected the proposal that he should have a number of loyalist ballads produced under the aegis of Reeves's Association translated into Welsh, although translating fervour was widespread throughout the land, with editions of key English tracts and pamphlets making appearances in Welsh.[20] With the exception of two free-metre (or ballad-type) poems, one of which was sponsored by the aristocrat Paul Panton of Plas Gwyn in Anglesey, and neither of which appears to have been printed in ballad form, Welsh balladry seems to have been largely left to its own devices in the early years of the Revolutionary decade.[21]

The ballad tradition in Wales, as demonstrated in recent work by Siwan M. Rosser, shares many features with balladry in England and beyond.[22] The relaxation of restrictions on the printing trade in 1695 had a profound effect on the ballad trade in Wales as well as in England, enabling print culture to take an early hold on the genre.[23] Thomas Jones, a Welsh almanac-maker and printer resident in London at the time, was quick to see that a move to the town of Shrewsbury on the Welsh border would provide him with enhanced business opportunities.[24] Others joined him: Jones included, there were five active ballad printers in Shrewsbury at various times during the first half of the eighteenth century; at least two in Chester; and one in Hereford.[25] Two ballad printers ventured into west Wales during the same period, setting up presses at Trefhedyn in Cardiganshire and in the busy market town of Carmarthen.

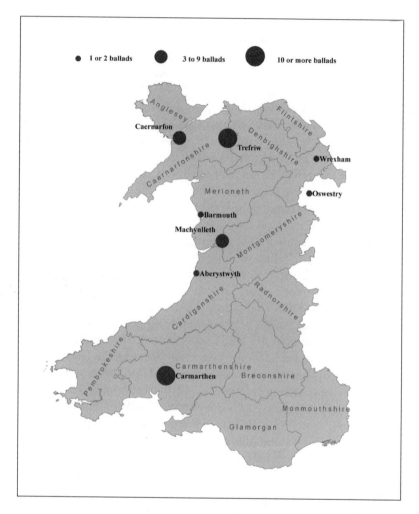

Figure 1. Towns where ballads in this anthology were printed

By the end of the eighteenth century there were presses involved in ballad printing in as many as eight towns, six of which were located in Wales itself, and five of these in the north of the country.[26] Commentators have often tried to account for the relative paucity of the ballad tradition in south Wales during the eighteenth century. J. H. Davies argued that the strength of a sequence of religious revivals in south Wales during the seventeenth and eighteenth centuries dampened the appetite for balladry, channelling creative energy into the production of hymns instead.[27] Rosser follows Thomas Parry's suggestion that the trade simply lent itself to the geographical features of the north, with the movement of itinerant tradesmen and drovers to and fro from England into the vales of Edeirnion, Uwchaled, Clwyd and Conwy, facilitating the dissemination of material suitable for ballads as well as providing a standard route for the distribution of ballad texts, once printed.[28] There is no doubt that a single printing family based in Trefriw near Llanrwst was also crucial to the development of the trade in the north. Dafydd Jones (Dewi Fardd; active during 1776–85), followed by his son, Ishmael Davies (1785–1816), and grandson, John Jones (Pyll Glan Conwy; 1817–65), established a buoyant business, to which balladry was central.[29] The youngest member, John Jones, argued for the importance of producing accessible poetry in ballad-style in the preface to an anthology of poetry in 1812. His words might be taken as the manifesto of three generations of his family:

[Yr wyf] wedi bod yn fwy gofalus am foddhau pobl y wlad yn gyffredin gyda Charolau, Cerddi, &c nag yn chwilio allan Awdlau &c, i foddhau y rhodresgar: yr wyf yn meddwl mae Carolau a Cherddi sydd fwyaf gwasanaethgar yn yr amser presenol na dim arall o waith Prydyddion. O ba lês y bydd Awdl clogyrnaidd i'r werin, na fedrant ddeall (ond odid) air o ddeg ynddo?[30]

(I have been more careful to satisfy the ordinary people of the country with carols, songs, &c. than to look for *awdlau*, &c. to satisfy the conceited. I believe that carols and songs are more useful at the present time than anything else produced by poets. Of what benefit will a bungling *awdl* be to the common people, who can barely understand one word out of ten in it?)

Central to the early success of the Trefriw press were a small number of re-nowned ballad writers (or 'prydyddion') whose sellers (known as the 'baledwyr') relied heavily upon it for their printing needs.[31] Paramount among these was Ellis Roberts (Elis y Cowper), who spent most of his life living in the nearby village of Llanddoged. Although, as we have already seen, figures such as Ellis Roberts were subjected to the scorn of higher-ranking poets, their ballads were not without considerable craft. Whereas ballads in England remained metre- and rhyme-driven alone, Welsh ballad writers (in the north in particular) adopted a form of writing loosely based on the highly complex art of *cynghanedd*, where consonance and internal rhyme played a vital part in the construction of individual lines and couplets. This art was cross-bred with the art of popular music, as ballad writers structured their effusions to the metres of a variety of tunes, often imported from England.[32] The emphasis both on *cynghanedd* and on music means that the sound produced by word and note is often central to the appeal of Welsh ballads, and words or phrases within them which are difficult to appreciate (and seem merely to serve the purpose of filling up a line, adding nothing to its meaning) are more easily accounted for when they are heard set to music.[33] This is particularly true of syntax and punctuation, which can often only be truly understood by giving due attention to the musical structure of the tunes which lie behind the texts.[34] The importance of the sound of the ballads suggests that ballad performers (or sellers) were crucial figures in the world of Welsh (as of English) balladry. In a 1779 text, Ellis Roberts envisions a world where the seller ('Y Baledwr') is deceased, leaving angry old women, unable to read, frustrated by the inaccessibility of the printed text.[35] Elsewhere, Roberts enjoyed poking fun at the figure of the ballad seller and singer, using his removed and privileged position as a poet to satirize this dependent.[36] As the eighteenth century drew to its close, the triangular association between poet, seller and printer appears to have changed, with ballad writers becoming increasingly involved in the process of performing and distributing their own work, especially in south Wales. Here, the tradition, as suggested, grew along different lines. In the prosperous printing town of Carmarthen no single printer held dominance over the ballad trade, and up to four different printers were involved in it, often in competition, during the period 1793–1815. Likewise, there were no obvious leading horses among ballad writers. The metres used by writers (with the exception of some of the ballads printed in relation to the Fishguard invasion) were simpler than the 'carol' metres of the north, as described above; this may have reflected the strength of an oral ballad and song tradition in southern regions. Balladry did not lend itself to print as early as in the north, and did not appear to need cross-fertilization with print culture to sustain and enhance it.[37]

The development of ballad singing in the Wales of the period was contained and controlled by the factors outlined above relating to printing, geography and tradition. Some of these factors were unique to Wales or to particular areas within Wales; others can be identified with developments in English balladry. There is one current within Welsh ballad writing which sets it widely apart from its English equivalent, however: the ubiquitous nature of biblical reference and imagery within it. Welsh writers from all areas of the country appear to have been obsessed with the nature of sin and redemption and, although Thomas Parry described the underpinning religiosity of the ballad writers as 'remarkably simple and unquestioning' ('crefydd fach seml ac unplyg ryfeddol'), its pervasiveness means that it makes an indelible impression on the mind of a reader today, as it would have done for contemporaries who read and heard the ballads.[38] A morality based on this 'simple' religion colours attitudes among ballad writers towards a wide variety of subjects, as Rosser has demonstrated in the case of Welsh ballads dedicated to the representation of women. For the ballad writers of north Wales, the mindset conditioned by religion and reliance upon the Bible, coupled with the stylistic parameters set out by the alliterative, tune-based metres, often resulted in a 'lingua franca', where the individual poet's voice and perspective were lost.[39] Yet, ballad writers themselves, from the eighteenth-century 'prydyddion' to the early nineteenth-century balladeers proper, were evidently aware, at times at least, of their own unique status or personalities, and in some cases prepared to use their fame to enhance interest in (and the sale of) their ballads.[40] The writers' own sense of self serves as a reminder that Welsh balladry is not in fact as monochrome as might be expected, but offers a variety of perspectives on and insights to the experiences of the ordinary people whom it served.

Even if balladry in Wales was not seen as a threat to social stability at the turn of the 1790s, exploration of the ballad corpus which has survived suggests that ballads paid at least some attention to issues of social gradation and class tension. In fact, ballad writers in the earlier eighteenth century could be scathing in their portrayal of ruling class exploitation of ordinary people. This is the case in 'Ymddiddan rhwng Lloegr a Ffraingc ar y mesur a elwir Leave Land neu adel Tir' (A dialogue between England and France on the metre called Leave Land or Gadael Tir), a poem by Ellis Roberts published at the height of the Seven Years' War in October 1758.[41] This ballad shows the collusion of the British ruling classes, impersonated as 'England', with their equivalent social class in France over the question of corn imports. 'France', in her desire to reap the rewards of agricultural labour in Britain at the expense of a starving native population, advises a mercenary 'England' to shoot anyone who protests against the exportation of corn from Britain; 'England' concedes to having already done so the previous year when rioting against this practice took place and now plans to send its produce to France surreptitiously via the Isle of Man, promising death to anyone who attempts to frustrate its plans. In allowing his audience to listen in on this shameful sell-out of their own livelihoods, Ellis Roberts was certain to stir anger and indignation.[42]

Further dialogue poems (regrettably not always datable) pit members of different social classes against each other, thus providing a forum for exploring the representation of social tension in Welsh balladry. There appear to be two strands to such ballads: a landowner/tenant dialogue, and a tenant/beggar dialogue. The tenant is thus the consistent character, attacked from two different perspectives, a fact which suggests that the ballad audiences had a particular interest in his social position. This may have been because some of them hailed from the tenant class, aspired to it or were in close contact with it. Tenants are typically criticized in the ballads from the perspectives of both pauper and landlord for their decadent lifestyle (especially that of their offspring and womenfolk) and for social climbing.[43] Beggars are also typically reviled, although, of course, the genre ensures that they are granted a voice to put across their own viewpoint. They appear to be a source of anxiety to the tenants with whom they converse on account of their dependence on parish relief (the poor rate being one of several taxes cited in these poems). In two poems by Robert Morris, one probably dating from 1788, the other possibly originating in the 1790s, the dialogue ends as the beggar is taken away from the scene.[44] This happens in a more sympathetic manner in the earlier ballad than in the later, where the tenant savagely threatens to tie up the beggar's legs unless he immediately leaves the county. In the later text, there is concern about taxation and about the dependence not only of paupers but also of the wives of soldiers, suggesting that the poet was writing (during years of war) for an audience that was self-sufficient but far from well off. Even though the end of the poem favours the tenant, the beggar makes the point that the tenant is better off during the current period than generally on account of raised prices for goods, a fact attested to in the 1790s.[45] The scuffling between these two groups suggests a working out of tensions, but no threat to social stability, and not a hint of an alliance between traditional popular balladry and a reformist or radical message. Only in one ballad does the formula of chasing off one speaker turn against a landowner. A poem published by Richard Marsh, active as a printer in Wrexham between 1772 and 1792, ends with a threat of physical violence against the landowner:

> A ninne ar ôl blino a godwn i foppio,
> Cei[ff] llawer eu pwnnio yn eu Penn;
> Y Gŵr mwŷa a welwn, tuag atto cyfeiriwn,
> Mi tresiwn, mi laeniwn i Lenn.[46]

> (And we, having had enough, shall rise up to mob,
> many shall be beaten in the head;
> we shall head for the most illustrious man that we can see –
> we shall thrash him, we shall beat his mantle.)

This is a provocative ending for a ballad sung on 'God Save the King', a tune sometimes used in a sardonic mode by radicals in the 1790s.[47] Use of the melody by Welsh ballad writers in 1779, 1784 and 1788 is largely unprovocative, which suggests that the text published by Marsh may date from the early 1790s.[48] Even if this inference regarding dating is correct, however, it remains the case that, in a decade in which popular protest was on the increase throughout Wales, there is very limited reference to protest or social unrest within Welsh balladry. Riots in the north Wales coal-field in the summer of 1789, corn riots in Swansea and protests against enclosure in Hope, Flintshire, in 1793, and riots in Denbigh and Haverfordwest in 1795 left no mark on the output of Welsh ballad singers.[49] This may have reflected a sense among ballad writers that the traditional occasional foray into protest which was a feature of balladry earlier in the century was no longer an open avenue. Evidence shows that Thomas Edwards (Twm o'r Nant), a popular dramatist, poet and ballad writer, was unable fully to represent private feelings of sympathy for mob violence in Denbigh in 1795 in his poetic work.[50] This in turn suggests that at least some ballad writers in Wales were aware of the novelty of the period which was hailed by the fall of the Bastille in 1789, and of their entry into territory where previous markers regarding the permissibility of protest could no longer be relied upon.

Responding to Revolution

This anthology includes poetry published between 1793 and 1815. The earlier date represents the first clear responses in Welsh ballads to the events of the Revolution in France. The exhilaration of the initial years of the Revolution does not appear to have struck the ballad poets; neither did the vociferous debate among pamphlet writers stemming from the publication of Richard Price's *A Discourse on the Love of our Country* in 1789, at least not immediately. In England, conversely, Edmund Burke's *Reflections on the Revolution in France* (1791), composed in answer to Price's *Discourse*, sparked a huge pamphlet debate (which extended to the production of ballads and songs) and lead to 'the growth of a popular press and the evolution of a popular political literary style' which spanned the divide between loyalists and radicals.[51] The death of two of the most productive among Welsh ballad writers may be a factor in the silence of Welsh balladry in reaction to the very early years of the Revolutionary period: Huw Jones of Llangwm died *c.*1785, Ellis Roberts during 1789 itself.[52] Many of the known ballad writers represented in this anthology are 'new voices' of the 1790s and beyond, with little footing in the previous decades and no experience of singing in 'political' contexts such as the Seven Years' War or the American War of Independence.[53] Earlier eighteenth-century poets had fully engaged with the debates emanating from the conflict between Britain and her American colonies and, in spite of being what Gwyn A. Williams described as 'non-political Tories' for the most part, were 'temporarily unhinged' by the conflict, '[s]ome even [showing] a transient sympathy for errant brethren across the water'.[54] During 1793, however, a largely new wave of Welsh ballad writers began to respond to the cataclysmic events in France and their political and social ramifications in their own communities. Untypically, in the context of this anthology, in 1793 there were voices straddled along the divide between Church-and-King loyalism on the one hand and reforming Dissent on the other. The following discussion turns to these two contrasting standpoints, beginning in Dissenting south-west Wales, before moving northwards to the 'Tory' territory described by Williams.

The voices of Dissent: the ballads of south-west Wales (1793)

Two of the earliest texts presented here hail from Carmarthenshire in south-west Wales. They are almost unique in this anthology in that they clearly represent the voices of Dissenters – very little heard elsewhere.[55] Different from each other in attitude and stance – the first apparently conciliatory and deferential to the status quo, while the second is outraged and pugnaciously defensive – they are both framed by a prose narrative which sets them in context and perhaps betrays a certain anxiety as to their reception. The first, no. 1 in this anthology, was produced as a result of a meeting of Protestant Dissenters from the three denominations of Baptists, Independents and Presbyterians, held in Newcastle Emlyn in February 1793. Although no author's name is appended to the ballad text itself, the name of the chairperson at the meeting, William Williams, is clearly set at the end of the prose text, giving it the authority of an official statement. The meeting, and indeed the declaration itself, can be seen in the context of the rush among Protestant Dissenters (and numerous other public bodies) during late 1792 and early 1793 to affirm loyalty to the king in a climate increasingly hostile towards Dissent.[56] Declarations in a similar vein (none of which venture into verse, however) sprang from Dissenters in towns all over Britain, including London, Manchester, Haverhill in Suffolk, and Leeds, and were published in the London papers.[57] They typically refer to the 'Three Essential Estates – the King, the House of Lords, and the free representation of the People in an Elective House of Commons', to the Glorious Revolution which established the British constitution, and to their 'abhor[rence of] all Riots and tumultuous Proceedings' along with their determination to support their suppression by the Civil Magistrates.[58] The declaration which resulted from the south-west Wales meeting is substantially longer and fuller than those published in the London papers. Its ostensible purpose is to ward off any suggestion that Dissenters harbour sympathy with the violent aims and ways of the Revolution in France, and it urges any French sympathizers to 'go off to France all at one stroke, / a deluge of equals' (lines 59–60). An outright dismissal of the French model ('without taking heed of France . . .', line 63) is coupled with the use of the image of a deluge sweeping away the supporters of French-style 'equality' as if they were the dregs of the earth punished by God for their sins (but leaving the godly – the Welsh or the British – safe in their ark-like island). The author or collective authors clearly wanted to show that the ideals represented by the Revolution were rejected by the Dissenting community. Nonetheless, this poem appears to have a two-tier message. Not only does it speak to the greater public of the loyalty of Protestant Dissenters, it also speaks to Dissenting congregations themselves, seeking to provide them with guidance on how to negotiate the difficulties of their current situation.

Even at a remove of more than three years, the ballad was clearly inspired by Price's *Discourse on the Love of our Country*. Price's sermon was delivered to the Society for Commemorating the Revolution in Great Britain, and urges Protestant Dissenters 'to celebrate [that event] with expressions of joy and exultation'.[59] It also propagated a strongly reformist agenda, however, arguing for the pursuit of greater liberty of conscience, a more perfect toleration and more equal representation.[60] The celebrations of 1688, for Price, must on no account be a point of stasis, where men look backwards with satisfaction but fail to question whether any thing 'is left deficient'. Price's generation need to be 'transmitting the blessings obtained by [the Glorious Revolution] to our posterity, unimpaired and *improved*' (my emphasis).[61] The south-west Wales ballad likewise poises between past and future, and is no more a static celebration of 1688 than Price's work. In its description of the passing on of blessings from generation to generation and its strongly visionary outlook, picturing the blessings of future years, it shows (in spite of its rejection of the French ideal of equality) an almost missionary zeal for the Christianization of the world. The Particular Baptist Missionary Society for Propagating the Gospel among the Heathen had been established in 1792, and the first missionary, William Carey, sent out to India. This, together with the campaign to abolish slavery, which gained strength from the end of the 1780s, is evoked in the poem in a way which suggests a real commitment to a Dissenting agenda. Not only are 'the black people' (line 94) and the natives of India part of a vision of transformation through the power of the Gospel towards liberalization, the text also envisages a world in which all kinds of sinners, or men believed otherwise wanting (from the proud to the drunken, the miserly, oppressors and cruel masters) are rendered godly. The poem ends with an affirmation of what it seemingly denied in its introductory prose message – another Revolution:

> Yn ddilys mae i Dduwiolion
>   Ail oes a Refoliwsion,
> Pan caffon uno'n llon eu llef
>   Yn felys â nefolion.[62]

> (Godly people will surely
> have a second age and a Revolution
> when they shall join, with happy cry,
> sweetly with heavenly beings.)

A clear message is thus given not only of Dissenter loyalty and patriotism (couched in 'citizens of the world' terms, as in Price's *Discourse*) but also of the need for Dissenters to strive for a better world. The framing prose section which appears at the end shows a keen awareness of the limitations on Dissenters. It mentions their 'exclusion from the common rights of citizens', but counsels that the way forward lies in putting their faith in the still-evolving and ever self-perfecting constitution ('an excellent constitution, which has been improving for ages, and from its very principles has power, without violence or tumult, to correct every remaining imperfection'). Like Price, who urges upon his listeners the importance of tendering their 'patriotic service' to change the society in which they live, the ballad counsels that fear of failure should count for nothing: the reward 'of soon becoming members of a perfect community in the heavens' is sustenance in itself.[63]

The prose introduction to the ballad mentions the figure of the Pretender (it is not specified whether that of 1715 or of 1745). In the second ballad produced in Carmarthenshire, also probably in February 1793 (no. 2), the Pretender figures again, rather more colourfully, as the poet remembers how the Dissenting community 'drove [him] like a traitor before them'.[64] This text is a response to the publication of a Welsh translation of *One Penny-worth of Truth from Thomas Bull to his Brother John*, which, from the evidence of contemporary correspondence, we know was circulating in Carmarthenshire in February 1793.[65] Although Dissent is not mentioned in the original English *One Penny-worth*, the ballad is an exercise in self-defence carried out on behalf of the Dissenting community, to which it makes numerous references. It begins pugnaciously by accusing the author and translator of the text either of ignorance or of being enemies to the king and the truth. It then accuses them of putting forth arguments which resurrect the cause of the Pretender and his attempts at a tyrannous rule. '[I]f Thomas had printed his ill-intentioned letter in the year 1745, when the Pretender landed in this island, he would certainly have died on the gallows, according to his desert', claims the author, echoing the words of Charles James Fox in a House of Commons speech on 13 December 1792. Fox had claimed that *One Penny-worth* contained 'assertions, concerning the divine right of anointed Kings, and such other matter, as, if published in the year 1715, or 1745, would have been held treason', and 'would have been supposed to defend the right impiously called divine by the Pretender, in opposition to that, which was so much better, the right resulting from the affection and loyalty of the People to the House of Brunswick, upon whom they so deservedly relied'.[66]

Like the previous ballad (no. 1), this poem delves into the history of Dissent in order to establish the lineal descent of Dissenting loyalty. It ventures as far back as the Restoration in its historical reference, claiming that 'it was the

Dissenters who brought King Charles the Second to the Crown in the year 1660', a potentially controversial claim in view of the established tradition in Welsh literature that Dissenters were strongly connected with the downfall of Charles II's father, Charles I, executed in 1649.[67] The author avoids any qualification of this claim (perhaps signalling his confidence in his own version of history) but is at greater pains to deal with claims directly raised in *One Penny-worth* about more recent Dissenting history. The pamphlet claims that:

> Our National Debt for which we are now paying such heavy taxes, was doubled by the troubles in America. Yet those people who fomented and brought those burdens upon us, are they that rail most at the expensiveness of our Government, and use it as a handle for overturning it . . .

The ballad writer saw this as a direct accusation against Dissenters, who, although they opposed going to war against the American colonists, could be viewed as 'fomenters' of the conflict in view of the support which they lent the colonists to stand their ground against a British executive which refused them parliamentary representation.

More central to the ballad (as to the pamphlet itself), however, is the Revolution currently underway in France. Of the three slogan-words promoted by the French – 'liberté', 'égalité' and 'fraternité' – the second probably instilled the greatest fear into the bosoms of the propertied classes in Britain.[68] It is the doctrine of equality which receives *One Penny-worth*'s initial attention:

> The Clerk is not equal to the Parson; the Footman is not equal to the Judge upon the Bench. If it were as they say, then the Clerk might get up into the Pulpit; the Footman might sit at the top of the table; the Thief might take his place upon the Bench and try the Judge; and the Coachman might get into the coach and set his Master upon the box, who, not knowing how to drive, 'tis ten to one but he overturns him.[69]

The ballad tackles this view, attributed to 'those conceited monkeys the French . . . and some Englishmen at home, who hate this country as bad as the French do', by arguing that Dissenters never harboured plans to turn the social hierarchy upon its head (lines 53–60). Yet, when the poet devotes a stanza to define what Dissenters believe and strive towards, his meaning is not immediately apparent, in spite of the gusto of the initial couplet:

> Yr hyn mae'r diwygwyr yn sicr yn ddal
> Yn wyneb mab Siencyn a phawb o'r rhai bal,
> Fod hawl gan gardotyn fel brenin, heb freg,
> I chwarae dros ffortun â'i fywyd yn deg.[70]

(What the reformers certainly believe
in the face of Jenkin's son and all the other stupid ones,
is that a beggar, like a king, without guile,
has the right to play his life out for fortune's sake.)

The ideal of equality expressed here may draw on notions of new beginnings
such as those increasingly sought by Welsh Dissenters in the New World. In
May 1793 the Welsh magazine *Y Cylchgrawn Cynmraeg* published a letter
from the expatriate John Evans of Waunfawr in Caernarfonshire, who had
left Wales for America in search of the descendants of the legendary Welsh
prince, Madog. Evans wrote that 'this is the most wonderful country I have
ever seen; the poor people here live better than the farmers in Wales' ('Dyma
y wlad hyfrydaf a welais erioed; y mae y bobl dlodion yn y wlad yma yn
byw yn well na'r ffarmwyr yn Nghymru').[71] This sentiment was later reflected
in a Welsh ballad composed by an emigrant to America, which mentioned
the equality of status among the population in the New World.[72]

As in the case of the first Dissenting ballad discussed (no. 1), 'Sylwiad byr'
(no. 2) also apparently addresses two audiences. It is aware of (and wishes to
profit from) the potential of cheap print to influence a popular audience, and
attempts to anticipate the response to its arguments. It claims that the verdict
of ordinary people on *One Penny-worth* is that 'Thomas and his lines are
certainly too costly' (line 88), and it attempts to deflate the pamphlet's arguments by maintaining that its main spokesman is a 'tongue-less bell' (line 72).
Throughout, it repeatedly accuses Thomas of lying, and attempts to attribute
to him the blame for disruption and disturbance in public order, turning on
its head the argument that Dissenters are disloyal to the Crown. Its concluding
stanza, however, is a prayer-like plea for strength, imploring God to grant
the necessary 'patience and nourishment' for the Dissenting community to
shoulder the cross put upon them by society:

O, Arglwydd da! dyro amynedd a maeth
I'th lesg bererinion er gwell ac er gwaeth;
Trwy bob gwradwyddiadau a chroesau o hyd,
Ein henaid ddyrchafo Iachawdwr y byd.[73]

(Oh, good Lord! give patience and nourishment
to Your weary pilgrims for better and for worse;
through all dishonours and afflictions always,
may the Redeemer of the world raise our soul.)

'Faithful Britons': the loyalist response (1793–4)

The two ballads hitherto discussed present rather lone voices within this anthology in their portrayal of the Dissenting and reforming response to growing public mistrust as the Revolutionary decade proceeded. They are likely to be the work of educated authors: the first emanated from a meeting chaired by William Williams, a highly literate and influential member of the Baptist community in Cardiganshire, and the second shows evidence of acquaintance with views expressed by Charles James Fox, the leader of the Whigs in Parliament at this time.[74] In a third ballad produced in 1793 we move northwards into a terrain firmly established as the preserve of Gwyn A. Williams's 'Tory' ballad singers during the course of the eighteenth century; a terrain where, although ballad writers were prepared to make complaint about aspects of social life, they tended only to draw attention to 'where the shoe pinched' as R. T. Jenkins succinctly put it.[75] A new voice here in the 1790s is that of Richard Roberts, initially a ballad seller who probably realized his own talent for composition and became involved in producing and, most probably, selling his own work. Roberts had a predilection for choosing themes related to the troubles of the time and is, as a result, fairly well represented in this anthology.

Roberts's two earliest ballads in this volume (nos. 3 and 7) relate to the executions of Louis XVI in January 1793 and his wife, Marie Antoinette, in October of the same year. In the background to both poems is the spectre of war, France having commenced hostilities against Britain in February 1793. This links the poems with English ballads on the deaths of Louis XVI and Marie Antoinette, which also invoke the Europe-wide conflict that was quickly emerging early in 1793. In 'A New Song, called, The French King's Blood Crying for Vengeance', the 'ruffian' French are confronted by 'vast thunder / From Portugal and Spain; / From Austria and from Russia, / And Prussia more renown'd', let alone the 'Warriors of Great Britain', Brunswick and Holland. In 'The Lamentation of the French Queen, in Prison, with the moving Discourse of the Princess Royal, and the young Dauphin', the incarcerated Marie Antoinette (who, awaiting certain death at the hands of the Revolutionaries, rather clumsily characterizes herself as 'Hamlet's Ghost') envisages a France 'in great confusion, / By glittering swords, and cannon balls', and warns that 'It will end in dissolution'.[76] For both ballads, war is the answer to the outrage of regicide. For the author of the former, the Revolutionaries have 'made a blot in history, / By [their] infernal rage' and must be supplanted. The theatrical imagery implies that men are responsible for the actions of war: 'The combin'd drum beats come, come, come! / To lop you up the stage'.[77] In Richard Roberts's songs, the picture is somewhat less straightforward. Although his work shares with contemporary English ballads an abundance of pathos at the fate of Louis's wife, it is also more reflective upon the British position in the narrative of the Revolution in France.[78] The ballad on the king's execution (no. 3) opens with an address to the Britons which invokes war, but immediately diminishes human agency in its vicissitudes by maintaining that 'God Himself is the arbiter / on sea and land'.[79] This leaves all to be played for. Since God is greater than all the Britons' enemies, worship of and faith in Him are the crucial factors in saving Britain from destruction.[80] Engagement in war is for Richard Roberts a matter for reflection not simply on the evil of the opposing country but also on the potential failings of the mother country.

Roberts envisages disaster in Britain on two counts. Unlike the English ballads on the death of the French monarchs, which make no mention of the possibility of an invading force from France landing on British soil, this possibility is keenly imagined in Roberts's work.[81] This, as Mary-Ann Constantine has noted in papers on Welsh balladry of the period, may be the result of the emphasis in Welsh historiography on the inbred sinfulness of the ancient Britons (who are amalgamated with the British subjects of the late eighteenth century in Roberts's and others' work) and the arrival of punishment for this wickedness reaching the Isle of Britain from overseas.[82] Yet, the 'bloody enemy' (no. 3, line 83) feared by Roberts is not solely an external force. 'Treachery' (of a particularly violent and bloodthirsty nature) is portrayed as rife within Britain itself. Popular radicalism is the immediate threat: Roberts expresses the hope that Britain's internal enemies will be kept away from his audience's hearing (no. 3, line 93), which suggests that the permeation of a popular radical message is a cause for anxiety for him as for the ruling elites elsewhere. The association of popular radicalism with Dissent is only fleetingly made, as Roberts refers to Britain's enemies as 'sham Christians' (no. 3, line 111), and asks for the support of a Trinitarian God in the battle against them (no. 7, lines 87–8).

Central to both ballads, as promised in their titles, is the narration of the stories of the French monarchs' executions. Both make use of the *memento mori* theme, which expresses bewilderment at the transience of human life, for kings and beggars alike. Louis himself is the subject of this astonishment in one ballad, his children in the other. Whereas the children's frailty is invoked for the sake of pathos in a poem devoted to the fate of their mother (no. 7, lines 60–1), Louis's is part of a portrayal which occasionally dips into a less sympathetic representation:

> Fe ganodd ffárwel ar ddydd Llun
> Ac fe ddwedodd wrth ei fab ei hun,
> "Bydd fyw yn dy le yn dda dy lun,
>   Rhag terfyn dy oes.

to the latter's representation of Louis XVI's final moments (no. 3), we find an implication that the king himself instigated a conflict with his people:

> Fe aeth brenin Ffrainc yn anghytûn
> I roi dial hy ar ei deulu'i hun;
> Fe a'i trowd o'i le yn ddrwg ei lun –
>   Cadd derfyn du;
> Am ei groes faterion mowrion maith
> Cadd ddiodde loesion, creulon graith,
> Sef torri ei ben ar fyr daith –
>   Heb obaith bu.[89]

> (The king of France went contentiously
> to effect a bold vengeance upon his own family;
> he was turned out of his seat in a cruel fashion –
> he had a calamitous end;
> for his great, numerous perverse actions
> he had to suffer agonies, a cruel scar,
> namely the severing of his head in a short time –
> he was without hope.)

In view of the varied and confused lexicon of this opening stanza, it is very difficult to determine how Roberts intended the 'vengeance' enacted by Louis XVI upon his own family, or possibly his own nation, to be interpreted.[90] The king's treatment is seemingly decried as 'cruel' and agonizing, yet he is charged with having conducted 'numerous perverse actions' and, in a later stanza, with being an 'unwise man under the firmament' (line 51). This lack of precision opens up the possibility of viewing Louis as either a God-like figure wreaking revenge on a disobedient people, or alternatively as a king who showed a deplorable lack of sympathy in his (unspecified) actions against his own subjects. He also at times takes on the mantle of a misunderstood prophet, 'struck in his own country' (line 21). Roberts's ballad on the death of Marie Antoinette contains none of this ambiguity. Even while describing her attempt to secure foreign aid against Revolutionary France, an action generally seen in France as highly duplicitous, Roberts has nothing but sympathy. He is likewise clearly unaware of the monstrous charges made against her at her trial regarding her surviving son, the Dauphin, and simply draws on her status as a mother to elicit his audience's sympathy (no. 7, lines 55–6).[91] As in Roberts's ballad on Louis XVI's death, a great deal of the energy of the text is channelled into describing the physical torment inflicted on the queen, his listeners and readers' disgust at the Revolutionaries' actions and heart-felt sympathy with the pair ensured by the depiction of Louis's scalded corpse, treated 'like animal

skins in our country', or Marie Antoinette's 'little arms bound'.[92] The simile
in the first instance brings the picture home in cruel starkness, whereas the
placing of the endearing adjective 'bach' (little) speaks powerfully in the second
instance. In neither case is the guillotine clearly invoked, yet Roberts's tortured
attempts at conveying the manner of Louis's death suggests that he may have
been aware of its existence. Louis is said to have had his head placed 'Ar y
siaffer dyner denn' (on the gracious, neat chafing-dish, line 50), perhaps in
an attempt to evoke the bucket-like structure into which the head would
have rolled once chopped off.[93] A minor textual variant in the Machynlleth
and Wrexham imprints of Roberts's ballad to Louis suggests an effort by the
printer-compositors to describe execution by the guillotine, or otherwise
reflect a process of interpretation carried out during the transmission of the
text; the words 'tan fur' (underneath a wall) in these imprints may suggest
the movement of a wall-like contraption downwards on the neck. Marie
Antoinette is said, literally, to have had her throat cut – an inexact description
of the process of execution by guillotine. The reference to 'corn ei gwddw'
(literally, her throat or windpipe, line 47) once again reverts to animal imagery:
hens are frequently killed by twisting their necks in this way. The sense that
Roberts is searching hard both for precise terminology and for more round-
about ways of describing both deaths suggests the novelty of the world which
he attempts to portray in these texts in all its stark horror.[94]

Richard Roberts's emphasis on an internal enemy, as early as the initial days
of the Revolutionary Wars, is not an isolated phenomenon among the ballads
included in this anthology. It is further developed in a 1794 ballad by Roberts
(no. 8), where the war against France is envisaged as a religious war against the
forces of Catholicism. As in his ballads on the deaths of the French monarchs,
there is a certain amount of confusion between the war fought against Revolutionary France and an internal battle against a host of representative animal
figures, including 'gwiberod' (vipers), 'bleiddied' (wolves) and 'seirff' (serpents),
the latter clearly stated to be present in England (line 61). Other Welsh sources,
including the interlude by Hugh Jones (mentioned above) and *Y Cylchgrawn
Cymraeg* (published in 1793 and 1794) saw the Revolution itself as a scourge
for Catholicism.[95] In spite of the widespread prejudice against Dissenters suggested by the south-west ballads of 1793, it is this anti-Catholic strain that
Roberts takes up here. He wages a war on what appears at least in part to be
the forces of British Catholicism, who are intent, he claims, 'were they to

receive aid' (line 63), upon bloodletting. The ballad's 1794 date is too early for this to be a reference to the activities of the United Englishmen, an association of radicals with strong links to the United Irish (who were themselves only truly taking shape under that name in the latter part of 1794).[96] It is more probable that the background to the ballad lies with William Pitt's efforts to steer an Irish Catholic Relief Act in 1793, in preparation for the 1800/1801 Acts of Union between Ireland and mainland Britain.[97] Roberts, and the community in which he lived, may also have been aware of the considerable numbers of Catholics living in large English towns including Birmingham, Liverpool and Manchester as the eighteenth century drew to its close. Manchester and Salford, for instance, had a Catholic population of eight per cent in 1793, and Lancashire as a whole was plagued by anti-Catholicism in the 1800s in particular.[98]

An anonymous ballad (no. 6), again dated 1794, also evokes the presence of an 'internal enemy', but shows considerable ambiguity regarding the identity of this foe. Written 'in consideration of the times', it adopts the simple 'hen bennill' metre characteristic of poetry written with a leaning towards home-spun wisdom and moral counsel. It describes with poignant simplicity the succession of happy times and troubled ones, with peace succeeded by war just as birth is by death or laughter by tears. The evoking of the rhythms of existence lends an inevitability to war, yet the poet wishes to advise his listeners to exhibit faithfulness to their country and to avoid criticism of each other (lines 21–32). The 'evil, turbulent men' initially blamed for raising commotion in the homeland (line 23) are here gradually amalgamated with the poem's individual listeners in an effort to impress upon each one the need to examine their conscience and their behaviour, regulating their almost canine urge to 'gibe and judge' ('Cnoi a barnu', line 31) others, driving them into corners in an attempt to outdo them. The poet calls instead for a reformation of manners and behaviour and for repentance before God, his tendency to blame the Britons' own behaviour for their predicament during this period of war indicative of the mood of this ballad corpus as a whole.

The Fishguard invasion (1797): loyalty, identity and the hand of God

The tension between an enemy within and the external forces of Revolutionary France, together with the self-critical soul-searching signalled by the earlier poetry, all come to a head in the ballads produced in the aftermath of the Fishguard invasion in February 1797. Threats of invasion, feared by the ballad writers of north Wales since 1793 (and in previous wars, including the conflict against the American colonies in the 1770s and 1780s), were

Goodwick Sands.

Figure 2. 'Goodwick Sands', from J. Baker, *Picturesque Guide through Wales* (1797)

now realized and, just as Roberts had worried about internal enemies prepared
to lend the French a hand, the inhabitants of Pembrokeshire and neighbouring
Carmarthenshire, in the aftermath of the scare, exhibited angst about the
possibility that local people might have colluded with the enemy. The story
of what happened when four shiploads of soldiers (many of them French
convicts, others Irishmen, some trained soldiers) landed in Cardigan Bay on
22 February 1797 has been revisited by countless commentators and scholars
and is still the subject of widespread debate. As Roland Quinault has suggested,
in one of the most recent explorations of the landing, there was an early streak
of commentary which aimed to deflate the significance of the experience.
Jonathan Lovett, an Englishman present in Pembrokeshire soon after the event,
made a strong case by letter to the duke of Portland on 3 March 1797 that
'some evil minded people [were bent on] lessen[ing] the merits of the Welch
upon the French landing in Pembrokeshire by presenting their numbers as
only two or three hundred and absolutely without *any sort of arms* not even
sticks'.[99] Iolo Morganwg, a confirmed radical, also belittled the invasion and
what he considered the hyperbolic response which it elicited. It was, in his
view, no more than the landing of 'a thimble-full of French men . . . on our
coast'.[100] The Cardiganshire-based brothers of John Jenkins (Ifor Ceri) were

slow to communicate to him what had happened. Jenkins, who was employed as a curate in Whippingham on the Isle of Wight at the time, 'waited with anxiety for every post, after the Country was invaded, but in vain for a Letter from my Brothers', and berated them for 'trifl[ing]' with him.[101] Further north, the ballad writers active around the printing hubs of Wrexham and Oswestry in the north-east, Trefriw in the north-west, and Machynlleth in mid-west Wales, were peculiarly reticent regarding the event. Only two ballads emanated from printing houses in these areas. The anonymous ballad no. 15 has survived only in an imprint produced by Ishmael Davies in Trefriw; records indicate the existence of another imprint by Edward Prichard of Machynlleth which is no longer extant. This poem gives a comprehensive account of the invaders' pranks and, although it is impossible to be certain about its provenance, the detail in itself suggests a more localized inception. The only other ballad on the landing to emanate from the north Wales presses is the work of Richard Roberts (no. 20). Compressed into two stanzas, it relates how a terrifying invasion took place in Pembrokeshire, leading to chaotic scenes of rape and a mass exodus of the region's inhabitants from their homes. The danger, however, was swiftly deflated as soldiers came from England to imprison the French. The poem concludes with an expression of faith in God's ability to conquer 'our' enemies. In view of Richard Roberts's earlier ballads on the Revolution and on the threat to stability presented by internal enemies and by the sin of the Britons more generally, this is a some- what disappointing text, which fails fully to engage with the concept of infiltration from abroad and its consequences (other than the sensationalist claims mentioned) for the community involved.

To find such engagement we must turn to the ballads composed either in Pembrokeshire (Thomas Francis's, no. 21) or in the neighbouring counties of Cardigan and Carmarthenshire (nos. 18, 19, 22, by Nathaniel Jenkin, Phillip Dafydd and George Stephens). These were all printed (almost exclusively by John Evans) in the market town of Carmarthen, some thirty miles from the scene of the landing.[102] Other texts were published anonymously, one with no imprint, but are likely to have been produced in the area (nos. 12, 14, 15). Whereas some observers played down the significance of the invasion, for these poets it was a notable threat to life and limb, from which they were graciously 'delivered' by God. In no instance do the ballads mock the serious- ness of the French's intentions; in this respect they differ from loyalist songs produced in the wake of the sister invasion of Bantry Bay in Ireland, only two months before, in December 1796. In 'General Wonder', an anonymous contemporary piece, the French general, Hoche, is confronted with a host of other abstract 'generals', including 'General gale' who provided a forceful wind to frustrate the plans of the invaders.[103] 'On the late Invasion, 1797', published in *A collection of constitutional songs* (1799–1800), teasingly relives the invasion attempt from the perspective of the French, suggesting that, after long deliberation on 'which way they should steer', they 'at last . . . bethought 'em of our Christmas cheer'. In view of their trite objective of 'lick[ing] their lank lips' and thinking 'to regale / On . . . Carberry mutton and old bottled ale', it is perhaps no surprise that the 'French gluttons' are easily defeated by a benign Saint Patrick, who, with the assistance of Æolus, conjures up a storm to drive them away.[104]

The 1796 Bantry Bay attempt was, of course, an abject failure for the French, and this certainly colours the representation of the event in contemporary song.[105] In spite of the rather jovial tone of some of these loyalist effusions, however, a degree of seriousness prevails. One song, 'The Invasion. (Written in January 1797)', attributes Ireland's deliverance from Hoche's men to a combination of providential winds and the efforts of local people:

> Oh! where was Hood? and where was Howe?
> And where Cornwallis then?
> Where Colpoys, Bridport, or Pellew,
> And all their gallant men?
>
> Nor skill nor courage aught avail
> When providence gainsays;
> The storm arose and closed our ports,
> A mist o'erspread the seas.
>
> For not to feeble mortal man
> Did God his vengeance trust;
> He raised his own tremendous arm –
> All-powerful and all-just.
>
> . . .
>
> The sons of Themis proudly drew
> The sword of Justice bright,
> And thirty thousand Yeomen blades
> Reflected back its light.
>
> Now, firm and bold, her hardy troops
> To Erin's coast repair;
> With ardent zeal they march along,
> Their banners fill the air . . .[106]

In the conspicuous absence of the heroes of the British navy, it is the storm itself to which victory is attributed. Vividly portrayed as an all-engulfing mêlée, its 'billows mounting o'er [the enemy's] heads, / To kiss the bending sky', the moment at which it strikes is one 'When Earth beheld her God'. This interpretation of the Bantry Bay invasion is echoed in one of the Welsh texts to emanate from the Fishguard landing, in what is a relatively rare reference in the ballads to Ireland:

> Nid cryfdwr llongau ar y moroedd
> A'u rhwystrodd mewn i Iwerddon dir,
> Ond gair o'i enau a orchmynnodd,
> "Tyred wyntoedd, na fydd hir!
> Chwytha longau rhai dinistriol,
> Canons mawr a bwlets trwm,
> Powdwr du ac arfau glowion
> Lawr i'r môr fel pelen blwm!"[107]

> (It was not the strength of ships upon the seas
> that prevented them from entering the land of Ireland,
> but a word from His mouth did command,
> "Come, winds, do not be long!
> Blow the ships of the pernicious ones,
> large cannons and heavy bullets,
> black powder and shining weapons
> down into the sea like a lead ball!")

Although storms at sea did not feature in the defeat of the invaders at Fishguard, a belief in God's ability to prevent harm to a population threatened by invasion is echoed in every one of the ballads composed in the wake of the event, and often signalled in the titles, with their ubiquitous references to the Lord's deliverance. It is implied that a near-miraculous agency was at work on the occasion in the description of their surrender in the anonymously-published ballad no. 12:

> Rhyfeddod ar ryfeddod! Ryfeddod daear lawr,
> Wrth weled creulon filwyr yn bwrw'u harfau lawr
> O flaen y Saeson glewion a'r Cymry mwynion triw;
> Dewch, holl drigolion Brydain, i foli'r Seilo byw.[108]

> (Wonder upon wonder! Wonder upon the surface of the earth,
> seeing cruel soldiers putting down their arms
> in front of the valiant English and the noble, loyal Welsh;
> come, all the inhabitants of Britain, to praise the living Siloh.)

In Nathaniel Jenkin's depiction of the events, the Christian faith of the local army, led by parsons and priests and carrying the symbolical armaments of 'the shield of faith and the sword of the Spirit, / and the helmet of tender Salvation' (no. 18, lines 74–5), lends them a masque-like presence in their march to meet the French. Their confidence is evident in their complete lack of fear; God's power in the way in which He makes possible their victory 'without conflict or a fight' (line 93). Like the Syrians of the Old Testament (albeit in a rather less bloody manner), the enemy are rendered powerless. For the Methodist exhorter, Phillip Dafydd, the faithful Britons' cry for God's help pierced the heaven above, whereupon God 'arranged' a host of instruments, foremost among them Lord Cawdor, leader of a six-hundred-strong army against Tate's men.[109] And, even if God's war waging cannot be easily amalgamated with the physical forces of nature (as in Bantry Bay), Phillip Dafydd is at pains to evoke such a phenomenon when he calls to mind the Israelite Barak and prophetess Deborah's song of praise to God for His assistance in defeating the Canaanite Sisera.[110] Thomas Francis, in yet another ballad attributing the victory to God and reducing human agency in its outcome to the action of those who prayed for His assistance, simply evokes the 'storm' in a metaphorical sense.[111]

In their confidence in the power of God to deliver Ireland from the French, Protestant songs published after the Bantry Bay expedition of 1796 present hardly a hint of the complexity of the Irish society thus 'saved'.[112] 'General Wonder' in its insistence on an all-encompassing, universal response draws both 'rich' and 'poor' through a range of emotions in reaction to the event, among them 'disaffection', 'woe', 'dread', 'joy', 'ease', 'horror', 'praise' and 'love', all claimed to have been 'general'. 'The Invasion. (Written in 1797)' ends by expressing a hope that 'never more may foe presume / To dare this Christian land', thus glossing over the acute internal religious tensions within Ireland. In its attempt to perform the same feat, the hope for Ireland in 'On the late Invasion, 1797' is that 'no feuds or discord [may] her united sons sever'. In the effort to claim unity, and to reclaim the term 'united', such a line risks calling to mind the militant United Irish organization, in full flow in 1797, whose response to invasion by French hosts differed widely from that of loyalist Protestant Irishmen. The Fishguard ballads repeatedly affirm their loyalty to king and country, maintaining a staunch Protestant front in reaction to the invasion and eschewing the slightest degree of sympathy towards the French. They also, however, whether wittingly or not, provide a commentary on the tension which surfaced following the invasion, when a number of Protestant Dissenters (mostly Baptists) were accused of connivance with the enemy.

A quatrain from Phillip Dafydd's ballad prompted the Baptist minister William Richards of Lynn to compose a prose tract, *Cwyn y Cystuddiedig*, vigorously defending his brethren from attack. Dafydd had written of his astonishment at the connivance of enlightened men with the French enemy:

Mi ryfeddais fil o weithiau
I fod dynion hardd eu doniau
Gwedi'u dallu mor dywylled,
Yn margenna â'r fath fegeried.[113]

(I have wondered a thousand times
that men of decent moral virtue
should be so greatly blinded
as to bargain with such beggars.)

In a ballad which runs to 220 lines this is only a very brief reference. It none-theless contains an unquestioned assumption of the guilt of the Nonconformists involved, and may well have contributed to the process of prejudicing the local population (potential jurors) in advance of the trial of two of the men taken up by the authorities on suspicion of colluding with the enemy. It was the injustice of this that incensed Richards, who argued 'Peth ciaidd a barbar-aidd, dros ben, yw ceisio duo a rhagfarnu carcharorion cyn y caffo eu hachos ei brofi mewn brawdle, a cheisio rhagfeddiannu y wlad yn eu herbyn; gan na oddef y gyfraith iddynt hwy, druain, gynnyg cyfiawnhau neu amddiffyn eu hunain, cyn eu treial' (It is an extremely cruel and barbarous thing to attempt to blacken and condemn prisoners before their case has been tried in a court of law, and to attempt to prejudice people against them, since the law does not permit them, wretches that they are, the opportunity to justify or defend themselves before their trial).[114] Other ballads do not draw attention to the charge against the two men awaiting trial, and are rather at pains to demonstrate the loyalty of the local population. They make only passing references to the French doctrines of equality and liberty in an effort to diffuse them of any possible attraction to an audience.[115]

The demonstration of loyalty to king and country emerges as one of the prime concerns of the Fishguard ballads. Linda Colley and others have drawn attention to the complexity of the question of identity within the constituent 'countries' of Great Britain during the eighteenth century.[116] The peoples of the Celtic countries, in view of the troubled histories of their relations with England, might well be expected to feel divided loyalties between their love of their native countries and their allegiance to an all-British monarch. Ballads composed in England during the Revolutionary and Napoleonic wars often reduced the British entity to the three nations of England, Scotland and Ireland.[117] Welsh ballad writers and poets were adept at adjusting the perspective to include or exclude their own nation as the case might be, and had been so for some time. Poetry from the 1640s, a period when the official *lingua* of royal and parliamentary declarations emphasized the presence of 'three nations' within the conflict of civil war, shows that, in adapting directly from English balladry, Welsh poets could write in or write out references to their own country. In 'Y Letani Newydd', adapted from the English poem 'A New Litanie', for instance, a derogatory reference to 'Welsh hubbub-men' is deliberately left out.[118] Welsh ballads commemorating recruitment to the regular forces and the militia may well have partially reflected English texts, and often include English-language refrains. Whereas similar refrains in English ballads make no mention of Wales, Welsh poets invariably write Wales into the picture, even when using the (foreign) English language. The English refrain to a ballad by Edward Pugh (no. 4), for instance, runs:

> Brave Welsh and English, Scots and Irish,
> We'll finish them all of hand;
> We'll rise through England, Wales, Scots and Ireland,
> To be under the duke's command.

A corresponding English ballad mentions only 'the British lads of England', almost claiming the British entity in its entirety to the English nation. Like Edward Pugh, Jonathan Hughes in a militia poem originally composed in the mid-1750s (no. 11) mentions 'England and Wales' in the patriotic English-language refrain.

The negotiations of Welsh versus British identities is immediately evident in the Fishguard ballads' titles, several of which make reference to the 'Brytaniaid', 'yr hen Frytaniaid', or the 'Cymry' (Britons, the old Britons or the Welsh). Their audiences would have a legacy of viewing themselves as 'Brutaniaid' or 'Brytaniaid' (Britons), emanating from the 'Brutiau', the medieval chronicle texts which rendered the work of Geoffrey of Monmouth accessible to Welsh audiences. This period, however, brought with it an increasing awareness of the other 'Britain' to which the Welsh, or ancient Britons, must now show their loyalty. A dual identity is clearly signalled in one of the anonymous ballads (no. 12) when the poet mentions Britain under the name 'Ynys Brydain Fawr' (line 31), thus amalgamating the ancient, legendary Welsh name for Britain (Ynys Brydain, the Isle of Britain) with the name of the emerging political entity of 'Prydain Fawr' (Great Britain).[119] The composition of the forces assembled to confront the French is given in detail in the ballad: cavalry led by Lord Cawdor, the Cardiganshire militia and Pembroke and Newport volunteers led by Major Ackland and Colonel Knox, together with sailors, possibly from Solva near St David's, and colliers from the Haverfordwest area. Following these armed men, says the ballad, came 'many a thousand of the Welsh' (line 28); whether or not this number included women (as accounts soon afterwards claimed) is unspecified.[120] These forces, 'the valiant English and the noble, loyal Welsh' (line 35) are all lauded for their gallant efforts. This account of the repelling force suggests that the armed men were viewed as Englishmen, whereas the Welsh were supporting amateurs, an assessment which rings true in view of the linguistic divide between largely Welsh-speaking north Pembrokeshire and the 'Little England' beyond the *Landsker* line.[121] Moreover, the military presence is described as led by prominent landowners, none of whom were native Welshmen, and whose 'otherness' is conveyed by the use of English-language terminology to represent their titles or offices (lord, major, colonel). In its efforts to fuse these two disparate linguistic and national groups into a single force, the ballad displays its anxiety to project a loyalty to Great Britain and to 'the arms of England' (line 56) in the context of the war being fought beyond the confines of Pembrokeshire, maintaining a united front in opposition to the threat posed by 'the old destroyer', France (line 1).

Other poems make similar reference to the duality of the repelling force (no. 14, lines 29, 41–2), but not all are as clearly concerned with commemorating the part played by the Anglicized establishment and the English component of Pembrokeshire life to the defeat of the French. A ballad by Nathaniel Jenkin (no. 18) presents self-reflective and semi-autobiographical features, most notably in its final stanza, where the poet refers to his own predicament:

> Er bod llawer wedi gweithio
> Ar y testun hwn, rwy'n tystio,
> Cymerwch hwn gan hen ddyn trwstan
> Pymtheg mlwydd a thrugain oedran.
>   Â'r hen awen wedi rhewi
>   A Nathaniel
>   Yn ddwys dawel yn distewi;
>   Ond bod y bywyd eto'n para –
>   Nid oes hefyd
> Ond afiechyd yn fynycha'.[122]

> (Although several have laboured
> on this topic, I declare,
> take this from a bungling old man
> aged seventy-five years.
> The old muse has frozen
> and Nathaniel,
> sober and quiet, holds his peace;
> but that life yet remains –
> there is, however,
> only ill health most frequently.)

Figure 3. Thomas Rowlandson, 'Castellnewydd Emlyn [1794]'

In his awareness of the multiple offerings on the subject of the invasion, Nathaniel Jenkin displays his peculiarly personal interest in singing on the topic. This is further shown at a point in the text where the third-person narrative of the repelling forces of 'hen Frytaniaid' (old Britons, line 52) is momentarily exchanged for a first-person plural account ('Seeing us so confident / and our truthful utterance giving us such comfort', lines 81–2). This intensifies the impression of Nathaniel's involvement: he adds to our knowledge of the composition of the local Welsh presence which confronted Tate's men in noting that 'zealous people' from his home town of Newcastle Emlyn were among their number (line 64). Although, aged seventy-five, as he acknowledges in the final stanza, he is perhaps unlikely to have been present in this host, his reference to his own home town suggests how local people (from beyond Pembrokeshire itself) invested themselves in the event and its aftermath, an impression corroborated by William Richards's vivid account of Thomas John and his neighbours' movements from the moment they heard of the invasion until the French had been safely incarcerated in Haverfordwest on 24 February.[123] As well as satisfying an impetus to tell a story which touched his own community, Nathaniel Jenkin also plays the role of a wise exhorter, passing on his sense of the danger of sin, and his particular concern for 'the kindred of Gomer' (line 102) – a name which, unlike that of the 'Brytaniaid', refers uniquely to the Welsh people. The opening stanzas of the ballad cry for an improvement in the morals of the inhabitants of Wales before whom

God's rod is to be seen in punishment for long sinfulness. These stanzas show the influence of the popular Welsh poet and vicar, Rees Prichard, whose homely and well-loved poems on simple metres (including the 'hen bennill' which forms the initial quatrain of each stanza in Nathaniel Jenkin's ballad) made frequent references to God's impending judgement together with exhortations to enhanced godliness.[124] In spite of a nod to the conventions of loyalist balladry in the penultimate stanza, the note upon which Nathaniel Jenkin's poem closes tends to corroborate Quinault's view that 'It was primarily self-interest, rather than loyalty to "king and country", which made the people of Pembrokeshire oppose the French'.[125]

The anonymous ballad no. 15 is the most vivid account of the invasion preserved in Welsh balladry, written on a brisk metre which contrasts with the lilting movement of the lines in Nathaniel Jenkin's poem. Although it places itself within a familiar framework which envisages warfare as divine punishment, it soon launches into the narrative proper, describing the antics of the French themselves in a way which suggests the proximity of its author to the location of the invasion (lines 13–30). Balancing this portrayal of mindless destruction by the French is the response of the local population, to whom the defeat of the invaders is almost exclusively attributed. The poet has little to say of the military, whom he reduces to 'a few soldiers' (line 43), utterly blanking from the record the names and titles of the nobles in command. Instead, he portrays 'a true army' (line 48) made up of ordinary inhabitants armed with 'scythes and sickles' and 'pitchforks' (lines 45, 46), alongside the colliers of south Pembrokeshire with their 'pointed sticks' (line 53), who are here easily absorbed into the fabric of a popular resistance in spite of the linguistic divide. The rallying cry of this army is 'Duw gadwo'r brenin!' (God save the king!, line 47), and the ballad writer revels in the all-British commendation of the Welsh for their bravery and loyalty:

> Gwych gwŷr sir Benfro, am fileinio,
>   A ddarfu g'weirio'r gwaith.
> Trwy Frydain cawsant glod,
>   Wych Gymry, am eu bod
> Yn bur i'r Coron, wŷr howddgara',
>   Yn rhwydda' dan y rhod . . .[126]

(it was the gallant Pembrokeshire men, by being resolute,
that set the matter to rights.
Throughout Britain they were praised,
noble Welsh, because they were faithful
to the Crown, most willing men,
readiest under the firmament . . .)

Loyalty to Britain is actively proclaimed here alongside a pride in Welshness which demonstrates the possibility of a dual identity and allegiance. At the same time, this sense of pride sets aside the controversy regarding Nonconformist collusion with the enemy suggested in Phillip Dafydd's poem, and overrides the sometimes heavy religiosity found in the other ballads.

The ballads composed in the aftermath of the Fishguard invasion thus display a variety of viewpoints, even while they are all concerned to some degree with portraying a community loyal to the British crown. Some do this by deferring the victory to the military, while others claim it for the people with an astounding confidence that has an appealing freshness. Others yet again, sometimes prefaced with a psalm of praise (nos. 14, 19, 21), highlight the divine agency of God in the victory, sometimes severely reducing the narrative, as in Thomas Francis's ballad (no. 21) in which the account of the event is limited to the first five stanzas in a twelve-stanza ballad. Many of these, even, are thin on the ground in terms of factual narrative: stanza 4, for example, is devoted to imagining the mayhem which might have occurred (the murder of children, the rape of wives, and the killing of menfolk by the sword, besides the takeover of the land by the invaders) had God not intervened for the benefit of the British people. It is the relationship of his audience with God, not their worldly loyalties, which most concerns Thomas Francis, as he builds a text firmly rooted in biblical territory. He shows the dire consequences of sin, arrogance and self-aggrandizement, ushering his listeners instead into the safety of a metaphorical ark.

Taking up arms: ballads of the militia, the volunteers and the army (1793–1815)

For Thomas Francis, war is 'a kind of wise providence / above the knowledge of men', ordained by God 'to answer some end or other' (no. 21, lines 113–14, 116). As war against Republican France loomed, Welsh ballad singers turned their attention to the experience of taking up arms, not only among those recruited to join the regular army or militia, but also within individual communities, where voluntary corps were raised with increasing ardour as the conflict progressed. Roland Quinault has argued that the experience of the 1797 invasion gave rise to increased volunteering in the Fishguard area. The effusions of Dafydd Evan Morgan from the Carmarthenshire parish of Tre-lech and Betws on the topic of the Teifi-side voluntary forces lends weight to his claim. Dafydd Morgan's ballad (no. 24) portrays as the work of God the deliverance of the Welsh from the French invaders, who, like the renegade Belshazzar, were found wanting when weighed in His scales. Whereas the ordinary people who defeated them were simply 'a few weak soldiers' (line 35), used by God as instruments, the nobles who led them are portrayed as having been moved in their hearts by the Lord to bring about victory. It is as an appendage to printed eulogies of Lord Cawdor and others that Dafydd Morgan offers this ballad, wishing to make known the names of Cardiganshire and Carmarthenshire leaders such as Colonel Lloyd of Bronwydd, Major Brigstocke of Blaen-pant, Captain Parry of Gernos and Captain Bowen of Waunifor, all of whom may have been inspired by Cawdor's example.[127] His deferential stance towards these men is suggested in his humble acknowledgement that if he were 'endowed with better talents' he 'would sing more clearly' in their praise (lines 141–2). Two 1799 ballads by George Stephens (nos. 22 and 23), the first of which makes reference to Fishguard, turn to the subject of their author at the end, playing with the poetic conceit of withholding the poet's name while yet edging ever-closer towards revealing his identity. This, together with the metre of the ballads, suggests that George Stephens may have been a more prolific poet within the oral ballad tradition than his small number of printed ballads would lead us to suppose.[128] In ballad no. 23, which eulogizes the same volunteer leaders as those praised by Dafydd Morgan, he closes by stating his expectations of financial reward and his hope that his humble offering will not weigh too heavily upon anyone (lines 77–88). His words suggest his efforts to carve out for himself a career as a ballad writer, using the medium of print and building up a repertoire centred on the increased mobilization in his neighbourhood. It is a reminder, perhaps, that it was not simply radical poets who stood back from revealing their identity in print. As in the case of pamphleteering, loyalist ballad writers were also sometimes reluctant to reveal their names in full, perhaps out of modesty or prudence.[129] A comparable example of this kind of reticence is found in the case of an English poet writing about a review of the Kent volunteers by George III in 1799. The poet explains that he used 'A fictitious name . . . to screen himself till his composition on this most charming subject had stood the public investigation'.[130] Reticence or humility may have been caused by different factors in the case of the two authors in question here: George Stephens aims at the cautious self-projection of a poet emerging into print, whereas Dafydd Morgan (who openly attaches his name to his printed ballad) is more likely to be conditioned by social deference.

In fact, praise of the gentry, whose virtue has led them to 'unite entirely / in order to sustain society / in the cause of our kingdom' (no. 24, lines 129–31), is a striking feature of Dafydd Morgan's ballad. Only briefly does he turn to the ordinary men who have enlisted in the corps, praising them for their 'virtuous manners' and 'military knowledge' (lines 158, 159) and wishing that they should possess the grace 'to remember their end' (line 178). The question of obsequiousness towards the leaders of the militia and volunteers is an important factor in locating the viewpoints of various ballads regarding militarization in this period. Was militarization along the lines provided by volunteering and, from 1808, the local militia, an opportunity for poetical panegyric (a vital aspect of Welsh tradition) in a more popular vein, and if so, does this help gauge the character of popular loyalism among Welsh communities? Or did the ballad writers show a more complex range of attitudes towards volunteer corps and militia membership, with corresponding consequences for our reading of popular sentiment? Unlike some of the other themes treated by the ballad writers in this period (including actual invasion and the execution of monarchs, at least within living memory), the militia had a pedigree as a topic that was both reasonably long and fairly accessible within Welsh balladry.[131] The earlier Welsh 'militia ballads' date from the Seven Years' War and relate to the regular militia, which had been reformed in 1757. With its use of ballots to fill its ranks, offering better-off recruits the opportunity to pay for a substitute, this was clearly a very different institution from both the volunteers (active from 1794, and re-established under new regulations in 1803) and the local militia (a less democratic replacement for the latter corps, put in place in 1808).[132] It was open to abuse and met with resistance, whereas membership of the volunteers and local militia was often eagerly sought.[133] Ballads relating to the regular militia have a continued relevance during 1793–1815, since the institution remained active throughout the period and ballad singers continued to produce songs to and about its members, alongside songs (such as Dafydd Morgan's) fêting the voluntary forces. The dividing lines between the various types of corps are at times very faint, with poetry from a regular militia context subjected to free adaptation into what may be a volunteering context in some cases.

The earliest militia ballads suggest that there was a notable degree of social resistance to taking up arms.[134] This is the case in a 1756 ballad by Jonathan Hughes, a poet from the Llangollen area in Denbighshire, which addresses the old-style 'trained bands' (no. 11). The poem ran into repeated reincarnations during the course of the eighteenth century, initially as a 'militia' ballad in 1763.[135] It remained a viable text as late as the mid-1790s, with only the minor substitution of 'Lewis' (the French monarch Louis XV) for 'anghred' (atheism, line 44) to render it contemporary. Its reference to the French as '[g]wŷr ffri' (free men, line 7) may even have accrued added ironic resonance upon its reissue. No change was made to a section which describes the typical 1750s response to militia armament, a fact which may suggest the continued relevance of Hughes's riposte to it:

Rhai ddywed fel hyn, yn swrth ac yn syn,
Fod ymladd yn ddychryn rhy ddwys;
Ond dychryn mwy drud pe doent yma i gyd –
Dau mwy fydde'n penyd a'n pwys.[136]

(Some say like this, wearily and in fright,
that fighting is too awful a terror;
but there would be a more dire alarm should they all come here –
twice as great would our tribulation and burden be.)

The song's English-language refrain strikes a confident, patriotic note with its challenge to '*the French in every town*', as it encourages its militia host to '*be merry, very glad, / In the face of our mad enemies*' (lines 19–20, 23). Perhaps inspired by English-language militia songs (a song with a comparable refrain was produced in nearby Shropshire in the same period),[137] the use of English within this text is a feature found elsewhere within the body of Welsh militia songs. It suggests both the essential foreignness of the armament process for the Welsh and the effort made by the poets to forge a new pan-British identity among their audiences.[138] English-language militia songs were created in Wales itself by the late eighteenth century, often in border regions. They typically fêted corps' noble founders and their officers, revelled in descriptions of the men's handsomeness and consequent effect on the ladies, threw in the odd derogatory reference to Jacobins, or set a challenge to 'these blustering blades of France' on patriotic tunes such as 'The Vicar of Bray'.[139] Welsh ballad writers of the latter eighteenth century freely used English vocabulary and phrases in militia and volunteer songs in a way which may simply have reflected a growing identification with the parallel processes of militarization and gradual Anglicization within Welsh communities. There is a natural vividness to the language of the following stanza from a ballad to a voluntary corps composed by John Thomas of Penffordd-wen, the adaptation of English verbs (roar, exercise) fitting into the pattern of the rhyme with an ease worthy of some twenty-first-century linguistic corruptions:

Mae bechgyn glân Trefaldwyn – O! mor *neat*, &c.,
Mewn coch yn gwic eu cychwyn, &c.;
A'r ffeifs a'r drums yn roario
A'r arms yn hardd ddisgleirio,
A nhwythe yn acseseisio
A'u cariad yn yspïo – O! mor *neat*, &c.[140]

(The fair lads of Montgomeryshire – Oh! how smart, &c.,
in red are quick to stir, &c.;
and the fifes and drums roaring
and the arms shining beautifully
and they exercising
and their sweethearts looking on – Oh! how smart, &c.)

In ballad no. 28 the regular county militias of all twelve Welsh counties are praised, stanza-by-stanza and although it is only the lads of Denbighshire that are considered to be Englishmen ('Saeson', line 51), in view of the Anglicized nature of their border-land county, the descriptions of most of the corps end with a rousing final line in English, expressing the stark determination of the men to 'kill the foes', to 'fire on', or to 'bravely fight for George the Third' and the Prince of Wales.[141] Somewhat incongruously, however, Welsh legend and lore maintain a hold upon this ballad: it evokes the story of Caswallon's pursuit of Julius Caesar, as preserved in the Welsh Triads, and names 'Milfford Hafen' as a possible site for an enemy landing. In the latter case, although it rejects the Welsh name for Milford Haven, Aberdaugleddau, it makes the connection between the port and battles for Protestant and Welsh supremacy in the tradition of prophetic song.[142] The popularity of this material, set to a simple, sing-song metre, is suggested by the fact that George Stephens may have borrowed several lines from it for one of his ballads (no. 23). The bathos of the final stanza, which seems to hinge these brave men's prospects on the hope of a favourable wind (presumably to blow away the enemy before contact is achieved) appears to be unintentional.

Whereas ballad no. 28 suggests a readiness among Welsh audiences to embrace a popular patriotism, other songs saw militia membership as a heavy duty, even while embracing it. Robert Davies's song to the Denbighshire regular militia (no. 37) may be a reworking of an earlier song to the militias of Wales in their entirety, now adapted to include two stanzas celebrating the leadership of the Denbighshire corps.[143] Sung on the doleful tune of 'Trymder' (Heaviness), it evokes the pain of separation, as militia members, whose voices present the ballad in the first-person plural, leave Wales for London and 'the depths of England'. Reminiscent of the way in which earlier ballads represented the cause against the militia, the song shows the effect of mobilization on families and friends left behind, asking them to pray on their men's behalf.[144] In so doing, they will provide the soldiers with a 'mindful commemoration' (line 80), vital since the latter will be incapable of singing while away from their parishes (line 81). The concept of 'losing voice' expressed here (in a poem which contains no hint of the macaronic nature of some of the other militia ballads) has a peculiar resonance. The poem ends soberly commending the militia men to God's keeping in the next world, thus enacting the finality of military service for countless numbers of men during this period.[145] This is a climax building on the gradual withdrawal of the certainty of return in the final stanzas of the poem, where 'when we come back' (line 84) mutates into the much more tentative 'who knows . . . that we may not come / back alive?' (lines 87–8).

The heavy burden of joining up is explored in two ballads associated with the figure of James Turberville (Siemsyn Twrbil). These texts present a different angle on Welsh balladry, since they are closely linked to an oral ballad tradition, of which there is sadly very little remaining evidence. According to the historian D. Rhys Phillips:

> At the end of the Eighteenth century, no itinerant bard in Glamorgan was better known than James Turberville, the bearer of a celebrated Norman-Welsh name. While roaming around Llangyfelach, he was pressed for military service, served in the wars on the Continent, and died as a prisoner in the fortress of Sedan, 1812.[146]

Phillips's reference to Llangyfelach elucidates an undated ballad text published in Trefriw by Ishmael Davies (no. 5), which describes the recruitment of an unnamed young man into the army of the Duke of York at Cowbridge in Glamorgan. Further versions of the ballad have been preserved, containing variations and interpolations of the kind to be expected where transmission occurs through oral channels. A quotation from the ballad by Phillips includes a reference to Turberville by the familiar form of his Christian name, 'Siemsyn', but Phillips's evidence contradicts the trend in modern literary scholarship of attributing the ballad to Turberville. He suggests instead that it was the work of a fellow-itinerant poet, Shôn ap Ifan.[147] A second ballad relating to the experience of taking up arms is attributed to Turberville. 'Milisia Morgannwg' (The Glamorgan Militia) is of an uncertain date, and may well not fall within the chronological range of this anthology.[148] Read alongside ballad no. 5, which has here been tentatively dated to 1793, it provides intimate testimony to the experience of joining the militia, something that is unique within the Welsh ballad corpus.[149] The ballads share a first-person singular narrative perspective and suggest a strong attachment to their main protagonist's home county of Glamorgan. 'Milisia Morgannwg' recounts the history of what is most probably the regular militia of Glamorgan, whose training takes them out of their region and to large-scale meetings involving other militia corps. In the midst of all, the poet insists that 'Gwlad Morgannwg sy'n cario'r dydd' (It is the land of Glamorgan that carries the day). Ballad no. 5 shows its narrator singing farewell to his native parish of Llangyfelach in Glamorgan, having been recruited into the army in nearby Cowbridge. As the ballad was recycled and redistributed in later years, the sense of taking leave of one's home town became central to its appeal: its title is often given in later imprints as 'Ffarwél i Langyfelach Lon' (Farewell to Merry Llangyfelach).[150] Another feature of both ballads is the interest in the process of recruitment, or in the point where an ordinary man makes the commitment to become a soldier. This process is only sketchily described in 'Milisia Morgannwg', which portrays a bewildered young man's arrival in a military camp ('tre o ganfas', a canvass town), where he is persuaded to remain by the flattering welcome of a group of noblemen. In ballad no. 5, the young man's enlistment to the Light Dragoons is prompted by the pomp and ceremony of the recruitment process: the music of fifes and drums, together with the ready exchange of money, lifts him out of the drabness of everyday life, and makes him the object of admiration to the womenfolk present at the scene. Yet, in both cases, the allurement of recruitment time is soon replaced by an awareness of the hardship of military life, lived ''n annedwydd ar ben y mynydd / Mewn tre o ganfas' (unhappily on the hilltop / in a canvass town, 'Milisia Morgannwg') or spent training under 'heavy duty' ('*duty* caled', no. 5, line 18) in London, in preparation for embarking for the Continent. The attitude of the female onlookers to the recruitment of the men and their subsequent disappearance from the community is also shown to be ambivalent, upon reflection. The women who greet the Glamorgan militia when they enter the town of Cardiff ('Milisia Morgannwg') are a mixed bunch of the happy and the sad, some of whom the poet envies for their freedom, others who are admitted to be adversely affected by the loss of their menfolk (''n troi mewn trafel bob nos a dydd', wandering in care every night and day). In ballad no. 5, the initial euphoria of the women upon seeing their men raised into the ranks of the military is questioned by the literary device placed at the end of the poem:

> Os gofyn neb pwy wnaeth y gân,
> Dywedwch chwi mai merch fach lân
> Sydd yn dymuned nos a dydd
> I'w hannwyl gariad gael rhodio'n rhydd.[151]

> (If anyone asks who made the song,
> tell them that it was a fair little lass
> who wishes night and day
> that her dear love should be able to walk free.)

This attempt to claim, in a woman's voice, the authorship of a poem which has throughout been narrated in the voice of a male protagonist is perhaps best seen as a spurious attempt to write in the responses of the women left at home to this story of military recruitment rather than as a further complicating factor in the question of the poem's authorship.[152] It suggests how this poem may have affected different audiences in various ways as it evolved and circulated within the community in Glamorgan and beyond. The soldier's ambivalent conclusion regarding military service – that, having joined up he may now decide for himself which is best, his home country or distant ones (lines 23–4) – was clearly open to a variety of interpretations. In view of the story of Turberville's own death on the Continent, it speaks volubly of the lure of change to a young man and the bitterness of the realization that enlistment, in the heat of the moment, was a decision badly made.[153]

Poets in north Wales were equally aware of the allure of militarization. In an undated poem which probably belongs to the nineteenth century, Robert Morris, a Baptist from Caernarfonshire, addresses the militia of Gwynedd, away from Wales on active duty (no. 38). This song is largely one of consolation to those remaining behind, acknowledging the pain of separation, praising the Welsh for their part in the defence of the realm (lines 49–50), encouraging the men's reliance in providence, and looking forward to peace. Yet, even though Robert Morris's evident intention is to reconcile his listeners with the realities of warfare, he also shows a certain discernment about the trappings of war: the appeal of smart, red uniforms, and of the rousing music of drums and pipes (lines 73–82). Elsewhere, these trappings are fêted. For Griffith Williams (Gutyn Peris), commemorating the advancement of the Caernarfonshire militia, who were promoted a rifle corps in 1812 in recognition of their dedicated contribution to the military, the changes which accompanied this promotion are seen as a cause for celebration (ballad no. 33). Williams lists the change in uniform, custom, arms, way of life and name (lines 25–36). Notably, he sees the process of advancement as one in which the bondage of 'a restricted scope' is exchanged for 'an ardent course', as the men's increased investment in the defence of their country leads them onto a path controlled by their personal passions alone. A manuscript copy of this ballad in its author's own hand provides brief notes to accompany the first stanza, in which a number of the (former militia) corps's members are named. These notes link them to their homes: Officer Edwards hails from Nanhoron, Captain Jones from Cefn y coed, Master Hughes from Penmynydd, and Master Price is described as 'nai i Humphreys Rhyd lanfair' (nephew to Humphreys, Rhyd Lanfair). Although these notes did not find their way into the printed ballad, the fact that the poet conceived of the men in these terms suggests one of the reasons why militia ballads interested audiences. These men are now in Ireland, and greeted from their home county. Some may have already evolved in their personalities beyond the recognition of their neighbours of old; the very fact that they are now known by military titles rather than in the traditional Welsh way (linking them either to their household name or to better-known relatives) distances them and confers upon them a new identity. Making the connection between their fame and their beginnings (as in the manuscript notes) ensures the involvement of the audience for this ballad in the process of militarization.

Naming individual soldiers is a prime feature of ballad no. 29, published in 1810, and once again the work of Robert Morris. This time, we return to a ballad dedicated to a volunteering force rather than a regular militia or indeed an army corps (as in nos. 5, 11, 33, 37 and 38). Morris fills two and a half stanzas on the brisk but lengthy metre of 'Belisle March' with the names of the members of this corps, showing a detailed knowledge which suggests that he may have used an official, published military list as a source.[154] Like such lists, Morris also stops short of naming the most ordinary members of the corps, even though he describes these men as 'faithful old friends, / ones very dear to me' (lines 61–2), claiming lack of time as an excuse. Yet, having regaled his audience with the names of the more prominent members of the corps, he then turns his attention to offer the ordinary members a word or two of advice on how to conduct themselves during training, cautioning them against grumbling, moaning and complaining, and explaining that:

> Os ŷnt yn gwasgu wrth eich dysgu,
>   Rhaid iddynt felly fod;
> Mae eu swyddau hwy fel chwithau
>   A'u rhwymau dan y rhod.[155]

> (If they are harsh while teaching you,
> they must be so;
> their offices like yours
> have obligations under the heavens.)

The men's boon in joining the corps lies in their involvement in the spectacle of volunteering, which grants them a status as 'The new servants of George the Third' (line 125) and puts them at the centre of attention in training exercises and parades through local villages.[156] The military music sweeps all before it, with nature itself adding the voices of thunder claps and echoing rocks to an orchestra of sound (lines 97–120). The vivid picture given of the effect of military music on the Caernarfonshire parish of Llanbeblig shows that Robert Morris, unlike his counterpart Dafydd Morgan in south Wales, is concerned not with the elevation of the county's great and good but with the effect of militarization on ordinary people. His ballad shows the entire community's relationship with the process and is significantly less deferential. Although it retains a framework of reverence, acknowledging that every individual must fall into the position given him by birthright (lines 77–8), the ballad's evocation of the excitement of local militarization means that it offers evidence, keenly sought by historians, of the reasons for volunteering.[157]

War-reporting (1794–1815)

Poets writing in 1815, when Napoleon's capture finally brought more than twenty years of war to an end, make reference to the physical distance of their audiences from scenes of battle. A ballad by Thomas Jones (no. 36) insists on the huge number of casualties at Waterloo, urging his listeners not to doubt him even though they are in Wales and not in Belgium (lines 77–8). Another anonymous ballad states:

> Nid oes fawr tu fewn i Gymru,
> Yn gwybod beth yw cael eu sathru,
> Gan y gelynion ffyrnig creulon,
> Sy'n hiraethu am waed yn gyfan.[158]

> (Not many within Wales
> know what it is to be trampled upon
> by the fierce, cruel enemy,
> thirsting for blood.)

In spite of the large-scale militarization brought about by recruitment to militia and volunteer forces and notwithstanding the invasion episode of 1797, this statement doubtless holds true for many communities throughout Wales. Welsh exploits in the face of the French threat were in no way comparable to the experiences of soldiers and civilians drawn into the conflict in Continental Europe or indeed in the Ireland of 1798, and so there are no songs corresponding to those vaunting the heroism of the rebel Irishmen, for instance. English-language Irish texts arising from the 1798 rebellion abound in imagery of a brutal, masculine heroism, which takes as reference points the classical figures of Caesar and Alexander the Great, the Celtic warrior-hero, Arthur, and biblical warriors such as David and Joshua, and evoke the ritual drinking of the soldiers in a manner reminiscent of Old Irish society. They are often brutal in their portrayal of murder and execution, even when depicting the death of their own heroes, foremost among them the 'blessed priest', Father Murphy.[159]

In the absence of a vivid experience of the violence and devastation of war,
Welsh ballad writers were largely confined to the role of reporting on the
commotion of war in Continental Europe, playing the part of newsmongers
in spreading the word about battles fought on land and sea. In a period which
saw an increased production and circulation of newspapers, with Wales particularly well-served by the border-town journals of Hereford, Shrewsbury
and Chester, the ballad writers were simultaneously aware of the papers as
sources of information and fearful of their hold on their own audiences.[160]
As far westward as Ystrad in Cardiganshire, the diarist John Davies had access
to the Chester-printed Welsh journal, *Y Geirgrawn*, in 1796, and admitted in
his entry for 30 November 1797 to have 'little done except reading newspapers'
all day.[161] On other occasions, in spite of the radical leaning of Davies's reading
(he copied songs from *Y Geirgrawn* and notes that he spent time on 31 December
1798 'making a pair of Pocket book Clasps and reading the Age of reason'),
he would go to church to celebrate 'A Day of Publick Thanksgiving'.[162] Both
these phenomena – newspaper reading and Church celebratory dates – are
subject to attack by Welsh ballad writers. A 1794 ballad by Richard Roberts
(no. 8), a poet whom we have already seen was fearful of the spread of radical
ideas among his fellow-Welshmen, suggests that news culture could be viewed
as a particularly dangerous phenomenon:

> Mae'r papur newydd bob yn ail dydd
> (Hyd y gwledydd beunydd bydd)
> Yn dweud fod rhai dan glo
> A'r lleill yn rhodio'n rhydd.
> Nid gwir yw'r cwbl, rwyf i'n meddwl,
> A roed yn fanwl ynddo fe –
> Mae anwiredde ar dro
> Yn llithro i'r un lle.[163]

> (The newspaper every other day
> (it goes daily throughout the lands)
> says that some are imprisoned
> and others walk free.
> Not everything, I think,
> that has been detailed in it
> is true – falsehoods now and again
> slip into that same place.)

Roberts's reference to newspaper claims that some are 'imprisoned' while
others 'walk free' suggests a concern about the influence of the papers on
the ideological battle between radicals and loyalists. He is anxious about the

message of political radicals whom he sees as intent on encouraging ordinary people to take up principles of liberty on the model of those adopted in France. Roberts also maintains that finding out the latest news from the war has become an obsession among his compatriots, threatening their faith in God's ability to rule events in the human world. Conditioned by the urge to inquire continuously (line 37) they are plunging into secularism, lured by voices recounting contrasting news of success and failure. Richard Roberts is not alone among the ballad writers in expressing concern about the effect of military success on the British psyche. In a ballad commemorating the victory of John Jervis in a crucial battle against the Spanish fleet in February 1797, Edward Pugh also attacks the celebratory culture which basks in the glory of human victories, forgetting that they are all in fact attributable to God:

> Nid sŵn tincian clychau na hunan chwyddiadau
>   (Mae'n dost fod fath bethau'n cael bod)
> Yn lle gweddi howddgara' a diolch hyfryda'
>   I'r Arglwydd Dduw'n benna' sy'n bod.[164]

> (Neither the sound of ringing bells nor the puffing up of ourselves
> (it is pitiful that such things are allowed to exist)
> in place of the sweetest prayer and the loveliest thanks
> to the Lord God almighty.)

The comments of these two ballad writers suggest a degree of unease regarding both the manner of reporting military and naval victories and the way in which such victories were subsequently celebrated. For both poets, a failure to set the conflicts of the period in the context of God's providence was a crucial flaw.

There is no doubt that, in spite of the misgivings suggested by Richard Roberts, the culture of war-reporting did leave its mark on Welsh balladry. Earlier ballad writers had limited access to knowledge about naval battles or military campaigns. In as recent a conflict as the American War of Independence, ballads responding directly to specific battles were rare, even though Welsh ballad writers sang over fifty songs on the subject of the war and even though newspapers were already increasingly available during the first half of the 1770s.[165] Within the period 1793–1815, however, a modest number of ballads relating to specific heroes, battles or campaigns have been preserved. They begin with the 1793 and 1794 campaigns of the Duke of York in Flanders, proceed to the naval battles which brought lords Howe, Jervis and Nelson to fame in 1794, 1797 and 1805 respectively, and end with the huge upheavals of the Napoleonic campaigns in mainland Europe during 1812–15. Exploration of the nature of the portrayal of war in these ballads shows a gradually increasing interest in news and in its accurate representation as the period progressed.

The Duke of York (1793, 1794)

The ballads reporting on the campaigns of the Duke of York belong to the earliest years of the two decades of war in which Britain and large parts of Continental Europe became embroiled in the 1790s. The ballad writers appear to be aware that they are entering a new period of uncertainty as the fighting begins, Robert Roberts noting:

> Ni bu ers oesoedd, hir flynyddoedd,
> Mo'r fath ryfeloedd cyhoedd cas . . .[166]

> (There have not been for ages, many years,
> such notorious, cruel wars . . .)

It may be the novelty of war which accounts for the lack of generic clarity in a ballad by Edward Pugh (no. 4) which is part recruitment song and part news ballad. Its reporting on the heroism of the Duke of York aids the ballad's effort to engender support for the war effort, as do its references to the dangers of not responding in kind to the French ('In the kingdom of France / there are countless enemies, unrestricted; / the duke and his army are defeating them / and preventing them from entering our country', lines 9–12) and its jingoistic English refrain, which carefully ensures a place for the Welsh among the other British nations involved in the defence of the realm.[167] Turning to consider the Welsh soldiers already on the Continent in the duke's army, Edward Pugh offers a striking description of Welsh blood flowing over French territory (lines 73–4). Unlike the later ballad writers and singers, who wish to highlight the distance between their audience's experiences and the carnage dominating Continental Europe, Pugh attempts to map the Welsh onto the foreign territory of the war, describing them as 'the Welsh French-men'. Rather than bringing the news to his audience, it is as if he were taking his audience, metaphorically and through their intimate connection with their fellow-Welshmen abroad, to the scene of the news. The process of mapping the audience onto foreign territory is enhanced in the ballad's description of one of the key moments of the duke's campaign in Flanders during 1793, the successful siege of the north-eastern French town of Valenciennes. Edward Pugh renders the place-name as both 'Valenseina' and 'tre' Caerseina' (lines 26, 39): the latter is based on the Welsh formula for naming walled towns from the period of the Roman conquest of Britain, using 'Caer-' as a prefix.

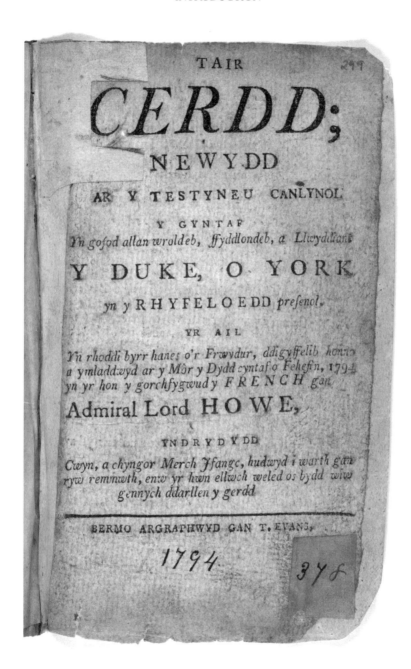

TAIR

CERDD;

NEWYDD

AR Y TESTYNEU CANLYNOL.

Y GYNTAF

Yn gosod allan wroldeb, ffyddlondeb, a Llwydiant

Y DUKE, O YORK

yn y RHYFELOEDD *presenol.*

YR AIL

*Yn rhoddi byrr hanes o'r Frwydur, ddigyffelib honno
a ymladdwyd ar y Môr y Dydd cyntaf o Fehefin,* 1794
yn yr hon y gorchfygwud y FRENCH *gan*

Admiral Lord HOWE,

YN DRYDYDD

*Cwyn, a chyngor Merch Jfangc, hudwyd i warth gan
rywe remmwth, enw yr hwn ellwch weled os bydd wiwe
gennych ddarllen y gerdd*

BERMO ARGRAPHWYD GAN T. EVANS.

1794   378

Figure 4. Title page of a ballad pamphlet including poems on the Duke of York's Flanders campaign and on Lord Howe's Glorious First of June victory (nos. 9 and 10)

The coining of the name furthers the ballad's imaginary colonization of this corner of Continental Europe.

The portrayal of the duke himself suggests a colossal presence with both paternal and youthfully heroic attributes. As he saves his men from the fire, he is a 'radiant, flourishing scion' (line 90) who has no care for his own safety or indeed his life. The second ballad devoted to the duke's exploits, the work of Robert Roberts (no. 9), echoes this portrayal throughout, not least in a vivid description of an episode relating to the duke's escape from his enemies across the Espierres brook (lines 49–60).[168] An officer who accompanied him at the time wrote a poem commemorating the escape and praising the duke for his negotiation of the stream, describing him as 'a second Leander' who 'beat back the billows' and 'plunged in the tide' in order to cross.[169] Although a search for further poetry commemorating this event has not proved fruitful, Robert Roberts's ballad suggests how this story circulated, with his use of the device of *sangiadau* (interpolations) which draw attention to the miraculous behaviour and deliverance of the duke on the occasion. These *sangiadau* appear to mimic the possible response of the ballad's audience:

> Gwych ryfelwr, meitha' milwr,
> Concwerwr, lladdwr llu.
> Bu lawer batel heb dynnu'i fwties
> *(Mae'r hanes heno am hyn)*;
> I lawr tan draed, roedd gwŷr mewn gwaed –
> *Mae'r siarad yma'n syn.*
> Fe gadwodd Duw ei fywyd
> Er bod mewn penyd pur,
> A'r plwm o'u cwmpas fel y cenllysg,
> Fawr derfysg arfau dur.[170]

> (. . . a brilliant warrior, the wisest soldier,
> a conqueror, a killer of a host.
> He has been through many a battle without taking his boots off
> *(the story about this is here tonight)*;
> down underfoot, there were men in blood –
> *there is stunned talk here.*
> God protected his life
> although he was in great peril,
> with the lead around them like hail,
> the great tumult of steel weapons.) (My emphasis.)

Reports of the duke's campaigns appeared in Welsh in *Y Cylchgrawn Cynmraeg* under columns headed 'Arwyddion yr Amserau' and 'Newyddion' (Signs of the Times and News), but they were very general accounts of his progress, lacking in colourful detail of the kind found in Robert Roberts's ballad.[171] The London newspapers of the period likewise make no mention of this story. It does not feature in reports from *The London Chronicle* on 20 May, nor *The World (1787)* on 23 May, which give accounts of the movement of the opposing forces in Flanders on Sunday, 18 May; neither is it mentioned in the duke's own letter to Henry Dundas, dated 19 May 1794 and published in *The Oracle and Public Advertiser* on 24 May.[172] This would suggest that this was a story which spread beneath the 'official' currents of war-reporting, a fact which conditions our impression of the journalism represented in Robert Roberts's ballad.

The Glorious First of June and Cape St Vincent (1794, 1797)

1794 was also the year in which the British navy under Admiral Lord Howe defeated the French in an action off the Island of Ushant in the Atlantic Ocean. Only one surviving Welsh ballad tells of this battle, although it was the subject of several English songs.[173] An interesting point of comparison exists within a Welsh context, however. The Dolgellau-based Elizabeth Baker kept a copy of a letter sent from John Morris, a local man who served with Howe on 1 June, to his parents, describing his experience of this battle. In an unpunctuated rush ('Theres but one comma in the letter, but the sense is evident', Baker noted), John Morris gives a description of the movement of Howe's navy from its departure from Portsmouth on 1 May until contact was made with the French, reaching a climax on 1 June. The clarity of the account means that it is perfectly possible to date various parts of the narrative. Morris also gives details of the wounded and deceased, together with the condition of the two navies and the length of the main action (which, he claims, lasted from around nine in the morning until three in the afternoon on 1 June). The writing is at times extremely graphic, as when Morris describes how he and his fellows boarded one of the defeated enemy ships on Howe's command:

> So we borded another and put 30 men on bord of her and I am one of em when we first borded her the Decks was Coulard with blood and dead bodys and limps of men and her mas[t] and rigings laining over the Decks we Could not walk there was upwards 400 men killed on bord of her.[174]

This report shows a very detailed awareness of the progression of events. It is not known what its author's precise status in the fleet was, but the description of his boarding an enemy ship on Howe's command and in the company of thirty others suggests that he may have been one of the rank and file. If so, he was remarkably knowledgeable, a fact which indicates the degree of involvement of ordinary naval personnel.[175]

It is unlikely in view of geographical factors that Robert Roberts, who hailed from Llannor in Caernarfonshire, composed his ballad (no. 10) using the eyewitness account of John Morris. The detail presented in Morris's account, however, implies that direct experience of conflict, unfiltered through the periodical press, could form the basis of very detailed and 'journalistic' reports.[176] The poet introduces his material in the ballad's opening lines as something that he 'heard' (line 7), a fact which suggests the importance of oral news streams in the transmission of this story. Much of his account corresponds to the kind of detail transmitted by John Morris. He notes how two days passed before the opposing fleets engaged (lines 9–10), and that the action took place on 1 June, beginning at ten in the morning and continuing for more than five hours, statistics which again correspond fairly closely to those given by Morris (lines 5, 17–18, 21). The factual reporting, however, is firmly placed within a celebratory framework, which, from the first stanza, leaves no doubt as to the successful outcome of the action (lines 23–4). Dramatic tension is created within this framework from the second stanza onwards, when the account plunges *in medias res*. The folly of the overconfident French is contrasted with the determination of Howe, whose speech to his men rivals that of the sixth-century poet Taliesin's Urien Rheged ('"Prysurwch! Lladdwch! Nac arbedwch, / A llwyddwch ar fôr llaith!"', "Make haste! Kill! Do not spare, / and prevail on the watery sea!", lines 47–8).[177] The frequent use of pauses within the tune of 'King George's Delight', to which this ballad was most probably sung, also serves to build suspense, as in the following lines, where the opponents eye each other in preparation for engagement:

> Yn sbio o bob tu, ⌒ bawb o'r ddau-tu, ⌒
> Cyn dechreu plannu plwm.[178]

> (looking in every direction, all from both sides,
> before beginning to scatter lead.)

With the publication of two ballads on the battle of Cape St Vincent, in which Lord Jervis crushed the Spanish fleet, Welsh ballads begin to show an increased engagement with the more official voice of war-reporting found in the newspapers. This is tangentially so in a ballad by Edward Pugh (no. 16)

who, as we have seen above, expresses concern about the culture of celebration attendant upon the war, attempting instead to ground his response to Jervis's victory in 'sweetest prayer and the loveliest thanks / to the Lord God almighty' (lines 27–8). Hugh Jones of Glan Conwy's involvement with the official channels of newspaper reporting is much more directly in evidence in his poem on the same battle (no. 17). The detail of his casualty and other figures is almost certainly the result of reading a newspaper report of the event, a fact further suggested by his evocation of 'counting' ('cyfri') ('Against the men of Britain, that is on the side of savage Spain, / there were twenty-seven ships all in a row; / little, sprightly England had fifteen ships then, / *and those are the numbers I got*', lines 13–16; my emphasis). A similar suggestion rises from the reference to 'accounts' ('they injured two hundred and twenty-seven / of our men, honest lads, *according to accounts*', lines 71–2; my emphasis).[179] Jones revels in a dramatic presentation of the conflict between the two sides, making creative use of the stock ingredient of the enemy's hubris before battle (present in the English ballad, 'Jervis taking the Spanish Fleet', which mentions 'The haughty Spaniards Boasting').[180] Early insults against the Britons, depicting them as 'wretches like sheep upon the waves', 'dross' and 'old curs' (lines 18, 23, 24), are transformed into acknowledgement of their superiority ('"The Britons are not / sheep but are savage, cruel demons"', lines 39–40). The poet enjoys the vision of the Spanish's retreat, 'with their arses on fire' (line 41) and their men thrown into the sea 'like old porpoises' (line 36). An element of black humour is further developed by an extended metaphor suggested to Jones by the date of the battle. This date was simply 'The fourteenth day of February' for the ballad writer who composed 'Jervis taking the Spanish Fleet'; it was 'Valentine's day' for another English writer who sang of a series of British naval victories in the period.[181] To Hugh Jones, the date 14 February 1797 was notable for being Shrove Tuesday, and in view of that, the lead bullets which plummeted towards the Spaniards were 'pancakes', heavy enough to sit in the Spaniards' stomachs forever. The light-hearted reference to the concept of fasting (a lengthy period of which the Spaniards were now entering, according to Jones) suggests a distancing from the general tone of self-inspection suggested by Pugh's ballad, when it counsels prayer and fast as antidotes to excessive celebration (no. 16, lines 23–4). Together with the allusion to the story of the Spanish Armada, a main-stay of English naval pride, this suggests a certain secularization on an English model in this ballad.[182] Yet, Hugh Jones is unable to leave his audience with-out the customary reference to the 'hand of mighty God' in the victory (line 75) and the realization that England in fact has long deserved failure rather than fame (lines 79–80).

Nelson ballads (1805)

Horatio Nelson, the subject of as many as ninety songs in English, was also commemorated in Welsh ballads and poems.[183] In a study of English-language Nelson songs, Mark Philp analyses the difference between street ballads (or traditional naval ballads) on the one hand, and songs sung by educated members of the elite in the interest of promoting loyalism on the other hand. Among the characteristics of elite ballads he notes a lack of specificity regarding the actual events of battles and a heavy focus upon the figure of Nelson himself and especially on his death. In spite of these features, Philp argues that the gap between elite song and traditional ballad is greatly narrowed in the case of Nelson poetry. There are no texts critical of his actions and the loyalist response to his victory at Trafalgar appears to have coloured and lead the way in which all kinds of songs portray him, denying any ambiguity even in traditional-style ballads' depiction of his character. A typical elite response to Nelson's death is gauged from the pages of the Swansea newspaper, *The Cambrian*, established in the early years of the nineteenth century.[184] Several poems commemorating his death were published in the paper from November 1805 onwards, and in the 23 November issue a competition for composing a song on the subject was announced.[185] It may have been a song inspired by the competition which appears in the manuscript of John Morgans from the parish of Llanfihangel Genau'r-glyn in Cardiganshire.[186] As late as 1869, John Jones (Talhaiarn) busied himself with composing an imitation ('Efel-ychiad') of an English poem entitled 'The death of Nelson'.[187] It appears, then, that there were channels through which an elite and Anglicized reaction to Nelson's career might have flourished within Wales and influenced represen-tation and reaction.

Evidence of such an approach to the subject of Nelson and Trafalgar is found in the surviving three Welsh ballads commemorating Nelson's death. Two of the three texts are remarkably unspecific in their commemoration of the battle. A ballad by the radical pamphleteer John Jones (Jac Glan-y-gors) gives no information whatsoever on the whereabouts of the battle which it discusses, on the numbers of ships and men involved, nor does it even name the enemy.[188] Instead, using the tune of 'Trymder' (literally 'Heaviness') with its mournful connotations, it constructs an elegiac mood, turning from the initial celebration of victory to face the sad fact of Nelson's death. Appreciation of Nelson in the second stanza gives place to a more general mourning in the third stanza, as the poet turns to consider the wives of the sailors killed in the action (a feature of the English ballad 'Jervis taking the Spanish Fleet') and prays for peace.[189] It may be felt that a gestural loyalty to king and naval hero in the second stanza merely lulls the listener of this poem into a third stanza which disapproves of British war-time policy, so that the model 'elitism' of the ballad is to some extent a cloak behind which a more critical viewpoint on the war is expressed. The author clearly harbours anti-war views, and wishes to link gratitude for victory with an agenda for peace rather than with the habitual jingoism. At the same time, however, there is no reason to doubt Glan-y-gors's sincerity in his opening praise of the navy and expression of George III's loss upon Nelson's death.[190]

Glan-y-gors's ballad was published as the second in a ballad pamphlet, preceded by another poem on Trafalgar, composed by John Thomas, Pen-fforddwen (no. 26).[191] It may have been the popularity of John Thomas's poem which ensured the significant sales of Glan-y-gors's ballad noted by Richard Griffith (Carneddog).[192] Although Thomas's poem displays features of what might be characterized as an 'elite' ballad style, it retains a punchiness which might well have attracted a typical ballad audience, and claims its place as the most detailed contemporary battle narrative of Trafalgar extant in Welsh. It names the enemy with characteristic gusto and proceeds to develop the stock feature of their pre-battle hubris, an element already noted in the poem on Cape St Vincent by Hugh Jones, Glan Conwy (no. 17):

> Fe gasglodd Ffrainc giedd i'w dilyn mewn dialedd
> Holl berfedd (naws bonedd) Ysbaen;
> I'n tanio cytunant mewn balchder a thrachwant,
> Derchafant, ymledant ymlaen.
> Tua phymtheg ar hugien o longau'n llawn cynnen,
> Cychw'nen (air milen) i'r môr,
> A deuddeg cant weithie o wŷr ar eu byrdde,
> Am ladd ar eu siwrne wŷr Siôr . . .[193]

> (Cruel France gathered together to follow them in vengeance
> the entire guts of Spain (noble nature);
> they agree in pride and greed to fire on us,
> they rise up, they extend themselves forwards.
> Around thirty-five ships full of hostility,
> they set out (loathsome word) to sea,
> and some twelve hundred men on board,
> intending to kill George's men on their journey . . .)

The poet adds to this picture of enemy pride details of the numbers of ships and men who opposed the Britons, and continues in the next stanza to report the claims made by the enemy admirals that they would capture every British ship they could see before them, together with Nelson and his men, whom they would take prisoner and deposit in France or Spain.

The start of the narrative of the battle displays the folly of such boasting, as the British provide 'a hundred kisses of lead and quick fire' (line 45), tearing the enemy ships' rigging, and answering the threat of imprisonment with real capture and the killing of around thirty thousand men (a grossly exaggerated figure).[194]

In the entire eight stanzas of this poem, Nelson is named only three times, twice in conjunction with his men (lines 31, 39–40), and once in commemoration (lines 71–2). This forms a point of contrast with the third printed Welsh-language Nelson ballad, the work of the Baptist miller Robert Morris (no. 27). Nelson is named fifteen times in its nine stanzas, ensuring that he is the constant focus of attention throughout, although the poem also makes space to attribute the essence of the victory to God, claiming that it was He, and not the power of 'our' ships or number of 'our' arms, nor human skill that ensured triumph. Traditional elements such as the typical pre-battle repartee of the enemy is almost absent in Morris's ballad (with merely a passing reference to such banter in lines 19–20) and, although there are graphic portrayals of thundering cannon-balls and skilful wielding of sword, they figure as vignettes, not clearly placed within a specific battle narrative. In fact, the poem provides an overview of the main campaigns of Nelson's career, focusing on Trafalgar initially and primarily, yet also looking back onto the battles fought in Copenhagen and Egypt, and noting Nelson's involvement in as many as a hundred and twenty-four battles for Britain. Like Hugh Jones, Glan Conwy, in his narrative of Cape St Vincent, Morris names the numbers of opposing ships at Trafalgar (27 British to 33 French, lines 49–52), and the traditional hostility between France and Britain is evoked in the description of the French opponents, 'from the race of Louis', arising 'like flies, worthless ones, on a journey' to meet Nelson (lines 53, 54). Nonetheless, it is harder to imagine this ballad placing itself in the hearts of an ordinary Welsh-speaking audience. Its commemorative framework distances it of its own accord, and this distance appears to be emphasized by a feature of the printing (carried out by Thomas Roberts of Caernarfon) which underpins the poem with footnotes detailing the exact geographical locations of the places named in the text. For instance, Cádiz is said to be 'a town of Spain, 5 miles in length, 2 in breadth, 4[?5] w. of Gibralter, and 90 w. by s. of Malaga. Lon. 6, 11, w. Lat. 36, 31, n.' When a reference to Caledfwlch is footnoted in English 'King Arthur's sword', the impression given is that this poem may even have been aimed in part at least at an elite audience. It differs from most ballad products of the period in Welsh, too, in that it is printed singly on a broadsheet, a feature which would have made it appropriate as a wall hanging, and which underlines its commemorative nature.

Napoleon ballads (1812–15)

The final group of news ballads relate to Napoleon's downfall – to the initial abdication which took place in Paris on 4 April 1814, and the final dénouement of Waterloo in June 1815. Historians of the English ballad tradition have argued that Napoleon ballads took two different forms, either as propaganda literature, sponsored by the elite, or as an underlying 'folk' tradition (which surfaced after 1815) where Napoleon was seen more in the light of a flawed hero, a response easily understood in view of the British reaction to the great man as he briefly docked in Plymouth before his voyage to St Helena in 1815.[195] There is little evidence of a similar reworking of the figure of Napoleon in the Welsh folk-song tradition of subsequent years.[196] What survives in the printed ballad tradition reflects a flurry of excitement at the announcement of final victory in June 1815. A ballad by Thomas Jones (no. 36) ran to at least four imprints (an unusually high number for a Welsh ballad), two of which came from Ishmael Davies's Trefriw press. The versions printed by an unspecified printer or printers included five additional stanzas, which suggests that the song may have been hastily published by Davies in the immediate aftermath of the battle and later expanded. The additions (which are rather carelessly placed in the scheme of the poem) largely centre on the presence of women on and near the battlefield, showing their plucky defiance of Wellington's command that they passively stand back from the conflict, only to return later to bury their dead. The women insist:

> "Ni safwn ni yn ôl 'r un lathen;
> Os ydyw'r Arglwydd Dduw yn rhannu,
> Ni gawn ein gwŷr yn fyw o'r armi."[197]

> ("We shall not stand back a single yard;
> if the Lord God judges,
> we shall have our husbands alive from the army.")

The interpolation (or the restitution) of these stanzas may be a reflection of a certain printer or seller's awareness of the market potential implicit in recounting this example of female strength: female listeners and readers may well have enjoyed this particular section of the ballad. At the same time, it is clear that the metre chosen (that of the 'hen bennill') readily admits the introduction of new material (often only loosely related to what has gone before). The poem revisits Bonaparte's career, but is more clearly focused on drawing out a moral message from the story, in accordance with the norms of its 'hen bennill' metre. The moral lesson is aimed directly at the French, who are seen as heroes fallen from greatness. They are warned to restrain themselves from warmongering in future, and not to put their faith in the Pope ever again (lines 57–72).

Research by A. Cynfael Lake has demonstrated that, in the eighteenth century, there was a clear distinction between the 'prydydd' (the poet, who composed ballad poetry) and the 'baledwr' (the 'balladeer', who was responsible for its dissemination).[198] Although one eighteenth-century 'baledwr', Richard Roberts, appears also to have been a 'prydydd', suggesting that change was already afoot in the late eighteenth century, the transition which led to the development of balladeer-poets appears properly to belong to the nineteenth century.[199] Two further ballads on the downfall of Napoleon by Ioan Dafydd from the parish of Llandeilo Tal-y-bont in Glamorgan (nos. 34 and 35) show a transition in the manner of ballad production in Wales. Ioan Dafydd's style in both ballads shows his acute awareness of performance features. In ballad no. 35 he interpolates the narrative with references to his own role as narrator (lines 61, 101–2, 111), and ends with the crucial matter of payment:

> Gan fod y gân oll yn wirionedd
> Ac yn tynnu tua'i diwedd,
> Brysiwch, bobl, i'ch pocedi
> I chwilio am geiniog goch amdani.[200]

> (Since the whole song is true
> and draws towards its conclusion,
> hasten, people, to your pockets
> to search for a single penny for it.)

In ballad no. 34, Dafydd ends similarly, noting that he must now stop lest he should tire anyone with his singing, and asking for a penny in payment for 'the little piece of paper' (line 89) which should be respected when being read. His unease about lack of control of the ballad as printed material is suggested by a warning at its foot, 'Let no one sell this song without the author's permission'. Ioan Dafydd's work thus suggests how war-reporting may have entered marketplace and fairground, the ballad-maker (and, probably, singer) becoming an oracle for the news, and using his performance to put across a mixture of fact (naming a catalogue of allied leaders and key campaigns), gleeful anti-Napoleonic propaganda, Christian faith, moralizing, vignettes designed to elicit pathos for suffering (e.g. among women and children), and celebration. With this hotchpotch of responses to what the balladeer recognizes to have been over twenty years of war between Britain and France, he aims to produce poetry capable of attracting the attention and sympathy of a roving market audience.

✧ ✧ ✧ ✧

Exploration of Welsh printed ballad texts which relate to specific military figures and battles during 1793–1815 reveals a development in the manner of reporting warfare. Earlier texts, commemorating the successes of the Duke of York in the opening campaigns of the war in Flanders, show a legendary basis for the reporting. They lack the detail of regular journalism, and appear to rely heavily instead on perceptions of heroism. These perceptions are used in part to shore up the recruitment efforts of the British military at the beginning of the wars and to ensure a place for Wales within the British entity (nos. 4 and 9). Later ballads, focusing on naval battles, are built on narrative and dramatic bases, using dialogue to expand upon a set pattern of pre-battle boasting by the enemy, followed by their debasement by the British and their realization of their failure. This pattern is particularly prevalent in Hugh Jones, Glan Conwy's ballad on Jervis's Cape St Vincent victory in 1797 (no. 17). Jones's work also shows the increasing relevance of newspaper journalism to ballad writers, and their increasing acceptance of the importance of factual reporting. The Nelson ballads were composed at the height of state intervention in popular cultural perceptions of the war, and they can be interpreted as negotiating between popular preconceptions about war-reporting in ballad material on the one hand and the expectations of the status quo on the other. The Nelson portrayed by the Baptist ballad writer Robert Morris is a very different hero from the Duke of York of the earlier ballads – in an attempt at conforming to an elite perception of Nelson's heroism, Morris's hero loses the natural colour and haphazard heroism of the Duke of York and evolves into a saint-like figure, whose name is monotonously repeated throughout the poem (no. 27). Finally, ballads on the defeat of Napoleon enact their own popularity as performances. We know of the widespread distribution of one of these ballads, that of Thomas Jones (no. 36); a second balladeer, Ioan Dafydd, displays overt concern over the dissemination of his material, suggesting that news-bearing ballads, spanning events as long as the twenty-years' war between Britain and France, had a strong popular currency among Welsh audiences (nos. 34 and 35). Such popularity suggests that the ballad was, at this stage, evolving into a strong competitor with the periodical press in Wales. Welsh-language newspapers and journals were few and far between in the earlier decades of the 1800s, and ballad historians have suggested that nineteenth-century balladeers reigned supreme as newsmongers until at least the mid-1850s.[201] Richard Roberts's concern about the traditional ballad audience's preoccupation with 'news' and 'newspapers' during the 1790s was in some respects premature (no. 8). The balladeer (now, I would suggest, firmly evolving into the one-man-act of nineteenth-century Wales) increasingly held the key to distributing information of this kind, and could ensure the continuation of a homely mix of news and interpretation, and promote a traditional Welsh obsession with faith, sin and the hand of God in human action. The ballads of the period 1793–1815 offer crucial evidence of change and development in Welsh balladry, as it began negotiating with the still comparatively new phenomenon of the periodical press in Wales.

Conclusion

In 1797 the Carmarthen printer John Evans brought out a ballad recounting the eventful journey of a group of emigrants who left Milford Haven for America in April 1795 or 1796 (no. 13). Its triumphant final stanza, with its praise of the peaceful egalitarianism of American society, suggests why they left:

> Nid oes dynion â boliau mawrion
> Blonegog tewion yma'n bod;
> Nid oes chwaith gardotyn llymrig,
> Ond pawb yn debyg, i'r un nod;
> Pe bai tlodion Cymru'n gallu
> Croesi'r werlig donnog draw,
> Trwy weithio byddent byw'n gysurus
> Mewn gwlad heddychol, fro di-fraw.[202]

> (No men with large, greasy,
> fat bellies exist here;
> neither is there a wretched beggar,
> but everyone is similar, of the same status;
> if the poor of Wales could
> cross the billowy ocean yonder,
> by working they would live comfortably
> in a peaceful country, a land without fear.)

Emigration proved to be a way out of the constrictions of life in Britain for a considerable number of Dissenters during the 1790s.[203] Suffering under increased surveillance and mistrust, let alone fundamental restrictions on civil and religious liberty, they saw escape to America, with its promise of a new beginning, as the better option. Yet, the skeletal nature of the reformist-radical voice in ballads composed in Wales, as across the border in England during this period, cannot be fully attributed either to repression or emigration. As suggested already, popular radicalism was almost certainly much less widespread than its loyalist counterpart. Moreover, what did exist in terms of radical song may not have survived, largely since much of it never reached the printing presses. An intriguing stanza in a poem by 'J.P.', published in Caernarfon in 1804, poses the troubled question:

Paham mae Protestaniaid, gwŷr llygon a gwŷr llên,
Yn gwgu ar ei gilydd a rhoddi sen am sen?
'Sgrifennu llyfrau a chanu, a hyn mewn chwerwedd mawr?
O, gochel, Brydain, gochel, rhag tynnu barn i lawr![204]

(Why do Protestants, lay men and clergymen,
scowl at each other and throw insult for insult?
Write books and sing, and this in great bitterness?
Oh, beware, Britain, beware, lest judgement should be drawn down!)

It may surprise to hear of polemical material circulating in conservative Caernarfonshire and it is unclear precisely what the nature of the books and singing mentioned may have been. Since it did not involve Catholics it was probably either the result of disputes between fellow Dissenters or between the Anglican Church and Dissent. [205] Lack of radical balladry means, of course, that this anthology is mostly concerned with a conservative and loyalist response to the upheaval caused by the French Revolution and the decades of war which followed upon its heels. In spite of a relative lack of dialogue between what may crudely be described as the 'two sides' of the political divide, this does not mean that the material represented here is uniform and colourless. In fact, it offers a valuable opportunity to gauge the nature of popular loyalism in one of the constituent parts of Great Britain, showing it to be an extremely nuanced phenomenon, as others have claimed for different geographical areas.[206] The ballad writers sometimes respond enthusiastically to British victory in naval battles, at other times question the culture of celebration; they are intensely aware of their enemies, both foreign and home-grown, but often turn an eye inwards towards the moral characteristics of their own audiences; they enjoy the patriotic spectacle of volunteering with its potential for expressing local civic pride, but also regret the human cost of militarization.

The chronological span of the texts ensures an awareness of the development of popular balladry over the entire length of the Revolutionary and Napoleonic wars, a feature which has not tended to be the case in the historiography of the period in general.[207] In adopting this broader range of dates, we are able, for example, to see the way in which the theme of the 'internal enemy' is concentrated in texts produced in the 1790s, but finds echoes in later ballads, such as no. 25, printed in 1804 (lines 75–6). Whereas Dissenters are at the very least defensive of their position towards the status quo in 1793, by the early 1800s they are able to express their patriotism more confidently. Although the anonymous author of ballad no. 31, evidently a Dissenter, courts controversy with his comments on Church and tithe in 1811, the early nineteenth-century ballads by the Baptist Robert Morris show a dedicated and confident patriotism. Morris's two ballads addressing the militia mention the hope of future peace in terms which demonstrate his commitment to his area and to Wales: emigration, believed to be the answer by Dissenters in the 1790s, is firmly absent from his vision of the future (no. 29, lines 141–2; no. 38, lines 105–20). We also see the continued relevance of the Fishguard invasion, as the balladry of south-west Wales demonstrates an increased commitment to volunteering in its wake. The event continued to be fêted as an example of courage and virtue by poets in north Wales as late as 1813.[208] The bewildered stance of Richard Roberts and Robert Roberts as the wars begin, sparked by the executions of Louis XVI and Marie Antoinette in 1793, can be contrasted with the more confident effusions of Ioan Dafydd and Thomas Jones in 1815. Using simpler metres (more characteristic of poetry emanating from south Wales than from the north) and, in Ioan Dafydd's case, writing his own presence into the narrative in a manner more tentatively demonstrated in the work of George Stephens at the turn of the century, their ballads show a self-assurance regarding their own status as balladeers and their grasp of their chosen subjects. In spite of what might be characterized as an elite influence on ballads commemorating the career and death of Nelson, by the end of the period the voices of the balladeers display a remarkable degree of autonomy – conditioned by the demands of their marketplace audiences, they essentially serve their own communities, without excessive obsequiousness towards higher-ranking members of society.

Notes

[1]   Hester Lynch Piozzi to Mrs Pennington, Denbigh, 11 September 1794, in Oswald G. Knapp (ed.), *The Intimate Letters of Piozzi and Pennington* (London, 1914; 2nd edn., Stroud, 2005), p. 120. I am grateful to Dr Elizabeth Edwards for drawing my attention to this reference.

[2]   'The Chapter of Kings[:] A Favorite Historical Song Sung by Mr. Collins in the Evening's Brush', printed source preserved in NLW, Llanelwy 2379, pp. 134–5.

3   Piozzi confides in a letter to Mrs Pennington, dated 7 February 1793, that she 'sent a sheet to the Crown and Anchor for distribution this morning . . .' She was also among the writers of anti-Napoleonic broadsides in 1803. Knapp (ed.), *The Intimate Letters of Piozzi and Pennington*, p. 87; Stuart Semmel, *Napoleon and the British* (New Haven, 2004), pp. 41, 264.

4   Letter to John Reeves, 4 December 1792, quoted by Christopher Marsh, 'The Sound of Print in Early Modern England: The Broadside Ballad as Song', in Julia Crick and Alexandra Walsham (eds.), *The Uses of Script and Print, 1300–1700* (Cambridge, 2004), p. 172.

5   Mark Philp, 'Music and Politics: Section 1', in *idem* (ed.), *Resisting Napoleon: The British Response to the Threat of Invasion, 1797–1815* (Aldershot, 2006), p. 173. For reformist songs in England in the period, see Michael Scrivener, *Poetry and Reform: Periodical Verse from the English Democratic Press 1792–1824* (Detroit, 1992).

6   Mary-Ann Constantine, '"The French are on the sea!": Welsh and Irish Songs of French Invasion in the 1790s', in Louis Grijp (ed.), *Proceedings of the International Ballad Conference, Terschelling, 2010* (Trier, forthcoming); and further Tom Dunne, 'Popular Ballads, Revolutionary Rhetoric and Politicisation', in Hugh Gough and David Dickson (eds.), *Ireland and the French Revolution* (Dublin, 1990), pp. 139–55.

7   H. T. Dickinson suggests that there was a natural, spontaneous popular bent towards loyalism, something that the masses of loyalist propaganda could only serve to confirm. H. T. Dickinson, 'Popular Conservatism and Militant Loyalism', in *idem* (ed.), *Britain and the French Revolution 1789–1815* (Basingstoke, 1989), pp. 119–20. This is also the theory which informs the tremendously influential study by Linda Colley, *Britons: Forging the Nation 1707–1837* (New Haven, 1992).

8   Frank J. Klingberg and Sigurd B. Hustvedt (eds.), *The Warning Drum: The British Home Front Faces Napoleon. Broadsides of 1803* (Berkeley, 1944), p. 24.

9   See NLW, Elizabeth Baker, nos. 97 (27 August 1794, 'The Patriots Prayer', copied from *The Sun*); 98 (27 February 1794, 'To Opposition', copied from *The True Briton*); and 454 (11 June 1797, extracts from *The Sun* relating to Grey's reform resolution and the mutiny in the fleet).

10 Ibid., no. 456, is 'A note on Jacobinism' which Baker notes was 'transcribed to strengthen common sense, and inscribed to Lieut. Anwyl of the Merioneth Militia'. This suggests an interest in passing on material. Her links with the community are further suggested by the presence of copies of letters sent by serving naval personnel to contacts in the Dolgellau area. See nos. 395 (copy of a letter from John Morris, Portsmouth, to his parents, 14 June 1794), further discussed below; 403 (copy of a letter from William Lloyd, on board HMS *Belliquex*, to Revd Francis Parry, Llanaber, 21 July 1798).

11 David Eastwood, 'Patriotism and the English State in the 1790s', in Mark Philp (ed.), *The French Revolution and British Popular Politics* (Cambridge, 1991), pp. 151–2.

12 Robin Ganev, *Songs of Protest, Songs of Love: Popular Ballads in Eighteenth-Century Britain* (Manchester, 2010), p. 186; Kevin Gilmartin, '"Study to be Quiet": Hannah

More and the Invention of Conservative Culture in Britain', *ELH*, 70 (2003), 493–540.

[13]   Anne Stott, *Hannah More: The First Victorian* (Oxford, 2003), p. 170, quoting from a More manuscript.

[14]   Susan Pedersen, 'Hannah More Meets Simple Simon: Tracts, Chapbooks, and Popular Culture in Late Eighteenth-Century England', *Journal of British Studies*, 25 (1986), 87; Gilmartin, '"Study to be Quiet"', 504–8.

[15]   Ganev, *Songs of Protest, Songs of Love*, pp. 187–8.

[16]   Ibid., pp. 191–8.

[17]   Ibid., chapter 2.

[18]   The best summary of scornful attitudes towards balladry and other forms of popular Welsh culture is found in Thomas Parry, *Baledi'r Ddeunawfed Ganrif* (1935; 2nd edn., Llandysul, 1986), pp. 1–17. Parry quotes the words of Goronwy Owen from J. H. Davies (ed.), *The Letters of Goronwy Owen (1723–1769)* (Cardiff, 1924), p. 140.

[19]   E. Wyn James, 'Rhai Methodistiaid a'r Anterliwt', *Taliesin*, 57 (1986), 8–19.

[20]   Hywel M. Davies, 'Loyalism in Wales, 1792–1793', *WHR*, 20, no. 4 (2001), 687–716. For the reference to Poole and the ballads, see 701.

[21]   The two loyalist free-metre songs are 'Cân Twm Paen' by David Thomas (Dafydd Ddu Eryri), in *idem* (ed.), *Corph y Gaingc* (Dolgellau, 1810), pp. 196–201; and 'Carol plygain, i'w ganu ar fesur newydd a wnaed yn amser Tho. Payne, pa un a fygyth-iodd godi terfysg yn y llywodraeth, trwy annog y bobl i an-ufudd-dod, ac yn wrth-wynebiad i hyny, y gelwir y mesur canlynol yn Ufudd-dod, neu Ufudd-dod i'r Llywodraeth' by John Thomas, in *idem, Telyn Arian: sef Llyfr Barddoniaeth; yn cynnwys Carolau, Cerddi, Awdlau, ac Englynion, &c. Ar amryw Destynau, ac hefyd, Cerddi a phenillion, yn gymysgedig o Gymraeg a Saesonaeg, Ond y cwbl ar gynghayedd* [*sic*] *a mesurau a arferir yn Gymraeg* ([1806]; 3rd edn., Llanrwst, 1823), pp. 32–4. The former is included in Cathryn Charnell-White (ed.), *Welsh Poetry of the French Revolution 1789–1805* (Cardiff, forthcoming).

[22]   Siwan M. Rosser, *Y Ferch ym Myd y Faled: Delweddau o'r Ferch ym Maledi'r Ddeunawfed Ganrif* (Caerdydd, 2005). The study of Welsh ballads is now better-served than ever, with the recent launch of a comprehensive and searchable data-base of ballads printed in the eighteenth century, 'Cronfa Baledi', at *http://www. e-gymraeg.org/cronfabaledi*, and the complementary 'Welsh Ballads Online', at *http:// cat.llgc.org.uk/ballads*. The latter includes scanned texts of ballads preserved in the collections of the National Library of Wales and the Salisbury Library at Cardiff University.

[23]   As many as twenty-eight presses were set up outside London and the towns of Oxford and Cambridge between 1695 and 1728. See William St Clair, *The Reading Nation in the Romantic Period* (Cambridge, 2004), p. 87 n. 18.

[24]   Geraint H. Jenkins, *Thomas Jones yr Almanaciwr 1648–1713* (Caerdydd, 1980), pp. 12, 14.

[25]   Jones was succeeded as a ballad printer in Shrewsbury during the first half of the eighteenth century by Thomas Durston (1712–62), John Rhydderch (1715–28),

John Rogers (1707–24) and Richard Lathrop (1740–57). Welsh material was printed in Hereford between 1721 and 1748, and two ballads printed here probably date from the same period. Roger and Elizabeth Adams were active in Chester between 1731 and 1771. See *BWB*, pp. 3, 14, 74–8, 96, 233.

[26] They are the border towns of Chester and Oswestry, together with the Welsh towns of Wrexham, Trefriw, Machynlleth, Barmouth, Caernarfon and Carmarthen. This information is based on *BWB, passim*. On the printing towns and printers involved in producing the texts represented in this anthology, see Fig. 1, p. 4.

[27] *BWB*, pp. v–vi.

[28] Rosser, *Y Ferch ym Myd y Faled*, pp. 2–3; Parry, *Baledi'r Ddeunawfed Ganrif*, pp. 24–7.

[29] Gerald Morgan, 'Baledi Dyffryn Conwy', *Canu Gwerin*, 20 (1997), 2–12.

[30] John Jones, preface to *Blwch Caniadau* (1812), quoted in Glyn M. Ashton, 'Arolwg ar Brydyddiaeth Gymraeg 1801–25 (Parhad)', *Llên Cymru*, 15, nos. 1 and 2 (1984–6), 118–19.

[31] For the distinction between 'prydydd' and 'baledwr' see note to no. 3, Author, and the discussion below.

[32] On the tunes used by Welsh free-metre poets, see Phyllis Kinney, 'The Tunes of the Welsh Christmas Carols (I)', *Canu Gwerin*, 11 (1988), 28–57; *eadem*, 'The Tunes of the Welsh Christmas Carols (II)', *Canu Gwerin*, 12 (1989), 5–29. Settings of the tunes involved in this anthology are found in the appendix.

[33] Rosser makes a similar case in *Y Ferch ym Myd y Faled*, p. 2.

[34] Note that in some cases, however, the structure of sentences militates strongly against the dictates of the tune, making satisfactory punctuation very difficult. See, for example, no. 35, stanza 8.

[35] 'Rhên wragedd aflawen sy heb fedru darllen, / [S]y'n rhegi'n bur [fil]en' (The unhappy old women who are unable to read / curse very severely). Ellis Roberts, 'O gwynfan i'r Cymry o golled am yr arian cochion, oedd yn peru llawenydd oi derbyn; ag i chwanegu ar eu galar mae'r hên chwecheiniog yn myned ar fyr i Lundain iw hail gweinio' (Trefriw, 1779; JHD 317). For the performances of English chapmen, see St Clair, *The Reading Nation in the Romantic Period*, p. 344.

[36] See Ellis Roberts, '[Cerdd] o gyngor ir merched rhag priodi'r un dyn di ana yn y flwyddyn hon. Rhag iddo flino ar ei gwmpeini a myned i b[r]eifetirio neu'n filisia neu'r maniwar neu ryw le anghyspell arall' (Trefriw, 1778; repr. Aberhonddu, 1781; JHD 307ii). This is discussed in Ffion Mair Jones, '"Gwŷr Lloeger aeth benben â'u brodyr eu hunen": Y Baledwyr Cymraeg a Rhyfel Annibyniaeth America', *Y Traethodydd*, CLXVI, no. 699 (2011), 197–225, esp. 213.

[37] Iolo Morganwg, the famous Glamorgan literary forger, wrote perceptively (if not without bias) of the differences between the 'alliterative lines of mere nonsense' produced in north Wales and the 'little stanzas too natural and simple to be called epigrams in the modern acceptation of the term, but infinitely better', produced in the south and 'found chiefly in the mouths of the common people'. Cathryn Charnell-White, *Bardic Circles: National, Regional and Personal Identity in the Bardic Vision of Iolo Morganwg* (Cardiff, 2007), p. 258.

38   Parry, *Baledi'r Ddeunawfed Ganrif*, p. 16.
39   Rosser, *Y Ferch ym Myd y Faled*, p. 140, and for inbred attitudes towards women, often
      based on scriptural representation, see, for example, p. 104. Note that Rosser briefly
      considers the possibility that female ballad writers were able to offer alternative
      perspectives on female experience. Ibid., pp. 5–7.
40   Huw Jones of Llangwm makes reference to himself in 'Breuddwyd y prydydd ar
      Hitin Dincar' (Mwythig, 1765; JHD, 715ii), in the autobiographical 'Annerchiad
      Hugh Jones y Prydydd or Mwythig at y Cymry iw ganu ar Lea Land' (Mwythig,
      n.d.; JHD 155biii) and on the title page of a dialogue poem 'Fel y digwyddodd i'r
      prydydd fod mewn tŷ tafarn pan ddaeth ysgowl-wraig flîn i nôl y gŵr adre; a'r
      ymddiddan a fu rhyngddynt: ar Lân medd-dod mwyn'. Note that the latter was
      published by Ishmael Davies, Trefriw, in 1813.
41   Ellis Roberts, 'Ymddiddan rhwng Lloegr a Ffraingc ar y mesur a elwir Leave Land
      neu adel Tir' (Mwythig, 1758; JHD 71ii).
42   A 1760 ballad by Roberts's contemporary, Huw Jones of Llangwm, celebrates the
      end of the practice of exporting wheat to France as the Seven Years' War progressed.
      Although its focus lies in a gleeful portrayal of French suffering, it also strikes out
      at the corn dealer Richard Colley, whose behaviour had sparked corn riots in
      1740. Alaw Mai Edwards and A. Cynfael Lake (eds.), *Detholiad o Faledi Huw Jones:
      'Llymgi Penllwyd Llangwm'* (Aberystwyth, 2010), pp. 48–51.
43   See, for example, Hugh Jones, 'Ar ddull ymddiddan rhwng Mr Tir a'r T[enant]'
      (n.p., 17--; JHD 834i); anon., 'Cerdd ar ddyll ymddiddan rhwng y Mr. Tir a'r
      Tenant . . . ar . . . God Save the King' (Wrexham, n.d.; JHD 281ii).
44   Robert Morris, '[Y]mddiddan rhwng y cardotyn, ar cerlyn, sef Sion Siwrwd a
      Thwm Dew' (n.p., [1788]; JHD 626ii); *idem*, 'Ymddiddan rhwng y tenant ar
      cardottyn' (Trefriw, n.d.; JHD 413ii). The latter was sold by Robert Prichard,
      who is known (from other ballad imprints) to have been active in 1795 and
      1797. See Cronfa Baledi.
45   David Howell, *The Rural Poor in Eighteenth-Century Wales* (Cardiff, 2000), p. 76. The
      beggar cites the increased prices paid for animals (for meat provision) and butter.
      This corresponds with the escalation of prices noted by Howell in Llanferres,
      Denbighshire, and Wrexham at the end of 1795, when beef, mutton and bacon
      together with both salt butter and fresh butter were more dear. By 1813 the prices
      of provisions in north Wales were almost twice their pre-war levels.
46   Anon., 'Cerdd ar ddyll ymddiddan rhwng y Mr. Tir a'r Tenant . . . ar . . . God Save
      the King' (Wrexham, n.d.; JHD 281ii).
47   For radical uses of 'God Save the King' during the 1790s, see Michael T. Davis, '"An
      Evening of Pleasure Rather than Business": Songs, Subversion and Radical Sub-
      Culture in the 1790s', *Journal for the Study of British Cultures*, 12, no. 2 (2005),
      115–26; and, in a Welsh context, Mary-Ann Constantine and Elizabeth Edwards,
      'Bard of Liberty: Iolo Morganwg, Wales and Radical Song', in Michael Brown,
      Catriona Kennedy, John Kirk and Andrew Noble (eds.), *United Islands? Multi-lingual
      Radical Poetry and Song in Britain and Ireland 1770–1820* (London, forthcoming).
      See further notes to no. 3.

48   See Hugh Jones, '[Cerdd] O gwynfan am y byd helbylus sydd ar for a thir' (Trefriw, 1779; JHD 314ii); Ellis Roberts, '[Cerdd] Yn rhoi byrr hanes dynes a wnaeth weithred ofnadwy ym mhlwy Llansantffraid Glyn Conwy, sef diheunyddio ffrwyth ei bry ai ado fe rhwng bwystfilod y ddaear' (Trefriw, 1784; JHD 360i); Robert Morris, 'Carol plygain newydd ar don Duw gadwo'r Brenhin' (n.p., [1788]; JHD 626i). Other eighteenth-century ballads set to the tune are undated.

49   For protests and riots in Wales at this time, see W. Lloyd Davies, 'The Riot at Denbigh, 1795', *BBCS*, IV, part I (1927), 61–73; Sharon Howard, 'Riotous Community: Crowds, Politics and Society in Wales, *c.*1700–1840', *WHR*, 20, no. 4 (2001), 656–86; David J. V. Jones, *Before Rebecca: Popular Protests in Wales 1793–1835* (London, 1973); *idem* (= D. J. V. Jones), 'The Corn Riots in Wales, 1793–1801', *WHR*, 2, no. 4 (1965), 323–50.

50   Thomas Edwards was urged by a fellow-poet, Robert Davies of Nantglyn, to respond in verse to the suppression of the 1795 corn and anti-militia riot in Denbigh. The resulting poem was peculiarly non-committal, even though Edwards was prepared to vilify the elite in a private letter to the radical John Jones (Jac Glan-y-gors). Glyn Ashton, *Hunangofiant a Llythyrau Twm o'r Nant* (Caerdydd, 1962), pp. 18–19. See also, however, a manuscript poem by Thomas Edwards, describing the bitter experience of serving in the militia. 'Rhyddhad o'r Milisia', in Dafydd Glyn Jones (ed.), *Canu Twm o'r Nant* (Bangor, 2010), pp. 182–4, 307.

51   Mark Philp, 'Introduction', in *idem* (ed.), *The French Revolution and British Popular Politics*, p. 5. English ballads which respond enthusiastically to the new conditions in France brought about by the Revolution include the anonymous 'Millions be free. A new song' (n.p., n.d.), and 'A song' ("The records of France, from the earliest age") (n.p., n.d.), both on 'Bodleian Library Broadside Ballads: The *allegro* Catalogue of Ballads' at *http://www.bodley.ox.ac.uk/ballads/ballads.htm*.

52   G. G. Evans, *Elis y Cowper* (Caernarfon, 1995), p. 12; A. Cynfael Lake, *Huw Jones o Langwm* (Caernarfon, 2009), p. 49.

53   Exceptions include Evan James, who was active as a poet in the 1770s, but whose productivity as a ballad writer cannot be compared with that of Ellis Roberts or Huw Jones of Llangwm. For details of the work and lives of the ballad writers whose work is included in this anthology, see the notes. Evan James is discussed in the notes to no. 30.

54   Gwyn A. Williams, *The Search for Beulah Land: The Welsh and the Atlantic Revolution* (New York, 1980), p. 7. Further comments by Williams in this vein are found in *idem*, *When Was Wales? A History of the Welsh* (1985; paperback edn., London, 1991), p. 167. He appears to be echoing R. T. Jenkins, *Hanes Cymru yn y Bedwaredd Ganrif ar Bymtheg: Y Gyfrol Gyntaf (1789–1843)* (Caerdydd, 1933), p. 5. Further on the ballad writers and the American War of Independence, see Jones, '"Gwŷr Lloeger aeth benben â'u brodyr eu hunen"'.

55   Exceptions include the work of the Baptist, Robert Morris (nos. 27, 29, 38), and the anonymous ballads nos. 13 and 31.

56   Scrivener, *Poetry and Reform*, p. 12.

57 *The World (1787)* (London), issue 1861 (15 December 1792); *The Courier* (London), issue 87 (1 January 1793); *The World (1787)* (London), issue 1892 (21 January 1793); *St. James's Chronicle or the British Evening Post* (London), issue 5002 (28–30 March 1793).

58 Quotations taken from *St. James's Chronicle or the British Evening Post* (London), issue 5002 (28–30 March 1793).

59 Richard Price, *A Discourse on the Love of our Country* (1789), in D. O. Thomas (ed.), *Price: Political Writings* (Cambridge, 1991), p. 188.

60 Ibid., pp. 189–93.

61 Ibid., pp. 192–3.

62 No. 1, lines 97–100.

63 Price, *A Discourse on the Love of our Country*, in Thomas (ed.), *Price: Political Writings*, pp. 194, 195.

64 No. 2, line 28.

65 See no. 2, note. For the text, see [William Jones], *One Penny-worth of Truth from Thomas Bull to his Brother John*, in *Liberty and Property Preserved against Republicans and Levellers: A Collection of Tracts Number I* (London, 1793), pp. 1–5.

66 Report of meeting in the House of Commons, 13 December 1792, in the London paper, the *General Evening Post*, issue 9240 (13–15 December 1792).

67 This is a particularly strong historical tradition in the popular literature of north Wales. See Ffion Mair Jones, 'Pedair Anterliwt Hanes' (unpublished University of Wales PhD thesis, 2000), pp. 72–4. In 1810, William Williams of Llandygái in Caernarfonshire, an antiquary, author and quarry official, wrote scathingly of the connection between Dissent and the mid-seventeenth-century regicide. See Dafydd Glyn Jones, '"Y Misoedd", gan William Williams, Llandygái', *Llên Cymru*, 22 (1999), 93–107. The tradition may have been less evident in other Welsh regions.

68 'Liberty' was a well-rehearsed concept in English discourse, dating from Magna Carta, and increasingly appropriated by the loyalist elite. See, for example, John Dinwiddy, 'England', in *idem* and Otto Dan (eds.), *Nationalism in the Age of the French Revolution* (London, 1988), p. 64.

69 *One Penny-worth of Truth*, p. 2.

70 No. 2, lines 61–4.

71 'Taith at y Madogion', a copy of a letter from John Evans to his brother, 1792, in *Y Cylchgrawn Cynmraeg*, II (May 1793), 115.

72 See no. 13, lines 65–8.

73 No. 2, lines 93–6.

74 For Williams, see notes to no. 1, and for Fox, see *ODNB*, s.n. Charles James Fox (1749–1806).

75 'Gweiddi lle mae'r esgid yn gwasgu': R. T. Jenkins, *Hanes Cymru yn y Ddeunawfed Ganrif* (Caerdydd, 1928), p. 131. Comments in a similar vein are found in *idem*, *Hanes Cymru yn y Bedwaredd Ganrif ar Bymtheg*, pp. 21, 28.

76 Anon., 'A New Song, called, The French King's Blood Crying for Vengeance' (n.p., [1793]); anon., 'The Lamentation of the French Queen, in Prison, with the

moving Discourse of the Princess Royal, and the young Dauphin' (n.p., [*c*.1793]). The texts are found on BLBB.

77 Anon., 'A New Song, called, The French King's Blood Crying for Vengeance', BLBB.

78 For English ballads emphasizing the pathos of Marie Antoinette's demise, see, for example, anon., 'The Lamentation of the French Queen, in Prison', and anon., 'A New Song, On the Cruel Usage of the French Queen' ([London], [1793]). The latter is found on BLBB.

79 No. 3, lines 5–6.

80 See ibid., lines 95–8.

81 Nos. 3 and 7, lines 119–20 and 79–80 respectively. Fears of a French landing were prevalent in Britain from February 1793, and English ballads which mention invasion include anon., 'A New Song Called Old England Dry' (Liverpool, n.d.); anon., 'The French Invasion' (n.p., 1794); anon., 'The Voice of the British Isles' ([London], n.d.). See Alexandra Franklin and Mark Philp, *Napoleon and the Invasion of Britain* (Oxford, 2003), p. 8.

82 The narrative impetus to this trend in the historiography lies with the successive Anglo-Saxon invasions of the Brythonic kingdoms of north-east Britain, culminating with their defeat in the late sixth and the seventh century. Representation of the invasions as a punishment for British sin begins with Gildas's *De Excido Britanniae*, and is still vividly present in Theophilus Evans, *Drych y Prif Oesoedd* (1716, 1740). For this theme in the ballads, see Mary-Ann Constantine, 'Welsh Ballads of the French Revolution' (unpublished paper delivered at the International Ballad Conference, Cardiff, July 2008); *eadem*, '"The French are on the sea!"'. The substantial literature on this topic includes Dafydd Glyn Jones, *Gwlad y Brutiau* (Abertawe, 1991).

83 No. 3, lines 35–42.

84 Hugh Jones, *Gwedd o Chwareyddiaeth sef Hanes Bywyd a Marwolaeth, Brenhin, a Brenhines Ffraingc: Ac amryw eraill o'u Deiliaid. Hefyd Darluniad o Grefydd Babaidd: A'r modd y darostyngwyd y Pabyddion yn y Tymestl diweddar* (Trefriw, 1798), pp. 45–6. See the forthcoming edition of the play, Huw Jones, *Hanes Bywyd a Marwolaeth Brenin a Brenhines Ffrainc*, ed. by Ffion Mair Jones; and *eadem*, '"Brave Republicans": Representing the Revolution in a Welsh interlude', in Mary-Ann Constantine and Dafydd Johnston (eds.), *'Footsteps of Liberty and Revolt': Essays on Wales and the French Revolution* (Cardiff, forthcoming).

85 Huw Morys, *Y Rhyfel Cartrefol*, ed. by Ffion Mair Jones (Bangor, [2008]), pp. 143, 145; Ffion Mair Jones, 'Huw Morys and the Civil Wars', *Studia Celtica*, XLIV (2010), 190–2. See also, Luned Davies, 'The Tregaer Manuscript: An Elegy for Charles I', *NLWJ*, XXXI, no. 3 (2000), 243–70.

86 It is not clear what awareness the ballad singers of the late eighteenth century had of the regicide of Charles I. Although poetry on the Civil Wars was published in the popular and influential anthology, *Blodeu-gerdd Cymry* (reissued in 1779), none of the poems included made direct reference to the regicide. See 'Carol gwiliau er coffa am yr hen Frutaniaid yn amser Oliver Crwmwel' and 'Ymddiddan rhwng

y Gwir Brotestant a'r Eglwys', both by Huw Morys; and 'Adroddiad fal y bu gynt' by Rowland Vaughan, in David Jones (ed.), *Blodeu-gerdd Cymry* (Mwythig, 1759), pp. 46–9, 49–52 and 52–5 respectively.

[87] See Jones, "'Gwŷr Lloeger aeth benben â'u brodyr eu hunen'", 210–11.

[88] Michel Delon and Paul-Édouard Levayer, *Chansonnier révolutionnaire* ([Paris], 1989), pp. 102–4.

[89] No. 3, lines 7–14.

[90] The Welsh word 'teulu' may also indicate the meaning 'nation'.

[91] In this respect, Roberts reflects the general state of knowledge in Britain about the charges made against Marie Antoinette at her trial and circulated in France during the years leading up to the Revolution and to her death. See Colley, *Britons: Forging the Nation,* pp. 269–70.

[92] Nos. 3 and 7, lines 64 and 44 respectively.

[93] See further note to no. 3, line 50.

[94] A comparison may be made with reference to the execution of Charles I in a Welsh interlude on the seventeenth-century Civil Wars. 'Ystaffle' is the term used, perhaps in an attempt to render in Welsh the English 'scaffold', and in some confusion with 'ystafell' (room), as if the dramatist were unsure whether this was a public execution or one conducted in private, or otherwise harboured anxiety about re-enacting the death on a public stage. See Huw Morys, *Y Rhyfel Cartrefol,* pp. 145, 232.

[95] See, for instance, anon., 'Hanes y Grefydd Grist'nogol o Ran ei Llwyddiant', in *Y Cylchgrawn Cymraeg,* I (February 1793), 14; and Jones, "'Brave Republicans'".

[96] Note that the United Irish was in any case not an exclusively Catholic sectarian organization. Further on its development, see R. B. McDowell, 'The Age of the United Irishmen: Reform and Reaction, 1789–94', and *idem*, 'The Age of the United Irishmen: Revolution and the Union, 1794–1800', in T. W. Moody and W. E. Vaughan (eds.), *A New History of Ireland. IV. Eighteenth-Century Ireland 1691–1800* (Oxford, 1986; paperback edn., 2009), pp. 289–338, 339–73.

[97] Iain McCalman (ed.), *An Oxford Companion to the Romantic Age: British Culture 1776–1832* (Oxford, 1999), p. 446.

[98] Colin Haydon, 'Religious Minorities in England', in H. T. Dickinson (ed.), *A Companion to Eighteenth-Century Britain* (Oxford, 2002), p. 242; Katrina Navickas, *Loyalism and Radicalism in Lancashire, 1798–1815* (Oxford, 2009), pp. 109–17, esp. 114.

[99] Roland Quinault, 'The French Invasion of Pembrokeshire in 1797', *WHR,* 19, no. 4 (1989), quoted, 619.

[100] Geraint H. Jenkins, Ffion Mair Jones and David Ceri Jones (eds.), *The Correspondence of Iolo Morganwg* (3 vols., Cardiff, 2008), II, p. 19, letter 446, Iolo Morganwg to William Owen Pughe, 7 March 1797.

[101] NLW 1897E II, no. 105, John Jenkins to his mother, 25 April 1797. The brothers, in all fairness, claimed to have written on 9 March, but Jenkins only received a letter dated a month later, 9 April 1797.

[102] Note that the Solva imprint of Thomas Francis's ballad was printed during the 1850s or 1860s. See notes to no. 21.

103 Terry Moylan (ed.), *The Age of Revolution: 1776 to 1815 in the Irish Song Tradition* (Dublin, 2000), p. 23.

104 Anon. (ed.), *A collection of constitutional songs. To which is prefixed, a collection of new toasts and sentiments written on purpose for this work*, I (Cork, 1799–1800), pp. 78–80.

105 For a comparison of the Fishguard ballads and those composed in the aftermath of the 1798 landing and subsequent rebellion in County Wexford, see Constantine, '"The French are on the sea!"'.

106 'The Invasion. (Written in January 1797)', in anon. (ed.), *A collection of constitutional songs*, I, pp. 80–2.

107 No. 14, lines 49–56.

108 No. 12, lines 33–6.

109 No. 19, lines 27–8, 31–40. For an account of the response of a Nonconformist congregation (busy at worship when news of the invasion reached them), see Geraint H. Jenkins, 'Glaniad y Ffrancod yn Abergwaun ym 1797', in *idem, Cadw Tŷ Mewn Cwmwl Tystion: Ysgrifau Hanesyddol ar Grefydd a Diwylliant* (Llandysul, 1990), p. 263. Since Phillip Dafydd was a Methodist, his ballad is unlikely to be referring to this precise instance of a call for God's help. It is nonetheless certain that Methodists also used prayer to quell their fears during the time of the greatest threat.

110 See note to no. 19, lines 163–4.

111 No. 21, lines 43–4, 79.

112 See 'The Invasion. (Written in January 1797)', in anon. (ed.), *A collection of constitutional songs*, I, p. 82.

113 No. 19, lines 81–4. Further on the link between these lines and Richards's pamphlet, see John James Evans, *Dylanwad y Chwyldro Ffrengig ar Lenyddiaeth Cymru* (Lerpwl, 1928), p. 178.

114 [William Richards], *Cwyn y Cystuddiedig a griddfanau y carcharorion dieuog, neu, ychydig o hanes dyoddefiadau diweddar Thomas John a Samuel Griffiths, y rhai goddef gorthrymder tost a chaethiwed caled . . . yn ddi-achos, a gawsant eu rhyddhau . . . yn Hwlfford . . .* (Caerfyrddin, 1798), p. 19. The translation is my own. Although an English translation of the pamphlet, under the title *Triumphs of Innocency*, was advertised as forthcoming at the end of the Welsh original, it appears that this was never completed. *Ex inf.* Dr Marion Löffler.

115 See Ffion Mair Jones, '"The silly expressions of French Revolution . . .": The Experience of the Dissenting Community in South-West Wales, 1797', in David Andress (ed.), *Experiencing the French Revolution* (Oxford, forthcoming).

116 For example, in the discussion of 'John Wilkes and Englishness', in Colley, *Britons: Forging the Nation*, pp. 112–22.

117 The chorus to an anonymous poem, 'The Sons of Albion' ([London], [?1814]), is a case in point: 'Neither rebels, French, or Sanscullote, / Nor the dupes of tyranny boast, / Shall conquer the English the Irish, nor the Scotch, / Nor shall land upon our coast'. BLBB. Note that there are several other imprints of this ballad on BLBB. See further note to no. 4.

118 Nesta Lloyd (ed.), *Blodeugerdd Barddas o'r Ail Ganrif ar Bymtheg*, I (Barddas, 1993), pp. 284–6, 422–3. The 'Ymddiddan rhwng Rowndyn a Merch', which appears in

the same anthology and is dated by Lloyd to 1642–9, may be a translation of the work of the ballad-writer Laurence Price. It includes a reference to Wales which, if this was a translation, may well have been added to the original poem. See ibid., pp. 423. On the period and the continued historiographical trend towards glossing over Wales, see Morys, *Y Rhyfel Cartrefol*, pp. 38–47; Jones, 'Huw Morys and the Civil Wars', 186–7.

[119] Britain is described in the same way in no. 23, line 68.

[120] For stories of female involvement in repelling the French at Fishguard, see no. 21, note to lines 37–8, and further Quinault, 'The French Invasion of Pembrokeshire in 1797', 629.

[121] On the sharp linguistic divide in Pembrokeshire, see Russell Davies, 'Language and Community in South-west Wales *c.*1800–1914', in Geraint H. Jenkins (ed.), *Language and Community in the Nineteenth Century* (Cardiff, 1998), pp. 106–8.

[122] No. 18, lines 111–20.

[123] Richards, *Cwyn y Cystuddiedig*, pp. 36–46.

[124] Cf. Rees Prichard, 'Achwyn Mr. Prichard ynghylch Tre' Llanddyfri a'i rybudd a'i gyngor ef iddi', in Lloyd (ed.), *Blodeugerdd Barddas o'r Ail Ganrif ar Bymtheg*, I, pp. 280–3.

[125] Quinault, 'The French Invasion of Pembrokeshire in 1797', 628.

[126] No. 15, lines 63–8.

[127] Further on these leaders see the notes to nos. 23 and 24.

[128] See note to no. 22, Author, and footnote no. 152.

[129] Amanda Goodrich comments on the large number of anonymous pamphlets published between 1790 and 1796, many of which were loyalist. The evidence suggests that 'anonymity was not primarily a refuge for radicals avoiding pros-ecution'. 'Surveying the Ebb and Flow of Pamphlet Warfare: 500 Rival Tracts from Radicals and Loyalists in Britain, 1790–1796', *British Journal for Eighteenth-Century Studies*, 30, no. 1 (2007), 7.

[130] William Pinn, 'A Novel Description of His Majesty's Review of the Kentish Volunteers, August 1st, 1799', in *idem, Poems, on various subjects: in which is a most beautiful and novel description of His Majesty's review of the Kentish Volunteers* (Chatham, 1800), p. 66.

[131] The accessibility of earlier militia ballads is suggested by the print history of ballad no. 11.

[132] The most complete study of the regular militia remains J. R. Western, *The English Militia in the Eighteenth Century: The Story of a Political Issue 1660–1802* (London, 1965). For the development of volunteering from the 1790s onwards, see Kevin B. Linch, '"A Citizen and Not a Soldier": The British Volunteer Movement and the War against Napoleon', in Alan Forrest, Karen Hagemann and Jane Rendall (eds.), *Soldiers, Citizens and Civilians: Experiences and Perceptions of the Revolutionary and Napoleonic Wars, 1790–1820* (Basingstoke, 2009), p. 209.

[133] For a reaction to cases of abuse within Welsh regular militia corps in 1781, see Thomas Pennant, *Free Thoughts on the Militia Laws . . . addressed to the Poor Inhabitants of North Wales* (London, 1781), and the discussion in Jones, '"Gwŷr Lloeger aeth

benben â'u brodyr eu hunen'", 214–15. For the excessive numbers of men who offered to serve as volunteers in Merionethshire in 1803, see Hugh J. Owen, *Merioneth Volunteers and Local Militia During the Napoleonic Wars (1795–1816)* (Dolgelley, [1934]), pp. 58–60.

134 See, for example, Rosser Llwyd, 'Carol, anogol gynigiad, ar Frydain hyfrydol erfyniad' (Caerfyrddin, 1759; JHD 508). Further on this and other Welsh militia ballads dating from the 1750s to the early nineteenth century, see Ffion Mair Jones, '"A'r Ffeiffs a'r Drums yn roario": Y Baledwyr Cymraeg, y Milisia a'r Gwirfoddolwyr', *Canu Gwerin*, 34 (2011), 18–42.

135 See notes to no. 11.

136 No. 11, lines 37–40.

137 Anon., 'A new song calld the Militia-Man', in NLW, Bodwenni 246, *The Militia-Men's Garland, containing 4 new songs*, pp. 2–4. The printed pamphlet is undated, but other internal evidence suggests a late 1750s–early 1760s date.

138 On Jonathan Hughes's firm commitment to his native tongue but simultaneous readiness to write clumsy English verse on occasion (often in deference to English patrons including the Ladies of Llangollen and the Chirk Castle family), see Siwan M. Rosser (ed.), *Bardd Pengwern: Detholiad o Gerddi Jonathan Hughes, Llangollen (1721–1805)* (Barddas, 2007), p. 17.

139 Anon., 'A New Song in Praise of the Loyal Holywell Volunteers' (1797), quoted in R. Paul Evans, 'The Flintshire Loyalist Association and the Loyal Holywell Volunteers', *Flintshire Historical Society Journal*, 33 (1992), 65–6; a stanza on the tune of 'The Vicar of Bray', quoted from an unnamed source by Owen, *Merioneth Volunteers and Local Militia*, pp. 55–6. Other English-language poetry relating to volunteer forces emanated from the border town of Oswestry. See anon., 'A song, presented to the Lady of Owen Ormsby, Esq; at Porkington, February 5th, 1798', and 'British Toasts. Porkington. Nov.r 14. 1799 (Tune Gen.l Toast)', NLW, Brogyntyn Estate Records, PQH1/5, unpaginated. See also the untitled song beginning 'General Hill's gone to sea, hey boys, ho boys!' (1808) which sings the praises of the 'Shropshire Militia Boys', in Michael Peele, *Shropshire in Poem and Legend* (Shrewsbury, 1923), pp. 124–5.

140 John Thomas, 'Cerdd newydd i annerch volunteers Gwynedd' (Trefriw, n.d.; JHD 806ii).

141 For dating issues relating to this ballad, see notes to no. 28.

142 On Caswallon, see note to no. 28. On Milford Haven in the 'canu brud', see Margaret Enid Griffiths, *Early Vaticination in Welsh with English Parallels*, ed. by T. Gwynn Jones (Cardiff, 1937), p. 151. See also the 1768 ballad by an Anglican clergyman, George Owen, 'Rhyfeddol Broffwydoliaeth Myrddin' (n.p., [1768]; JHD 672), which was reprinted in 1796 (n.p., [1796]; JHD 792). It contains a reference to the ruddying of the river Tywi on account of an English presence at 'Aber Milffort', and describes a full-scale battle in the same location, in which a Protestant force shall be victorious.

143 Anon., 'Cerdd a wnaed i filitia Cymru, i'w chanu ar Drymder' (Dolgelleu, [1799]; JHD701ii). See notes to no. 37.

[144] On this aspect of earlier militia songs, see Jones, '"A'r Ffeiffs a'r Drums yn roario"'.

[145] Note that members of the regular militia were not obliged to serve outside Great Britain, so that their chances of survival would be considerably higher than those of soldiers serving in the regular army, for whom life 'too frequently proved brutal and short'. Significant numbers of militia men would transfer their service to the regular forces during the Napoleonic wars, however, partially making up for the shortage in numbers due to the unprecedented scale of casualties incurred. Bryn Owen has suggested that the Denbighshire militia became an 'Army of Reserve capable of supplying the regular Army with a steady stream of well trained re-inforcements' following the victory at Trafalgar in 1805. See David Gates, 'The Transformation of the Army 1783–1815', in David G. Chandler and Ian Beckett (eds.), *The Oxford History of the British Army* (Oxford, 1994; paperback edn., 2003), pp. 133, 137, 138; Bryn Owen, *History of the Welsh Militia and Volunteer Corps 1757–1908: Denbighshire & Flintshire (Part 1)* (Wrexham, 1997), pp. 28, 31.

[146] NLW, D. Rhys Phillips, 321, p. iii.

[147] Ibid., p. iii, and, further, see notes to no. 5.

[148] It may date from the period of the American War of Independence, but was not published until well into the nineteenth century, which suggests that it enjoyed a lengthy circulation within oral tradition. A degree of confusion in the narrative of the preserved text also suggests a history of oral transmission. The ballad is found in imprints by William Morris, Aberdare, n.d. (Bangor 28 (18)); and by T. Howells, Glebeland, Merthyr [Tydfil], n.d. (NLW, 'Baledi a Cherddi', 19, no. 61).

[149] For other examples of itinerant writers (often ballad writers) connected with the military, see Michael Harris, 'A Few Shillings for Small Books: The Experience of a Flying Stationer in the 18th Century', in Robin Myers and Michael Harris (eds.), *Spreading the Word: The Distribution Networks of Print 1550–1850* (New Castle, Delaware, 1998), pp. 105–6, note 44.

[150] See notes to no. 5. An adaptation of the ballad in north Wales during the 1870s exchanged the place-name Llangyfelach for Caernarfon. See D. Rhys Phillips, 231, p. iv; and for the text, anon., 'Bachgen yn ymadael a'i enedigol wlad. Hen gerdd a gyfansoddwyd gan' mlynedd yn ol' (Caernarfon, n.d.), Cardiff City Library, Ballads and Fugitive Pieces, I, f. 152.

[151] No. 5, lines 29–32.

[152] On the use of a closing stanza referring to the poet in ballads composed by women, see Rosser, *Y Ferch ym Myd y Faled*, pp. 5–7. Rosser notes the popularity of such formulaic endings (by male as well as female poets) in early free-metre Welsh poetry, and suggests that it is essentially connected to oral rather than printed balladry.

[153] Cf. the story of Joseph Mayett, a Buckinghamshire farm servant, who 'enlisted in his county's militia in 1803 because he was taken out of himself for once by the recruiting party's brass band, led to his doom by music quite as much as the children who followed the Pied Piper of Hamelin'. Colley, *Britons: Forging the Nation*, p. 325.

[154] See notes to no. 29.

[155] No. 29, lines 73–6.

[156] For examples of a contemporary onlooker's response to the volunteers, see notes to no. 29, line 111.

[157] For comments on the difficulty of assessing the nature of the experience of volunteering for the volunteers themselves, see Linch, '"A Citizen and Not a Soldier"', pp. 207–8.

[158] Anon., 'Can newydd yn dangos fod bradwriaeth ar droed; ac yn golygu y bydd terfysg rhwng gwledydd a'u gilydd yn yr amser presennol' (Trefriw, 1815), Bangor 9 (28).

[159] See anon., 'Come all you warriors', and anon., 'Some Treat of David', both dated 1798, in Georges-Denis Zimmerman (ed.), *Songs of Irish Rebellion: Political Street Ballads and Rebel Songs 1780–1900* (Dublin, 1967), pp. 142–8. For a discussion of 'the often violent and destructive everyday experience' of the Napoleonic wars, drawing on primary documents including letters, diaries and memoirs relating to the Battle of the Nations, fought at Leipzig, 16–19 October 1813, see Karen Hagemann, '"Unimaginable Horror and Misery": The Battle of Leipzig in October 1813 in Civilian Experience and Perception', in Forrest, Hagemann and Rendall (eds.), *Soldiers, Citizens and Civilians*, pp. 157–78. For a Welsh ballad which attempts to invoke a heroism in some ways comparable to that shown in the Irish texts, see ballad no. 30 by Evan James, which conjures up the names of Welsh heroes of the past and attacks both a brutish, butcher-like Napoleon and the 'false' Irish.

[160] By the mid-1780s Wales and the East Midlands were among the areas best served by the newspaper industry. Hannah Barker, *Newspapers, Politics and Public Opinion in Late Eighteenth-Century England* (Oxford, 1998), pp. 122, 124. The periodical press in Wales is discussed in a new study by Marion Löffler, *Welsh Responses to the French Revolution: Press and Public Discourse 1789–1802* (Cardiff, forthcoming).

[161] NLW 12350A, 'Diary . . . of John Davies, Ystrad, 1796–9', pp. 24, 81.

[162] Thanksgiving was celebrated on 29 November in 1797 and 1798. In the latter year, Davies noted that he had seen 'the following lines stuck up on the church door of Ystrad church' on this day:

> Vile Hereticks are these your Pranks
> To murder men and give god thanks
> Vain Hypocrites Proceed no further, –
> For god accepts no thanks for murder.

See ibid., pp. 81, 109. The reference to reading Paine's *Age of Reason* (parts 1 and 2, 1794, 1795) is in ibid., p. 83. For Davies's handwritten copies of radical poetry (some taken from printed sources, others circulated in manuscript), see ibid., pp. 6–7, 88–9, 103, 128–9.

[163] No. 8, lines 25–32.

[164] No. 16, lines 25–8.

[165] Huw Jones's 'Ychydig o hanes y fattel fu'n ddiweddar mewn ynys a elwir Gansi lle darfu ir Ffrangcod feddwl ei bod wedi ei hynill hi, a thrwy ryfedd Ragluniaeth

Duw fel y darfu i ychydig nifer o wyr Lloegr eu gorchfygu nhw' (Trefriw, 1781; JHD 329i) is an exception in the case of the American War, but relates to a battle in nearby Guernsey rather than to any of the battles fought in North America itself. It would be misleading to suggest that no ballads reporting on warfare were sung during the earlier eighteenth century. For one example, see the 1758 poem by Huw Jones, 'Dechrau cerdd o goffadwriaeth am orfoleddus lwyddiant brenin Prwsia ar ei holl elynion gyda chywir hanes am gymaint a laddodd a chymaint oedd i'w erbyn', in Edwards and Lake (eds.), *Detholiad o Faledi Huw Jones*, pp. 46–7.

[166] No. 9, lines 5–6. It is unlikely that either Robert Roberts or Edward Pugh had published ballads before the 1790s, so that they would have had no personal experience of singing on the theme of war. See 'Cronfa Baledi', s.n. Edward Pugh and Robert Roberts.

[167] See above, under 'The Fishguard invasion (1797): loyalty, identity and the hand of God'.

[168] See notes to no. 9, lines 53–60.

[169] A. H. Burne, *The Noble Duke of York* (London, 1949), pp. 144–7. The poem's source is *An Accurate and Impartial Narrative of the War, by an Officer of the Guards* which, although undated, Burne considers to have been contemporary. See ibid., p. 342.

[170] No. 9, lines 35–44.

[171] *Y Cylchgrawn Cynmraeg*, II (May 1793), 120; III (August 1793), 179, 234, 235; [IV] (January/February 1794), 287, 288.

[172] *The London Chronicle*, issue 5899 (20 May 1794); *The World (1787)*, issue 2310 (23 May 1794); *The Oracle and Public Advertiser*, issue 18705 (24 May 1794).

[173] See, for example, anon., 'A new song, called Lord Howe's Glorious Victory over the French' [?1800]; anon., *Four New Songs, viz. 1. Howe's defeat of the French fleet, on June the 1st, 1794 . . .* [1805]; Stephen Storace, *The Glorious First of June: The Favorite Airs, Duett, Glees, & Chorusses in the New Musical Entertainment, call'd The Glorious First of June, as Performed . . . for the Benefit of the Widows and Orphans of the Brave Men who fell in the Late Engagements under Earl Howe* (London, [1794]). All three sources are housed at the British Library. No ballads prioritizing this battle are included on BLBB.

[174] NLW, Elizabeth Baker, no. 395, John Morris to William Morris, 14 June 1794.

[175] Cf. the correspondence of members of the Jenkins family of Cardiganshire, who spent many years in the navy during this period. See e.g. NLW 1897E i, no. 16, Jeremiah Jenkins to John Jenkins, 2 February 1804, which contains detailed information about the position of the enemy fleet. Morris's letter to his parents, in spite of its grisly detail, gives the impression of his own pride in serving with Howe and his personal investment in the action. This perhaps challenges what N. A. M. Rodger has described as 'a common opinion, derived in considerable measure from Masefield's *Sea Life in Nelson's Time*, that naval discipline was harsh and oppressive, officers frequently cruel and tyrannical, ratings drawn from the dregs of society, ill-treated and starved'. N. A. M. Rodger, *The Wooden World: An Anatomy of the Georgian Navy* (London, 1986), pp. 11–12.

[176] Note, however, that copies of letters from naval officers to government officials often served as the first sources of information about battles in contemporary newspapers.

[177] Cf. 'Gweith Argoet Llwyfein', where Urien prepares his men for battle with a string of first-person plural verbs in the imperative mood:'dyrchafwn' (let us raise), 'porthwn' (let us consume),'[c]yrchwn' (let us attack) and finally 'lladwn' (let us kill). Ifor Williams (ed.), *The Poems of Taliesin*, English version by J. E. Caerwyn Williams (Dublin, 1987), pp. 6–7.

[178] No. 10, lines 11–12. For the tune, see notes to nos. 8 and 9, and the setting included in the appendix.

[179] Jones's interlude, *Hanes Bywyd a Marwolaeth Brenin a Brenhines Ffrainc*, also suggests that he was a keen reader of several sources, including newspapers.

[180] Two copies of 'Jervis taking the Spanish Fleet' are preserved on BLBB, one printed in Dumfries (n.d.) and the other without an imprint.

[181] See footnote no. 180 for 'Jervis taking the Spanish Fleet'; and for 'Naval Victories', see John Holloway and Jean Black (eds.), *Later English Broadside Ballads, Volume 2* (London, 1979), p. 164: 'But Valentine's day next and great Jervis / No pen can describe, nor no lingo can speak'.

[182] A catalogue of British heroes, including Elizabethan ones, are named in 'On the threatened invasion', anon. (ed.), *A collection of constitutional songs*, I, pp. 26–7. Note that the Spanish Armada was the subject of an early Welsh ballad-style poem. Tegwyn Jones, 'Brasolwg ar y Faled Newyddiadurol yng Nghymru cyn y Cyfnod Argraffu', *Canu Gwerin*, 25 (2002), 8–9.

[183] Mark Philp, 'Politics and Memory: Nelson and Trafalgar in Popular Song', in David Cannadine (ed.), *Trafalgar in History: A Battle and its Afterlife* (Basingstoke, 2006), p. 99. The following discussion only considers the three printed Welsh ballads relating to Nelson. A Nelson poem is included in both Thomas (ed.), *Corph y Gaingc*, pp. 201–4, and Jonathan Hughes, *Gemwaith Awen Beirdd Collen* (Croesoswallt, 1806), pp. 179–82.

[184] The paper was intended from its inception in 1804 to serve Wales in its entirety. See Louise Miskell, *'Intelligent Town': An Urban History of Swansea, 1780–1855* (Cardiff, 2006), pp. 53–4.

[185] See the untitled stanza ("When England's Fleet, resistless on the main") by William Davies of Cringell, Neath; 'On Nelson's Victory and Death' by 'Cymro' (a Welshman); and 'On Nelson's Death' by J.A. of Swansea in the *Cambrian*, 16 November 1805, 3, 4; the anonymous stanza 'On Nelson's Death', in ibid., 23 November 1805, 3; an 'Acrostic' (spelling out 'Nelson') by Tyro; and 'On the Death of Lord Nelson' by the seventeen year old R.W. of Swansea in ibid., 21 December 1805, 4. For the poetry competition see ibid., 23 November 1805, 1.

[186] Morgans's manuscript, Cwrtmawr 370A (unpaginated), contains a lengthy poem on Nelson dated 1 May 1806. It also includes an eight-stanza poem entitled 'On the Death of Admiral Lord Nelson'. On the provenance of the manuscript, see B. G. Owens, Rhiannon Francis Roberts and R. W. McDonald, *A Catalogue of the Cwrtmawr Manuscripts Presented and Bequeathed by John Humphreys Davies*, II (Aberystwyth, 1993), p. 425.

[187] NLW 192B (unpaginated). The poem is said to have been written for S. Allen Jones, Mold, and clearly hails from a song original, since it is divided under the headings 'Recitative' and 'Air'.

[188] For a modern edition of the text, see E. G. Millward (ed.), *Cerddi Jac Glan-y-gors* (Barddas, 2003), pp. 132–3.

[189] 'Jervis taking the Spanish Fleet' reports the events of the battle of Cape St Vincent in a typically patriotic manner, but turns in the final lines to the question of the women and children left destitute by British losses.

[190] Reformist as well as loyalist poets could demonstrate this kind of patriotism, as Mark Philp has shown to be the case with John Freeth, the Birmingham ballad-writer. See Philp, 'Politics and Memory', p. 96. Freeth composed celebratory ballads on the victories of Howe in June 1794 and Nelson at the battle of the Nile; see 'On Admiral Nelson's Victory Britannia Triumphant' and 'The Tars of Old England (Written on the day the news came of Lord Howe's victory)', in John Horden, *John Freeth (1731–1808): Political Ballad-writer and Innkeeper* (Oxford, 1993), pp. 197–8, 200. See also the patriotic 'Ode to the Glamorgan Volunteers' (1798) by the radical stone-mason and poet, Iolo Morganwg, in Jenkins, Jones and Jones (eds.), *The Correspondence of Iolo Morganwg*, II, pp. 556, 716; III, pp. 84, 85–7.

[191] See *BWB*, p. 149, no. 459.

[192] See Millward (ed.), *Cerddi Jac Glan-y-gors*, p. 133.

[193] No. 26, lines 13–20.

[194] Millward (ed.), *Cerddi Jac Glan-y-gors*, p. 133, notes that the combined French and Spanish fleets lost almost 4,500 men in the action at Trafalgar.

[195] Vic Gammon, 'The Grand Conversation: Napoleon and British Popular Balladry', at *http://www.mustrad.org.uk/articles/boney.htm*; Philp, 'Politics and Memory', p. 117; and for typical ballads, see BLBB and notes to nos. 34, 35 and 36. On Napoleon's reception in Plymouth, see F. M. H. Markham, *Napoleon and the Awakening of Europe* (London, 1954), p. 164.

[196] Waterloo is remembered in a small number of folk songs and ballads, but Napoleon goes unmentioned. See Dafydd Jones, 'Rhyfel-gerdd Twrci a Rwssia; a llaw-gymorth Prydain, i achub Twrci rhag Rwssia', in Mary Lilian Parry-Jones, 'Astudiaeth o Faledi Dafydd Jones, Llanybydder: Eu Cefndir a'u Cynnwys' (unpublished University of Wales MPhil dissertation, 1990), pp. 129–32; and 'Gwn Dafydd Ifan', in Mrs Herbert Lewis, *Folk Songs Collected in Flintshire and the Vale of Clwyd* (Wrexham, 1914), pp. 34–5; *Cylchgrawn Cymdeithas Alawon Gwerin Cymru*, IV, part 4 (1954), 102.

[197] No. 36, lines 18–20.

[198] See notes to no. 3.

[199] On nineteenth-century practice, where balladeers usually sang their own work (although borrowing was also very much in vogue), see Tegwyn Jones, 'Baledi a Baledwyr y Bedwaredd Ganrif ar Bymtheg', in Geraint H. Jenkins (ed.), *Cof Cenedl VI: Ysgrifau ar Hanes Cymru* (Llandysul, 1991), pp. 101–34. Note, however, the case of Robert Jones (Callestr Fardd), who wrote poetry for a specific impoverished balladmonger, John Lloyd, during the 1830s, suggesting that the eighteenth-century

practice dividing 'prydydd' from 'baledwr' was not entirely extinct by this stage. See ibid, pp. 105–6.

[200] No. 35, lines 121–4.

[201] For the gradual increase in the numbers of Welsh-language journals and newspapers during the first half of the nineteenth century, see Huw Walters, *A Bibliography of Welsh Periodicals 1735–1850* (Aberystwyth, 1993); and on the threat posed by the periodical press to Welsh balladry, see Tegwyn Jones, 'Welsh Ballads', in Philip Henry Jones and Eiluned Rees (eds.), *A Nation and its Books: A History of the Book in Wales* (Aberystwyth, 1998), p. 249.

[202] No. 13, lines 65–72.

[203] Hywel Davies notes that Bob Owen of Croesor claimed that 1,340 (elsewhere 1,349) Welsh people emigrated to the United States between 1794 and 1801. Davies advises caution in the use of these figures, however, since Owen did not 'cite his authorities' in presenting them. Hywel M. Davies, '"Very different springs of uneasiness": Emigration from Wales to the United States of America during the 1790s', *WHR*, 15, no. 3 (1991), 381.

[204] No. 25, lines 45–8.

[205] The poet may have intended a reference to the controversy between Methodists and churchmen which was in full flow in the early years of the nineteenth century and resulted in an intense pamphlet war between attackers of Methodism and its defenders. See David Erwyd Jenkins, *The Life of the Rev. Thomas Charles, B.A., of Bala, promoter of Charity and Sunday Schools, founder of the British and Foreign Bible Society, etc.* (3 vols., Denbigh, 1908), II, pp. 355–93. For Welsh radical song in the period, see Constantine and Edwards, 'Bard of Liberty'. 'Breiniau Dyn', a radical song composed by Iolo Morganwg in 1798, was not printed as a ballad until the 1840s, when it was used by the Chartists. See 'Breiniau Dyn. Can Newydd' (n.p., n.d.), Salisbury Library, Cardiff University (T. J. 5023 (Sal). 1/86). On another copy in the same library (David John, Ieu., and Morgan Williams, Merthyr [Tydfil], T. J. 3664), apparently identical, a pencil note reads 'Published as a supplement to "Udgorn Cymru", Oct. 1, 1841'. See further Geraint and Zonia Bowen, *Hanes Gorsedd y Beirdd* (Abertawe, 1991), pp. 40–1; and E. Wyn James, 'Welsh Ballads and American Slavery', *The Welsh Journal of Religious History*, 2 (2007), 59–86.

[206] Navickas, *Loyalism and Radicalism in Lancashire*, pp. 6–7.

[207] Ibid., pp. 1–2.

[208] See Robert Davies, 'Cân yn achos y rhyfel', in *Dwy Gerdd Ddiddan Gyntaf* [*sic*] *yn dangos fel y siomodd Merch y prydydd Can yn achos y Rhyfel, gan Robert Davies o Nanglyn* (Trefriw, [?1813]), in Bangor 9 (12).

Texts and
Translations

Editorial principles

In editing the ballads in this anthology, the following practices have been adopted, with a view to presenting a Welsh-language text that is accessible to modern readers but simultaneously preserves the distinct eighteenth- and early nineteenth-century idiom of the ballads, in its informality and dialectal nature. Translations into English are set on parallel pages. These aim to represent as literally as possible the meaning of the Welsh text, and those conversant with both languages should be able to compare text and translation with relative ease. Where more than one imprint of a ballad has survived, the imprint containing the better readings has been selected as the main text, although, in some cases, other imprints have dictated the placing of individual ballads within the chronology of the anthology (e.g. nos. 11, 28). Further imprints (and in some cases manuscript and printed book versions) are listed underneath, together with variant readings (where significant). The vast majority of eighteenth-century Welsh ballads were catalogued by the collector and scholar J. H. Davies in his *Bibliography of Welsh Ballads Printed in the Eighteenth Century* (London, 1911). Davies numbered the texts and, following his death, further texts discovered were likewise given 'JHD numbers'.[1] These are crucial finding aids for the student of these ballads and have been included at the foot of each text, together with information (where known) about the publisher, the seller, the publication date of the ballad, and the title of the document in which it was printed, if different from the individual ballad title. Sources of all texts, including variants, are also included. In several cases, the most accessible source is 'Welsh Ballads Online', a database including full ballad texts found on the National Library of Wales's website (*http://cat.llgc.org.uk/ballads*). The sources used on the database are also named, if given there. Further information is provided where relevant: for example, references to woodcuts or other decorations, notes on the relationship of various imprints, and the titles of the pamphlets where the texts were published (given in their original form, unedited).

Punctuation and capitalization have been standardized fully. An attempt has been made to synchronize the punctuation of the edited Welsh version as far as possible with the English translation. Printers' errors have been corrected silently, but a note is made underneath the Welsh text if a ballad has been particularly badly composed (e.g. no. 12). Errors typically include placing a 'u' for an 'n' and vice versa, or joining words together haphazardly. Variant readings between texts, where the variation may impinge upon the meaning of a word or phrase, are given in a section headed 'Variants' at the bottom of the edited Welsh versions, and significant editorial changes are likewise signalled in a section headed 'Textual readings', also placed below the edited Welsh text, which gives the original readings of the text. Missing or illegible sections and doubtful readings are presented using square brackets. An illegible section is represented by a line enclosed in square brackets ([---]), the length of the line corresponding to the length of the section that is missing. When it is possible to hazard a guess at what is illegible, this is done by using square brackets, in which the guess-reading is placed, preceded by a question mark ([?A'r]). The question mark is omitted if it is possible to guess a reading beyond reasonable doubt ([A'r]). When a slight change is needed to a word in order for a line to scan, or to render the meaning clear, these have been added in italics (e.g. 'briw-ŵyr', 'Ysbaen').

The issues of spelling, orthography, dialectal forms and grammar present the greatest challenges to the editor of these ballads. Orthographical features have been standardized: e.g. accents (the latter mostly circumflex accents) have been inserted or taken away; use of the letters 'y' and 'u', often diverging from modern practice in these texts, have been standardized; and letters have been doubled according to modern practices ('n' is doubled in modern Welsh in certain places, whereas 't' never is, although the ballad writers or their printers were fond of doubling it in words such as 'eto').

The epenthetic 'h' (e.g. in 'brenhin') has been omitted, although the 'h' at the beginning of a word (e.g. 'henwaf', 'hefo', both listed as variant forms in *GPC*) has been retained. The 'g' inserted to represent the 'ng' sound (un-necessarily according to current orthographical practices) has also been omitted (e.g. in 'Ffraingc'), whereas the 'th' in 'bytho' (< byddo) (also in 'thyne' and ''tholodd') has been retained. Cases where the 't' of the standard form is softened to a 'd' (as in 'adgyweirio' or 'melldigedig') have been left unchanged with the exception of the term 'Ymneillduwyr' which is found within close proximity to the standard form of 'Ymneilltuwyr' in no. 2, and has for that reason been standardized throughout. The hardened 'p' has likewise been softened to a 'b' except in the word 'papist'. Words divided or brought together in a non-standard way have been adapted (e.g. 'ynghanol' is rendered as 'yng nghanol' and 'yngwyneb', although properly 'yn wyneb', as 'yng ngwyneb').

Dialect endings remain unchanged: e.g. 'genedlaetha' (< genedlaethau), 'galonne' (< galonnau). Where adding an apostrophe for a missing letter or letters is a straightforward task, this has been done (e.g. 'cry' > 'cry', 'e' – > 'e"). Epenthetic vowels are ubiquitous in these texts, and have been retained (e.g. 'powdwr' (< powdr), 'eger' (< egr), 'hoedel' (< hoedl/hoeddl), 'brwydyr' (< brwydr)), and sometimes even added, in italic script, if their presence is necessary to the scansion of a line (e.g. 'Ymguddio yn y dwf*w*n fôr' or 'Fo'n cymryd Llyf*y*r Duw yn rheol'). Loss of the diphthong is also common, as in 'gwcha' (< gwycha'), 'nerthodd' (< nerthoedd), or 'degryn' (< deigryn). Diphthongs are also occasionally changed (e.g. 'gowsant' < gawsant) or added ('sybwyll' < sybwll). These forms have been retained, with the exception of the added diphthong in 'ei' and 'ein' in 'ei gyd' and 'ein magasoch', which have been changed to 'i gyd' and 'y'n magasoch' in the interest of clarity. The loss of the diphthongs 'ae' and 'oe' is a particular feature of the language of the texts composed in south-west Wales. In these cases an apostrophe has been included to designate the lost letter (e.g. 'bla'n', 'gro's'). The ballad writers' own use of apostrophes calls for attention, too: they regularly apostrophize verbal nouns such as 'rho'i', 'c'odi', 'gwel'd', 'myn'd', or nouns such as 'Crist'nogion' or 'cym'dogaeth', all of which derive from lengthier word forms (rhoddi, cyfodi, gweled, myned, Cristionogion, cymydogaeth), but are rendered in their shortened forms in today's standard language ('rhoi', 'codi', 'gweld', 'mynd', 'Cristnogion', 'cymdogaeth'). The apostrophes used in the ballads have thus been omitted, in the interests of providing an accessible text for the modern reader, with some exceptions where it was felt that retaining them might aid comprehension (e.g. 'bon'ddigion', 'ddae'ren', 'g'reuddyd', 'ieu'nctid', 't'ranau').

Some word forms are unexpected to the modern ear. We have, for instance, 'duc' or 'duwc' for 'dug'; 'calyn', usually rendered as 'canlyn'; 'cynfigen', usually 'cenfigen'; 'rhydd-did' or 'rhydid', usually 'rhyddid'; or 'tywyllwg', usually 'tywyllwch'. All of these are included as variants in *GPC* and there is no justification for changing them. Some additional word forms, not listed as variants in *GPC*, but sometimes seen in its examples of usage, are also included (e.g. 'rhegu', listed in an 1803 example in *GPC*, '[c]wsglyd', 'haulwen', '[m]orwyodd'). Plural forms of nouns not listed in *GPC* are also included (e.g. 'ffryndiau', 'ffrynds', 'gelynod', '[p]laue'). Plural forms ending '-iad' instead of the standard '-iaid', common in the oral and written language of this period, have also been retained (e.g. 'Bapistiad', 'penaethiad'). Only very occasionally have word forms been changed: e.g. 'gwiaill' to 'gwiail' (no. 15, line 53), or 'gwincio' to 'gwencio' (ibid., line 88). Such changes are signalled in the section headed 'Textual readings', previously mentioned.

A jostling between a literary or standard language and the oral dialect is apparent throughout these texts. This dual linguistic culture is nowhere more apparent than at the point of the rhyme. The ballad writers move fluidly from literary to oral in their attempts to find satisfactory rhymes. Nonetheless, the printed texts often do not record the word forms necessary for a satisfactory rhyme. Ballad no. 18, for example, includes the following rhymes: 'dwylaw' / 'distrywio'; 'ofn' / 'gelynion'; 'chaethiwed' / 'Syriaid'. By adjusting one word in each pair either to a literary or to an oral form, all of these pairings could be made to yield correct rhymes: 'dwylo' / 'distrywio'; 'ofon' / 'gelynion'; 'chaethiwed' / 'Syried'. The poets and printers' inability to regularize such features testifies to the fluidity of the language in this period – poised between the influences of local dialect and the literary language promoted largely by the Bible. In this anthology, the decision to change words so that they secure a satisfactory rhyme has been made on a case-by-case basis, taking issues such as the likely provenance of the poem and the general gist of a particular section within it to account.[2] Complicated changes involving several words and less-than-satisfactory word forms have been avoided.

Issues relating to grammar include faulty mutations (e.g. 'Am doethder', 'i'r coron', 'yn liwgar', 'Saith ddeg', 'Yr ail dydd'), which have been retained unless the demands of alliteration dictated otherwise, and how to present pronouns (e.g. ''i' < 'ei' is often given instead of the plural form ''u' < 'eu'). The latter have been standardized. Other issues include the use of sub-standard forms such as 'ac heb', 'ac hefyd' and 'cymeryd' (< cymryd) still common in the spoken and written language today; and the omission of the definite article before 'rheini' (those) (e.g. 'a rheini' < a'r rheini) or of the 'c' in 'nac' in 'na ymddiffyn'. These features have been reproduced as in the original texts. The insertion of an 'i' before the conjunction 'bod' in 'i fod' is a feature of the oral language of some of the south-west poets, and has likewise been retained. The relative pronoun 'a' in 'a fu' or 'a ddarfu' is sometimes rendered by the poets as a 'y' ('y fu', 'y ddarfu'), and the definite article or preverbal particle 'y' as 'i' ('ir cyfle' < yr cyfle; 'i mae' < y mae). These features have been standardized.

Elision of vowels at word boundaries has been standardized (e.g. 'fe ei' > 'fe'i'; 'eto yn' > 'eto'n'; 'llwyddo yn llawn' > 'llwyddo'n llawn'), with a few exceptions where retaining the lengthier form (without the elision) benefits the requirements of the metrical line. Occasional editorial additions have been made to improve the metre or to clarify the meaning within any given line; these are placed in italics.

The texts include a sizeable number of words borrowed from English. Where such Anglicizations are included in *GPC* with a standardized Welsh spelling, this has been adopted (e.g. 'army' > 'armi'; 'sentry' > 'sentri'; 'militia'

> 'milisia'). Where the form of a word given clearly reflects its English origin, the English form has been used, placed in italics (e.g. *soldiers*, *officer*, *fleet*, *sailors* (> 'sealers')). Borrowings are sometimes less straightforward, since the orthography used reflects the transitional state of a word, partially retaining its English spelling, partially taking on features relating to its pronunciation by Welsh speakers (e.g. 'Bony Parti', poised between 'Bony Party' and 'Boni Parti', or 'folunteer', which is in transition from 'volunteer' to 'foluntîr'. Issues relating to the borrowing and adaptation of English terms surface strongly in place-names (as the ballad writers venture singing about Germany, Peru, Plymouth, Prussia, Russia and Spain, and about 'Frenchmen') and in vocabulary relating to the military, including titles such as 'Major', 'Lord', 'Admiral' and 'Colonel' (the latter of which has several variant forms in the texts). So as to retain the flavour of this period of expanding horizons, these names have been presented in their original form. This is sometimes simply the English form (e.g. Russia, Major), here given without italicization, and at other times a more transitional name (e.g. Plymouth, in a mutated form, is given as 'Mhlimouth', the French as 'Frensh' or 'Ffrenshman', but also as 'French'). Welsh names for places in Wales have been standardized, as have biblical names and personal names where standardization was straightforward (e.g. Blucher is given as Blücher, Campbel as Campbell, Cowdor as Cawdor and Welington as Wellington). In some cases, the ballad writers play with names in a creative way: Valenciennes is rendered as both 'Valenseina' and 'tre' Caerseina'. These have been retained in the original, the translation offering the standard form for 'Valenseina' and attempting a translation of 'tre' Caerseina' as 'the walled town of Valenciennes'.

Note that tune names are given in the language of their appearance in the original Welsh ballad texts under the titles of the edited ballads. In the headings to the translations, the titles have been retained in their Welsh form unless they were also known by an English name in the period (e.g. in the case of 'Duw Gadwo'r Brenin', or 'God Save the King').

Notes

1   Note that there are no JHD numbers for nineteenth-century ballads.
2   For useful comments on this problem, see Dafydd Glyn Jones (ed.), *Canu Twm o'r Nant* (Bangor, 2010), p. 30.

1793

*1. Dienw, 'Y brenin a'r llywodraeth, neu, y Refoliwsion yn 1688 wedi
gwneuthur ail Refoliwsion yn afreidiol i'r Brutaniaid'*

Sylwer,

Mai wrth y Refoliswion y meddylir y cyfnewidiad llywodraeth a fu yn yr
ynys hon yn y flwyddyn 1688, pan y darfu i'r deiliaid o un fryd ddiarddelu
Siames yr Ail am deyrnasu trwy ben-arglwyddiaeth yn ôl ei ewyllys anwadal
ei hun ac nid yn ôl rheol a chyfreithiau sefydlog y Parliament; a dewis a
choroni William, tywysog Orange, yn frenin yn ei le. Y cyfnewidiad hwnnw
a ddygodd deulu Hanover, sef y Siorses, brenhinoedd goreu Brydain, i mewn
i'r orsedd, yn lle'r Pretender ac etifeddion Siames yr Ail. Rhaid i bob dyn
sy'n parchu'r brenin ac yn caru ei wlad ddiolch i Dduw am gyfnewidiad a
fu gymaint er gwell, a gweddïo yn erbyn ail gyfnewidiad a fyddai yn sicr er
gwaeth.

Pan oeddym yn ochneidio dan orthrymder, yr Arglwydd a roddes Refoliwsion ac a'n gwnaeth ni yn genedl hapus hyd heddiw. Achwyned caethion eto, a
Duw a'u rhyddhao trwy'r byd. Dangoswn ninnau ddiolchgarwch, a defnyddiwn
ein rhydd-did trwy addoli Duw, anrhydeddu'r brenin, cadw y cyfreithiau, a
gwneuthur daioni i bob dyn.

Fe fu amseroedd blinion
 Yn hir ar Gymry a Saeson,
Gan fod pob gŵr o'n gwlad yn gaeth,
 Nes daeth y Refoliwsion.

Pob enw o Gristnogion   5
 Gyd-unent mewn achwynion;
Y gwŷr, waith maint y cur a'r cam,
 Gyd-leisiai am Refoliwsion.

Diswyddwyd Siames yn gyfion
 Am arglwyddiaethu'n greulon;   10
Coronwyd William yn ei le −
 O, lwysaidd Refoliwsion!

Gŵr oedd yn haeddu'r goron;
 E rôi Arglwyddi mawrion

1793

*1. Anon., 'The king and the government, or, the Revolution of 1688 having
made a second Revolution unnecessary for the Britons'*

Note,

That by the Revolution what is meant is the change of government which
took place in this island in the year 1688, when the subjects unanimously
expelled James the Second for reigning through tyranny according to his
own unstable will and not according to the established rule and laws of the
Parliament; and chose and crowned William, prince of Orange, as king in
his place. It was that change which brought the Hanover family, namely the
Georges, Britain's best kings, onto the throne, instead of the Pretender and
the heirs of James the Second. Every man who respects the king and loves
his country must thank God for a change which was so much for the better,
and pray against a second change which would certainly be for the worse.

When we were groaning under oppression, the Lord gave a Revolution
and made us a happy nation to this day. Let slaves complain again, and may
God liberate them throughout the world. Let us show gratitude, too, and let
us use our liberty by worshipping God, honouring the king, keeping the
laws, and doing good to every man.

There were troublesome times, long-lasting,
to the Welsh and the English,
because every man in our country was enslaved,
until the Revolution came.

Every denomination among the Christians   5
joined together in complaints;
the men, on account of the extent of the pain and the wrong,
cried out together for a Revolution.

James was justly taken from office
for ruling cruelly;   10
William was crowned in his place –
Oh, fair Revolution!

He was a man who deserved the crown;
he put great lords

A'r werin wael i gyd dan iau   15
    Yr un cyfreithiau union.

Fe gadwai gyfoethogion
    Rhag ginio gwarrau'r gweinion,
Ac yn y llwch, y gwanna' llanc
    Rhag crafanc cewri cryfion.   20

Hael roes in dolerasion,
    Na naga i neb Cristnogion
Gael mynd yn llu bob Sul i'r llan,
    Neu addoli man y mynnon'.

Byth cofir am y cyfion: 25
    Ei goffadwriaeth dirion
Pan êl y tadau o'r byd i bant
    A gair gan blant ac wyron.

In daeth yr un bendithion,
    Hwy lifant in fel afon;   30
Ni gawn yn siŵr o hyd gan Siôr
    Wir flas o'r Refoliwsion.

Y penna' o'n pendefigion
    A'r gwaelaf oll o'n gweision
A gyd-fwynhan' o dan y nef   35
    Fawr les y Refoliwsion.

Nid all ond rhyw rai deillion
    A deiliaid hanner-dylon,
O chwilio'n llwyr, weld mewn un lle
    Ail eisiau Refoliwsion.   40

Pan cawn ni ddweud ein cwynion
    A symud beichiau trymion
Heb lid na thrais mewn gwlad a thref,
    Pwy les wnâi Refoliwsion?

Heb rith, dymunai Brython   45
    Na welo neb o'u meibion

and the common people all under the yoke   15
of the same just laws.

He prevented the wealthy
from flaying the backs of the weak,
and, in the dust, kept the weakest lad
from the claws of mighty giants.   20

He generously gave us toleration,
which does not prevent any Christians
from going in a crowd every Sunday to the church,
or worshipping wherever they wish.

The just one will forever be remembered: 25
the happy memory of him
when the fathers go from the world to the grave
will be held by children and grandchildren.

The same blessings came to us,
they flow towards us like a river;   30
we shall surely still have from George
the true taste of the Revolution.

The most elevated of our lords
and the lowliest of all our servants
enjoy together under the heaven   35
the great benefit of the Revolution.

Only some blind people
and half-witted subjects,
from a thorough search, can see anywhere
the need for a second Revolution.   40

When we are allowed to voice our complaints
and remove heavy burdens
without anger or violence in town and country,
what good would a Revolution do?

Without illusion, Britons would wish   45
that none of their sons

Mwyach fyth tu yma i fôr
    Ail oes o Refoliwsion.

Tra fyddo brenin tirion
    A iawn lywodraeth union,   50
Mae'n ddigon siŵr na bydd un Sais
    Â'i lais am Refoliwsion.

Aed Ellmyn* fel y mynnon,
    Heb wân rhwng pen a chynffon;
Byth dan un monarch mawr yr a'   55
    Ein gwerin a'n goreuon.†

Os 'does i'n *constitution*
    Deg-lanwedd, neb gelynion,
Aent ffwrdd i Ffrainc ar gainc i gyd,
    Yn ddilyw o gydraddolion.   60

Cyd-unwch Gymry mwynion,
    Â'i gilydd, o un galon,
Heb hidio Ffrainc, mewn cadarn ffrwd
    O gariad brwd i'r Goron.

Hwyr wisged Siôr y goron –   65
    Pan gado hi, aed yn union
O dad i fab, o fab i ŵyr,
    O'r ŵyr byth i'r orwyron.

Y brenin byth fo cyfion,
    A'r deiliaid bawb yn ffyddlon,
Y tlawd yn rhydd, a'r cryf yn fwyn,   70
    I wrando ar gŵyn y gweinion.

A phob un o'r esgobion
    Yn oleu seren wiwlon,
Yn harddu'i swydd a haelrwydd ffel,   75
    Fel Tilots neu fel _____

Llu ffôl yr annuwiolion,
    Feilch, meddwon, glwth, cybyddion,

should ever more on this side of the sea
witness a second age of Revolution.

While there is a gracious king
and a true, righteous government, 50
it is quite certain that no Englishman
will raise his voice for a Revolution.

Let Dutchmen* do as they please,
without distinction between head and tail;
our common people and our nobles will ever go 55
under one great monarch.†

If our constitution,
fair and pure its appearance, has any enemies,
let them go off to France all at one stroke,
a deluge of equals. 60

Join together, gentle Welshmen,
with one another, of one heart,
without taking heed of France, in a steady torrent
of zealous love to the Crown.

May George long wear the crown – 65
when he leaves it, may it go directly
from father to son, from son to grandson,
from grandson always to the great-grandsons.

May the king always be just,
and the subjects all faithful, 70
the poor free, and the strong kind,
to listen to the complaint of the weak ones.

And each one of the bishops
a bright, kindly star,
gracing his office with wise generosity, 75
like Tilots or like _____

The foolish host of the ungodly,
proud ones, drunkards, gluttons, misers,

A gwŷr y trais trwy gyrrau'r tir
  A ddelo'n wir Dduwiolion. 80

Na weler meistriaid creulon,
  Na threiswyr byth na thrawsion,
Na chynnen mwy, na chlwy na chledd,
  Yn brathu hedd y Brython.

Ond mwynlais heddwch mwynlon 85
  A dyw'no rhwng pob dynion,
Rhwng gwlad a gwlad, rhwng bryn a bro –
  A'r India gano'r undon.

Od oes un wlad o ddynion
  Yn aros eto'n gaethion, 90
Y Duw roes gymaint braint i'n bro
  A'u rhoddo hwythau'n rhyddion.

Yr Un ddôi â'r hen Iuddewon,
  A ddaw â'r bobol dduon
O gaeth hyll erchyll dywyll dai 95
  I oleu rydd-did gwiwlon.

Yn ddilys mae i Dduwiolion
  Ail oes a Refoliwsion,
Pan caffon' uno'n llon eu llef
  Yn felys â nefolion. 100

* Trigolion Holland, megis Venice, America a Ffrainc, ydynt heb na brenin
na gwahanol raddau o ddinasyddion.
† Ein constitiwsion neu ein corffoliad gwledig ni ym Mhrydain a wnair i
fyny o dair rhan, sef brenin, arglwyddi a'r bobl gyffredin.

Pen-y-bont, Castellnewydd, Chwefror 13, 1793

Mewn cyfarfod cyffredinol o weinidogion yr Ymneilltuwyr Protestannaidd
o'r tri enw, yn sir Aberteifi, sir Gaerfyrddin a sir Benfro, a'r Parch. W. Williams
yn y gadair,

and the men of violence throughout the land,
shall become truly godly. 80

May cruel masters not be seen,
nor oppressors nor wicked ones,
nor strife any more, nor wound nor sword,
piercing at the peace of the Briton.

But may the soothing voice of a gentle peace 85
shine between all men,
between country and country, between hill and vale –
and may India sing the same tune.

If there is any country of men
who still remain captive, 90
may the God who gave such a privilege to our country
make them free too.

The One who brought the old Jews
will bring the black people
from confined, repulsive, hideous dark houses 95
to the light of excellent liberty.

Godly people will surely
have a second age and a Revolution
when they shall join, with happy cry,
sweetly with heavenly beings. 100

* *The inhabitants of Holland, like those of Venice, America and France, are without a king or different ranks of citizens.*
† *Our constitution or body politic in Britain is made up of three parts, namely king, lords and the common people.*

[The following prose text is the original English declaration which arose from the meeting. Material omitted in comparison with the Welsh text is substituted in square brackets.]

Salutation Tavern, Newcastle, February 13th, 1793

At a general meeting of Protestant Dissenting ministers, of the three Denominations, in the counties of Cardigan, Carmarthen and Pembroke, the Rev. W. Williams in the chair,

Cytunwyd,

Mai cymwys ac angenrheidiol ar yr amser hwn o anair a drwg-dyb, ydyw i ni, megis un corff, yn y modd mwyaf agored, ddatgan ein ffyddlondeb a'n glyniad diwahân wrth y ffurf-lywodraeth trwy frenin, arglwyddi a chyffredin, ac a gafas ei mawr hadgyweirio a'i chadarnhau ar y Refoliwsion, sef y mawr gyfnewidiad a fu yn y deyrnas hon yn y flwyddyn 1688.

Y bydd i ni gofleidio pob cyfleusdra i wasgu ar feddyliau ein pobl a'n cymydogion, ffyddlondeb i'r brenin a pharch i'r cyfreithiau, a gwrthwynebu pob terfysg ac anffyddlondeb, pe byddai i'r fath ddrygau byth gyfodi o fewn cylch ein cydnabyddiaeth a'n gweinidogaeth ni.

A than effeithiolaeth gorchymynion crefydd a'i hegwyddorion o weithrediad, heb olwg ar fantais nac anrhydedd bydol i'n denu, yn fyddar i bob barn anghariadus ac anair anhaeddiannol oddi wrth bob enw a gradd o ddynion, ac heb ein siglo ychwaith gan ddifreiniad o swyddi gwledig a breintiau dinasyddion, y bydd i ni siriol barhau yn ein hufudd-dod i'n llywiawdwyr ac yn ein sêl dros y drefn ragorol honno o lywodraeth ag sydd wedi bod yn ymddiwygio yn gyson dros yr oesoedd aeth heibio, ac yn meddu llawn awdurdod eto i wellhau pob gweddillion o amherffeithrwydd, heb drais na therfysg.

Cytunwyd,

I'r bwriadau uchod gael enw y blaenor yn y gadair wrthynt, dros holl aelodau y cyfarfod, a'u cyhoeddi unwaith yn un o bapurau Llundain, papur Bristol a phapur Henffordd, a'u dosbarthu trwy'r dalaith yn Gymraeg ac yn Saesonaeg.

William Williams, Blaenor yn y gadair

JHD no.: 541

Source: Welsh Ballads Online (Cwp LlGC)

Publication: John Ross, Carmarthen, 1793

Resolved,

That at this crisis it is proper and necessary for us, as a body, without reservation, to express our loyalty and adherence to the constitution under the Revolution, 1688, consisting of king, lords and commons [that was greatly reformed and perfected at the Revolution, namely the great change that happened in this kingdom in the year 1688].

That we shall embrace every opportunity to impress on the minds of those connected with us, loyalty to the king and reverence for the laws, and to discountenance every tumult or sedition, should such evils spring up within the circle of our influence.

That under the influence of the precepts of religion and those impressions it leaves on our minds as motives of action, having no secular interest or honours to decoy us, deaf to every illiberal and uncandid reflection from every description of men, and unshaken by an exclusion from the common rights of citizens, we shall cheerfully persevere in our obedience to government and our zealous attachment to an excellent constitution, which has been improving for ages, and from its very principles has power, without violence or tumult, to correct every remaining imperfection.

Resolved,

That the above resolutions be signed by the chairman, [on behalf of all those present at the meeting] and inserted in the English *Chronicle*, the Bristol and Hereford papers [, and circulated through the province in Welsh and in English].

William Williams, Chairman

2. Dienw, 'Sylwiad byr ar y papuryn a ddaeth allan yn ddiweddar dan yr enw
Un-geiniogwerth o Wirionedd, mewn anerchiad gan Tomas ap
Siencyn i'w frawd Siôn, *amcan a diben pa un ydoedd ceisio drwgliwio'r*
Ymneilltuwyr yng ngolwg y werin anwybodus'

Hysbysiad

Digwyddodd i bapuryn ddyfod i'm llaw, dan ddull o anerchiad Tomas ap
Siencyn i'w frawd Siôn, yr hwn sy gyfieithiad o lythyr Thomas Bull i'w
frawd Siôn. Diau fod yr awdwr a'r cyfieithwr naill ai'n hollol anwybodus o
gyfreithiau'r tir ac o hanes y wlad, neu'n elynion i'r brenin ac i'r gwirionedd.
Y maent yn gwrthwynebu y rheol trwy ba un y mae y teulu brenhinol
presennol yn llywodraethu'r deyrnas hon, ac am hynny gellir meddwl eu bod
yn gyfeillion i'r Pretender. Ac yn eu gwaith yn rhoi drygair i'r Ymneilltuwyr,
y mae'n eglur eu bod am gyfodi terfysg yn y wladwriaeth ac am annog
erledigaeth a thywallt gwaed eu cyd-ddeiliaid fel y gwnaeth y paganiaid a'r
papistiaid gynt. Nid gwir yw fod yr Ymneilltuwyr yn groes i lywodraeth
frenhinol, eithr i lywodraeth gaethiwys hiliogaeth y Pretender. A diau pe
buasai Tomas yn argraffu ei lythyr drwgfwriadus yn y flwyddyn 1745, pan
diriodd y Pretender yn yr ynys hon, y cawsai yn ôl ei haeddiant farw wrth
grocpren. Y mae yn ddiamau mai'r Ymneilltuwyr a ddygodd y Brenin Siarl
yr Ail i'r Goron yn y flwyddyn 1660, ac iddynt uno yn galonnog gyda'r
Whigiaid i ddwyn y Brenin William i mewn yn y flwyddyn 1688, a Brenin
Siors y Cyntaf yn y flwyddyn 1714; a'u bod hyd y dydd hwn yn ufudd i'r
llywodraeth ym mhob peth, ac na unasant unwaith â gwrthryfelwyr yr Eglwys
Sefydledig o blaid y Pretender.

Mi welais bapuryn yn tramwy drwy'r tir,
A'i enw'n gyffredin, *Ceiniogwerth o Wir*;
Gwaith Tomas ap Siencyn oedd at ei frawd Siôn,
Gŵr suredd ei siarad – amdano rwy'n sôn.

Fe luniodd ei leiniau yn gwbwl ar gam   5
Wrth ganmol ei hunan a chanmol ei fam;
"Gŵr didwyll ac onest," medd Tomas, "yw'n tad,
A'i gyfri'n synhwyrol gan bobl y wlad."

Beth bynnag oedd synnwyr onestrwydd ei dad,
'Does fawr o ganmoliaeth i Tomas trwy'r wlad;   10
Ond ganddo fe'i hunan, yn llydan ar led,
Fe rodd i'r wladwriaeth geiniogwerth o'i gred.

2. Anon., 'A brief observation regarding the pamphlet which appeared recently under the name One Penny-worth of Truth, *in an address by Thomas son of Jenkin to his brother John, the intention and purpose of which was to try and misrepresent the Dissenters in the eyes of the ignorant populace'*

Announcement

A pamphlet happened to come to my hand, in the form of an address by Thomas son of Jenkin to his brother John, which is a translation of the letter of Thomas Bull to his brother John. The author and the translator are doubtless either completely ignorant of the laws of the land and the history of the country, or are enemies to the king and to the truth. They oppose the rule through which the current royal family rules this kingdom, and for that reason it might be thought that they are friends to the Pretender. And by denigrating the Dissenters, it is clear that they wish to raise disorder in the state and want to encourage persecution and shedding of the blood of their fellow-subjects like the pagans and papists in former times. It is not true that the Dissenters are opposed to monarchical rule, only to the oppressive rule of the Pretender's lineage. And if Thomas had printed his ill-intentioned letter in the year 1745, when the Pretender landed in this island, he would certainly have died on the gallows, according to his desert. There is no doubt that it was the Dissenters who brought King Charles the Second to the Crown in the year 1660, and that they valiantly joined with the Whigs to bring King William to power in the year 1688, and King George the First in the year 1714; and that they are to this day obedient to the government in everything, and that they never once joined the rebels from the Established Church in favour of the Pretender.

I saw a pamphlet travelling through the land,
and its common name was *One Penny-worth of Truth*;
it was the work of Thomas son of Jenkin to his brother John,
a man of sour speech – it is of him that I speak.

He put his lines together utterly unjustly   5
in praising himself and praising his mother;
"Our father," says Thomas, "is a guileless and honest man,
and considered sensible by the people of the country."

Whatever his father's sense of honesty was,
there is not much praise for Thomas through the land;   10
but on his own behalf, far and wide,
he gave the state a pennyworth of his belief.

Mae Tomas ddysgedig, anniddig ei ddawn,
Yn sôn am drefniadau llywodraeth yn iawn;
Ond eto mae'n wrthun i neb is y nen
Rhoi'u cred i waith un dyn dotiedig ei ben.

15

Ei amcan yn gyfan trwy'r gorchwyl i gyd –
Drwgliwio'r Neilltuwyr yng ngolwg y byd
A'u dodi nhwy allan, o fychan hyd fawr,
Yn bobl aflonydd ar wyneb y llawr.

20

Fe geulodd ar gelwydd annedwydd, heb fraw,
Wrth sôn am ryfelodd America draw;
Fe haerodd hyn allan yn llydan mewn llid,
Gan ddweud mai'r Disenters fu'r achos i gyd.

Pwy fu yn fwy ffyddlon i'r Goron erio'd
Dros bennaeth derfynol na rhain dan y rhod?
Pwy safai greulondeb yn wyneb y tân
Nes gyrru'r Pretender fel bradwr o'u bla'n?

25

Ai Tomas ap Siencyn anniddig a gawn,
Neu ryw rai o'r Toris, wŷr llidus a llawn?
Ni welwyd (ni welir, gobeithio, mewn bod)
Neb dynion mor greulon i'r Goron erio'd.

30

Dan rith o ffyddlondeb ac wyneb go hardd,
Fel sarff pan yr hudodd hi Efa'n yr ardd,
Mae Tomas fel rhingyll am ennill y tir
I gredu drwg araith *Geiniogwerth y Gwir*.

35

Ond gwir nid oes ynddo fe nemawr yn bod!
Mae'n llawnach o gelwydd (annedwydd yw'r nod!),
'Fod Tomas yn agos yn un dymer â'i dad,
Am godi gwrthryfel a thrafel trwy'r wlad.

40

Mor gwsglyd yw 'gasgliad a'i sylwiad di sail –
Ymwisgodd mewn llurig mor denau â'r dail;
Ei amcan i'r gwaelod, fe'i gwelwyd trwy'r wlad,
Oedd sathru'r Disenters fel dom dan ei draed.

Learned Thomas, with his discontented nature,
mentions correctly the arrangements of government;
but yet it is ridiculous that anyone under the heaven   15
should believe the work of a man whose head is dotish.

His entire intention throughout the undertaking –
to disparage the Dissenters in the eyes of the world
and to give out that they are, from little to great,
an unruly people on the face of the earth.   20

He brewed up an unhappy lie, without fear,
by mentioning the wars of America, yonder;
he proclaimed this out extensively in indignation,
saying that the Dissenters were the entire cause.

Who was ever more faithful to the Crown   25
in favour of a limited ruler than these under the heaven?
Who faced cruelty in the face of fire
until they drove the Pretender like a traitor before them?

Is it irritable Thomas son of Jenkin that we have here,
or some from among the Tories, men full of wrath?   30
No men have ever been seen (none ever shall be, let us hope)
so cruel towards the Crown.

Under a facade of loyalty and a fair countenance,
like the serpent when it lured Eve in the garden,
Thomas, like a sergeant, wishes to win the land over   35
to believe the false oratory of *One Penny-worth of Truth*.

But there is hardly any truth in it!
It contains more by the way of lies (it is a wretched feature!),
since Thomas is almost of the same disposition as his father,
wanting to raise rebellion and trouble throughout the country. 40

How foolish is his conclusion and his unfounded observation –
he has dressed himself in armour as thin as the leaves;
his intention to the core, it was seen through the country,
was to trample on the Dissenters like manure under his feet.

Fe wyrodd y leiniau oedd olau ar lawr   45
Ynghylch gogyfuwchder rhwng bychan a mawr;
Nid [?sôn] maent am gyfoeth, ŵr annoeth, heb wall,
Na rhannu meddiannau y naill rhwng y llall.

'Does sôn gan ddiwygwyr gwiw gywir a gawn
Am berson na chlochydd, forauddydd na nawn,   50
Na barnwr na ysgwïer, na lleidr na gwas,
Ond Tomas ap Siencyn osododd hyn ma's.

Ni luniodd diwygwyr erioed y fath blan,
Na thaflu'r fath wradwydd o'i herwydd i'r llan;
Rhoi'r clochydd i'r pylpud a'r person i'w le,   55
Na barnwr na lleidr i newid eu lle.

Na thynnu'r pendefig o'i gerbyd i lawr,
A rhoddi ei was fynydd, annedwydd fae'r awr;
Byth boed y fath drefn (heb drafod) is nen,
Rhag ofn yr aiff Tomas ap Siencyn yn ben.   60

Yr hyn mae'r diwygwyr yn sicr yn ddal
Yn wyneb mab Siencyn a phawb o'r rhai bal,
Fod hawl gan gardotyn, fel brenin, heb freg,
I chwarae dros ffortun â'i fywyd yn deg.

Ond och, y drwg liwio ar 'nurddo sy'n awr   65
Ar gorff o Ddisenters dros wyneb y llawr;
Â geiriau mor chwerw, pob enw, pob gradd,
Mae Tomas ap Siencyn yn llwyr am eu lladd!

Mor rhyfedd y cablodd y cablydd heb ball,
Â'i anian yn union fel meibion y fall;   70
Er cymaint yr haerodd, ni lwyddodd e' fawr
Â'i gloch heb un tafod, hyll suredd ei sawr.

Ymdanwyd, fe ddywedwyd, fe lygrwyd y wlad,
A'n bod ni yn erbyn y brenin heb wad;
'Dyw hyn ond y celwydd annedwydd i gyd   75
Gael duo'r Disenters yng ngolwg y byd.

He perverted the lines which were clearly set out 45
about equality between great and small;
they do not mention wealth, foolish man, I am without error,
nor sharing of possessions between one another.

The apt, correct reformers that we have do not mention
parson or sexton, neither morning nor afternoon, 50
neither judge nor esquire, neither thief nor servant,
but it was Thomas son of Jenkin who set this out.

Reformers never came up with such a plan,
nor threw such insult upon the Church on its account;
put the sexton in the pulpit and the parson in his place, 55
nor swapped the places of judge and thief.

Nor pulled the nobleman down from his carriage,
and raised up his servant, it would be an unhappy hour;
let there never be such an order (without discussion) under the heaven,
in case Thomas son of Jenkin should become leader. 60

What the reformers certainly believe
in the face of Jenkin's son and all the other stupid ones,
is that a beggar, like a king, without guile,
has the right to play his life out for fortune's sake.

But alas, the disparaging and the disgracing that there now is 65
of a body of Dissenters over the face of the earth;
with such bitter words, for every name, every class,
Thomas son of Jenkin wishes to kill them entirely!

How excessively did the slanderer revile without cessation,
his temperament exactly like the sons of the devil; 70
in spite of the extent to which he reproached, he had little success
with his tongue-less bell, ugly and sour his aroma.

It was spread aboard, it was said, the country was corrupted,
to believe that we are against the king, without denial;
this is nothing but miserable untruth 75
in order to blacken the Dissenters in the eyes of the world.

Mae meibion Sersia hyd yma'n y byd
Yn blino eneiniog yr Arglwydd o hyd;
Darostwng eu balchder, eu llawnder a'u llid –
Gwna'r deiliad yn ffyddlon i'r Goron i gyd!   80

Duw cadw ein brenin ar Brydain o'r bron,
Ein gwlad a fo'n llonydd a'n llywydd yn llon;
Diddyma gynghorion rhai creulon eu cais
Mae'n dda ganddynt ryfel a thrafel a thrais.

Dymunwn lonyddwch, tawelwch trwy'r tir,   85
Yn groes i egwyddor *Ceiniogwerth y Gwir;*
Meddyliau cyffredin y werin ynghyd
Fod Tomas a'i leiniau yn ddiau rhy ddrud.

Doed pob rhyw ymryson yn gyson i lawr,
A chariad fo'n llanw holl wyneb y llawr;   90
Tangnefedd a lifo fel afon ar led,
Brenhinoedd a deiliaid fo i gyd o iawn gred.

O, Arglwydd da! dyro amynedd a maeth
I'th lesg bererinion er gwell ac er gwaeth;
Trwy bob gwradwyddiadau a chroesau o hyd,   95
Ein henaid ddyrchafo Iachawdwr y byd.

JHD no.: 673

Source: Welsh Ballads Online (Col 1793 LlGC)

Publication: n.p., 1793

The sons of Sersia thus far in the world
are molesting the Lord's anointed always;
cast down their pride, their plenitude and their anger –
make the subjects all faithful to the Crown!   80

God keep our king over the whole of Britain,
may our country be tranquil and our leader happy;
destroy the machinations of men of cruel endeavour
who like war and trouble and violence.

We wish for tranquillity, peace throughout the land,   85
in opposition to the principle of *One Penny-worth of Truth*;
the general opinions of the populace together
are that Thomas and his lines are certainly too costly.

May every dispute fall down without fail,
and may love fill all the face of the earth;   90
may peace flow like a river all round,
may kings and subjects all be of a true creed.

Oh, good Lord! give patience and nourishment
to Your weary pilgrims for better and for worse;
through all dishonours and afflictions always,   95
may the Redeemer of the world raise our soul.

3. Richard Roberts, 'Ychydig o hanes y g[wrthr]yfel a [fu] rhwng brenin Ff[rainc] [a'i deyrnas ei hun, ac] y to[rasant ei] be[n ef;] ac fel y maent yn a[wr] yn sychedu am waed yr hen Fryt[a]niaid; ond gobeithio y tagant o [s]yched yn gyntaf, ac na chânt mo'u hewyllys arn[om] ni. Duw a safo gy[d]a Brenin George III [a]c Eglwys [L]oegr'
Tune: 'Duw Gadwo'r Brenin'

Brytaniaid ffyddlon, rwyddlon ryw
A'i theulu doeth, rhai a 'tholodd Duw,
   O, clyw di'n glir!
Sŵn rhyfeloedd ydyw'r stŵr,
Ond Duw Ei Hun yw'r canol ŵr   5
   Ar ddŵr a thir.
Fe aeth brenin Ffrainc yn anghytûn
I roi dial hy ar ei deulu'i hun;
Fe a'i trowd o'i le yn ddrwg ei lun –
   Cadd derfyn du;   10
Am ei groes faterion mowrion maith
Cadd ddiodde loesion, creulon graith,
Sef torri ei ben ar fyr daith –
   Heb obaith bu.

Ni chlywodd neb yn ein hamser ni   15
Fath driniaeth caeth ar bennaeth bu –
   Mae'i deulu'n drist;
Fe gadd hir garchar, dyfnder dwys,
Tan fawr ofid, penyd pwys,
   Cyn y gwys na'r gist;   20
Fe'i trawyd o yn ei wlad ei hun
Am ei droeau a'i blaeau blin;
Nhw wnaen' yn euog, lidiog lun,
   Eu brenin brau,
A chyn ei lwyr ddibennu o'r byd   25
Fe wnawd ei rw[m]o'n ddu i gyd,
A'i hilio hi ar dro â hilyn drud
   Gofid a gwae.

Pan ddaeth y dydd a'r awr i ben,
'Ddatodai ei hun ei goler wen   30
   Cyn diben ei daith;
Fe wnaeth ei 'wyllys, medd y wlad,

3. Richard Roberts, 'A little of the history of the insurrection which took place
between the king of France and his own kingdom; and that they cut off his head;
and how they are now thirsting for the blood of the ancient Britons; but let us hope
that they will die of thirst first, and that they will not see their will fulfilled
upon us. May God stand with King George III and the Church of England'
Tune: 'God Save the King'

Faithful Britons, a liberal lineage
and its wise family, ones who worshipped God,
Oh, listen clearly!
The commotion is the sound of war,
but God Himself is the arbiter   5
on sea and land.
The king of France went contentiously
to effect a bold vengeance upon his own family;
he was turned out of his seat in a cruel fashion –
he had a calamitous end;   10
for his great, numerous perverse actions
he had to suffer agonies, a cruel scar,
namely the severing of his head in a short time –
he was without hope.

No one in our time heard   15
of such grievous treatment of a king –
his family are mournful;
he was in prison for a long time, deep abyss,
under great affliction, a heavy punishment,
before the grave or the coffin;   20
he was struck in his own country
for his evil tricks and destructions;
they found their fragile king guilty,
an indignant figure,
and before dispatching him fully from the world,   25
he was tied up, all in black,
and covered with the grievous covering
of affliction and woe.

When the day and the hour came to an end,
he undid his white collar himself   30
before the end of his journey;
he made his will, says the country,

Trwy gennad Duw a'i ganiatâd
   (Caled fu'r gwaith);
Fe ganodd ffârwel ar ddydd Llun   35
Ac fe ddwedodd wrth ei fab ei hun,
"Bydd fyw yn dy le yn dda dy lun,
   Rhag terfyn dy oes.
Cymer siampl ohono' i nawr –
Cei weld yn llif fy ngwaed i'r llawr –   40
Bûm i fel mur yn frenin mawr,
   Ond ar lawr mae'm loes."

Fe dynnai'i fodrwy oddi am ei fys,
Fe yrre honno i'w wraig ar frys
   O'i lys a'i le;   45
Fe ddweude'i fod o'n maddau'n rhwydd
I bob gelyn yn eu gŵydd,
   Trwy'r Arglwydd nef.
Ar hynny o boen fe roed ei ben
Ar y siaffer dyner denn;   50
I'r dyn annoeth dan y nen
   Bu diben tost –
Torri'i wallt a'i rannu a wnaed,
A gwlychu ei napcyn yn ei waed,
Heb feindio'n gl[i]r mewn tre' na gwlad   55
   Mo'u gwastad g[o]st.

Bron bedair llath fe dorrwyd lle
Yn y ddaear greigaidd gre'
   (Cadd droiau drud);
Yn lle gwneud iddo fe dair arch   60
Tywalltwyd arno ddŵr a chalch
   Heb barch yn y byd.
Cadd ei scaldio (heb boen) i ei groen yn gri
Fel crwyn anifeiliaid ein gwlad ni,
A'i godi o'n llipryn, delpyn du,   65
   I fyny o'r fan.
Fe a'i claddwyd efo ffrindiau'i dad
(Mae'r gair ar led ar hyd y wlad) –
Na ddelo i'n bro ni byth mo'r brad
   Trwy gwynian gwan.   70

by God's leave and permission
(it was a harsh deed);
he said farewell on Monday   35
and he said to his own son,
"Live within your condition, in a commendable manner,
lest your life should be ended.
Take an example from me now –
you shall see in the flow of my blood to the ground –   40
I was a great king, like a rampart,
but my agony is on the ground."

He took the ring from his finger,
he sent it to his wife in a hurry
from his court and position;   45
he said that he freely gave his forgiveness
to every enemy in their presence,
through the Lord of heaven.
With that degree of pain his head was placed
on the gracious, neat chafing-dish;   50
to the unwise man under the firmament
there was a bitter end –
his hair was cut and shared out,
and his napkin dipped in his blood,
utterly without heeding in town or country   55
about their continual cost.

A space of almost four yards was dug
in the stony, tough earth
(he had harsh vicissitudes);
rather than making three coffins for him   60
he was covered with water and lime
without any kind of respect.
He was scalded (without pain) to his raw skin
like animal skins in our country,
and he was raised, a drooping black lump,   65
up from the place.
He was buried with his father's friends
(the word is abroad throughout the country) –
may treachery never come to our land
through feeble complaint.   70

Yr unfed dydd ar hugain daeth
O fis Ionawr (cynnwr' caeth,
   Â'i drafferth drud)
Un mil saith gant tair ar ddeg
A phedwar ugain, ffri iawn deg   75
   (Yr oedd lled yn y llid).
Bu fyw ddeugain mlwydd onid dwy;
Ni chae fo aros dim yn hwy.
Fe gadd ei gladdu yn wael ei glwy
   Mewn plwy o'u plith;   80
Yr unfed Lewis, ddyrys ddyn,
Ar bymtheg oedd, medd pob rhyw un.
Gelynion Lloegr, egr wŷn,
   Na ddoed un byth.

Gwnawn fawl ar dôn, gan foli Duw   85
Fod brenin Lloegr eto'n fyw,
   Hoff wiw ddyn ffraeth.
Mae pob un sydd yn perchen ffydd
Yn gweiddi'n daeredd nos a dydd
   Rhag cerydd caeth.   90
Mae gwaedgwn duon, greulon griw,
Yn llawn o frad am roi i ni friw;
Ni ddoe' nhw'n agos byth i'n clyw
   Trwy Dduw a'i ddawn;
Mwy ydy'r Hwn sydd drosom ni   95
Na'n holl elynion, lewion lu;
Os rhown ni'n cred yn Nuw sydd gry'
   Ei gwmni a gawn.

Mae gormod, 'sywaeth, yn ein plith
O elynion noeth am wneud eu nyth   100
   Mewn rhagrith rhwydd.
Duw chwyno Ei winllan burlan bêr
O bob pren sur sydd dan y sêr
   Yn gynnar o'n gŵydd.
Un Tomi Paen gadd dwymyn boen –   105
Llosgi ar frys ei grys a'i groen;
Daeth mwg yn ffri trwy ddwy ffroen
   Mewn du-boen dân;

It happened on the twenty-first day
of January (grievous strife,
with its painful turmoil)
one thousand seven hundred and ninety-three,   75
very bold and complete
(the fury was widespread).
He lived for forty years minus two;
he was not permitted to stay longer.
He was buried in wretched sickness
in a parish from their midst;   80
he was the sixteenth Louis,
everyone says, unfortunate man.
May there never come any of England's enemies,
severe trouble.

Let us sing praise upon a tune, extolling God   85
that the king of England is yet alive,
beloved, worthy, spirited man.
Every one who possesses faith
shouts fervently night and day
against grievous chastisement.   90
Evil bloodhounds, cruel mob,
are full of treachery, wishing to cause us injury;
may they never come near our hearing
by the grace of God and His blessing;
He who is on our side is greater   95
than all our enemies, valiant throng;
if we put our trust in God who is strong
we shall have His company.

There are, alas, among us, too many
shameless enemies who wish to make their nest   100
in slick falseness.
May God soon weed His uncorrupted, sweet vineyard
of every sour tree that is under the stars
from our sight.
A certain Tommy Paine underwent a feverish torment –   105
his shirt and his skin swiftly burnt;
smoke came freely through his two nostrils
in a fire of black anguish;

Mae eto ormod o'r un fath
O elynion croesion, sythion saeth,   110
Fel rhith Gris'nogion fyddo'n ffraeth –
    Oer waith a wnân'.

Duw gadwo'n brenin, riddyn radd,
Na chaffo'i elynion byth mo'i ladd
    Mewn dialedd du;   115
I'n parlament bo llwyddiant llawn,
A'i holl gynghorion, doethion dawn,
    Gwellhawn, bob llu;
Mae Ffrainc a'i *fleet* am ddod ymlaen
I mewn yr cyfle cynta' gaen';   120
Er maint eu stŵr ni ddaw mo'u staen
    Na'u paen i ben;
Fe â milwyr Lloegr cyn bo hir
A'u llonge a'u stôr ar fôr a thir;
Duw, cadarn Ŵr, fo gyda'n gwŷr   125
    Fel mur, Amen.

JHD nos., sources, publication details and document titles:

A: Bangor 7 (30); Trefriw, 1793; *Dwy Gerdd Ddiddan Y gyntaf A gymerwyd or
11 Ben. [o] Hebread yn dangos ma'i trwy ffyd[d] y mae'r Nef iw chael. Yn ail,
Ychydig o hanes y g[wrthr]yfel a [?fu] rhwng Brenhin Ff[raingc a'i ddeil]iaid, ar
modd y to[rasant ei] be[n], ac fel y maent yn aw[r] y[n] sychedu am waed y[r] [h]
ên Frytaniaid, ond gobeithio y tagant o [s]yched yn gyntaf, ac na chant mo'u hewyllys
arn[om] ni. Duw a safo gy[da] Brenin George III, [a]c Eglwys [L]oegr.*

B: JHD no. 490i; Welsh Ballads Online (Cwp LlGC); Titus Evans, Machynlleth,
1793; *Dwy o gerddi newyddion: Y Gyntaf. Yn rhoi ychydig o hanes am y gwrthryfel
a fu rhwng Brenin Ffraingc a'i deyrnas ei hun, ac y torrasant ei ben ef; ac ymhellach
y modd y maent yn sychedu am waed yr hen Frytaniaid; ond gobeithio y tagant o
syched yn gyntaf, ac na chant mo'u hewyllys arnom ni. Duw a safo gyd a Brenin
George y IIIydd, ac Eglwys Loegr. Yr Ail. Am gwymp Dyn yn yr Adda cyntaf, a'i
gyfodiad yn yr Ail.*

C: JHD no. 295ai; Welsh Ballads Online (Cwp LlGC); A. Hughes, Wrecsam,
17--. C is very closely related to B. It consists of the same two ballads in the
same order, but is much more poorly composed.

there are yet too many of the same kind
of perverse enemies, unbending arrow,   110
like sham Christians who are glib –
they do wicked deeds.

God keep our king, a core of dignity,
so that his enemies shall never be able to kill him
in calamitous vengeance;   115
may there be full success to our parliament,
and all its councillors, wise and gifted,
let us improve, every throng;
France and its fleet want to come on
and invade at the first opportunity that they might have;   120
in spite of the extent of their bustle, neither their stain
nor their pain will succeed;
England's soldiers will before long
take their ships and their reserve on land and sea;
may God, steadfast One, be with our men   125
like a rampart, Amen.

Variants: Title. B, C – ac fel y maent yn a[wr] > ac ymhellach y modd y maent; 13. B, C – tan fur daith; 50. B, C – siasser; 53. C – rannau; 66. C – o'r fant; 70. B, C – gwuniad; 85. B, C – ar don; 98. C – gwm a ni gawn; 110. C – G elynion.

4. Edward Pugh, '[Cerdd] o ganmoliaeth i'r Duke o' York, a diolchgarwch i
Dduw, am gael y ffafr o orchfygu ein gelynion, sef y Ffrancod'
Tune: 'Belisle March'

Holl brydyddion dethol doethion,
    Yn fawrion ac yn fân,
Sy ag awen rywiog, giwrus gaerog,
    Odidog, g'lonnog, glân;
O, clodforwn a chanmolwn   5
    A rhoddwn yn un rhyw
Y gwrol d'wysog Yorc ardderchog
    (Calonnog, enwog yw).
Yn nheyrnas Ffrainc yn ffri
    Gelynion sydd heb ri';   10
Y duc a'i armi sy'n eu gorchfygu
    A'u nadu nhw i'n gwlad ni.
O! moliant, moliant a gogoniant
    I Dduw, yn bendant bur,
Am gadw'r gweddol dduc grasusol   15
    A'i ragorol wrol wŷr.
A'i annwyl frawd a fu
    Rhwng pedwar gelyn cry' –
Duw oedd yn mynnu iddo'u gorchfygu
    Er hynny, gwn, yn hy.   20
Brave Welsh and English, Scots and Irish,
    We'll finish them all of hand;
We'll rise through England, Wales, Scots and Ireland,
    To be under the duke's command.

Y duc oedd benna' rheolwr gwcha'   25
    Yn Valenseina, 'n siŵr,
A Hood, ŵr union, a'u lladde'n feirwon,
    Rai dewrion, ar y dŵr;
Y canans yno oedd yn rhwygo,
    A'u cwartorio nhw ar y tir,   30
Ond mawr fu lladdfa gwŷr Val'seina,
    Y golla' yma'n wir.
Y duc a ddaeth i'r dre'
    Yn awr â'i fyddin gre',
A'u cleddyfau noethion yn torri'n gelynion,   35
    Oedd yn llawnion ym mhob lle;

4. Edward Pugh, 'A song of praise to the Duke of York, and of thankfulness to God, for granting the favour of vanquishing our enemies, namely the French'
Tune: 'Belisle March'

All pre-eminent, wise bards,
great and small,
who have a genial, skilful, mighty muse,
splendid, courageous, virtuous;
Oh, let us extol and praise   5
and portray in the same manner
the valiant, excellent prince of York
(he is high-spirited and distinguished).
In the kingdom of France
there are countless enemies, unrestricted;   10
the duke and his army are defeating them
and preventing them from entering our country.
Oh! praise, praise and glory
to God, emphatically pure,
for protecting the worthy, gracious duke   15
and his excellent, valiant men.
And his dear brother
who found himself between four strong enemies –
God insisted that he should defeat them
in spite of that, I know, undaunted.   20
Brave Welsh and English, Scots and Irish,
    We'll finish them all of hand;
We'll rise through England, Wales, Scots and Ireland,
    To be under the duke's command.

The duke was the chief and most excellent ruler   25
in Valenciennes, it is certain,
and Hood, upright man, struck them dead,
brave ones, on the water;
the cannons hacked, there,
and quartered them on the land,   30
but great was the loss of the men of Valenciennes,
the most damaging here indeed.
The duke came to the town
now with his strong army,
and their bared swords chopping our enemies   35
who were numerous everywhere;

A'n gwŷr ceffyle â'u gloyw arfe –
    F' a'u rhwyge bob yn rhes,
Nes ildio'n benna' tre' Caerseina
    I'r duc, ŵr llawna', er lles.   40
Y rhyfel, drafael drud,
    Gwaith pechod yw fo i gyd;
Oni ddoir yn gynnar o'r Aifft i Ganan
    Fe fag ryw lydan lid.
Brave Welsh and English, Scots and Irish,   45
    We'll finish them all of hand;
We'll rise through England, Wales, Scots and Ireland,
    To be under the duke's command.

Duw gadwo Brydain rhag cynfigen
    Yn siŵr, na chynnen chwith,   50
Ond fel brodyr ar bob prydie,
    Na ddêl dwys blaue i'n plith.
O, Ffrainc ddiofal! Cymrwch siampal
    (Anwadal â'i ddrwg wŷn):
Baich o bechod, dwyn dial trwmnod   55
    Yn hynod arni'i hun.
Duw a safo'n bur
    Efo'r duc a'i wŷr,
Gan ei fod o yleni ymhlith gelynod,
    Y Ffrancod, sorod sur.   60
A Duw o ddifri fo'n rheoli
    Yleni ar ei lu,
Gan gadw'n dirion Duc Yorc hyfrydlon,
    O, Arglwydd cyfion cu!
Clod i Dduw bob awr   65
    Am rydid Brydain Fawr;
Byddwn oll drwy gariad yn bur i'r Goron,
    Gristnogion wiwlon wawr.
Brave Welsh and English, Scots and Irish,
    We'll finish them all of hand;   70
We'll rise through England, Wales, Scots and Ireland,
    To be under the duke's command.

Mae ein gwaed, ddie, yn ffynhonne,
    Yn ffrydie yn nhir Ffrainc;

and our cavalry with their shining arms –
they tore them row by row,
until the walled town of Valenciennes had yielded
to the duke, generous man, it was for the better.⠀⠀⠀⠀⠀⠀40
The war, costly trouble,
it is all the work of sin;
unless we come quickly from Egypt to Canaan
it will breed a widespread wrath.
Brave Welsh and English, Scots and Irish,⠀⠀⠀⠀⠀⠀45
⠀⠀*We'll finish them all of hand;*
We'll rise through England, Wales, Scots and Ireland,
⠀⠀*To be under the duke's command.*

May God keep Britain safe from envy
and from unfortunate dissension,⠀⠀⠀⠀⠀⠀50
but let us be like brothers at all times,
so that grievous plagues come not among us.
Oh, careless France! Take an example
(fickle with its evil whim):
a burden of sin drawing revenge with a heavy mark⠀⠀⠀⠀⠀⠀55
strikingly upon itself.
May God stand purely
with the duke and his men,
because he is this year among enemies,
the French, sour dregs.⠀⠀⠀⠀⠀⠀60
And may God truly rule
His host this year,
gently protecting the delightful Duke of York,
Oh, righteous, precious Lord!
Praise to God every hour⠀⠀⠀⠀⠀⠀65
for the freedom of Great Britain;
may we all through love be pure to the Crown,
Christians of excellent hue.
Brave Welsh and English, Scots and Irish,
⠀⠀*We'll finish them all of hand;*⠀⠀⠀⠀⠀⠀70
We'll rise through England, Wales, Scots and Ireland,
⠀⠀*To be under the duke's command.*

Our blood is, without a doubt, like fountains,
streams in the land of France;

Gwaedd fawr erchyll ddigwydde i'r gweddill   75
 Wrth ymgynnull ym mhob cainc.
A'r Cymry Ffreinig sy'n gystuddiedig –
 Bu rhain dan ddirmyg dwys –
Mae rheini'n dyner efo Lloeger,
 Mawr bywer, nid tan bwys.   80
Holl filwyr Brydain fach
 Sy'n awr mewn calon iach,
Sy mewn ymrafel â Ffrainc, gwnaent ryfel,
 Rhag dêl rhyw uchel wach;
Duc Yorc yn syful y fo a'u safiodd,   85
 A'u tynnodd hwynt rhag tân;
Gydag ef o ddifri y cwyd y rheini
 Yleni oll yn lân.
Mawr glod sy'n bod trwy'r byd
 I'r impyn claerwyn clyd,   90
Sydd yn mentro heb hidio'i hoedel
 I'r rhyfel, drafael drud.
Brave Welsh and English, Scots and Irish,
 We'll finish them all of hand;
We'll rise through England, Wales, Scots and Ireland,   95
 To be under the duke's command.

JHD no.: 454

Source: Welsh Ballads Online

Publication: Trefriw, [?1793]

Document title: *Balad Newydd Yn Cynwys Tair o Gerddi Y cyntaf, O ganmoliaeth i'r Duke o York, a diolchgarwch i Dduw, am gael y ffafr o orchfygu ein gelynion sef y Ffrangcod. Yn ail Hymn o ddeisyfiadau Gwyr Brydain Yn drydydd Carol am ddydd y Farn.*

a great, hideous clamour befell the rest   75
as they gathered for every attack.
And the Welsh Frenchmen who are afflicted –
these suffered intense disdain –
those are affectionately with England,
a great power, not under pressure.   80
All the soldiers of little Britain
who are now hale and hearty,
who are in a conflict with France, they made war,
lest some loud screech should come;
the Duke of York graciously saved them,   85
and took them from the conflagration;
they will rise with him in earnest
this year, every single one.
There is great praise throughout the world
for the radiant, flourishing scion,   90
who ventures without care for his life
to the war, costly trouble.
Brave Welsh and English, Scots and Irish,
  We'll finish them all of hand;
We'll rise through England, Wales, Scots and Ireland,   95
  To be under the duke's command.

5. [?Shôn ap Ifan], 'Ffarwél gŵr ieuanc i'w wlad oedd wedi listio i'r armi hefo'r
Duwc o' Yorc'

Ffarwél i Langyfelach lon
A'm holl gymdogion i gyd o'r bron;
Rwy'n mynd i weld pa'r un sy well,
Fy ngwlad fy hun ai'r gwledydd pell.

Martsio'r ffordd wnawn i'n 'y mlaen   5
Nes imi fyned i dre'r Bont-faen;
I roen nhwy yno'n fawr eu sbort
Yn listio gwŷr gyda'r Duwc o' Yorc.

Troi fy mhen wnawn i ryw dŷ
A'r aur a'r arian oedd yno'n ffri,   10
A'r *drums* ar ffeiffs yn cario'r sŵn –
Mi listiais gyda'r *Light Dragoon.*

Roedd yno ferched yr holl sir
A 'nghariad inne, a dweud y gwir;
I roen hwy yno'n fawr eu sbort   15
Yn ein gweld ni'n mynd gyda'r Duw[c] o Yor[c].

Landio wnaen i Lundain fry,
A *duty* caled oedd arnom ni
I handlo'r gwn a'r cledde noeth
A'r bwleds plwm a'r powdr poeth.   20

Martsio wnaen ni yn ein bla'n
Gael treio'r Ffrens o fawr i fân;
Yn awr rwy'n gweld p'run sy well,
A'i 'ngwlad fy hunan ai'r gwledydd pell.

Ffarwél fo 'nhad a f'annwyl fam   25
Sy wedi fy magu a 'nwyn i'r lan
Mewn sens ac oedran o flaen y tân,
A chan ffarwél fo i'r merchaid glân.

Os gofyn neb pwy wnaeth y gân,
Dywedwch chwi mai merch fach lân   30

5. [?Shôn ap Ifan], 'The farewell of a young man, who had enlisted with the Duke of York's army, to his country'

Farewell to merry Llangyfelach
and all my neighbours every one;
I am going to find out which is best,
my own country or the distant lands.

I was marching along the road 5
until I reached the town of Cowbridge;
they were having great fun there
enlisting men to go with the Duke of York.

I turned into some house
and the gold and silver flowed freely there, 10
and the drums and the fifes made a noise –
I enlisted with the Light Dragoon.

The girls of the whole county were there
and my sweetheart too, to tell the truth;
they were having great fun there 15
watching us go with the Duke of York.

We landed in London, yonder,
and there was heavy duty upon us
to handle the gun and the unsheathed sword
and the leaden bullets and the hot powder. 20

We marched forward
to try the French from great to small;
now I see which one is best,
whether my own country or the distant lands.

Farewell to my father and my dear mother 25
who have raised me and brought me up
in sense and years in front of the fire,
and may there be a hundred farewells to the fair girls.

If anyone asks who made the song,
tell them that it was a fair little lass 30

Sydd yn dymuned nos a dydd
I'w hannwyl gariad gael rhodio'n rhydd.

Sources, publication details and document titles:

A – NLW, BC, vol. 12, no. 14; I. Davies,Trefriw, n.d.; *Dwy o Gerddi Diddanol,*
Y GyntafYn gosod allan ddymuniad y Credadyn mewn golwg ysprydol at Grist
Ymhrynnedigaeth y Bŷd: a'r Sailor's Bold. Yn ail. Ffarwel Gwr Ieuangc iw wlad
oedd wedi listio i'r Army hefo'r Duwc o york.

B – Cardiff City Library, Ballads and Fugitive Pieces, vol. 2, W.7.162, ff. 15,
141, 189; NLW, BC, vol. 2, no. 71; n.p., n.d. (this version shows clear signs of
belonging to the nineteenth century); no title – 'Can Ffarwel i Llangyfelach
lon; SefAm Fachgen yn Ymadael a'i Wlad Enedigol' is followed by 'Myfyrdod
ar Lanau Conwy. Ar y Mesur "Earl of Moririah"', and 'Liza Lan'; a black and
white image of two hands meeting in a handshake is included at the head
of the ballad, and a black and white image of a steam ship at its end.

C – NLW, D. Rhys Phillips 231 (quotes one couplet in the original Welsh,
and provides a translation of the 'additional' stanza (stanza 2) of version B
only).

Variants: Title. B – 'Can Ffarwel i Langyfelach lon; Sef Hanes am Fachgen
yn Ymadael a'i Wlad Enedigol'; 2. B – A'r merched ieuainc oll o'r bron; B
– additional stanza included after the first stanza: Ond llythyr ddaeth yn foreu
iawn, / Ac un arall y prydnawn, / Fod yr English Fleet yn hwylio i macs /
A minnau dros y cefnfor glas; 11. B – Y ffeiffs a'r drwm; 15. C – Roedd
Siemsyn yno'n fawr ei sport; stanzas 6 and 7. B – in reverse order; 31. B –
gweddîo.

who wishes night and day
that her dear love should be able to walk free.

1794

Chwi Frutaniaid oll yn gryno,
Dewch ynghyd, rhowch glust i wrando
Tra bwy'n adrodd hyn o eiriau
Am ddiwygiad ein bucheddau.

Cawsom amser hir o heddwch,   5
Brenin tirion a dedwyddwch;
Amser haf ac amser medi,
Fe allai daw yr amser c'ledi.

Cawsom amser braf i blannu,
Amser llwydd i adeiladu;   10
Amser chwerthin, amser dawnsio,
Amser eto sydd i wylo.

Cawsom amser i ymgofleidio,
Amser caru, amser gwnïo,
Amser iechyd, amser cadw,   15
Amser geni, amser marw.

Yn awr hi ddaeth yn amser rhyfel,
Amser galar ac ymrafel,
Amser lladd ac amser colli,
Amser dwys ac amser tewi.   20

Yr ŷm ni oll y dyddiau yma
Yn ofni i'r Ffrancod gael y trecha'
Ac i ddynion drwg, aflonydd
Wneuthur cynnwrf yn y gwledydd.

Pe bae pawb o'r wlad yn ffyddlon   25
O un genau ac un galon,
Fyth ni fyddai raid in ofni
Dim yn fwy nag ofni pechu.

Yn lle bod fel brodyr dedwydd
Bawb o'r bron yn caru'i gilydd,   30

1794

6. Anon., 'New rhymes in consideration of the times, in the year 1794'

You Britons all together,
gather round, give an ear to listen
while I recite these few words
about the reformation of our lives.

We had a long period of peace,   5
a mild king and felicity;
a time for summer and a time for reaping,
it may be that the time of hardship will come.

We had a pleasant time to sow,
a time of prosperity to build;   10
a time to laugh, a time to dance,
there is yet time to weep.

We had time to embrace one another,
a time to woo, a time to stitch,
a time for health, a time to preserve,   15
a time to give birth, a time to die.

Now has come a time for war,
a time for grief and strife,
a time for killing and a time to suffer loss,
a solemn time and a time to be silent.   20

We are all these days
fearful lest the French should be victorious
and that evil, turbulent men
should cause commotion in the lands.

If everyone in the country were faithful   25
with one assent and of one heart,
we should never have to fear
anything more than the fear of committing sin.

Instead of being like happy brothers
every single one loving each other,   30

Cnoi a barnu'r ydym ninnau
Bawb ei gilydd mewn cornelau.

Tyngu a rhegu a melltithio
A wneir yn hyfach na gweddïo;
Dywedyd celwydd, adrodd chwedlau,   35
Sydd fynychach na gweddïau.

Gormod sydd o bob gloddesta,
Meddwi budr a phuteindra,
Campiau drwg o bob rhywogaeth
Sy'n cynyddu ym mhob cymdogaeth.   40

Os daw dial ar ein teyrnas,
Cledd y gelyn, oer alanas,
Llwyth pechodau'n gwlad yn ddiau
Sydd yn hogi min y cleddau.

Weithian, Brydain, edifara   45
Yn y llwch wrth draed Jehofa,
Llef am bardwn am dy bechod
A chais hedd yng ngwaed y cymod.

Arglwydd, cadw Dy eneiniog,
Siors y Trydydd, ben coronog,   50
Ar ei orsedd hardd mewn urddas,
Yn ben trefnwr ar ein teyrnas.

JHD no.: 701aii

Source: Welsh Ballads Online

Publication: n.p., 1794

Document title: No title is given, but this poem is printed alongside 'Myfyrdod ar fywyd a marwolaeth, a phwy fydd ein cyfeillion gwedi angau'.

we gibe and judge
each other in corners.

Cursing and swearing and blaspheming
is done more boldly than praying;
telling lies, relating stories,   35
is more frequent than prayers.

There is too much of all kind of revelling,
vile drunkenness and whoring,
evil pursuits of every kind
are on the increase in every neighbourhood.   40

If vengeance should come upon our kingdom,
the enemy's sword, cold slaughter,
it is certain that it is our country's burden of sin
that is whetting the blade of the sword.

Henceforth, Britain, repent   45
in the dust at the feet of Jehovah,
cry for pardon for your sin
and seek peace in the blood of the atonement.

Lord, protect Your anointed one,
George the Third, crowned head,   50
on his beautiful throne in honour,
chief ruler of our kingdom.

7. Richard Roberts, 'Ychydig o hanes brenhines Ffrainc; y modd y cafodd ei
difetha, sef torri ei phen a rhwymo ei dwy fraich ar ei chefn, Hydref 17, 1793'
Tune: 'Gwêl yr Adeilad'

Pob un sy â theimlad ynddo,
Yn gywreindeg dowch i wrando –
   Rwy'n cwyno ar ganiad;
Ni bu mewn gwlad na theyrnas
Rai milain gwaeth eu malais,   5
   Drwy ddiras doriad.
Mae Ffrainc heb frenin ar ei mainc,
Na chwaith frenhines. (On'd tost yw'r hanes? –
   Wrth goffa ar gyffes mae'n abl crugo craig!)
Nhw laddai'r ddau yn farw,   10
   Roedd hynny'n sorw saig.
Fe ddaw rhyw ddial oddi draw –
Mae Duw yn ddiau yn hogi'i gleddau;
   Nhw ddôn' i'r ddalfa o waith eu briwiau braw;
Gwaed gwirion sydd yn gweiddi   15
   Am eu rhoddi'n rhych y rhaw.

Y frenhines a gadd garchar
Dros flwyddyn hir a chwartar
   Mewn siambar sybwyll;
Bu arni lawer eisiau   20
Mewn tywyllwch ar amserau,
   Heb gynnau cannwyll.
Hi wnaeth, pan oedd dan gyflwr caeth,
Danfonai'i hunan at emprwr German
   Swm mawr o arian, a hyn mewn ffwdan ffraeth,   25
I gario ymlaen y rhyfel,
   Rhag mynd mewn gafel gwaeth.
Mae Sbaen yn gryno efo'n graen,
A Holand hwytha', ac empres Russia,
   A brenin Prussia, a Lloegr (siwra' sain),   30
Er lladd rhai miloedd yno –
   Mae'n anhawdd rhifo rhain.

Ni chadd brenhines Louis
Mo'i diwedd fel bai'n dewis

7. Richard Roberts, 'A little of the story of the queen of France; the manner in which she was slain, namely by severing her head and tying her two arms onto her back, October 17, 1793'
Tune: 'Gwêl yr Adeilad'

Everyone who is capable of feeling,
wisely and fairly come and listen –
I make my lament in song;
there were never in country nor kingdom
cruel ones of greater wickedness,   5
through an infamous stroke.
France is without a king upon its throne,
nor yet a queen. (Is it not a pitiful story? –
Commemorating it in a confession is enough to afflict a rock!)
They killed both dead,   10
that was a sorrowful dish.
Some vengeance will come from yonder –
God is doubtlessly whetting His sword;
they will be brought to prison on account of their dreadful wounds;
innocent blood is calling out   15
for their being put in the shovel's ditch.

The queen was imprisoned
for more than a long year and a quarter
in the depth of a chamber;
she suffered many needs   20
in darkness at times,
no candle being lit.
She did, while she was in a confined condition,
herself send to the German emperor
a great sum of money, and this with ready speed,   25
to continue the war,
so as to prevent a situation of greater adversity.
Spain as one shares our aspect,
and Holland also, and the Russian empress,
and the king of Prussia, and England (the most certain report),   30
even though many thousands have been killed there –
it is difficult to number them.

Louis's queen did not have her end
as she would have chosen

(Anhwylus alwad).   35
Mis Hydref y pymthegfed
Y seiniwyd warthus weithred
     (Heb gelu'n galed);
'R ail dydd, rhoen' arni farn ddi-fudd,
I'w dwyn drwy drafel hyd at y sgaffel   40
     I gael dioddau dial, lliw'r grafel ar ei grudd.
Fe allai'i bod hi heno
     (Heb ffaelio) ar aden ffydd.
Pan ddaeth, ei breichiau bach yn gaeth,
Cyn ei dibennu hi ddwedai'i gweddi,   45
     Â dwyfron ddifri cyn soddi ynddi'r saeth.
Fe dorrwyd corn ei gwddw,
     Ac felly marw a wnaeth.

Cyn iddi gael ei diben
Ni adwaenai ei phlant ei hunan,   50
     Rai gwiwlan gowled.
Pan basiai'r ferdid arni,
Ei phen nid allodd godi,
     Dan gwlwm caled.
Pob dyn sy'n perchen plant ei hun,   55
Fe all hwn gonsidro ei hunan heno –
     Na ollyngo'n ango' ond cofio yn bur gytûn,
Mae'i phlantas bach yn salw,
     Yn byw dan sorw syn.
Peth mawr fod y rhain mor lwyr ar lawr,   60
Sef plant y brenin, o raddol ruddin,
     Heb help na ymddiffyn, bob munud ennyd awr.
Y sawl a ystyrio'n ffyddlon,
     Gall dorri calon cawr.

Ei phen pan gadd ei dorri   65
(Truanaidd, trwm drueni),
     Heb gelu, coeliwch,
Ac wrth ei gwallt fe'i codwyd –
Ddigasaidd a ddangoswyd
     Mewn golau, gwelwch.   70
Rhyw bryd rhaid inni fynd i gyd,
I gyd-gyfarfod; ni cheiff undyn wybod
     Yr awr na'r diwrnod y barniff Duw y byd.

(unfortunate summons).   35
On the fifteenth of October
was the despicable deed signed
(hardheartedly, without concealment);
the second day, they gave verdict upon her without blessing,
to take her wretchedly as far as the scaffold   40
to suffer vengeance, her cheek the colour of the gravel.
It may be that tonight
she is (without fail) on the wing of faith.
When she came, her little arms bound,
she said her prayer before being executed,   45
with sombre heart before the blade was plunged into her.
Her neck was severed,
and thus did she die.

Before she met her end
she did not know her own children,   50
beautiful darlings.
When the verdict was passed upon her,
she was not able to raise her head,
it being under a hard knot.
Every man who has children of his own   55
may tonight himself consider –
let him not forget but remember full well,
her little children are sickly,
living in senseless sorrow.
A terrible thing that they, the king's children,   60
of such high-born nature, should be so utterly set low,
without help or protection at any time.
Whosoever faithfully considers this,
it can break the heart of a giant.

When her head was severed   65
(a deplorable, heavy affliction),
without concealment, believe me,
and by her hair it was raised –
the gentle one was displayed
clearly, you see.   70
We must all go at some time,
to meet together; no man may know
the hour nor the time that God will judge the world.

Rho ras, O! Arglwydd cyfion,
   Na ledion dan Dy lid.   75
Rŷm ni, dan enw ffraethlon ffri,
Sef gwir Gristnogion, wŷr Brydain brydlon,
   Dan George a'i goron a'i Eglwys, radlon ri;
Er hyn, mae Ffrainc a'i theulu
   Am ei llenwi hi yma'n lli.   80

Duw a gadwo George ein brenin
A'i ddeiliaid sy'n ei ddilyn
   Rhag gelyn gwaedlyd.
Mae'r gwaedgwn melltigedig,
Fuleiniaid rhy fileinig,   85
   Am ein cael i'r gofid.
Duw Tri a safo'n hochr ni
Rhag pob bradwriaeth (ddiffawd ddiffaith,
   Sy'n riwlio'n helaeth) ysywaeth heddiw sydd;
A rheini'n llwyr, pe gallen',   90
   A ollyngai'n gwaed ni'n lli.
Duw'n ben a'n cadwo'n siŵr rhag sen.
Mae'n mawr bechodau'n eu galw yma
   I'n rhoi mewn poenau a'n cael mewn dalfa don.
Duw gadwo inni'n rhyddid   95
   Bob munud bawb, Amen.

JHD no.: 732i

Sources: copies of the same imprint are found in Bangor 14 (13); Bangor 19(8); Bangor 19(9). Bangor 14 (13) is very slightly damaged; the other two copies present clearer readings.

Publication: W. Edwards, Croesoswallt, 1794

Document title: *Dwy Gerdd Newydd, Y Gyntaf, Ychydig o hanes Brenhines Ffraingc; y modd y cafodd ei difetha, sef torri ei phen, a rhwymo ei dwy fraich ar ei chen, Hydref 17, 1793. Yr Ail, Rhybudd i bawb gofio am awr Angau, y Bedd, a'r Farn ddiweddaf. gan Richard Roberts.*

Give grace, Oh! just Lord,
that we may not spend a life in Your wrath.   75
We, under a resounding free name,
as true Christians, the fair men of Britain,
are under George and his crown and his Church, gracious king;
in spite of this, France and its host
wish to fill it here in a flood.   80

May God save George our king
and his subjects who follow him
from a bloody enemy.
The cursed bloodhounds,
excessively fierce villains,   85
want to bring us to grief.
May the Trinity stand on our side
against every treachery (without blessing and wicked,
which rules extensively) that exists, alas, today;
and they would, if they could, completely   90
let out our blood in a stream.
May God as head keep us safe from abuse.
Our great sins call them here
to put us in torment and bring us to a tight prison.
May God protect our liberties for us all   95
every minute, Amen.

8. Richard Robert[s], '[Cerdd newydd] yn gosod allan y moddion am y
rhyfeloedd presennol rhyngom a'r Ffrancod, a dull y grefydd babaidd'
Tune: 'King George's Delight'

Ow'r hen Frutanied, bur eu bwriad,
Gwael eu synied – gwyliwch sen!
Os ydyw Duw yn ddig,
Daw peryg' am eich pen.
Mae'n mawr bechode fel cymyle   5
Yn galw am ddialedde a'i lid;
Mae'n rhyfedd iawn gan rai
Fod Duw yn godde' cyd.
Ond eto mae'i fygythion
Ar droion drymion draw;   10
Mae barn wrth linyn cyn yleni,
A hynny'n peri braw.
Mae'r cledde noeth a'r powdwr poeth
Yn well na'r coeth aur cu,
Trwy Dduw ein Tad ar faes y gwaed   15
(Hyll fwriad felly fu).
Er bod ein pur elynion
Yn greulon ac yn groes
(Mae bryd cythreulig Ffrancod ffyrnig
I'n rhoi dan lewyg loes),   20
Bydd Duw ar ran pob Cristion gwan;
Rhag pob rhyw lydan lid
Yn drist fe droen' – fe wrendy'r Oen
A'u dwyn o boen y byd.

Mae'r papur newydd bob yn ail dydd   25
(Hyd y gwledydd beunydd bydd)
Yn dweud fod rhai dan glo
A'r lleill yn rhodio'n rhydd.
Nid gwir yw'r cwbl, rwyf i'n meddwl,
A roed yn fanwl ynddo fe –   30
Mae anwiredde ar dro
Yn llithro i'r un lle.
Amlach hyd y gwledydd
Y coelir celwydd noeth
Na'r Bibl pur sy'n dweud y gwir –   35
Un gore ar dir, air doeth.

8. Richard Robert[s], 'A new song setting out the features of the current wars
between us and the French, and the manner of the popish religion'
Tune: 'King George's Delight'

Oh, the old Britons, of faultless resolution,
humble their thoughts – beware of censure!
If God is angry,
danger will come upon you.
Our great sins are like clouds   5
calling for vengeances and for His wrath;
some find it very extraordinary
that God should suffer so long.
But still His threats are heavy
on occasions yonder;   10
judgement has been hanging upon a string before this year,
and that has caused fear.
The bare sword and the hot powder
(such a hideous intention there was)
are better than the fine, precious gold,   15
through God our Father on the field of battle.
Although our mortal enemies
are cruel and surly
(the devilish intention of the fierce Frenchmen
is to subject us to death's agony),   20
God will be on the side of all poor Christians;
from every great fury
they would anxiously turn – the Lamb listens
and takes them away from the torment of the world.

The newspaper every other day   25
(it goes daily throughout the lands)
says that some are imprisoned
and others walk free.
Not everything, I think,
that has been detailed in it   30
is true – falsehoods now and again
slip into that same place.
Barefaced lies are more often believed
through the lands
than the pure Bible which tells the truth –   35
the best on earth, wise word.

Rhyw holi o hyd sy 'mhlith y byd
(Bob ennyd adfyd yw)
Heb feddwl fawr rhwng lloer a llawr
Am doethder mawr ein Duw.   40
Gwir yw fod gwaed yn colli
A hynny'r dyddiau hyn –
N'w'ddion caled gallwn goelio,
Mae'n swnio'n fater syn.
Clyche Lloeger a diwnie'n dyner   45
Trwy bleser mawr a blys;
Pob newydd da a'n llwyr well*h*a,
Ac a'n llonna ni'n ein llys.

Fe ddaeth gwiberod buchedd bechod,
I blith colomennod, hynod yw;   50
Mae rheini'n rhodio'n rhwydd
Yn groes i'r Arglwydd Dduw.
Y mae'r bleiddied mewn crwyn defaid
(Yr hyll babistiad, brofiad prudd);
Duw wnelo ar fyr o dro   55
Na chaen' mo'r rhodio'n rhydd.
Rw' i['n] chwennych cael eu chwnnu
Rhag mygu'r lili lân;
Os felly a fydd trwy Dduw a'i ffydd
Mi lunia' ar gynnydd gân.   60
Mae'r seirff â'u ffalster eto'n Lloegr,
Fawr nifer efo ni,
Yn llawn o frad; pe cae' nhw aed
Nhw ollynge'n gwaed ni'n lli.
Ond eto rwy'n gobeithio   65
Na chaent mo'r llwyddo'n llawn,
Er maint 'u dyfes, filen fales,
A'u proffes, ddiras ddawn.
Mae'r holl babistiad dienwaediad
Â'u tyniad yn gytûn   70
Yn erbyn crefydd Crist –
Mae'r Gair yn dyst ei hun.

Duw a dro'i galonne rhag gelyniaeth
I addoli'n berffaith Duw yn bur,

There is constant inquiring among the people
(every moment is a crisis)
with little thought given between the moon and the earth
to the great wisdom of our God.   40
It is true that blood is being shed,
and that in these days –
news that is hard to bear we may believe,
it sounds like an astonishing matter.
England's bells sweetly sounded   45
with great pleasure and delight;
every good news restores us completely
and brings us joy in our court.

The vipers of sinful life have come
among doves, it is evident;   50
they wander unhindered
in opposition to the Lord God.
The wolves are in sheep's clothing
(the hideous papists, grim experience);
may God ensure within a short time   55
that they may not roam freely.
I long for them to be weeded
lest they should stifle the pure lily;
if it shall be thus through God and His faith
I shall hold forth in song.   60
The serpents and their falsehood are yet in England,
in great numbers among us,
full of treachery; were they to receive aid
they would make our blood flow in streams.
But yet I hope   65
that they shall not succeed in full,
in spite of their malicious scheme, cruel malice,
and their profession of faith, graceless gift.
The unregenerate papists
are all drawn in the same direction   70
against Christ's religion –
the Word itself is proof.

May God turn hearts away from enmity
to worship God perfectly and faultlessly,

Yn lle y delwau aur   75
(Fe dodde D'air Di'r dur).
Mae'n arw 'u gweld nhw ar 'u glinie
Yn addoli'r prenie a'r delwe trist,
A gwrthod yn ei swydd
Yr Arglwydd Iesu Grist.   80
Er cymaint sydd o filoedd
Ar dir a moroedd maith
Yn colli'u bywyd a'u holl olud
(Nid gwynfyd ydi'r gwaith);
Annuwiolion trymion sydd yn tramwy,   85
A hynny'r dyddiau hyn.
Nid oes neb yn fyw, am hynny, clyw,
A'u atalie ond Duw Ei Hun.
Duw gadwo George ein brenin,
A'i fuddiol fyddin fawr,   90
Ein gwŷr a'n llonge rhag gwall ange,
Hwn a'n malurie i lawr.
Holl Frydain, clyw, a galw ar Dduw,
Tra foch di byw yn ben,
I'w cadw i gyd rhag brad a llid   95
Bob munud bawb, Amen.

JHD nos., sources, publication details and document titles:

A: JHD 631i; Welsh Ballads Online (Cwp LlGC) and Bangor 7 (31); n.p.,
n.d.; *Dwy Gerdd Newydd Y Gyntaf yn gosod allan y moddion am y Rhyfeloedd
presennol rhyngom a'r Ffrangcod, a dull y grefydd Babaidd ar King George Delight.
Yn ail Cyffes ymadrodd neu Eiria Diweddaf Robert Owen o blwyf Llanrwst yn Sir
Ddimbych; yr hwn a ddioddefodd yn haeddedigol ar pren dioddef yn yr hen waun
neu old Heath yn ymyl y Mwythig 17. Ebrill ar Loath to Depart.*

B: JHD 270ii; Welsh Ballads Online; W. Edwards, Croesoswallt, 1794; *Dwy
Gerdd Newydd, Y Gyntaf, Rhybudd i bawb gofio am awr Angau, y Bedd, a'r Farn
ddiweddaf. Yr Ail, Yn Achos y Rhyfel presennol. Gan Richard Roberts.*

Variants: Tune. B – 'King Charles's Delight'; 2. B – syniad; 4. B – ein; 8. B – Ei
fod; 10. B – droeau'n; 18. B – gryfion; 19. B – [M]ae eu bryd cythreulig,
Pharaoh ffyrnig; 43. B – [N]ewyddion galant; 44. B – swnio ar; 64. B – lyngcai;
73. B – Duw tro ein calonau; 75. B – Yn lle eu; 79. B – yn eu swydd;

rather than the golden images 75
(Your word would melt steel).
It is grievous to see them upon their knees
worshipping the sad crosses and the images,
and refusing the authority
of the Lord Jesus Christ. 80
In spite of the numbers
who, on land and wide seas,
are losing their life and all their wealth
(the work is no bliss);
Godless forces come and go, 85
and that in these days.
There is no one alive, therefore, listen,
who could prevent them save God Himself.
May God protect George our king
and his great, beneficial army, 90
our men and our ships from death's snare,
which batters us down.
The whole of Britain, listen, and call on God,
while you live as chief,
to keep them all from treachery and wrath 95
each one every minute, Amen.

85. B – Rhybuddion trymion; 86. B – amser hyn; following the text, B – *englyn*: Lluniais a rhoddais yn rhwydd – rigl / Oreuglod i'r Arglwydd: / Dïau hael yw Duw hylwŷdd, / Rhoi doniau i saint dyna ei swydd.

9. Robert Roberts, '[Cerdd] yn gosod allan wroldeb, ffyddlondeb a llwyddiant y Duke o' York yn y rhyfeloedd presennol' Tune: 'King Charles's Delight'

Gwrandewch a 'styriwch, mae'n dosturi,
Fe aeth trwy boeni lawer byd
O ddynion meirch a thraed
I gadw'n gwlad yn glyd.
Ni bu ers oesoedd, hir flynyddoedd,   5
Mo'r fath ryfeloedd cyhoedd cas;
Fe gollwyd gwŷr a'u stôr
Ar dir a'r cefnfor glas.
Y Duk' o' York a safodd
O'i wirfodd efo'i wŷr;   10
Cadd lawer brwydyr o ochor Brydain,
Mae'n para eto'n bur.
Er ynnill gwledydd draw a'r trefydd
(Gwir beunydd felly bu),
Rhaid mynd yn ôl fel dynion ffôl   15
I forol am a fu.
Bu llawer batel eger
Rhwng Ffrainc a Lloeger llawn,
A sathru'r meirw'n gelanedde
O'r bore i'r prydnhawn.   20
Y plwm a'r powdwr, canons cynnwr',
Mawr drwbwl, swmbwl syn –
Aeth mil i lawr mewn llai nag awr
A'u gwaed i'r llawr fel llyn.

Y brenin Pryssia a holl Germania,   25
Yr empres Russia, droua drud,
A llawer heblaw rhain
Wnae ddechre llydain lid;
A chwedyn cilio heb osio canlyn
Yn erbyn Ffrenshmyn, fyddin fawr,   30
Ac ofni'u lladd i gyd
Bob munud ennyd awr.
Mae Fredrick, mab ein brenin,
A'i fyddin, gwreiddyn cry',
Gwych ryfelwr, meitha' milwr,   35
Concwerwr, lladdwr llu.

9. Robert Roberts, 'A song setting out the valour, loyalty and success of the
Duke of York in the current wars'
Tune: 'King Charles's Delight'

Listen and reflect, it is a cause for sorrow,
a great many cavalry and foot soldiers
have departed anxiously
in order to keep our country safe.
There have not been for ages, many years,   5
such notorious, cruel wars;
men and their supplies have been lost
on land and on the blue ocean.
The Duke of York stood
readily with his men;   10
he fought many a battle on Britain's behalf,
and he still remains virtuous.
In spite of having won lands yonder and the towns
(it is true that it was ever thus),
they had to return like foolish men   15
to take care of what was left.
There have been several harsh battles
between France and proud England,
and the corpses of the dead stamped underfoot
from morning to afternoon.   20
The lead and the powder, roaring cannons,
great trouble, astonishing scourge −
a thousand fell in less than an hour
and their blood flowed to the ground like a lake.

The king of Prussia and the whole of Germany,   25
the empress of Russia, terrible crises,
and many apart from these
began a widespread wrath;
and then retreated without daring to pursue
against the great army of the Frenchmen,   30
and fearing every minute lest they should all be killed
in the space of an hour.
Frederick, the son of our king,
and his army, a strong nucleus,
is a brilliant warrior, the wisest soldier,   35
a conqueror, a killer of a host.

Bu lawer batel heb dynnu'i fwties
(Mae'r hanes heno am hyn);
I lawr tan draed, roedd gwŷr mewn gwaed –
Mae'r siarad yma'n syn.　　　　　　　　40
Fe gadwodd Duw ei fywyd
Er bod mewn penyd pur,
A'r plwm o'u cwmpas fel y cenllysg,
Fawr derfysg arfau dur.
Trwy Dduw a'i gledde mae'n galonnog,　　45
Ŵr enwog, serchog sydd;
Er lladd mewn llid gryn bart o'r byd,
Mae e' mewn rhyddid rhydd.

Fe ddihange'n lanwaith rhag ei elynion
Trwy'r Arglwydd, cyfion dirion Dad;　　50
Roedd llawer mil mewn llid,
Â'u bryd am wneud ei frad.
Nhw a'i gyrason' i lan afon
(Gore'i galon, union ŵr);
Ei geffyl pallu wnaeth　　　　　　　　55
Â mentro'r traeth na'r dŵr.
Fe fentrodd nofio'n wisgi
Heb foddi yn y fan;
Ei goese a'i freichie oedd ei rwyfe,
Fe ledie rhyngtho a'r lan.　　　　　　60
Cadd lawer treial am ei hoedel
Pan oedd ar drafel drud;
Fe'i cadwodd Duw rhag brad a briw,
Mae eto'n byw'n y byd.
Mae rhai yn mentro'u bywyd　　　　　　65
A gado'u golud gwael,
Â'u bryd fel brodyr eto i'r frwydyr,
Heb feindio faint fo'r fael.
Duw bendigedig, llwydda Ffredrig
Yn erbyn ffyrnig Ffrainc,　　　　　　70
A chadw ei wraidd* rhag blinder blaidd,
Yn fwynaidd ar ei fainc.

* sef George y III.

He has been through many a battle without taking his boots off
(the story about this is here tonight);
down underfoot, there were men in blood –
there is stunned talk here.   40
God protected his life
although he was in great peril,
with the lead around them like hail,
the great tumult of steel weapons.
Through God and his sword he is courageous,   45
the famous, charming man that he is;
even though he has killed in fury through a great part of the world,
he remains in unrestricted freedom.

He would escape unscathed from his enemies
through the medium of the Lord, kind, righteous Father;   50
there were many thousands in anger,
intent upon betraying him.
They drove him to a river bank
(honest man with the best of hearts);
his horse refused to venture   55
onto the shore or in the water.
He dared to swim quickly
without drowning on the spot;
his legs and arms were his oars,
he led the way to the bank.   60
He had many trials for his life
while on his bold course;
God protected him from treachery and hurt,
he is still alive in the world.
Some risk their lives   65
and leave their wretched possessions,
intent like brothers for the battle again,
not minding what the reward might be.
Blessed God, give success to Frederick
against ferocious France,   70
and keep his root* from the tribulation of wolves,
kindly upon his throne.

* *namely, George III.*

JHD no.: 495i

Source: Welsh Ballads Online (CGPLE, 378)

Publication: T. Evans, Bermo, [1794]

Document title: *Tair Cerdd; Newydd Ar y Testyneu Canlynol Y Gyntaf Yn gosod allan wroldeb, ffyddlondeb, a Llwyddiant Y Duke, O York yn y Rhyfeloedd presenol, Yr Ail Yn rhoddi byrr hanes o'r Frwydur, ddigyffelib honno a ymladdwyd ar y Môr y Dydd cyntaf o Fehefin, 1794, yn yr hon y gorchfygwud y French gan Admiral Lord Howe, Yn Drydydd Cwyn, a chyngor Merch Ifangc, hudwyd i warth gan ryw remmwth, enw yr hwn ellwch weled os bydd wiw gennych ddarllen y gerdd.*

Textual readings: 47. o'r bart byd.

10. Robert Roberts, '[Cerdd] yn rhoddi byr hanes o'r frwydyr ddigyffelyb honno a ymladdwyd ar y môr y dydd cyntaf o Fehefin 1794, yn yr hon y gorchfygwyd y French gan Admiral Lord Howe'
Tune: 'King Charles's Delight'

Pen comander llongau Lloeger
A wnaeth rymusder (gwychder gwaith!),
Lord Howe, ymladdwr pur,
Wrth nofio'r llwybyr llaith
Y diwrnod cynta' o fis Mehefin, 5
Yleni yw'r flwyddyn (erwin floedd) –
Os gwir a glyweis i
Am y rheini, felly roedd.
Nhw fuont am ddau ddiwrnod,
Cyn taro dyrnod trwm, 10
Yn sbio o bob tu, bawb o'r ddau-tu,
Cyn dechreu plannu plwm.
'Mhen dau ddiwrnod y bu'r cyfarfod,
Â syndod mawr yn siŵr –
Saethu a rhwygo, lladd a llarpio, 15
A'u darnio lawr i'r dŵr.
Deg o'r gloch y bore
Bu dechre'r chware chwith,
Â chyrff y dynion dan y tonnau,
Oer frawiau yno'n frith. 20
Dros bump o oriau bu'r ymladdfa,
Yn curo'u goreu glas,
Ond Ffrainc a gollodd a ninneu enillodd
Ac a siwrodd hynny o sias.

Y Frensh a dyngen' cyn mynd allan, 25
A'u dull yn llawen, dalla' llu,
Na chymren' freib na thâl
Nes treio'u hoedel hy.
A phawb a safodd yno o'i wirfodd,
Ac felly ffaeliodd dynion ffôl – 30
'Nôl myned tros eu nyth,
Nid aethant byth yn ôl.
Roedd pedair llong ar hugain
O'r Frensh trwy lydain lid;
Nid oedd ond deuddeg o longau a dynion 35

10. Robert Roberts, 'A song giving the brief history of that incomparable battle
that was fought on the sea on the first day of June 1794, in which the French
were defeated by Admiral Lord Howe'
Tune: 'King Charles's Delight'

The chief commander of England's ships,
Lord Howe, a virtuous fighter,
achieved a mighty work (the valour of the deed!),
while swimming along the watery path
on the first day of June   5
of the current year (terrible cry) –
if what I heard
about those was true, so it was.
They remained for two days,
before striking a heavy blow,   10
looking in every direction, all from both sides,
before beginning to scatter lead.
The battle took place after two days,
with great astonishment it is certain –
shooting and ripping, killing and tearing to pieces,   15
and mangling them down into the water.
At ten o'clock in the morning
did the awful game begin,
with the men's bodies under the waves,
dreadful terrors all around.   20
The fight took more than five hours,
pounding for all they were worth,
but it was France that lost and us who won
and claimed that victory.

The French swore before setting out,   25
all carefree, blindest of hosts,
that they would take neither bribe nor payment
until they had put their audacious life to the test.
And everyone stood there of their free will,
and so did foolish men err –   30
having left the nest,
they never returned.
There were twenty-four ships
of Frenchmen ready for battle;
there were only twelve manned ships   35

O Frydein (frydlon fryd).
Yn erbyn Lloeger daeth eu gwychder,
A'u llawnder diwellhad;
Tros bum awr bu ryfel mawr
A'n curo lawr a wna'd.   40
Lord Howe oedd ben comander
O ochor Ll[o]eger lon;
Fe ddywede'n ffyddlon wrth ei weision
Oedd dirion uwchlaw'r don:
"Yn awr yw'r amser, heb ddim ffalster,   45
Gwŷr Lloeger, mwynder maith!
Prysurwch! Lladdwch! Nac arbedwch,
A llwyddwch ar fôr llaith!"

Admiral Lloegr enilleu'r treial,
Er colli'n y rhyfel hoedel rhai;   50
Er clwyfo llawer un
Mae rheini â llun gwellhau.
Mae'r Frensh ym Mhlimouth ac yn Falmouth,
Oerion dylwyth, adwyth yw,
Mewn carchar, trymder trist,   55
Heb 'ddoli 'Christ na Duw.
Mae amser pur ryfeddol
Rhwng pobol yn y byd –
Lladd a sbeilio, llusgo a llarpio,
Rhai eto'n cwyno cyd.   60
Rhoed pawb ei weddi'n fwyn i fyny
Ar Dduw wir ffynnu'n ffydd;
Fe haedde glod gan bawb sy'n bod
Am ddifa'r sorod sydd.
Mab Duw a dorro'r rhyfel   65
Rhag peri gafel gwaeth,
A chadw'n teyrnas mewn cadernid
A'i phur hoff ryddid ffraeth.
A llwydda 'th 'Fengyl rhagddi'n rhigyl,
Naws syful, ni ddaw sen;   70
Rho ras mewn pryd i bawb trwy'r byd,
Bob munud byth, Amen.

JHD no.: 495ii

from Britain (steadfast intent).
Against England came their gallantry
and their full force, not to be bettered;
for over five hours there was a great conflict
and we were beaten down.   40
Lord Howe was the chief commander
on mighty England's side;
he said faithfully to his servants
who were cheerful above the wave:
"Now is the time, without any flattery,   45
men of England, great gentility!
Make haste! Kill! Do not spare,
and prevail on the watery sea!"

England's admiral won the trial,
even though some lives were lost in the war;   50
although many were wounded,
they look to be on the mend.
The French are at Plymouth and Falmouth,
a wretched tribe, it is a misfortune,
in prison, a sad hardship,   55
worshipping neither Christ nor God.
It is a very extraordinary time
among the people of the world –
slaughter and plunder, hauling and mangling,
some yet complaining so long.   60
May everyone meekly raise up his prayer
to God that He should truly prosper our faith;
He deserves praise from everyone alive
for destroying the dregs which exist.
May the Son of God put an end to the war   65
lest greater adversity should be caused,
and keep our kingdom in strength
and her pure, admirable, generous freedom.
And promote Your Gospel to go forth eloquently,
a civil spirit, no censure shall come;   70
give grace in time to everyone through the world,
every minute for ever, Amen.

Source: Welsh Ballads Online (CGPLE, 378)

Publication: T. Evans, Bermo, [1794]

Document title: see no. 9

1795

*11. Jonathan Hughes, '[Cerdd] o galondid i'r milwyr gwladychaidd yr
ydys yn godi yn y deyrnas hon i gadw porthladdoedd, pa rai a elwir yn
gyffredin milisia'*
Tune: 'Tempest of War'

Pob gŵr ifanc glân, da 'i gywer a'i gân,
Da 'i amcan a mwynlan i'n mysg –
Fe ddaeth ordinhad y brenin (â'i rad)
I'n galw ni ddŵad dan ddysg,
A rhaid in 'n rhwydd, bawb sefyll i'r swydd   5
Yn ebrwydd, er [llwydd a] gwellhad,
Rhag y Ffrancod, wŷr ffri, sy'n nesu atom ni,
Â'u byddin yn codi fel cad.

Na chymrwn wan ffydd, na chalon ry brudd,
Ni gadwn y dydd gyda Duw;   10
Mae gwŷr da ar ein tu, yn llewyrch i'n llu,
I'n dysgu, rheoli'n un rhyw;
Tra caffom gryfhad penaethiad ein gwlad,
Marchogion, mewn cariad mwyn cu,
Rhaid ymladd yn llon dros Loegr, gaer gron –   15
Nid oes ond anffyddlon a ffy.

Byrdwn:
We will go along all through every throng,
With trumpets and song of all size;
Believe every lad, be merry, very glad,
In the face of our mad enemies.   20
We men of train band at King George's command
At hand in all England and Wales,
Will give a new gown to the French in every town
With the sword and cut down all their tails.

Tros farw yma'n glir, na chollwn mo'n tir –   25
Nyni a fynnwn yn hir ei fwynhau;
Er gwaetha' drwg wŷn, os byddwn ni'n un
A Duw yn gytûn ganiatáu,
Mae'n harfau ni'n siŵr ar dir ac ar ddŵr,
Er dwndwr a chynnwr' rhy chwyrn;   30

1795

*11. Jonathan Hughes, 'A song of encouragement to the patriotic soldiers
that are being raised in this kingdom to protect harbours, who are generally
called the militia'
Tune: 'Tempest of War'*

Every honest young man, whose disposition and song is good,
well-intentioned and genial in our midst –
the king's ordinance has come (by his grace)
to call us to come under training,
and we must readily, each one, stand to the task   5
quickly, for the sake of success and reform,
against the French, free men, who are drawing nearer to us,
their army rising like a throng.

Let us not be weak in faith, nor downhearted,
we shall win the day with God;   10
there are good men on our side, radiant in our host,
to teach us, rule us in unity;
while we have the strength of our country's rulers,
knights, in noble, amiable love,
we must fight gladly for England, round fortress –   15
only the disloyal flees.

Refrain:
We will go along all through every throng,
With trumpets and song of all size;
Believe every lad, be merry, very glad,
In the face of our mad enemies.   20
We men of train band at King George's command
At hand in all England and Wales,
Will give a new gown to the French in every town
With the sword and cut down all their tails.

Even if we must die, let us not lose our land –   25
we will insist upon enjoying it for a long time;
in spite of wretched trouble, if we will be one
and God willing,
our arms are sure on land and on water,
in spite of most violent clamour and tumult;   30

Os unwn ni ynghyd, rhown godwm i gyd
I'r Ffrancod er cyhyd eu cyrn.

Pob Cristion ar droed sy'n ifanc mewn oed,
I'w frenin ymroed mewn iawn rym;
Gwell ymladd â'r gad na'i gollwng i'n gwlad,   35
Rhag ofn y bydd lladdiad mwy llym.
Rhai ddywed fel hyn, yn swrth ac yn syn,
Fod ymladd yn ddychryn rhy ddwys;
Ond dychryn mwy drud pe doent yma i gyd –
Dau mwy fydde'n penyd a'n pwys.   40

Byrdwn: *We will go along, &c.*

Dowch, filwyr, gerbron! Rhaid cadw'r wlad hon,
Hen Frydain goch dirion, wych deg;
Gwell George mewn gwir gred yn aer ar 'i lled
Nag anghred agored 'i geg.
Ni phrisiwn ni ddraen er Ffrainc nac Ysbaen   45
Tra bo Duw'n blaen inni'n blaid;
Ni safwn ni'n ôl ar faes nac ar ddôl,
Er allo un hudol ddrwg haid.

Gore cyngor, gair cu, er llwyddiant i'n llu,
Yw peidio â hyderu ar un dyn;   50
Mae rhyfel o hyd er seiliad y byd,
Ar ddwylaw Duw hefyd 'i Hun.
Gweddïwn am ras, da fwriad di-fas,
Fel Josiwa, gwas i Dduw gwyn;
Pob duwiol fe a'i dysg, fe fydd yn eu mysg   55
Er dyfod oer derfysg yn dynn.

Byrdwn: *We will go along, &c.*

Rhown ffárwel ar ffo i'n brodyr o'n bro –
Rhaid myned i draenio at y drwm;
Rhaid dysgu pob gŵr ar dir ac ar ddŵr
I fflamio, trin powdwr a phlwm;   60
A dysgu'r un wedd, boed rhyfel boed hedd,
Ymarfer â'r cledd ar fodd clau,

if we unite together, we shall throw down
all the French, no matter how long their horns.

Every upright Christian who is young in years,
let him devote himself to his king in true might;
better to fight against the army than to let it into our country,   35
lest there should be a more severe slaughter.
Some say like this, wearily and in fright,
that fighting is too awful a terror;
but there would be a more dire alarm should they all come here –
twice as great would our tribulation and burden be.   40

Refrain: We will go along, &c.

Stand forth, soldiers! This country must be preserved,
red, gracious, splendid, fair old Britain;
better George in true belief as heir all over it
than atheism with its gaping mouth.
We shall not give a fig for France or for Spain   45
while God is plainly on our side;
we shall not stand back on field or on meadow,
no matter what any deceitful, cruel throng can do.

The best advice, precious word, for the success of our host,
is not to rely on any man;   50
there has always been war since the foundation of the world,
at God's own hands, too.
Let us pray for grace, a good, sagacious intention,
like Joshua, servant of blessed God;
He will teach every godly one, He will be amidst them   55
even if wicked strife should fiercely come.

Refrain: We will go along, &c.

Let us say farewell as we leave to our brothers from our land –
we must go to the drum to train;
every man on land and on water must be taught
to blaze, to handle powder and lead;   60
and learn just the same, whether there be war or peace,
to practise with the sword in a swift manner,

I sefyll gerbron os digwydd o'r don
I elynion â'u swynion nesáu.

Dymuno ar ein glân rieni nad ân'   65
I duchan neu riddfan ar ôl;
Mawr achos sy i ni, ond fe allai'ch bod chwi
Yn ei chyfri'n rhyw ffansi rhy ffôl.
Ond rheitiach yw rhoi gelynion i ffoi
Na theilo na throi – ymroi yr ŷm ni;   70
Rhowch weddi ar Dduw Tad am ein rhwydeb a'n rhad,
A'n cadw rhag brad yn ein bri.

Byrdwn: We will go along, &c.

JHD nos., sources, publication details and document titles:

A: JHD 750ii; Bangor 14 (16); n.p., [?1796], tros Robert Prichard; *Dwy Gerdd Newydd Yn gyntaf [O] annogaeth i bob Cymro Diledryw a garo lwyddiant ei wlad ai genedl, i ddewis Cymro o gyd-wladwr yn Farchog, neu Ben-Swyddog, yn y Dadleu-dy Cyffredin yn yr Etholiad nesaf i ddyfod. Yn ail O galondid ir Milwyr gwladychaidd, yr ydis yn godi yn y Deyrnas hon i gadw Porthladdoedd, pa rai a elwir yn gyffredin Militia.*

B: JHD 766ii; Bangor 15 (2); Stafford Prys, Amwythig, 1763, tros Thomas Roberts; *[D]wy Gan Am Geiniog, Y gyntaf yn dangos fel mae Plant y Byd hwn yn cwyno mwy am ffrwyth y Ddaear nag am Iesu Grist. Yr ail: Cerdd o Galondid ir Milwyr Gwladychaidd, yr ydis yn ei godi yn y Deyrnas hon I gadw'r Porthladdoedd pa rai a elwir [---]din y Militia, neu Train Bands.* This document is incomplete and paper edges are damaged; the text begins at line 19.

C: NLW MS 18B, pp. 453–4, 'Cerdd yn Amser Rhyfel', dated 1756. The text is incomplete and ends with line 52. This manuscript is in the hand of David Ellis, Cricieth (1736–95), and was compiled between 1779 and 1794. See Daniel Huws, 'Repertory of Welsh Manuscripts and Scribes' (2 vols., unpublished), I, pp. 5–6.

D: JHD 491i; E. Prichard, Machynlleth, 1795. The text has not survived but is listed in *BWB*, p. 162, the reference taken from William Roberts, *Cambrian Bibliography containing an account of books printed in the Welsh language, or relating to Wales,* edited and enlarged by D. Silvan Evans (Llanidloes, 1869; facs. reprint,

to stand in the front if enemies and their spells
should happen to draw nearer by sea.

We wish that our good parents   65
should not grumble and groan after us;
there is great need for us, but it may be that you
consider it some very foolish fancy.
But it is better to make our enemies flee
than to spread dung or plough – we are doing our bit;   70
pray to God the Father for our success and our blessing,
and to keep us safe from treachery.

Refrain: We will go along, &c.

Amsterdam, 1970), p. 695; *Tair Gerdd* [*sic*] *Newydd Tra rhagorol. 1. Cerdd o Galondid i'r Milwyr Gwladychaidd yr ydys yn codi yn y deyrnas hon i gadw'r Porthladdoedd, pa rai a elwir yn gyffredin Militia neu'r Train Band. II. Myfyrdod Duwiol rhwng Dyn ac ef ei hun cyn dydd ar ei wely* [*sic*]. *III.Ymddiddan rhwng hen Wr, a Llanc ieuangc oedd yn myned i garu: bob yn ail bennill.*

Variants: 1. C – da gywir ei; 6. C – llwydd; 12. C – a'n rheolu; 13. C – pennaethiaid; 15. C – Rhag; 17. C – Chorus neu Byrdwn; 18. C – songs; 21. C – train'd; 26. C – Ni; 28. B – yn cydturn; 31. C –'nghŷd; 35. B – ein g'lad; 38. C – dychryn rhai dwys; 39. B – pe ddont; 43. C – ein lled, B – i led; 44. B, C – Na Lewis; 45. B –Yspaen, C – yn Ffraingc; 46. C – 'n y blaen; 48. B, C – ddraig; 51. B – y rhyfel, C – Mae'n Rhyfel; 56. B – or derfysg; 60. C – a thrin; 70. C – theilio.

Textual readings: 23. Frence.

1797

12. Dienw, 'Cân newydd am y waredigaeth fawr a gafodd yr hen Frytaniaid trwy law Duw [a] Lord Cawdor, oddi wrth lu o ladron Ff[rein]ig yn y flwydd 1797'

Hir iawn bu'r hen ddinistrydd yn bwgwth dod i'n tir
A'r gelyn hyll dinistriol i ladd â'r cleddau clir;
Er cy[maint] waeddodd pechod, trugaredd ddaeth i lawr –
Ffrwyth peraidd eiriolaeth ein Harchoffeiriad mawr.

Saith gant ddwy waith o filwyr a ddaeth i'r lan i'n tir,5
Oll wedi dysgu handlo y dryll a'r cleddau dur;
A[?'u] diben yn ddrygionus (plant angall, pwy a'u câr?) –
Och! braf yr oe'nt yn swaeo 'r hyd cernydd mân Penca'r.

[N]es dyfod o Lord Cawdor a'i bum can gŵr ar lawr,
A phum deg o farchogion, yn debyg iawn i'r wawr;10
Duw wnaeth yr olwg arnynt i'r anferth lu wa[n]ha[u],
Pan ddaethant i'w eu golwg am ddau o'r gloch ddydd Iau.

Ar [?la]swellt faes Trele[te]rt, fe ddarfu Cawdo[r] lew
I ffrontio'i filwyr ieuainc dan faner gref y llew,
Nes ofni'r hen ŵr penllwyd, a dweud yn oleu deg,15
"Nis gallaf dim o'u sefyll â phedwar cant ar ddeg."

Yn hardd, aeth Cawdor wrol a'r Cornel Colby mwyn
A'r Major Ac[?k]land grymus a Knox tuag Abergwaun;
A chant o'r glân filisia o Aberteifi sir
Ddilynai'r gwŷr ceffylau yn gywir ac yn glir.20

A chan gŵr glew o Benfro ddilynai sodlau rhain,
Dan gario'r mwsged gloyw a'r dager llym bla'n main;
A milwyr Knox y cornel oedd nesa' ymlaen at rhain –
Gwŷr glewion, gwn o'r goreu, glân sawdwyr Abergwaun.

Gwŷr Trefdraeth ar ôl hynny a gadwai ymlaen yn glos,25
A llawer iawn o Hwlffordd rows ysgwydd dan y gro's;
A'r morwyr glân o Hagan a'r coliers chwerwon du,
A llawer mil o'r Cymry ddily[n]ai'r arfog lu.

1797

12. Anon., 'A new song on the great deliverance which the old Britons received through the hand of God and Lord Cawdor, from a host of French thieves in the year 1797'

For a long time did the old destroyer threaten to come to our land
and the hideous, pernicious enemy to kill with the bright sword;
however much sin cried, mercy did descend –
the fragrant fruit of the advocacy of our great Archpriest.

Two times seven hundred soldiers came to land on our soil,   5
all having learnt to handle the gun and the steel sword;
evil their intention (foolish children, who loves them?) –
alas! finely did they sway along the little cairns of Pencaer.

Until Lord Cawdor and his five hundred men came down,
and fifty cavalrymen, much resembling the dawn;   10
God made their appearance cause the great host to waver
when they came to their sight at two o'clock on Thursday.

On the pasture of the plain of Letterston, valiant Cawdor
drew up his young soldiers under the bright banner of the lion,
until the old grey-haired man took fright, and said quite plainly,   15
"I cannot oppose them with fourteen hundred."

Nobly, valiant Cawdor and the gentle Colonel Colby
and the mighty Major Ackland and Knox went towards Fishguard;
and a hundred of the honest militia of Cardiganshire
followed the cavalry men loyally and purely.   20

And a hundred courageous men from Pembroke followed upon their heels,
carrying the shining musket and the pointed, slender-tipped dagger;
and the soldiers of Colonel Knox were closest behind these –
valiant men, I know full well, the honest soldiers of Fishguard.

The men of Newport after that tightly pressed on,   25
and a great many from Haverfordwest put their shoulder under the cross;
and the honest mariners of Hagan and the surly black colliers,
and many a thousand of the Welsh followed the armed host.

Lord Cawdor gadwai'r bla'n (gŵr haeddai barch
    heb ble) –
Ond cofied y Brytaniaid mai Duw cynhaliodd e';   30
Duw safodd gyda'n byddin yn Ynys Brydain Fawr,
Nes gwnaeth yr olwg arni i'r French roi'u harfau [lawr].

Rhyfeddod ar ryfeddod! Ryfeddod daear lawr,
Wrth weled creulon filwyr yn bwrw'u harfau lawr
O flaen y Saeson glewion a'r Cymry mwynion triw;   35
Dewch, holl drigolion Brydain, i foli'r Seilo byw.

Nid oen' hwy o rifedi ond pum can gŵr a saith,
A phum deg o farchogion, yn mynd â rhain yn gaeth;
A hwythau o wŷr arfog yn saith can gŵr ddwy waith!
O, diolch, diolch, diolch, i'r Hwn a'u rhodd yn gaeth!   40

'Dyw rhyddid gore Ffrancod ond rhyw gaethiwed du –
Duw gadwo'r hyll elynion rhag dod i'n trethu ni;
Rwy'n credu caem ni hynny, a heddwch cyn bo hir,
Oni bai fod Gog a Magog yn llidiog yn y tir.

Gwŷr rhyddion yw'r Brytaniaid, hiliogaeth Gomer, sydd   45
Yn caru eu hannwyl frenin yn ffyddlon nos a dydd;
A boddlon iawn i'r gyfraith (nid oes mo'i gwell hi'n bod) –
Amdani mi ddymunwn i'r Arglwydd gael y clod.

Trugaredd i fy mrenin a heddwch ar ei ben –
Ymborthi wnelo'n helaeth ar ddail y Bywiol Bren;   50
'Run modd, yr waedoliaeth, yn fawrion ac yn fân,
Cwrdd wnelont ar foreuddydd yn nhref Caersalem lân.

Ei drethwyr fyddo'n gyfiawn a'i swyddwyr ar fôr a thir
Fo'n ffyddlon dros y Goron yn tynnu'r cleddau du[r];
'R holl filwyr fyddo'n ffyddlon a gwrol bônt hwy i [g]lyd –   55
Duw lwyddo arfau Lloegr yn ddychryn i'r holl fyd.

Duw roddo edifeirwch am bechod trwy ein gwlad
A ffydd yn enw Iesu fu farw yn Ei wa'd;
A l[l]wydded air y deyrnas i ddryllio Babel fawr;
Nesáu mae'r hyfryd foreu cawn weled hon ar lawr.   60

Lord Cawdor kept to the van of battle (a man who deserved respect
    without argument) –
but let the Britons remember that it was God who sustained him;   30
God stood with our army in the Great Isle of Britain,
until the view it presented made the French put down their arms.

Wonder upon wonder! Wonder upon the surface of the earth,
seeing cruel soldiers putting down their arms
in front of the valiant English and the noble, loyal Welsh;   35
come, all the inhabitants of Britain, to praise the living Siloh.

They were in number but five hundred and seven men,
and fifty cavalrymen, who took these away as prisoners;
and they two times seven hundred armed men!
Oh! thanks, thanks, thanks to the One who made them captive!   40

The best freedom of the French is but some dark bondage –
may God keep the hideous enemies from coming to tax us;
I believe that we would have that, and peace before long,
were it not that Gog and Magog are raging in the land.

The Britons, the race of Gomer, are free men   45
who love their dear king faithfully night and day;
and are very satisfied with the law (there is no better one in existence) –
for it I would wish the Lord to receive the credit.

Mercy to my king and peace upon his head –
may he feed plentifully on the leaves of the Tree of Life;   50
in the same way, may his kindred, both great and small,
meet upon a morning in the holy town of Jerusalem.

May his tax collectors be just and may his officers on sea and land
be faithful in support of the Crown while drawing the steel sword;
may all the soldiers be faithful and valiant –   55
may God speed the arms of England to the terror of the entire world.

May God give repentance for sin through our country
and faith in the name of Jesus who died in His blood;
and may the word of the kingdom shatter great Babel;
the joyful morning when we shall see it on earth is drawing nearer.   60

Duw gadwo Ynys Brydain rhag min y cleddyf glas
A rhag i arfau Lloeger byth, byth i golli'r ma's;
A rhodded i ni heddwch – gweddïed pawb am hyn –
Er mwyn yr Hwn fu farw ar ben Calfaria fryn.

JHD no.: 759

Source: Welsh Ballads Online (Cwp LlGC (gwaelod))

Publication: n.p., [?1797]

Notes: A vertical decorative border separates the two columns of the text. The quality of the printing is very poor.

Textual readings: 11. wa[.]han; 12. yw ei; 13. Ruswellt, Treleiort; 17. Cowd r, Coldy; 18. Ac[?k]lana, K ox, Abergwain; 19. Abertifi; 21. ddilynau; 23. Kn x; 24. Aberwain; 27. col ers; 32. Fre ch; 36. hwll, Bry ain; 37. c n'; 38. gaith; 40. h n; 44. yu; 46. hanwy; 52. C rdd; 58. Iesu u; 60. c wn; 61. r ag; 62. bytd byth; 63. pawd; 64. fanw.

May God protect the Isle of Britain from the edge of the deadly sword
and from England's arms ever, ever being overcome;
and may He give us peace – let everyone pray for this –
for the sake of the One who died upon the hill of Calvary.

13. Dienw, 'Cân newydd o America, a ysgrifennwyd gan un o'r rhai a aeth i'r wlad honno yn ddiweddar, yr hon sy'n cynnwys y llwyddiant a'r aflwyddiant a gawsant ar eu taith, ynghyd ag ychydig hanes o'r wlad eang honno'

Yn ôl fy addewid, mi 'sgrifennais
I chwi hanes fer o'm taith,
Oddi ar yr amser darfu 'n fadael
Â Chymru dir i'r cefnfor maith.
Gwedi bod yn aros wythnos   5
Ar yr afon cyn mynd i ma's,
Nos Iau, y seithfed dydd o Ebrill,
Gael dechreu'n taith i'r cefnfor glas.

Am naw ar gloch yn gadael Milffwrdd,
A myned ffwrdd wrth oleu'r nos,   10
I gael rhoi ffarwél wrth ymadael,
Dros byth, i Gymru, ein daear glos.
Ymhen diwrnodau, rhai ae'n gleifion,
A rhai mewn iechyd, goreu'u gra'n,
A'r wythnos gyntaf yn llwyddiannus   15
O ran y gwynt yn gyrru ymla'n.

Amffion ar adenydd cyflym
Yn rhwygo tonnau'r dyfroedd mawr;
Hi red mor ebrwydd gyda'r awel
Â naw milltir yn yr awr.   20
Wyth o'r dyddiau cyntaf gawsom
Y gwynt yn gyson gyda'n taith;
Dauddeg wedyn yn ein herbyn,
Heb un eflyn lawer gwaith.

Weithiau'r gwyntoedd yn cyfodi   25
Ac yn cynhyrfu'r tonnau draw,
Weithiau'n chwyddo fel mynyddau,
Â'r olwg arno'n peri braw.
Gwedi bod rhyw dalm o ddyddiau
A rhai wythnosau arno fe,   30
Nid oedd dychryn arnom gwedyn,
Mwy nag ar y tir yn nhre'.

13. Anon., 'A new song from America, written by one of those who recently went to that country, which recounts the good fortune and the adversity that they encountered on their journey, together with some account of that vast country'

According to my promise, I have written
for you a brief account of my journey,
from the time that we left
the land of Wales for the wide ocean.
Having waited for a week   5
on the river before setting out,
on Thursday evening, the seventh day of April,
we were able to begin our journey to the blue ocean.

At nine o'clock we departed from Milford,
and went away by the evening light,   10
so that we could say farewell to Wales, our beautiful land,
in leaving her forever.
Within days, some became ill,
and others were in health, their condition the best,
and the first week was successful   15
in so far as the wind drove us forwards.

Amphion upon swift wings
tearing the waves of the great deeps;
she runs as quickly with the breeze
as nine miles per hour.   20
On eight of the first days that we had
the wind was favourable for our journey;
on twelve afterwards it was against us,
without the slightest breeze several times.

The winds sometimes rose   25
and agitated the waves yonder,
the sea sometimes swelled like mountains,
its appearance causing fear.
Having been for many days
and some weeks upon it,   30
we were not afraid then,
any more than on land at home.

Maes yn rhodio ar dywydd tirion
Bwrdd yr *Amffion* oeddem ni,
Weithiau'n gweled golwg hynod   35
O fawrion bysgod heb ddim rhi';
Gweld y porpys yn neidio fynydd
Yn lluoedd dirifedi maith,
A'r pysgodyn bach hedfanog
A'r siarcs a'r twmblers lawer gwaith.   40

Seithfed o Fai bu'r storom fwya'
A gawsom ni ar y môr,
Yn dywyll nos mewn dŵr anniben
Heb oleu haulwen, sêr, na llo'r.
Nid ofni dŵr nac ofni gwyntoedd,   45
Ond ofni'r creigiau gerllaw'r tir,
Ac ofni brynoedd mân dywodydd
Oedd ddigon dryllio'n llong, *yn* wir.

Ymhen pum wythnos ryfedd hynod,
Cawsom waelod cynta'r môr,   50
A'r prest fyddin aeth â'n bechgyn
I fwrdd llong ein Brenin Siôr.
Yr un diwrnod gwelsom hefyd
Diroedd hyfryd, coedydd draw,
Yr Ynys Hir yn dweud heb ryfyg   55
Fod America gerllaw.

Dydd Sadwrn wedyn ar ôl hynny
Heibio Sandyhook ymlaen
A gweld y coedydd sedar gwyrddon
O bob tu'r afon, Athen lân!   60
Am ddau ar gloch ni welsom ddinas
(Noddfa a gawsom ni yn awr)
Caerefrog-newydd, dinas ryddid,
Lle nid oes llid mewn ergyd mawr.

Nid oes dynion â boliau mawrion   65
Blonegog tewion yma'n bod;
Nid oes chwaith gardotyn llymrig,
Ond pawb yn debyg, i'r un nod;

We were out in fair weather
wandering the deck of the *Amphion*,
sometimes seeing a wondrous sight   35
of countless large fish;
seeing porpoises leaping up
in countless, large multitudes,
and the little flying fish
and the sharks and the tumblers many a time.   40

The greatest storm that we experienced at sea
took place on the seventh of May,
in the darkness of night in troubled water
without the light of sun, stars, nor moon.
We did not fear water nor fear winds,   45
but feared the rocks adjacent to the land,
and feared the mounds of fine sands
which were enough to wreck our ship, indeed.

After five most extraordinary weeks,
we touched the seabed for the first time,   50
and the press-gang took our lads
on board the ship of our King George.
The same day we also saw
delightful lands, forests yonder,
Long Island announcing truly   55
that America was close by.

The next Saturday after that
we went onwards past Sandyhook
and saw the green cedar trees
on either side of the river, fair Athens!   60
At two o'clock we saw the city
(we now had a sanctuary)
of New York, the city of liberty,
where there is no great stroke of wrath.

No men with large, greasy,   65
fat bellies exist here;
neither is there a wretched beggar,
but everyone is similar, of the same status;

Pe bai tlodion Cymru'n gallu
Croesi'r werlig donnog draw,   70
Trwy weithio byddent byw'n gysurus
Mewn gwlad heddychol, fro di-fraw.

JHD no.: 557

Source: Welsh Ballads Online

Publication: I. Evans, Caerfyrddin, dros I. Thomas, 1797

if the poor of Wales could
cross the billowy ocean yonder,   70
by working they would live comfortably
in a peaceful country, a land without fear.

14. Dienw, 'Cân o ddiolchgarwch i'r Arglwydd am Ei waredigaeth hynod, yn
ein cadw rhag fflangell ein gelynion pan tiriasant yn ein tir'

'Cenwch i'r Arglwydd ganiad newydd'

Mae'n argoeli'n amser enbaid
Ar bererinion Sion ddewr;
Mae'r French a'r Sbaniards am orchfygu
Holl drigolion Brydain Fawr.
Rŷm mewn dychryn mawr gan ofnau   5
Bradwriaeth gas gelynion cry';
'Does neb ond Duw byddinoedd Israel
A saif o blaid ein milwyr ni.

Mae'n holl elynion hyll a chreulon
Mewn cadwyn gan ein Brenin mawr;   10
Fe saif yn gryf o blaid Ei bobl
Mewn gorthrymderau ar y llawr.
Ymwrolwn mewn cyfyngder,
Mae'n cyfaill goreu ar ein rhan;
Fe fydd yn flaenor i handlo'r cleddyf   15
Oddi amgylch Sion ymhob man.

Mae'n gwŷr bon'ddigion yn ffyddlon ddigon
(Ni fedraf nawr eu henwi i gyd),
Er bod rhyw ffyliaid am ddringo fynydd
Gog'uwch â'r rhain yn hyn o fyd.   20
Dau well fod cariad yn llenwi Brydain
('S dim diffyg arall yma'n bod):
Llywodraeth burion, Efengyl dirion,
Y famaeth oreu fu erio'd.

Y mae Lord Cawdor a Lord Milffrwd   25
Yn weision ffyddlon i'r deyrnas hon,
A Churnel Colby, fu'n wynebu
Ein gelynion, lu o'r bron!
Y Cymry, ynghyd â Saeson Penfro,
Fu'n driw o blaid ein Coron wiw;   30
Dymunai'r rhain i gael gwirionedd
A'r goron auredd gyda Duw.

14. Anon., 'A song of gratitude to the Lord for His remarkable deliverance, keeping us from the scourge of our enemies when they landed on our land'

'Sing to the Lord a new song'

It promises to be a fearful time
for the pilgrims of brave Zion;
the French and Spaniards wish to defeat
all the inhabitants of Great Britain.
We are greatly alarmed by fears   5
of cruel treachery by strong enemies;
there is no one but the God of Israel's hosts
who will stand in support of our soldiers.

All our hideous and cruel enemies
are chained by our great King;   10
He stands firmly on the side of His people
who are under oppressions upon earth.
Let us take heart in affliction,
our best friend is on our side;
He shall be a leader to handle the sword   15
all around Zion.

Our noblemen are faithful enough
(I cannot now name them all),
although there are some fools who wish to climb up
as high as them in this world.   20
Twice better that love should fill Britain
(there is no other deficiency here):
perfect government, sweet Gospel,
the best nurse that ever was.

Lord Cawdor and Lord Milford   25
are faithful servants to this kingdom,
and Colonel Colby, who faced
our enemies, an entire host!
The Welsh, together with the English of Pembroke,
were loyal in support of our worthy Crown;   30
they wished for truth
and the golden crown with God.

O, frodyr, rhowch help eich gweddïau
A'ch caniadau o fawr glod
Yn ddiolchgarwch i'r Oen a brynodd   35
Fywyd miloedd cyn ein bod.
Fe roddodd eiriau fel cleddyfau
Yng ngenau'i weision i anturio ymlaen,
A llwfwrdra i'n gelynion,
Nes iddynt lowro'u harfau'n lân.   40

Cymry'n wrol safodd fynydd
Yn hynod dros yr ynys hon;
Os cawn ni eto'r fath wahoddiad,
Na lwfrhaed ein calon drom.
Awn ymlaen â diben cywir –   45
Fe wrendy'n Tad ar lef Ei blant,
Y Duw fu gadarn gyda Dafydd
Pan dorrodd ben Golia bant.

Nid cryfdwr llongau ar y moroedd
A'u rhwystrodd mewn i Iwerddon dir,   50
Ond gair o'i enau a orchmynnodd,
"Tyred wyntoedd, na fydd hir!
Chwytha longau rhai dinistriol,
Canons mawr a bwlets trwm,
Powdwr du ac arfau glowion   55
Lawr i'r môr fel pelen blwm!"

Gyfeillion, p'odd y gallwn dewi
Heb weiddi'n uwch mewn bro a bryn,
"Bendigedig fyddo'r Arglwydd
Am Ei waredigaethau in!"   60
Fe fydd o hyd yn ostyngedig
I wrando ein hannheilwng lef;
Gobeithiwn eto cawn ein cadw –
Digonol allu ydyw Ef.

Ein Bugail da, bendithia'n brenin   65
A'n holl flaenoriaid, fawr a mân,
A'i hardd gydmares (fwyn ei fynwes)
A'i deulu i gyd yn ddi-wahân.

Oh, brothers, give your prayers in aid,
and your songs of great praise
in thanksgiving to the Lamb who bought   35
the lives of thousands before we were born.
He gave words like swords
in the mouths of His servants to venture forth,
and cowardliness to our enemies,
until they lowered their arms completely.   40

The Welsh bravely stood up
splendidly for this island;
if we should have such an invitation again,
may our heavy heart not turn coward.
Let us go forward with true intent –   45
our Father will listen to His children's cry,
the God who was steadfast with David
when he struck off Goliath's head.

It was not the strength of ships upon the seas
that prevented them from entering the land of Ireland,   50
but a word from His mouth did command,
"Come, winds, do not be long!
Blow the ships of the pernicious ones,
large cannons and heavy bullets,
black powder and shining weapons   55
down into the sea like a lead ball!"

Friends, how can we stay silent
without shouting more loudly on hill and dale,
"Blessed be the Lord
for His deliverances to us!"   60
He will always deign
to listen to our unworthy cry;
we hope that we shall yet be preserved –
He is of sufficient might.

Our good Shepherd, bless our king   65
and all our leaders, great and small,
and his beautiful wife (he whose spirit is gentle)
and all his family, without distinction.

Ni gawsom ryddid yn eu dyddiau
Gael Dy addoli yn ddi-baid;   70
Na ad i'r Ffrancod draw gyfyngu
Ein breintiau gwerthfawr – bydd o'n plaid.

Parhad o hyn yw'n herfyniadau
(Gael moli'n Prynwr gwerthfawr byth) –
Tro'n gelynion 'nôl yn fwynion,   75
'Th Efengyl dirion rho'n eu plith.
Cyflawna'th air i ben yn fuan –
"Cyrrant gleddyfau'n sychau mwy,
A'u gwaywffyn oll yn bladuriau,
Heb neb yn cario arfau'n hwy."   80

Fe fydd gorfoledd mawr rhyfeddol
Pan welir Sion wan dylawd
Yn dod i'r lan o'r cystudd yma,
Dan adain ein hanwylaf Frawd;
Heb un gwahanglwyf yn ein blino   85
A'n pwys ar ein Hanwylyd gwiw,
Fu'n prynu'n bywyd ar Galfaria –
Ein Priod annwyl yw a'n Duw.

Os gofyn neb o'r byd neu'r Eglwys
Pwy rows y geiriau hyn ar gân,   90
Un a ddymunai ddiwygio Brydain
Heb dwrf y meirch na swn y tân;
Efengyl Iesu yn ei phurdeb
Yn torri pob heresïau lawr,
A Siors y Trydydd yn gwisgo'r goron   95
Heb un gwrthnebwr, fach na mawr.

JHD no: 560i

Source: Welsh Ballads Online (Cwp LlGC)

Publication: I. Evans, Heol-y-prior, Caerfyrddin, 1797

Document title: *Cân o ddiolchgarwch i'r Arglwydd, am ei waredigaeth hynod yn ein cadw rhag ffalngell* [sic] *ein gelynion, pan tiriasant yn ein tîr: ynghyd â marwnad*

We found freedom during their days
to be able to worship You incessantly;   70
do not let the Frenchmen yonder
limit our precious privileges – be on our side.

Our prayers are a continuation of this
(so that we may praise our precious Redeemer for ever) –
turn our enemies meekly homewards,   75
spread Your gracious Gospel among them.
Bring about Your word soon –
"They will turn swords into ploughshares
and all their spears into scythes,
without anyone bearing arms any more."   80

There will be extraordinarily great jubilation
when mild, impoverished Zion is seen
coming to the shore following this tribulation,
under the wing of our most dear Brother;
without any leprosy to vex us   85
and our weight upon our worthy Loved One,
who bought our lives upon Calvary –
He is our dear Spouse and our God.

If anyone from they lay-world or the Church
asks who put these words to song,   90
it was someone who wished to reform Britain
without the clamour of the horses or the sound of the fire;
Jesus's Gospel in its purity
striking down every heresy,
and George the Third wearing the crown   95
without any opponent, great or small.

Daniel Dafydd, ysgol-feistr Gymraeg yn Meidrim, yr hwn a ymadawodd â'r byd, yr 11eg o fis Mawrth, 1797, yn 51 blwydd o oedran.

15. Dienw, 'Clod i'r Cymry, gwŷr sir Benfro, am gymeryd y rheibus
elynion cythreulig, ysglyfyddwyr mileinig, sef Ffrancod, pan diriasant yn
Abergwaun'
Tune: ['Belisle March']

Sŵn rhyfeloedd sy mor filen
   Yn magu cynnen cas;
Nid yw hynny ond gwaith pechu,
   Eisiau deisy' ar Iesu am ras.
Mae rhai yn bwgwth daw Gog a Magog –   5
   O! lu cyndyniog dwys
O rai moethus – i'n difetha
   (Yn benna', arwa' bwys).
Gweddïo gwnawn ar Dduw,
   Fe'n ceidw i fyny i fyw   10
Rhag llu mileinig melltigedig
   O rai crwydredig ryw.
Dwy long forwyodd, yn daer a diriodd,
   Cywirodd yn Abergwaun,
I ysglyfaetha neu ladrata,   15
   A'r rhai mileinia' ymlaen.
Y Ffrancod, sorod sur,
   Oedd yn llawn o arfa dur –
O! rai llidiog, lu cynddeiriog,
   Anhrugarog wŷr.   20
Dwyn a difa moch a defed,
   Y dynged aeth yn dost;
Berwi a rhostio'n ffast a ffestio,
   Cestio heb hidio'r gost.

Dwyn yr yde o'r ysguborie   25
   A gwartheg a'r lloie'n llu;
Mynd i'r seleri (naws hwyl arw)
   [I] gael cwrw croyw cry';
'R ôl yfed eu gore o'r bir y bore
   Nhwy ollynge'r rest i'r llawr.   30
Gwŷr sir Benfro'n dechreu mileinio,
   Yn chwennych c'weirio'u gwawr.
Nhwy losgen' ddodrefn tai
   [?I] ferwi bwyd (roedd bai);
Nhw wersylle â'u pabelle   35

15. Anon., 'Praise to the Welsh, the men of Pembrokeshire, for seizing the
voracious, fiendish enemies, savage plunderers, namely the French, when they
landed in Fishguard'
Tune: ['Belisle March']

The clamour of war is so savage,
breeding cruel strife;
it is nothing but the product of sin,
for want of beseeching Jesus for grace.
Some threaten that Gog and Magog will come –   5
Oh! grim, perverse host
of voluptuous ones – to ruin us
(the greatest, most dire burden).
We will pray to God,
He shall sustain us alive   10
against a ferocious, accursed host
of vagabonds.
Two ships sailed, landed brazenly,
kept their appointment in Fishguard,
to pillage or steal,   15
and the most loathsome of them at the front.
The Frenchmen, sour dregs,
were teeming with steel weapons –
Oh! irascible, furious host,
merciless men.   20
They stole and destroyed pigs and sheep,
it was a pitiful fate;
they boiled and roasted swiftly and feasted,
drank greedily without care for the cost.

They stole the corn from the barns   25
and the cattle and calves in droves;
they went into the cellars (a spirit of great merriment)
to get fresh, strong beer;
having drunk their fill of the beer in the morning
they poured the rest on the ground.   30
The men of Pembrokeshire began to become furious,
wanting to thrash their hides.
They burnt the furniture of houses,
to boil food (they were at fault);
they camped with their *pabellau*   35

(Neu'u tentie, rhodde rhai),
Gan ysbeilio'r wlad o'i heiddo,
    Ymgeisio yn un gainc;
Llu gwrthnysig, cad mileinig,
    Rhai ffyrnig, milwyr Ffrainc.   40
Y Cymry a gode'n gad
    I ymladd am eu gwlad;
Pawb yn eglur, a 'chydig filwyr,
    [F]el brodyr i wneud eu brad.
Hel pladurie a chrymane,   45
    Picwarche a garie'r gwŷr,
Gan floeddio'n sydyn, "Duw gadwo'r brenin!"
    Megis byddin bur.

Y Cymry ffyddlon a danie'n union
    Rai ergydion croes –   50
Dychryn calon i'r Ffrancod ladron,
    Yn union, am eu hoes.
A'r coliars enwog â'u gwiail pigog
    Yn rhywiog doen' yn rhanc,
Gan ddymuno caen' cwartorio   55
    Neu'u blingo ar ryw blanc.
A'r rheibwyr drwg yn awr
    Y roent eu harfau i lawr;
Ymroi yn union yn garcharorion,
    Rhai surion, drwg eu sawr.   60
Y mae'r hagr wŷr mewn carchar,
    Bu edifer am eu taith;
Gwych gwŷr sir Benfro, am fileinio,
    A ddarfu g'weirio'r gwaith.
Trwy Frydain cawsant glod,   65
    Wych Gymry, am eu bod
Yn bur i'r Coron, wŷr howddgara',
    Yn rhwydda' dan y rhod;
Ni ddaw i Gymru o Ffrainc ond hynny
    I bentyrru fyth i'n tir,   70
'Te, caen' fynd adre' heb eu penne,
    Fel y gwedde, i ddweud y gwir.

(or their tents, some would say),
plundering the country of its possessions,
greedy for everything;
vile host, a savage throng,
fierce ones, the soldiers of France.   40
The Welsh formed an army
to fight for their country;
everyone plainly, and a few soldiers,
like brothers to put paid to them.
They gathered scythes and sickles,   45
pitchforks did the men carry,
shouting suddenly, "God save the king!"
like a true army.

The faithful Welsh fired at once
a few opposing shots –   50
a terrible fright to the French thieves,
truly, for their lives.
And the famous colliers with their pointed sticks
nobly they came in rank,
wishing they would be able to send them packing   55
or flay them on some griddle.
And the evil ravagers now
put down their arms;
they surrender at once as prisoners,
sour ones of a bad odour.   60
The ugly men are in gaol,
there was regret for their journey;
it was the gallant Pembrokeshire men, by being resolute,
that set the matter to rights.
Throughout Britain they were praised,   65
noble Welsh, because they were faithful
to the Crown, most willing men,
readiest under the firmament;
none from France save they shall come into Wales
ever to flock into our land,   70
if so, they might go home without their heads,
as would be fitting, if truth be told.

Pob perchen awen, gwnawn gyduno
    I egluro clod
I wŷr sir Benfro am iddyn' fentro   75
    Heb hidio dan y rhod.
Duw, cadw'r Senedd rhag dim llygredd,
    Yn buredd heb ddim bai,
A'r Cymry tirion yn bur i'r Goron,
    Yn ffyddlon, rwyddlon rai.   80
O, Arglwydd, dedwydd Dad,
    Dod nerth i ni gadw'n gwlad;
Rhag nerthodd cryfion ein gelynion
    Dod inni arwyddion rhad.
Gwasgara'r cwmwl, tor y swmbwl,   85
    Dod iddyn' drwbwl tranc,
Fel na ddelo i Gymru i reibio
    Neu gwencio drwg eu gwanc.
Diogelwch, heddwch hir,
    Fo i dario yn ein tir,   90
Heb ddim gelyniaeth i'w ystyriaeth,
    Ond cariad perffaith pur.
Arglwydd cyfion, Frenin Sion,
    Y gwir Dduw cyfion coeth,
O, sa'n dragwyddol efo'n brenin breiniol,   95
    O, Arglwydd dethol doeth!

JHD nos., sources, publication details and document titles:

A. JHD 426i; Bangor 8 (5) and Bangor 14 (17); Ishmael Davies, Trefriw, [1797], dros R. Prichard; *Tair o Gerddi, Newydd: Y gyntaf Clod ir Cymry gwyr sir Benfro am gymeryd y Rheibus Elynion Cythreulig, ysglyfyddwyr mileinig, sef Ffrancod pan diriasant yn Abergwaen. Yn ail diolch i Dduw am y rhydd-did a gafodd Lloegr i ymladd a'r Spaniards a'u gorthrechu a chymeryd eu Llongau ar y môr, gan y Llywydd Arglwydd Jervis. Yn drydydd Mawl i Ferch.*

B. JHD 493i; the text has not survived but is listed in *BWB*, p. 163; Rowlands, *Cambrian Bibliography*, p. 710; and Jones, 'Gwaith Argraffwyr Machynlleth', 29–30; Edward Prichard, Machynlleth, n.d.; *Tair o Gerddi. Y cyntaf Clod i'r Cymry gwyr Sir Benfro am gymeryd y Rheibus Elynion Cythreulig ysglyfyddwyr mileinig sef Ffrancod pan diriasant yn Abergwaen. Yn ail diolch i Dduw am y*

Every owner of a muse, let us come together
to proclaim praise
to the men of Pembrokeshire for having ventured   75
without a care in the world.
God, keep Parliament from any corruption,
purely without any fault,
and the gracious Welsh faithful to the Crown,
loyal, liberal ones.   80
Oh, Lord, blessed Father,
give us strength to protect our country;
against the strong powers of our enemies
give us gracious signs.
Scatter the cloud, break the spur,   85
give them the trouble of destruction,
so that ones of evil greed do not come to Wales
to ravage or to fight.
May safety, long peace,
tarry in our land,   90
without any enmity to be heeded,
but perfect, pure love.
Just Lord, King of Zion,
the true, just, pure God,
Oh, may You stand everlastingly with our anointed king,   95
Oh, precious, wise Lord!

rhydd-did a gafodd Lloegr i ymladd a'r Spaniards a'u gorthrechu a chymeryd eu Llongau ar y mor, gan y Llywydd Arglwydd Jervis. Yn drydydd Hymn.

Textual readings: 53. gwiaill; 88. gwincio.

16. Edward Pugh, '[D]iolch i Dduw am y rhydd-did a gafodd Lloegr i ymladd
â'r Sbaniards a'u gorthrechu a chymeryd eu llongau ar y môr, gan y llywydd,
Arglwydd Jervis'
Tune: *'Duw Gadwo'r Brenin'*

Duw, Tad trugaredde, Brenin nef ole,
    I Loegr y rhodde fe'n rhwydd;
Y gwir Dduw yw'r rhoddwr, y Fe yw'r cymerwr,
    Rhyfelwr, dadleuwr da lwydd.
Mawr rydd-did cadd Lloeger gan Dduw o'r uchelder   5
    I ymladd yn eger yn awr;
Ar y môr yn ddiweddar, *fleet* Sbaen oedd ystrowgar –
    Syrthiodd yn liwgar i lawr.

A gwych longau Lloeger a ganfu ar fyrder
    Fleet Sbaen ar 'u cyfer yn gu.   10
Fe ddwede Lord Jervis, "Byddwch filwyr ofalus!
    Mae Ysbaniards, wŷr grymus, yn gry'."
Er amled eu llonge, gwŷr Lloegr a'i mentre,
    Ac yno fe danie'r ddau du,
Blant Jervis o ddifri'n gweld llong Sbaen yn soddi   15
    A'r môr yn cau arni yno'n hy.

A pheder o'u llonge Lord Jervis cymere
    (Dyne iddyn' chware go chwith)
A'r lleill a ddiangodd o'r golwg – nis gwelodd –
    Gyrrodd, anrheithiodd eu rhith.   20
Clod i Dduw cyfion am y rhydid a gawson
    I drechu'n gelynion mor glau;
Ni ddylem weddïo bob pryd ac ymprydio,
    Cyd uno heb gwyno, nac-hau.

Nid sŵn tincian clychau na hunan chwyddiadau   25
    (Mae'n dost fod fath bethau'n cael bod)
Yn lle gweddi howddgara' a diolch hyfryda'
    I'r Arglwydd Dduw'n benna' sy'n bod.
Rhown glod i'r Gorucha' am gadw Britania
    A'i llywodraethwyr pura' mewn parch;   30
A'n Brenin George hefyd – dymunwn bob munud
    I Dduw gadw'i iechyd hyd arch.

*16. Edward Pugh, 'Thanks to God for the deliverance which England
had to fight the Spaniards and vanquish them and take their ships
upon the sea, by the commander, Lord Jervis'
Tune: 'God Save the King'*

God, Father of mercies, King of bright heaven,
He provided for England generously;
the true God is the bestower and He is the One who takes away,
a warrior, an advocate of good prosperity.
England had great freedom from God from on high   5
to fight vigorously now;
on the sea recently, Spain's fleet was scheming –
it fell dramatically downwards.

And the mighty ships of England soon found
Spain's fleet sitting pretty opposite them.   10
Lord Jervis said, "Be careful, soldiers!
Spaniards, stout men, are strong."
In spite of the abundance of their ships, England's men took their chance,
and there the two sides fired,
Jervis's children with steadfast resolution seeing Spain's ship sinking   15
and the sea inexorably closing upon it.

And Lord Jervis took four of their ships
(that was a very nasty game for them)
and the others fled from sight – he did not see them –
he drove, he destroyed their pretence.   20
Praise to the righteous God for the liberty we were given
to defeat our enemies so swiftly;
we ought to pray at every meal and fast,
join together without complaining or refusing.

Neither the sound of ringing bells nor the puffing up of ourselves   25
(it is pitiful that such things are allowed to exist)
in place of the sweetest prayer and the loveliest thanks
to the Lord God almighty.
Let us give praise to the Most High for preserving Britannia
and her purest rulers in respect;   30
and our King George, too – let us wish every minute
that God should preserve his health until he reaches the grave.

O! Dduw trugarocaf, y Tad galluocaf,
    Fel hyn y gweddïaf yn ddwys –
Cadw wlad Bryden rhag gelynion aflawen,   35
    Dod rhai sy am gynnen dan gwys.
Dod nerth, O! Dad cyfion, i'n milwyr yn ffyddlon
    (Milisia – mae'n burion eu bod)
I gadw ein teyrnas rhag un gelyn diras –
    Mae hyn yn gyfaddas i fod.   40

JHD no.: 426ii

Sources: Bangor 8 (5); Bangor 14 (17)

Publication: Ishmael Davies, Trefriw, [1797], dros R. Prichard

Document title: see no. 15A

Oh! most merciful God, the most able Father,
thus do I earnestly pray –
keep the country of Britain from loathsome enemies,   35
put those who wish for strife under the sod.
Give strength, Oh! just Father, to our soldiers faithfully
(the militia – it is a good thing that they exist)
to keep our kingdom from any wicked enemy –
it is right and proper that it should be so.   40

17. Hugh Jones, '[Cerdd] yn rhoi hanes brwydr a fu rhwng Lloegr a Hisbaen,
y 14 o Chwefror 1797, a'r modd y gorchfygwyd yr Ysbaeniaid gan Syr John
Jervis, admiral Lloegr'
Tune: 'Duw Cadw'r Brenin'

Llawenwn oll unwaith trwy burffydd yn berffaith;
   Mae odiaith deg araith ar goedd.
'N mis Chwefror, yn ddiau, bu brwydr rhwng llongau,
   Cewch glywed mai chwarae gwych oedd.
Cychwyne'r Ysbaeniaid tu 'g at y Ffrainconiaid   5
   Fel diawlaid a bleiddiaid rhag blaen,
Ar feddwl cysylltu i gael ein gorchfygu,
   A'u llid oedd yn cynnu fel caen.
Un Admiral Serfus, pan glywodd yn hysbys,
   Ae 'n ddirus a hwylus o'u hôl;   10
Ymhen tridiau, hefyd, sef ar ddydd Mawrth Ynyd,
   Fe wele'r wâr enbyd, ddi-rôl.

Yn erbyn gwŷr Prydain, sef gan Ysbaen filain,
   Roedd saith llong ar hugain yn rhes;
Gan Loegr bach wisgi roedd pymtheg llong wedi,   15
   A hynny o gyfri 'ma ges.
Fe ddwede'r Ysbaeniaid, "Wel, dacw'r Brutaniaid,
   Trueiniaid fel defaid ar don!"
Troi'n ôl yn llawn balchder i'r frwydr, ar feder
   Lladd nifer bach Lloeger yn llon.   20
Llawenant o'r achos; nis gallant mo'r aros
   I ddyfod yn agos i ni,
Ond dwedyd, "Hai! Taniwn, a'r sothach a saethwn,
   Hen gorgwn! Ni a'u lladdwn fel lli!"

A'n hadmiral ninnau a fforddiodd ei longau   25
   Cyn dechrau rhoi'r gynnau ar 'u gwaith,
Gan ddwedyd, "Fal yma mae inni ryfela
   Yn erbyn y dyrfa sy ar daith."
[R]oedd llongau mawr erchyll Ysbaen 'rôl ymgynnull
   Yn edrych fel cestyll o'u co';   30
Ond llongau bach Lloeger, pan ddaethant ar gyfer,
   A'u rhoddodd mewn trymder bob tro.
Ymladde'n gwŷr tyner dros bum awr a hanner
   Er nifer iselder yn siŵr,

17. Hugh Jones, 'A song giving the story of a battle which took place between England and Spain on 14 February 1797, and how the Spanish were vanquished by Sir John Jervis, England's admiral'
Tune: 'God Save the King'

Let us all rejoice at once, faultlessly through true faith;
there is an exceptional, fair account to be conveyed publicly.
In the month of February, undoubtedly, there was a battle between ships,
you shall hear that it was a gallant sport.
The Spaniards started out towards the French   5
like devils and wolves forthwith,
intending to unite so as to get the better of us,
and their fury ignited like a cane.
A certain Admiral Jervis, when he heard about this,
went directly and swiftly after them;   10
within three days, too, namely on Shrove Tuesday,
he reached the perilous, unruly conflict.

Against the men of Britain, that is on the side of savage Spain,
there were twenty-seven ships all in a row;
little, sprightly England had fifteen ships then,   15
and those are the numbers I got.
The Spaniards said, "Well, the Britons are over there,
wretches like sheep upon the waves!"
They turned back to the battle full of pride, with the intention
of killing England's small host merrily.   20
They rejoice at the chance; they cannot wait
to come near us,
but say, "Hey! We shall fire, and we'll shoot the dross,
old curs! We'll kill them in droves!"

And our admiral walked about his ships   25
before beginning to put the guns to their task,
saying, "It is like this that we shall fight
against the host which is underway."
The great, frightful ships of Spain after gathering together
looked like raging castles;   30
but England's little ships, when they came to face them,
put them in hardship every time.
Our good men fought for more than five and a half hours
despite their small numbers indeed,

Nes gweld Ysbaen ddynion [?ar] dop y môr eigion   35
　　Fel hen lamhidyddion yn dŵr.

Pan wele Sbaen erwin eu llongeu mor gregyn,
　　Gwybuont mae cethin eu cost.
Dywedant yn unblaid, "Nid ydyw'r Brutaniaid
　　Yn ddefaid ond diawlaid blin, tost."   40
Rhedasant tu' chartreu â'r tân 'n eu tinau
　　A'u llongau (oer foddau) [a]r feth.
Aeth cantoedd, trwy drallod, o'u dynion i'r g[w]aelod –
　　Yn fwyd i'r hen bysg[od] am [?be]th.
Eu hadmiral ffyrnig â'i long fawr, gythreulig,   45
　　Oedd ysig, fethedig ei thop;
Bu gorfod i'w longe ei llusgo hi â rhaffe
　　Am gartre', myfyrie'r hen fop.

Fe gymre'n gwŷr ninnau toc beder o'u llongau
　　Ar wyneb y tonnau drwy'r tân;   50
Dau cant, triugain union ac un oedd yn feirwon
　　O'u dynion, rhwng mowrion a mân.
Tri chant dau a deugain o friw-wŷr yn ochain
　　Ar y pedair llong filain ar fôr;
Pwy ŵyr pa faint hefyd a gollodd eu bywyd   55
　　O'r lleill ddarfu symud rhag Siôr?
Os ar ddydd Mawrth Ynyd y daeth y llu gwaedlyd
　　Lladronllyd i'n symud yn syth,
Nhw gafodd grempogau o blwm a thân golau
　　A sâi yn eu boliau dros byth.   60

Fe gâdd yr Ysbaenaidd, do, gan y Brutanaidd,
　　Bryd ffiaidd, wawr blymaidd o'r blaen.
Elisabeth hyfryd a'i rhoddodd o, hefyd,
　　Pan drechodd weis bowlyd Ysbaen.
Os darfynt ymprydio er yr egwyl honno   65
　　Roedd yn amser cael cinio mewn cell,
Ac felly 'r tro yma, 'rôl cymryd eu rhedfa,
　　Hwy gowsont eu gwala'n ddau gwell.
Saith ddeg a thri union o'n gwŷr a lladdason'
　　Yn y frwydr hell, greulon o graith;   70
Dau gant, medd hanesion, ac ugain brifason'
　　O'n dynion, weis union, a saith.

until they saw the men of Spain on the surface of the ocean   35
like old porpoises in the water.

When harsh Spain saw their ships in such tatters,
they knew that their losses were severe.
They said with one voice, "The Britons are not
sheep but are savage, cruel demons."   40
They ran for home with their arses on fire,
and their ships ruined (sorry state).
Hundreds of their men, through calamity, went to the bottom –
food for the old fish for a while.
Their fierce admiral's great, fiendish ship,   45
was shattered, its upper part ruined;
his ships had to haul it with ropes
towards home, pondered the old fop.

Our men soon took four of their ships
on the surface of the waves through the fire;   50
exactly two hundred and sixty-one of their men
were dead, great and small taken into account.
Three hundred and forty-two wounded men groaning
on the four dreadful ships upon the sea;
who knows how many others lost their lives   55
from among the ones who fled from George?
If the bloodthirsty, thieving host came upon Shrove Tuesday
to put us to flight,
they received pancakes made of lead and blazing fire
which would remain in their stomachs for ever.   60

Indeed, the Spaniards were given a loathsome meal
of a leaden cast by the Britons before.
It was lovely Elizabeth who bestowed it, too,
when she defeated the filthy slaves of Spain.
If they happened to fast since that period   65
it was time for them to have dinner in a cell,
and so this time, having taken their run,
they had their fill twice as well.
They killed exactly seventy-three of our men
in the ugly battle, a cruel scar;   70
they injured two hundred and twenty-seven
of our men, honest lads, according to accounts.

Ond cofiwn ni'n ddiau mai nid nerth ein harfau
    A rwygodd eu llongau mewn llid,
Ond llaw Duw galluog, pen Brenin trugarog,   75
    A'u gwnaeth nhw mor garpiog i gyd.
Mawr, mawr yw amynedd Duw Tad a'i drugaredd
    Sy'n cadw'n glân annedd i ni;
Haeddasom ers amser wrth gwrt y cyfiawnder
    Droi Lloeger i brudd-der o'i bri.   80
Philistiaid anraslon a aeth i dŷ Dagon
    'Rôl caffael i Samson fawr sen;
Rhag ofn ein dibennu, na wnawn ni mo hynny,
    A Duw ddelo i'n maethu ni, Amen.

JHD no.: 417i

Source: Bangor 8 (4)

Publication: Ishmael Davies, Trefriw, [1797]

Document title: *Dwy o Gerddi Newydd Yn gyntaf Yn rhoi hanes Brwydr, a fu rhwng Lloegr â Hisbaen; y 14 o Chwefror 1797 a'r modd y gorchfygwyd yr Ysbaeniaid gan Sir John Jervis Admiral Lloegr. A genir ar Duw Cadw'r Brenhin. Yn ail Carol Plygain, ar Derfyn y Dyn byw.* An *englyn* by Hugh Jones is included at the end of the pamphlet.

But let us remember well that it was not the strength of our arms
that tore their ships in anger,
but the hand of mighty God, the merciful chief King,   75
who made them all so ragged.
Great, great is the patience of God the Father and His mercy
that keep our pure habitation for us;
we have deserved for a long time according to the court of justice
to find England turned to sorrow from its prestige.   80
Graceless Philistines went to Dagon's house
having caused Samson great abuse;
lest we should be terminated, let us not do that,
and may God come to nourish us, Amen.

18. Nathaniel Jenkin, 'Annerch i'r Cymry, i'w hannog i edifarhau am eu
pechodau a dychwelyd at Dduw, ac i'w glodfori am ein gwared o grafangau'r
Ffrancod didrugaredd'

Salm 124: 6, 'Bendigedig fyddo'r Arglwydd, yr Hwn ni roddodd ni yn
ysglyfaeth i'w dannedd hwynt'

Deffro, Gymru, bydd barodol,
Mewn da fwriad edifeiriol;
Ymlanha, cyhoedda ympryd,
Gad dy feiau, gwella'th fywyd;
    Gosod wylwyr ar dy gaerau,   5
        Deisyf gymod
    A bydd barod hwyr a borau.
    Dyrchafa'th lef, gweddïa lawer,
        Gwêl y drygfyd
    Mawr a'r gofid sy ar dy gyfer.   10

Mi debygwn, wrth iawn synied
Y nodau gwael, fy mod yn gweled
Y meysydd oll yn wynion allan
A chwedi crymu lawr i'r cryman;
    A'r cynhaeaf mawr cyffredin,   15
        Wrth bob nodau,
    Wedi dechrau, er ein dychryn;
    Ac er ein bygwth, gwelir bagad
        Mewn tywyllwg,
    Dan nod amlwg, yn ddideimlad.   20

Mae gwialen Duw'n ymddangos
Am hir bechu – dyna'r achos –
Ac yn ysgwyd uwch ein pennau
Ac yn ein bygwth â dyrnodiau,
    Ond hyd yn hyn yn cael ei dala;   25
        A hyn a ddengys
    Fod Duw â'i ewyllys inni wella.
    Os hir erys Duw heb daro,
        Trwm o'r diwedd
    Fydd y dialedd pan y delo.   30

18. Nathaniel Jenkin, 'An address to the Welsh, to urge them to repent
of their sins and return to God, and to praise Him for delivering us
from the claws of the merciless French'

Psalm 124: 6, 'Blessed be the Lord, who hath not given us as a
prey to their teeth'

Awaken, Wales, be ready,
with a penitent, virtuous resolution;
cleanse yourself, declare a fast,
leave your faults, improve your life;
place watchmen on your citadels,   5
ask for atonement
and be ready evening and morning.
Raise your cry, pray a great deal;
see the great affliction
and the trouble that face you.   10

I would think, from correctly examining
the humble signs, that I see
the fields outside all white
and stooped downwards for the sickle;
and the great, general harvest,   15
according to every sign,
having started, causing us alarm;
and so as to threaten us, a callous host
is seen in the dark,
under a conspicuous sign.   20

God's rod appears
because of lengthy sinning – that is the cause –
and shakes above our heads
and threatens us with blows,
but has hitherto been withheld;   25
and this shows
that it is God's will that we should mend our ways.
If God waits for long without striking,
the vengeance will be heavy
when at last it comes.   30

O! mor isel y bu'r Iesu
Mewn mwyn agwedd yn mynegi
Y pethau welwn ni eglura'
Yn ddiamau'r dyddiau yma:
    Cariad brawdol wedi oeri,   35
      Llid a rhagfarn
    Mewn modd cadarn wedi codi;
    Garw falais a rhyfeloedd
      A gofidi
    Yn taer ysu rhwng teyrnasoedd.   40

Fe ddarfu i'r Ffrancod dewrion dirio
Wrth Abergwaun o fewn sir Benfro,
Ac yn treisio 'nôl eu pwrpas
Fel ellyllon dewrion diras;
    Ac yn gwneuthur aml ddrygau   45
      A cholledion
    I amryw ddynion o'u meddiannau;
    Â'u peiriannau yn eu dwylo,
      Mewn llawn fwriad
    Ar ddwys darawiad i ddistrywio.   50

Wrth weled bwriad y barbariaid,
Fe gyffrôdd gwaed yr hen Frytaniaid.
Wrth y miloedd nhwy godason',
Fel Brytaniaid diriaid dewrion;
    Yn un asgwrn ac un ysgwydd,   55
      Fel Cristnogion
    O un galon efo'i gilydd;
    Gan fentro 'mlaen yn bur galonnog,
      Gyda'i gilydd,
    Yn enw'r Llywydd mawr galluog.   60

Roedd gwŷr cedyrn wedi codi
O Benfro sir ac Aberteifi,
Yn gapteniaid ac yn filwyr;
O Emlyn dref daeth pobl bybyr
    Gyda'i gilydd, am y cynta',   65
      Yn finteioedd,
    Amryw filoedd am ryfela,
    Heb na meddwl na gwybodaeth

Oh! how lowly did Christ
with mild aspect point out
the things that we see most clearly
without doubt these days:
brotherly love cooled,   35
anger and prejudice
raised up strongly;
bitter malice and wars
and fears
fiercely devouring between kingdoms.   40

The brave French did land
near Fishguard within the county of Pembroke,
and pillaged according to their intention
like bold, wicked demons;
and inflicted numerous evils   45
and losses of their possessions
upon many men;
with their instruments in their hands,
fully bent
on destruction at a heavy stroke.   50

Upon seeing the design of the barbarians,
the old Britons' blood was aroused.
By the thousand they rose,
as terrible, brave Britons;
shoulder to shoulder,   55
as Christians
of one heart all together;
venturing forwards very valiantly
together,
in the name of the great, mighty Lord.   60

Strong men had been raised
from Pembrokeshire and Cardigan,
captains and soldiers;
zealous people came from the town of Newcastle Emlyn,
all together, vying to be first,   65
they formed into companies,
several thousands wishing to fight,
without thought or certainty

Y caent eu bywyd
I ddychwelyd yn iach eilwaith.   70

Yn eu mysg yr oedd personiaid
(Mwyn hoff auraidd) ac offeiriaid,
A chyda rhain roedd arfau hyfryd –
Tarian ffydd a chleddy'r Ysbryd,
    A helm yr Iechydwriaeth dirion.   75
      Dyna'r arfau
    Âi trwy galonnau'r drwg elynion;
    Ni allai'r gwilliaid godi erfyn
      Nac un bicell
    Yno o hirbell yn ein herbyn.   80

Wrth ein gweled mor hyderus
A'n gwir siarad mor gysurus,
Heb ddim dychryn, braw nac ofon,
Fe ddigalonnodd y gelynion,
    Ac a aethant i gyfyngdra   85
      A chaethiwed
    Fel y Syried yn Samaria,
    A bodloni mynd i garchar
      Rhag eu damnio
    A'u hanffurfio yn ddi-ffafar.   90

Dyma ryfedd waredigaeth
A'r tro glanaf trwy ragluniaeth,
Heb na rhyfel nac ymladdfa,
Ond trefn uchel y Gorucha'.
    Cymeryd pymtheg cant o ladron   95
      Ar un borau,
    Ar fyr eiriau, 'n garcharorion;
    A chymeryd eu holl arfau
      A thermigion,
    Mewn modd union, i'n meddiannau.   100

O, Dduw! rho nerth i deyrnas Lloeger,
Yn enwedigol epil Gomer,
I gadw'n brenin grasol mwynedd
Yn ddiarswyd ar ei orsedd;
    I amddiffyn braint y ffydd Gristnogol   105

that they would be in possession of their lives
to return healthily again. 70

Among them there were parsons
(noble, praiseworthy, virtuous) and priests,
and these had fine arms –
the shield of faith and the sword of the Spirit,
and the helmet of tender Salvation. 75
These were the arms
that would go through the hearts of the evil enemies;
the brigands could not raise a weapon
nor a single pike
there from a distance against us. 80

Seeing us so confident
and our truthful utterance giving us such comfort,
without any fear, dread or trepidation,
the enemies lost heart,
and went into tribulation 85
and bondage
like the Syrians in Samaria,
and resigned themselves to going to gaol
lest they should be damned
and disfigured ruthlessly. 90

This was a wonderful deliverance
and the loveliest outcome through the medium of providence,
without conflict or a fight,
only the exalted plan of the Almighty.
Fifteen hundred thieves 95
were in one morning
taken prisoners, to put it briefly;
and all their weapons
and every item were brought
directly into our possession. 100

Oh, God! give strength to the kingdom of England,
especially to the kindred of Gomer,
to protect our gracious, mild king
fearless upon his throne;
to defend the privilege of the Christian faith 105

A'i pherthnasau
A phob rhadau angenrheidiol;
Ac einioes fer a chur anorffen
   Ac anghysur
Ym mysg bradwyr Ynys Bryden.   110

Er bod llawer wedi gweithio
Ar y testun hwn, rwy'n tystio,
Cymerwch hwn gan hen ddyn trwstan
Pymtheg mlwydd a thrugain oedran.
   Â'r hen awen wedi rhewi   115
      A Nathaniel
   Yn ddwys dawel yn distewi;
   Ond bod y bywyd eto'n para –
      Nid oes hefyd
   Ond afiechyd yn fynycha'.   120

JHD nos., sources, and publication details:

A: JHD 819; Bangor 19 (13); I. Daniel, Caerfyrddin, 1797. A woodcut showing two flowers is found at the end of the text.

B: John Howell (ed.), *Blodau Dyfed; Sef, Awdlau, Cywyddau, Englynion, a Chaniadau, Moesol a Diddanol, A Gyfansoddwyd Gan Feirdd Dyfed, Yn y Ganrif Ddiweddaf A'r Bresennol* (Caerfyrddin, 1824), pp. 281–5.

Variants: 37. B – sydd yn codi; 39/40. B – A gofid felly, / taer yn ysu; 48. B – 'n egr yno; 52. B – Brydeiniaid; 54. B – Prydeiniaid; 58. B – fyn'd y'mlaen; 99. B – Herwyr creulon; 117. B – ar ddystewi.

and its connections
and all essential bounties;
and give a short life and endless pain
and discomfort
to the traitors of the Isle of Britain. 110

Although several have laboured
on this topic, I declare,
take this from a bungling old man
aged seventy-five years.
The old muse has frozen 115
and Nathaniel,
sober and quiet, holds his peace;
but that life yet remains –
there is, however,
only ill health most frequently. 120

19. Phillip Dafydd, 'Anogaeth i foliannu Duw am y waredigaeth
fawr a gafodd y wlad pan tiriodd 1,400 o'r Ffrancod echryslon yn
Pencaer yn sir Benfro, i oresgyn ein tir trwy ladd a llosgi ein
cyd-wladwyr'

'O ddaioni'r Arglwydd y mae, na ddarfuasai am danom. Molwch yr Arglwydd,
canys da yw.'

Rwyf yn eich annerch chwi, Frytanied –
Dewch yn nes, rhowch glust i glywed!
Mi adroddaf i chwi'n gryno
Fel digwyddodd yn sir Benfro;
Fel y cadwodd Duw Ei bobol   5
Rhag y ffyrnig lu uffernol!
　　　Dyma'r gad sydd am wa'd,
　　A'u bwriad am fyrddiwn;
　　Fel y cenllif maent yn cynllwn –
　　Achub, Iesu, rhag y nasiwn.   10

Ar ddiwrnod, hynod hanes,
Fe ddaeth arswyd yn fy mynwes;
Newydd trist a ddaeth i'm clustiau
(Fe ddaeth aeth a briw i'm bronnau),
I fod y Ffrancod wedi landio   15
Ar Bencaer, a phawb yn crio.
　　　Ysbeilio tai a wnaent bob rhai,
　　Nes ydoedd gwae a gofid,
　　A'r trigolion yn anhyfryd
　　Yn gorfod gadael 'nôl eu golud.   20

Pan ddaeth y gelynion yma
Mewn i ynys fach Brytania,
Sarnu'n bwyd a rhwygo'n dillad,
Dechreu treisio'n ddigon anllad;
Llosgi'n Biblau, lle mae bywyd,   25
Wnae'r paganiaid melldigedig,
　　　Nes aeth llef groyw gref
　　I mewn i'r nef uchod;
　　Dyma dristwch a mawr drallod
　　A ddaeth i ni yn ddiarwybod.   30

19. Phillip Dafydd, 'Encouragement to praise God for the great deliverance which the country had when 1,400 fearsome Frenchmen landed at Pencaer in Pembrokeshire, to conquer our land by murdering and burning our fellow-countrymen'

'It is of the Lord's mercies that we are not consumed. Praise ye the Lord for he is good.'

I greet you, Britons –
come nearer, lend an ear to hear!
I shall relate to you concisely
how things came about in Pembrokeshire;
how God preserved His people   5
from the fierce, hellish host!
This is the army who wants to draw blood,
and whose intention is to take a myriad;
they ambush like a torrent –
Jesus, may You protect us from the race!   10

One day, a remarkable story,
dread came to my breast;
sad news came to my ears
(sorrow and hurt came to my bosom),
that the French had landed   15
on Pencaer, and that all were weeping.
They were pillaging houses, all of them,
causing woe and distress,
and the inhabitants grievously
had to leave their wealth behind.   20

When these enemies
came into the little island of Britannia,
they ruined our food and tore our clothes,
started to rape very wantonly;
the cursed pagans   25
burnt our Bibles, where life is,
until a strong, clear cry
went into the heaven above;
this was a sorrow and a great affliction
that came upon us unexpectedly.   30

Y mae Duw yn arfer gwrando
Ar Ei bobl annwyl eto;
Fe wrandawodd [ar] Hezeciah
Pan yr oedd dan boen a gwasgfa;
Fe wrandawodd ar sir Benfro   35
A'i rhai miloedd oedd ar ddeffro.
  Trefnu wnaeth foddion maith
  Ar eu taith ddyrys;
  Daeth Lord Cawdor yn gysurus
  Cyn i'r Ffrancod gael eu hwllys.   40

Yn Ei law fe gymrodd Campbell
I fyddino ymlaen y rhyfel
A'n cymhwyso â gwiw ddoniau
Nes gwanychodd eu calonnau.
Pedwar cant ar ddeg o Ffrancod   45
Ar eu gyrfa gadd eu gorfod;
  Rhoddi lawr eu harfau nawr,
  O! dyma awr ddedwydd;
  Rhown ogoniant yn dragywydd
  A rhyw fawrglod fyth i'n Harglwydd.   50

Yr oedd Cawdor yn offeryn
Â'i wŷr meirch a'u harfau cedyrn;
Colonel Colby yn galonnog
I dorri lawr y ffyrnig Ffrancod;
A milisia sir Aberteifi   55
A'r *trainbands* oedd gyda hynny –
  Pawb ynghyd, o'r un fryd,
  I gymryd yn union
  Gleddeu'r Arglwydd a Gideon,
  Dorri lawr ein holl elynion.   60

Major Bowen ddaeth yn arfog
A Cadpen James, y milwr enwog,
A'r holl wlad i gyd yn codi
Â'u hen arfau gyda'i gily',
A'u pladuriau a'u ffyn ddwybig   65
A'r crymanau, i gymeryd;
  Pawb yn fyw, yn enw Duw,
  I roddi briw marwol.

God is still wont to listen
to His dear people;
He listened to Hezeciah
when he was burdened with pain and hardship;
He listened to Pembrokeshire   35
and its several thousands who were awake.
He arranged extensive means of support
on their difficult journey;
Lord Cawdor came to the rescue
before the French got their will.   40

He took Campbell in His hand
to marshal for the battle
and prepare us with excellent skills
so that their spirits weakened.
Fourteen hundred Frenchmen   45
were set on their way;
they now put down their arms,
Oh! this is a happy hour;
let us give glory everlastingly
and some great praise for ever to our Lord.   50

Cawdor was an instrument
with his cavalry and their powerful arms;
Colonel Colby valiantly came
to cut down the fierce French;
and the militia of Cardiganshire   55
and the trained bands were with them –
everyone together, of the same mind,
righteously to take
the sword of the Lord and of Gideon,
to cut down all our enemies.   60

Major Bowen came in arms
and Captain James, the famous soldier,
and the whole country rising up
together, with their ancient arms,
and their scythes and their pitchforks   65
and the reaping hooks, to seize the enemy;
everyone eager, in God's name,
to deal out a mortal wound.

Hynod wyrthiau sy mor nerthol –
Aeth pawb o'i babell i ddal y bobol.   70

Abergwaun, di gest ddihengi
O law dynion didosturi;
Rho di'r clod i gyd yn gryno
I Frenin Sion am dy safio.
Er i'r Ffrenchman ddweud yn olau   75
'Fod mewn gwaed dynion dros ei 'sgidiau,
    Fe ddaeth cryd trwyddo i gyd
    (O, hyfryd yw'r hanes!);
    Rhows Duw arswyd yn ei fynwes
    Nes gwanychodd cwpla'i neges.   80

Mi ryfeddais fil o weithiau
I fod dynion hardd eu doniau
Gwedi'u dallu mor dywylled,
Yn margenna â'r fath fegeried.
Lladd a llosgi ffordd y cerddon',   85
Dyma fwriad ein gelynion!
    Cadw ni, Arglwydd cu,
    Rhag y llu yma
    (Sydd yn bygwth i'n difetha),
    Er mwyn y Gŵr fu ar Galfaria.   90

Fe ddaeth yr Efengyl dirion
Yma'n gynnar, medd hanesion;
Ac er gwaetha' pob heresïau
Daeth ei sŵn i mewn i'n clustiau.
Fe'n dyrchafwyd hyd y nefoedd   95
Gan ein Llywydd mawr y lluoedd.
    Dyma fraint fawr ei maint –
    O, gymaint yw'n gwynfyd
    Ein bod yn meddiannu rhydd-did!
    O, am afael ar wir fywyd!   100

Mae ugain mil a mwy na hynny
O werth gwaed yr Arglwydd Iesu
O hiliogaeth y Brytanied
Yn y wlad yn awr i'w gweled.
Ysbryd gweddi ddelo'n gymwys,   105

Remarkable miracles are so powerful –
everyone departed from his tent to catch the people.   70

Fishguard, you escaped
from the hands of merciless men;
take care to give all the praise properly
to the King of Zion for saving you.
Although the Frenchman plainly said   75
that he was over his shoes in men's blood,
a dread came all through him
(Oh, the story is delightful!);
God put dread in his bosom
until he was deprived of strength to fulfil his business.   80

I have wondered a thousand times
that men of decent moral virtue
should be so greatly blinded
as to bargain with such beggars.
To murder and burn wherever they go,   85
this is the intention of our enemies!
Protect us, beloved Lord,
from this host
(who threaten to ruin us)
for the sake of the Man who was on Calvary.   90

The sweet Gospel
came here early, accounts say;
and in spite of every heresy
its sound came into our ears.
We were raised as far as the heaven   95
by our great Lord of hosts.
This is an enormous privilege –
Oh, how great is our blessedness
that we are in possession of freedom!
Oh, to take hold of true life!   100

There are twenty thousand and more
from among the race of the Britons
now to be seen in the country
by virtue of Lord Jesus's blood.
May the spirit of prayer come directly,   105

Yn oleu eglur yn yr Eglwys,
    Nes bo'n llef yn y nef
  Gydag Ef Ei Hunan,
  Ac yn Ei allu gadw allan
  Dreigiau gwancus, drwg eu hamcan.   110

Y mae eisieu ffydd iachusol
I gredu'r Bibl arnom bobol,
Ac mae eisiau edifeirwch
Nawr o'r nef a duwiol dristwch.
Gwir ufudd-dod a fo'n tarddu   115
A gwir gariad yn rhagori;
    Dyma le tan y ne'
  Gyd ag E', gwedyn.
  Nid oes arall a'n hymddiffyn
  Ond ein tirion Arglwydd Frenin.   120

Er bod cyfoeth yn yr India,
Aur Peru gan Sbaen eu gwala
A holl longau'r Dutch a'r Ffrancod,
Mae yma allu mwy rhyfeddod.
Iechydwriaeth ydyw'r muriau,   125
Angeu'r Groes yw'r trysor gorau!
    Cyfiawnder hael Adda'r ail,
  O, dyma sail hynod!
  Nid oes arfau gan y Ffrancod
  All ei dorri fyth na'i ddatod.   130

Y mae Duw yn hogi'i gleddau –
Mae e'n hongian uwch ein pennau
Ac yn bygwth taro'r ergyd
Fel nas gallwn droi na symud,
Am ddibrisio yr Efengyl   135
A throi ati'n gwar a'n gwegil.
    Os dial ddaw yn drwm o draw
  Fe fydd braw enbyd;
  Hi fydd yma yn ddychrynllyd
  Os i'n gwlad daw'r cleddyf gwaedlyd.   140

Os i'n gwlad y daw y cleddau
I gael yfed gwaed calonnau,

manifestly clear in the Church,
until our cry is in heaven
with Jesus Himself,
who has it in His power to keep out
voracious dragons of evil intention. 110

We people need a redeeming faith
to believe in the Bible,
and we need repentance
now from heaven and pious sorrow.
May true obedience flourish 115
and true love excel;
this is then a place
in His company under heaven.
There is no one else who will protect us
but our gracious Lord King. 120

Although there is wealth in India,
Spain have their fill of Peru's gold
and the Dutch and French all their ships,
there is here a more wondrous might.
The walls are Salvation, 125
the death on the Cross is the best treasure!
The generous justice of the second Adam,
Oh, this is a remarkable foundation!
The French do not have arms
that can ever break or untie it. 130

God is whetting His sword –
it is hanging above our heads
and threatens to strike the blow
so that we shall be unable to turn or move,
for neglecting the Gospel 135
and turning our backs on it.
If vengeance should come heavily from yonder
there will be terrible fright;
it will be dreadful here
if the bloody sword comes to our country. 140

If the sword comes to our country
in order to drink the blood of hearts,

Tost yw gweled bechgyn Cymru
Yn eu clwyfau'n mynd i'w claddu;
Tost yw gweled gwragedd diwair   145
Yn cael eu treisio yn dra hagar,
    A'r plant bach yn ddigon iach
    Bellach yn pallu —
    Ond eu distrywio'n ddidosturi,
    Heb gael cymorth eu rhieni.   150

Arglwydd grasol, Tad tosturi,
'R Hwn wyt erioed yn gwrando gweddi,
Clyw ein cwyn ac achub ninnau
Rhag y cyfryw aeth ddialau.
Cofia, Arglwydd, am drugaredd,   155
Yr hon sy nawr yn un â'th fawredd;
    Dyma'n ple o flaen y ne' —
    Sef clwyfe Calfaria
    I gadw'th annwyl bobl yma
    Rhag fath ddistryw blin a gwasgfa.   160

Fe waredodd Duw Ei bobol
Ym mhob oes, mewn modd rhyfeddol;
Afon Ceision yn rhyfela
A'r sêr yn sarnu lluoedd Sisra.
Nawr yn ein dyddiau ninneu   165
Mae rhagluniaeth fawr yn chwareu.
    Y clod i gyd, nawr bob pryd,
    Yn hyfryd i'n Harglwydd,
    Fel bo'n beraidd ein lleferydd
    Heb droi'n geiriau yn dragywydd.   170

Mil o fendithion ddelo beunydd
Yn gryno ar gorun Siors y Trydydd;
Trysorau gras o'r nefoedd uchod,
Bendithion Iesu ar ddaear isod.
Delw Duw fo ar ei deulu,   175
Cywir gariad yn rhagori;
    Mawr yw'r fraint, y siriol saint —
    O, gymaint sy i'r cyfion
    Gael meddu'r anllygredig goron,
    Heb sôn am ryfel, draw i'r afon!   180

it will be painful to see the lads of Wales
being buried with their wounds;
it will be painful to see chaste wives   145
being most violently raped,
and the young children, once healthy enough,
now perishing –
just being destroyed mercilessly,
without the help of their parents.   150

Gracious Lord, Father of mercy,
You who have always listened to prayer,
listen to our complaint and save us too
from such grievous reprisals.
Remember mercy, Lord,   155
that which is now one with Your greatness;
this is our plea before heaven –
that the wounds of Calvary
should protect Your beloved people here
from such dire destruction and affliction.   160

God has delivered His people
in every age, in a wondrous way;
the river Kishon making war
and the stars despoiling the hosts of Sisera.
Now in our days   165
great providence plays a part.
All the praise, now at every time,
joyfully to our Lord,
so that our utterance be ever sweet
and our words unbending.   170

May a thousand blessings come every day
heaped upon the head of George the Third;
the treasures of grace from heaven above,
the blessings of Jesus upon the earth below.
May God's image be upon his family   175
and may true love excel;
great is the privilege, joyful saints –
Oh, so great it is for the just
to have possession of the uncorrupted crown,
without mention of war, on the other side of the river!   180

Hir oes hefyd, heddwch gaffo,
A'r goron ar ei ben yn gryno,
A'i gynghoriaid heb anghariad –
Undeb ysbryd fyddo'n wastad;
A holl filoedd maith ei filwyr   185
Fyddo'n concro'r French ysbeilwyr.
      Os Un yn Dri fydd gyda ni,
    Er eu lledu nhwy yn llydan,
    Os yn Ei allu y daw allan
    Fe gyll y gwancwn oll eu hamcan.   190

Mi ddymunwn lwyddiant helaeth
I Efengyl Iechydwriaeth,
A phob rhyfel wedi darfod,
Ond â buchedd gas o bechod,
A phawb heb roeso un heresïau,   195
Egwyddorion afiach Priestley.
      Iesu mawr, dere nawr,
    Fel bo gwawr hynod;
    Holl deyrnasoedd daear isod
    Fo mewn heddwch pur oddi uchod.   200

Un fil saith cant oedd y flwyddyn,
Naw o ddegau a saith gwedyn;
Ddwyfed dydd ar hugain gryno
O fis Chwefror y bu'r taro.
Dyma'r flwyddyn o oedran Iesu   205
Y gadd y Ffrancod eu gorchfygu.
      Yn lle ein lladd ni bob gradd
    Trwy ymladd a'n hymlid,
    Nhwy i garchar gadd eu cyrchyd
    A ni gael drylliau'r rhai dychrynllyd.   210

Nawr fy mrodyr, rwyf yn rhoi ffarwél –
Gobeithio na ddaw mwyach ryfel;
Ac os rhaid myned i ryfela,
Enw Duw *a* fyddo ymlaena'.
Gyda'n gilydd bawb i godi,   215
Oll o'n bronnau, heb ymrannu;
      Cymry glân, awn ymla'n
    Ac allan, trwy allu

May he have a lengthy life too, and peace,
with the crown firmly upon his head,
and his advisers without uncharitableness –
may there be unity of spirit at all times;
and may the vast thousands of his soldiers   185
conquer the French plunderers.
If the One in Three shall be with us,
even if the enemy should be spread out far and wide,
if He comes forth in His might
the voracious creatures will all fail in their purpose.   190

I wish extensive success
to the Gospel of Salvation,
and for every war to be ended,
except against an evil life of sin,
and everyone without a welcome   195
to any of the heresies, the unwholesome principles of Priestley.
Great Jesus, come now,
so that there should be a splendid dawn;
may all the kingdoms of the earth below
be in pure peace from above.   200

One thousand seven hundred
nine tens and seven again was the year;
on precisely the twenty-second day
of the month of February did the attack occur.
This was the year of Jesus's age   205
that the French were defeated.
Rather than killing us of all ranks
by fighting and chasing us,
they were taken to gaol
and we had the rifles of the terrible ones.   210

Now, my brothers, I say farewell –
let us hope that war does not come any more;
and if we must go to war,
may God's name lead the way.
Let us rise all together,   215
every single one, without parting;
pure Welshmen, let us go forth
and out through the might

Y Duw hwn oedd gyda Dafy'
Pan gadd pen Golia'*i* dorri.   220

JHD no.: 558

Sources: Welsh Ballads Online (Col 2894 LlGC); LlGC Col 230; CaerLD

Publication: Ioan Evans, Heol-y-prior, Caerfyrddin, 1797

of this God who was with David
when Goliath's head was severed. 220

20. Richard Roberts, 'Dau bennill yn rhoi ychydig o hanes y gelynion a
diriasant i borthladd Abergwaun yn sir Benfro'
Tune: 'Ffansi'r Milwr'

[R]howch glust ymwrandawiad
Mewn ffair ac mewn marchnad,
[S]y'n clywed cryn siarad, yn siŵr;
[Ma]e sŵn am ryfeloedd
Ers amryw flynyddoed[d]   5
[Drw]y'r siroedd, ar diroedd a dŵr.
[Ma]e'r bobl gyffredin
Yn dechre cael dychryn
[Rha]g ofn y daw'n gelyn i'n gwlad;
[Mae']r Ffrancod am ddŵad,   10
Heb gelu (mae'n galad!)
A thyne ydi'u bwriad a'u brad.
Daeth rhai i sir Benfro,
Do, drosodd i dreisio,
Gan chwilio ac yn pluo pob plwy;   15
A'r bobl, rhan amle,
Yn gado'u trigfanne
Rhag myned tan gloie, tyn glwy.

I Abergwaun, meddant,
Daeth mil a phedwar cant,   20
Ar ôl myned o'u *frigate* am ffrae;
Mawr golled wnae'r gwilliad,
Yn dwyn anifeiliad –
Er hynny, fe a'u dofad, bob dau.
Daeth sawdwyr o Loegar   25
[I'w] cyrchu nhw i'r carchar,
[Na] chawson' fawr bleser o'u blys.
[----] rhagor rw' i'n clywed
[----------------] [?iddi] gweled
[------------------] mewn brys.   30
[M]ae'r Ar[gl]wydd Dduw cyfion
[Yn] drech na['n] gelynion,
[Ga]ll gadw inni'n llownion ein lle,
Na chaffo'r gwŷr gwaedlyd
Mo'n manne mewn munud   35
I'n rhoi mewn tyn ofid tan ne'.

20. Richard Roberts, 'Two stanzas giving a little of the story of the enemies
who landed in the harbour of Fishguard in Pembrokeshire'
Tune: 'Ffansi'r Milwr'

Give an attentive ear
in fair and in market,
where a great deal of chattering is heard, to be sure;
there has been talk about wars
for many years   5
throughout the shires, on land and on sea.
The common people
are beginning to take fright
lest our enemy should come to our country;
the French wish to come,   10
there is no denying (it is hard to bear!)
and that is their intention and their conspiracy.
Some came to Pembrokeshire,
yea, came over to conquer,
searching through and despoiling every parish;   15
and the people, most of the time,
leaving their dwellings,
lest they should be locked up, harsh pain.

To Fishguard, they say,
came one thousand and four hundred,   20
having left their frigate for a fight;
the brigands caused great loss,
stealing animals –
nonetheless, they were overpowered, every pair.
Soldiers came from England   25
to take them to the gaol,
so that they did not get much pleasure from their lust.
[----] more I hear
[---------------] to see
[------------------] in a hurry.   30
The righteous Lord God
is mightier than our enemies,
He can keep our place for us, replete,
so that the bloody men
should not take our positions in a minute   35
to put us in heavy affliction under heaven.

JHD no.: 738ii

Source: Bangor 14 (12)

Publication: Ismael Dafydd, Trefriw, [?1797]

Document title: *Dwy o Gerddi, Da Rhagorol yn nadal ir un edliw ar ol yn gyntaf Yn dangos pa mor wageddus yw i ddyn roi ei hyder ar y byd, o blegid mae Awdwr y gan hon wedi [-----] nad oes un ffrind ag y gall o roi ei ymddiried ynddo ond un, sef Iesu Grist. Yn ail Dau Benill yn rhoi Ychydig o hanes y Gelynion a Diriasant i Borthladd Abergwaen yn Sir Benfro iw chanu ar fesur a elwir ffansi'r Milwyr o Waith Richard Roberts.*

Woodcut: small design including suns and tiny circles.

Condition: torn along left hand side of recto page.

21. Thomas Francis, 'Cân am y waredigaeth a gafodd y Brytaniaid o ddwylaw'r Ffrancod gwaedlyd'

Salm 126: 3, 'Yr Arglwydd a wnaeth i ni bethau mawrion, am hynny yr ydym yn llawen'

O! Brydain, hoff ei breintiau braf,
Deffro a saf mewn sobrwydd,
A gwêl y waredigaeth faith
A rhyfedd waith yr Arglwydd.
Fe ddaeth y gelyn cas i'n golwg,   5
Ar feddwl ymladd, hyn oedd amlwg;
Ni chafodd gennad wneud ei gynnig –
Duw'n gwaredodd ni'n garedig
Rhag mynd dan ddwylaw'r Ffrancod ffôl,
Alltudion hollol herllug.   10
I Bencaer sydd yn sir Benfro
Daeth y rhai drewllyd drwg i dreio,
Ond aeth eu gobaith yn anniben –
Awd â hwy i garchar, fawr a bychen;
Ni chawsant gennad dywallt gwa'd   15
Na gwneuthur brad i Bryden.

Oddi wrth yr Arglwydd y daeth hyn
Yn rhybudd i ni'n hynod
I ymadael mwy o hyn i ma's
Â'n buchedd gas o bechod.   20
Brydain, dos! Na phecha mwyach,
Rhag ofn y cei di gerydd garwach.
Di gest dy arbed y tro yma;
O dy wagedd nawr diwygia,
A dyro'r clod i gyd heb gêl,   25
Yn uchel i'r Gorucha'.
Yno (rhifwyd hwynt yn rhyw fan,
Oedd dan eu harfau i gyd yn gadarn),
Bedwar cant ar ddeg a rhagor
Wedi tramwy o wledydd tramor   30
Ar feder ein difetha ni –
Llaw uchel fu o'n hochor.

21. Thomas Francis, 'A song on the deliverance that the Britons had from the hands of the bloody French'

Psalm 126: 3, 'The Lord hath done great things for us; whereof we are glad'

Oh! Britain, renowned for her ample privileges,
awake and stand in sobriety,
and see the great deliverance
and the extraordinary work of the Lord.
The cruel enemy came into our sight,   5
intending to fight, this was clear;
he did not have leave to carry out his attempt –
God kindly delivered us
from falling into the hands of the foolish French,
utterly brazen-faced foreigners.   10
To Pencaer which is in Pembrokeshire
did the foul, wicked ones come to contend,
but their hopes became vain –
they were taken to gaol, great and small;
they were not given leave to shed blood   15
nor to cause the ruin of Britain.

This came from the Lord
as a warning to us, strikingly,
to abandon from henceforth
our cruel life of sin.   20
Britain, go! Sin no more,
lest you should have harsher punishment.
You were saved this time;
reform from your vanity now,
and give all the praise openly,   25
resoundingly to the Most High.
There (they were numbered somewhere,
all strongly armed),
fourteen hundred and more
who had travelled from foreign lands   30
with the intention of destroying us –
an exalted hand was on our side.

Nid llu o wŷr â'u harfau llym,
Er maint eu grym, wy'n gredu,
A'u rhwystrodd hwynt ymlaen yn hy   35
A'n taro'n ddidosturi;
Na chwaith rifedi'r dynion erill
Oedd yn syml yno'n sefyll,
Ond llaw ddirgelaidd y Duw tirion
A wan-galonnodd ein gelynion,   40
Fel nas gallsent dreio ma's
Fel oedd eu cas amcanion.
Os clod i ddynion sy, 'n ddiamau,
Y rhai fu'n gweddïo'n daer a haeddai,
Gan mai rheini'n lân a lwyddodd,   45
Trwy Dduw, 'n ufudd, fry o'r nefoedd,
I wrando ar eu llef a'u llais,
Ac, yn ôl eu cais, atebodd.

Gallasem nawr i fod yn friw
Dan ddwylaw'r griw greulonaf,   50
Heb ganfod cysur yn y byd,
O'r lleiaf hyd y mwyaf;
Gweld lladd y plant serchogaidd hawddgar,
Treisio'r gwragedd, a'u rhwygo'n hagar!
Gwŷr a meibion union heini,   55
Eu lladd â'r cleddeu, ac yna'u claddu,
Ac eraill, a gâi fyw yn fwy,
Wneud fel bôn' hwy'n rheoli;
Neu ffoi, meddaf, i'r mynyddoedd,
A gado'n teiau i gyd a'n tiroedd   60
I'n gelynion eu meddiannu,
A ninneu yno yn newynu.
Ond Brydain brofodd Dduw yn dda –
Mae heddwch yma heddy.

Dewch, lân Frytaniaid o bob rhyw,   65
Rhown glod i Dduw yn gyson
Am ein gwaredu ni mor ddwys
O law rhai cyfrwys creulon;
Gwedi'n bygwth am ein trosedd,
Mewn barn, fe gofiodd am drugaredd,   70
Fel na chafodd yr holl Ffrancod

It was not a host of men with their sharp weapons,
in spite of their power, I believe,
that prevented them from going forwards intrepidly 35
and striking us mercilessly;
nor yet the abundance of the other men
who simply stood there,
but the mysterious hand of the gracious God
that discouraged our enemies, 40
so that they could not seek to act
according to their cruel intentions.
If there is praise to men, doubtlessly,
it is those who prayed fervently that deserve it,
since it was those who utterly prevailed, 45
because of God, readily, above from heaven,
listening to their cry and their voice,
and, according to their request, He answered.

We could now have been shattered
under the hands of the cruellest mob, 50
unable to find a comfort in the world,
from the smallest to the greatest among us;
seeing the loving, amiable children being killed,
the wives being raped and hideously mutilated!
Honest, vigorous men and lads 55
being killed with the sword, and then buried,
and others, who would be allowed to live after that,
doing as they should rule;
or we should have had to flee, I say, to the mountains,
and leave all our houses and our lands 60
for our enemies to possess them,
while we should be starving there.
But Britain proved that God was good –
there is peace here today.

Come, honest Britons of every lineage, 65
let us consistently give praise to God
for delivering us so profoundly
from the hand of crafty, cruel ones;
after threatening us for our transgression,
in judgement, He remembered mercy, 70
so that all the French were not able

Ddim ein difa, er eu dyfod.
I garchar cyrchwyd hwynt yn rhwydd –
I'r Arglwydd rhoddwn fawr-glod;
Ond boneddigion da eu doniau
Fu'n ddiffael gan Dduw'n offerynnau,
I dawelu'r cwthwn cethin
Ddaeth heb arbed yn ein herbyn;
Gostegodd grym y storom gref
A throwd ein llef yn chwerthin.

75

80

Mae gelyn arall yn y wlad
Wna fwy o frad na Ffrancod;
O achos hwn mae'r swae a'r stŵr,
Ac enw'r gŵr yw pechod.
Mae'r bwystfil yma'n feistr caled –
Peidiwn groesaw hwn mor nesed;
Os gwasnaethwn ef yn rhywiog
Ni gawn yn gyflawn iawn y gyflog;
A'i gyflog ef, marwolaeth yw,
Medd Gair y Duw galluog.
Brydain dirion, gloywa d'arfau,
Bydd yn barod hwyr a borau
Gweddi'r ffydd a chariad ffyddlon
Pan agosáu bo dy gaseion;
Rhoi gweddi at Dduw yw'r goreu dryll
I ladd dy hyll elynion.

85

90

95

Yr Arglwydd sydd ryfelwr triw
(Yr Arglwydd yw Ei enw),
A'r neb a dreio ag Efe,
Fe ddaw ei chwareu'n chwerw.
Efe wareda'r neb a gredo
Neu roddo ei ymddiried Ynddo,
A rhai rhyfygus sy'n mynd rhagddynt
Yn eu henwau'u hun a'u helynt,
Gall Ef eu llwyr orchfygu'n lân
Fel us o fla'n y corwynt.
Mewn cyfyngder eitha' caled,
Fe roes i Israel wir ymwared
Pan oent o flaen y Pharao creulon
Rhwng Pihahiroth a Baal-seffon;

100

105

110

to destroy us, even though they came.
They were quickly taken to gaol –
let us give great praise to the Lord;
but gentlemen of good grace 75
were without fail instruments of God,
to quieten the hideous storm
that came against us unsparingly;
the strength of the mighty storm subsided
and our cry was turned to laughter. 80

There is another enemy in the country
who will cause greater treachery than Frenchmen;
it is on account of this one that there is tumult and commotion,
and the fellow's name is sin.
This monster is a cruel master – 85
let us not welcome him so closely;
if we genially serve him
we shall have the payment very fully;
and his wage is death,
says the word of the mighty God. 90
Gracious Britain, burnish your arms,
be ready evening and morning
the prayer of the Christian faith and loyal love
when your foes draw nearer;
to direct a prayer to God is the best gun 95
to kill your ugly enemies.

The Lord is a faithful warrior
(the Lord is His name),
and anyone who contends with Him
his play will turn sour. 100
He delivers whoever believes
or puts his trust in Him,
and arrogant ones who go forth
in their own names and their own way,
He can vanquish them completely and utterly 105
like chaff before the tornado.
In most cruel affliction,
He gave Israel true deliverance
when they were before the cruel Pharaoh
between Pihahiroth and Baalzephon; 110

Cadd Israel fynd trwy'r môr heb goll,
A'r Aifftiaid oll a foddon'.

Mae rhyfel yn rhyw drefen ddoeth
Uwchlaw gwybodaeth dynion;
A'r Hwn 'hordeinodd hi yw Duw   115
I ateb rhyw ddibenion.
Fe allsai'n rhyfedd trwy ryfeloedd
Agoryd drwsau'r pell deyrnasoedd
I'r Efengyl fanol fwynaidd
I 'hedeg yno a chael gogonedd.   120
Os felly yw 'wyllys Brenin nef,
Ei allu Ef yw'r allwedd.
Y mae'n rhaid i fod rhyfeloedd,
Medd ein Biblau, rhwng y bobloedd,
A dechreuad o ofidiau   125
Ydyw'r aethlyd boethlyd bethau;
Ac yma yng Nghymru'r dyddiau hyn
Mae'r dychryn wedi dechrau.

Ond gwelwch – na chyffroer chwi,
Ganlynwyr Iesu grasol –   130
Ar ôl y rhyfel chwi gewch hedd
A hyfryd wledd dragwyddol.
Daliwch ati hyd y diwedd
Yn ddiarswyd wrth yr orsedd;
Yn ddiderfyn gyda'r dyrfa   135
Chwi gewch seinio i gyd "Hosanna!"
I'r Hwn a'ch golchodd chwi mor wyn
Trwy farw ar fryn Calfaria.
Y mae rhybudd ar ôl rhybudd
Yn ein galw efo'n gilydd   140
Fel gwlad a chenedl i ddychwelyd;
On'd e, daw cerydd gwaeth i'n cwrddyd –
Am hynny ffown ar aden ffydd
Cyn delo'r dydd dychrynllyd.

Mor barod ŷm ni, ddynion gwag,   145
Yn fawrion ac yn fychain,
I weled eraill ar y bai
A chyfiawnhau ein hunain!

Israel was allowed to go through the sea without loss,
and all the Egyptians drowned.

War is a kind of wise providence
above the knowledge of men;
and God is the One who ordained it   115
to answer some end or other.
Through the medium of wars He could wondrously
open the doors of the distant kingdoms
so that the fair, mild Gospel
could fly there and find glory.   120
If the King of heaven's will is thus,
His might is the key.
There must be wars,
say our Bibles, between the peoples,
and the dreadful, inflamed affairs   125
are the beginnings of hardships;
and here in Wales in these days
the terror has begun.

But see – do not be disturbed,
followers of gracious Jesus –   130
after the war you shall have peace
and a joyful, everlasting feast.
Keep at it until the end
without consternation beside the throne;
ceaselessly with the host   135
you shall all sound "Hosanna!"
to the One who washed you so white
by dying upon the hill of Calvary.
Warning after warning
calls us together   140
as a country and nation to return;
otherwise, greater chastisement shall come and meet us –
for that reason let us flee upon the wing of faith
before the terrible day should come.

How ready are we, vain men,   145
great and small,
to see the fault in others
and to justify ourselves!

Os bydd bai yn bod, yn ddiball,
Fe'i cyfrifir ef i arall;   150
Os bydd clod yn bod yn rhyw fan,
Fi a'i haeddai hwn fy hunan!
Ac felly rŷm ni ar hyd y wlad
Am gael dyrchafiad Haman.
Fe ddechreuodd hyn, yn gywren,   155
Gan Adda ydoedd draw yn Eden.
O! Adda, pam y gwnest di'r cynnig
Fwyta'n ffri o'r ffrwyth gwarddedig?
"Y wraig a roddest baro'r tro,
A hi a nhwyllo' i'n herllug."   160

Wel, bellach, Arglwydd, trwy bob bro,
Dymunaf, rho dangnefedd,
A phlygu'n isel wrth Dy dra'd
I geisio rhad drugaredd.
Cadw Siors ein tirion frenin   165
Eto goron ar ei gorun,
A hir oes iddo ef deyrnasu –
Duw a'i dalio ef a'i deulu.
A'n bradwyr oll ar dir a dŵr
A gaffo'n siŵr eu siomi;   170
Llwyddo wnelo'r fwyn Efengyl,
Ac yn rhagor elo hi'n rhigyl
I ymofyn plant afradlon adrau
Sydd eto gyda'r moch a'r cibau,
I godi a mynd tua thŷ eu Tad   175
'Gael torri'n rhad eu heisiau.

Pan daeth y terfysg hyn i'n [tir]
Oed Crist yn gywir goffaf,
Rhoi'r blwyddi i gyd mewn lein ar lawr
Heb golli nawr os gallaf;   180
Saith o gantoedd enwa' i gynta',
Saith o ddegau mi fenega',
Saith pedwar ugain a saith trigain
Yn dra chyflawn ro' i drachefen,
A saith a deugain at y rhi'   185
I wneud y cyfri'n gyfain.
Nac aed angeu mwy yn ango' –

If fault there is, without fail,
it is attributed to somebody else;   150
if praise is to be had somewhere,
I would deserve that myself!
And thus do we throughout the country
wish for Haman's exaltation.
This began, precisely,   155
with Adam who was yonder in Eden.
Oh! Adam, why did you carry out the proposition
to eat freely of the forbidden fruit?
"It was the woman that You gave that caused the crisis,
and she who impudently deceived me."   160

Well, henceforth, Lord, through every region,
I wish, give peace,
and humble supplication at Your feet
to seek gracious mercy.
May George our gracious king   165
yet keep a crown upon his head,
and may he have a long life to rule –
may God sustain him and his family.
And may all our traitors on land and sea
be surely undone;   170
may the gentle Gospel prosper,
and may it henceforth swiftly go
to fetch prodigal children home
who are still with the pigs and the husks,
to rise and go towards their Father's house   175
so as to end their destitution freely.

I shall make a correct record of the age of Christ
when this strife came to our land,
and put all the years down in a line
without losing any now if I can;   180
I shall first name seven hundreds,
seven tens shall I mention,
seven eighties and seven sixties
shall I very completely give in addition,
and seven and forty to the number   185
to make the count complete.
May death no longer be forgotten –

Rhoddodd rybudd, fe ddaw heibio
Holl drigolion gwlad Brytania;
Nawr cyn delo'r dilyw *i*'n dala,   190
Rhown bawb i Dduw briodol barch
Ac awn i'r arch fel Noa.

JHD nos., sources, publication details and document titles:

A: JHD 559; Welsh Ballads Online (Cwp LlGC); I. Evans, Caerfyrddin, 1797; *Can am y Waredigaeth a Gafodd y Brytaniaid O Ddwylaw'r Ffrangcod Gwaedlyd. Gan Thomas Francis, Fachongle, o Blwyf Nevern.*

B: NLW, BC, vol. 34, no. 107; John Williams, Solva, n.d.; *Tiriad y Ffrancod yn Mhencaer, ger Abergwaun, ar yr Ailfed dydd ar ugain o Chwefror, 1797.*

C: CaerLD, Ballads and Fugitive Pieces, vol. II, f. 205; Thomas Ellis, n.p., n.d.; *Tiriad y Ffrancod yn Bencar, Ger Abergwaun, Ar yr ailfed dydd ar ugain o Chwefror, 1797.* Incomplete (ends at line 144).

Variants: B, C – Psalm quotation not included; 1. B, C – Britain hoff; 6. B, C – Ar fedr; 10. B, C – haerllug; 11. B – Yn Bencar, C – Yn Bencâr; 28. B, C – dan arfau / yn gyfan; 35. B, C – A'u rhwystrai hwynt fyn'd 'mlaen yn hy'; 53. B, C – Lladd ein plant; 54. B – Treisio'n gwragedd; 57. B, C – yn hwy; 58. B, C – baint; 60. B, C – teiau gyda'n; 76. B, C – Fu'n ddyfal gyda Duw; 82. B, C – Wnaeth; 83. B – mae *sway* a stwr, C – mae *sway* a stŵr; 95. B, C – yw gorau dull; 97. B, C – ryfelwr *true*; 109. B, C – oedd; 110. B, C – Pahiroth a Balsephon; 117. B, C – Fe allai; 118. B, C – Agorir; 142. B, C – Cyn daw; 160. B – hi nhwyllodd i yn haerllug; 161. B – bob tro; 163. B – phlyg ni; 176. B – A thori; 177. B – tir *supplied in print*; 179. B – leiniau ar.

he gave a warning, he shall come by
all the inhabitants of the land of Britannia;
now, before the deluge should come to catch us,   190
let us all give due respect to God
and let us go into the ark like Noah.

1799

22. G[eorge] S[tephens], 'Cân o glod i'r Arglwydd am ein holl fuddugoliaethau
ar fôr ac ar dir'

Mae llawer wedi canu cainc
Am uwchder ffroen a balchder Ffrainc,
A minnau'n dweud, os Duw a'i myn,
Na chario'r môr hwy'r ochr hyn.

Er dod o'r Ffrancod, wŷr di-ras,   5
Ar hyd y môr, yn tannu ma's
Mewn hyder mawr caent ddod i'r lan
I dir Iwerddon mewn rhyw fan;

Hwy fuont yno'n hwylio'n hir,
Yn ffaelu'n deg â mentro i dir;   10
Daeth cennad Duw trwy'r stormydd mawr,
Ac a'u dymchwelodd hyd y llawr.

Hwy ddaethant eilwaith ar fyr o dro
I'r lan, i dir, yn sir Benfro,
Islaw Llanwnda – dyna'r fan   15
Y dôi'n gelynion dig i'r lan.

A chwedyn cododd pawb o'r wlad
Fel cewri cedyrn ar eu tra'd;
Yr hen a'r ieuainc yn gytûn
Am ladd a llarpio'r bleiddiaid blin.   20

Dôi'r Arglwydd Cawdor, cywrain call,
A'i lu 'gael cwrdd â phlant y fall,
A chydag ef hwy ddoent i ddews,
Fel y 'Syriaid gydag Eliseus.

Gofynnai'r brenin yn ddi-nâd,   25
"A darawa' i hwy, fy annwyl Dad?"
"Na wnei; bydd di'n hawddgarach gŵr –
Arlwya iddynt fara a dŵr.

1799

22. G[eorge] S[tephens], 'A song of praise to the Lord for all our victories on sea and on land'

Many have sung a song
about the haughtiness and pride of France,
while I say that, if it is God's will,
the sea may not carry them to this region.

Even though the French, vile men,   5
came along the sea, spreading out
in great hopes that they should be able to come to the shore
in the land of Ireland in some place;

they were sailing there for long,
utterly unable to venture to the land;   10
God's message came through the great storms,
and overthrew them along the ground.

They shortly came a second time
to shore, to land, in Pembrokeshire,
below Llanwnda – that is the place   15
where our wrathful enemies came to the shore.

And then everyone in the country arose
upon their feet like powerful giants;
the old and the young in agreement
wishing to kill and devour the vicious wolves.   20

Lord Cawdor, skilful and wise,
and his host came to meet the children of the devil,
and with him they came to their senses,
like the Assyrians with Eliseus.

The king asked freely,   25
"Shall I strike them, my dear Father?"
"No; be a more kindly man –
provide them with bread and water.

Na feddwl ddim am dywallt gwa'd,
Ond gyr hwy bant tua thir eu gwlad,   30
A, rhag eu cwilydd, ni ddônt hwy
I'th flino di na minnau mwy."

Sydd i'w cyffelybu fel y rhain –
Gwnâi gwŷr Pencaer ac Abergwaun
Roi bwyd a diod yno'n faith   35
I gael eu cynnal hwy ar eu taith.

Mi glywais ddweud fod ambell un
Yn fawr ei frad i'w wlad ei hun;
Am hyn o dro, 'doedd hwn ond drel,
Ail gyngor ffôl Ahitoffel.   40

Mae gyda ni lyngesau'n stôr
A milwyr maith ar dir a môr;
Nac ofnwn ddim o'r waedlyd griw,
Gan ddodi ein pwys yn ddwys ar Dduw.

Braf Hood yn siŵr, a Jervis sydd,   45
A Bridport, Duncan, nos a dydd;
Gwnaeth Nelson ddychryn mawr a braw
I'r Ffrensh wrth Alecsandria draw.

Daeth pymtheg mil o'r Ffrancod ma's
Mewn hyder i goncro'r cefnfor glas;   50
I gael tirio yng Iwerddon oedd eu chwant,
A'u bryd ar ladd pob Protestant.

John Bourlass Warren, ffyddlon ŵr,
A'i fechgyn dewrion ar y dŵr;
Byrhaws eu neges – fe'u trowd i lawr   55
O dan lifeiriant dyfroedd mawr.

Syr Richard Strachan, trwy Dduw'n faith,
Ag un long fechan a sincodd saith;
Fe gymerth ddwy, dihangodd tair –
Braf Richard Strachan, gario'r gair.   60

Do not consider shedding blood,
but drive them away towards the land of their country,   30
and, for shame, they shall not come
to trouble you nor me any more."

Which is to be likened to these –
the men of Pencaer and Fishguard
gave food and drink there extensively   35
in order to sustain them on their journey.

I heard it said that one or two
did great treachery to his own country;
for this act, he was but a numskull,
similar to the foolish counsel of Ahithophel.   40

We have ready navies
and numerous soldiers on land and sea;
let us not fear any of the bloody throng,
and rely devoutly upon God.

Fine Hood, certainly, and there is Jervis,   45
and Bridport, Duncan, day and night;
Nelson caused great alarm and fear
to the French near Alexandria, yonder.

Fifteen thousand Frenchmen came out
in the hope of conquering the blue main;   50
their desire was to land in Ireland,
their intent to kill every Protestant.

John Bourlass Warren, faithful man,
and his brave men on the water;
he shortened their mission – they were cast down   55
under the deluge of great waters.

Sir Richard Strachan, through God's wisdom,
with one small ship sank seven;
he took two, three escaped –
fine Richard Strachan, may he win renown.   60

Ond y milwyr penna' (coelia, clyw!)
Yw gweinidogion tirion Duw;
Yr arfau ffeina' yn ddiffael
Sydd gyda rheini *i* gyd i'w gael.

Sef, cleddeu'r Ysbryd, tarian ffydd,   65
A heddwch lân, gydwybod rydd,
A helm yr Iechydwriaeth gref
Trwy saethau o weddi *i* fyny i'r nef.

Ni ro' i fy mhwys ond ar fy Nuw,
Cans Fe all ladd a chadw'n fyw,   70
Yr Un yn Dri, a'r Tri yn Un –
Tad, Mab ac Ysbryd Sanctaidd ŷn'.

Gall ladd ein pechod o bob rhyw,
A chadw'r enaid bach yn fyw,
A'u maddeu i gyd mewn munud awr   75
A'u claddu ym môr Ei gariad mawr.

Duw gadwo George ein brenin ni,
A phawb yn ffyddlon iddo sy'
Ro*'u* golwg fry am gyrraedd braint,
'Run modd â'r nefol siriol saint.   80

Os gofyn neb pwy ganodd hyn,
G.S. – mae'n byw rhwng bro a bryn
Y ffordd yr ewch chwi'n gymwys pur
O Emlyn dref tua'r gogledd dir.

JHD no.: 568

Source: Welsh Ballads Online (LlGC Amr Crd W2.4296 (24))

Publication: Ioan Evans, Caerfyrddin, 1799

But the principal soldiers (believe me, hear!)
are God's gracious ministers;
all the finest weapons without fail
are to be had with them.

Namely, the sword of the Spirit, the shield of faith,   65
and honest peace, a free conscience,
and the helmet of powerful Salvation
acquired by means of prayer shot up into heaven.

I shall put my weight on God alone,
since it is He who can kill and keep alive,   70
the One in Three, and the Three in One –
They are the Father, Son and Holy Ghost.

He can kill every kind of sin of ours,
and keep the little soul alive,
and forgive them all in an instant   75
and bury them in the sea of His great love.

May God protect George our king,
and may everyone who is faithful to him
set their sights upwards to reach for freedom,
in the same way as the heavenly, joyful saints.   80

If anyone asks who sang this,
G.S. – he lives between hill and dale
on the way that you take directly
from the town of Newcastle Emlyn towards the land of the north.

23. [George Stephens], 'Cân o ganmoliaeth i *volunteers y tair sir, sef sir*
Benfro, sir Aberteifi a sir Gaerfyrddin'

Dewch, lân brydyddion, bawb ynghyd,
O gywir fron ac uniawn fryd,
I ganmol pawb o'r bobl bur
Sydd gwedi codi'n *folunteer.

Rhown barch mewn hedd i'n bonedd call,   5
Bob un yn llon 'run wedd â'r llall,
Am iddynt feddwl yn ddi-nâd
Am godi gwŷr at gadw'n gwlad.

Mawr barch i rhain, ond clod i Dduw –
Fe'n cadwodd ni hyd yn hyn yn fyw   10
Er amled ein gelynion cas,
Un rhyw o fewn a'r llall o fa's.

Mor hardd yw 'u gweled ar y banc
Yn martsio a thraino'n llawer rhanc;
A'r gwŷr bon'ddigion, mwynion maith,   15
Sydd yn flaenoriaid ar y gwaith.

Wyth cant dan arfau, 'n deg eu gwawr,
Sy o gyfer Llanybydder lawr;
Ar ddwy lan Teifi, dyna'r gwir,
Ar fryn a phant, mae'r folunteer.   20

Ac os daw taro ar ein tir,
Mae'r rhain o'r bron yn ffyddlon wŷr
Â chalon hy i fentro 'mla'n
Mewn gwrol ffydd trwy fwg a thân.

Daw Curnel Llwyd yn flaenaf un   25
A'r Cadpen Lewes, ddawnus ddyn,
A'r Cadpen Parry o flaen y gwŷr,
Gan drin yn galant eu folunteer.

Daw'r Major Brigstocke o'r Blaen-pant
A'r Cadpen Taylor gyda'i gant   30

*23. [George Stephens], 'A song of praise to the volunteers of the three counties,
namely Pembrokeshire, Cardiganshire and Carmarthenshire'*

Come, fair poets, all together,
with true heart and just intent,
to praise all the faithful people
who have risen up as volunteers.

Let us pay tribute peacefully to our wise gentry,   5
each one merrily the same as the next man,
because they thought without denial
of raising men to protect our country.

Great respect to these, but praise to God –
He has kept us thus far alive   10
although our cruel enemies are so numerous,
one kind within and the other outside.

How noble it is to see them on the bank
marching and training in many ranks;
and it is the gentlemen, obliging and numerous,   15
who are the leaders of the work.

There are eight hundred bearing arms, fair to behold,
this side of Llanybydder;
on the two banks of the Teifi, that is the truth,
on hill and in dale, there are volunteers.   20

And if our land should be attacked,
these are all faithful men
with a bold heart to venture forth
in manly faith, through smoke and fire.

Colonel Lloyd comes first of all   25
and Captain Lewes, talented man,
and Captain Parry before the men,
gallantly handling their volunteers.

Major Brigstocke from Blaen-pant comes
and Captain Taylor with his hundred   30

A Griffiths o Benwenallt-fawr
O flaen ei gwmni megis cawr.

Daw'r Major Llwyd, Llangoedmor glân,
A'i holl gwmpeini *i* gyd ymlaen;
A'r ddau ganwriad o Glwyd Jack,   35
Sy'n siŵr o sefyll at eu tac.

A'r Cadpen Bowen lawen lon
A Meistr Davies, hardd ar don,
A Jones a Saunders gyda'u gwŷr –
East Teify Side y folunteer.   40

Mae yn sir Benfro filwyr ffein,
Yn Nhrefdraeth ac yn Abergwaun,
A Hwlffordd, Penfro'n traino'n grand
Wrth arch y gwŷr sy'n rhoi'r cománd.

Mae yng Nghaerfyrddin fechgyn braf,   45
Mor hardd â'r *tulip* yn yr haf;
Pob un o'r rhain, heb ronyn braw,
Ag arf niweidiol yn ei law.

O! annwyl fechgyn, byddwch ddoeth,
Cyn mynd i'r frwydyr bybyr boeth;   50
Roi'ch dwylaw i ymladd, â chalon llew,
A'ch bysedd i ryfela'n lew;

Fel, os daw gelyn byth i'n gwlad,
Na chaffo ddim o'i waith yn rhad;
Mae'r Cymry'n awr yn dysgu'n bur   55
Drin gwn o dde a'r cleddeu'n glir.

Mae 'Nghymru lawer bachgen smart –
Pe hapiai i gwrdd â Buonaparte
Â chwtshel dderwen yn ei law,
Gwnaiff iddo dreiglo oddi yma draw.   60

Boed bendith ar ein bonedd syw
A'r gwŷr sy ar ddwy lan Teifi'n byw

and Griffiths of Penwenallt-fawr
before his company like a giant.

Major Llwyd of fair Llangoedmor
and all his company come forward;
and the two captains from Clwyd Jack,   35
who are sure to keep to their tack.

And joyful, merry Captain Bowen
and Master Davies, splendid on the sea,
and Jones and Saunders with their men –
the East Teifi Side volunteers.   40

There are in Pembrokeshire fine soldiers,
in Newport and in Fishguard,
and Haverfordwest and Pembroke training in style
according to the order of the men who give command.

There are fine lads in Carmarthen,   45
as handsome as the tulip in the summer;
each one of them, without a glimmer of fear,
bearing a dangerous weapon in his hand.

Oh! dear boys, be prudent,
before you go to the hot, fierce battle;   50
put your hands to fight, with a lion's heart,
and your fingers to wage war bravely;

so that, if an enemy ever comes to our country,
he does not find his work easy;
the Welsh are now faithfully learning   55
how to handle a gun and the sword properly.

There is in Wales many a smart lad –
if he should come across Bonaparte
with a cudgel of oak in his hand,
he will make him flee from here back yonder.   60

A blessing upon our elegant gentry
and the men who live on either side of the Teifi

(Na chaffo Satan ynddynt wall
I gwympo maes y naill a'r llall),

Gan roddi eu bryd, i gyd o'r bron,   65
Am gadw'r gelyn draw i'r don,
Na chaffo le *i* roi'i droed ar lawr
O fewn i Ynys Brydain Fawr.

Gwŷr Ffrainc a Spain a Holand sydd
Am ddifa'n heinioes nos a dydd;   70
Nac ofnwn ddim, gan gredu'n gry'
Fod Brenin Alffa gyda ni.

Ac Ef â'i law, alluog Iôr,
Oedd gyda'n milwyr ar y môr
Pan foddodd ein gelynion lawr,   75
Tua godreu'r hen fynyddoedd mawr.

Tair hatling fychan yw fy rhodd
Ger bron y byd i gyd ar go'dd;
Os cânt dderbyniad (hyn sydd wir)
Bydd mwy'n fy marn na darn o dir.   80

Mi a gesglais hyn ar fesur hir
Mewn bwriad pêr a meddwl pur,
Na welai neb yn ormod fwyth
I seinio cân ar wyth ac wyth.

Fe ganwyd hyn heb unrhyw ffors   85
Gan Siors, fab Stephen Thomas Siors;
Mae'r pedwar enw'n gryno 'nghyd,
Wel, dyma fo – mae'n Gymro i gyd.

* *volunteers.*

JHD no.: 567

Source: LlGC (Amr Crd) W2.4296 (30); CaerLD

Publication: I. Evans, Heol-y-prior, Caerfyrddin, 1799

(may Satan find no defect in them
to make them fall out with one another),

putting their whole hearts, all of them together,   65
into keeping the enemy the other side of the sea,
so that he shall get no place to set his foot down
within the Island of Great Britain.

The men of France and Spain and Holland
wish to destroy our lives day and night;   70
let us fear nothing, believing strongly
that King Alpha is with us.

And it was He and His hand, mighty Lord,
who was with our soldiers on the sea
when our enemies sank down,   75
towards the skirts of the old mountains.

Three small half-farthings is my tribute
before the whole world in public;
if they are accepted (this is the truth)
it will be more in my mind than a piece of land.   80

I put this together on the long metre
with a sweet intention and pure mind,
so that nobody would see it too much of an indulgence
to sound out a song on eight and eight.

This was sung without any compulsion   85
by George, son of Stephen Thomas George;
those are the four names all joined together,
well, there he is – a pure Welshman.

1800

24. Dafydd Evan Morgan, 'Cân o glod i foluntiers Glan Teifi
a'u hoffisers'

Trigolion gwlad Brydain,
Clywch, fawrion a bychain,
Heb ango' – mae'n angen ich wrando
Ar lais y Jehofa,
'R Hwn eto hyd yma   5
Sy'n dirion yn para i rybuddio.
Trwy Ei air a'i fwyn genhadon
A'i ragluniaethau llariaidd tirion,
Mae Ef yn galw ar bawb (heb gelu)
Ymado â'u buchedd ddrwg o bechu   10
A llefain am drugaredd
Cyn delo dydd dialedd.
Mae'n Hiesu ar yr orsedd
Hyd yma am drugarhau.

Ni glywsom am wledydd,   15
Dinasoedd a threfydd
Oedd gadarn eu caerydd, ddistrywiwyd;
March coch o'r cyflyma'
Gas redeg ei yrfa –
Gwlad Brydain hyd yma ddiogelwyd.   20
Mawr yw'r rhwymau sy arnom, Gymry,
A phawb o'n teyrnas i felys foli
A chanmol Duw, 'r Hwn fu mor dirion,
A'n cadwodd, do, rhag llu o elynion
A diriodd i sir Benfro   25
Mewn bwriad i'n distrywio;
Ond gorfu arnynt yno
Mewn braw roi'u harfau lawr.

Er cael o'r llu hagar
Roi traed ar ein daear,   30
Mawr ddychryn Belsassar ddaeth arnynt.
Eu calon a wywodd
A'u cluniau a flin grynodd,
Duw'r nefoedd a gododd fath gorwynt;

1800

24. Dafydd Evan Morgan, 'A song of praise to the volunteers of Glan Teifi and their officers'

Inhabitants of the land of Britain,
hear, great and small,
without forgetfulness – it is necessary for you to listen
to the voice of the Jehovah,
He who thus far   5
kindly continues to give warning.
Through His word and His sweet messengers
and His gentle, kind providences,
He calls on everyone (without concealment)
to leave off their evil lives of sin   10
and cry for mercy
before the day of reckoning should come.
Our Jesus on the throne
thus far wishes to show mercy.

We heard about countries,   15
cities and towns
strongly fortified, which were destroyed;
the speediest red steed
was allowed to run his course –
the land of Britain has thus far been safeguarded. 20
Great are the ties upon us, Welshmen,
and everyone from our kingdom to worship
and praise God sweetly, He who was so kind,
who kept us, indeed, from a swarm of enemies
who landed in Pembrokeshire   25
with the intention of destroying us;
but they were forced there
in fear to put down their arms.

Even though the ugly host
were able to set foot on our land,   30
the great terror of Belshazzar came upon them.
Their courage wilted
and their knees shook fearfully,
such a hurricane did the God of heaven raise;

Fel, trwy ychydig filwyr gweinion   35
(Pa rai nid gwell na gwŷr Gideon),
Cawsom ninnau'r fuddugoliaeth
Mewn gwyrthiol fodd (bur oruchafiaeth).
Rhown glod i'n Harglwydd hawddgar
Amdan Ei nefol ffafar;   40
Ni gawsom ddedwydd gydmar
I goncro'r Ffrancaidd hil.

Fe ddarfu'n Duw tirion
Eu *h*arddel fel moddion;
Calonnau'n gwŷr mawrion gynhyrfodd.   45
Lord Cawdor yn benna' –
Ie, 'n barchus mi a'i henwa' –
Trwy nerth y Jehofa gorchfygodd;
Ac amrywiol gyda hynny
O foneddigion allwn enwi,   50
Pa rai sy â'u henwau a'u clod yn hynod,
Yn argraffedig, wedi'u gosod.
Am hynny minnau frysia'
I ddweud am eraill, medda',
Pa rai sy o'r rhyw ffyddlona'   55
I sefyll dros ein gwlad.

I'r diben o amddiffyn
Ein teyrnas a'n brenin,
Pob graddau'n gyffredin gynhyrfodd;
Mewn ysbryd milwraidd,   60
[---]
'N enwedig, ein bonedd gyd-unodd
I guro maes am *volunteers*
A'u gwisgo'n hardd â lifrau *soldiers*
A'u traino'n ddoeth yn y *train* milwrol   65
A'u gwneud, fel Arthur, yn filwyr nerthol.
Gobeithio bydd hyn yma,
Trwy gymorth y Jehofa,
Er lles i wlad Brytania
A choron Brydain Fawr.   70

Yng ngoror glan Teifi
(Y ddwy ochor rwy'n barchu)

so that, with a few weak soldiers   35
(who were no better than Gideon's men),
we took the victory
in a miraculous way (thorough mastery).
Let us give praise to our kind Lord
for His heavenly favour;   40
we found a blessed partner
to conquer the French race.

Our kind God
adopted them as a means;
He excited the hearts of our great men.   45
Lord Cawdor foremost –
yes, I shall respectfully name him –
through the might of Jehovah he overcame;
and several gentlemen with him
that I could name,   50
whose names and praise
have been famously set out in print.
For that reason, I shall hurry
to tell of others, I say,
who are of the most faithful kind   55
to stand up for our country.

For the purpose of defending
our kingdom and our king,
every order of men alike stirred themselves;
in a military spirit   60
[---------------------------------------]
our gentry in particular united
to strike forth for volunteers
and to dress them finely in soldiers' uniforms
and train them wisely in the military discipline   65
and make them mighty soldiers like Arthur.
Let us hope that this,
through the assistance of the Jehovah,
will be of benefit to the land of Britannia
and the crown of Great Britain.   70

In the region of the Teifi's banks
(I honour both sides)

Mae bonedd i'w henwi'n wych hynod;
Pa rai sydd, o'u calon,
Yn gywir i'r Goron,   75
Dan arfau o blaid Brydain yn barod;
A chwedi rhoi er mwyn 'r Efengyl
Feddiannau lawer (nid yn gynnil)
At gadw'u gwlad a'u ffryns a'u cene'l,
A'u bywyd, os bydd raid, mewn rhyfel.   80
Boed bendith fawr y nefoedd
Er llwyddiant gyda'n lluoedd
Ar diroedd ac ar foroedd –
Hyn yw'm dymuniad i.

Yn flaena' ga' i enwi   85
Sy'n addfwyn flaenori
Gwych *soldiers* glan Teifi, glyn tawel:
Yw'r Colonel Lloyd enwog
O Fronwydd ardderchog.
Dros foroedd bu'n fywiog mewn rhyfel,   90
Ond yn awr mae e' yma 'ng Nghymru,
Yn hardd ei osgedd, yn addysgu
Ein hieuenctid ninnau i iwso'u harfau,
Mewn cyflym fodd, y gwn a'r cleddau;
Fel ffyddiog Brotestaniaid   95
I wrthsefyll llu'r Atheistiaid,
Pa rai sy'n wyneb galed,
Heb barch i Dduw na dyn.

Ym mhalas Llangoedmor,
Lle teg ar bob tymor,   100
Mae colonel yn rhagor i'w enwi:
Pen bonedd, mwyn beunydd,
Brawd Colonel Lloyd, Bronwydd –
Eich deuoedd maent filwyr pur heini,
A chwedi bod mewn trwm ryfeloedd   105
Lle lladdwyd Ffrancod wrth y miloedd,
A'r Sbaniards gwaedlyd didrugaredd
Trwy gymorth nef gas yno'u diwedd.
Ond nawr mae e'n blaenori
Hardd *soldiers* Aberteifi,   110

there are nobility to be named with splendid fame;
who, from their heart,
are true to the Crown,   75
ready under arms on Britain's behalf;
and who have given for the sake of the Gospel
many possessions (not scantily)
towards the protection of their country and their friends and their nation,
and their lives, if need be, in war.   80
Let the great blessing of heaven
be with our troops for success
on land and sea –
this is my wish.

First of all may I name   85
he who gently leads
the splendid soldiers of the banks of the Teifi, a quiet vale:
famous Colonel Lloyd
from excellent Bronwydd.
Overseas he has been active in war,   90
but he is now here in Wales,
handsome his mien, teaching
our youth to use their weapons
in a swift manner, the gun and sword;
as faithful Protestants   95
to resist the host of the Atheists,
those whose faces are hard,
without respect for God nor for man.

In the mansion of Llangoedmor,
a lovely place in every season,   100
there is another colonel to be named:
the head of the gentry, always gentle,
the brother of Colonel Lloyd, Bronwydd –
the pair of them are fine, sprightly soldiers,
and have been in heavy wars   105
where Frenchmen were killed by the thousands,
and the bloody, merciless Spaniards
through the help of heaven met their end there.
But now he is leading
the fair soldiers of Cardigan,   110

O'i galon yn ddigulni
Dros goron Brydain Fawr.

Yn flaenor gwych enwog
Mae Major fwyn Brigstocke –
Blaenpant yw 'i ardderchog gartrefle.   115
Mae yntau'n blaenori
Ar regiment o'r Cymry
Sy'n traino ar lan Teifi, dan arfe.
A Chapten Taylor dewr o 'Stradmor,
Pendefig mwyn, a doeth ei gyngor;   120
A Chapten Wells o'r Gellidywyll,
Sy'n hollol groes i'r Ffrancod erchyll.
Gwnaed Duw hwy *i* gyd fel Samson
Gael concro'u holl elynion,
I ymddiffyn achos Sion   125
A choron Brydain Fawr.

Mae eto hardd fonedd
Gas feddu'r fath rinwedd
Â'u bod yn gyfanedd gyduno
I gynnal cymdeithas   130
Yn achos ein teyrnas –
Pur gymwys ac addas i'w cofio.
Capten Lewes o'r Llysnewydd
(Mae'n fawr ei barch mewn gwlad a threfydd)
A Chapten Parry dewr o'r Gernos   135
(Pendefig cymwys at yr achos).
Eich dau maent hardd flaenoried
I flaenori'r Protestanied
I ryfela â'r Ffrancod di-gred
Sy'n waedlyd am ein gwlad.   140

Pe meddwn well doniau
Mi ganwn 'n fwy golau
(Mae'm gwllys, pe gallai, wneud felly)
O barch i'r pendefig
Mwyn doniol da diddig   145
A duwiol arbennig, wy'n gredu –
Capten Bowen o Weinifor,
Mae'n flaenor hardd o fewn i'n goror;

from his heart without narrow-mindedness
on behalf of the crown of Great Britain.

There is noble Major Brigstocke,
a splendid, famous leader –
Blaen-pant is his excellent home.   115
He also leads
a regiment of the Welsh
who train on the banks of the Teifi, under arms.
And brave Captain Taylor of Stradmore,
a noble gentleman of wise council;   120
and Captain Wells of Gellidywyll,
who is utterly opposed to the terrible French.
May God make them all like Samson
to conquer all their enemies,
to defend the cause of Zion   125
and the crown of Great Britain.

There are further noble gentry
who possess such virtue
so as to unite entirely
in order to sustain society   130
in the cause of our kingdom –
very deserving and fitting of remembrance.
Captain Lewes of Llysnewydd
(he is greatly revered in countryside and towns)
and brave Captain Parry from Gernos   135
(a gentleman fit for the cause).
The two are splendid chiefs
to lead the Protestants
to war against the godless French
who are bloodthirsty for our country.   140

If I were endowed with better talents
I would sing more clearly
(my will, if I were able, is to do so)
out of respect to the noble, gifted,
good, genial   145
and, I believe, particularly godly gentleman –
Captain Bowen of Waunifor,
he is a handsome leader within our area;

Mae e'n blaenori ar gant o filwyr,
Rheini o'u gwaelod bawb yn gywir.   150
Rhoed Duw 'ddo ffydd fel Dafydd
A gras fo ar gynnydd beunydd,
Fel gallo mewn llawenydd
Ymado â hyn o fyd.

A chwithau'r dewr fechgyn,   155
Hardd weision ein brenin,
A listiodd yn gytûn dan arfau;
I'ch moesau rhinweddol
A'ch addysg milwrol
Mae'ch clod yn rhagorol trwy'n parthau.   160
Gobeithio cewch chwi'n fwyn gynyddu
Mewn duwiol fodd ym mhob daioni,
Fel byddo'ch llwyddiant o'r rhyw orau
Wrth iwso'r tanllyd wn a'r cleddau.
Os felly, gellwch fentro   165
I faes y gwaed yn gryno;
Mae'n Harglwydd wedi addo
Bod yno ar eich rhan.

O'm gwaelod, heb gulni,
Dymuna' i ddaioni   170
I bawb sy'n cyd-dynnu dan arfau:
Pob *officer* bywiog
Sy o dymer galonnog
I iwso'r gwn enwog a'r cleddau,
A phob soldier is ei alwad –   175
Mawr lwyddiant iddynt yw'm dymuniad.
Fy ngwyllys yw i Dduw'r trugaredd
Roi iddynt ras i gofio'u diwedd,
Fel y galloch fyw'n gysurus
Yn hyn o fyd trafferthus,   180
Ac hefyd fod yn hapus
'N ôl mynd tu draw i'r bedd.

I George ein pen-llywydd
(O'r enw mae'n drydydd –
'Mddiffynnwr i'r grefydd Gristnogol),   185
Mawr lwyddiant fo iddo

he leads a hundred soldiers,
who are all thoroughly true.   150
May God give him a faith like David's
and grace increasing daily,
so that he can leave this world
in joy.

And you, the brave lads,   155
the noble servants of our king,
who enlisted as one man under arms;
for your virtuous manners
and your military knowledge
your praise is glorious throughout our region.   160
Let us hope that you will thrive nobly
in a godly way in every virtue,
so that your success be of the best kind
while using the fiery gun and the sword.
If so, you can venture   165
to the field of blood all together;
our Lord has promised
to be there on your behalf.

From the bottom of my heart, without meanness,
I wish goodness   170
to every one who works together under arms:
every lively officer
with a hearty disposition
to use the splendid gun and sword
and every soldier of a lower rank –   175
great success to them is my wish.
My will is that the God of mercy
should give them grace to remember their end,
so that you can live in comfort
in this troublesome world,   180
and also be happy
after going to the other side of the grave.

To George our sovereign
(he is the third of that name –
a defender to the Christian faith),   185
may he have great success

Ym mhob da, rwy'n dymuno;
Ie, 'r fendith a gaffo'n dragwyddol.
A phob un o'r lein frenhinol,
Gwnaed Duw nhwy o'r bron yn deulu duwiol;   190
A rhoed Ei Ysbryd Glân i 'fforddi
Ein holl flaenoriaid mewn daioni.
Boed Brydain mewn diogelfa
Dan adain y Jehofa,
Lle mae iddi sicr noddfa   195
Tra paro hyn o fyd.

Source: LlGC (Amr Crd) W2.4296 (33)

Publication: I. Evans Caerfyrddin, 1800

Textual readings: 40. Am dan; 44. I arddel

in every good thing, I wish;
yes, may he be blessed everlastingly.
And each one of the royal line,
may God make them all a godly family;   190
and give His Holy Spirit to guide
all our leaders in goodness.
May Britain be in a safe place
under the wing of the Jehovah,
where there is certain protection for her   195
while this world lasts.

1804

25. J.P., 'Cân sylweddol, [y]n annog Brydain i gofleidio eu breintiau gwladol a chrefyddol a diwygio am eu beiau'

Ow, Frydain aml freintiau, beth ydyw'r cwmwl du
Sy'n crogi'n hyll ei agwedd uwchben dy diroedd di?
Dy bechod, och, yw'r achos o'r farn arswydus sydd,
Gan hynny edifara, galara amdano'n brudd.

'Does ardal dan yr haulwen sydd uwch ei braint a'i bri,   5
Ond och! ei chamddefnyddio – O, Brydain! – 'r ydwyt ti
A byw yn anniolchgar am freintiau uchel ryw,
Diystyru a chablu enw yr Hollalluog Dduw.

Mae 'Fengyl gras yn seinio o fewn dy furiau llo[n],
Ac eto rwyt ti'n sathru pêr genadwri hon;   10
Trwy hon mae Duw yn galw – O, Frydain fyddar, clyw! –
[R]hag cael dy daro â dyrnod dieithrol iawn ei rhyw.

Mae gennyt frenin tirion sy'n dadmaeth mwyn i'r wlad,
Mae gennyt ben-cynghoriaid sy'n ffyddlon a di-frad,
Mae gennyt bob rhagorfraint sydd eisiau o bob rhyw;   15
O, Frydain, gwir ddiwygia – na themtia'th dirion Dduw.

Pechodau o bob graddeu sy'n galw am farn i lawr;
'Fu pechod ar y ddaear nad yw e' yn Brydain Fawr:
*Bradwriaeth, trais, gorthrymder, cenfigen, lladrad, lladd –
'Does bosib enwi pechod nad groeso gennym gadd.   20

Mae balchder yn ei gerbyd, a'r holl werinos ffôl
Yn rhedeg wrth y miloedd, yn wallgof, ar ei ôl;
Godineb a chynhennau sydd yn cynyddu'n fawr –
Pa ryfedd fod Duw cyfiawn yn bygwth barn i lawr?

Mae llawer o broffeswyr yn anodd iawn eu trin –   25
'Ddioddefant mo'r gwirionedd, gan chwydd a chwerwedd blin;
'Does a[r]nynt am eu beiau un gwae na gwasgfa nawr –
Pa ryfedd fod Duw cyfiawn yn bygwth barn i lawr?

1804

25. J.P., 'A substantial song, urging Britain to embrace its secular and religious privileges and to correct its faults'

Oh, Britain of many privileges, what is the black cloud
which hangs, ugly its aspect, above your lands?
Your sin, alas, is the cause for the awful judgement that there is,
because of that repent, weep for it earnestly.

There is no region under the sun that has higher privilege and renown,   5
but alas! – Oh, Britain! – you are misusing it
and living without giving thanks for privileges of a high order,
disregarding and blaspheming the name of the Almighty God.

The Gospel of grace resounds within your joyful walls,
and yet you trample upon her sweet tidings;   10
through her God calls – Oh, deaf Britain, hear! –
lest you should be struck with a blow of a most exceptional kind.

You have a gracious king who is a gentle foster father to the country,
you have chief counsellors who are loyal and without treachery,
you have every privilege that is wanted of all kinds;   15
Oh, Britain, truly reform – do not tempt your gracious God.

Sins of every order call for judgement to come down;
there was no sin on earth that it is not in Great Britain:
*treachery, violence, oppression, envy, theft, murder –
it is impossible to name a sin that has not been welcomed by us.   20

Pride is in his chariot, and all the foolish populace
are running by the thousands, insanely, after him;
adultery and disputes are greatly increasing –
what wonder that righteous God is threatening judgement down?

Many who profess religion are very difficult to handle –   25
they will not submit to the truth, on account of pride and angry bitterness;
they do not now suffer any remorse or qualms for their sins –
what wonder that righteous God is threatening judgement down?

Ac hefyd y mae gormod o ragfarn corniog cas
Rhwng dynion gwir sylweddol, sef etifeddion gras;   30
Dieithrwch, oerfelgarwch, a surni, ffiaidd sawr –
Mae hyn yn temtio'r nefoedd i dywallt barn i lawr.

Mae eto ryw ddrycholaeth, fel lledrith ei oer nâd,
'N crochweiddi mai yn ofer *y* tywalltodd Crist Ei waed;
Yn haeru fod mewn fflamiau werth gwaed yr Aberth mawr –   35
Mae hyn yn arwydd eglur fod barn bron dod i lawr.

Mae eilwaith [ra]i a ddylai ofalu am borthi'r praidd,
Yn dangos fod gelyniaeth a chwerwedd yn eu gwraidd;
Â'u diflas 'sgrifenadau, mae iddynt anghlod mawr –
Nid yw'n beth rhyfedd gennym fod Duw yn gwgu nawr.   40

Fe amcanwyd chwerwi'r mawrion yn erbyn gwŷr y w[lad],
I'w poeni am eu breintiau, mae'n brenin yn rhoi'n rhad,
Sef rhydd-did i addoliad drwy Tolerasion fawr –
Pa ryfedd pe disgynnai rhyw ddrygfarn ar y llawr?

Paham mae Protestaniaid, gwŷr llygon a gwŷr llên,   45
Yn gwgu ar ei gilydd a rhoddi sen am sen?
'Sgrifennu llyfrau a chanu, a hyn mewn chwerwedd mawr?
O, gochel, Brydain, gochel, rhag tynnu barn i lawr!

Cofleidiwn bawb ein breintiau, heddychlon byddwn byw,
Am George ein tirion frenin, diolchwn bawb i Dduw;   50
Diogeled Brenin nefoedd eneiniog Brydain Fawr,
Yr Hollalluog Dduwdod wrandawo'n llef yn awr.

Blodeuo wnelo teulu brenhinol Brydain gu
Mewn rhinwedd, gras a phurdeb, o'm calon ddyweda' i;
Bendithion rif y tywod ddihidlo lawr o'r nen   55
Ar deulu George y Trydydd, a dyweded pawb "Amen".

Paid Brydain â dychrynu – gweddïa ar dy Dduw;
Tor ymaith, trwy 'difeirwch, dy bechod o bob rhyw;
Fe 'ddawodd Duw dy wrando a'th arbed wna Fe'n llyn
Er mwyn yr Iesu a hoeliwyd ar ben Calfaria fryn.   60

And also there is too much horned, hateful prejudice
between truly important men, namely the heirs of grace;   30
estrangement, lack of zeal, and sourness, abhorrent its stench –
this tempts heaven to pour down judgement.

There is yet some spectre, its screech like a phantom,
bawling that Christ spilt His blood in vain;
claiming that the worth of the great Sacrifice's blood is in flames –   35
this is a clear sign that judgement is about to come down.

There are, then, some who should be attending to nourishing the flock,
but who show that enmity and bitterness are at their very root;
with their loathsome writings, there is great dishonour to them –
we find it no strange thing that God is frowning now.   40

An attempt was made to embitter the great against the men of the country,
to make them worry about their privileges, which our king gives freely,
namely freedom to worship through the great Act of Toleration –
what wonder if some evil judgement should descend on earth?

Why do Protestants, lay men and clergymen,   45
scowl at each other and throw insult for insult?
Write books and sing, and this in great bitterness?
Oh, beware, Britain, beware, lest judgement should be drawn down!

Let us all embrace our privileges, let us live peacefully,
for George our gracious king, let us all thank God;   50
may the King of heaven protect the anointed one of Great Britain,
may the Almighty Godhead listen to our cry now.

May beloved Britain's royal family flourish
in virtue, grace and purity, I say it from my heart;
may countless blessings flow down from heaven   55
upon the family of George the Third, and let everyone say "Amen".

Do not tremble, Britain – pray to your God;
break off, through repentance, your sin, of every kind;
God promised to listen to you and He will save you thus
for the sake of Jesus who was nailed on top of the hill of Calvary.   60

Gweddïa am helaeth lwyddiant i filwyr môr a thir;
Gweddïa ar Dduw y lluoedd fynd allan gyda'n gwŷr;
Gweddïa am ddiogelu porthladdoedd Brydain Fawr;
Gweddïa ar Dduw ddarostwng dy elynion oll i lawr.

Duw, gwrando weddi Brydain, a gwared trwy Dy ras   65
Rhag llid gelynion gwaedlyd, sef Ffrancod caethion cas;
Er amled eu rhifedi, gall Duw eu difa
      ar daith,
Fel byddin Zeres Ethiop, oedd fil o filoedd maith.

Beth yw pum cant o filoedd, O, Arglwydd, o Dy flaen?
Ond megis peiswyn ysgafn neu haid o wybed mân?   70
Un angel sydd yn ddigon mewn llai na munud awr
I goncro'r Ffrancod ffroenwyllt fel byddin Syria fawr.

O, Arglwydd, maddeu'n beiau a gwared ni rhag brad,
A llwydda'th 'Fengyl dirion trwy holl derfynau'n gwlad;
Duw cadw i ni'r rhydd-did, rhag ein gelynion pell   75
A rhag gelynion gartre', nad ŷnt un gronyn gwell.

Rho fwy o ysbryd cariad ac ysbryd gweddi ddwys,
Rho rym i wlad ac Eglwys roi arnat Ti eu pwys;
Ond in gael nerth a llwyddiant o flaen Dy orsedd fawr,
Fe sethrir Bonaparte a'[i] Ffrancod ffôl i lawr.   80

* *This was composed with a view to the desperate plot of Despard, and his tools.*

Sources: BC, vol. 32, no. 119; Bangor 25 (121). The latter is damaged.

Publication: T. Roberts, Carnarvon, 1804

Textual readings: 70. peiswyr

Pray for extensive success for the soldiers of sea and land;
pray the God of hosts to go out with our men;
pray for the safeguarding of the harbours of Great Britain;
pray God to strike down all your enemies.

God, listen to Britain's prayer, and deliver through Your grace   65
from the wrath of bloodthirsty enemies, namely the slavish, cruel French;
in spite of the magnitude of their numbers, God can destroy them
          on their way,
like the army of Zerah the Ethiop, which was a thousand thousands strong.

What are five hundred thousands, Oh, Lord, before You?
Just like light chaff or a swarm of midges?   70
One angel is enough in less than an instant
to conquer the rash French like the army of great Syria.

Oh, Lord, forgive us our faults and deliver us from treachery,
and speed Your gracious Gospel through every part of our country;
God, protect our freedom for us, against our distant enemies   75
and against enemies at home, who are not a shred better.

Give more of the spirit of love and the spirit of solemn prayer,
give power to country and Church to put their weight upon You;
as long as we have strength and success before Your great throne,
Bonaparte and his foolish Frenchmen will be trampled down.   80

* *This was composed with a view to the desperate plot of Despard, and his tools.*

1805

26. John Thomas, '[Cerdd] o ddiolchgar goffadwriaet[h] am y gorfoleddus
fuddugoliaeth a dderbyniasom yn ddiweddar ar ein gelynion'
Tune: 'Duw Gadwo'r Brenin'

Pob geneu cydganed am wrol ymwared
    Dderbynied drwy nodded Duw'r ne'!
Am nad ydym feirw, bawb union, bob enw,
    Rhown ddiolch drwy groyw ffydd gre'!
Er cymaint ein pechod, mae'r Arglwydd nef uchod   5
    Yn canfod ein trallod bob tro;
Pan gryfa' ein gelynion 'c erchylla'u dichellion,
    Gwna'u hanfon (wŷr ffeilsion!) ar ffo;
Sef Ffrancod, wŷr gwaedlyd, godasant yn embyd,
    A gwŷr Ysbaen hefyd ae'n hy,   10
Â llonge o fawr gryfder yn nofio, gryn nifer,
    Ac ynddyn' nhw lawer o lu.

Fe gasglodd Ffrainc giedd i'w dilyn mewn dialedd,
    Holl berfedd (naws bonedd) Ysbaen;
I'n tanio cytunant mewn balchder a thrachwant,   15
    Derchafant, ymledant ymlaen.
Tua phymtheg ar hugien o longau'n llawn cynnen,
    Cychw'nen' (air milen) i'r môr,
A deuddeg cant weithie o wŷr ar eu byrdde,
    Am ladd ar eu siwrne wŷr Siôr –   20
'Ran 'piniwn 'r hen Boni yw'n llusgo ni a'n llosgi
    A chymryd ein llestri mewn llid,
A dŵad i'n daear i'n cyrchu ni i garchar
    A'n rhoi ni mewn galar i gyd.

Dwy genedl oedd unfryd ar y môr i'n cymeryd   25
    (Wŷr gwaedlyd, am g'reuddyd pob gradd),
A'u hadmirals enwog oedd ddewrion, gynddeiriog,
    Â'u bwriad yn llidiog i'n lladd;
Gan ddeudyd yn eger y cymrent bob llester
    A welent wrth bleser o'u blaen;   30
A Nelson a'i wŷr hefyd a gymran' nhw'n gaethglud
    I Ffrainc, drwy naws benyd, neu Sbaen;

1805

26. John Thomas, 'A song of thankful commemoration for the triumphant
victory which we received recently over our enemies'
Tune: 'God Save the King'

Let all mouths sing together about a splendid deliverance
which came to pass through the support of the God of heaven!
Let us give thanks through a sweet, strong faith
that we are not dead, each and every one!
In spite of the extent of our sin, the God of heaven above   5
sees our calamity every time;
when our enemies are at their strongest and their stratagems most awful,
He puts them to flight (false men!);
namely, the French, bloodthirsty men who arose terribly,
and the men of Spain also became bold,   10
with ships of great strength sailing, a large number,
and a great host of soldiers within them.

Cruel France gathered together to follow them in vengeance,
the entire guts of Spain (noble nature);
they agree in pride and greed to fire on us,   15
they rise up, they extend themselves forwards.
Around thirty-five ships full of hostility,
they set out (loathsome word) to sea,
and some twelve hundred men on board,
intending to kill George's men on their journey –   20
for the whim of old Boney is to haul us and burn us
and to take our vessels in anger,
and to come to our land to take us to prison
and put us all in grief.

There were two nations on the sea intent to take us   25
(murderous men, wanting to reach every rank),
and their famous admirals were brave and furious,
their intention fiercely to kill us;
impudently saying that they would take every vessel
that they saw before them, at their pleasure;   30
and Nelson and his men also will they take prisoners of war
to France, as a punishment, or Spain;

Ac y gwyntia' nhw'n gynta' i randir East India
   I ddygyd ein breintia ni a'n bri;
Ac wedyn, ar fyrder, y cae' nhw'u holl bleser,   35
   Sef gwaed pobl Lloeger yn lli.

Fel hyn cychwynason', yn iach ac yn wchion,
   Â'u calon yn greulon iawn gry';
Fe'u gwelodd Nelson dirion a'i ddoniol iawn ddynion,
   Oedd ddewrion wiw loywon, iawn lu.   40
Troe'r Ffrancod i'w llyncu mewn gorchest a 'mgyrchu,
   Ac atyn' nhw nesu'n o neis.
Ein brodyr o Bryden ag ysgwydd y'u gwasgen'
   Fel cecsen neu fesen mewn feis.
Gwn cawson' gan cusan o blwm a thân buan,   45
   Nes teimlan' neu clywan' nhw'i glais;
A'u rigins nhw'n rhwygo, 'r hen ganon yn cwyno
   Nad oedden' nhw'n leicio mo'i lais.

Ni chowson' nhw o'n llongau ond benthyg bwledau,
   Fel t'ranau, 'c o'n gynnau caen' gainc.   50
Y chwilod pan chwalwyd, treiasant trwy arswyd
   Gael dianc o'r ffrwgwd i Ffrainc.
Eu dwylo mewn dalfa roe dynion Brytania,
   Bywioca' wŷr dewra' ar y dŵr;
Ein gwynion wŷr gonest a dorrodd eu dirwest,   55
   Er maint oedd eu gorchest bob gŵr.
Ein canans a'n gynnau, ein peics a'n cleddyfau,
   Ein bagnets i'w bronnau fu'r braw,
A'[r] [S]ais efo'r Cymro, rai gwych, yn eu handlo,
   A Duw yn eu llwyddo [------]   60

Tua thri deg o filoedd o'u dynion ae danodd
   Neu gwympodd i'r moroedd oer mawr,
Ac felly, Ffrainc erwin, a Sbaen yno i'w chalyn,
   A dorrwyd, yn llurgyn, i'r llawr.
'R Ysbaenod drwy boene ollyngwyd i'w cartre',   65
   Yn llarpie tan friwie, tyn fraw,
Tan rwymiad tra chelfydd am fod inni beunydd
   Yn ufudd a llonydd rhagllaw.
Y Ffrancod ysgeler a ddygwyd i Loeger
   Yng ngharchar, tyn drymder tan draed.   70

and that they will speed first to the territory of East India
to steal our privileges and our renown;
and then, shortly, that they would have their whole pleasure, 35
namely, to see the blood of the people of England flowing.

Thus did they set out, healthily and gallantly,
their hearts very cruel and strong;
gracious Nelson and his very gifted men,
who were a very brave, worthy, bright host, saw them. 40
The French turned to gobble them up in triumph and to fall upon them,
and drew closer to them quite precisely.
Our brothers from Britain crushed them with their power
like a reed or an acorn in a vice.
I know that they received a hundred kisses of lead and quick fire, 45
until they could feel or sense its bruising;
and their riggings torn, the old cannon complaining
that they did not like his voice.

They got nothing but borrowed bullets from our ships,
like thunderbolts, and they had a tune from our guns. 50
When the beetles were shattered, they tried out of dread
to escape from the fray to France.
The men of Britain bound their hands,
the liveliest, bravest men on the water;
our blessed, honest men put an end to their fast, 55
never mind how great each man's feat.
Our cannons and our guns, our pikes and our swords,
our bayonets were a fright to their breasts,
and the Englishman with the Welshman, splendid ones, handling them,
and God speeding them [------]. 60

Around thirty thousand of their men went under
or fell into the great, cold seas,
and so, terrible France, and Spain following her there,
was struck down, a carcass, to the ground.
The Spaniards were sent off home in pain, 65
torn to pieces with wounds, heavy fear,
on the most clever condition
of being always obedient and peaceable towards us.
The villainous French were taken to England,
to prison, tight oppression under foot. 70

Os Nelson gadd farwolaeth, cadd gyflawn fudd'goliaeth
  A'i selio hi'n odiaeth â'i waed.

Llaw Duw oedd yn eglur yng ngwyneb y frwydyr
  Na chowsem ni a'n brodyr ein brad.
Diolched pob Cymro a Sais gydag efo   75
  I'r Un sydd yn llwyddo i'n gwellhad,
Ein dyfod mor hyfryd a chaffael ein bywyd,
  Ein rhyddid a'n golud i gyd
Yn lle bod yn gaethion yn nwylo'n gelynion,
  Mor greulon yw'r lladron a'u llid.   80
Y Ffrancod digrefydd sy flinion aflonydd –
  I wledydd maent beunydd yn boen;
Ond Saeson a Chymry a ddarfu'u dychrynu –
  Mae Boni'n darn grynu'n ei groen.

Rhown glod ar ein glinie i Frenin uchel-ne'   85
  A gadwodd ein llonge rhag llid,
A'n tirion lân frenin, wiw fuddiol, a'i fyddin,
  Ein bonedd a'n gwerin i gyd.
Blaenoriad ein pobl eglwysig a gwladol
  Synhwyrol fo'n wrol fyw'n hir;   90
Un sylwedd i'n *sailors* iawn saildeg a'n *soldiers*
  A holl *volunteers* ein tir.
Wel, safwn yn wrol – gweddïwn *ar* Dduw nefol
  Am sefyll i'w bobol yn ben.
I Frydain hyfrydwch; a garo howddgarwch   95
  Am heddwch dymunwch, Amen.

Source: Bangor 7 (21)

Publication: Trefriw, [1805]

*Document title: Dwy Gerdd Newydd I. O ddiolchgar goffadwriaeth am y gorfoleddus
Fuddygoliaeth a dderbyniasom yn ddiweddar ar ein Gelynion. II Cân Newydd a
wnaed mewn perthynas ir Frwydur ddiweddar ar Môr [sic], y mha un y lladdwyd y
gwych Ryfelwr Arglwydd Nelson.*

If Nelson died, he had a complete victory
and sealed it splendidly with his blood.

God's hand was clear before the battle
that we and our brothers should not be betrayed.
May every Welshman and Englishman with him give thanks   75
to the One who promotes our betterment,
that we prospered so well and that we kept our lives,
our liberty, and all our riches
instead of being enslaved in the hands of our enemies,
so cruel are the thieves and their wrath.   80
The unreligious Frenchmen are savage and merciless –
they are constantly troublesome to countries;
but the English and the Welsh gave them a fright –
Boney is shaking in his skin.

Let us give praise on our knees to the King of high heaven   85
who protected our ships from wrath,
and our kindly, blessed, most beneficial king and his army,
our nobility and all our common people.
May the wise leaders of our men of Church and state,
live long and bravely;   90
the same substance to our well-founded sailors and our soldiers
and all the volunteers of our land.
Well, let us stand valiantly – let us pray to the heavenly Father
to stand as a leader for His people.
Joy to Britain and may he who loves kindliness   95
wish for peace, Amen.

27. Robert Morris, 'Cân newydd am y bu[ddugoliaeth]au clodfawr yn erbyn
llyngesau cysylltiedig Ffrainc a Sbaen a marwolaeth y digymar a'r llwyddiannus
lywydd, Arglwydd Nelson'
Tune: 'Duw Gadwo'r Brenin yr hen ffordd'

Wel, wel, Ynys Brydain, un gaerog wen gywrain,
　　A guddiwyd dan adain Duw nef!
Mae'n amser in geisio iawn offrwm yn effro,
　　Gweddïo i fwy leisio'i fawl Ef.
Mi gadd Ynys Prydain, fel Rahab y butain,　　　　　　　　　5
　　Ei hachub a'i harwain o hyd;
Tan adain rhagluniaeth, trugaredd fawr helaeth
　　A gafodd gan bennaeth y byd.
Er cymaint ei phechod, trugaredd fwyn barod
　　A ddaeth i'w chyfarfod ar fôr;　　　　　　　　　　　　10
O flaen Bony Parti e redodd yn wisgi
　　Drugaredd, dosturi da stôr.

Roedd Brenin brenhinoedd, yng nghanol ein lluoedd,
　　O'n plaid ni ar diroedd a dŵr.
Arddelodd yn dirion y llywydd gwych, Nelson,　　　　　　15
　　Cynhaliodd ei galon fel gŵr.
Nid oedd tan un goron un ail i'r gwych Nelson
　　Am dorri gelynion i lawr;
Er maint oedd yn ffrostio ein lladd a'n difreintio,
　　Roedd Nelson yn curo pob cawr.　　　　　　　　　　20
Dros Frydain wlad hyfryd, fe seliodd yn waedlyd
　　Hardd goron ei fywyd i farn;
Er maint oedd yn ceisio ein lladd a'n distrywio
　　Ni chafwyd mo'n sigo ni'n sarn.

Ni welwyd yn olau ar fôr â'i fawr furiau,　　　　　　　　25
　　Chwyddedig wyllt donnau, well dyn,
Rhag Boney bob ennyd a'i luoedd anhyfryd,
　　Rai enbyd a gwaedlyd eu gwŷn.
O ganol y gynnau bu lidiog bwledau,
　　Pellennau, ryw dyrrau o dân,　　　　　　　　　　　　30
A'u lleisiau lluosog fel t'ranau terwynog
　　Dan Nelson, galonnog ŵr glân.
Bu ef yn odidog (tro annwyl, tra enwog),
　　Yn filwr calonnog â'i lu;

27. Robert Morris, 'A new song about the celebrated victories against the united fleets of France and Spain and the death of the peerless and successful commander, Lord Nelson'
Tune: 'God Save the King the old way'

Well, well, Isle of Britain, a fine, bright fortress,
hidden under the wing of the God of heaven!
It is time for us to awaken and seek a proper offering,
to pray that more people should voice His praise.
The Isle of Britain, like the whore Rahab,   5
was saved and led always;
under the wing of providence, a great, magnanimous mercy
did it receive from the ruler of the world.
In spite of the extent of its sin, sweet, ready mercy
came to meet it on the sea;   10
before Bonaparty quickly ran
mercy, compassion in good supply.

The King of kings, in the midst of our hosts,
was on our side on lands and sea.
He graciously championed the brilliant leader, Nelson,   15
He upheld his courage like a man.
There was none like the noble Nelson under any crown
for cutting down enemies;
no matter how much he bragged that he would murder and despoil us,
Nelson vanquished every giant.   20
On behalf of the delightful country of Britain, he sealed bloodily
the beautiful crown of his life to righteousness;
in spite of the numbers who were trying to kill and destroy us
we were not crushed underfoot.

A better man was not manifestly seen on the sea,   25
with its great walls, swelling, wild waves,
protecting every moment from Boney and his horrible hosts,
destructive and murderous in their rage.
From the midst of the guns there came fiery bullets,
balls, like heaps of fire,   30
and their multiple voices like fervent thunderbolts
under Nelson, valiant, honest man.
He was outstanding (a very dear deed, much talked of),
a courageous soldier with his host;

Duw oedd yn ei lwyddo rhag Ffreinig wŷr ffroenio –   35
 Roedd Nelson yn taro o'n tu.

Nid cryfder ein llongau, nid amledd ein harfau,
 Nid sgil ac nid doniau cnawd dyn
A barodd y llwyddiant i'n milwr na moliant,
 Na dim yn ei haeddiant ei hun;   40
Ond Duw roddodd ysbryd i'n milwr i 'maelyd
 A rhoddi ei fywyd hyd fedd.
E gafodd ein Nelson ryw ysbryd a chalon
 I ladd ein gelynion â'i gledd –
Y Sbaenwyr a'r Ffrancod a ddaeth i'w gyfarfod,   45
 Hwy gawsant ryw ddiwrnod go ddu;
Ein milwyr gwych celfydd, o dan Siôr y Trydydd,
 A Nelson yn llywydd i'n llu.

Saith lestr a'r hugain buredig o Brydain
 Gan Nelson, y cywrain wŷr cu;   50
I'w erbyn o'r Ffrancod, roedd tair ar ddeg hynod
 Ar hugain, fel llewod yn llu.
E gododd o *Gadis hil lawer o Lewis,
 Fel gwybed, rai dibris, ar daith.
Er gwyched rhyfelwyr oedd Ffrancod, Ysbaenwyr,   55
 Daeth arnynt drwm wewyr tra maith.
Ym mhenrhyn †Trafalgar bu Nelson digymar
 Yn ymladd yn llidgar fel llew;
Â'i gleddyf yn rhwygo, eu gwaed oedd yn lliwio,
 Yn cwympo o dano fe'n dew.   60

Yn ‡Copenhagan ymladdodd yn gyfan
 Un Nelson, wŷr gwiwlan ar goedd;
E lwyddodd Duw tirion y llywydd gwych Nelson
 Yn erbyn rhai blinon eu bloedd.
Ei olwg i'w elyn yn 'r Aifft a fu'n ddychryn,   65
 Er uched oedd corun pob cawr;
Yng ngallu Duw'r nefoedd y torrodd fyddinoedd
 Estroniaid yn lluoedd i'r llawr.
Cant pedwar ar hugain o frwydrau tra milain
 Ymladdodd tros Frydain, ei fro;   70
Tros Frydain a'i choron ymladdodd hen Nelson
 Hyd ddiwedd, yn ffyddlon, heb ffo.

it was God who preserved him from the haughty Frenchmen – 35
Nelson struck on our side.

It was not the strength of our ships, not the abundance of our arms,
not the skill and not the genius of human flesh
that caused the success or the praise for our soldier,
nor anything connected with his own merit; 40
But God gave spirit to our soldier to grapple
and give his life as far as the grave.
Our Nelson found some spirit and heart
to kill our enemies with his sword –
The Spaniards and Frenchmen who came to meet him 45
had a rather gloomy day;
our splendid, skilful soldiers, under George the Third,
and Nelson as commander of our host.

Nelson, the dear, ingenious man,
had twenty-seven ship-shape vessels from Britain; 50
against him, there were a remarkable thirty-three
of the French, like a host of lions.
From *Cádiz there rose many from the race of Louis,
like flies, worthless ones, on a journey.
In spite of the might of the French and Spanish as warriors, 55
very long, heavy anguish came upon them.
On the cape of †Trafalgar the incomparable Nelson
fought wrathfully like a lion;
his sword hacked, their blood stained,
falling abundantly under him. 60

In ‡Copenhagen a certain Nelson,
a right-living man, I declare, fought soundly;
gracious God sped the brilliant commander Nelson
against ones whose battle-cry was terrible.
His appearance was a terror to his enemy in Egypt, 65
notwithstanding the height of each giant's crown;
in the power of the God of heaven he cut down
the armies of foreigners in throngs to the ground.
He fought a hundred and twenty-four very fierce battles
for Britain, his land; 70
for Britain and its crown old Nelson fought
to the end, faithfully, without fleeing.

Un milwr mor ffyddlon â'r llywydd gwych Nelson
    Dros Frydain a'i choron ni chaed;
Yn ollawl enillodd bob brwydr gynhygiodd,   75
    Gelynion a gollodd eu gwaed.
Mwy laddodd hen Nelson, wrth farw fel Samson,
    O erchyll elynion ei wlad;
Mwy ydoedd, mae'n eglur, na ||Ch'ledfwlch hen Arthur,
    I wared ei frodyr o frad.   80
Yn llaw'r Hollalluog bu'n filwr calonnog
    Dros Frydain, flodeuog ei dawn.
Rhagluniaeth fawr olau fu ar fôr â'i hen furiau,
    Hi gaeodd y llwybrau yn llawn.

Os lladdwyd hen Nelson, oedd i ni fel moddion   85
    Yn erbyn gelynion ein gwlad,
Mae gan ein Duw ddigon yn fuddiol o foddion –
    Ei gariad a'r rhoddion yn rhad.
Mellt, t'ranau a gwyntoedd, haul, lleuad Duw'r lluoedd,
    Y moroedd a'u dyfroedd fel dyn,   90
A 'mladdodd mewn rhyfel, rai gochwyrn brig uchel,
    A Duw yn eu harddel Ei Hun;
Duw'r nefoedd yn llwyddo pob peth i gydweithio
    Fel dynion o dano bob dydd;
Rhai'n sefyll, rhai'n syrthio, i'w ogoniant heb gwyno,   95
    Ac felly a fynno fe fydd.

Os pechi'n ddigwilydd yn fwy na'th chwiorydd,
    Hen Frydain, cei gerydd o gur.
Ti golli dy freintiau os bychan dy ffrwythau,
    Deui allan o'r peiriau'n fwy pur.   100
Darfydded effeithiau baich adwyth bechodau,
    Sy'n galw ryw farnau ar fyd;
Teyrnased dedwyddwch, llawn addas llonyddwch,
    O fôr i fôr – heddwch o hyd.
Duw buro Ei Eglwys, Ei briod hardd gymwys,   105
    Fel byddo hi'n wiwlwys hardd wen;
Â Siors ar ei orsedd, trwy goron trugaredd,
    Yn moli Duw'r mawredd, Amen.

* *Cadiz, a town of Spain, 5 miles in length, 2 in breadth, 4[?5] w. of Gibralter, and 90 w. by s. of Malaga. Lon. 6, 11, w. Lat. 36, 31, n.*

There was never any soldier so faithful as the noble commander Nelson
to Britain and her crown;
he won outright every battle which he attempted,   75
enemies lost their blood.
Old Nelson killed more, in dying like Samson,
of the awful enemies of his country;
he was greater, it is apparent, than the ||Caledfwlch of old Arthur,
in delivering his brothers from treachery.   80
In the hand of the Almighty he was a hearty warrior
for Britain, of thriving favour.
Great, shining providence was present on the sea with its ancient walls,
it blocked the paths fully.

If Nelson, who was like a medicine to us   85
against the enemies of our country, is killed,
our God has plenty of effective medicines –
His love and the gifts freely given.
The lightening, thunderbolts and winds, sun, moon of the God of hosts,
the seas and their waters like a man   90
have fought in war, some waves very swift with a high crest,
and God Himself championing them;
the God of heaven promoting everything to work together
like men underneath Him every day;
some standing, some falling, to His glory without complaint,   95
and so what He wills comes to pass.

If you should sin shamelessly more than your sisters,
old Britain, you shall have affliction as a rebuke.
You shall lose your privileges if your fruits are small,
you shall come out of the melting-pots more pure.   100
May the effects of the burden of grievous sins,
that call certain judgements upon the world, cease;
may happiness rule, fully fitting tranquillity,
from sea to sea – peace always.
May God purify His Church, His beautiful, proper spouse,   105
so that she shall be lovely, beautiful and blessed;
with George upon his throne, through the crown of mercy,
praising the God of greatness, Amen.

* *Cádiz, a town of Spain, 5 miles in length, 2 in breadth, 4[?5] w. of Gibralter, and
90 w. by s. of Malaga. Lon. 6, 11, w. Lat. 36, 31, n.*

† *Trafalgar, a cape of Spain, in Andalusia, 30 s. e. from Cadiz, Lon 6, 1, w. Lat. 36, 11, n.*
‡ *Copenhagen, the capital of Denmark, 500 n. e. of London, Lon. 12, 40, e. Lat. 55, 41, n.*
‖ *King Arthur's sword.*

Source: LlGC (Ffol. 192)

Publication: T. Roberts, Caernarfon, [1805]

Textual reading: 47. milwr

† *Trafalgar, a cape of Spain, in Andalusia, 30 s. e. from Cadiz, Lon 6, 1, w. Lat. 36, 11, n.*
‡ *Copenhagen, the capital of Denmark, 500 n. e. of London, Lon. 12, 40, e. Lat. 55, 41, n.*
|| *King Arthur's sword.*

?1807

28. Dienw, 'Cân o glod i'r milisia deuddeg sir Cymru'

Milisia Cymru, oll o'r bron,
Dymunai'n dda i'r deyrnas hon;
George y Trydydd yw ein pen,
O! llwyddiant iddo byth, Amen.

Ffrainc a Sbaen a Holand sydd   5
Mewn bwriad llawn o gario'r dydd;
O! cy[m]rwn galon, Gymry, nawr –
E fynnwn weld eu pennau i lawr.

Hwylio'u llongau maent yn awr
'Gael dyfod dros y cefnfor mawr   10
I Milfford Hafen cyn bo hir,
Lle treia rhain eu landio i dir.

Sir Aberteifi ddaw'n ddi-frad,
Wrth *notes* y *drums* y bydd eu tra'd;
And always ready by the word,   15
"I'll bravely fight for George the Third!"

Sir Gaerfyrddin ddaw i lawr
Yn fechgyn glana', teca'u gwawr;
A rheini'n siriol fel y sêr –
With hearts of steel they'll never fear.   20

Sir Forgannwg ddaw fel tân
Heb un yn blino yn y bla'n;
A rheini'n fechgyn heini llon –
"With muskets clean, we'll fire on!"

Sir Frycheiniog gyda'r wawr   25
A fyddant yno'n gwmp'ni mawr;
A rhain fel mur ar lan y môr –
They'll never fear when cannon roar.

Sir Faesyfed ddaw'n ddi-stŵr,
Yn fechgyn glew tua glan y dŵr;   30

?1807

28. Anon., 'A song of praise to the militia of the twelve counties of Wales'

The militia of Wales, all together,
wishes well to this kingdom;
George the Third is our leader,
Oh! may he ever prosper, Amen.

France and Spain and Holland   5
fully intend to win the day;
Oh! let us Welshmen now take heart –
we wish to see their heads brought low.

They are now sailing their ships
to come over the great ocean   10
to Milford Haven before long,
where they will try to come to land.

Cardiganshire comes without treachery,
their feet will move to the notes of the drums;
And always ready by the word,   15
"I'll bravely fight for George the Third!"

Carmarthenshire comes down,
lads of the fairest and most handsome appearance;
and they are cheerful like the stars –
With hearts of steel they'll never fear.   20

Glamorganshire will come like fire
without a single one getting tired at the front;
and they are sprightly, happy lads –
"With muskets clean, we'll fire on!"

Breconshire will be there at dawn,   25
a large company;
and they will be like a rampart on the sea shore –
They'll never fear when cannon roar.

Radnorshire will come without tumult,
brave boys, to the edge of the water;   30

E fyn y rhain eu treio i ma's –
They loose their blood for Prince of Wales.

Sir Benfro ddaw i lan y traeth –
Ni enwyd eto neb o'u bath;
A rheini'n sowndion ar y sand –   35
Against the foes they'll steady stand.

Mae'n sir Drefaldwyn fechgyn smart
Pe'u hapient gwrdd â Bonobarte;
A'r ffyn o dderw yn eu llaw
A wnae iddynt dreiglo yma a thraw.   40

Mae 'n sir Feirionnydd fechgyn braf,
Mor hardd â'r *tulip* yn yr haf;
Pob un o'r rhain sy'n ffyddlon wŷr –
Ar fryn a phant yn *volunteer.*

Sir Gaernarfon ddaw'n ddi-o'd,   45
A rheini'n glau, 'gael cario'r glod;
Heb un o'r cwmp'ni'n tynnu'n gro's –
With bloody fight they'll kill the foes.

Sir Ddimbych ddaw, yn fechgyn gwych,
A sŵn eu cloion fel y clych;   50
A rheini'n Saeson o'r un *size* –
By word command they'll fire twice.

Fe ddaw bechgyn sir y Fflint –
Nhwy 'mladdant fel Caswallon gynt,
Fel gorfu i Caesar, fawr ei *roar,*   55
Ymguddio yn y dwfwn fôr.

Sir Fôn a ddengys wrol fryd
Yn erbyn ymgyrch trawsion byd;
Yn filwyr cedyrn safant hwy –
Fe rônt i'r gelyn farwol glwy.   60

Fe glywsom gan ryfelwyr gynt
Mai cymorth mawr fuasai'r gwynt;

they wish to try the enemy out –
They'll lose their blood for Prince of Wales.

Pembrokeshire shall come to the edge of the beach –
none like them have yet been named;
and they will stand firmly upon the sand –   35
Against the foes they'll steady stand.

There are in Montgomeryshire smart lads
should they happen to meet Bonaparte;
and the cudgels of oak in their hand
would make the enemy flee here and there.   40

In Merionethshire there are fair lads,
as handsome as the tulip in the summer;
each one of these are faithful men –
volunteers on hill and in dale.

Caernarfonshire comes without delay,   45
and they are swift, so as to deserve the praise;
without any of the company being awkward –
With bloody fight they'll kill the foes.

Denbighshire come, brilliant lads,
and the sound of their locks like bells;   50
they are Englishmen of the same size –
By word command they'll fire twice.

The lads of Flintshire will come –
they will fight like Caswallon of old,
so that Caesar, great his roar,   55
had to hide in the deep sea.

Anglesey will show a manly intention
against the campaigns of the evil ones of the world;
steadfast soldiers they will stand –
they will give the enemy a deadly injury.   60

We heard from warriors in former times
that the wind had been of great assistance;

Gweddïwn ninnau'n awr yn llym
To have the end – God save the king.

JHD nos., sources and publication details:

A: JHD 386; Welsh Ballads Online; Ishmael Davies, Trefriw, [17--]

B: Bangor 8 (19); I. Davies, Trefriw, [?1807]

The two versions are extremely similar, the use of italics being the only factor which distinguishes one from the other.

Textual readings: 2. Dymuna'i'n; 50. cloiou.

let us now pray passionately
To have the end – God save the king.

1810

29. Robert Morris, 'Cerdd i milisia cartrefol sir Gaernarfon'
Tune: 'Mynediad i'r Ynys Deg'

Gyda'ch cennad (fon'ddigaidd ddygiad),
    Cewch glod trwy glymiad glân,
Yn ôl eich swyddau gwir rwydd a graddau,
    Ag enwau rhai ar gân.
Lord Bulkeley'n bennaf un a henwaf   5
    Yn gyntaf yn y gwaith;
Mae'n aelod puredd yn y Senedd,
    Mewn clod a mawredd maith.
Mae'r Cyrnal Assheton-Smith,
    Rhag troeon chwerwon chwith;   10
A Williams, wedyn, Llangwstenyn,
    Dda rosyn – yn ddi-rith,
A'r Capten Haslam doniol dinam,
    Gywirlam yn eu gŵydd,
A'r Capten gwiwbert John Roberts,   15
    Ŵr llonbert er eu llwydd.
Capten Robert Roberts sydd,
    John Jones yr ail ŵr rhydd
(Capteniaid gwiwber, mwynion dymer),
    Yn drydydd Beaver bydd.   20
Thomas Jones ufudd yn bedwerydd
    Yn gelfydd eto gawn;
Edward Roberts pumed, William Roberts chweched,
    A'r seithfed Humphreys iawn.

Lifftenants – henwaf Oakes yn gyntaf,   25
    Hugh Jones a gaf yn gu;
John Hughes meddaf, Robert Jones nodaf,
    Pugh, llonaf yn y llu;
William Payne y pennir, Robert William welir,
    Owen Prichard cywir cawn;   30
A William Parri sydd i'w gyfri'
    Er llenwi rhanc yn llawn.
Mae gŵr eglwysig glân,
    Jones Bodffordd heb wahân,
A Jones y Doctor, iachus gyngor,   35

1810

29. Robert Morris, 'A song to the local militia of Caernarfonshire'
Tune: 'Belisle March'

With your leave (dignified behaviour),
you shall be praised in fair melody,
according to your truly generous occupations and status,
with the names of some in song.
Lord Bulkeley do I name as the chief one,   5
the first in the work;
he is a faithful member in Parliament,
in extensive praise and greatness.
There is Colonel Assheton-Smith,
to guard against bitter, unfortunate events;   10
and then Williams of Llangystennin,
a good rose – it is no illusion,
and talented, faultless Captain Haslam,
true his pace in their presence,
and the worthy and fine Captain John Roberts,   15
a jolly, handsome man who will promote their success.
There is Captain Robert Roberts,
the second free man is John Jones
(lovely captains of a kind temper),
Beaver will be the third.   20
Obedient Thomas Jones is the fourth
that we have, skilful too;
Edward Roberts the fifth, William Roberts the sixth,
and the seventh, true Humphreys.

Lieutenants – I first of all name Oakes,   25
and Hugh Jones, pleasantly;
John Hughes I say, Robert Jones I note,
Pughe, the jolliest in the host;
William Payne is appointed, Robert Williams is seen,
we have true Owen Prichard;   30
and William Parry must be counted
so as to fill the rank fully.
There is a fair churchman,
Jones of Bodffordd, without discrimination,
and Jones the doctor, healthy his advice,   35

Ag onor yn y gân;
A'r Doctor Curry i'w cynghori
　　Rhag poeni yn y pwys –
Milisia llesol, rhai cartrefol,
　　Rhai doniol o wŷr dwys.　　　　　　　　　　40
Ensigns yn deg eu dawn,
　　Rai mwynaidd lluniaidd llawn;
Nid oes cwmpeini mwy hardd a gwisgi,
　　A'u nodi'n deg a wnawn.
Llanciau tirion sir Gaernarfon,　　　　　　　　45
　　Rai dewrion oll ar dir,
Eirfeilch arfog, gwŷr coronog,
　　Sy enwog yn ein sir.

Dau William Owen, dau *ensign* llawen,
　　T. Hughes 'r un diben dwys,　　　　　　　　50
Mae Efan Efan', William Jones gwiwlan,
　　Wŷr purlan dan 'r un pwys;
Yn ddiatal mae un eto
　　Ddylaswn 'i gofio ar gân –
William Robert', oreubarch Rubert,　　　　　　55
　　Gŵr o galonbert glân.
Y sarjeant major mwyn,
　　Mae'n ddoniol 'i ymddwyn,
Mewn dysg a chariad at ei alwad,
　　Mewn dygiad hardd ar dwyn.　　　　　　　60
Mae eto ffyddlon hen gyfeillion,
　　Rai mwynion iawn i mi –
E balla amser gan ei fyrder
　　I henwi'ch hanner chwi.
'Rof i chwi er hyn i gyd　　　　　　　　　　65
　　Ddyledus barch ynghyd;
Mae'n glod a chysur eich gweld yn eglur,
　　Yn frodyr o unfryd.
Na rwgnechwch na thuchanwch,
　　Na chwynwch fawr ychwaith;　　　　　　　70
Rhaid i'r swyddogion fod yn ffyddlon
　　Neu gyfion yn eu gwaith.

Os ŷnt yn gwasgu wrth eich dysgu,
　　Rhaid iddynt felly fod;

is honoured in the song;
and Doctor Curry to advise them
lest they should suffer under the burden –
beneficial militia, the local ones,
gifted, earnest men.   40
Ensigns of fair talent,
kindly, full of comeliness;
there is no company more splendid and sprightly,
and we shall note them fairly.
The kind lads of Caernarfonshire,   45
all brave ones upon land,
magnificent, armed, crowned men,
who are famous in our county.

Two William Owens, two happy ensigns,
T. Hughes of the same solemn purpose,   50
there is Evan Evans, handsome William Jones,
faultless men under the same burden;
there is one more that I should remember
in song, without impediment –
William Roberts, a Rupert of the best respect,   55
a man with a beautiful, fair heart.
The gentle sergeant major,
he is beneficent in his conduct,
in learning and love towards his calling,
in conspicuously noble behaviour.   60
There are yet more faithful old friends,
ones very dear to me –
time runs out, it is so short,
for me to name half of you.
I will give to you together, in spite of all this,   65
the respect that you deserve;
it is a credit and a comfort to see you clearly,
brothers of one mind.
Do not grumble or moan,
nor complain much, either;   70
the officers must be faithful
or just in their work.

If they are harsh while teaching you,
they must be so;

Mae eu swyddau hwy fel chwithau 75
　　A'u rhwymau dan y rhod.
Pawb i'w alwad 'n ôl ei drefniad
　　A'i osodiad yn ei swydd,
Mewn brawdgarwch mwyn a heddwch –
　　Diogelwch yn eu gŵydd. 80
A byddwch bawb yn bur
　　Mewn cariad heb un cur
(Rhag gelynion o galonnau)
　　O dan eich arfau dur.
Cewch ganmoliaeth, parchedigaeth, 85
　　Yn helaeth iawn o hyd,
A byddwch wrol yn wastadol,
　　Yn freiniol iawn o fryd
Dros Arfon (wiwlon wedd) –
　　Yn barchus hyd eich bedd; 90
Na chaffo estron Ffrancod hyllion,
　　Gelynion, ddim o'n gwledd.
Dymunwn heddwch a llonyddwch,
　　Dedwyddwch yn ein dydd,
A charcharorion sydd yn gaethion 95
　　I rodio'n radlon rydd.

Cenwch fiwsig (hoenwych fesur),
　　Yn eglur iawn eich nod,
Nes byddo'r creigiau yn rhoi lleisiau
　　A thyrfâu'n rhannau'r rhod. 100
Doed naturiaeth i gyd-daro,
　　I byncio'i dawn yn bêr;
Coded nwydau yno i neidio
　　I seinio dan y sêr.
Y miwsig oll ynghyd, 105
　　Hyfrydol o unfryd –
Codwch faner Siôr i fyny
　　I'w barchu a'i harddu o hyd;
Dadseiniwch allan (unwedd anian)
　　Yn gyfan (wiwlan waith); 110
Dysgwch droedio, saethu a tharo,
　　A mwrdro'r gelyn maith.
Dadseiniad George y drwm
　　Nes codo pawb o'u cwm,

their offices like yours   75
have obligations under the heavens.
Each one to his calling according to his ordering
and his place in his office,
in gentle fraternity and peace –
there is safety in their presence.   80
And may you all be true
in a spirit of love without any anxiety
(for fear of bold enemies)
under your steel arms.
You shall have praise, respect,   85
very extensively always,
and be manly at all times,
very dignified in your intention
on behalf of Arfon (of a worthy and cheerful appearance) –
respectful until you come to your grave;   90
so that no ugly, foreign Frenchmen,
enemies, should have any of our feast.
We wish peace and tranquillity,
happiness in our day,
and that prisoners who are captive   95
should walk happily to freedom.

Play music (on a fine, lively metre),
very clear in your intention,
until the rocks lend voices
and thunder claps in parts of the firmament.   100
May nature come to strike with you,
to warble her virtue sweetly;
may passions rise there and leap up
to sound out under the stars.
The music all together,   105
beautifully harmonious –
raise up George's banner
to honour and grace him always;
strike out (single-minded spirit)
flawlessly (fitting and fair work);   110
learn to step, to shoot and strike,
and to murder the widespread enemy.
May George strike the drum
until everyone raises from their vale,

Wrth glywed lleisiau a gweled goleu   115
    Y fflamau tân a phlwm;
Na chlywodd pobloedd trwy Lanbeblig
    Erioed fath fiwsig fwyn –
Adlais odlau, lwysedd leisiau,
    A doniau gwych ar dwyn.   120

Deg cant (yn ddibrin) ydyw'r fyddin,
    Iawn egin yn eu nwy,
Dilesg deulu, blodeu Cymru,
    Rhai'n caru medru mwy.
Gweision newydd Siôr y Trydydd,   125
    Yn gelfydd iawn i gyd,
Llanciau Eryri, hardd a gwisgi,
    Rai heini iawn o hyd.
Boed llwyddiant (mwyniant mawr)
    I guro pob rhyw gawr;   130
Cymerwch galon, milisia ffyddlon
    Gwlad Arfon, wiwlon wawr.
Llwydd i'n brenin ynghyd â'i fyddin
    A'i lin o fewn ei wlad;
'N ôl ei ddiweddu, rhain fo'n teyrnasu,   135
    Yn tynnu fel eu tad.
Ar orsedd Frydain fro
    Hyd byth, hyd byth y bo
Ei blant a'i wyrion i gario'r goron
    Tra byddo'n 'r afon ro.   140
Hil y Cymry fo'n cartrefu
    A glynu yn eu gwlad,
A boed llonyddwch a brawdgarwch
    Er heddwch inni'n rhad.

Source: LlGC (Amr Crd) 162 (8)

Publication: T. Roberts, Caernarfon, 1810

Document title: Cerdd i Milisia Cartrefol Sir Gaernarfon, Ar y Dôn a elwir Mynediad i'r Ynys dêg, Belisle March. Ynghyd A Dychymyg: I'w chanu ar y Mesur a elwir Ymdaith Monach.

hearing the voices and seeing the light   115
of the flames of fire and lead;
people through Llanbeblig
never heard such sweet music –
the echo of rhymes, beautiful voices,
and splendid talents everywhere to be seen.   120

There are ten hundred (no less) in the army,
true buds in their passion,
a spirited family, flowers of Wales,
ones who would love to do more.
The new servants of George the Third,   125
all very skilful,
the handsome and swift lads of Snowdonia,
always very sprightly.
May there be success (great joy)
to defeat every giant;   130
take heart, faithful militia
of the land of Arfon, worthy and cheerful your appearance.
Success to our king together with his army
and his line within his country;
after his death, may they rule,   135
taking after their father.
On the throne of the land of Britain
for ever, for ever
may his children and grandchildren carry the crown
while there shall be gravel in the river.   140
May the race of the Welsh make their homes
and remain in their country,
and may there be tranquillity and fraternity for us
freely, for the sake of peace.

30. Evan James, 'Anogaeth i bawb fentro'n galonnog i'r rhyfel yn erbyn y Ffrancod, yn enw Arglwydd Dduw byddinoedd Israel, ac nid yn unig mewn gall[u] dynol'
Tune: 'Belisle March'

Holl wŷr a bechgyn, dowch i'r fyddin,
    Cyffredin mewn cyffroed
O blaid, heb gwynfan, hen Ynys Brydan,
    Rai'n burlan o bob oed.
Er alltud gaethedd, hyll fygythiad,   5
    Baganiad, deiliaid Doeg,
Drwy Frenin Sion ni chânt yr awron
    Ddim un o'u 'mcanion coeg.
Gwaed *Rhys ap Tewdwr mawr
    O'r deheu, goreu gwawr –   10
Yr hen Frytaniad, rhwydd cytunwch,
    Na arswydwch ddim o'u sawr.
Hil *Owen Tudur, o Fôn di-ddadel,
    I'r rhyfel dowch yn rhes,
I wneud y Ffrancod, surion sorod,   15
    Fel llygod heb ddim lles.
Hilogaeth *Beli Mawr
    A *Gruffudd Cynan cawr,
Dowch i'r unman, fawr a bychan,
    I'w sathru'n lân i lawr –   20
Boneparti ynfyd, cigydd gwaedlyd
    (Swyn hefyd ni saif yn hir).
Ym mhlaid ein byddinoedd bydd gallu'r nefoedd
    Ar goedd mi greda'r gwir.

Mae'n ein teyrnas wiwdda addas,   25
    Messias enw a sâi;
Er mwyn hwnnw gwneiff ein cadw,
    Pur henw sy'n parhau.
Â chledde'r Ffrancod ni haeddem ddyrnod
    Oherwydd pechod pwn;   30
Os cawn Ei gymod bydd rhyfeddod
    Da hynod y dydd hwn.
Ond er Ei fwyn Ei Hun
    Arbedodd Mab y Dyn
Genhedlaetha mewn cyfyngdra,   35

30. Evan James, 'Encouragement for all to venture valiantly to the war against the French, in the name of the Lord God of the hosts of Israel, and not only in human strength'
Tune: 'Belisle March'

All men and lads, come to the army,
all with a common impulse
on behalf of the old Isle of Britain, without complaining,
fine ones of every age.
In spite of foreign bondage, a ghastly threat,   5
pagans, vassals of Doeg,
through the King of Zion they shall not this hour achieve
a single one of their vain aims.
The blood of great *Rhys ap Tewdwr
from the south, the best leader –   10
old Britons, unite swiftly,
do not be at all dismayed by their stench.
The race of *Owen Tudor, from Anglesey without a doubt,
come in ranks to the war,
to make the French, sour dregs,   15
like helpless mice.
The race of *Beli the Great
and the mighty *Gruffudd son of Cynan,
come to the same place, great and small,
to tramp him cleanly to the ground –   20
mad Bonaparty, bloody butcher
(a spell that will not stand for long, either).
In the cause of our armies shall be the power of heaven
I publicly give credit to the truth.

There is in our good and deserving kingdom   25
the name of the everlasting Messiah;
for its sake He will preserve us,
a pure name which lasts.
We would deserve a blow from the sword of the French
on account of a burden of sin;   30
if we receive His atonement there shall be
a remarkable miracle this day.
For His own sake alone
did the Son of Man save
nations in distress,   35

Er Adda lawer un.
Yr un yw eto – nesawn ato,
   Ymddiriedwn Iddo'n iawn;
Mae ganddo ryfedd fawr drugaredd,
   Er maint y llygredd llawn.   40
Gall dorri hundeb, Tad tragwyddoldeb,
   A'u troi i ddallineb llwyr,
Fel llu Sodom, lle arswydus –
   Rhyfygus, ffawtus ffwyr.

Pe baem ni heddiw mewn llwch a lludw   45
   Yn galw ar Dduw gwyn,
Arbedid eto Sais a Chymro,
   Rwy'n coelio heno hyn.
Ond i'r Gwyddelod ffals eu gwaelod
   A'r Ffrancod hyll eu ffroen,   50
Ni fyddem felly drwy Grist Iesu
   I'w dychrynu, cig a chroen.
Pe doem heb feddu dim
   Rhoe inni ryfedd rym,
Â ninne'n gnawdol a hunanol   55
   Ac afresymol syn.
Hawdd mynd yn bwyllig i gyrchu meddyg
   I'r difriwedig fron,
Iach ei donnen sy'n byw'n ddiangen,
   Â'i grechwen llawen, llon.   60
Trigolion Sion sydd
   Yn barchus berchen ffydd;
Mewn gorthrymdera gwnewch ganiada –
   "Hosanna", dyma'r dydd!
O blaid 'r Efengyl ar bob egwyl   65
   Yn rhugl dowch bob rhai;
Yn enw'n bendant 'r Iesu oreusant –
   Ni bydd eich llwyddiant llai.

Er maint yw dyfais pob pendefig,
   Cythreulig, ffyrnig ffôl,   70
Mae Brenin dirfawr â'i allu tramawr
   I'w cadw'n awr yn ôl.
Maent hwy fel teirw mawr, hyderus,
   Rhyfygus, ffawtus ffau;

many a one since Adam.
He is still the same one – let us draw nearer to Him,
let us truly put our trust in Him;
He has wonderful, great mercy,
in spite of the abundant corruption.   40
He can break an alliance, the Father of eternity,
and turn them to sheer blindness
like the host of Sodom, a dreadful place –
arrogant, false terror.

If today we were in dust and ashes   45
calling upon blessed God,
the Englishman and the Welshman would yet be saved,
I believe this tonight.
But as for the Irishmen of false roots
and the ugly-faced Frenchmen,   50
we should thus through Jesus Christ
be able to scare them, flesh and skin.
If we came possessing nothing
He would give us a wonderful power,
even though we are carnal and selfish   55
and senseless without reason.
It is easy to go leisurely to fetch a doctor
for one whose breast is unwounded,
whose skin is healthy and who lives without want,
derisively laughing, happily and merrily.   60
The inhabitants of Zion
are respectfully possessed of a faith;
in tribulations may you sing hymns –
"Hosanna", this is the day!
In the cause of the Gospel at every opportunity   65
come forth each one volubly;
clearly in the name of Jesus, the best saint –
your success will not be any less.

However great the stratagems
of all fiendish, fierce foolish leaders,   70
there is now a very great King with enormous might
to hold them back.
They are like great, audacious bulls,
an ostentatious, false lair;

Rhag eu cyrn hirion a'u dannedd llymion   75
  Iôr cyfion sydd yn cau.
Teyrnasu ymhob lle
  Mae'n union Frenin ne';
Rhown ninne'n bendant holl ogoniant
  Neu foliant iddo Fe,   80
Nid â'n gwefuse ond ein buchedde
  A phur galonne glân;
Rhoddwn fawrglod i'r holl Drindod,
  Dda hynod, ddi-wahân.
A'n harglwydd frenin, Siôr,   85
  Hwn ydyw'n pen a'n pôr,
O tan y nefoedd fe deyrn[as]oedd
  Flynyddoedd, iawnfodd iôr;
A'i hepil eto a deyrnaso,
  A llwyddo bo'r gwŷr llên;   90
I'r Brenin breiniol, Tad tragwyddol,
  Y bytho'r mawl, Amen.

* Hen dywysogion Cymru.

JHD nos., sources, publication details and document titles:

A: JHD 460ii; Welsh Ballads Online (Cwp LlGC); Trefriw, n.d.; *Dwy Gerdd Newydd, Y gyntaf o ddeisyfiad am gynnorthwy yr Hollalluog i'r Brytaniaid, orthrechu'r Ffrangcod gormeslyd y nghyd a chyngor i bawb beidio a hyderu yn eu nerth eu hun; ond yn yr hwn yn hyttrach sydd yn gallu pob peth. Yn ail o annogaeth i bawb fentro yn galonnog i'r rhyfel yn erbyn y Ffrangcod; yn enw Arglwydd Dduw byddinoedd Israel Ag nid mewn gallu dynol.*

B: Welsh Ballads Online (CGPLE, 212), and BC, vol. 12, no. 13; I. Dafies, Trefriw, [?1810]; *Dwy gerdd newydd. Y gyntaf, Hanes y Ty a'r Bobl a losgodd sef gwraig a phlentyn bâch iddi a'i thad, yn Nhref Caernarfon y 5ed o Fai, 1810 Yn ail annogaeth i bawb fentro yn galonog i'r Rhyfel yn erbyn y ffrangcod, yn enw Arglwydd Dduw Byddinoedd Israel, ac nid yn unig mewn gallu dynol: i'w datgan ar Belisle March.*

against their long horns and their sharp teeth   75
the rightful Lord defends.
The righteous King of heaven
rules in every place;
let us emphatically give
every glory or praise to Him,   80
not with our lips but with our lives
and pure, blessed hearts;
let us give great praise to the entire Trinity,
marvellous and inseparable.
And our lord and king, George,   85
who is our head and our chief,
beneath heaven he reigned
for years, genuine lord;
and may his progeny reign yet,
and may the clergymen prosper;   90
praise be
to the high King, everlasting Father, Amen.

* *Ancient Welsh princes.*

Variants: 26. B – Messeis; 40. B – ein llygredd; 41. B – dorri ei hundeb; 44. B – gwarthus gwŷr.

Textual readings: 56. sym

1811

31. Dienw, 'Marwnad i'r degymau yn Ffrainc, a ganwyd gan ŵr
eglwysig o brofiad galarus ar eu hôl'
Tune: [? 'Mentra Gwen']

Mae'r degwm mewn peryglon, beth a wnawn? Beth a wnawn?
Mae gofid ar ein calon, beth a wnawn?
Mae'r bobol yn ei erbyn
A'u golwg fel y gelyn;
Ni cheir mo'r gwenith melyn, beth a wnawn? Beth a wnawn?   5
Mae hyn yn fyd anhydyn! Beth a wnawn?

Wel, dyma dro echryslon, newydd drwg, newydd drwg!
I wŷr y gynau duon, &c.;
Rhai gadd eu boliau'n llawnion,
Ficeriaid a churadion,   10
Trwy gael degymau mawrion, &c., &c.,
A bwyta chwys tylodion! &c.

Ni welso[m] ddyddiau hyfryd, amser braf, amser braf,
'R offeiriaid yn segurllyd, &c.;
Cael dilyn cŵn a chardiau   15
A darllain ar y Suliau
A photio'r cwrw gorau, &c., &c.;
Hyn oll oddi wrth ddegymau! &c.

Bu amser da'r offeiriaid, darfod wnaeth, darfod wnaeth,
Â'u cyfri'n wŷr diniwaid, &c.;   20
Ag arian lond eu pyrsau
I ddal ar draed ceiliogau;
Roedd hynny'n fyd o'r gorau, &c., &c.,
A'i gael oddi wrth ddegymau! &c.

Yn awr mae'r byd yn gallach, dyna'r drwg, dyna'r drwg,   25
Ni cheir mo'r ddegfed bellach, &c.;
'R offeiriaid sydd yn groenllwm
Yn cwyno ar ôl y degwm
A'r hoffaidd arian offrwm, &c., &c.;
Och! ddyddiau blin a welwn, &c.   30

1811

31. Anon., 'An elegy for the tithes in France, sung by a
churchman in mournful experience after them'
Tune: [? 'Mentra Gwen']

The tithe is in danger, what shall we do? What shall we do?
There is distress upon our heart, what shall we do?
The people are against it
and their appearance is hostile;
the white wheat shall not be had, what shall we do? What shall we do?   5
This is an intractable world! What shall we do?

Well, this is an atrocious turn, bad news, bad news!
For the men of the black robes, &c.;
the ones who had their bellies full,
vicars and curates,   10
by having great tithes, &c., &c.,
and eating the sweat of the poor! &c.

We saw delightful days, halcyon time, halcyon time,
the priests idle, &c.;
able to indulge in dogs and cards   15
and to read on Sundays
and to tipple the best beer, &c., &c.;
all this from tithes! &c.

The good time of the priests has been, it came to an end, it came to an end,
when they were considered harmless men, &c.;   20
with their purses full of money
to wager on the feet of cockerels;
that was the best of worlds, &c., &c.,
and to be had from tithes! &c.

The world is now wiser, that's the trouble, that's the trouble,   25
the tenth part is no longer to be had, &c.;
the priests are poor
complaining after the tithe
and the pleasant money of the offertory, &c., &c.;
alas! the hard times that we see, &c.   30

Mae Babel fawr yn syrthio, drwg yw'r peth, drwg yw'r peth,
Ei sylfan sydd yn siglo, &c.;
Mae'r pab nawr bron yn gelain
Yng ngharchar, och! fath ddamwain;
Monachod sydd yn ochain, &c., &c.;   35
Mae cwyno mawr ym Mhrydain, &c.

'Does tâl am faddeu pechod, gwae sy'n dod, gwae
          sy'n dod!
Ni phrynir mwy 'sgymundod, &c.;
Ceir clywed crio enbaid
Gan fil o gardinaliaid,   40
Esgobion ac offeiriaid, &c., &c.,
A hen glochyddion gweiniaid, &c.

Fe ddaeth gweddïau fyny, amser drwg, amser drwg,
Rhônt heibio'n lân aberthu, &c.;
Yn awr 'dyw'r arian llydain   45
I neb o deulu Rhufain;
Mae miloedd mewn wylofain, &c., &c.,
Fu'n bwyta ar bwys y butain, &c.

'Does mwyach barch i'w arfer, beth a wnawn?
          Beth a wnawn?
Ar hyll ddefodau lawer, &c.;   50
'Does geiniog mwy am ddarllen,
Fe gaewyd ffwrdd y gacen,
Mae gwaedd o Fôn i Lunden, &c., &c.;
Yn ffiaidd 'r aeth ein 'fferen, &c.

Mae'r dydd yn dechreu gwawrio, dyna'r drwg, dyna'r drwg,   55
Y dywyll nos aeth heibio, &c.;
Ar fyr hi fydd yn olau,
Fe dderfydd coel grefyddau,
Rhônt heibio'r hen ddefodau, &c., &c.,
A'r pabaidd osodiadau, &c.   60

Rhaid bellach fyw yn gynnil, beth sy' *i'w* wneud? Beth sy' *i'w* wneud?
A gado'r babaidd epil, &c.;
Fe ddarfu byw'n afradlon
Ar bwys llafurwyr tlodion;

Great Babel is falling, it is a wretched thing, it is a wretched thing,
its foundation is quaking, &c.;
the pope is now almost dead
in gaol, alas! such a mishap;
monks are bewailing, &c., &c.;   35
there is great complaint in Britain, &c.

There is no payment for forgiving sin, affliction is on its way, affliction
      is on its way!
Excommunication can no longer be bought, &c.;
fearful weeping shall be heard
from a thousand cardinals,   40
bishops and priests, &c., &c.,
and feeble old sextons, &c.

Prayers have come to an end, a harsh time, a harsh time,
they shall give up sacrifice entirely, &c.;
now there are no large sums of money   45
for anyone from the family of Rome;
thousands are in lamentation, &c., &c.,
who formerly ate beside the whore, &c.

There is no longer any respect for their custom, what shall we do?
      What shall we do?
For many hideous rites, &c.;   50
not a penny is to be had any more for reading,
the cake has been cut off,
there is outcry from Anglesey to London, &c., &c.;
our mass has become loathsome, &c.

The day is beginning to dawn, that's the misfortune, that's the misfortune, 55
the dark night has gone by, &c.;
shortly it will be light,
false religions will come to an end,
they will put aside the old rites, &c., &c.,
and the popish decrees, &c.   60

We must henceforth live frugally, what can be done? What can be done?
And leave the popish brood, &c.;
living extravagantly
on the backs of poor labourers has come to an end;

O, 'r amser braf a welsom! &c., &c.,   65
Mae gofid ar ein calon, &c.

Ffarwél i'r holl ddegymau, byth y mwy, byth y mwy,
Ni welwn ddim fath ddyddiau, &c.;
Mae miloedd yn galaru
I'w weld e'n cael ei gladdu   70
A mynd i'r bedd i bydru, &c., &c.,
Heb obaith daw e' i fyny, &c.

Source: BC, vol. 10, no. 18

Publication: James a Williams, Aberystwyth, 1811, dros D. Amos

Oh, the pleasant time that we saw! &c., &c.,   65
There is misery in our hearts, &c.

Farewell to all the tithes, ever more, ever more,
we shall not see such days, &c.;
thousands are mourning
seeing it being buried   70
and going to the grave to rot, &c., &c.,
without hope that it shall come back, &c.

32. John Thomas, 'Cerdd newydd ar ddull ymddiddan rhwng rhieni
a'u plant, pa rai sydd allan yn y rhyfel presennol'
Tune: 'Y Dôn Fechan'

Rhieni
O! fechgyn Cymru, liw-gu olygon,
Blodeu gwŷr sy o blaid y Goron,
Cofio amdanoch mewn daioni,
Wycha' rhinwedd, mae'ch rhieni.

Plant
Ein tad a'n mam, on'd trist ŷm trostoch,   5
Mor ddigysur y'n magasoch;
Gado Cymru a'n teulu talog,
Gado'n gwlad a'n tai goludog.

Rhieni
Dymunem ichwi bob bendithion
I 'mddwyn yn g'lonnog at y g'lynion;   10
Digonoldeb da 'c anwylder,
Heb ddim gofid ar eich cyfer.

Plant
Er in gael ymbell awr o esmwythder,
Weithiau lendid, weithiau lawnder,
Rhaid dwyn anhunedd, gwaeledd gilwg,   15
Pan fo'n gelyn yn ein golwg.

Rhieni
O! annwyl blant, gochelwch faswedd,
Puteindra, medd-dod, geiriau cabledd;
Mae ymddiddanion drwg anrasol
Yn llygru moesau dynion duwiol.   20

Plant
Mae'n wir fod gwyniau a drygioni
I'w enwi ormod yn yr armi;
Er hyn, mae rhai yn cadw'n wisgi,
Eu cyrff yn liwgar, heb eu halogi.

*32. John Thomas, 'A new song in the form of a dialogue between
parents and their children, who are out in the current war'
Tune: 'Y Dôn Fechan'*

Parents
Oh! lads of Wales, lovely faces,
the flowers of men who support the Crown,
your parents, noblest virtue,
remember you in kindness.

Children
Our father and mother, so sad are we on your behalf,   5
so comfortlessly did you raise us;
leaving Wales and our cheerful family,
leaving our country and our prosperous houses.

Parents
We would wish you every blessing
to conduct yourselves courageously in the face of the enemy;   10
good competence and affection,
without any grief for you.

Children
Even though we have a few hours of tranquillity,
sometimes brightness, sometimes plenty,
we must suffer anxiety, wretched hatred,   15
when our enemy is within our sight.

Parents
Oh! dear children, shun wantonness,
prostitution, drunkenness, words of blasphemy;
evil, graceless conversations
corrupt the morals of godly men.   20

Children
It is true that there are lusts and evils in the army
too many to be mentioned;
in spite of this, some remain pure,
their bodies clean and undefiled.

Rhieni
Mae tad a mam yn drwm eu calon,   25
Yma'n isel aml noson,
Yn ffaelu cysgu wrth gofio'u plentyn
Sy 'r nos yn effro'n gwylio'r gelyn.

Plant
Rhaid mowntio'r *guard*, rhaid sefyll sentri,
Dydd a hirnos diodde'u hoerni,   30
A gwylio malais gelyn milain
Sy'n osio brad i Ynys Brydain.

Rhieni
Gwae – Ow! ryfel, garw ofid –
Fod raid i'n plant ni ddiodde 'u hymlid;
Oerfel, blinder, gwres a syched   35
Ac 'wyrach newyn, er eich niwed.

Plant
Gan fod gelynion yn sychedu
Am olchi'u traed yng ngwaed y Cymry,
Mae'n haws i'r ieunctid wylio rheini,
A'r henaint gwiwddoeth rhônt eu gw[eddi].   40

Rhieni
Rhowch chwithe 'ch goglud yn yr Ar[glwydd]
I gadw'ch calon, gyda'ch gilydd;
Fel Joshua a'r hen Gideon,
Digalonnwch y gelynion.

Plant
Er inni rodio'n wyneb uchel,   45
Mae ein dagrau ni'n y dirgel
Yn aml dreiglo hyd ein gruddiau
Wrth gofio'n hannwyl dad a'n mamau.

Rhieni
Rŷm ninnau'n tywallt aml ddegryn
Wrth fanwl gofio am ein bechgyn,   50
Am wyddom ni, sy'n llawr y beddrod
Neu 'ngwaelod môr yn fwyd i bysgod.

Parents
There is a father and a mother with a heavy heart,   25
abject here on many a night,
unable to sleep as they remember their child
who is awake at night watching the enemy.

Children
We must mount the guard, we must stand sentry,
day and long night suffer their coldness,   30
and watch the malice of a vicious enemy
who attempts to bring ruin to the Isle of Britain.

Parents
Alas – Oh! war, cruel affliction –
that our children must suffer being persecuted;
cold, tiredness, heat and thirst   35
and perhaps famine, to harm you.

Children
Because there are enemies thirsting
to wash their feet in the blood of the Welsh,
it is easier for the young to keep watch over those,
and for the wise old people to offer their prayer.   40

Parents
May you also put your trust in the Lord,
to keep your courage, all together;
like Joshua and Gideon of old,
dishearten the enemy.

Children
Although we walk with our faces held high,   45
our tears in private
often flow along our cheeks
when we remember our dear fathers and mothers.

Parents
We also shed many a tear
when we carefully remember our boys,   50
who, for all we know, are on the floor of the cemetery
or in the bottom of the sea, food for fish.

Plant
O! newydd trwm os clyw ein mamau,
Fu'n ein magu â llaeth eu bronnau,
Fod y canons yn ein torri   55
Oddi ar ein traed, a'n gwaed yn colli.

Rhieni
Mae'n alar meddwl magu bachgen
Trwy boen a gofid; pan dry ei gefen
Ym maes y gwaed y ceir ef gwedi,
I'w rwygo'n 'lodau rhwng bwledi.   60

Plant
Ffarwél, ffarwél, ni a fyddwn berffaith
I gadw'n breintiau, 'n tir a'n cyfraith;
Pan fynno Duw, dychwelwn adre',
Er dur a thân, er dŵr a thonne.

Source: BC, vol. 12, no. 11

Publication: I. Davies, Trefriw, 1811

Document title: *Dwy o Ganiadau Newyddion. Yn gyntaf. Carol Plygain I'w ganu ar y mesur a elwir "Ymadawiad y Brenhin" Yn ail. Cerdd, Ar ddull ymddiddan rhwng Rhieni a'u Plant, pa rai sydd allan yn y Rhyfel presennol: i'w chanu ar y Dôn Fechan.*

Textual readings: 5. ond

Children
Oh! heavy news should it be heard by our mothers,
who suckled us with the milk of their breasts,
that the cannons are cutting us down   55
and our blood flowing.

Parents
It is grief to think of raising a boy
in pain and care; when he turns his back
he is then found on the field of battle,
to be torn limb from limb by all the bullets.   60

Children
Farewell, farewell, we shall be perfect
so as to protect our privileges, our land and our law;
when God wills, we shall return home,
in spite of steel and fire, in spite of water and waves.

1812

*33. Griffith Williams (Gutyn Peris), '[P]enillion i annerch milwyr cartrefol
swydd Gaernarfon, pan flaenorasant ar holl filwyr Brydain i wasanaethu i'r
Iwerddon, a chynnig eu gwasanaeth yn erbyn y Ffrancod yn yr Hisbaen yn y
flwyddyn 1812. Am yr hyn bethau gwnaed oll yn rifl corps'*
Tune: 'Belisle March'

At filwyr Arfon i'r Iwerdd'
    Anerchion fyrdd yn awr,
A chymeriad, parch a mawredd
    Gan fonedd Brydain Fawr,
Am eich cynnig a'ch amcanion   5
    I lewion fynd ymlaen
O blaid y Goron, yn dra gwrol
    (Weis buddiol), i Ysbaen.
Y swyddog Edwards sydd,
    Filwriad radlon rhydd,   10
A'r Cadpen Jones a'r Cadpen Showell,
    Yn dawel yn eu dydd;
A Meistr Price a Hughes a Churchill,
    Ddiwreiddiol wŷr o ddysg –
Y rhaglawiaid dewr a glewion,   15
    A mwynion yn eich mysg.
Anrhydedd a mawrhad
    I'r gwŷr sy'n blaenu'r gad,
A'r Doctor Carreg, mawr y'i cerir,
    Fe'i cofir heb nacâd.   20
Eich gwŷr (un galon) a'ch câr yn ffyddlon,
    Flaenorion cyfion cu,
Mae'ch tirionwch at y rheini
    Yn llonni pawb yn llu.

Rhoes y llywodraeth i chwi uchafiaeth,   25
    Yn helaeth, mewn mwynhad,
Am eich purder a'ch gwrolder
    A'ch glewder dros eich gwlad.
Cael newid dull a lliw eich dillad
    Am wisgiad ydoedd well,   30
A newid eirf a newid arfer
    Er mwyn eich purder pell;

1812

33. Griffith Williams (Gutyn Peris), 'Stanzas to address the county soldiers of Caernarfonshire, when they took the lead over the soldiers of the whole of Britain to serve in Ireland, and offered their service against the French in Spain in the year 1812. For these reasons they were all made a rifle corps'
Tune: 'Belisle March'

To the soldiers of Arfon in Ireland
myriad greetings now,
and esteem, respect and veneration
from the nobility of Great Britain,
for your offer and your intentions 5
bravely to go forward
in the cause of the Crown, very courageously
(useful servants), to Spain.
There is officer Edwards,
a good-natured, free colonel, 10
and Captain Jones and Captain Sewell,
calm in their day;
and Masters Price and Hughes and Churchill,
uprooted men of learning –
the brave and valiant majors, 15
amiable in your midst.
Honour and veneration
to the men who lead the host,
and Doctor Carreg, greatly is he loved,
he is remembered without denial. 20
Your men (of one heart) and your faithful kinsmen,
just, beloved leaders,
your kindness towards them
gives joy to one and all.

The government gave to you a pre-eminence, 25
magnanimously, in satisfaction,
on account of your purity and courage
and bravery on behalf of your country.
You were permitted to change the style and colour of your clothes
for uniform that was better, 30
and change arms and change custom
on account of your far-reaching purity;

A newid rhodiad rhwym
   Yn llwyr am rediad llym,
A newid enw i nod union –   35
   Arwyddion mwy o rym.
Yn glod i'n gwlad a rhad fawrhydi,
   I'n cenedl ni a'n iaith,
A drych ydych (orwych aerwyr)
   I filwyr Brydain faith.   40
Mawr sôn amdanoch sydd
   A chofio eto fydd,
Gan hir goffáu eich enwau hynod
   'N ôl darfod am eich dydd.
Llanciau Eryri i gyd sydd gwedi   45
   Blaenori ar bawb yn awr;
Am hyn yr erys eich arwyrain
   O fewn i Frydain Fawr.

Cadwraeth rhoed erioed ar Frydain
   (Glas Merddin gain ei gwedd)   50
Er cadw i ddynion eu meddiannau
   A chadarnhau ein hedd.
Er y Derwyddon, mae adroddiad
   Am fynych gad a fu,
Ac am ein tadau a maint eu dewrder   55
   Yn ymlid llawer llu.
N[i] fu hen Frydain Fawr
   [F]wy gwerth na gwell ei gwawr
I haeddu'i chadw ar ran y rheini
   Yn well na ni yn awr.   60
Pa well cyfreithiau, pwy uwch eu breintiau
   O'r tywysogaethau i gyd
Na Brydain, maenol dawn a mwyniant,
   Sydd ben gogoniant byd?
Tirionwch un Duw Tri   65
   Sy'n llenwi'n ynys ni
Ac yn ben moliant gyda'n milwyr,
   Ei hamddiffynwyr hi.
Boed (heb beidiaw) Ei law yn loyw
   I gadw hon heb goll,   70
Nes troi arfogaeth Ei filwriaeth
   Yn arfau amaeth oll.

and change a restricted scope
entirely for an ardent course,
and change your name for a proper title –   35
signs of further power.
A credit and a gracious dignity to our country,
to our nation and our language,
and you are a mirror (superb warriors)
for the soldiers of wide Britain.   40
There is great talk about you
and you will yet be remembered,
your renowned names long commemorated
after your days have passed.
The lads of Snowdonia have all   45
taken precedence over everyone now;
for this reason your praise will remain
throughout Great Britain.

A watch was ever kept upon Britain
(Merlin's Close, fair its appearance)   50
to protect men's property for them
and reinforce our peace.
From the time of the Druids, there are accounts
of frequent battles taking place,
and of our fathers and the extent of their bravery   55
chasing off many a host.
The Great Britain of old
was not more valuable or better in her aspect
to deserve to be guarded on their behalf
than on ours now.   60
Where are there better laws, which is higher in her privileges
among all the principalities
than Britain, land of grace and pleasure,
which is the pinnacle of the world's glory?
The kindness of the God of the Trinity   65
fills our island
and is the height of praise among our soldiers,
her protectors.
May His hand be bright (without desisting)
to keep her without loss,   70
until the weaponry of His soldiery
is all transformed into tools of agriculture.

Sources, publication details and document titles:

A: BC, vol. 32, no. 117; T. Roberts, Caernarfon, 1812; *Dwy o Cerddi, O Hanes Yn Gyntaf Am yr echrydus Lofruddiaeth a wnaeth Thomas Edwards, (alias Hwyntw mawr,) ar ferch yn y Penrhyn deudraeth Sir Feirionydd, gyda byr hanes am ei golledigaeth. Yn Ail Penillion i annerch Milwyr Cartrefol Swydd Gaernarfon; pan flaenorasant ar holl filwyr Brydain i wasanaethu i'r Iwerddon, a chynnyg eu gwasanaeth yn erbyn y ffrangcod yn yr Hispaen yn y flwyddyn 1812; Am yr hyn bethau gwnaed oll yn Rifl Corps.*

B: manuscript version in NLW 10257B, pp. 46–8; 'Penillion ar Bilile march, i annerch Milwyr cartrefol swydd Gaer'narfon, pan ddarfu iddynt flaenori holl filwyr Brydain, i wasanaethu yn Iwerddon, a chynnyg myned yn erbyn y Ffrangcod i'r Hispain yn y fln. 1812. am yr hyn bethau y gwnaed hwy oll yn Rifl Corps'. The manuscript is in the hand of Griffith Williams (Gutyn Peris), was compiled between 1800 and 1833, and contains, among other things, poetry composed by Williams himself during 1802–16. See Huws, 'Repertory of Welsh Manuscripts and Scribes', I, p. 179.

Variants: 1. B – Iwerddon; 7. B – yn deg, wrol; 12. B – ein dydd; 14. B – Ddi eiddil; 21. B – Eich is swyddogion a'ch câr; *underneath stanza 1. B has note, reading* 'Edwds Nanhoron. Jones Cefn y coed Hughes Penmynydd Price nai i Humphreys Rhyd lanfair'; 37. B – Mawr glod; 47. A. – arwyrion; 55. B – hen Dadau mawr eu dewrder; 63. A – Brydaen; 71. B –Y Filwriaeth.

1815

Wel, wel, rhaid canu eto, gwir yw'r gair, gwir yw'r gair,
Fe gaethiwyd yr hen gadno, gwir yw'r gair;
Sef Bonaparte y filen,
Fe'i daliwyd ef drachefen;
Mae llawer gŵr yn llawen, gwir yw'r gair, gwir yw'r gair,   5
Ar ddŵr ac ar y ddae'ren, gwir yw'r gair.

Fe haeddsai gael ei grogi, &c., &c.,
Heb achos *judge* na *jury*, &c.;
A thorri'i ben ar blocyn
A'i lusgedd lusgo wedyn   10
A'i ddryllio bob yn ddernyn, &c., &c.,
A'i gladdu'n nhwlc y mochyn, &c.

Bu'n achos ac yn foddion, &c., &c.,
I ladd y General Picton, &c.;
Mae miloedd yn galaru   15
Yn Lloegr ac yng Nghymru
Waith iddo gael ei golli, &c., &c.,
A safio bywyd Boni, &c.

Mae'r diafol gwedi'i hala, &c., &c.,
Mewn llong tua Sant Helena, &c.;   20
Ni ddaw ef mwy drachefen
I ddrygu Ynys Bryden;
Fe gaiff ei gardo'n gywrain, &c., &c.,
Nes bo fe marw'n gelain, &c.

Mae rhai â gruddiau gwlybion, &c., &c.,   25
O dadau a mamau tirion, &c.;
Ac uchel gri eu clywed
Gan weddwon ac ymddifaid,
Waith colli ffrynds mor nesed, &c., &c.,
Heb obaith byth eu gweled, &c.   30

1815

*34. Ioan Dafydd, 'A new song on the retaking of Bonaparte,
together with his sending to St Helena'
Tune: [? 'Mentra Gwen']*

Well, well, we must sing again, so it is, so it is,
the old fox has been taken into captivity, so it is;
namely Bonaparte the villain,
he has been caught again;
many a man is happy, so it is, so it is,   5
on the sea and on land, so it is.

He had deserved to be hung, &c., &c.,
without need for judge nor jury, &c.;
and to have his head struck off on a block
and be slowly drawn afterwards   10
and cut up piece by piece, &c., &c.,
and be buried in the pigsty, &c.

He was the cause and the means, &c., &c.,
of the killing of General Picton, &c.;
thousands are grieving   15
in England and in Wales
because he has been lost, &c., &c.,
and Boney's life saved, &c.

The devil has sent him, &c., &c.,
in a ship towards Saint Helena, &c.;   20
he shall come no more
to do evil to the Isle of Britain;
he shall be closely guarded, &c., &c.,
until he is a dead carcass, &c.

Some have wet cheeks, &c., &c.,   25
among kindly fathers and mothers, &c.;
and loud cries are to be heard
from widows and orphans,
having lost such close friends, &c., &c.,
without hope of ever seeing them, &c.   30

Rhyw gannocdd maith eu cyfri', &c., &c.,
Gadd fynd trwy fin y cleddy', &c.,
Yng ngwyneb eu ffyddlondeb
I'r Farn a thragwyddoldeb,
A ninnau heb ystyried, &c., &c.,   35
Ddaioni Duw i'n harbed, &c.

Trwm iawn oedd gweld y gwragedd, &c., &c.,
Yn ffoi am ryw ymgeledd, &c.,
A'u plant bach yn eu breichiau
Ar hyd y ffyrdd a'r caeau,   40
Yn cael eu lladd yn lleibiau, &c., &c.,
Gan fwlets fel cawodau, &c.

Eu tai yn wenfflam olau, &c., &c.,
Eu dodren a'u trysorau, &c.;
A'r gwaed fel rhyw gornentydd   45
Yn llifo ar hyd y maesydd;
'Does yno fawr llawenydd, &c., &c.,
Ond och a galar beunydd, &c.

Pwy ddyn na ddôi o'i galon, &c., &c.,
Roi'r clod i Frenin Seion, &c.,   50
Am Iddo fod mor dyner
A chadw'r Farn o Loeger,
A rhoi i ni gael esmwythder, &c., &c.,
Hyd yma drwy ein hamser, &c.

Rhof gyngor i chwi'n dawel, &c., &c.,   55
Ymdrechwn [a]m gael gafel, &c.,
Yng ngodrau'r gŵr o Idde';
Fe faeddodd Bonaparte,
'Doedd neb ond Ef a allsai, &c., &c.,
Ei roi ef mewn cadwynau, &c.   60

Ond cofiwn hyn yn wastod, &c., &c.,
Mai dyma ffrwythau pechod &c.,
A'i gyflog yw marwolaeth,
'Nôl gair Duw yn ddiweniaeth,
A'i rym Ef ydyw'r gyfraith, &c., &c.,   65
Ni thorrir un iot ymaith, &c.

Many hundreds were their number, &c., &c.,
who met their end at the sword's edge, &c.,
in the face of their loyalty
to the Judgement and to eternity,
and we had not considered, &c., &c.,   35
God's goodness in delivering us, &c.

It was very sorrowful to see the wives, &c., &c.,
fleeing for some protection, &c.,
and their young children in their arms
along the roads and the fields,   40
being killed in droves, &c., &c.,
by bullets like showers, &c.

Their houses blazing bright, &c., &c.,
their furniture and their treasures, &c.;
and the blood like torrents   45
flowing along the fields;
there is not much joy there, &c., &c.,
only woe and grief every day, &c.

What man would not from his heart, &c., &c.,
come and give praise to the King of Zion, &c.,   50
for being so gracious
as to keep the Judgement away from England,
allowing us to remain in comfort, &c., &c.,
up to this point in our lives, &c.

I will quietly give you advice, &c., &c.,   55
let us attempt to get a hold, &c.,
on the hem of the Jewish man's garment;
He defeated Bonaparte,
There was none but He, &c., &c.,
Who could have put him in chains, &c.   60

But let us always remember this, &c., &c.,
that these are the fruits of sin, &c.,
and its wages are death,
according to God's word without flattery,
and His might is the law, &c., &c.,   65
not a jot shall be struck away, &c.

Dymunaf i bob enw, &c., &c.,
Gael modd wrth fyw i farw, &c.,
Fel gallont hwy pryd hynny
Gael palmwydd yn lle cleddy',   70
A thelyn aur i ganu, &c., &c.,
Byth gyda'r Oen a'i gwmp'ni, &c.

Mae Wellington a Blücher, &c., &c.,
Yn rhodio Ffrainc yn glyfer, &c.;
Mae'r rhai oedd yno'n gyndyn   75
Yn byw yn awr mewn dychryn;
'Does fawr yn gwrychio'i gydyn, &c., &c.,
Cawn heddwch bob yn ronyn, &c.

Hir oes a gras ar gynnydd, &c., &c.,
Ddymuna' i Siors y Trydydd, &c.,   80
A heddwch a thrugaredd
Tra bo fe ar ei orsedd,
A'i dderbyn yn y diwedd, &c., &c.,
I'r nef, lle mae gorfoledd, &c.

Rhaid i mi'n awr ddibennu, &c., &c.,   85
Rhag blino neb wrth ganu, &c.,
Gan ddeisyf ar bob oedran
Roi ceiniog goch yn fuan
Am y papuryn bychan, &c., &c.,
A'i barchu wrth ei ddarllan, &c.   90

Source: Bangor 25 (12)

Publication: Jonathan Harris, Porth Tywyll, Caerfyrddin, 1815

Notes: followed by a hand sign with the warning: 'Na fydded i neb werthu'r gân hon heb gennad yr awdur' (Let no one sell this song without the author's permission).

I wish every person, &c., &c.,
to find a means in life to die, &c.,
so that they at that time
can have palm leaves instead of a sword,   70
and a golden harp to sing, &c., &c.,
evermore with the Lamb and His company, &c.

Wellington and Blücher, &c., &c.,
are cunningly roaming France, &c.;
those who were stubbornly there   75
now live in fear;
hardly anyone sets up his locks in bristles, &c., &c.,
we shall have peace little by little, &c.

I wish to George the Third, &c., &c.,
a long life and increasing grace, &c.,   80
and peace and mercy
while he should be on his throne,
and that he should be accepted in the end, &c., &c.,
to heaven, where glory is found, &c.

I must now conclude, &c., &c.,   85
lest I should tire anyone by singing, &c.,
by asking those of all ages
to give a single penny swiftly
for the little piece of paper, &c., &c.,
and to respect it while reading it, &c.   90

*35. Ioan Dafydd, 'Cân o anogaeth i bawb i olygu Duw yn flaenor i'r
cynghreirwyr yn Ffrainc'
Tune: 'Ymadawiad y Brenin'*

Dewch yn fwynaidd, foneddigion,
Gwŷr a gwragedd a gwyryfon,
Hen ac ifanc, canol oedran –
Rwyf yn eich galw *i* gyd yn gyfan,
Ac yn teilyngu arnoch beunydd   5
Ddymuno llwydd yn rhwydd i'r prydydd
I ddweud y gwir trwy bob sir,
Yn gywir ar ganiad,
Fel y gallo gael derbyniad
Ym mhob rhyw ffair a phob rhyw farchnad.   10

Â fy nghalon rwyf yn amcanu
Yn dra thirion i draddodi
Y newyddion yn wythnosol
Sy'n dod i ni yn dra rhagorol,
Er eu bod yn dristwch beunydd   15
I lawer un sy'n flin trwy'r gwledydd.
A thyma'r nod, oherwydd bod
Eu hynod ffryndiau gorau
Fry yn Ffrainc yn sefyll brwydrau
Yn sŵn y drwms a'r gwns a'r cleddau.   20

Mae'n gynwysedig yn y newydd
Eto lawer o lawenydd.
Gwragedd rai fu'n wylo dagrau
Gaiff rodio â'u priod wrth eu hochrau,
A llawer tad a mam oedrannus   25
A llawer merch fu'n byw'n alarus
Fydd yn ddible'n mynd i ryw dre',
Cael gweld eu ffryndiau gorau
Yn dod adre' o'u carcharau,
Wedi gorffen cario'r cleddau.   30

Ni gydunwn bawb yn gyfan
I foli'r Gŵr sy â phlaniad gwinllan,
Ag Ef Ei Hun yn ei bugeilio
Rhag i'r ba'dd o'r coed i durio.

35. Ioan Dafydd, 'A song of encouragement for everyone to
regard God as leader of the allies in France'
Tune: 'King's Farewell'

Come obligingly, gentlemen,
men and women and virgins,
old and young, middle aged –
I call upon you one and all,
and deem you worthy every day   5
to wish the poet a plentiful prosperity
to tell the truth through every county,
correctly in song,
so that it will be well-received
in every fair and every market.   10

With my heart I aim
very courteously to deliver
the news on a weekly basis
that comes to us very splendidly,
although they are a cause of sadness daily   15
to many a one who is weary throughout the lands.
And this is the mark, because
their excellent, best friends
are yonder in France standing their ground in battles
in the noise of the drums and the guns and the swords.   20

Included in the news
there is yet a great deal of happiness.
Some wives who have wept tears
shall walk with their husbands by their sides,
and many an elderly father and mother   25
and many a girl who lived sorrowfully
shall doubtless go to some town,
to see their best friends
coming home from their prisons,
having ceased to carry the sword.   30

We shall all unite faithfully
to praise the One who is responsible for planting the vineyard,
keeping guard of it Himself
lest the boar from the woods should come rummaging.

Ac er fod Bonaparte a'i armi　　　　　　　　　　35
Cyhyd â'i fryd am ddyfod iddi,
Ni faidd e' – clyw! – tra Iesu'n fyw,
I sathru mo'i grawnsypiau.
Mae gwerth y gwaed o fewn i'r muriau
Na chaiff byth brofi min y cleddau.　　　　　　　40

Roedd Buonaparte, pan ddaeth e' gynta'
Tua'i fyddin fawr i Russia,
Yn goganu trwy i gynnwr'
Fod ar y byd i gyd yn emprwr.
Ond fe ddaeth Brenin y brenhinoedd　　　　　　45
I eu luddio ef a'i luoedd;
Mewn ennyd awr fe orfu i'r cawr
A'i wŷr, er dirfawr dristwch,
Ffoi ar ffrwst am ddiogelwch,
Ond er ei wae ni chas lonyddwch.　　　　　　　50

Mae'r Arglwydd Wellington â'i ddoniau,
Yn denu'r French wrth y miliynau;
Y rhai gynt oeddynt yn elynion
Heddiw elwir yn gyfeillion.
Cleddau'r Arglwydd a Gideon　　　　　　　　　55
Gwympa'r cewri mwyaf creulon
O bob gwlad lawr wrth dra'd
Y Meddyg rhad sy'n maddau
Ac yn gwisgo'r noeth yn ddiau
Â'i gyfiawnder gwyn difrychau.　　　　　　　　60

Ni allaf lai na choffa Blücher –
Rowland Hill sy *still* mewn pryder –
[W]edi mentro eu bywydau
[?Yn] wyneb mwg a thân a chleddau.
Eu cymorth hwy yw Ceidwad Israel,　　　　　　65
Gŵr cyfarwydd iawn mewn rhyfel;
Â'i air fe wna yn glau i'r iâ
A'r eira i ryfela.
Fe haeddai gael y mawl ym mlaena'
Am gadw'r cleddau draw oddi yma.　　　　　　70

And although Bonaparte and his army 35
has had it in mind to come into it for so long,
he shall not dare – hark! – while Jesus is alive
to stamp upon its bunches of grapes.
There is a worth of blood within the walls
that shall never taste the sword's edge. 40

Bonaparte, when he first came
with his great army towards Russia,
claimed through his passion
to be emperor of the entire world.
But the King of kings came 45
to hinder him and his hosts;
in a moment the giant and his men,
to their great sadness,
had to flee in haste to safety,
but in spite of his affliction he did not find tranquillity. 50

Lord Wellington with his talents
is attracting the French by the millions;
those who were formerly enemies
are today called friends.
The sword of the Lord and Gideon 55
shall topple the most cruel giants
from every country at the feet
of the gracious Healer who forgives
and clothes the naked without doubt
with His blessed, spotless justice. 60

I can do no less than call Blücher to mind –
Rowland Hill is still in distress –
having ventured their lives
in the face of smoke and fire and sword.
Their aid is the Saviour of Israel, 65
a man very familiar with war;
with His word He swiftly makes the ice
and the snow wage war.
He should deserve to have the foremost praise
for keeping the sword away from here. 70

Mae mwy nag ugain mlynedd barod
Er pan ddechreuodd yr anghydfod
Rhyngom ni a'r French ysgeler.
Er eu rhif ac eu cryfder,
Er cyd maent wedi dala ati,   75
Fe gafodd Buonaparte ei faeddu.
Teyrnasodd [I]ôn a Wellington,
Fu'n ffyddlon yn ei erlid
Nes daeth y dydd i'w oddiweddyd
A chael y fuddugoliaeth hyfryd.   80

Os cas Buonaparte ddihangfa
Rhag cael ei ladd yn rhyfel Russia,
Fe ddaeth y dydd i ben er hynny
I'r cadno gael ei gyflawn faeddu.
Er iddo fod fel Pharo greulon,   85
Yn ymgyndynnu yn ei galon,
Dangosodd Duw Ei fod yn fyw
Ac yntau'n rhyw ddyn egwan.
Yn y gadwyn ceir e'n gadarn
Gan y cynghreirwyr dewr yrŵan.   90

Brenin Spain a brenin Prussia,
Y Cossacks dewr ac emprwr Russia,
Sweden hefyd, â'u byddinoedd
A joinodd Wellington a'i luoedd,
A Duw y nefoedd yn blaenori –   95
Fe gawd pen ar Bonaparti
A heddwch llawn mwyach gawn,
Heb angen dawn rhyfela.
Dewch i ganu am yr uwcha',
Canu mawl y Brenin Alffa.   100

O! na feddwn dafod angel
Fel y gallwn ganu'n uchel
A chael fy llais fel clychau Aaron –
Mi rown fy mryd o hyd yn gyson.
Ni fyddai 'ngwaith trwy'm taith ond hynny –   105
Dymuno ffydd bob dydd i foli
Y Brenin gwiw sy'n gadarn Dduw
I gadw'n fyw Ei eiddo.

More than twenty ready years
have passed since the contention began
between us and the villainous French.
In spite of their number and their strength,
in spite of the length of time they have kept at it,   75
Bonaparte has been vanquished.
The Lord and Wellington have ruled,
who faithfully pursued him
until the day came to overtake him
and seize the delightful victory.   80

If Bonaparte had an escape
from being killed in the Russian war,
the day came to pass in spite of that
for the fox to be utterly beaten.
Even though he behaved like cruel Pharaoh,   85
becoming obstinate in his heart,
God showed that He was alive
and that Bonaparte was only some weak man.
He is soundly held in chains
by the brave allies now.   90

The king of Spain and the king of Prussia,
the brave Cossacks and the emperor of Russia,
Sweden too, with their armies
joined Wellington and his hosts,
and the God of heaven leading –   95
an end was had to Bonaparty
and we shall henceforth have complete peace,
without need for the art of war.
Come to sing each louder than the other,
to sing the praise of the Alpha King.   100

Oh! that I might possess the tongue of an angel
so that I could sing loudly
and find my voice like the bells of Aaron –
I would always devote my mind without ceasing.
My work throughout my journey would be nothing but that –   105
to wish for faith every day to praise
the excellent King who is a powerful God
to keep those who belong to Him alive.

Afradloniaid, deuwch ato –
Chwi gewch wledd mewn hedd a groeso.   110

Nid wyf eto am ddibennu
Heb yn hollol i fynegi
Fod Paris gaerog wedi'i goresgyn
Trwy allu Duw oedd gyda'r werin.
A thyma'r Gŵr rows fuddugoliaeth   115
Heb achos profi braw marwolaeth.
Gwirionedd yw; mae'n gadarn Dduw
I gadw'n fyw mewn taro.
Er Ei fod yn Dduw'n ymguddio,
Fe fyn i'r gwan yn gyfan goncro.   120

Gan fod y gân oll yn wirionedd
Ac yn tynnu tua'i diwedd,
Brysiwch, bobl, i'ch pocedi
I chwilio am geiniog goch amdani.
A dymuned pawb trwy'r gwledydd   125
Hir oes a gras i George y Trydydd,
A choron wen fo fyth ar ben
Braf Louis y Deunawfed.
Heddwch, llwyddiant ar ei ganfed,
[F]o i frenhinoedd ac i ddeilied.   130

Source: JDL 20a

Publication: n.p., [?1815]

Come to Him, prodigals –
you shall have a feast in peace and welcome. 110

I do not yet wish to finish
without having expressed exactly
that walled Paris has been overwhelmed
through the might of God who was with the people.
And this was the One who gave victory 115
without a cause to experience the terror of death.
It is the truth; He is an immovable God
to keep alive in need.
Even though He is a God who hides Himself,
He wishes the weak to conquer utterly. 120

Since the whole song is true
and draws towards its conclusion,
hasten, people, to your pockets
to search for a single penny for it.
And may everyone throughout the lands wish 125
a long life and grace to George the Third,
and may there ever be a blessed crown upon the head
of brave Louis the Eighteenth.
May there be peace, prosperity a hundredfold,
to kings and to subjects. 130

36. Thomas Jones, 'Cân newydd am y llwyddiant a gafodd ein milwyr ar Bonaparte a'i fyddin yn Ffrainc, y 16, 17 a'r 18 o Fehefin diweddaf'

Brydain! Brydain! Mawr yw'th lwyddiant!
Dod i Frenin ne'r gogoniant!
Efe Ei Hun – nid dyn nac angel –
A barodd lwydd i'n gwŷr o ryfel.

'Ddeutu canol mis Mehefin   5
Dacw'n dechreu sŵn a dychryn
Draw yn Ffrainc rhwng miloedd lawer,
Pawb â'u harfau'n ôl eu harfer.

[Roedd pum cant o wragedd tirion
Gyda Wellington a'i ddynion;   10
Wel, dyma'r lle roedd galar galon,
Wrth glywed llef a gwaedd y gweddwon.

Wellington yn ddiau ddweda,
"O, wragedd mwynion, sefwch chwitha
Yn ôl i gyd o'r waedlyd frwydyr,   15
Gael i chwi gladdu cyrff y meirwyr."

Ac yna'r gwragedd i gyd ateben',
"Ni safwn ni yn ôl 'r un lathen;
Os ydyw'r Arglwydd Dduw yn rhannu,
Ni gawn ein gwŷr yn fyw o'r armi."   20

Am saith o'r gloch ar forau Duwsul
Y dechreuwyd y waedlyd orchwyl;
Cyn pen y pedwar ugain munud,
Fe aeth pymtheg mil i dragwyddolfyd.

Rhowch chwi bawb trwy wledydd Cymru   25
Barch a chlod i Earl of Urbri';
Fe gadd nerth ac ysbryd gwrol
I gadw Wellington a'i bobol.]

Fe feddyliwyd nad oedd ddoethach
Bonaparte – ond cawd ei bertach;   30

36. Thomas Jones, 'A new song about the success which our soldiers had over Bonaparte and his army in France on the 16th, 17th and 18th of last June'

Britain! Britain! Great is your success!
Give the King of heaven the glory!
It was He Himself – neither man nor angel –
who caused success to our men of war.

Around the middle of the month of June   5
lo, there begins a clamour and alarm
yonder in France between many thousands,
all with their arms according to their wont.

[There were five hundred gentle women
with Wellington and his men;   10
well, that is where there was heart's grief,
hearing the cry and wailing of the widows.

Wellington said indeed,
"Oh, gentle wives, stand back,
all of you, from the bloody battle,   15
so that you can bury the bodies of the dead men."

And then the wives all answered,
"We shall not stand back a single yard;
if the Lord God judges,
we shall have our husbands alive from the army."   20

At seven o'clock on Sunday morning
was the bloody task begun;
before eighty minutes had passed,
fifteen thousand had gone to eternity.

All of you through the lands of Wales,   25
give respect and praise to the Earl of Uxbridge;
he found strength and manly spirit
to preserve Wellington and his people.]

It was thought that there was none
wiser than Bonaparte – but someone more quick-witted was found;   30

Yr enwog Wellington a Blücher
Aeth yn gywir ar ei gyfer.

Ac er bod Bone, y *villain* aflan,
Yn ei wlad a'i dir ei hunan,
Gorfu iddo droi ei gefen –   35
Pwy gariai'r dydd ond arfau Pryden!

Fe fu llawer gynt yn ofni
Draw yn Lloegr ac yng Nghymru,
Buasai Bone (heb fodd i'w luddias)
A'i wŷr yn darnio hyn o deyrnas.   40

Aeth o drais i wledydd erill,
A'i wŷr wrth arch yn trin yn erchyll;
Ond, clod i Dduw, ni chas ef ddyfod
I'n gwlad â'i dyrfa i beri difrod.

Offerynnau oedd y dynion,   45
Er mor ddethau ac er mor ddoethion;
Duw Ei Hun a gadwodd Bryden,
Er mwyn Ei eiddo –
            er na haedden'.

Daeth y bwystfil nawr mewn gafel
(Clod i'r Iesu), â'i ben yn isel;   50
Gwelsom bellach hyd ei gadwyn –
Byth na fyddo ganddo [f]yddin.

Rhew ac eira'n Russia, meddant,
A ddechreuodd ei aflwyddiant;
Collodd filwyr yno filoedd,   55
Nid trwy saethu, ond Duw a'u sythodd.

Ffrancod, Ffrancod! P'le mae'ch emprwr?
P'le mae'ch cawr a'ch pen rhyfelwr?
P'le mae'r gŵr fu gynt yn meddwl
Concro'r byd i gyd yn gwbwl?   60

Clywaf rywun yno'n ateb,
Dan e[i] gŵyn, gan guddio'i wyneb:

the famous Wellington and Blücher
loyally faced him.

And although Boney, the dirty villain,
was in his own country and land,
he had to turn his back —   35
who carried the day, but the arms of Britain!

Many formerly worried
yonder in England and in Wales,
that Boney (without any way of stopping him)
and his men would dismember this kingdom.   40

He went by force to other countries,
and his men by order meting out terrible treatment;
but, praise to God, he was not able
to come to our country with his company to cause destruction.

The men were instruments,   45
even though they were so dexterous and so wise;
it was God Himself who protected Britain,
for the sake of those who belonged to Him —
          although they were not worthy.

The monster has now come to hand
(praise to Jesus), his head brought low;   50
we have now seen the length of his chain —
may he never have an army.

Ice and snow in Russia, they say,
began his failure;
he lost thousands of soldiers there,   55
not by their being shot, but God froze them.

Frenchmen, Frenchmen! Where is your emperor?
Where is your giant and your chief warrior?
Where is the man who once meant
to conquer the whole world entirely?   60

I hear someone there answering,
in his grief, hiding his face:

"Cas ci anfon gynt i Elba,
Ac eto eleni *i* Sant Helena."

O[s] felly, Ffrancod, aeth eich blaenor,   65
Peidiwch chwithau byth yn rhagor
Â rhifo'ch gwŷ[r] i faes y rhyfel,
Ond dysgwch dewi a byddwch dawel.

A Duw a roddo ichwi rywun
Yn ôl Ei feddwl Ef yn frenin,   70
Fo'n cymryd Llyfyr Duw yn rheol,
Heb goelio'r pab sy'n twyllo pobol.

Gobeithio bydd y meysydd cochion
A rhifedi'r lladdedigion
Yn peri i bawb ffieiddio rhyfel   75
A chadw Bone mwy mewn gafel.

Yn Waterloo bu llef a llad*d*fa,
Peidiwch ameu, er bod yma;
Lladdwyd yno, medd hanesion,
Bedwar ugain mil o ddynion!!!   80

[Nid haeddu gwg, ond torri'i gegen
A haeddai bradwr Ynys Bryden;
Fe fu'n achos lladd myrddiynau
Yn awr ers ugain o flynyddau!]

Ond yn lle cwyno, ddynion, cenwch!   85
Mae gwawr heddiw yr aiff yn heddwch.
Aed Efengyl gras trwy'r gwl[ed]ydd,
Heb neb yn galw am ladd ei gilydd.

Bu i luoedd Napoleon,
Gelynion creulon cras,   90
Ddisbinio gwlad Hisbania
A'r fro o Italia fras
A mynnu holl Germania
Â Phrwsia wych ei gwedd

"He was sent before to Elba,
and again this year to Saint Helena."

If your leader departed thus   65
do not ever more, Frenchmen,
muster your men to the battlefield,
but learn to hold your peace and be silent.

And may God give you someone
according to His judgement as king,   70
who takes God's Book as a rule
without believing the pope who deceives people.

Let us hope that the red fields
and the sum of the slaughtered
shall cause everyone to abhor war   75
and to keep Boney captive evermore.

At Waterloo there was a roar and a massacre,
do not doubt, even though you are here;
stories say that eighty thousand men
were killed there!!!   80

[The betrayer of the Isle of Britain
deserves not a scowl but to have his windpipe broken;
he has been the cause of the death of myriads
for twenty years now!]

But instead of lamenting, men, sing!   85
It appears today that peace will come.
May the Gospel of grace go through the lands,
without anyone calling for the killing of each other.

Napoleon's hosts,
cruel, harsh enemies,   90
pillaged the land of Spain
and the boundary of fertile Italy
and claimed the whole of Germany
and magnificent Prussia,

Yn hylaw gyda Holand,   95
Heb warant glau ond cledd.

Sources, publication details and document titles:

A: BC, vol. 12, no. 17; I. Davies, Trefriw, [1815]

B: Bangor 9 (24); I. Davies, Trefriw, [?1815]

C: Bangor 10 (18); Bangor 25 (132), incomplete; n.p., [?1815]; *Dwy o Gerddi Newyddion. 1, Ychydig o Hanes am Parry Bach, Cefnder i Ddic Sion Dafydd. [2,] Am y llwyddiant a g[afo]dd ein Milwyr ar Bonaparte A'i fyddin, yn Ffraingc.*

D: Bangor 25 (11); n.p., n.d.

Variants: stanzas 3–7 included in C and D only; stanza 21 included in B only.

dexterously together with Holland, 95
without true authority but a sword.

Undated

37. R[obert] Davies, 'Cân milisia Dinbych'
Tune: 'Trymder'

Milisia Dinbych, gwych eu gwedd,
 Gwlad Wynedd wen,
Bu gorfod inni godi o'n parth
 I gadw'n pen.
Ar ôl rhoi unwaith arfau i lawr   5
Mewn heddwch megis hanner awr,
Daeth uchel floedd i Brydain Fawr
 Barodol fyw;
A pharotoi cyffroad hir,
Arfau a thân ar fôr a thir,   10
Yn erbyn sain gelynion clir
 Sydd yn ein clyw.

Yr ordinhad a roed yn hy
 I gasglu gwŷr,
Rif y dail, aneirif dorf,   15
 Dan arfau dur;
I gario cleddau goleu a gwn
Trwy ofal hir y rhyfel hwn.
Mae pennau'r byd i gyd yn grwn
 Am godi'n gwraidd –   20
A'r rhain yw'r Ffrancod, anhoff ryw,
Sy am ddwyn ein lle a'n llongau a'n llyw;
Ond gyda Duw tra bo ni byw,
 Nid neb a faidd.

O'n gwlad yn awr y'n galwyd ni   25
 Er gwylied nerth,
I gadw'n tir a'n coron wir –
 Rhai cywrain werth.
Yn iach i'n clau fynyddau ni,
Llwyni a bronnydd llawn eu bri;   30
Gwlad Cymry hen nis gwelwn ni
 Rhawg drwyddi dro.
I waelod Lloegr, mewn pellhad,
Teithiasom ni dan g'ledi o'n gwlad,

Undated

37. R[obert] Davies, 'Song of the Denbighshire militia'
Tune: 'Trymder'

The militia of Denbigh, splendid their appearance,
blessed country of Gwynedd,
we had to get up from our patch
to protect our leader.
Having once put our arms down   5
in a peace which lasted as if half an hour,
a loud cry came to Great Britain
to live in preparation;
and prepare for a long agitation,
arms and fire on sea and land,   10
against the clear sound of enemies
which is in our hearing.

The order was boldly given
to raise men
in large numbers, a countless crowd,   15
under steel arms;
to carry bright sword and gun
through the long anxiety of this war.
The leaders of the whole wide world
wish to uproot us –   20
and these are the Frenchmen, a nasty breed,
who wish to take our place and our ships and our leader;
but God being with us as long as we live,
no one will dare do so.

From our country we have now been called   25
in order to watch for a host,
to defend our land and our true crown –
most valuable things.
Farewell to our outstanding mountains,
shrubs and hill-sides of great renown;   30
we shall not see the old country of the Welsh
for a very long time.
To the depths of England, distancing ourselves,
did we travel in hardship from our country,

I gyffwrdd gelyn, blaena' brad,   35
    Sy'n blino'n bro.

Wel, gyda Duw ein Ceidwad, awn,
    Yn llawn un llu;
Ar dir a môr, byddinoedd Siôr
    Llwyddiannus sy.   40
Daeth drwy dre' Lundain (glodsain glir)
Dros dri ugain saith o flodau'n sir –
Planhigion harddwych Dinbych dir
    Gaiff hir goffâd;
Ac yn blaenori â'i gleddyf noeth   45
Ein colonel oedd (un cyhoedd, coeth) –
Syr Watkin Williams Wynn, naws doeth,
    O Wynnstay.

Ein Colonel Lloyd Salusbury lân,
    Gallt Faenan fwys,   50
A'n Major Foulkes, oedd hyfryd lawn
    O Briviate lwys;
A'n deuddeg cadpen, lawen ddrych,
A'n meddyg Hughes, un moddog gwych,
A'n pen swyddogion megis clych   55
    Mewn ymgais clwm.
Sergentau, corpols, gwŷr ynghyd,
Cymry un fron – cymerwn fryd
I deithio'r byd, â'i loesau drud,
    Wrth lais y drwm.   60

Gwŷr ieuainc Cymru, hyfion lu,
    Mae'n harfau'n lân,
Wedi ymroi i ymbarotoi
    Yn erbyn tân.
Dangoswn beth yw'n swydd i'r byd   65
Mewn parodrwydd pur o hyd;
Os na bydd eisiau, gorau i gyd,
    Mewn c'ledfyd clwy.
Mae gobaith mab o ryfel, medd
Y geiriau gynt, gywiraf gwedd;   70
Ond nid oes gobaith neb o fedd,
    Ac ni bydd mwy.

to meet an enemy, greatest treachery,   35
who threatens our land.

Well, with God our Saviour we go,
fully as a single force;
on land and sea, George's armies
are successful.   40
Through the town of London (clear sound of praise)
over seven times three score of the flowers of our county came –
the splendid plants of the land of Denbigh
will long be remembered;
and leading with his unsheathed sword   45
was our colonel (a refined public figure) –
Sir Watkin Williams Wynn, wise nature,
of Wynnstay.

Our virtuous colonel, Lloyd Salusbury
of fair Gallt Faenan,   50
and our Major Foulkes, full of cheerfulness
from lovely Priviate;
and our twelve captains, fair spectacle,
and our doctor Hughes, a fine-mannered man,
and our chief officers like bells   55
working in harmony.
Sergeants, corporals, men together,
Welshmen of one heart – let us make up our minds
to travel the world, with its heavy pains,
to the voice of the drum.   60

The young men of Wales, a bold host,
our arms are fair,
dedicated to prepare
against fire.
Let us show what our role is to the world   65
in true readiness always;
if there should be no need, all the better,
in a world of hardship and injury.
A son of war has hope, say
the old words, quite rightly;   70
but there is no hope for anyone from the grave,
nor shall there be any more.

Pob geneth ifanc wych a chall,
    Yn iach i chwi,
Mae rhyfel mawr a blin iawn awr   75
    O'n blaenau ni!
A'r rhai adawsom yn ein gwlad,
Gweddïwch gyda ni'n ddi-wad –
Chwiorydd, brodyr, mam a thad,
    Coffâd di-ffôl.   80
Nid allwn ganu 'mhell o'n plwy',
Ond yn ein gwlad, mewn hedd di-glwy,
Ni ganwn fwy, trwy ddawn ein nwy,
    Pan ddown yn ôl.

Ymlaen yr awn mewn diau dawn   85
    Er dued yw;
Pwy ŵyr, dan rhod, nad allwn ddod
    Yn ôl yn fyw?
Cydsobrwn, teimlwn, ar ein taith –
O'n blaenau mae myrddiynau maith   90
(Nid esgus chwaith, argoelion llaith)
    Y gelyn llym.
Os trefnwyd ni gan Ti, Dduw'r Tad,
I roddi ein bywyd dros ein gwlad,
O! derbyn ni i'th drugaredd rad,   95
    Dragywydd rym.

Sources, publication details and document titles:

A: BC, vol. 2, no. 122; J. Jones, Llanrwst, n.d.

B: Welsh Ballads Online (Cardiff University); J. Jones, Llanrwst, n.d.

C: JDL 116a; n.p., n.d.

Variants: 5. C – un waith rhoi; 31. C – Gwlad Cymru.

Every beautiful and sensible young girl,
farewell to you,
a great war and a very painful hour   75
lies ahead of us!
And those whom we left in our country,
pray with us willingly –
sisters, brothers, mother and father,
a mindful commemoration.   80
We cannot sing far away from our parish,
but in our country, in time of peace and security,
we shall sing more, through the power of our passion,
when we come back.

Forward we go, in certain grace   85
even though it is so dark;
who knows, under the firmament, that we may not come
back alive?
Let us become earnest and feel together on our journey –
ahead of us lie the countless scores   90
(not sham ones either, cold forewarnings)
of the fierce enemy.
If we were destined by You, God the Father,
to give our lives for our country,
Oh! receive us into Your generous mercy,   95
everlasting power.

38. *Robert Morris, 'Cerdd i filisia Cymru'*
Tune: *'Mynediad i'r Tir Teg'*

Milisia ffyddlon Gwynedd dirion,
    Rai dewrion yn eu dydd,
[B]yddin arfog dan Siôr enwog,
    Chwi ddynion serchog sydd;
[E]ich anrhegu rwyf i o Gymru   5
    A gyrru hyn o gân,
[F]y hen gymdeithion gwiwlon golau,
    Â gwir galonnau glân.
[R]hof glod a nod yn awr
    I'r fyddin enwog fawr,   10
[I] chwi, milisia, sydd yn hardda',
    Rai llonna' ar y llawr –
[M]yned drosom, er maint y dryswch,
    Gael inni heddwch hir;
[Rh]wystro estron hen elynion,   15
    Rai taenion, ddod i'n tir.
[--] ni sydd gartre', heb gur,
    Cael llawndra o'r bara a'r bur;
[Ch]witheu'n buredd, hwyr a borau,
    Yn dal yr arfau dur;   20
[-] mae milwyr, brodyr Brydain,
    Rai cywrain o wŷr call,
[Rh]ag i'r Ffrancod roddi dyrnod
    Gyda gormod gwall.

[--] bod tadau gyda mamau   25
    Yn wylo dagrau dwys,
[A]eth llawer bachgen, yn oer ei ddichwen,
    Oddi wrth fun loerwen lwys;
Er bod gwragedd salw'u sylwedd,
    Â'u gwedd yn ddigon gwael,   30
Cymerwch galon – mae pawb yn foddlon
    A ffyddlon yn ddiffael.
Er bod y Ffrancod ffrost
    Yn bygwth yn eu bost,
Lle byddo gafal Duw, mae'n atal,   35
    Ni ddaw un dial tost.
Mae rhagluniaeth Duw yn helaeth,

38. Robert Morris, 'A song to the militia of Wales'
Tune: 'Belisle March'

The faithful militia of sweet Gwynedd,
brave ones in their day,
an armed host under glorious George,
you are amiable men;
I offer you a gift from Wales   5
and send this song,
my old excellent, bright companions,
with truly honest hearts.
I give praise and renown now
to the great, famous army,   10
to you, the militia, who are the most splendid
and vigorous ones on earth —
going on our behalf, despite the difficulty,
to secure a long-lasting peace for us;
preventing old, foreign enemies,   15
from spreading to our land.
So that we who are at home, without affliction,
should have an abundance of bread and beer;
you, on the other hand, faithfully, evening and morning,
hold the lead arms;   20
[-] are the soldiers, brothers, of Britain,
skilful, sensible men,
lest the French should strike a blow
causing great destruction.

[--] that fathers and mothers   25
are crying grave tears,
many a lad, dejected his countenance, has gone
from a fair girl of moon-like beauty;
although there are wives in an unhealthy condition,
their countenance wretched enough,   30
take heart — everyone is ready
and faithful without fail.
Even though the bragging French
threaten in their boast,
where God's hold remains, He prevents   35
so that no bitter revenge comes.
God's providence is extensive,

I'r diffaeth gael un darn;
Nid yw Ei 'wllys Ef na'i allu
      Ddim ond addfedu'r Farn.   40
Y chwi yw'r gweis a gaed,
      Rai trefnus o wŷr traed,
I gadw'n ffyddlon ein teyrnas dirion
      Rhag colli'n wirion waed;
Os daw'r Galiaid, wallus williaid,   45
      Fel bleiddiaid mawr eu blys,
Gwnawn eu curo, fel rhai cywrain,
      O Frydain oll ar frys.

Mae clod nodidog fod Cymry'n llidiog
      Ac yn enwog iawn,   50
A da osgo rai diysgog
      Am bob ardderchog ddawn.
Am hyn diolchwn – ymostyngwn
      Ac na falchïwn chwaith;
Mae Duw, â thyner da ddoethineb,   55
      Ag wyneb ar bob gwaith.
Rhag unrhyw gynnen gainc,
      Sef erchyll ffrewyll Ffrainc,
Boed Siôr yn eistedd mewn gwirionedd
      Trwy fawredd ar ei fainc.   60
Doed awdurdod oddi uchod
      I dreiddio'r Ffrancod draw,
A ninnau'n unol, rai ufuddol,
      O dan ei lesol law.
Chwi, gwŷr a llanciau glân,   65
      Rhaid tynnu'n nesa' i'r tân;
Dymuno llwyddiant rwyf i'n ddiffuant
      A mwyniant fawr a mân,
A gras 'n [?rym] heb groes etifedd
      Tu fewn i'w annedd ef;   70
Ond purdeb calon i Siôr a'i goron
      Yn union dan y nef.

Mae dillad cochion yn arwyddion
      Fod creulon fywyd croes;
Yr heddwch mwynlan a rhydd-did purlan   75
      'N druan iawn a droes.

so that the wicked get one part;
neither His will nor His might
are anything but the fulfilment of the Judgement. 40
You are the servants that were found,
orderly infantry,
faithfully to protect our gracious kingdom
lest innocent blood should be shed;
if the Gauls, sinful brigands, should come 45
like ravenous wolves,
we will beat them all, like skilful ones,
out of Britain in a hurry.

There is a notable reputation that the Welsh are fierce
and very worthy of praise, 50
and it is good that there are untrembling ones
for each excellent blessing.
For this let us give thanks – let us stoop
and let us not grow proud either;
God, with good, gentle, wisdom, 55
keeps an eye on every action.
Against any attack of contention,
namely the hideous scourge of France,
may George remain in truth
through greatness upon his throne. 60
May authority come from above
to pierce the French, yonder,
and we united, obedient ones,
under his beneficial hand.
You, virtuous men and lads, 65
must draw right up to the fire;
I sincerely wish success
and joy to great and small,
and grace as a power without an opposing heir
within his dwelling; 70
but purity of heart to George and his crown,
righteously under heaven.

Red uniforms are signs
that this is a time of cruel adversity;
the pleasant peace and faultless liberty 75
have turned very wretched.

Os rhaid curo'r drwm i ruo
   Er deffro llawer llun,
A phibau miwsig a phob mesur
   Er denu natur dyn –   80
Na ddigalonwch, chwaith,
   Y milwyr, mwynwyr maith;
Byddwch foddlon ym mhob gorchwylion,
   Rai tirion, ar eich taith.
Na thynnwch aflw'dd oddi wrth yr Arglwydd   85
   Oherwydd aflan haid,
[W]rth hyderu yn eich gallu
   Ac Ef yn peri paid;
A byddwch oll i gyd
   Dros Frydain o un fryd,   90
A rhowch grediniaeth yn rhagluniaeth,
   Hen bennaeth mawr y byd.
Nid eill arfau, er dull eurfodd,
   Er gwirfodd, wared gŵr;
Ym mhob dialedd mawr a dilyw,   95
   Mae enw Duw yn dŵr.

Daw amser eto i flodeuo,
   I chwi gael rhodio'n rhydd;
Pan ddelo'r amser, chwi gewch bleser
   Trwy fwynder mawr a ffydd;   100
Os rhaid curo yn erbyn cawri
   Mae gweddi'n oreu gwaith –
Mae gan yr Arglwydd arwydd euraid
   Wrth weled llygad llaith.
Ceir heddwch cyn pen hir,   105
   Tawelwch yn ein tir;
Dowch eto'n oleu at eich hanwylyd,
   Heb symud dim o'ch sir.
Er bod gelynion yn ymryson
   Am gael y goron gu,   110
Mae Iôr uchelder yn Ei burder,
   Un tyner, eto o'n tu.
Y rhydd-did gyda'r hedd
   A safo yn ei sedd,
Gan ymledu a chartrefu   115
   Drwy Gymru, wiwgu wedd;

If the drum must be beaten to roar
in order to awaken many a figure,
and the pipes of music and every metre sounded
in order to arouse man's nature –   80
do not dishearten, either,
soldiers, noble host;
be satisfied in every task,
gracious ones, upon your journey.
Do not draw adversity from the Lord   85
on account of a vile hoard,
by presuming upon your might
while He causes you to stop;
and may you one and all
be unanimous on Britain's behalf,   90
and put your trust in providence,
the great, old ruler of the world.
Arms cannot, despite a grand manner,
however willing, give deliverance;
in every great vengeance and deluge,   95
God's name is a tower.

A time will come again to prosper,
so that you can roam freely;
when the time comes, you shall have pleasure
through great tenderness and faith;   100
if we must contend with giants
prayer is the best act –
the Lord has a golden sign
when He sees a wet eye.
There will be peace before long,   105
tranquillity in our land;
you shall yet come brightly to your dear one,
without moving at all from your county.
Although enemies contend
for possession of the precious crown,   110
the Lord on high in His purity,
gentle one, is yet on our side.
May freedom together with peace
stand upon his throne,
spreading and settling   115
throughout the lovely land of Wales;

Poed cariad brawdol yn wastadol
   A siriol, yn ddi–sen,
A doed cytundeb hardd ei gwyneb
   Am undeb mwy, Amen   120

Source: Welsh Ballads Online (LlGC, JHD xii.121)

Publication: n.p., n.d.

Document title: *Dwy Gerdd Ddiddan, Yn Gyntaf Hanes un Sian Niclason merch i Farchog yn Llundain yr hon drwy demptiad Satan a amcanodd wenwyno ei thâd a'i Mam, ond Duw a ddanfonodd ei Angel attynt i ddatguddio'r dirgelwch, Yn ail Cerdd i Filittia cymry ar don a elwir Mynediad i'r tîr teg neu Belisle March.*

Textual readings: 51. osgei; 75. rhydid; 100. fydd

may there be brotherly love continually
and cheerfully, without abuse,
and may fair-faced agreement come
for unity henceforth, Amen.					120

Notes to the Texts

1.

Publication:
John Ross (1729–1807) was trained as a printer in London, and moved to Carmarthen to follow his trade in 1763, initially working in partnership with Rhys Thomas. Other partnerships followed: with John Daniel during 1791–4 and possibly also in 1800, and with a printer named Lewis in 1799. Compared to his contemporaries, Ross's output was impressively large. It included the publication in 1770 of the controversial Methodist Peter Williams's edition of the Bible, an achievement involving much labour and expense. *DWB*, s.n. John Ross; Peter Williams (1723–96); *LW*, II, pp. 870–1.

Prose introduction:
the change of government which took place in this island in the year 1688 The reign of James II, between 1685 and 1689, proved a turbulent one in Great Britain. James attempted to transform his country into a modern Catholic state, on the model of France, but in so doing found himself at odds with revolutionary opponents, intent on creating a less absolutist and more tolerant state on the model of the Dutch Republic. Although the traditional account, promoted by Macaulay in the mid-nineteenth century, claimed that the Glorious Revolution was a bloodless affair and in fact hardly a revolution at all, modern historiography questions this, suggesting instead that it was the first modern revolution, which had resonances beyond Britain, not least in the France of the pre-Revolutionary years. Steve Pincus, *1688: The First Modern Revolution* (London, 2009); Keith Michael Baker, *Inventing the French Revolution* (Cambridge, 1990), pp. 173, 175, 207.

The Glorious Revolution was celebrated among Dissenters as a triumph over Stuart tyranny and for providing a starting point for religious toleration for communities of worshippers outside the Church of England. Richard Price's *A Discourse on the Love of our Country* was delivered to the Society for Commemorating the Revolution in Great Britain in November 1789, yet found occasion to criticize the limitations of the 1688 Revolution, noting that the repressive Test Laws were still in force and continued to discriminate against Dissenters. Price and others saw the Revolution in France as an opportunity to bolster support in Britain for efforts to correct the deficiencies of the British constitution. D. O. Thomas (ed.), *Price: Political Writings* (Cambridge, 1991), pp. 176–96; Mark Philp, 'Introduction', in *idem* (ed.), *The French Revolution and British Popular Politics* (Cambridge, 1991), pp. 2–3.

Pretender This may refer to either James Edward Stuart ('The Old Pretender'; 1688–1766) or his son, Charles Edward Stuart ('The Young Pretender'; 1720–88). The former staged an invasion of Scotland in 1715, eliciting support there and in northern England; while the latter invaded Britain in 1745, marching southwards to within 140 miles of London in an attempt to overthrow the Hanoverian king, George II. Both died in exile, their dynastic ambitions unfulfilled. *ODNB*; Linda Colley, *Britons: Forging the Nation 1707–1837* (New Haven, 1992), pp. 77, 82–3.

line 53 (ballad's note to) Louis XVI was granted the title 'King of the French' by the 1791 Constitution (which he himself ratified on 13 September that year). It severely limited his powers, but was not deemed radical enough for the sweep of revolutionary fervour gripping France during the early 1790s: Louis was suspended from office on 10 August 1792 and the monarchy abolished on 21–2 September the same year. By the time the next Constitution had been created in June 1793, declaring France a republic, Louis had been executed. Colin Jones, *The Longman Companion to the French Revolution* (Harlow, 1988), pp. 66–71; and for Louis XVI's execution, see further note to no. 3.

Holland, known as the United Provinces, was invaded by France in February 1793, and further in 1794–5. Only at the Treaty of the Hague on 16 May 1795 was it transformed into the Batavian Republic, a 'sister republic' to France, ruled and occupied by it. Venice retained its neutrality in the Europe-wide conflict brought about by the Revolution, recognizing France as a republic in late 1793. It was nonetheless divided between France and other republican states in October 1797. Ibid., p. 135.

The American colonies declared their independence from Great Britain in 1776. More than a decade later, in 1787, representatives from each of the states of the new country came together at the Federalist Convention to create a Constitution for the United States of America. A general mistrust of a monarchical government on the one hand, and of excessive popular rule (or democracy as characterized by Aristotle) on the other, prevailed. The delegates instead showed a preference for the creation of a republic, which would involve the formation of a representative government unbounded by a hereditary executive. Ralph Ketcham (ed.), *The Anti-Federalist Papers and the Constitutional Convention Debates* (London, 1986), pp. 1–12.

line 76 'Tilots' is a reference to John Tillotson (1630–94), a Low Churchman whose voice was among those critical of the absolutism of the Stuart regime. A fervent anti-Catholic, Tillotson had strong Nonconformist sympathies and was much loved by Nonconformists. He was a favourite of the new king, William III, who appointed him archbishop of Canterbury in 1689, a post which he only reluctantly took up out of a sense of duty. He had argued that there was full justification for removing James II from power, since he had 'threatened our religion and laws, and the very constitution it self of our ancient government'. *ODNB*; Pincus, *1688: The First Modern Revolution*, pp. 167, 410, 416–17.

line 88 Missionary societies, promoting the spreading of the Gospel both domestically and abroad, were prominent in Britain from the middle of the eighteenth century. By *c.*1760, Methodists, Anglicans and Dissenters had created such societies. When the Baptists established a society originally named the Particular Baptist Missionary Society for Propagating the Gospel among the Heathen in 1792, the missionary society reached a new stage in its development. This society instigated professional practices, including the provision of training for their workforce, who included William Carey (1761–1834), their first missionary to Serampore in India in 1792. Further societies on the same model were established by Methodists and Anglicans during the 1790s. *ODNB*, s.n. William Carey (1761– 1834); Iain McCalman (ed.), *An Oxford Companion to the Romantic Age: British Culture 1776–1832* (Oxford, 1999), s.n. missionaries and missionary societies; H. Cernyw Williams, *William Carey, D.D, a chan'mlwyddiaeth cenadaeth y Bedyddwyr* (Llangollen, 1891).

Concluding prose section:
a general meeting of Protestant Dissenting ministers Meetings intended to display the loyalty of Nonconformists (especially those involved in the work of the Reform Societies) were held in every part of Wales during 1793. John James Evans, *Dylanwad y Chwyldro Ffrengig ar Lenyddiaeth Cymru* (Lerpwl, 1928), pp. 120–2.

William Williams A Pembrokeshire-born Anglican, William Williams (1732–99) became attracted to the Baptist faith in his late twenties and was soon afterwards preaching in the Baptist cause. By 1774 he had moved to Cardigan where he founded two Baptist chapels (in 1775–6 and 1797 respectively) and, despite

being a Nonconformist, managed to secure himself a seat on the benches of
both Pembroke and Cardiganshire quarter sessions. In 1792 he assisted Morgan
John Rhys in his plan to send Bibles to France, but when war broke out in 1793,
he was one of the foremost arrangers of the meeting of Protestant Nonconformists
from which this ballad emanated. He was a keen pamphleteer and a contributor
to *Y Cylchgrawn Cymraeg*. He also appears to have written at least one poem,
which refuted the practice of ranting among the members of his first congregation
at Ebenezer chapel in Llanfair Nantglyn, Pembrokeshire. It is possible that he
was the author of the ballad in question here, although this cannot be proven.
DWB, s.n. William Williams (1732–99).

inserted in the English Chronicle, *the Bristol and Hereford papers* The report of the
meeting appeared in the *Hereford Journal* on 27 February 1793. I am grateful to
Dr Marion Löffler for this information.

2.

The pamphlet named in the title of this ballad was *One Penny-worth of Truth from
Thomas Bull to his Brother John* (1792), the work of the High Anglican cleric,
William Jones of Nayland (1726–1800). Jones's *One Penny-worth* was only one
of a flood of counter-revolutionary pamphlets published between November
1792 and January 1793, following the establishment in London by John Reeves
of the Association for Preserving Liberty and Property against Republicans and
Levellers. The Association promoted and financed the publication of pamphlets
designed to reveal the iniquities of the Revolution in France and the essential
superiority of the British constitution. Jones's pamphlet has been described as
one of the 'cruder' products of this whirl of activity, deliberately intended to
reach and influence the lower classes. Robert Hole, 'British Counter-revolutionary
Popular Propaganda in the 1790s', in Colin Jones (ed.), *Britain and Revolutionary
France: Conflict, Subversion and Propaganda* (Exeter, 1983), pp. 53–69.

The pamphlet was translated into Welsh probably in early 1793, and distributed
in Carmarthenshire, a fact which reflects the anxiety of civic leaders about the
possible influence of Painite sentiments on ordinary people in the county. Its
circulation is signalled in the following from a letter, dated 25 February 1793,
from David Thomas, Llwynwermwnt, to his brother Benjamin at Wellington in
Somerset:

Mae'n debig fod rhyw gyffroad mawr yn gyffredin trwy'r wlâd ynghylch y Revolution
ag mae'n debig fod llawer o Argraffu papurau bychain o amriw fâth yn Saesonaeg
a Chymraeg gwelais dri mâth o rai Cymraeg titl un ydoedd C[nio]gwerth o wirionedd

mewn ffordd o Lythyr yn canmol trefn y Llywodraeth ag yn dangos ffolineb Fraingc yn gw[n]euthur Revolution ai bod wedi dechreu y's 4 blynedd ag heb fawr argol i ddibenu etto a llawer mwy traulfawr na chadw'r Brenin &c.

(There seems to be some great commotion common throughout the country regarding the Revolution, and there are apparently a great deal of little pamphlets of various kinds in English and Welsh being published. I saw three Welsh ones. The title of one was *One Penny-worth of Truth* in the form of a letter praising the form of the government and showing France's folly in having a Revolution, and that they had started it four years ago and were without the slightest indication that it will yet come to an end; and it is much more costly than keeping the king, &c.)

NLW 7166D, no. 300.

On the letter and the translation of the pamphlet (which has not survived), see Hywel M. Davies, 'Loyalism in Wales, 1792–1793', *WHR*, 20, no. 4 (2001), 687–716.

In view of the widespread paranoia at the time regarding 'radical' thinking, it is no surprise that the ballad contains no imprint citing place and agent of publication. There is every reason to suppose, however, that it also originated in Carmarthenshire. Some features of the language confirm this view, suggesting a south Wales provenance, e.g. 'bla'n', 'erio'd'.

lines 7–9 'Our father, you know, always maintained the character of a blunt, honest, sensible man; and our mother was as good a sort of woman as ever lived.' [William Jones], *One Penny-worth of Truth from Thomas Bull, to his Brother John*, in *Liberty and Property Preserved against Republicans and Levellers: A Collection of Tracts Number I* (London, 1793), p. 1.

lines 17–18 The defensive stance of the poet in relation to Dissenters is a firm indication that he was himself a Dissenter. There is no direct reference to Dissenters in Jones's pamphlet, and it only turns to contemplate those voices within Britain which oppose its own views and allegedly support the Revolution at the end, with a diatribe against those who, he claims, brought about the American War of Independence (1775–83). See lines 21–2.

line 77 The reference to 'Sersia', possibly 'Serfia', is difficult to explain.

3.

Author:

It is probable that there were two eighteenth-century ballad writers of the name Richard Roberts, one working during the 1740s, and the other, with whom this anthology is concerned, working in the late 1780s and the 1790s. The latter may have originally worked as a ballad seller, later beginning to capitalize on the opportunities offered by this itinerant trade to compose and distribute (perhaps even to sing) his own work. He describes himself at the foot of the Trefriw imprint of this ballad as a 'baledwr', a term which recent research by A. Cynfael Lake reveals to have related during the eighteenth century to the seller of ballads rather than the poets ('prydyddion') who created them. Roberts's output includes nos. 3, 7, 8 and 20 in the current anthology, all on topical subjects relating to the upheaval of the 1790s. He also sang religious poems, which were printed in [1787], 1792 and 1794 (JHD nos. 451i, 294i and 270i). His publishers were almost exclusively based in north and mid Wales and in the border town of Oswestry, which strongly suggests that he hailed from these regions. Cronfa Baledi; A. Cynfael Lake, 'Evan Ellis, "Gwerthwr llyfrau a British Oil &c."', *Y Traethodydd*, CXLIV, no. 613 (1989), 204–14; *idem*, 'William Jones a'r "ddau leidir baledae"', *Llên Cymru*, 33 (2010), 124–42, esp. 125.

Publication:

Ishmael Davies (1758–1817) succeeded his father Dafydd Jones (Dewi Fardd), to a printing business in Trefriw in the Vale of Conwy, upon the latter's death in 1785. Thomas Parry maintained that Ishmael Davies's work excelled that of his father. In a more recent survey of the work of three generations of printers from this family, however, Gerald Morgan disputed this claim, arguing that the standard of printing from the Trefriw press only improved when Ishmael's son, John Jones, returned home to work for the business in 1810–11. During the years of collaboration between Ishmael and his son, work by a great variety of poets was published, this in contrast to the practice of Dafydd Jones, who, at least from the ballad perspective, published the work of a rather limited spectrum of poets. *LW*, II, p. 849; Gerald Morgan, 'Baledi Dyffryn Conwy', *Canu Gwerin*, 20 (1997), 2–12.

Titus Evans was probably not brought up to the printer's craft and his work is generally considered to be poor in quality. He was the first to set up a press in Montgomeryshire, at Machynlleth, his earliest known imprint dating from the year 1789. He simultaneously worked as an excise officer and was promoted to a post in Barmouth in June 1793, where he continued also to work as a printer until his dismissal from office in May 1796. It has been suggested that he thereafter emigrated to America, possibly because of fear of persecution for the promotion of radical views, but there does not appear to be a consensus on this point. James

Ifano Jones, *A History of Printing and Printers in Wales to 1810, and of Successive and Related Printers to 1923: Also, A History of Printing and Printers in Monmouthshire to 1923* (Cardiff, 1925), pp. 136–7; Richard Jones, 'Gwaith Argraffwyr Machynlleth o 1789 Ymlaen', *JWBS*, XI, no. 1 (1958), 25–8; Gwyn A. Williams, *The Search for Beulah Land: The Welsh and the Atlantic Revolution* (New York, 1980), p. 65.

Anna Hughes (née Aldford) printed in Wrexham between 1793 and 1824, succeeding her husband, John Hughes (d. 1792), previously a bookseller and printer in the town. She married Joseph Tye, who was also a printer, in 1794, but was widowed again during 1796. *LW*, II, pp. 856, 875. Anna Hughes's lack of experience in directing print work may account for the poor quality of the printing of this ballad. Jones, *A History of Printing and Printers in Wales*, pp. 122–3.

Tune:

'Duw Gadwo'r Brenin' or 'God Save the King' originated among supporters of the Stuart dynasty, exiled from Britain at the Glorious Revolution. When Charles Edward Stuart invaded Britain in 1745, however, the song was taken up by the staunchly Protestant subjects of the reigning Hanoverian king, George II. It was widely distributed in newspapers, monthly magazines and broadsides and sung in church services and by ballad singers, and aided in rallying support for the protection of Britain against the Catholic threat of the Stuarts. Its popularity waned thereafter, with no more than four scheduled performances in the London theatres between 1760 and 1781. The next twenty years saw yet another reversal in its fortunes, with more than ninety performances and, by the early 1800s, it was being described as the British 'national anthem'. Not only was it sung by conservative loyalists, however, but radicals also claimed their share of it, sometimes with ironic intent.

In Wales, the tune 'Duw Gadwo'r Brenin' was adapted rhythmically to fit the metre of the poetry composed to it. Three different metres claimed the name, and the tune became popular from the late eighteenth century onwards. Almost all the examples of 'Duw Gadwo'r Brenin' found in this anthology can be set to a single version of the song (in triple time). This is the version named as 'God Save the King the old way' in ballad no. 27. The exception in this anthology is ballad no. 3, which calls for a different tune. It corresponds to the metre described by Hugh Hughes (Tegai) in *Gramadeg Barddoniaeth* (1862) as 'Duw Gadwo'r Brenin (Ffordd Gwynedd)' (God Save the King (the Gwynedd Way)), and can be set to a melody more closely corresponding to the English national anthem, such as the mid-Victorian 'Duw Gadwo'r Frenhines' (God Save the Queen) published in J. D. Jones's *Caniadau Bethlehem*. D. Roy Saer, 'Carol y Cymro ac Anthem y Sais', *Welsh Music*, VII, no. 9/10 (1985), 6–19; Phyllis Kinney, 'The Tunes of the Welsh Christmas Carols (II)', *Canu Gwerin*, 12 (1989), 7–8; Colley,

Britons: Forging the Nation, pp. 46–7, 224, 357; J. D. Jones, *Caniadau Bethlehem; yn Cynnwys Carolau Nadolig, Gan Brif Feirdd Cymru; Gyda Thonau Priodol, Wedi eu Cynganeddu a'u Trefnu i Wahanol Leisiau* (Rhuthun, 1857), p. 16.

line 32 'Louis made a will, in which he asked the pardon of God' for his own connivance with the Civil Constitution of the Clergy. Anon., *Massacre of the French King* (London, 1793), p. 1.

lines 43–4 '[H]e asked the valet to give his wedding ring to the Queen.' Simon Schama, *Citizens: A Chronicle of the French Revolution* (1989; London, 2004), p. 565.

lines 46–7 'I pardon those who have brought about my death', words quoted by Schama, in ibid., p. 566.

line 50 The reference to 'siaffer' may be an attempt at describing the guillotine, envisioning it as a 'chafing-dish', perhaps since it was a raised contraption upon which stood the circular shaped 'lunette' (into which the victim would place his or her neck prior to its being severed by a descending blade). Note that Hugh Jones, Glan Conwy, in an interlude set in Revolutionary France, did not name the guillotine as instrument of execution in the cases of Louis and his wife. They are placed on their stomachs, and their heads cut off. In Louis's case the instrument of cutting is specified as an axe. See Hugh Jones, *Gwedd o Chwareydd-iaeth sef Hanes Bywyd a Marwolaeth, Brenhin, a Brenhines Ffraingc* (Trefriw, 1798), pp. 44, 46, 51. The writers of *Y Cylchgrawn Cynmraeg*, on the other hand, did know of the guillotine, reporting the execution of the French queen, 'Y dywysoges anffortenus hon a ddioddefodd dan gyllell y guillotine dydd merchur yr unfed ar bymtheg o Hydref' (This unfortunate princess suffered under the knife of the guillotine on the sixteenth of October). *Y Cylchgrawn Cynmraeg*, III (August 1793), 237.

lines 53–4 Louis 'asked . . . if Cléry might not cut his hair to spare him the indignity of being cropped on the scaffold', but his request was not granted and he underwent a haircut in full view of the crowd. Accounts of spectators dipping their handkerchief in his blood have survived. Schama, *Citizens: A Chronicle of the French Revolution*, pp. 565, 566, 567.

lines 57–62 Louis's head and body were transported to the Madeleine, placed in a plain wooden coffin, as for the burials of the poorest, covered with quicklime and buried in a ten foot deep grave. Ibid., p. 568. Richard Roberts's four yards' grave is slightly deeper, corresponding to twelve feet.

line 67 The significance of these words is not clear. They may be interpreted as meaning that Louis was buried with the friends of God, his Father (rather than his human father) – that is, the poorest of the poor.

lines 71–5 The ballad writer notes the exact date of the execution, 21 January 1793. Inserting dates into metrical forms within free-metre Welsh poetry was a very common feat by ballad-writers and other poets. Cf. no. 21, lines 179–86.

lines 81–4 Having portrayed with sympathy the death of the French monarch, Richard Roberts now recalls the typical Welsh attitude to Britain's foremost enemy. Described as the slave of Belial by Ellis Wynne in the classic prose text *Gweledigaetheu y Bardd Cwsc* at the beginning of the eighteenth century, he was also lambasted in the popular tradition of the Welsh almanac, spearheaded by the first almanac printer, Thomas Jones. Ellis Wynne, *Gweledigaetheu y Bardd Cwsc*, ed. by Aneirin Lewis (Caerdydd, 1976), p. 10; Geraint H. Jenkins, 'Almanaciau Thomas Jones 1680–1712', in *idem, Cadw Tŷ Mewn Cwmwl Tystion: Ysgrifau Hanes-yddol ar Grefydd a Diwylliant* (Llandysul, 1990), p. 67. In spite of Louis's death, the enmity between Britain and France needs to be upheld, Richard Roberts praying that no French king (or French ruler as things now stand) should ever reach the shores of Britain. The fear of invasion is reiterated in the final stanza.

lines 85–98 The voices of the faithful, rejoicing that Britain's king is alive and well by shouting intensely day and night are contrasted with very different voices who, the ballad writer hopes, will never come within his and his audience's hearing. The 'Evil bloodhounds' to whom he refers appear to be political radicals within Britain itself, an impression which is confirmed at the opening of stanza 8.

line 105 This refers to reactionary burnings of Tom Paine effigies in several Welsh towns, including Cardiff on 29 December 1792, Llanymddyfri, probably during February 1793, and Carmarthen. Davies, 'Loyalism in Wales, 1792–1793', 693–4. This followed the establishment of numerous loyalist associations across Wales. See ibid. For an account of the Cardiff burning, see Evans, *Dylanwad y Chwyldro Ffrengig ar Lenyddiaeth Cymru*, p. 115.

4.

Author:
Edward Pugh is named as 'ap fyllin fardd' three times in *BWB* (see pp. 97, 149, 151). The name suggests family origins in the area of Llanfyllin in Montgomeryshire.

His printed ballads include, in addition to the two presented in this anthology, 'Cerdd, o hanes mab i wr bonheddig, o Lancashire aeth i drafaelio . . .' (A poem recounting the story of the son of a gentleman from Lancashire who went travelling . . .). This was printed in Oswestry in 1791 (JHD 265), with two further Trefriw imprints, both undated (JHD 458ii and JHD 463i).

Publication:
For Ishmael Davies, Trefriw, see note to no. 3.

Tune:
'Belisle March', also known in other examples in this collection by the Welsh names of 'Mynediad i'r Ynys Deg' and 'Mynediad i'r Tir Teg' (Entry to the Fair Island and Entry to the Fair Land; see nos. 29 and 38), attained almost instant popularity in Wales following its first appearance in 1763, at the end of the Seven Years' War. A version from Cwrt Mawr Music MS 12, probably from Darowen in Montgomeryshire, *c.*1816, is reproduced in Phyllis Kinney, 'The Tunes of the Welsh Christmas Carols (I)', *Canu Gwerin*, 11 (1988), 49–50. This is difficult for the voice, perhaps not surprisingly in view of its origins as a military march. It does, however, fit the words of several ballads included in this anthology remarkably well.

Title:
Duke of York Frederick, duke of York and Albany (1763–1827), was the second son of George III and his wife, Charlotte. He was trained in the military abroad and, upon the outbreak of war against France in 1793, put in command of the British contingent in Flanders, who were to work alongside an Austrian army led by the prince of Coburg. The campaigns of 1793, 1794 and 1795 were military failures, and tended to prove the duke's inexperience and shortcomings as a commander. Nonetheless, he was appointed to further positions in the army in 1795, 1798 and 1799, none of which restored his reputation. In later years, the duke turned his attention to reforming aspects of army life. He was instrumental in establishing the Royal Military Asylum in Chelsea (1801–3), the Royal Military Academy in Woolwich, and a military school in High Wycombe. He worked to improve the lot of the common soldier, and to weed out favouritism and the promotion of incapable officers. *ODNB*, s.n. Frederick, Prince, duke of York and Albany (1763–1827); A. H. Burne, *The Noble Duke of York* (London, 1949).

The two ballads which mention the Duke of York in this anthology (nos. 4 and 5) portray him in a very favourable light. Welsh poets did not always represent the duke and his campaign thus, however. A certain William of Aber Llandyfodwg was brought before magistrates at Bridgend in Glamorgan for singing 'Cân i'r

Duwc o Yorc a brwydr yr Is-Almaen', a poem which included criticism of the recruitment effort:

'Roedd iraid gweled arwain
Dros fôr o Brydain Fawr
Ein gwŷr i diroedd dyrys
Dan ofal gelyn cyfrwys,
Lle lladdwyd miloedd, dyna'r modd,
Yn lluoedd 'r hyd y llawr.

Calonnau mewn gelyniaeth,
Arferiaeth trwy'r holl fyd,
Sy'n digwydd mae'n ddiogel
O achos dynion uchel,
Gan ddirwyn rhan o ddynolryw
I erch dreialon drud.

(It was woeful to see our men
being led overseas from Great Britain
to wicked lands
under the care of a cunning enemy,
where thousands were killed (that was the way)
in hosts along the ground.

Hearts become hostile –
a custom throughout the entire world –
because of important men
it is certain,
who draw a part of humankind
into awful, ruthless tribulations.)

Ben Bowen Thomas, *Drych y Baledwr* (Aberystwyth, 1958), p. 47. Thomas does not name his source.

line 17 This line probably refers to the duke's younger brother, Ernest Augustus (1771–1851), who was out in Flanders at the same time as him. After four years' study at the University of Göttingen, Ernest began a career in the military, entering the Ninth Hanoverian Hussars in 1790. He was later transferred to the Heavy Dragoons and then promoted major-general in the Hanoverian army in February 1794. He fought courageously in the Flanders and Netherlands campaign, reputedly carrying French officers off the field single-handedly in battles during August 1793 and November 1794, and sustaining a wound to his

arm at Tournai in May 1794. In later life, he became king of Hanover. *ODNB*;
Burne, *The Noble Duke of York*, pp. 64, 116, 136–7, 193, 195.

lines 21–4 The refrain can be compared with that of the English-language
recruitment song, 'The Valiant Hero' ([London], 1794): 'For the British lads
of England so merrily will go, / With the bold Duke of York, sir, that valiant
hero'. See BLBB. The choice of an English refrain suggests that the Duke of
York was entering the popular consciousness as a hero during 1793. Note also
that the Welsh are included in the roll-call of British nations. This is not always
the case in English-language poems, which tend to mention the three nations
of the English, Scots and Irish alone. See, for example, the ballad 'The Voice of
the British Isles', to be sung to the tune of 'Hearts of Oak', which names the
representative figures of Jack the Englishman, Pat the Irishman, and Sandy the
Scotsman, but omits any mention of a Welshman. Mary-Ann Constantine, 'Welsh
Ballads of the French Revolution' (unpublished paper delivered at the International
Ballad Conference, Cardiff, July 2008); anon., 'The Voice of the British Isles'
([London], n.d.), BLBB. Conversely, Robert Buchanan's anti-Painite text, 'A
Loyal Song', written in Scottish dialect, begins with an arousing exhortation
to 'Britons, ane an' a, / Wales, England, Scotia, / Loyally sing: / Lads o Hibernia's
isle, / In guid auld Scottish style, / Sing, wi' hearts free frae guile / God save
the King'. Robert Buchanan, *Poems on Several Occasions* (Edinburgh, 1797),
pp. 74–7.

line 26 'Valenseina' (later 'Val'seina' and 'tre' Caerseina') is the name coined by
Edward Pugh for the town of Valenciennes in north-east France. This was besieged
during July 1793 by joint Austrian and British troops under Frederick, duke of
York, and the prince of Saxe-Coburg. The former took a leading part in directing
the digging of trenches around the town walls and, after the town surrendered
on 28 July, was put in charge of the negotiations for surrender. He was handed
over the keys of the town and welcomed by its French inhabitants. See Burne,
The Noble Duke of York, pp. 55–60. Burne suggests that the siege 'attained world-
wide fame' as 'the most considerable operation carried out in the first campaign'.
Ibid., p. 57.

lines 27–8 A reference to Samuel Hood, first Viscount Hood (1724–1816), naval
officer, who was appointed commander-in-chief in the Mediterranean at the
outbreak of war in February 1793. Hood left Portsmouth in the *Victory* on
22 May 1793, with some talented protégés, including Horatio Nelson. He was
approached by French envoys from Marseille and Toulon asking for protection
against the Jacobin Parisian forces coming down from the north. On 23 August
1793 he offered Toulon military protection provided that it would proclaim

Louis XVII king. These terms were accepted, and on 27 August, after the sailors of the French Mediterranean fleet had also agreed to the same condition, the British fleet sailed into Toulon and coalition forces occupied the town, with no resistance. In September 1794, the French Republic began a three-and-a-half month long siege of Toulon, only attaining success on 17 December. The British staged a three-day evacuation of French Royalists and battleships from the town, but since Hood's fleet was scattered throughout the Mediterranean, only a third of it was present to assist. Hood came home in November 1794 and did not return after that to active service. *ODNB*, s.n. Samuel Hood, first Viscount Hood (1724–1816); William Doyle, *The Oxford History of the French Revolution* (2nd edn., Oxford, 2002), pp. 249, 254–5.

line 43 A reference to the departure of the Israelites from Egypt, as described in the Book of Exodus, following a sojourn of 430 years in the country under the oppression of its Pharaohs. Exodus 12: 40–1.

5.

Author:

The attribution of the ballad to Shôn ap Ifan, a poet from the lower Swansea valley, is made on the basis of the reminiscences of Llewelyn Llewelyn (Llewelyn Ddu), as recorded by D. Rhys Phillips. This counters the traditional attribution of the ballad to James Turberville (Iaco or Siemsyn Twrbil), reiterated by Ben Bowen Thomas in a 1951 publication. The story of the ballad's inception given by Phillips suggests that it was a ballad *about* rather than *by* Turberville. NLW, D. Rhys Phillips, 231; Ben Bowen Thomas (ed.), *Baledi Morgannwg* (Caerdydd, 1951), pp. 55–6, 117.

Publication:

For Ishmael Davies, Trefriw, see no. 3.

The earliest known imprint of this ballad is the undated text edited here, printed by Ishmael Davies, who was active at Trefriw between 1785 and 1817. The ballad became popular in the nineteenth century, and is found under the title 'Can ffarwel i Langyfelach lon; sef hanes am fachgen yn ymadael a'i wlad enedigol', printed alongside the song 'Myfyrdod ar lanau Conwy', which was composed by Ishmael Davies's son and his successor to the printing business, John Jones (Pyll Glan Conwy; 1786–1865). As many as sixteen imprints of 'Can ffarwel i Langyfelach lon' are listed on LlGC ISYS: Baledi at *http://isys.llgc.org.uk*. Only three of these record publication details – they were printed by W. Lloyd, Aberdare; Spurrell, Carmarthen; and T. Howells, Merthyr Tydfil.

Tune:

None is named. Penny Robinson, in an article on the genre of leave-taking poems, suggests that it may have originally been set to tunes from the 'Lisa Lân' family of songs. She offers a setting of the words on one such tune. See Penny Robinson, 'Caneuon Ffarwél', *Canu Gwerin*, 24 (2001), 60–3.

line 6 Cowbridge in the Vale of Glamorgan.

line 8 Recruitment into the army in this period was voluntary for most men, incarcerated debtors and felons, together with the vagrant unemployed and the idle excepted. Army recruiters frequented country fairs and public houses in urban areas in search of recruits, who would then commit themselves to seven, ten or twelve years or, more often, a lifetime's service. The conditions were not favourable in comparison with those of militia enlistment or of civilian life, and army recruiters frequently complained of being short of numbers. Nonetheless, a trend towards enlistment in the regular army after a period spent in the militia was apparent in the years 1807 to 1812. David Gates, 'The Transformation of the Army 1783–1815', in David G. Chandler and Ian Beckett (eds.), *The Oxford History of the British Army* (Oxford, 1994; paperback edn. 2003), pp. 133, 137–8; Stanley D. M. Carpenter, 'The British Army', in H. T. Dickinson (ed.), *A Companion to Eighteenth-Century Britain* (Oxford, 2002), p. 476.

This ballad may date from the earliest campaigns of the war against Revolutionary France. The Duke of York left for Flanders in February 1793; additional troops, numbering 10,000 men, were deployed to assist his efforts in July 1794. The existence of English recruitment songs such as 'The Valiant Hero' (BLBB), printed in 1794, which names the duke, suggests that recruitment efforts were particularly stepped up at that time and linked with the duke in public perception. However, York also shared command of the joint British and Russian corps who (unsuccessfully) fought in the 1799 Helder campaign, and it remains a possibility that the ballad relates to a later period.

line 11 Linda Colley notes the power of military music over ordinary people during this period. See Colley *Britons: Forging the Nation*, pp. 325–6. Volunteer companies would often have very limited musical resources. Research on music in Newcastle upon Tyne and its environs suggests that 'many seem to have consisted only of a drummer or a fife player or two' in that area, and ballad no. 29 (on the local militia of Caernarfonshire) mentions the presence of a drum only, although it implies that voices were raised in song in a typical corps' outing, too. Roz Southey, 'The Volunteer Band, Newcastle upon Tyne', in Mark Philp (ed.), *Resisting Napoleon: The British Response to the Threat of Invasion, 1797–1815* (Aldershot, 2006), p. 179.

Regular militia corps appear to have had greater variety of choice with regard to music. The Merionethshire militia were equipped with a military band, able to play the tunes of 'Boyne Water', 'Toriad y Dydd' and 'Taliesin's Prophecy' to delight the crowd as the corps left Bala for the south coast of England in 1815. Hugh J. Owen, *Merioneth Volunteers and Local Militia During the Napoleonic Wars (1795–1816)* (Dolgelley, [1934]), pp. 105–7. Records dated 1793–6 relating to the Denbighshire militia reveal that their musical resources were enhanced by the presence of a pedal harp, which suggests that regiments raised in Wales acquired a distinctly Welsh flavour. NLW, Chirk Castle: B Denbighshire Quarter Sessions Records 1. Manuscript volumes, no. 117. Further on Welsh cultural influences on militia regiments, see Glyn Ashton, 'Arolwg ar Brydyddiaeth Gymraeg, 1801–25', *Llên Cymru*, 14, nos. 3 and 4 (1983–4), 234, which notes that the subscription list to Robert Davies's *Barddoniaeth, yn cynnwys cerddi, cywyddau, ac ynglynion, ar amryw destunau* (Llundain, 1803) includes the name of the Denbighshire militia as subscribers for a hundred copies.

The ballad in question here, which centres on the presence of a regular army recruitment party, names only drum and fifes, but the presence of music is clearly a factor in persuading the young narrator to enlist.

line 12 The Light Dragoons, which originated in 1759, were cavalry regiments. They used smaller-sized horses and were intended to carry out reconnaissance and screening activity, and to help in the pursuit of enemies after the initial action against them carried out by the larger forces of the heavy cavalry. They would also dismount and fight as infantry during battle. Gates, 'The Transformation of the Army', p. 148; Carpenter, 'The British Army', p. 474.

6.

Sung on the metre of the 'hen bennill', used in the Welsh tradition for poetry expressing universal truths in a homespun manner, this is a general reflection on the onset of war against the French. It warns its audience against submitting to sins of many kinds, including swearing, blaspheming, lying, revelling, drunkenness and whoring, and suggests that it is sins such as these that incite God's wrath.

lines 21–4 These lines contribute to the prevalent theme of the 'internal enemy' found in several of the texts anthologized here. Although the poet does wish to raise the question of the internal enemy (probably to be characterized as the typical politicized radical Dissenter), he is also keen to put his greatest emphasis on the crucial importance of living a godly, sin-free life.

7.

Author:
For Richard Roberts, see note to no. 3.

Publication:
William Edwards was active as a printer in Oswestry between 1793 and 1810. *LW*, II, p. 893.

Tune:
Several versions of 'Gwêl yr Adeilad' are preserved in the John Jenkins (Ifor Ceri) manuscripts. See Daniel Huws, 'Melus-Seiniau Cymru: Atodiadau', *Canu Gwerin*, 9 (1986), 53–4. The tune is also included in the mid-eighteenth-century manuscript of the fiddler John Thomas. Its origins are English, and probably related to an early seventeenth-century ballad, which begins with the words 'See the building, / where whilest my mistris lived in, / was pleasure's essence'. Whereas it lost popularity in England after the mid-seventeenth century, it remained a favourite metre among Welsh poets from the seventeenth to the nineteenth centuries. They relished the challenge of its intricate metrical pattern. Kinney, 'The Tunes of the Welsh Christmas Carols (I)', 34–5; Cass Meurig (ed.), *Alawon John Thomas: A Fiddler's Tune Book from Eighteenth-Century Wales* (Aberystwyth, 2004), pp. 76, 147.

Title:
October 17, 1793 Marie Antoinette was in fact executed on Wednesday, 16 October. Antonia Fraser, *Marie Antoinette: The Journey* (2001; London, 2002), p. 526.

lines 17–18 This roughly dates the queen's imprisonment to 13 August 1792, when, together with her husband, sister-in-law and two children, she was placed in custody at the Temple in the Marais district of Paris, a location chosen by the Paris Commune following an attack on the Tuileries, the royal family's previous residence. The Temple included the prison-like structures of a Small and a Great Tower. Marie Antoinette had a particular fear of these, telling a friend upon their entry into the Temple, 'You will see that they will put us into the Tower. They will make that a real prison for us.' The family were duly sent to the Small Tower on their first evening at the Temple. Ibid., pp. 456, 457–8.

line 24 This refers to Marie Antoinette's brother, Leopold II, who had succeeded his elder brother Joseph to the throne during 1790. Jones, *The Longman Companion to the French Revolution*, p. 130. The queen's appeals to these brothers fell on deaf ears. François Furet and Mona Ozouf (eds.), *A Critical Dictionary of the French Revolution*, translated by Arthur Goldhammer (London, 1989), p. 261.

lines 28–30 Spain joined the First Coalition against France in May 1793, France having declared war upon her in March of that year. Belligerent relations continued until the Peace Treaty of Basle in September 1795. Holland, or the United Provinces, was invaded by France in February 1793 and again in late 1794–5. In May 1795, the United Provinces were renamed the Batavian Republic, and brought formally under French occupation. The Russian Tsarina, Catherine II ('the Great'; 1762–96), allied with Austria in July 1792, but did not offer much assistance in the west against France because of preoccupations in Poland, especially during 1793 and 1795. Prussia, under King Frederick William II (1786–97), showed early sympathy with Austria in the war against France, and played an important part in the fighting against her during 1792–4. Jones, *The Longman Companion to the French Revolution*, pp. 134, 135.

lines 39–40 Marie Antoinette was brought before the Revolutionary Tribunal on 14 October 1793. She was accused, among other things, of involvement in an incestuous relationship with her young son and assisting foreign powers by sending money to help finance their war effort against France. On the second day of her trial, 15 October, after submitting to a sixteen-hour interrogation, she was found guilty of all charges against her and sentenced to death. Fraser, *Marie Antoinette: The Journey*, pp. 512–21.

line 45 Marie Antoinette does not appear to have said a prayer at her last moment, as claimed here. She was not granted a Catholic priest to give her communion on the morning of her execution, unlike Louis, and climbed up to the scaffold in silence, making no attempt to greet the crowd, again unlike Louis. Schama, *Citizens: A Chronicle of the French Revolution*, pp. 565–6, 675; Fraser, *Marie Antoinette: The Journey*, p. 526. On the less humane treatment granted Marie Antoinette throughout her trial and in the hours leading to her death, in comparison with her husband, see further ibid., pp. 511–12.

lines 58–9 Louis XVI and Marie Antoinette had four children: Marie-Thérèse Charlotte (1778–1851); Louis Joseph Xavier François (Dauphin of France; 1781–89); Louis Charles (Dauphin, then King Louis XVII; 1785–95); Sophie Hélène Beatrice (1786–7). The two who survived early infancy were imprisoned in the Tower with their parents. Louis Charles died in imprisonment on 8 June 1795, probably from tuberculosis. His elder sister fared better: negotiations to free her in exchange for the release of French prisoners in Austria were successful in December 1795. She later married the Duc d'Angoulême, son of her uncle, the exiled Louis XVIII, but she was continually reminded of her lost family, especially in view of the persistent appearance of 'false Dauphins' – men who claimed to be her deceased brother, Louis Charles. Fraser, *Marie Antoinette: The Journey*, pp. 531–4; Deborah Cadbury, *The Lost King of France: Revolution, Revenge and the Search for Louis XVII* (London, 2002); Evelyne Lever, *Marie Antoinette: The Last Queen of France*, translated by Catherine Temerson (New York, 2000); Susan Nagel, *Marie-Thérèse: The Fate of Marie Antoinette's Daughter* (London, 2009). For the family's imprisonment in the Tower, see notes to lines 17–18.

line 65 No mention is made here of the guillotine.

lines 79–80 As in ballad no. 3, Richard Roberts is concerned about the threat of invasion following hard upon the heels of the demise of the French monarchy.

lines 84–6 The use of the word 'gwaedgwn' (bloodhounds) echoes Richard Roberts's concern about internal enemies, possibly of radical bent, in ballad no. 3.

8.

Publication:
For William Edwards, Oswestry (the publisher of the B text), see note to no. 7.

Tune:
Of English origin, the tune 'King George's Delight' was used in Wales in the eighteenth and nineteenth centuries, its title rendered in Welsh as 'Hyfrydwch y Brenin Siôr' by the latter century. Kinney, 'The Tunes of the Welsh Christmas Carols (II)', 18–19. Kinney notes that she took the notation from the carol collection of John W. Jones, Caerbache, dated 1857, rearranging the barring but leaving the time values of the notes unchanged. The natural 4/4 beat of the tune is frequently stretched with bars lengthened by pause marks, ideal for a dramatic presentation of the story of this (and other) ballads.

lines 25–6 Hannah Barker, in a study of the eighteenth-century British press, maintains that Wales and the English Midlands was a 'region which was well served by newspapers', with a 'concentration of papers ... probably as dense ... as anywhere else outside the capital' by the 1780s. Barker demonstrates that papers overlapped in areas of distribution, but in general terms it could be said that the *Hereford Journal* (founded 1773) served the towns of south-east and south-west Wales, and as far north as Llanymddyfri and Llandeilo, areas also within the territory of the *Gloucester Journal* and Bristol papers. North Wales was well served by the *Shrewsbury Chronicle* (established *c.*1771). This area, in which

Richard Roberts most probably lived and worked, was also served by two Chester newspapers, *Adam's Weekly Courant* (established in 1732) and the *Chester Chronicle* (established in 1775). Furthermore, Welsh-language newspapers were increasingly a feature of Welsh public life, with the publication of *Y Cylchgrawn Cynmraeg* during 1793–4. Huw Walters, *A Bibliography of Welsh Periodicals 1735–1850* (Aberystwyth, 1993), p. 20; Hannah Barker, *Newspapers, Politics and Public Opinion in Late Eighteenth-Century England* (Oxford, 1998), pp. 113, 122–4. For a new study of the influence and contents of the periodical press in Wales, see Marion Löffler, *Welsh Responses to the French Revolution: Press and Public Discourse 1789–1802.*

stanzas 3 and 4 The virulent anti-papist sentiments expressed in these stanzas reflect the viewpoint of *Y Cylchgrawn Cynmraeg*, which argued in its earliest issue that the downfall of the monarchy in France represented the downfall of papism. 'Hanes y Grefydd Grist'nogol o Ran ei Llwyddiant', *Y Cylchgrawn Cynmraeg*, I (February 1793), esp. 14, which notes that 'it is likely that papism has had its death wound there [in France]' ('y mae'n debyg fod Pabyddiaeth wedi cael ei farwol glwyf yno'). Animal and flower imagery is used extensively in stanza 3 to differentiate between the innocent (doves, sheep, lily) and the evil (vipers, wolves, snakes), the enemy believed here, as elsewhere in Richard Roberts's work, to be housed on British soil, awaiting foreign aid.

9.

Author:
This is probably Robert Roberts, Llannor, from the Llŷn peninsula in Caernarfonshire, who composed no. 10. In addition to the two poems anthologized here, his output as a ballad writer consists of three imprints of a religious poem based on Hebrews, chapter 11, which is concerned with the question of faith (JHD 295ii, 372i, 656i), and a ballad on the murder of a woman and her two children by her husband (JHD 656ii). All were published in 1793 in Wrexham, Oswestry or Trefriw.

Publication:
Titus Evans of Machynlleth later moved to Barmouth in Merionethshire. See further no. 3.

Tune:
'King Charles's Delight'. There appears to be some confusion regarding the two tunes known as 'King Charles's Delight' and 'King George's Delight'. In an article on songs accompanied by the fiddle in eighteenth-century Wales, Cass Meurig

notes that the tune name 'The King Shall enjoy his own Again' was translated into a Welsh context as 'Difyrrwch y Brenin Siôr' (King George's Delight). Since it was 'a song composed to bolster the case of Charles the First and the Royalists' ('cân a ysgrifennwyd er mwyn hybu achos Siarl y Cyntaf a'r Brenhinwyr'), however, it is more plausible that its original title would have been 'Difyrrwch y Brenin Siarl' (King Charles's Delight). It may be the case that the two names indicated the same tune, with the king's name changed as the Stuart kings, Charles I and II, were eventually replaced by the three Hanoverian Georges. In any case, this ballad fits perfectly on 'King George's Delight', for which see note to no. 8. Cass Meurig, 'Canu i Gyfeiliant Ffidil yng Nghymru'r Ddeunawfed Ganrif', *Canu Gwerin*, 24 (2001), 20–41, esp. 25; *eadem* (ed.), *Alawon John Thomas*, pp. 25, 150–1.

lines 25–9 'Germania' here, as elsewhere in the ballads, appears to signify Austria, upon which France had declared war as early as 20 April 1792. Prussia joined Austria to rebuff the threat posed by this declaration of hostilities. Catherine II ('the Great') of Russia was only persuaded to join in by the British (against whom France had declared war on 1 February 1793) on 25 March 1793. The ballad's accusation against these powers (that they began the war but were not prepared to pursue it whole-heartedly) is not without foundation. All three countries had interests in eastern Europe, where the reigning king of Poland, Stanislas, had surrendered to a joint Polish and Russian army. Prussia feared the loss of Polish territory to Russia; and Austria (in spite of the close relationship between her ruling family and the French queen) did not wish to lose out on the possibility of territorial gain in Poland to Russia and Prussia. Jones, *The Longman Companion to the French Revolution*, pp. 130, 133, 134; Doyle, *The Oxford History of the French Revolution*, pp. 190, 198, 201, 204.

lines 53–60 On 18 May 1794, while campaigning in Flanders, Frederick, duke of York, found himself in 'a dangerously isolated position'. He attempted to recover Guards which had been left behind in perilous territory, but soon found that he was surrounded by the enemy, his ally, Otto, having abandoned the towns of Tourcoing and Wattrelos, previously in allied hands. The duke turned towards Leers, where his ally now lay. As he made his way on horseback he was fired upon by the enemy, and his escape was further hampered by the presence of the Espierres brook. His horse refused to leap over or ford his way through it, so the duke had to dismount and make his way through on foot. He was accompanied by an Officer of the Guards who composed a poem describing the occasion. Burne, *The Noble Duke of York*, pp. 144–7.

10.

Author, Publication and Tune:
For Robert Roberts and the tune 'King Charles's Delight', see no. 9; and for Titus Evans, see notes to nos. 3 and 9.

Title:
the first day of June 1794 This poem commemorates Richard Howe's victory against the French west of the Island of Ushant in the Atlantic Ocean on 1 June 1794. In the spring of 1794, the French admiral Villaret-Joyeuse attempted to lure Howe away from an incoming French grain convoy. Howe pursued in poor weather, finally catching sight of Villaret-Joyeuse's fleet on 1 June. Seven of Howe's ships broke through the French line of battle, sustaining heavy damage. Although as many as 1,148 British sailors were killed or wounded, it was the French who suffered the heavier count of 7,000 losses, one of its ships, the *Vengeur de Peuple*, sinking during the conflict. In spite of this, Howe was not unambiguously praised for his leadership in the battle. He reputedly called back two British ships prematurely from chasing two dismasted French ships, and was criticized for not pursuing victory to the full. Nonetheless, the general public saw the Glorious First of June as a victory. *ODNB*, s.n. Richard Howe, Earl Howe (1726–99); Peter Le Fevre and Richard Harding (eds.), *Precursors of Nelson: British Admirals of the Eighteenth Century* (Rochester, 2000), pp. 295–6; Brian Lavery, *The Line of Battle: The Sailing Warship, 1650–1840* (London, 1992), pp. 183, 184.

Admiral Lord Howe Richard Howe, Earl Howe (1726–99), probably began his career on the sea aboard a merchant ship, entering the navy in 1739. He came to public attention during the early days of the Seven Years' War. As one of the most promising captains in the British navy, he spent most of this war working with the Channel Fleet on blockades of Brest and raids against the French coast. His indecisive action and conciliatory stance towards the colonists during the American War of Independence, however, earned him many critics and he was repeatedly obliged to defend his conduct as commander-in-chief of the North American station in parliament. During the early 1780s he returned to service in the Channel, and was involved in blockading the French fleet at Brest following his appointment as commander-in-chief of the Channel Fleet in 1793. *ODNB*; Le Fevre and Harding (eds.), *Precursors of Nelson*, pp. 278–99.

11.

Author:

Jonathan Hughes (1721–1805) hailed from Pengwern near Llangollen in Denbigh-shire. Although he was involved in the earliest Gwyneddigion eisteddfodau held at Corwen and Bala in May and September 1789 respectively, his major output was in the free metres, in which he produced carols and an unpublished interlude, entitled *Y Dywysoges Genefetha* (1744). His work is preserved in dispersed manu-scripts (he lamented that 'some was wrongly written, other parts faulty and foul, with every kind of confusion upon it' ('peth wedi ei gam ysgrifenu, peth arall yn gandryll ac yn fudr, ac arnaw bob mâth o annhrefn')); published in almanacs and in the form of printed ballads and, posthumously, through the labour of his son of the same name, appeared in the anthology *Gemwaith Awen Beirdd Collen* (1806). He has been the subject of critical attention in recent years, with the publication of Siwan Rosser (ed.), *Bardd Pengwern: Detholiad o Gerddi Jonathan Hughes, Llangollen (1721–1805)* (Barddas, 2007). He was also the subject of Rosser's 'Golwg ar Ganu Rhydd Jonathan Hughes, 1721–1805' (unpublished University of Wales MPhil thesis, 1998). See further *DWB*; G. G. Evans, 'Yr Anterliwt Gymraeg', *Llên Cymru*, I, no. 2 (1950), 83.

Publication:

This ballad belongs properly to the year 1756 and the outset of the Seven Years' War. It predates the Militia Act of 1757, a fact which is reflected in its use of the term 'train band' in the refrain. Once the Act had been passed, this term became anachronistic, and the first imprint of the ballad, the work of the Shrewsbury-based Stafford Prys, signalled the change in a newly-coined title, which referred to 'the Militia, or Train Bands'. The ballad was reprinted during the 1790s by E. Prichard, Machynlleth (for whom see note to no. 15); the undated text reproduced here may also date from the same decade. The poem's continued use signals that some of its features, at least, were still relevant to a 1790s audience. The pro-militia propaganda and the attempt to persuade may be one such element; the English-language refrain another. Further on this song and its context as a Welsh militia ballad, see Ffion Mair Jones '"A'r Ffeiffs a'r Drums yn roario": Y Baledwyr Cymraeg, y Milisia a'r Gwirfoddolwyr', *Canu Gwerin*, 34 (2011), 18–42.

The seller named for the A text may be identified with the Robert Prichard who worked in this capacity during the 1790s. He may or may not be the same as a Robert Prichards who is credited with selling many undated ballads. The fact that the text edited here was published together with a topical election poem dating from 1796 suggests that this may well have been a 1790s imprint. See *BWB*, p. 249; Cronfa Baledi.

Tune:
'Tempest of War'. Several versions of this are found in NLW, J. Lloyd Williams, AH 1/48, unpaginated, two set in parts. One of these (a four-part setting) has been used as the basis of the setting of the words found in the appendix.

line 54 It is the deceased Moses who is described as 'the servant of the Lord' in Joshua 1: 1–2, and in Deuteronomy 34: 5. Since Joshua was appointed by God to follow Moses as leader of the Israelites on their journey to the Promised Land (Joshua, chapter 1), the nomen may, by extension, have been associated with him, too.

12.

This is one of a number of ballads included in this anthology which relate to the French landing at Pencaer near Fishguard on 22 February 1797. The landing can be seen in the context of several attempts at invasion carried out by the French during the rule of the Directory (October 1795–November 1799). These included three attempts to invade Ireland. The first Irish expedition was directed by Lazare Hoche, whose fleet sailed for Bantry Bay in December 1796, but was prevented from landing by strong winds; a second attempt was made under Jean Joseph Amable Humbert, who landed just over 1,000 men in Killala Bay, County Mayo, in August 1798, and marched to within eighty miles of Dublin before having to surrender; the third expedition left Brest in September 1798, but was intercepted by and surrendered to a chasing British fleet on 12 October. In the latter expedition, a prime mover of the plan to invade Ireland, Wolfe Tone, was on board one of the French ships, and was captured and sentenced to death for his part in the action.

The expedition which landed in Pembrokeshire was planned as a 'buccaneering party', according to the testimony of Wolfe Tone. It was Tone who undertook the task of translating the Directory's detailed, highly ambitious and, indeed, unrealistic expedition aims for the leader of the invasion force, William Tate, who did not speak French. The convoy of four ships was destined for Bristol, a city which Tate was ordered 'to reduce to ashes', thereafter proceeding northward towards Chester and Liverpool, attempting to inspire a popular insurrection against the British government on his way.

In the event, the ships anchored in Cardigan Bay, and the landing of the troops together with their equipment at Carreg Wastad Point, west of Fishguard, took place between 5 p.m. on 22 February and 4 a.m. the following day. The convoy of ships had left the bay by 5.10 p.m. on 23 February, leaving Tate and his men no escape route.

During their brief sojourn on the soil of Pembrokeshire, the invaders caused fear and damage in the Pencaer area, pillaging farms and homesteads, and displaying sporadic violence against the inhabitants. Meanwhile, the leaders of militia, volunteer and yeomanry troops in Pembrokeshire and the surrounding counties mustered their men to combat the threat, their numbers reputedly augmented by local people incensed at the boldness of the French. Tate finally surrendered on 24 February, and his troops were incarcerated in Haverfordwest, Fishguard and Pembroke. John S. Kinross, *Fishguard Fiasco: An Account of the Last Invasion of Britain* (Tenby, 1974); Geraint H. Jenkins, 'Glaniad y Ffrancod yn Abergwaun ym 1797', in *idem, Cadw Tŷ Mewn Cwmwl Tystion*, pp. 256–72; Phil Carradice, *The Last Invasion: The Story of the French Landing in Wales* (Pontypool, 1992); Roland Quinault, 'The French Invasion of Pembrokeshire in 1797: A Bicentennial Assessment', *WHR*, 19, no. 4 (1999), 618–42; J. E. Thomas, *Britain's Last Invasion: Fishguard 1797* (Stroud, 2007). See further notes to individual references, and ballads nos. 14, 15, 18, 19, 20, 21, 22. Reference to the landing is also made in no. 24. On the Irish expeditions, see Hugh Gough, 'The French Revolution and Europe 1789–1799', in *idem* and David Dickson (eds.), *Ireland and the French Revolution* (Dublin, 1990), pp. 1–13; Kevin Whelan, 'Politicisation in County Wexford and the Origins of the 1798 Rebellion', in ibid., pp. 156–78; Marianne Elliot, 'The Role of Ireland in French War Strategy, 1796–1798', in ibid., pp. 202–19; R. B. McDowell, 'Parliamentary Independence, 1782–9', in T. W. Moody and W. E. Vaughan (eds.), *A New History of Ireland. IV. Eighteenth-Century Ireland 1691–1800* (Oxford, 1996; paperback edn., 2009), pp. 265–373.

line 5 Tate is commonly believed to have been accompanied on his expedition by 1,400 soldiers, known as the *Legion Noire*. A proportion, but by no means all, of these were convicts. Among them also there were professional soldiers, officers (some Irishmen, others former French aristocrats), and even a few minors. Thomas, *Britain's Last Invasion*, pp. 54, 61.

line 8 The parish of Llanwnda in which the Pencaer area is located includes numerous ancient *cromlechau*, stone circles and the hill-fort of Gaer Fawr (sometimes rendered as Garn Fawr). Richard Fenton noted that 'Remains of Druidical monuments and other ancient works meet you here at every turn', and believed that 'By the very strong fortifications crowning the summits of those rocky eminences which extend from Garnvawr, the western extremity of the parish of Llanwnda to Penyrhiw eastward, and form a chain of well-connected posts, evidently British, there is every reason to suppose that the country the French fixed on for making their descent was chosen for the same purpose by the earlier piratical invaders'. The Royal Commission on the Ancient and Historical Monuments and Constructions in Wales and Monmouthshire, *An Inventory of Ancient*

Monuments in Wales and Monmouthshire VII. County of Pembroke (London, 1925), pp. 182–9.

line 9 'Lord Cawdor' refers to John Campbell (Baron Cawdor), owner of the 16,000-acre Stackpole estate near Pembroke. He defected from the Whigs and was duly awarded a peerage by William Pitt, the serving Prime Minister, in 1796. It was Campbell who was put in charge of the Pembrokeshire Yeomanry as they prepared to face the invaders. He also assembled further forces, up to a total of around six hundred men. They included his own Castlemartin troop of yeomanry, detachments of the Cardigan militia, the Fishguard and Pembrokeshire Fencibles, a hundred and fifty seamen, and members of the local gentry. Although his army was considerably smaller than the French's, Campbell was ingeniously able to convey the impression that he was in possession of further manpower when Tate asked for surrender negotiations. It was Campbell whom the local community regarded as their saviour on the occasion of the invasion. Thomas, *Britain's Last Invasion, passim*; Quinault, 'The French Invasion of Pembrokeshire in 1797', 626–7; [Francis Jones], 'An echo of 1797', *The Pembrokeshire Historian*, 3 (1971), 81–2.

line 13 'Trele[te]rt' refers to the village of Letterston, around thirty miles directly south of Fishguard.

line 15 Described by one eye-witness of the invasion as 'an old grey-haired man', William Tate is commonly believed to have been upwards of seventy years old when he embarked on this expedition. His supposed advanced years have led some commentators to assume that the expedition was only half-heartedly under-taken by the Directory; yet, new evidence found in an official list of French prisoners of war released from Britain in December 1798 suggests that he may have been aged only forty-four years. This lends support to the view that the invasion was taken seriously by Tate's seniors in government. Tate was probably born in America, but there is reason to suppose that he was of Irish extraction. He was an officer during the War of American Independence, but after failed attempts to rid the southern states of Louisiana and the Floridas of their Spanish populations during the early 1790s, was forced to leave America. In 1795 he arrived in France in quest of refuge. His considerable experience as a soldier may have prompted his being chosen *chef de brigade* (a rank equivalent to a general's) for the expedition which eventually landed in Pembrokeshire. Thomas, *Britain's Last Invasion*, pp. 58–61; Quinault, 'The French Invasion of Pembrokeshire in 1797', 621.

line 17 John Colby (b. *c*.1751) was lieutenant colonel and commanding officer of the Pembrokeshire militia at the time of the invasion. The force were away

in Harwich in Essex at the time, but Colby happened to be on leave in Pembrokeshire. Colby was one of the landed gentry of the county, his family having bought
the old Pembrokeshire estate of Ffynone in 1752. He inherited it in 1779 and
built a new mansion on the site. Thomas, *Britain's Last Invasion*, pp. 22, 25–6.

line 18 James Ackland held estates at Llanion, near Pembroke, and was the owner
of Earwear or Amroth Castle, which he restored to grandeur and luxury. Ackland
led the Pembroke volunteers, ninety-three members strong, to counter the invasion
force. Ibid., pp. 22, 24–5, 73, 77.

Thomas Knox of Minwear near Haverfordwest was the son of William Knox,
who had bought the two substantial estates of Llanstinan and Slebech in Pembrokeshire following a career as under-secretary for America (1770–82). It was the
younger Knox who was the commanding officer of the Fishguard Fencibles, a
force founded by his father in 1793, at the time of the invasion. He was at a ball
in the farm of Tregwynt, around four miles away from the site of the landing,
when the news of the invasion broke, but appears to have been reluctant to
credit the account and was accordingly hesitant in taking action. His decision
to retreat from Fishguard to join other forces advancing from Haverfordwest was
later severely criticized, and he resigned as commanding officer of the Fencibles
in May 1797. Ibid., pp. 22, 72–3, 79–80; Quinault, 'The French Invasion of
Pembrokeshire in 1797', 620–1, 634.

line 21 A reference to the Cardiganshire militia, a force of one hundred men
who were stationed in Pembroke at the time of the landing, employed in guarding
prisoners of war. Pembroke also provided a ninety-three-strong volunteer force
(Fencibles). Thomas, *Britain's Last Invasion*, pp. 73, 79.

line 25 The Newport division of the volunteers, who were ordered by Knox,
once he had heard of the invasion force, to station themselves at Dinas, between
Fishguard and Newport. Ibid., p. 73.

line 26 A press-gang under the direction of a Captain Langford was drafted in
from Haverfordwest to repel the invaders. Ibid., p. 73.

line 27 Pembrokeshire colliers had been involved in serious scuffles with the
authorities in the years preceding the invasion. This may account for the description
of them here as 'chwerwon' (surly or embittered). On 18 August 1795, a large
crowd of colliers from the nearby village of Hook, accompanied by women and
children, aggrieved at the social injustice under which they suffered, arrived in
Haverfordwest High Street armed with oak clubs. They attacked the Carmarthen
militia, who had been tipped off about their intended attack, but dispersed when

the Riot Act was read to them. Ibid., pp. 33–4. The seamen mentioned here may have been those of Solva, who, under the leadership of a Liverpool engineer, Henry Whitesides, marched northwards towards the scene of the invasion, and 'were joined on the march by several hundreds'. These men according to some accounts shot and seriously injured two of the French. [H. L. Williams], *An Authentic Account of the Invasion by the French Troops, Under the Command of General Tate, On Cerrig Gwastad Point, Near Fishguard* (1842; 2nd edn., Haverfordwest, [1853]), pp. 7, 9–11; Jenkins, 'Glaniad y Ffrancod', p. 266; Thomas, *Britain's Last Invasion*, pp. 81–2.

line 32 Knox was advised by Colby to parade his troops along the high grounds in order to reveal their strength to the French and make them reluctant to attack. In Tate's dossier regarding the surrender, mention is made of the numbers of the opposing British forces, who had risen 'en masse with troops of the line amounting to several thousand'. As Thomas points out, however, this claim may well have been made in order 'to offset any reprisals . . . when [Tate] returned to France'. He suggests instead that Tate surrendered because of the mounting chaos in his camp, largely due to the intoxication of his soldiers. Thomas, *Britain's Last Invasion*, pp. 79, 87–8.

line 44 In the book of Ezekiel, chapters 38–9, it is prophesied that God will lead a great army against the land of Israel during a time of peace when Israel least expects such an attack. Gog will be defeated by God in a huge slaughter. See also Revelation 20: 7–8.

line 45 According to one origin myth, particularly promoted by the Breton abbé, Paul-Yves Pezron, in *L'Antiquité de la nation et de la langue des celtes* (1703), the Welsh were descended from the biblical figure of Gomer son of Japheth, the latter one of Noah's sons. Genesis 10: 1–2; Caryl Davies, *Adfeilion Babel: Agweddau ar Syniadaeth Ieithyddol y Ddeunawfed Ganrif* (Caerdydd, 2000), *passim*. References to the audiences of Welsh-language ballads and free-metre songs and carols as 'the race of Gomer' are ubiquitous in such texts. In this anthology, see also no. 18, line 102.

line 59 There is no mention of the destruction of Babel in Genesis 11: 1–9, which only states that those involved in building the city gave up their work once the language which they spoke had been confounded, and that they were then scattered across the face of the earth.

13.

Publication:
John Evans (Ioan Evans; 1774–1830) was a son of the Machynlleth- and later
Barmouth-based printer, Titus Evans. He established his printing business at
Carmarthen in 1795, operating from Priory Street (Heol-y-prior) until 1813
(with a brief sojourn at Heol Awst in 1808). His main source of income was
the printing of Welsh-language Bibles and New Testaments, but he also published
journals such as *Seren Gomer* (from 1825) and the *Carmarthen Journal*. Jones, *A
History of Printing and Printers in Wales*, pp. 137, 143–4; *LW*, II, p. 852.

The seller, I. Thomas (probably John Thomas), is associated only with this
ballad in Cronfa Baledi.

Gwyn A. Williams notes that there were two waves of migration during the
decade of the French Revolution, the first in 1794–7, and the second in 1799–
1801. Both were sparked by high prices and grain shortage, factors which led
to extreme disaffection with the status quo among Dissenters. The rural area
on the juncture between the counties of Pembroke, Cardigan and Carmarthen
in south-west Wales was among those hardest hit by these difficulties, and the
response here as in Montgomeryshire and Merionethshire further north was a
movement eastwards to the USA. The emigrants were usually artisans (small farmers
or tradesmen), and often monoglot Welsh speakers. The poorest people would
probably have been unable to afford the cost of migration, especially if they had
families. The Baptists, led by Morgan John Rhys and his American brethren, were
key to the organization of migrants and to the development of settlements for
Welsh people. On 1 October 1796 Rhys and his wife Ann bought a substantial
tract of land, situated between Philadelphia and Pittsburgh. The town of Beula
was to be the capital of this new Cambria. Williams, *The Search for Beulah Land*,
pp. 125–39; Hywel M. Davies, '"Very different springs of uneasiness": Emigration
from Wales to the United States of America during the 1790s', *WHR*, 15, no. 3
(1991), 368–98.

line 17 The *Amphion*, under a Captain Williams, left for America in early April
1795 (or, according to some accounts, 1796), reaching New York nine weeks
later. Its Welsh passengers included two influential Carmarthenshire men, Thomas
Phillips, who was following his sons out to America, and his friend, Theophilus
Rees, together with many neighbours who were unable to finance their passage
at the time but promised to pay after finding work upon their arrival. The Welsh
people who had sailed on board the *Amphion* went on to Philadelphia, to nearby
Chester County and the 'Great Valley', with a contingent progressing further in
the autumn of 1797 to the Western Pennsylvanian town of Beula where Morgan

John Rhys had bought 20,000 acres of land. Their experiment at creating a new community here was dogged with trouble, however, and the early years of 1797–8 saw very low morale among them. Williams, *The Search for Beulah Land*, pp. 146–7, 150–1; 'Simon James 1770s–1820s' on *http://www.werelate.org/wiki/Simon_James_1770s-1820s*; Isaac Smacker, 'Historical Sketch of the Welsh Hill, Licking County, O.' (in two parts), *The Cambrian*, I, no. 2 (March/April 1880), 46–53; no. 3 (May/June 1880), 81–6, accessed on *http://ohio.llgc.org.uk/erth-lick-h.php*. The author of the online material on Simon James laments that 'No one has yet located a passenger list or other contemporary data about the Amphion'. Although this ballad cannot name the passengers (sadly the author's name was not attached to the printed poem), it provides important information about the journey and the egalitarian ideals of some of the travellers.

line 40 The 'twmblers' mentioned in the Welsh text were porpoises. This meaning is recorded for the English word 'tumbler' during 1808–12. See *OED*.

lines 51–2 An echo of this story is found in the experience of an earlier party of emigrants. The *Maria*, which left Bristol during the summer of 1795, was fired upon while out at sea by British warships flying the French flag. Its passengers were confused as to whether they were to be taken prisoner by the French or impressed into the British navy. They were eventually allowed to continue on their journey. Williams, *The Search for Beulah Land*, pp. 126–7.

It appears that the impressment referred to in this ballad took place within view of the North American shoreline, a contentious area for the impressment of mariners involved in trade during the earlier eighteenth century. Impressment itself was, of course, a highly controversial practice. From 1740 anyone who 'used the sea' was liable to impressment into the navy: this ballad suggests that mere 'use' as passengers rendered men permissible prey for press-gangs.

The fact that the author refers to the impressed as 'our lads' suggests that the ballad may have been composed by a woman or by an older man. Perhaps the balance is tipped slightly in favour of a female author, since it appears that even men of more advanced years were of interest to press-gangs, with fourteen per cent of impressed men, according to a survey of twenty muster books dated 1777–97, aged forty or over. Nicholas Rogers, *The Press-gang: Naval Impressment and its Opponents in Georgian Britain* (London, 2007), pp. 8, 11, 86–90, 141 n. 55.

14.

Author:
The ballad is bound with a second text, entitled 'Marwnad Daniel Dafydd, ysgol-feistr Gymraeg yn Meidrim, yr hwn a ymadawodd â'r byd, yr 11eg o fis Mawrth, 1797, yn 51 blwydd o oedran' (An elegy for Daniel Dafydd, Welsh schoolmaster at Meidrim, who left the world on the 11th of the month of March 1797, aged 51 years). The latter is followed by the name Cetturah Thomas, and this has led to the first poem (the one edited here) also being ascribed to her, whether correctly or not it is difficult to prove. See Evans, *Dylanwad y Chwyldro Ffrengig ar Lenyddiaeth Cymru*, p. 178; Cronfa Baledi. The second poem is evidently the work of a Methodist: 'Sosiet' Meidrim mawr yw'th drymder, / Ti gollaist berl sy' nawr yn ddisglair' (The Society of Meidrim, great is your grief, / you have lost a pearl which shines now), laments Cetturah Thomas, describing the deceased Daniel Dafydd as a '[M]ilwr cywir' (true soldier), who had friends at the Methodist hub of Llangeitho. The author of the first poem, conversely, implies a desire to remain anonymous. He or she ends the poem with the common poetic formula 'If any one enquires . . . / who put these words into poetry . . .', but discloses very little personal information in this section, other than a wish to 'reform Britain'.

Publication:
For John Evans, Carmarthen, see note to no. 13.

Sing to the Lord a new song Psalms 96: 1; Isaiah 42: 10.

line 16 'Zion' refers to Jerusalem, and by extension the land of Israel in biblical accounts. See, for instance, Psalms 137: 3–8: 'For there they that carried us away captive required of us a song; and they that wasted us required of us mirth, saying, sing us one of the songs of Zion.'

lines 25–7 For Cawdor and Colby, see notes to no. 12. Richard Philips of Picton Castle near Haverfordwest had recently been created Lord Milford. Thomas, *Britain's Last Invasion*, p. 22.

lines 47–8 For the battle between David and Goliath, see 1 Samuel 17. 'This day the Lord will deliver you into my hand, and I will strike you down, and cut off your head,' claimed David before murdering the giant.

lines 49–50 A reference to the failed French attempt at landing in Bantry Bay in 1796. Administrative difficulties delayed the onset of the excursion, led by the talented and still-youthful Lazare Hoche. Having embarked from Brest in mid-December, about a third of Hoche's force had reached Bantry Bay by Christmas-day. Although, according to some sources, a small scouting party went ashore on Christmas-eve, heavy winds made a full-scale landing impossible and the ships were forced to make their way back to France. The part played by the gales in preventing Hoche's entire force from invading Irish soil is acknowledged in a contemporary loyalist poem on the event:

> General wonder in our land,
> And general consternation;
> General gale on Bantry strand,
> For general preservation.
>
> . . .
>
> General gale our fears dispersed,
> He conquered general dread;
> General joy each heart has swelled,
> As General Hoche has fled.

Conversely, other Irish songs prayed for 'the wind of Freedom' to bring 'young Boney o'er' to relieve Ireland from British rule. R. B. McDowell, 'The Age of the United Irishmen: Revolution and the Union, 1794–1800', in Moody and Vaughan (eds.), *A New History of Ireland. IV*, pp. 349–50; 'The Shan Van Vocht' (notes), 'General Wonder' and 'Green Upon the Cape', in Terry Moylan (ed.), *The Age of Revolution: 1776 to 1815 in the Irish Song Tradition* (Dublin, 2000), pp. 22, 23, 25–6.

lines 78–80 'They will beat their swords into plowshares and their spears into pruning hooks. Nation will not take up sword against nation, nor will they train for war anymore.' Isaiah 2: 4; Micah 4: 3.

15.

Publication:
For Ishmael Davies and the seller, R. Prichard, see notes to nos. 3 and 11. A version printed in Machynlleth by Edward Prichard has not survived (JHD 493). Prichard was apprenticed to Titus Evans, Machynlleth, and worked as a printer in that town between 1793 and 1806. *LW*, II, p. 867; William Rowlands, *Cambrian Bibliography containing an account of books printed in the Welsh language, or relating to Wales*, ed. by D. Silvan Evans (Llanidloes, 1869; facsimile reprint, Amsterdam,

1970), p. 710; Jones, 'Gwaith Argraffwyr Machynlleth o 1789 Ymlaen', 29–30. Although the known imprints of this ballad hail from north and mid Wales, it seems unlikely that a text with this degree of detail regarding the invasion should have originated at such a distance from the scene of the landing.

Tune:
No tune is named, but the ballad fits 'Belisle March', for which see note to no. 4.

line 5 For Gog and Magog, see note to no. 12.

line 53 For the role played by Pembrokeshire colliers in defeating the French invaders, see note to no. 12.

16.

Author: For Edward Pugh, see note to no. 4.

Publication:
For Ishmael Davies, Trefriw, and the seller, R. Prichard, see notes to nos. 3 and 11.

Tune:
'Duw Gadwo'r Brenin'. See note to no. 3.

This ballad, together with no. 17, commemorates the victory of the British fleet, under John Jervis, over the Spanish fleet at Cape St Vincent on 14 February 1797. Spain had declared war on Britain in October 1797 (despite previously being among her allies; see no. 7, note to lines 28–30), and a combined French and Spanish fleet sailed from Toulon in December 1797. Whereas the French went ahead to Lorient in Brittany, the Spaniards stopped at Cartagena to improve the condition of their ships. When they set off again, on 1 February 1797, however, they remained short of supplies and men. The fleet was inadvertently blown through the Strait of Gibraltar out into the Atlantic, but managed to return towards Cádiz. Meanwhile, Jervis had left Lisbon on 18 January and was patrolling off Cape St Vincent in south-western Portugal. Many sightings of the Spanish fleet were reported to him and he prepared for battle, only realizing on the morning of 14 February that his fifteen ships of the line were to be opposed by twenty-seven Spanish ships. When a gap appeared between the ships of the opposing fleet, however, Jervis exploited it, and managed to separate the Spaniards into two groups. Four of their ships were lost, and another four severely damaged when Jervis called off the action at 4.22 p.m. that day. News of the victory reached London on 3 March and helped boost public confidence in the navy. *ODNB*, s.n. John Jervis, earl of St Vincent (1735–1823).

Born in Staffordshire, John Jervis (1735–1823) entered the navy in 1749, somewhat against the wishes of his family. Active service came his way during the Seven Years' War, when he took part in the recovery of Newfoundland in 1762, and he was present at all three reliefs of Gibraltar in the early 1780s. In autumn 1793 he was appointed to command an expedition to the West Indies, and in 1795 once more sent to the Mediterranean, where he commanded the British fleet during the major victory against the Spanish on 14 February 1797. This earned him the title earl of St Vincent in June that year, together with the votes of thanks of both houses of parliament and a medal from the king. Thereafter, Jervis continued to serve in the Mediterranean and the Channel until 1800, but in 1801 accepted the post of first lord of the Admiralty in Addington's cabinet. He worked on reforming the civil administration of the navy, conducting inquiries into dockyards and rooting out corruption. His innovations were not to everyone's liking, however, and his policies were blamed by the opposition for a slow-down in naval mobilization. *ODNB*; Le Fevre and Harding (eds.), *Precursors of Nelson*, pp. 324–50.

17.

Author:

Hugh Jones probably hailed from the parish of Llansanffraid Glan Conwy in Denbighshire. His work is sparsely represented among the National Library of Wales's manuscripts. A marginalia *englyn* attributed to him is repeatedly inscribed in an eighteenth-century hand in a copy of Rhys Jones (ed.), *Gorchestion Beirdd Cymru* (1773) (Cwrtmawr 141C, pp. 266, 267, 268); and NLW 11999B, pp. 80–3, contains a matin carol by Jones, 'Carol plygain ar hir oes dyn' (A matin carol on 'The lengthy life of man'). His output of printed ballads consists of two further matin carols, together with '[Cerdd] yn achos y rhyfel presennol' ([A poem] regarding the current war), the latter probably relating to the Revolutionary wars. See JHD nos. 415i, 417ii and 627bii. He was also the author of a newly discovered interlude on the history of the Revolution in France. The interlude reveals him to be well-read, interested in the political upheavals of his period as presented in the newspapers of his day, and an acute anti-Catholic. See Huw Jones, *Hanes Bywyd a Marwolaeth Brenin a Brenhines Ffrainc*, ed. by Ffion Mair Jones (forthcoming). The 'Carol Plygain' alongside which the current ballad is printed includes the following lines, which might suggest a vein of anti-war sentiment:

Nid ydyw Crist yn Feddyg ond i'r drylliedig llwm!
Fo wedi gweld ei waeledd, ai agwedd trosedd trwm
A hwnnw gaiff oi gariad ddatodiad cloiad clwm,
Ni cheiff Herodiaid mono, er chwilio trystio troi,
Am iddynt fod mor uchel am Ryfel yn ymroi.

(Christ is only a healer for the broken destitute,
who has seen his abjectedness and his condition of heavy transgression;
and he shall have from Christ's love his tight constraint released.
Herods shall not have it, even though they search, rage, spin around,
because they so arrogantly set themselves for war.)

Publication:
For Ishmael Davies, Trefriw, see note to no. 3. The date 1797 is provided in ink,
and appears alongside a second handwritten date of 1787.

Tune:
'Duw Cadw'r Brenin'. See no. 3.

For the battle of St Vincent and Jervis's victory, see note to no. 16.

lines 61–4 The Spanish king Philip II's 'Enterprise of England', otherwise known
as the Spanish Armada, was planned in response to the threats which Elizabethan
England posed to Spanish imperial concerns from the late 1560s. The privateering
activities of Francis Drake, Elizabeth I's support of anti-Spanish factions in the
Netherlands and her promises or threats to help the Portuguese pretender all
contributed to Philip's decision to assemble a fleet to sail towards Britain. In
spite of the disorganized state of English defence plans, the Armada, which
eventually set sail on 21 July 1588, failed to exert any real pressure on Elizabeth,
and had returned (with heavy losses) to Santander by 23 September 1588. John
Roger Scott Whiting, *The Spanish Armada* (1988; new edn., Stroud, 2004).

lines 81–2 When the duplicitous Delilah had shaven off Samson's hair, thus de-
pleting him of his strength, he was taken by the Philistines, who took out his
eyes, bound him in fetters and put him in prison. They then gathered to offer a
sacrifice to their god, Dagon, in thanks for their delivery from Samson. Judges
16: 19–24.

18.

Author:
Nathaniel Jenkin (listed as Jenkins in Cronfa Baledi) hailed from Newcastle Emlyn, on the Cardiganshire/Carmarthenshire border. He was the author of 'Can o glod i gwn Crynga: ac hefyd, hanes helwriaeth fawr, pan y daliwyd 12 o lwynogod mewn tri diwrnod' (A song of praise to the dogs of Crynga; and also, the story of a great hunt, when twelve foxes were caught in three days) (Caerfyrddin, n.d.; JHD no. xiv.209). Its printer, J. L. Brigstoke, was active in Carmarthen between 1829 and 1858, which means that the song must have been posthumously published in view of Nathaniel's claim in his 1797 ballad to be aged seventy-five. This suggests that his work continued to circulate in manuscript or orally for some years after his death. Evans, *Dylanwad y Chwyldro Ffrengig ar Lenyddiaeth Cymru*, p. 178; Cronfa Baledi; National Library of Wales online catalogue at *http://www.llgc.org.uk* for J. L. Brigstoke; and 'Can o glod i gwn Crynga' on Welsh Ballads Online.

Publication:
John Daniel (1755–1823), the son of a farmer, was apprenticed to the printer John Ross and gained further experience of the trade through work in London. He began to print in his own right in Carmarthen in 1784, and was probably still active until as late as 1818, when he sold his stock to a fellow printer from the same town, John Evans (for whom see note to no. 13). He was an immensely productive and innovative printer, and has been highly rated by historians of print in Wales. *DWB*; *LW*, II, p. 849.

lines 73–5 'Above all, taking the shield of faith, wherewith ye shall be able to quench all the fiery darts of the wicked. And take the helmet of salvation, and the sword of the Spirit, which is the word of God.' Ephesians 6: 16–17.

line 87 The Syrians besieged Israel in 2 Kings 18: 9–10, but were subsequently defeated by God, who 'smote in the camp of the Assyrians an hundred fourscore and five thousand', rendering them all 'dead corpses'. 2 Kings 19: 35.

line 102 See note to no. 12.

19.

Author:

Phillip Dafydd (1732–1814) was a clog-maker, living in straitened circumstances in Newcastle Emlyn, Carmarthenshire. He also worked as a Methodist exhorter, and held meetings in his home for fellow Methodists in 1760 and 1774–5, on the latter occasion in anticipation of the opening of a Methodist chapel in the town. He composed (and printed) elegies upon the deaths of William Williams of Pantycelyn and Daniel Rowland, in 1791 and 1797 respectively. The poem edited here brought him into controversy on account of its insinuations about the assistance given the French invaders by (unnamed) Dissenters (lines 81–4). William Richards, Lynn, responded vehemently to the suggestion that members of the Baptist community had thus colluded with the enemy in his printed pamphlet *Cwyn y Cystuddiedig a griddfanau y carcharorion dieuog, neu, ychydig o hanes dyoddefiadau diweddar Thomas John a Samuel Griffiths, y rhai goddef gorthrymder tost a chaethiwed caled . . . yn ddi-achos, a gawsant eu rhyddhau . . . yn Hwlffordd . . .* (Caerfyrddin, 1798). *DWB*; Evans, *Dylanwad y Chwyldro Ffrengig ar Lenyddiaeth Cymru*, p. 178; R. T. Jenkins, 'William Richards o Lynn', *TCHB* (1930), 30–2; Rowlands, *Cambrian Bibliography*, pp. 660, 708.

Publication:

For John Evans, see no. 13.

It is of the Lord's mercies that we are not consumed. Praise ye the Lord for he is good This appears to be an amalgam of Lamentations 3: 22 ('It is of the Lord's mercies that we are not consumed') and Psalm 106: 1.

lines 33–4 On Hezeciah's sickness and miracle recovery, see 2 Kings 20: 1–7.

line 39 Baron Cawdor. See note to no. 12.

line 41 See note to no. 12.

line 53 See note to no. 12.

line 59 Gideon led three hundred Israelites against the Midianites. They marched on the enemy camp, blowing trumpets, shouting 'The sword of the Lord, and of Gideon', and then drawing their swords against their adversaries. Judges 7: 17–22.

line 61 George Bowen of the manor of Llwyngwair, near Fishguard, was in charge of the Newport division of the volunteers. Thomas, *Britain's Last Invasion*, pp. 73, 145.

line 62 A Colonel James is mentioned in an 1842 account of the landing, as one of a number of officers who took part in a meeting to discuss the invaders' terms of surrender at the Royal Oak in Fishguard. [Williams], *An Authentic Account of the Invasion*, pp. 17–18.

line 70 This line's reference to the Pembrokeshire inhabitants' 'tents' has clear biblical overtones. See, for example, Judith 8: 36, 'So they returned from the tent, and went to their wards'.

lines 91–2 In his 'Epistol at y Cembru', which prefaced the Welsh translation of the New Testament published in 1567, Bishop Richard Davies publicized the view that a specifically Protestant Christianity had been brought to the ancient Welsh by Joseph of Arimathea in the time of the apostles. This predated the arrival of St Augustine in 597 to convert the Anglo-Saxons. *ODNB*, s.n. Augustine (d. 604); ibid. s.n. Richard Davies (*c*.1505–81); T. D. Kendrick, *British Antiquity* (London, 1950), pp. 15–17.

line 121 The British began trading in Asia in the early seventeenth century. By the mid-eighteenth century, the East India Company (which held a monopoly of British trade to and from Asia) was running a lucrative business, importing Indian cotton cloth and silk together with Chinese tea from Bombay, Madras, Calcutta and Canton. After the decisive Seven Years' War battle of Plassey (1757) the British possession of Bengal was consolidated to the advantage of the Company. P. J. Marshall, 'The British Empire at the End of the Eighteenth Century', in *idem* (ed.), *Cambridge Illustrated History: British Empire* (Cambridge, 1996), pp. 20–3; John Keay, *The Honourable Company: A History of the English East India Company* (London, 1991); H. V. Bowen, *The Business of Empire: The East India Company and Imperial Britain, 1756–1833* (Cambridge, 2005). See also no. 26.

line 122 The Inca empire included territory from present-day Ecuador to northern Chile when it was conquered in 1532 by Francisco Pizarro. Spaniards residing in the Caribbean Islands and other parts of the South American Spanish colonies rushed to Peru immediately after this conquest, hoping to profit from the precious resources of the area, which included gold, silver and mercury ore. Although the benefit of this wealth was initially confined to Lima-based merchants, in the 1760s and 1770s Charles III of Spain substantially liberated trading conditions, allowing more than ten Spanish ports to conduct direct trade with authorized ports in the Americas. Philip Ainsworth Means, *Fall of the Inca Empire and the Spanish Rule in Peru: 1530–1780* (London, 1932), p. 226; James Mahoney, *Colonialism and Postcolonial Development: Spanish America in Comparative Perspective* (Cambridge, 2010), pp. 64–72.

line 127 Jesus Christ is referred to as 'the last Adam' in 1 Corinthians 15: 45.

lines 131–2 This reference has biblical undertones. See, for example, 'If I whet my glittering sword, and mine hand take hold on judgment; I will render vengeance to mine enemies, and will reward them that hate me' (Deuteronomy 32: 41); and the references to a sword, 'sharpened to make a sore slaughter' in Ezekiel 21: 9, 10, 11. It also evokes the story of the sword placed above the head of the courtier Damocles during a banquet. See Simon Hornblower and Antony Spawforth (eds.), *The Oxford Classical Dictionary* (3rd edn., Oxford, 2003), s.n. Damocles.

lines 145–6 Accounts of a small number of attacks against women during the invasion period have survived. Mary Williams of Caerlem was reputedly shot in the leg and raped in the presence of her husband; and two further women reported acts of violence. One of them was a sixty year old virgin, reputedly raped by one of the Irish officers. The apparent helplessness of women in these stories (and in the references to rape in both this ballad and no. 21) contrasts with accounts of female bravery and action during the invasion scare. Iolo Morganwg, stationed at his Flimston home in the Vale of Glamorgan, gave short shrift to the whole affair. Nevertheless, as early as the beginning of March 1797, he had clearly heard of female involvement in the repulsion of the French, mentioning in correspondence that 'the old women of Pembrokeshire had secured the damned republicans . . .'. Jenkins, 'Glaniad y Ffrancod', p. 265; Thomas, *Britain's Last Invasion*, pp. 84–5; Geraint H. Jenkins, Ffion Mair Jones and David Ceri Jones (eds.), *The Correspondence of Iolo Morganwg* (3 vols., Cardiff, 2008), II, p. 19: Iolo Morganwg to William Owen Pughe, 7 March 1797.

lines 163–4 The prophetess Deborah accompanied Barak, son of Abinoam, in an attack against Sisera, the captain of the king of Canaan's army. She arranged to lure Sisera and his host to the banks of the river Kishon, where Barak would meet him with a 10,000-strong army. God created havoc among Sisera's army and delivered them to the swords of Barak's men. In the song which Deborah and Barak sang in praise of the Lord following the victory, it is stated that 'They fought from heaven; the stars in their courses fought against Sisera. The river of Kishon swept them away, that ancient river, the river Kishon.' Judges 4 and 5: 20–1.

line 179 'Know ye not that they which run in a race run all, but one receiveth the prize? So run, that ye may obtain. And every man that striveth for the mastery is temperate in all things. Now they do it to obtain a corruptible crown; but we an incorruptible.' 1 Corinthians 9: 24–5.

line 187 Dispute regarding the Trinity dates back as early as the first centuries AD. Those who questioned the notion of the Trinity in Britain were labelled Socinians from the mid-seventeenth century; by the early eighteenth century, as their views developed, they became known as Arians; and by the middle of the century, their belief now centred on an insistence that Christ was fully human, they were styling themselves as Unitarians. Phillip Dafydd's insistence on the Trinitarian creed in this ballad reflects his awareness of the spread of Rational Dissent within parts of Cardiganshire and Carmarthenshire, and the particular notoriety of the so-called 'Black Spot' of Unitarianism in the old county of Cardigan. D. Elwyn J. Davies, *'They Thought for Themselves': A Brief Look at the History of Unitarianism in Wales and the Tradition of Liberal Religion* (Llandysul, 1982); McCalman, *An Oxford Companion to the Romantic Age*, pp. 740–1.

line 196 Joseph Priestley (1733–1804) was a prolific writer and thinker who practised and published in fields as diverse as theology, philosophy, political theory, grammar, rhetoric, history, electricity and pneumatic chemistry. His work in all these areas was underpinned by a deep commitment to intellectual enquiry, something that was nurtured in him by his Socinian belief in the humanity of Christ. He considered his ministry to be his vocation, and served congregations at Needham Market in Suffolk, Nantwich in Cheshire, Mill Hill Chapel in Leeds, the New Meeting in Birmingham, and the Gravel Pit in Hackney. He also held posts as a tutor and teacher, including a period at Warrington Academy during the 1760s. In 1791 he published *Letters to Burke: A Political Dialogue on the General Principles of Government*, a work which vindicated the French Revolution. His support of the Revolutionaries embroiled him in controversy, and on 14 July that year his home, laboratory and church in Birmingham were attacked and damaged by a mob. By 1794, Priestley felt that no avenue was open to him save emigration to the United States of America, where he was warmly received. Honours tendered him included membership of Benjamin Franklin's Philosophical Society in Philadelphia; yet, even though he continued to publish, his time in his new country was brief. He died on 6 February 1804. *ODNB*; Peter Miller (ed.), *Priestley: Political Writings* (Cambridge, 1993); Isabel Rivers and David L. Wykes (eds.), *Joseph Priestley, Scientist, Philosopher and Theologian* (Oxford, 2008); R. B. Rose, 'The Priestley Riots of 1791', *Past and Present*, 18 (1960), 68–88.

lines 209–10 On the invaders' surrender of arms, see no. 12, esp. note to line 32. The French were incarcerated in Haverfordwest castle and, briefly, in three local churches and at the Guildhall in Haverfordwest. Thomas, *Britain's Last Invasion*, p. 92.

lines 219–20 See note to no. 14.

20.

Author:

BWB, p. 245, notes that both poems in this ballad pamphlet were anonymously published, but the title clearly states that the author of the second (anthologized here), if not the first, was Richard Roberts.

Publication:

For Ishmael Davies, Trefriw, see note to no. 3.

Tune:

It has not been possible to trace the tune 'Ffansi'r Milwr', which makes no appearance in the major eighteenth- and early nineteenth-century collections of Welsh folk and ballad tunes. Examples of its use are found in the work of both Ellis Roberts and Evan James (see JHD 485i; 107i; and 171ii). It is worth noting that the current ballad fits perfectly the tune of 'Duw Gadwo'r Brenin', included in the appendix.

21.

Author:

Thomas Francis is stated in this printed ballad to have hailed from Fachongle in the parish of Nevern (Nyfer) in Pembrokeshire. No other ballads of his are listed in *BWB*. There is little further information available about him. Evans, *Dylanwad y Chwyldro Ffrengig ar Lenyddiaeth Cymru*, p. 178.

Publication:

For John Evans, Carmarthen, see note to no. 13. John Williams of Solva near St David's in Pembrokeshire was active as a printer between 1851 and 1865. National Library of Wales online catalogue at *http://www.llgc.org.uk.*

lines 37–8 J. E. Thomas's recent study of the Fishguard landing claims that 'One of the most enduring legends of the invasion is that of the parading of Welsh women in their traditional dress, and the invaders believing them to be soldiers'. There is a hint at a similar story in these lines, which mention the presumably passive role of those who stood within the Frenchmen's view, thus giving the impression that a large host was gathering to confront them. No mention is made here nor in any of the other ballads, however, of female involvement. Thomas, *Britain's Last Invasion*, p. 149.

lines 108–12 The Israelites encamped near Pihahiroth and opposite Baalzephon on the Red Sea on their way out of Egypt, but were pursued by the Pharaoh's men. Moses extended his hand over the sea and God caused it to part so as to create a path across for the Israelites. When the Egyptians followed, their chariots' wheels removed by God, Moses stretched out his hand once more, this time to bring the waters back together, thus drowning the pursuers. Exodus 14.

lines 117–20 For missionary work in this period, see note to no. 1. The Methodists, like other denominations, became involved in such work on a more professional basis during the 1790s.

lines 123–4 See, for example, Mark 13: 7, 'And when ye shall hear of wars and rumours of wars, be ye not troubled: for such things must needs be; but the end shall not be yet.'

lines 153–4 Haman, the Agagite, was promoted by Ahasuerus, king of the Persian empire, above all other princes, who were obliged to bow down in reverence to him. Esther 3: 1–2.

lines 155–60 On the forbidden fruit of the tree of knowledge, see Genesis 2: 16–17; and on Eve sharing the fruit with Adam, ibid. 3: 6.

lines 173–6 A reference to the parable of the Prodigal Son, recited by Jesus in Luke 15: 11–32.

lines 181–6 The calculation given is $700 + 70 + (7 \times 80) + (7 \times 60) + 47$, which gives a total of 1797.

lines 190–2 Mankind began to multiply upon earth, but the wickedness of men distressed God, and He brought about a huge deluge to wipe the surface of the earth clear of the evil of man. Noah, a just and godly man, was forewarned of

the flood, and told to build an ark to protect himself and his family from the
waters. Genesis 6.

22.

Author:
'G. Stephen' is named by Evans as one of the balladeers who sang about the
Fishguard landing. See Evans, *Dylanwad y Chwyldro Ffrengig ar Lenyddiaeth Cymru,*
p. 178. The name 'Stephen' is not given in the only imprint of this text consulted
for this edition. Evans may have had access to another copy or may have known
of a poet of this name working in south-west Wales during this period. Cf. also
JHD nos. 566, 567, 568, all of which are attributed to George Stephens, printed
by John Evans in Carmarthen in 1799, and sung on the same metre, described by
the balladeer as the 'mesur hir' (long metre) at the end of no. 23. 'Can o ddiolchgarwch i Dduw, am ei waredigaethau o ddwylaw ein gelynion' (JHD 566), gives
the following information about its author: 'G.S. mae'n byw ar ddwyrain dy /
I lydiad gwyn Trehedin gawr' (G.S., he lives on the eastern side / of the white
gate of Trefhedyn Gawr). The current ballad (no. 22) mentions in its final stanza
that the poet lived on the road leading north from Newcastle Emlyn, which
accords well with the reference to Trefhedyn, a village joined to Newcastle
Emlyn by a bridge across the river Teifi.

Publication:
For John Evans, Carmarthen, see note to no. 13.

lines 5–12 See note to no. 14.

lines 24–36 The prophet Elisha (also known as Eliseus) inflicted the Assyrian
host with blindness and led them away from Israel into Samaria. When the king
of Israel saw the enemy there he asked Elisha whether he should smite them,
but was answered, 'Thou shalt not smite them: wouldest thou smite those whom
thou hast taken captive with thy sword and with thy bow? Set bread and water
before them, that they may eat and drink, and go to their master.' When the
Assyrians had eaten, he sent them away, and Israel was troubled no more by
them. 2 Kings 6: 21–2.

After the invading French force had laid down their arms on Goodwick Sands,
and before they were marched to gaol in Haverfordwest, 'Provisions were sent,
in carts and on horses, from the country, both for the English and French'.
[Williams], *An Authentic Account of the Invasion,* p. 21.

line 40 'And David said, O Lord, I pray thee, turn the counsel of Ahithophel into foolishness.' 2 Samuel 15: 31.

line 45 Samuel Hood, see note to no. 4. John Jervis, see note to no. 16.

line 46 Alexander Hood, Viscount Bridport (1726–1814), was promoted Baron Bridport in the Irish peerage following the battle of 1 June 1794, and two years later was made Baron Bridport of Cricket St Thomas in the British peerage. He also became second in command to Howe at this point in time, a position which left much to be desired as time went on, since Howe continued to exercise the authority of a commander although health problems meant that he could only command from the shore. When a French expedition set sail for Ireland on 16 December 1796, Bridport was sent to foil the attack. He left Spithead on 3 January, but contributed little to the eventual failure of the French plan. In autumn 1799 he was in charge of thirty-two ships of the line at Brest. *ODNB*, s.n. Alexander Hood, Viscount Bridport (1726–1814).

Adam Duncan, Viscount Duncan (1731–1804), was born and educated in Dundee, and entered the navy in 1746. Punctured by periods of unemployment during peace time, his career included activity during the Seven Years' War and the war against the American colonies. His greatest contribution to naval history, however, was made after his appointment as commander-in-chief of the British fleet in the North Sea in February 1795. He was charged with surveying seas extending from northern Scotland to the Channel, but armed with inadequate resources. His major feat was a two-year-long blockade of the Texel (1795–7), intended to alleviate the Dutch threat to British trade in the Baltic and prevent a Dutch invasion of Ireland, which was, nonetheless, attempted in October 1797. Duncan, stationed at Yarmouth at the time, sighted the Dutch fleet on 11 October, forming its line of battle around 5 miles from the Dutch coast, and in between the villages of Egmont and Camperdown. He gave a signal to attack, and the fleets, both of which consisted of sixteen sail of the line, engaged in a lengthy and bloody conflict. Duncan was able to take nine severely damaged enemy ships, and was duly honoured by the public when news of the victory reached Britain. The official title granted him, Baron Duncan of Lundie and Viscount Duncan of Camperdown, nonetheless seemed to his supporters to fall short of his deserts. He remained in command in the North Sea until 1800, when he aided in an expedition to land British troops in northern Holland. *ODNB*.

line 47 Horatio Nelson (1758–1805) remains one of the most renowned of naval heroes. A rector's son from Norfolk, he entered the navy at the age of twelve, reaching the coveted position of captain before his twenty-first birthday. His career reached maturity with the oncome of the Revolutionary and Napoleonic wars, when he played crucial roles in the battles of the Nile, Copenhagen and Trafalgar (for which see notes to lines 47–8; no. 27, line 61; and no. 26 respectively). Success in his public life was somewhat overshadowed by his affair with Emma, the wife of the British envoy in Naples and a friend of Nelson's, Sir William Hamilton. Current scholarship emphasizes his unconventionality, his independence and his instinctive responses to challenges set in his path, but is at pains to put his reputation as a naval hero in the context of developments and innovations in the navy during his lifetime. *ODNB*; Colin White, *The Nelson Encyclopædia* (London, 2002).

lines 47–8 A reference to the battle of the Nile, fought between a French fleet under Vice Admiral François Brueys (who was killed in the conflict) and fourteen British battleships commanded by Horatio Nelson. John Jervis, by now Lord St Vincent, had sent Nelson to the Mediterranean in quest of the French in April 1797. On 1 August, Nelson sighted the French fleet, anchored in a defensive line in the Bay of Aboukir, a few miles' distance from Alexandria. Although the day was then drawing to a close, Nelson nonetheless decided to press on with an attack, and made the crucially important decision to begin by attacking the French van, which was where Brueys had placed his weaker vessels. The British were able to separate into two lines and surround the enemy fleet. So heavy was the damage inflicted on the French that only two of their ships escaped. Nelson was raised to international fame for his part in the victory. White, *The Nelson Encyclopædia*, pp. 192–8.

line 53 John Borlase Warren (1753–1822) was sent to pursue the French squadron bound for Killala Bay from Brest in September 1798, in command of three ships of the line, five frigates and other smaller vessels. His small fleet met the French near Lough Swilly and engaged in conflict with them on 12 October. Warren was highly commended for his behaviour. *ODNB*.

line 57 Sir Richard John Strachan (1760–1828) was appointed to a frigate named *Concorde* in 1793. During spring 1794 this was among the ships commanded by Sir John Borlase Warren in the Brest area. On 23 April 1794 Warren engaged a squadron of four French frigates, capturing three. During 1795 Strachan commanded five frigates, sailing off the coast of Normandy and Brittany and capturing boats belonging to the enemy, many containing stores of military material. *ODNB*.

lines 65–7 Cf. note to no. 18.

line 71 Cf. note to no. 19.

23.

Author:
For George Stephens, see note to no. 22.

Publication:
For John Evans, Carmarthen, see note to no. 13.

This is the first of two ballads commemorating the efforts of the gentry of Cardiganshire, Carmarthenshire and Pembrokeshire to raise volunteer forces *c.*1799–1800. Cf. no. 24. It also clearly bears some relationship to no. 28. The latter has been tentatively placed under the year 1807, on the basis of a handwritten date on one of its surviving imprints. Mark Philp notes that 'Songs hymning volunteers were often turned to laud the particular local regiment' during this period, thus suggesting a progression from the general (a song about volunteers) to the particular (a song to a certain regiment of volunteers). If this was the case here, no. 28 should pre-date the current poem, and this is perfectly possible in view of the uncertainty regarding its dating. Mark Philp, 'Music and Politics, 1793–1815: Section 1', in *idem* (ed.), *Resisting Napoleon*, p. 177; and notes to no. 28.

line 12 Note the pervasive nature of the theme of the 'internal enemy'.

line 25 Colonel Thomas Lloyd (1740–1807), the son of Thomas Lloyd of Bronwydd and his wife Anne, daughter and sole heiress of William Lloyd, Henllys and Penpedwast, was high sheriff of Cardiganshire in 1793. He was a keen agricultural innovator, who recognized the importance of issues such as soil fertility, crop rotation and the introduction of new breeds of cattle and sheep. Although he was reputedly lenient to old and impoverished tenants who failed to pay their rents during periods of hardship, he was also involved in enclosure. He extended his estate by enclosing common land near Newport, Pembrokeshire, and acquired *c.*400 acres of land from Llanfyrnach common in 1809. This ballad's 'Curnel Llwyd' can be identified with the 'Colonel Lloyd . . . / O Fronwydd' in no. 24. Leslie Baker-Jones, *Princelings, Privilege and Power: The Tivyside Gentry in their Community* (Llandysul, 1999), pp. 71, 82, 110, 117, 124, 335.

line 26 This probably refers to William Lewes (1746–1828), son of John Lewes of Llysnewydd and Llanllŷr and his wife Rebecca (née Price). He was high sheriff of Carmarthenshire in 1785, and his son, William (1789–1848), became an officer in the Horse Guard. Ibid., p. 334. See also no. 24.

line 27 Cf. 'brave Captain Parry of Gernos' in no. 24, line 135. Llywelyn Parry of Gernos (d. 1836) never married, and left his estate to an illegitimate daughter by a servant maid. Ibid., pp. 106, 207, 246.

line 29 The Brigstocke family came to possession of Blaen-pant in the parish of Llandygwydd, Cardiganshire, upon the marriage of William Brigstocke (d. 1723) to Elizabeth, daughter of William and Bridget Jenkins of Blaen-pant, in the early eighteenth century. Blaen-pant passed through William and Elizabeth's son, Owen Brigstocke (1741–78), to their grandson, William Owen Brigstocke (1761–1831), who also inherited Gellidywyll in the parish of Cenarth, and added considerable further lands to the estate. For Gellidywyll, see also note to no. 24. William Owen Brigstocke was high sheriff of Cardiganshire in 1794. Francis Jones, *Historical Cardiganshire Homes and their Families*, ed. by Caroline Charles Jones (Newport, 2000), pp. 25–6.

line 30 Cf. 'brave Captain Taylor of Stradmore' in no. 24, line 119. This was probably James Nathaniel Taylor of Stradmore Vale (Ystrad-mawr) in the parish of Llandygwydd, Cardiganshire. He was in the possession of the estate until 1801. Ibid., pp. 91, 250–1.

line 31 Penywenallt in the parish of Llandygwydd, Cardiganshire, was bought by the family of John Griffiths (d. 1818), previously resident in America, while he was a child, and remained in the hands of the Griffiths family until *c.*1840. John Griffiths became a surgeon in the Royal Navy. Ibid., pp. 234–5.

line 33 Llangoedmor, at the head of the Teifi valley, was bought by John Lloyd of Ffosybleiddiaid in 1758, and enlarged and improved. He sold the house, Plas Llangoedmor, to David Edward Lewis Lloyd of Dolhaidd near Newcastle Emlyn in 1786, and it is probably the latter to whom this ballad refers. By June 1801, the house had been sold once again, this time to Revd Benjamin Millingchamp. Ibid., pp. 167–8.

line 35 These were probably two of the five sons of Anne Lloyd, co-heiress of Clwyd Jack, and her husband John Davies of Maes (d. 1796). One son, David Davies (d. 1806), was a JP; another, named Thomas Davies, died at the age of 29 in 1806. The name of the house was later corrupted to 'Lloyd Jack'. Ibid., pp. 179–81.

line 37 This probably refers to the Anglican Revd Daniel Bowen of Waunifor, Llandysul, Cardiganshire. In the early 1800s, Bowen and his son provided £2,400 to endow schools in west Wales and a scholarship at St David's College, Lampeter.

In 1835 he supported the building of the Church of Dewi in Llandysul, in response to the increased numbers of Dissenters in the area, and he was among those who led a gentry and clergy campaign to petition parliament regarding Catholic Emancipation in the 1820s. Baker-Jones, *Princelings, Privilege and Power*, p. 229. See also no. 24.

lines 38–9 Lack of specific information about the homes or estates of the men named in these lines make it difficult to identify them. They may have been among the lesser gentry involved in the volunteer forces of the counties in question.

line 58 By 1799 the Corsican-born and still youthful Napoleon Bonaparte (1769–1821) already had a notable if not uncontroversial career behind him. In 1796 he had been appointed commander of the army of Italy, which conquered that country during 1796–7; in 1797–8 he was commander of the army of England, poised for invasion of British soil; and in 1799 he led an army to Egypt, eventually abandoning it, however, and returning to France. Upon his return, he was patronized by a faction within the ruling Directory, headed by Cambacérès, and took a prominent part in the bloodless coup of 1–10 November 1799. This resulted in the creation of the Consulate, a body of three ruling consuls, of which Napoleon was president. F. M. H. Markham, *Napoleon and the Awakening of Europe* (London, 1954); Michael Broers, *Europe Under Napoleon 1799–1815* (London, 1996), pp. 14–20; Mark Philp, 'Introduction: The British Response to the Threat of Invasion, 1797–1815', in *idem* (ed.), *Resisting Napoleon*, p. 1.

Dated 1799, this is the earliest mention of Bonaparte in the current anthology. Further references are to be found in nos. 25, 26, 27, 28, 30, 34, 35, 36. Stuart Semmel, in a study of attitudes to Napoleon in Britain, claims that British people were aware of Napoleon's earlier campaigns in Italy (1796–7) and Egypt (1798), and it seems likely that his appointment as commander of the army of England (in October 1797) would have drawn yet further attention to his progress within the French military. An anti-Bonaparte poem, 'The Little Island: A New Song', was published in 1797 (and made frequent reappearances); Napoleon's earliest appearances in British political cartoons were in March 1797, in two prints by Isaac Cruikshank. By February 1798 Cruikshank had turned his attentions to Napoleon's plans to invade Britain, in a cartoon entitled 'Intended Bonne Farte raising a South Wind or a sketch of the Invasion found at the door of Brooks's on St James's Street'. Although Simon Burrows argues that the origins of a Napoleonic Black Legend rested primarily in the Britain of the 1790s, he concedes that the earlier cartoons depicting Bonaparte tend 'to ridicule Napoleon's role rather than defame his character'. This ballad's reference to him likewise shows no particular hatred of a personal nature. Alexandra Franklin and Mark Philp, *Napoleon and the Invasion of Britain* (Oxford, 2003), pp. 50–1; Stuart Semmel,

Napoleon and the British (New Haven, 2004), p. 31; Simon Burrows, 'Britain and the Black Legend: The Genesis of the Anti-Napoleonic Myth', in Philp (ed.), *Resisting Napoleon*, pp. 142–3.

lines 75–6 This is a difficult reference to interpret, having no obvious biblical parallel nor clear relevance to major naval battles fought *c.*1799.

line 77 References to 'hatlings' (half-farthings) are found in Mark 12: 42, and in Luke 12: 59 and 21: 2.

24.

Author:
Dafydd Evan Morgan, according to the evidence of this poem, which is his only surviving printed ballad, hailed from the parish of Tre-lech and Betws in Carmarthenshire.

Publication:
For John Evans, Carmarthen, see note to no. 13.

The volunteer leaders named here correspond to a great degree to the names in no. 23.

lines 18–19 'In the first chariot were red horses; and in the second chariot black horses; And in the third chariot white horses; and in the fourth chariot grisled and bay horses.' Zechariah 6: 1–2.

lines 24–5 On the Fishguard invasion, see note to no. 12.

line 31 Belshazzar gave a feast, using sacred vessels stolen from the temple in Jerusalem to drink wine with his guests. Cryptic text appeared on the wall, which was finally interpreted by Daniel. It proclaimed, among other things, 'Thou art weighed in the balances, and art found wanting'. Belshazzar was slain later that evening. Daniel 5.

line 36 For Gideon, see note to no. 19.

line 46 See note to no. 12.

line 66 Arthur is mentioned in early historical records and is believed to have been a historical British chieftain who lived during the late fifth and early sixth centuries. In early medieval Welsh literature, however, he evolved into a legendary figure, accomplishing astonishing feats such as leading his men to the Otherworld. Once included in Geoffrey of Monmouth's *Historia Regum Britanniae*, where he was portrayed as a feudal lord whose might exceeded that of the Romans, Arthur was catapulted into Europe-wide fame, making appearances in the literature of England, France and Germany. Meic Stephens (ed.), *The New Companion to the Literature of Wales* (1986; Cardiff, 1998), s.n. Arthur.

lines 88–9 See note to no. 23.

lines 99–101 See note to no. 23.

lines 114–15 See note to no. 23.

line 119 See note to no. 23.

line 121 Gellidywyll, Cenarth, is situated 2½ miles west of Newcastle Emlyn. It was purchased by James Lewes of Abernantbychan, Cardiganshire, in 1589, and remained in the ownership of the Lewes family until the death of Captain Thomas Lewes, without issue, in 1795, whereupon it passed to the nearest of kin, William Owen Brigstocke. It remained in the Brigstocke family's possession until the latter nineteenth century. The Captain Wells named here may have been an occupant in 1800. Francis Jones, *Historic Carmarthenshire Homes and their Families* (new edn., Newport, 1997), pp. 68–9.

line 123 Samson was born during a period in which the Israelites were being oppressed by the Philistines, and his birth was intended to set off a renewal of the Israelites' fortunes. He was granted tremendous strength by God to combat his enemies. Judges 13–16.

line 133 See note to no. 23.

line 135 See note to no. 23.

line 147 See note to no. 23.

line 151 One expression of David's faith in God is found in Psalms 39: 1–3.

25.

Author:
No other ballads are attributed to 'J.P.' in *BWB* or on Cronfa Baledi.

Publication:
Thomas Roberts (1760–1811) ran a printing business at Caernarfon between 1796 and 1811. Records of upwards of seventy titles printed by him are preserved. He was succeeded by his widow, Mary (d. 1814), who initially worked alone, entering a partnership with Roberts's nephew, R. Williams, in 1814. *LW*, II, pp. 869, 870.

the desperate plot of Despard Edward Marcus Despard (1751–1803) was an Irishman, born to a military family. He became a member of the army in 1766, and was promoted lieutenant in 1772 and captain in 1780. 1781 brought the first in a string of appointments to posts in the region of Honduras, and by 1786 he was superintendant of Honduras itself. He was soon in conflict with the established British community there, however, because of his eagerness to accommodate settlers displaced from territory recently taken over by Spain, and the complaints made to London about him lead to his being suspended from his post and recalled to Britain. Over a year later, in October 1791, the case against him was dismissed, but anger at his maltreatment drove him to the company of members of the radical London Corresponding Society and the United Irishmen. In 1798, he was arrested on suspicion of involvement in efforts by the United Irishmen and the United Britons to arrange simultaneous risings in England and Ireland to coincide with a French invasion. He was imprisoned for three years before being released without charge. His retreat thereafter to his Irish estate was cut short by a request from the United Irishmen leader, William Dowdall, to return to London, where he worked to enlist militant Irishmen to the United Irish cause. Some of these men attempted a rising on 6 September 1802, against Despard's advice. On 16 November, he was arrested at Lambeth, believed to be involved in planning a coup d'état. Even though Nelson appeared as a character witness on his behalf at his subsequent trial for high treason, he was nonetheless found guilty, and hanged and beheaded, along with six others, in front of a crowd of 20,000 spectators. *ODNB.*

line 43 The 1689 Act of Toleration, although it exempted Protestant Dissenters from penalties against them under existing law, did not repeal any of those laws. Dissent remained illegal until 1767, when it was ruled that the Act was to offer Dissenters public protection for their Dissent. Dissenters were also restricted by the Test and Corporation Acts of 1673 and 1661 respectively, which were intended to curb their influence in local and central government, including the military. Repeated attempts by Dissenters to repeal these acts were defeated in 1787, 1789 and 1790, and did not succeed until 1828. John Spurr, 'The Church of England, Comprehension and the Toleration Act of 1689', *EHR*, CIV (1989), 927–46; McCalman, *An Oxford Companion to the Romantic Age*, pp. 729–31.

line 68 This may refer to the host of Zerah the Ethiopian, which numbered 'a hundred thousand thousand, and three hundred chariots'. 2 Chronicles 14: 9.

line 72 The Syrians were constant enemies of the Israelites in the Old Testament. They were defeated by God's chosen people on several occasions, including during the reign of King David. See, for example, 2 Samuel, chapters 8 and 10.

line 80 See note to no. 23.

26.

Author:
John Thomas (1757–1835), born in the parish of Llannor in Caernarfonshire, took up varied occupations during his lifetime, working as a weaver, a seaman, a schoolmaster and a customs officer (based in Liverpool). Most of his life was spent living in Penffordd-wen in the parish of Nantglyn in Denbighshire. He later moved to Llwynbidwal, Bryneglwys, also in Denbighshire, and died at Overton in Flintshire, where he was buried. He had an interest in astronomy, to which he gave some attention in his *Annerch Ieuengctyd Cymru, yn IV Rhan* (1795), and was involved in almanac-making. He also published an interlude, *Urania, neu Grefydd Ddadleuon* (1793); and two poetry collections, *Telyn Arian, sef Llyfr Barddoniaeth* (1806) and *Nabl Arian, sef Llyfr Barddoniaeth* (1827). *DWB*, s.n. John Thomas (1757–1835).

Publication:
For Ishmael Davies, Trefriw, see note to no. 3. The date 1805 is provided in ink.

Tune:
'Duw Gadwo'r Brenin'. See note to no. 3.

This poem was published in the aftermath of the battle of Trafalgar, fought off the Cape of Trafalgar in south-west Spain on 21 October 1805. By summer 1805, Napoleon had abandoned his plans to invade Britain, turning his sights instead towards Austria. The combined Franco-Spanish fleet, led by Vice Admiral

Pierre Villeneuve, were to support his land campaign from the Mediterranean. Eventually, they left Cádiz, where they had assembled, and travelled south towards the Strait of Gibraltar. Nelson was nearby with a fleet of twenty-seven battleships. The opponents sighted each other early on 21 October, but the battle did not begin until mid-day. Nelson's officers had been well-briefed regarding the battle plan. The larger part of the fleet was to attack the rear of the enemy's line at close quarters, thus taking full advantage of the superior gunnery of the British. Meanwhile, the remaining British ships were to concentrate on preventing the rest of the enemy's ships from coming to the aid of their fellow-seamen. The battle developed, according to Nelson's plan, as a 'pell-mell battle' or confused mêlée, and delivered the desired result. By 4.30 p.m. that day, one Franco-Spanish ship was wrecked, a further seventeen captured by the British, and only eleven ships made their way back to Cádiz. A further four escaped but were captured at the battle of Cape Ortegal on 4 November 1805. The only blight upon this success for the British naval forces was that Nelson had been injured on board the *Victory* at 1.15 p.m., and died just as the battle was coming to an end. White, *The Nelson Encyclopædia*, pp. 235–9, 241–6.

The battle acquired 'an iconic status' in later years, even though it was not a decisive battle in the war between Britain and Napoleonic France, which continued to be fought for another decade. Contemporaries attributed the British victory to the command of Nelson, yet current scholarship suggests that the relative quantity and, more importantly, quality of the respective Franco-Spanish and British fleets, played a significant part in the victory. The British government had invested in improving its navy ten years previously, and the quality of their ships remained superior, despite injurious efforts to reform naval administration by Lord St Vincent in the intervening years. The Spanish fleet, on the other hand, was already in decline in 1805. David Cannadine, 'Introduction', in *idem* (ed.), *Trafalgar in History: A Battle and its Afterlife* (Basingstoke, 2006), pp. 1–4; Roger Knight, 'The Fleets at Trafalgar: The Margin of Superiority', in ibid., pp. 61–77; N. A. M. Rodger, 'The Significance of Trafalgar: Sea Power and Land Power in the Anglo-French Wars', in ibid., pp. 78–89.

Trafalgar was the subject of numerous English printed ballads and songs, and inspired the publication of three Welsh ballads, two of which are included in the current anthology (nos. 26 and 27). For the third, composed by John Jones (Jac Glan-y-gors), see E. G. Millward (ed.), *Cerddi Jac Glan-y-gors* (Barddas, 2003), pp. 132–3. For English Trafalgar ballads and songs, see Mark Philp, 'Politics and Memory: Nelson and Trafalgar in Popular Song', in Cannadine (ed.), *Trafalgar in History*, pp. 93–120.

line 17 The combined fleets of France and Spain consisted of thirty-three ships at the battle of Trafalgar. White, *The Nelson Encyclopædia*, p. 245.

lines 21–3 Napoleon himself was not involved in the battle of Trafalgar, neither was he still intent on an invasion of Britain by October 1805, as these lines in the ballad suggest. In fact, his plan to lure British naval forces from the Channel, leaving it largely at the disposal of an invading French force had been thwarted during the summer of 1805, and he had decided to abandon it in favour of a land campaign against the Austrians. White, *The Nelson Encyclopædia*, pp. 246–8.

lines 33–4 It was recommended as early as 1759 that the East India Company, a private commercial organization with a monopoly over British trade in the east, should receive 'the nation's assistance' to rule Bengal, thus liberating it to concentrate on mercantile activity alone. In spite of the recommendation, the Company continued to act as administrators (or indeed as 'sovereigns', as one contemporary put it) in the region of Bengal as late as 1858. Since Bengal was not a British colony on the model of the American colonies, there was no pretence that the British tradition of liberty should be extended to include the native Indians, from whom taxes were collected without consent. This makes these lines' reference to 'privileges' in an Indian context loaded with (doubtless unintended) irony. Marshall, 'The British Empire at the End of the Eighteenth Century', p. 22; Keay, *The Honourable Company*, pp. 362–4; Bowen, *The Business of Empire*, pp. 1–11, 197–205. On the trade conducted by the East India Company, see further note to no. 19.

line 61 Millward (ed.), *Cerddi Jac Glan-y-gors*, p. 133, notes that the combined French and Spanish fleets lost almost 4,500 men in the action at Trafalgar.

27.

Author:

Robert Morris (Robin Ddu Eifionydd; *fl.*1767–1816), the son of Morris Roberts and Elin Williams, Pen-carth, Llanystumdwy, Caernarfonshire, worked as a flax-worker and later as a miller. He wrote poetry in the strict and free metres, publishing it in the form of ballads and in the anthology edited by David Thomas (Dafydd Ddu Eryri), *Corph y Gaingc* (Dolgellau, 1810). His published ballads include a 'Carol plygain' (Matin carol) and '[Y]mddiddan rhwng y cardotyn, ar cerlyn' (A dialogue between the beggar and the churl) (n.p., [1788]; JHD 626i and ii); 'Marwnad neu goffadwriaeth o farwolaeth y brawd Robert Roberts, o sir Gaernarfon' (An elegy or commemoration of the death of the brother Robert Roberts from Caernarfonshire) (Caernarfon, 1802); 'Hanes y ty a'r bobl a losgodd . . . yn nhref Caernarfon y 5ed o Fai 1810' (The story of the house and the people who were burnt . . . in the town of Caernarfon on 5 May 1810) (Trefriw,

[1810]); 'Cerdd newydd i Mr Madog, ar Dref a adeiladodd ar ei enw, sêf Trêf Madog' (A new poem to Mr Maddox and the town which he constructed in his name, namely Tref Madog) (Trefriw, 1811); 'Ymddiddan rhwng y tenant ar cardottyn' (A dialogue between the tenant and the beggar) (Trefriw, n.d.; JHD 413ii); and an elegy to Mari Salomon, a member of the Llanllyfni Baptist Church (Trefriw, 1814). He also published *Ffurf yr Athrawiaeth Iachus* (Caernarfon, 1816), where he defended his Baptist faith. He was buried (at an unknown date) in the Particular Baptists' burial ground, Garndolbenmaen, Caernarfonshire. He had at least two sons, Morris Roberts (Eos Llyfnwy; *c.*1797–1876), a miller a little of whose poetical work was published; and Robert Morris, a preacher who took part in founding the Welsh Baptist cause in Birmingham. His grandson, Ellis Roberts (Elis Wyn o Wyrfai; 1827–95), was a renowned poet. *DWB*, s.n. Ellis Roberts (Elis Wyn o Wyrfai; 1827–95); CGPLE, XIII, nos. 274, 374, 413, 212, 219, 242; Welsh Ballads Online.

Publication:
For Thomas Roberts, Caernarfon, see note to no. 25.

Tune:
The designation 'yr hen ffordd' (the old way) signals that the poet was aware of the various strands of 'Duw Gadwo'r Brenin' tunes current in Wales during the latter part of the eighteenth century and in the nineteenth century. See Kinney, 'The Tunes of the Welsh Christmas Carols (I)', 7. This ballad can be set to the same tune as the majority of the 'Duw Gadwo'r Brenin' ballads found in this anthology (the exception being no. 3).

Clearly composed after Trafalgar, like no. 26, this poem may have had more of a commemorative agenda in mind, published on a single, ornamented sheet of paper. It gives attention to the major phases of Nelson's career, including his campaigns in Copenhagen and Egypt, providing footnotes to offer further information on these campaigns.

line 5 The prostitute Rahab assisted Israelite spies in Jericho by hiding them from the authorities. In return, she was promised that she and her family would be saved during an imminent invasion of the city by Israelite soldiers. She was to hang a red cord from the window of her house as a signal that it should be left undamaged. When the invasion was over, and Rahab saved, she came to live in Israel. Joshua 2 and 6: 17–25.

line 11 See note to no. 23.

line 53 Following an encounter with a British squadron under Robert Calder off Cape Finistere in July 1805, the French admiral, Villeneuve, directed his fleet towards Cádiz in southern Spain. It was from here that they set out to sea prior to the battle of Trafalgar. White, *The Nelson Encyclopædia*, pp. 244, 255–6.

line 61 The battle of Copenhagen was fought in response to a trade embargo set upon the British by the Baltic states. Initial efforts to resolve the dispute through diplomacy failed, and the British fleet sailed towards Copenhagen to face the Danish. Nelson was soon aware that the rear ships were the most vulnerable among the enemy's fleet, and accordingly decided to deal with those first, before sending the troops who had accompanied the fleet to the Baltic to attack the fort known as the Trekroner Battery. The fighting began at 9.30 a.m. on 2 April 1801, with no sign of a resolution to the battle until around 1.45 p.m. At this point, in view of the huge numbers of casualties (and perhaps with an eye on further action in the Baltic against the Russians), Nelson decided to offer the Danish government terms of surrender. These were accepted and the battle ended at around 3 p.m. Although Nelson, second in command to Admiral Sir Hyde Parker at Copenhagen, was placed in chief command of his fleet after the battle, public celebrations of the victory were muted in tone, and Nelson never received an official medal for the part he had played in the attack. Ibid., pp. 99–105.

line 65 For Nelson's victory in the battle of the Nile, see note to no. 22.

line 77 Samson died in captivity to the Philistines, by whom he had been blinded in both eyes. He was set between two pillars in a temple, and called upon God to strengthen him so that he could be avenged upon his enemies. So much empowered was he by this request that he brought the pillars and the temple itself down, killing himself and all present there. Judges 16: 26–30.

line 79 Arthur's sword, Caledfwlch, is mentioned as one of his most prized possessions in the late eleventh or early twelfth-century tale *Culhwch ac Olwen*. The sword also made appearances in Irish legend as 'Caladbolg' and in Geoffrey of Monmouth's *Historia Regum Britanniae* under the name 'Caliburnus'. The latter is the root of the English name for the sword, 'Excalibur'. Stephens (ed.), *The New Companion to the Literature of Wales*, s.n. Caledfwlch.

28.

Publication:

Two imprints of this ballad have survived, both very similar and both from Ishmael Davies's Trefriw press (see note to no. 3). One (B) has been dated 1807 by hand (hence the ballad's placing in this anthology); the other (A) apparently belongs to the eighteenth century (hence its inclusion in *BWB*). Note that several lines are either reproduced in or taken from no. 23, a text published in 1799. Correspondences are found between lines 41–2 (no. 28) and lines 45–6 (no. 23), and lines 37–40 (no. 28) and lines 57–60 (no. 23). Some of the required rhyme-words ('bla'n', 'tra'd', 'gro's') suggest a southern origin; the fact that the roll-call of county militia names begins in south-west Wales tends to confirm this impression.

Most Welsh county militias had been embodied during the Seven Years' War. Only those of the counties of Anglesey, Cardigan, Merioneth, Montgomery and Radnor remained unembodied until the American War of Independence. J. R. Western, *The English Militia in the Eighteenth Century: The Story of a Political Issue 1660–1802* (London, 1965), pp. 449–50. For a chart showing the percentages of armed men (whether volunteers or militiamen) in the twelve counties of Wales (and Monmouthshire) in 1804, see Colley, *Britons: Forging the Nation*, p. 402.

line 38 See note to no. 23.

lines 54–6 Caswallon, son of Beli Mawr, is a character both in the Welsh triads, 'Trioedd Ynys Prydein', and in the Second and Third Branches of *Pedair Cainc y Mabinogi.* These sources suggest the existence of a narrative regarding the dominance of Beli Mawr and his sons over the Isle of Britain, now largely lost. Caswallon was later identified with Cassivellaunus, king of the Catuvellauni tribe, who led the Britons against Julius Caesar in 54 BC, and his portrayal in Geoffrey of Monmouth's *Historia Regum Britanniae* is influenced by the accounts of Caesar, Dio Cassius and Bede. In 'Trioedd Ynys Prydein', Caswallon is named as one who went 'across the sea in pursuit of the men of Caesar', a reference which may help explain this ballad's claims that Caesar had to hide from him in the deep ocean (see lines 55–6). Stephens (ed.), *The New Companion to the Literature of Wales*, s.n. Caswallon; Rachel Bromwich (ed.), *Trioedd Ynys Prydein* (3rd edn., Cardiff, 2006), pp. 305–6.

lines 61–2 Following the praise given to the county militias, there is bathos and irony in this statement, which suggests that the members' best defence lies not in their military prowess but in the hope that the wind will carry the enemy away from the shores of Wales. It may be an attempt to belittle militia members for their fake courage: songs in this vein include the 1766 poem, 'Sir Dilberry Diddle, captain of militia: an excellent new song', at the end of which the hero and his associates 'unarm, and strip off their Clothes', the battle being 'over, without any Blows'. See NLW, Brogyntyn Estate Records, PQH1/5, unpaginated. For satirical representation of the militia in a Welsh context, see Tegwyn Jones, 'Hiwmor yn y Baledi', *Canu Gwerin*, 24 (2001), 11–12. It is more likely, however, that this ballad's comments regarding the saving properties of the weather simply draw on accounts of favourable winds during other invasion scares of the period, notably the Bantry Bay excursion of 1796 (see nos. 12 and 14).

29.

Publication:
For Thomas Roberts, Caernarfon, see note to no. 25.

Tune:
'Belisle March', here given both its English and Welsh title, 'Mynediad i'r Ynys Deg'. See note to no. 4.

The subject of this ballad is the Caernarfonshire local militia. The detailed names and occupations given in the text correspond well with the 1810 militia list for the county, which suggests that the poet may have had access to a copy of this list when he was preparing the ballad. Bryn Owen, *The History of the Welsh Militia and Volunteer Corps: 1. Anglesey and Caernarfonshire* (Caernarfon, 1989), p. 127. Note that the standardized names given in the printed list have been used in the translation of the text.

line 5 The corps was lead by Thomas James Warren Bulkeley (d. 1822) of Baron Hill near Beaumaris in Anglesey, who became a member of the peerage of the United Kingdom in 1784. *DWB*, s.n. Bulkeley family, Anglesey, etc.

line 55 The Rupert to whom William Robert' is compared was probably Prince Rupert (1619–82), a nephew of Charles I who became an icon among the cavaliers during the First Civil War. Appointed president of Wales on 5 February 1644, his career was cut short by a disagreement with the king, which precipitated his departure for the Continent. *ODNB*, s.n. Rupert, prince and count palatine of the Rhine and duke of Cumberland (1619–82); Geraint H. Jenkins, *The Foundations of Modern Wales* (Oxford, 1993), pp. 13–16; Ronald Hutton, *The Royalist War Effort, 1642–1646* (2nd edn., London, 2003), pp. 129–42.

line 97 On the effect of military music, see further note to no. 5.

line 111 This seems to describe the performance of military exercises in public, for inspection and for the edification of a local audience. The young Robert Griffith, son of the Garn estate in Caernarfonshire, wrote enthusiastically to his father from school in Oswestry in June 1804 of the 'very good looking' Chester volunteers, adding 'I am just going to see all the Chester Volunteers exercise'. NLW, Garn Estate Records, FPB 1/5, Letters by Robert Griffith, no. 4. Young Griffith made a habit of viewing various volunteer troops carrying out their exercises, declaring in June 1805 that the Flint volunteers 'did their exercise very bad. nothing to be compar'd to the St Asaph they did their exercises uncommonly well, and left the town in the good graces of the people'. Ibid., no. 9, Robert Griffith to his father, Major Griffith, 17 June 1805.

30.

Author:
Evan James (d. 1804), from Llanfachreth in Merionethshire, was involved in the book trade in Wales. He distributed books for authors including Peter Williams and Evan Evans (Ieuan Fardd), and for the printer J. Eddows of Shrewsbury. He may also have been an agent for John Ross, the Carmarthen printer. James was not an entirely reliable figure, however: Evan Evans complained in a letter of 6 September 1776 to Eliezer Williams, 'That man has to me proved an uncommon rogue; and if I had not discovered it in time, he would have cheated me and my subscribers of a very considerable sum of money'. James also composed poems and ballads. Poems of his appear at the end of Evan Evans, *Rhybudd cyfr-drist i'r Diofal a'r Difraw* (1773) and *Udgorn dydd Grâs* (1773), the latter of which he was the seller. He printed five ballads in addition to the one anthologized here, among them an elegy on the death of one of the stalwarts of Welsh ballad singing in the eighteenth century, Ellis Roberts (Elis y Cowper), a matin carol ('Carol Plygain') for the year 1793, and a ballad based on material from the book of Ezekiel, chapter 4 (JHD 171ii, 216i, 413ai and aii, 458). Aneirin Lewis, 'Llythyrau Evan Evans (Ieuan Fardd) at Ddafydd Jones o Drefriw', *Llên Cymru*, I, no. 4 (1951), 239–58; Rowlands, *Cambrian Bibliography*, p. 538; *BWB*, p. 150; Cronfa Baledi.

Publication:
Both imprints emerged from Ishmael Davies's Trefriw press. See note to no. 3.

line 6 Doeg, an Edomite, was chief herdsman to Saul, king of Israel. During a period of conflict between Saul and his son-in-law, David, Doeg carried out Saul's request to kill eighty-five of the Lord's priests, whom the king believed loyal to David. See 1 Samuel 21: 7; 22.

line 9 Rhys ap Tewdwr (d. 1093) became ruler of Deheubarth, a kingdom in south-west Wales, in 1081 and reigned supreme for seven years. He was killed in battle near Brecon. *ODNB*; Kari Maund, *The Welsh Kings: The Medieval Rulers of Wales* (Stroud, 2000), pp. 78–82.

line 13 Owen Tudor (Owain ap Maredudd ap Tudur; *c.*1400–61) was a member of a prominent Welsh family, settled at Penmynydd, Anglesey, and descended from Ednyfed Fychan. Following the failure of the Glyndŵr rebellion, he is believed to have obtained a position at court, and in May 1421, he joined a retinue bound for service in France. It was during his time abroad that he met and married the widow of Henry V, Catherine of Valois, with whom he had four children. He later became involved in the dynastic struggle between the houses of York and Lancaster and fought and was captured at the battle of Mortimer's Cross in February 1461. He was beheaded at Hereford. *ODNB.*

line 17 Beli Mawr may have been a Celtic or British God, possibly corresponding to the Gaulish god Belinus or Belenos. He is believed to have been the last native ruler of Britain before the arrival of the Romans. Bromwich (ed.), *Trioedd Ynys Prydein*, pp. 416–17.

line 18 Gruffudd ap Cynan (1054/5–1137) was born in Dublin, of Welsh and Irish royal parentage. Descending on his father's side from Rhodri Mawr, he had inherited the right to rule the kingdom of Gwynedd, and undertook a twenty-five-year struggle against other Welsh dynasties and the Normans to achieve this. After spending twelve years imprisoned at the hands of Hugh, the Norman earl of Chester, his fortunes turned for the better and he was able to build up a power base in north Wales from 1099. In 1114, however, he was obliged to pay a large tribute to the English king, Henry I, in return for the right to rule Gwynedd. His death in old age spurred the composition of an elegy by the renowned poet, Meilyr Brydydd. *ODNB.*

line 21 See note to no. 23.

lines 25–44 Note that the second stanza has only 20 lines, as opposed to the 24 of the other stanzas.

line 43 The town of Sodom was destroyed by brimstone and fire sent by God. Genesis 19: 24–5.

line 45 '. . . I abhor myself, and repent in dust and ashes.' This expression of penitence is found in Job 42: 6, and elsewhere in both Old and New Testaments.

line 49 This may suggest a date closely following the 1798 Irish rebellion for the initial composition and publication of this ballad. See further note to no. 12.

31.

Publication:
John James (1777–1848), minister of Bethel Baptist chapel, was the first to set up a printing press in Aberystwyth. He entered into partnership with Samuel Williams (1782–1820) in 1809, continuing to work under this arrangement until 1814. *LW*, II, pp. 844, 857; Gerald Morgan, *Ceredigion: A Wealth of History* (Llandysul, 2005), p. 347.

Dafydd Amos was active as a ballad seller throughout south-west Wales during the first half of the nineteenth century. He commissioned work from poets, using printers in the towns of Aberystwyth, Cardigan, Carmarthen and Neath to print the sheets for him. Although he had clear Nonconformist leanings (one ballad pamphlet which he sold contained poetry by a former Dissenting minister in Neath, Noal Simmonds), one of his most successful and most frequently reprinted products was an anti-Socinian and Unitarian song by Owen Dafydd of Cwmaman. *LW*, II, p. 845 and *passim*; Owen Dafydd, *Cân sylweddol yn dangos fod Crist yn Dduw yn gystal ag yn ddyn, a bod ei aberth yn haeddu rhyddhad i bechaduriaid, mewn gwrthwynebiad i Sosiniaeth, tan yr enw Dwyfundodiaeth* (several imprints, including Aberteifi, 1828; Llanelli, 1833; Caerfyrddin, n.d.); *Dwy gân, Y gyntaf, dameg y Deg Morwyn. Yr ail, hunanymholiad y Pererin. Ar werth gan Dafydd Amos. Gan Noal Simmonds, gynt Gweinidog yr Ymneilltuwyr yng Nghastell-nedd* (Castell-nedd, [1830–47]); National Library of Wales online catalogue at *http://llgc.org.uk.*

Tune:
None is named, but this would fit on 'Mentra Gwen'. Phyllis Kinney has shown that this tune had many different incarnations, suggesting three variant metrical groups. Although it was named by Richard Morris of Anglesey in 1717, it only gained popularity in Wales from the end of the eighteenth century, thereafter frequently appearing in print. Kinney, 'The Tunes of the Welsh Christmas Carols (I)', 39–41.

It is only the title of this poem which links its contents explicitly to France, and within the text itself there are references to Britain, to Anglesey and London. This is not untypical of ballads sung in the voice of the French enemy. A 1760 ballad by Huw Jones, Llangwm, 'Cwynfan gwŷr Ffrainc am ychwaneg o luniaeth o Loegr' (The men of France's complaint for more food from England) is steeped in references to people and places from the poet's north Wales home region as it mockingly portrays the French suffering from hunger as a result of the vicissitudes of the Seven Years' War. Simultaneously with local and British references, however, the current ballad is clearly intent on describing a Catholic state – not entirely an anachronism in the case of France by 1811, since Catholicism remained the major religion there during the Napoleonic era. The situation of the clergy in France may have struck the author as a worthy topic, likely to arouse interest among his own audience in 1811. Methodists and Nonconformists were adept at criticizing aspects of Church organization throughout the eighteenth century (tithes were a frequent issue of contention) and at times saw a connection between the vicissitudes of the Church of England and those of the Catholic Church of Continental Europe. Alaw Mai Edwards and A. Cynfael Lake (eds.), *Detholiad o Faledi Huw Jones: 'Llymgi Penllwyd Llangwm'* (Aberystwyth, 2010), pp. 48–51; Clive Emsley, *The Longman Companion to Napoleonic Europe* (London, 1993), pp. 258–9; Jeremy Gregory, 'The Church of England', in Dickinson (ed.), *A Companion to Eighteenth-Century Britain*, pp. 225–6, 236.

line 1 The tithe had in fact been abolished in France since 1789. On the night of 4 August that year, the deputies of the National Assembly, spurred on by news of rural discontent vented against seigneurial property, turned the centuries' old French social order upon its head. The tithe was one of the features of the 'feudal' regime abolished that night. Furthermore, during the debates of 5–11 August 1789, where the decisions of the night of 4 August were formalized, it was decided that the tithe, unlike other dues, should be abolished without indemnity on the grounds that it was too much to pay for the services rendered to the public by the Church.

During the Ancien Régime, the clergy had been entitled to a fraction (between 1/15 and 1/20) of the harvest in payment in kind, an imposition which amounted to about 8 per cent of a peasant's gross product. In fact, however, the payment often did not reach the parish clergy but was instead taken up by monasteries or laymen. Doyle, *The Oxford History of the French Revolution*, pp. 11, 34, 35, 98, 114–15, 136–7, 353; Furet and Ozouf (eds.), *A Critical Dictionary of the French Revolution*, pp. 110, 449.

lines 33–4 The ballad may be a response to the longstanding dispute between Napoleon and Pope Pius VII over the control of the Church. The Concordat, an agreement which, although it acknowledged the pope as head of the Catholic Church, gave the French state control of the Church in France, had been signed in July 1801. Relations with the Papacy deteriorated further when Napoleon declared an annexation of Rome in May 1807. Pius VII attempted to excommunicate Bonaparte, but was arrested and exiled. In February 1810 Rome was formally annexed into the French empire. In 1811 Napoleon called a National Church Council in an attempt to reshape the government of the Church. The document, entitled 'Views on the organization of Catholic worship', produced as a result of the discussions recommended that the Church 'lend a hand in the eradication of superstitious practices, those shameful leftovers of medieval barbarism'. Napoleon's administrators worked hard to eradicate local festivities, reduce the number of saints' days celebrated and suppress pilgrimages. Broers, *Europe under Napoleon*, pp. 221–2; Emsley, *The Longman Companion to Napoleonic Europe*, pp. 51, 258–9; Suzanne Desan, 'The French Revolution and Religion, 1795–1815', in Stewart J. Brown and Timothy Tackett (eds.), *The Cambridge History of Christianity: Enlightenment, Reawakening and Revolution 1660–1815* (Cambridge, 2006), pp. 556–74.

32.

Author:

There were two poets of the name John Thomas active in Wales in this period: John Thomas of Penffordd wen (clearly named at the foot of the printed version of ballad no. 26) and John Thomas of Pentrefoelas. Either may have composed this ballad. John Thomas (Eos Gwynedd; 1742–1818) of Pentrefoelas in Denbighshire was a shopkeeper and farmer. He composed poetry relating to the Revolutionary and Napoleonic wars, some of which appeared posthumously in the anthology *Eos Gwynedd, sef Casgliad o Ganiadau, ar Destynau Crefyddol, Moesol, a Difyrol*. Of particular interest are the songs 'Danghosiad achos y blinder a'r drudaniaeth yn amser Rhyfel Ffrainc' (A declaration of the cause of the tribulation and scarcity in the time of the French War) and 'Anerch i'r Cymry yn amser y rhyfel, 1803' (An address to the Welsh in the time of war, 1803), on the tunes 'Mwynen Merch' and 'Britons Bold' respectively. Their attitude towards the war is typical of the ballads in general: they denigrate sin, are firmly couched within a biblical frame of reference, and urge the Welsh to stand up to the bragging of Bonaparte. See *DWB*, s.n. John Thomas (Eos Gwynedd; 1742–1818); John Thomas, *Eos Gwynedd, sef Casgliad o Ganiadau, ar Destynau Crefyddol, Moesol, a Difyrol, gan y Diweddar Mr. John Thomas, Pentre'r Foelas*, ed. by William Williams (Gwilym Caledfryn) (Llanrwst, [1845]), pp. 104–7, 115–17.

Publication:
For Ishmael Davies, Trefriw, see note to no. 3.

Tune:
The notation for 'Y Dôn Fechan', as sung in the Vale of Meifod in Montgomery-shire, is found in John Jenkins's manuscript, 'Per-seiniau Cymru'. NLW 1940Aii, f. 95ʳ., no. 101.

The 'ymddiddan' or dialogue poem is a popular genre throughout Welsh poetic tradition. It first appears in medieval sources such as the Red Book of Hergest and the Black Book of Carmarthen, which present 'Ymddiddan Llywelyn a Gwrnerth' and 'Ymddiddan Myrddin a Thaliesin' respectively. The 'ymddiddan' became one of the staple genres of free-metre poetry as it emerged during the second half of the seventeenth century, and printed Welsh ballads include dialogue poems on a range of topics (among them love, matrimony and drunkenness) and between various interlocutors (the living and the dead, the poet and an animal or bird, or warring countries, for instance). Stephens, *The New Companion to the Literature of Wales*, s.n. 'Ymddiddan Arthur a'r Eryr', 'Ymddiddan Llywelyn a Gwrnerth', 'Ymddiddan Myrddin a Thaliesin'; Cronfa Baledi.

lines 21–2 Drunkenness was a particular problem in the army of this period. In the view of Arthur Wellesley, duke of Wellington (see note to no. 34), the rank and file was 'composed of the scum of the earth . . . fellows who have enlisted for drink – that is the plain fact'. Wellesley's troops were guilty of severe in-discipline following the more successful moments of the Peninsular campaign (see note to no. 33). Once they had captured former French strongholds in the Peninsula, they would loot, pillage, and commit rape, causing terror and hardship to the civilians whom they were meant to be relieving. There were opposing opinions on how to tackle such behaviour. While some believed that a humane approach, which encouraged the men to think for themselves, worked best, others (including Wellesley) favoured strict discipline, coupled with adequate attention to the material needs of the troops. Gates, 'The Transformation of the Army', pp. 143–5.

line 43 For Gideon, see note to no. 19. Joshua succeeded Moses as leader of the Israelites, directing their first action after crossing the river Jordan – the siege of Jericho. Joshua 6.

33.

Author:

Griffith Williams (Gutyn Peris; 1769–1838) was born at Hafod Olau, Waunfawr, Caernarfonshire, and worked as a farm labourer and quarryman, eventually becoming a foreman at the Penrhyn quarry near Bethesda. He was tutored as a poet by Abraham Williams (Bardd Du Eryri) at Llanllechid, and later by David Thomas (Dafydd Ddu Eryri), and initiated into the Gorsedd of the Bards at the Dinorwig eisteddfod of 1799 by Iolo Morganwg. He won prizes at eisteddfodau held in 1803 and 1810, singing strict-metre *awdlau* on the subjects of the renowned poet Goronwy Owen and 'George III's Jubilee' respectively. He published a volume of his work, entitled *Ffrwyth Awen* in 1816. *DWB*, s.n. Griffith Williams (Gutyn Peris; 1769–1838).

Publication:

For Thomas Roberts, Caernarfon, see note to no. 25.

Tune:

'Belisle March'. See note to no. 4.

This ballad's title refers to the Peninsular War (1808–14), which began as a result of Napoleon's efforts to effect a Europe-wide boycott of exports from Britain, a plan which he described as the 'Continental System'. Austria, Russia and Denmark had all responded to Napoleon's demands by 1808, Sweden following suite in 1810. Spain, however, was only half-heartedly concurrent, and Portugal did not offer any embargo on British trade. Relations between Napoleonic France and Spain were strained from 1806, and by early 1807, Napoleon had placed an increased military presence along the Pyrenees. Although he then formed an alliance with Spain to enable him to proceed through its territories to Portugal, his troops, led by Jean-Andoche Junot, in fact occupied the Spanish fortresses of San Sebastien, Pamplona, Figueras and Barcelona, and by March 1808, French forces had entered Madrid. While the Spanish populace staged uprisings against French rule, the British responded by sending troops to Portugal under Arthur Wellesley (later duke of Wellington), landing at Mondego Bay on 1 August 1808 and thus instigating a six-year campaign to liberate the Iberian Peninsula from French rule. Emsley, *The Longman Companion to Napoleonic Europe*, pp. 12–16; David Gates, *The Spanish Ulcer: A History of the Peninsular War* (1986; London, 2002). Further on the campaign, see no. 34, notes to lines 73–4.

   The Caernarfonshire militia was originally raised in 1762, as a result of the passing of the 1757 Militia Act. Thereafter, they were regularly raised to serve in periods of war, and were re-embodied in 1803 following the collapse of the

Peace of Amiens. The regiment served at a distance from home, lodging in barracks on the South Coast and in the West Country. During service in Sussex in 1808, the members offered to take up duty in Ireland, and eventually set sail there in late 1810. In December 1812, while still stationed in Ireland, they were promoted to a rifle corps, with new arms supplied by the government and a change of uniform from scarlet to green. The members made repeated offers of service yet further afield, including a proposal on 20 November 1812 'to serve in Spain and Portugal or any other part of Europe'. This offer elicited them praise for their 'zeal and spirit' from the Prince Regent. Offers of service with regiments of the line were also frequently tendered by individual members of this regiment, which suggests a strong commitment among them to a military way of life. Owen, *The History of the Welsh Militia and Volunteer Corps: 1. Anglesey and Caernarfonshire*, pp. 47–54; NLW, Broom Hall, 1307, letters dated 20 November, 1 and 2 December 1812.

line 9 Richard Edwards of Nanhoron, Botwnnog, Caernarfonshire, was appointed commanding officer of the Caernarfonshire militia in 1793. Owen, *The History of the Welsh Militia and Volunteer Corps: 1. Anglesey and Caernarfonshire*, pp. 47, 71, 72.

line 11 Richard Jones became a captain in the regiment on 9 November 1807; J. T. Sewell, the 'Showell' of the original ballad, was promoted captain and adjutant on 20 December 1811. Ibid., pp. 71, 72.

line 13 T. Churchill, promoted first lieutenant on 25 September 1808; Hugh Hughes, promoted first lieutenant on 12 January 1814; no one of the name Price is included in the lists. Ibid., p. 72.

line 19 Edward Carreg (or Carrey) was a surgeon for the regiment from 23 July 1803 and still serving in September 1825. Ibid.

lines 29–30 'The brilliant uniforms they affected were a splendid piece of propaganda in themselves, impressive to the onlooker and tickling the vanity of the recruit.' J. R. Western, 'The Volunteer Movement as an Anti Revolutionary Force, 1793–1801', *EHR*, LXXI (1956), 607.

line 50 '[C]las Merddin' is an ancient name for the Isle of Britain in Welsh mythology. 'Clas' derives from the Latin 'classis', meaning enclosure, and is used in this case to refer to 'people of the same country.' Bromwich (ed.), *Trioedd Ynys Prydein*, p. 248.

34.

Author:

Ioan Dafydd, according to the evidence of this printed ballad, hailed from the parish of Llandeilo Tal-y-bont (also known as Llandeilo Fach) in Glamorgan. He typically frames his ballads in exhortations for his market- and fair-day audience's attention and in requests for payment for the printed sheets on which the ballads were published. This, together with his warning at the foot of this ballad, 'Let no one sell this song without the author's permission', suggests that he may have edged towards balladeering in nineteenth-century style, delivering his own material and receiving the financial reward for his work directly from its ad-hoc audience. The second stanza of no. 35 also refers to his aim to bring 'news' to his listeners on a weekly basis, reflecting perhaps an effort to channel newspaper-style information through a popular source. In an 1813 ballad, he sang:

> Pe doe Bonaparte ag army
> O wyth can mil i dir yng Nghymru
> Yn fuan trwyddo caent eu concro
> Fel yr wyth cant ddaeth i Sir Benfro.
> Yn awr 'rwy' yn rhoi heibio canu
> Dowch chwithau 'nghyd i gyd i brynu
> Mi wn fod gennyf lawn werth ceiniog
> I'r cybydd mwyaf annhrugarog.

> (If Bonaparte came with an army
> of eight hundred thousand to land in Wales,
> they would soon be entirely conquered
> like the eight hundred who came to Pembrokeshire.
> I shall now stop singing:
> may you all come together to buy.
> I know that I easily have a penny's worth
> for the most hard-hearted miser.)

Thomas, *Drych y Baledwr*, p. 47, source not named.

Publication:

Jonathan Harris (1784–1838) was a native of either Carmarthenshire or Glamorganshire. Apprenticed to William Collister Jones of Chester, he started printing at Carmarthen in 1807, working from premises in King Street until sometime in 1808, and thereafter at Dark Gate. He was also a bookseller and stationer, and sold patent medicines. His biggest printing venture was a quarto edition of Peter Williams's Bible (1823, 1824); in spite of the substantial extent of his output, however, he has been described as but an 'indifferent craftsm[a]n'. He retired in 1832, and was living at Llanegwad, Carmarthenshire, at the time of his death. Jones, *A History of Printing and Printers in Wales*, pp. 189–90; *LW*, II, pp. 855, 903.

Tune:
No tune is designated, but these words fit the metre of 'Mentra Gwen', with a slight adjustment to the placing of the phrase 'gwir yw'r gair' in the final two lines of each stanza. This change has been made in the text presented here. For the tune, see note to no. 31.

Title:
This ballad celebrates the recapture of Napoleon following the allied victory at the battle of Waterloo (for which see further notes to ballad nos. 35 and 36). Napoleon had already been defeated once by Blücher (see below), who entered Paris on 30 March 1814. Napoleon abdicated on 4 April 1814 and was imprisoned on the island of Elba until his escape on 1 March 1815. He then campaigned for a hundred days to regain not his entire empire but the throne of France, miraculously mustering a 100,000-strong army, which was, nonetheless, soon defeated by allied forces under Wellington and Blücher at Waterloo in Belgium. Broers, *Europe Under Napoleon*, pp. 257–9.

After the battle, Napoleon was brought to Torbay and later Plymouth on board the British warship, the *Bellerophon*. He was warmly received by hosts of British people at Plymouth in particular, and generally revered by Whigs and radicals. Tory fears that he would encourage a surge of pro-Jacobinism in Britain prevailed, however, as the decision was made to send him into permanent exile on the small island of St Helena in the South Atlantic Ocean (see line 20). Markham, *Napoleon and the Awakening of Europe*, chapter 11.

line 4 A reference to Bonaparte's recapture, following his initial exile to the island of Elba, for which see further note to no. 36.

line 14 Thomas Picton (1758–1815) began his military career in the West Indies, taking part in the capture of St Lucia in 1796. He was then promoted military governor of Trinidad, a post from which he was later recalled after charges of promoting torture had been made against him. Partially exonerated from these charges, he was raised to the rank of major-general in 1808 and in 1810 appointed to command a division in the Peninsula. A strict disciplinarian who administered physical punishment to his troops, he was also a courageous fighter, prepared to lead his men from the front. His contribution to the battle of Vitoria was particularly crucial. In spite of this, however, he did not gain a peerage, and briefly turned his thoughts to leaving the military and entering parliament. He was recalled, however, to take command of the Fifth Division during Napoleon's Hundred Days' Campaign, and was killed in action at the battle of Waterloo. As a Welshman, who hailed from Poyston in Pembrokeshire, he is understandably a subject of commemoration in this ballad. *ODNB; DWB;* Robert Havard, *Wellington's Welsh General: A Life of Sir Thomas Picton* (London, 1996); Mark Adkin, *The Waterloo Companion: The Complete Guide to History's Most Famous Land Battle* (London, 2001), pp. 104–5.

line 37 For the presence of women at Waterloo, see note to no. 36.

lines 73–4 Arthur Wellesley, first duke of Wellington (1769–1852) was born in Dublin. He fought under the Duke of York in the Netherlands in 1794, and undertook service in India during 1797–1805. Upon his return home, he accepted an administrative post in government as chief secretary for Ireland (1807–8), but, by mid-June 1808, had abandoned it in favour of a return to active service in the Spanish and Portuguese Peninsula. After close-run, defensive encounters at Vimeiro (1808) and Talavera (1809), Wellesley commanded a joint Anglo-Portuguese army to win a decisive victory at Busaco in September 1810. His troops entered Madrid in August 1812, and Wellesley was appointed generalissimo of the Spanish armies. By 1813 he was in command of a 100,000-strong army of British, Portuguese and Spanish soldiers. The French's army, conversely, was being depleted by Napoleon's call for men to refill the ranks of his main army following the disaster of the Russian campaign. Following the battle of Vitoria on 21 June 1813, Wellesley was able to establish himself in the north-eastern corner of Spain, and the last engagement of the war was fought in Toulouse in April 1814. Just over a week later, Wellesley had signed a convention for the cessation of hostilities and the removal of all French troops from Spain.

Wellington returned to active service in 1815, sharing command of the allied forces gathering against Napoleon in the Netherlands. His superbly organized defence was crucial in the ensuing victory against the French at Waterloo on 18 June 1815. After the battle, Wellington advanced into France, securing an armistice on 3 July. He remained there as commander-in-chief of an occupying allied force for five years. *ODNB.*

Prince Gebhard Leberecht von Blücher (1742–1819) began his military career as a teenager, commissioned into service with the Swedish army. In 1760, he was captured by the Prussians and persuaded to join their service. He became a successful cavalry officer, and commanded the Prussian army during the campaign which led to the invasion of France and the march on Paris in 1814. So depleted were Blücher's reserves after this success that he retired from the army, but he was recalled as commander-in-chief in 1815, his aggressive approach, coupled with his hatred of the French, making him ideally suited for the post despite his advanced years. Affectionately known as 'Papa Blücher' among his troops, Wellington famously described him as a 'Damned fine fellow' after first meeting him in Paris in 1814. Adkin, *The Waterloo Companion*, p. 109; Emsley, *The Longman Companion to Napoleonic Europe*, p. 162; Roger Parkinson, *The Hussar General: The Life of Blücher, Man of Waterloo* (London, 1975).

35.

Author:
For Ioan Dafydd, see note to no. 34.

Tune:
'Ymadawiad y Brenin', also known as 'King's Farewell', may have originated as a tune to accompany an English ballad of 1648, 'King Charles His Speech, and last Farewell to the World', but was adapted to fit the contours of the Welsh language. Its earliest notation is in John Thomas's 1752 fiddle manuscript. Kinney, 'The Tunes of the Welsh Christmas Carols (I)', 35–7; Meurig (ed.), *Alawon John Thomas*, pp. 54, 151.

This ballad again looks back over the highlights of the Napoleonic era, drawing attention to Napoleon's defeat in Russia and at Waterloo, and to the overthrow of Paris. See notes to nos. 34 and 36.

line 55 For Gideon and his sword, see note to no. 19.

line 61 See note to no. 34.

line 62 Rowland Hill, first Viscount Hill of Almaraz (1772–1842), was born to a Shropshire family of rising fortunes and had a distinguished career behind him by 1815. Well-loved by his troops, he was involved in the defence of Toulon in 1793, put in charge of the 90th Foot in Egypt in 1801, and was given a near independent command by Wellington in the Peninsula, where he took part in several battles, including those of Rolica, Corunna and Talavera. During Waterloo, he was in charge of a corps consisting of between 25,000 and 30,000 men, stationed at some distance from Wellington's main troops. As a result, Hill's duties in the battle were not particularly heavy, and accounts of Waterloo rarely mention him. In fact, he did lead one brigade from among his corps to battle against the French Imperial Guard on the evening of 18 June. His horse was shot underneath him, and he fell, suffering severe bruises and concussion. An English ballad devotes a stanza to his exploits:

> Brave General Hill so much renown'd commanded our left wing,
> And with our British hearts of gold destruction for to bring,
> As Hector like he did behave where thousands were laid low
> In verse sublime his deeds shall shine that day at Waterloo.

After Waterloo, Hill served as second in command of the Army of Occupation in France, and when Wellington was elected Prime Minister in 1828, he was promoted commander-in-chief of the British army. *ODNB*, s.n. Rowland Hill, first Viscount Hill (1772–1824); Adkin, *The Waterloo Companion*, p. 103; anon., 'The Battle of Waterloo' (London, [1815]; Johnson Ballads f. 112, BLBB).

lines 91–4 The alliance which Napoleon faced at Waterloo included, in addition to the British and Prussians, troops from the King's German Legion, and from Nassau, Brunswick and Hanover, together with Dutch and Belgian troops. Adkin, *The Waterloo Companion*, p. 37. There is no reason to suppose that Swedish, Spanish and Russian troops were involved in the battle, as this ballad claims.

line 103 In His colloquy with Moses on Mount Sinai, God decreed that Moses's brother, Aaron, should have a robe, the edge of which was to be decorated with blue, purple and scarlet pomegranates, interlaced with golden bells. Exodus 28: 33, 34.

line 128 Louis Stanislas Xavier (Comte de Provence and Louis XVIII; 1755–1824) was the son of Louis, Dauphin of France, and his wife, Princess Maria Josepha of Saxony, and the brother of Louis XVI. He fled Revolutionary France for Belgium in 1791, and remained in exile (largely in England) until 1814. In April of that year he returned to France to take the throne, which was again briefly taken away from him during Napoleon's Hundred Days' Campaign. Louis XVIII accepted many of the changes which had taken place in the France of the Revolutionary period, reigning as a constitutional monarch. Physically decrepit, he was described by Wellington as a 'perfect walking sore', and scorned by the ex-Bonapartist soldiers of his new royalist army as 'le cochon'. Adkin, *The Waterloo Companion*, p. 20; Emsley, *The Longman Companion to Napoleonic Europe*, p. 201; Philip Mansel, *Louis XVIII* (Stroud, 1999).

36.

Author:
The popularity of this ballad by Thomas Jones is suggested by the numerous imprints of the text, two of which are from the Trefriw press of Ishmael Davies,

the other two from unknown presses. A southern dialect is suggested by certain features of the text: the verbal forms '[ll]uddias' and 'Cas', the added epenthetic in '[c]efen' (< cefn), the use of the word '[p]ertach'. The choice of the simple 'hen bennill' metre (as opposed to the more ornate, tune-based metres generally favoured by poets in north Wales) may also suggest a southern provenance. In a five-stanza section added to the text in imprints C and D, however, there are hints of a northern dialect ('ddweda', 'chwitha'), and the possible reference to the earl of Uxbridge, later marquess of Anglesey (see note to line 26), may also suggest that the additions were of a different origin from the main text.

Publication:
Both A and B imprints were published by Ishmael Davies, Trefriw. See note to no. 3.

lines 9–20 Richard Roberts's 1794 ballad, 'Cerdd o fawl i filitia swydd Aberteifi, ynghyd a'r officers, gan roddi iddynt glod fel y maent yn ei haeddu' (A song of praise to the militia of Cardiganshire, together with their officers, praising them according to their desert) (Croesoswallt, 1794; JHD 271i) notes the presence of women as camp followers for Welsh militia regiments:

> Mae o'n gwragedd puredd parod,
> Wedi dyfod i'r hir daith,
> A gado eu hanwyl ffrindiau gartre,
> A mentro'r siwrne moddau maith:
> Mae Duw yn rhannu ar y rheini,
> Ni chant mo'r ll'wgu mewn un lle,
> Mae hynny'n ddigon i rannu rhyngddom,
> Os byddwn foddlon galon gre'.
>
> (Some of our pure, ready wives
> have come on the long journey,
> leaving their dear friends at home,
> and venturing on the lengthy journey.
> God decrees for them
> that they shall not starve at any point;
> that is enough to share between us,
> if we are satisfied and of good heart.)

Both British and French women were involved in the military campaigns of the Napoleonic wars. French regiments authorized the presence of women, wearing apparel of military style, who were employed in selling tobacco and spirits to the soldiers, together with tending to their wounds after battle. British regiments limited the number of wives permitted to accompany their husbands on active service to six, or sometimes only four. Many more followed their husbands and lovers, however, to military camps. When news of Napoleon's invasion of Belgium reached the British, some women followed their menfolk onto the battlefield. Others were on the scene after the event, searching for their loved ones and attending to the wounds of the soldiers. They included Jenny Jones, an Irishwoman who followed her Welsh husband, Lewis, to Belgium, and reputedly spent three days on the battlefield. The couple's daughter found her injured father on the field, and Jenny nursed him to recovery. Mary Corbett Harris, 'Wandering at Waterloo', *Country Quest*, 10, no. 9 (1970), 5–6; Roy Palmer (ed.), *The Rambling Soldier: Life in the Lower Ranks, 1750–1900, through Soldiers' Songs and Writings* (Harmondsworth, 1977), p. 246; Andrew Uffindell, 'Women at Waterloo' at *http://www.historynet.com/magazines/military_history/3031026.html*; Catriona Kennedy, 'From the Ballroom to the Battlefield: British Women and Waterloo', in Alan Forrest, Karen Hagemann and Jane Rendall (eds.), *Soldiers, Citizens and Civilians: Experiences and Perceptions of the Revolutionary and Napoleonic Wars, 1790–1820* (Basingstoke, 2009), pp. 137–56.

Women also feature in English-language Waterloo ballads. 'The Waterloo Hero' displays the pathos of the bereft girlfriend when news reaches her at home of her lover's death (Shaftesbury, n.d.; Harding B 25(2007), BLBB); 'Elwina' recounts the story of a soldier who lay wounded on the battlefield when 'A female most charming appear'd to [his] view', aided his recovery and consented to become his wife (London, n.d.; Harding B 16(80c), BLBB); in an English ballad, 'The Battle of Waterloo', a single couplet is devoted to the fate of widowed women and their children, urging their home country to 'Relieve their ... wants' (London, [1815]; Johnson Ballads f. 112, BLBB). None of these texts capture the resolute spirit of the women depicted in Thomas Jones's ballad.

lines 21–4 The hour of the commencement of the battle appears to have been subject to continuous rethinking from the French point of view. Napoleon had intended a very early start at around 6 a.m. He was later persuaded by a variety of circumstances to postpone the beginning of the event until 9 a.m., then until 1 p.m., but in fact the first shots were fired at around 11.30 a.m. The loss of life at Waterloo was on a substantial scale: Wellington lost 17,000 men, the Prussians 7,000, and Napoleon around 30,600. Ballads typically record details such as these. In 'Battle of Waterloo' (n.p., n.d.; Firth c.17(304), BLBB), it is recounted that:

> The number of the French that at Waterloo was slain,
> Was near to 60 thousand all laid upon the plain;
> Near 40 thousand of them fell upon that fatal day,
> Of our brave British heroes who their prowess did display.

Adkin, *The Waterloo Companion*, pp. 73, 77–8.

line 26 This may refer to Henry William Paget, earl of Uxbridge (1768–1854). His father was the fortunate begetter of a baronetcy and, later, of 100,000 acres of mining land in England and Ireland, factors which influenced Paget's education (at Westminster School and Oxford University). He served as MP for Caernarfon and Milborne Port (1790–1812), simultaneously pursuing a career in the military from 1793. He was involved in the Flanders campaign in 1794 and in the Peninsular War, but a certain distance was placed between him and Wellington when he eloped with the latter's sister-in-law. At Waterloo, he expertly commanded a 10,000-strong cavalry corps, only to be injured in his right knee by a shell splinter in the closing stages of the battle. His leg was later amputated. After Waterloo, he became marquess of Anglesey and, in 1828, lord lieutenant of Ireland. *ODNB*; Adkin, *The Waterloo Companion*, pp. 27, 106.

lines 53–6 The freezing temperatures of the Russian winter, which fell to -20° and sometimes even -30° in November 1812, are generally believed to have been a crucial factor in the defeat of Napoleon's *Grande Armée* during its Russian campaign. Michael Broers partly disputes this, claiming that the cold temperatures only set in during the very late stages of Napoleon's retreat from Russia, and that his army had in fact been severely reduced in numbers on its advance into Russia, as a result of disease caused by the heat and following the battles of Smolensk and Borodino. Broers, *Europe Under Napoleon*, pp. 235–6; Emsley, *The Longman Companion to Napoleonic Europe*, pp. 17–18.

line 63 Napoleon spent ten months as emperor of the island of Elba, 190 kilometres from France, following his defeat at the hands of Blücher in Paris in 1814. The escape from the island took place on 26 February 1815, when Napoleon, sailing in the *Inconstant* (which had been painted to look like a British ship) led a tiny fleet and army, landing in Golfe Juan near Antibes on 1 March. Adkin, *The Waterloo Companion*, pp. 11–20; Markham, *Napoleon and the Awakening of Europe*, pp. 127–33.

37.

Author:
Robert Davies (Bardd Nantglyn; 1769–1835), from the parish of Nantglyn in Denbighshire, is best-known as an eisteddfod poet. He was an active participant in the eisteddfodau held by the London-Welsh Gwyneddigion society in Wales during the 1790s, and his sojourn in London between 1800 and 1804 brought him into even closer contact with this society, whom he served as both secretary and official bard. He later competed and adjudicated in the provincial eisteddfodau

of the 1820s and 1830s. His poetry was published in several anthologies, including *Diliau Barddas* (1827). His output as a ballad writer consists of two (or possibly three) eighteenth-century poems (JHD nos. 414i (Trefriw, 1799), 750i and perhaps 863ii), the 1813 'Cân yn achos rhyfel' (A song in the matter of the war) (Trefriw, [?1813]; Bangor 9 (10)) and an 1815 poem on the Day of Judgement, 'Cerdd yn datgan ychydig hanes am ofnadwy farn Duw ar yr annuwiolion, yn y dydd olaf neu ddydd y farn' (A song setting forth some intelligence regarding God's terrible judgement upon the wicked, on the last day or the Day of Judgement) (Trefriw, 1815; Welsh Ballads Online).

Publication:
The dating of this ballad presents many problems. Two versions of the text have survived. The A text was published in Llanrwst by John Jones (Pyll Glan Conwy). Jones removed the family business inherited from his father, Ishmael Davies, and grandfather, Dafydd Jones, from Trefriw to the nearby town of Llanrwst in 1825. The second version, B, includes no imprint but has features which suggest a publication date of *c.*1850. This may mean that this ballad was not in fact published during the Napoleonic wars, although the details of the officers named suggest a composition date no later than 1811 (see notes to lines 49–50). It should also be compared with 'Cerdd a wnaed i filitia Cymru, i'w chanu ar Drymder' (A song made to the militia of Wales, to be sung on 'Heaviness'), published by Thomas Williams (1757–1841) of Dolgellau. Williams traded as a bookseller in Dolgellau from *c.*1794 and as a printer during 1798–1808, and the ballad is tentatively dated 1799 on Welsh Ballads Online and Cronfa Baledi. For Williams, see *LW*, II, p. 878. Note, however, that 1799 is problematic as a date if lines 5–6 do indeed refer to the Peace of Amiens, as suggested in the note to lines 5–6.

   The content of 'Cân milisia Dinbych' and 'Cerdd a wnaed i filitia Cymru' is very similar, with the exception of an additional two stanzas (stanzas 4 and 5) in the middle of the former ballad, which offer a roll-call of the names of the Denbighshire militia's officers. Both texts may have been inspired by Thomas Edwards, 'Cân ar ymadawiad militia swydd Ddinbych, Mai 29th, 1778' (A song on the departure of the Denbighshire militia, 29 May 1778) (Wrexham, n.d.; JHD 694), also on the tune 'Trymder'.

Tune:
The tune 'Trymder' is first mentioned in the 1760s and was first printed, alongside words by Robert Davies, in 1857. Several varying but related versions have survived, most originating in north Wales. Kinney, 'The Tunes of the Welsh Christmas Carols (I)', 38–9.

lines 5–6 This may refer to the short-lived Peace of Amiens, signed on 27 March 1802, but in preparation from February 1801, when William Pitt resigned as Prime Minister and was replaced by Henry Addington. Although Pitt had defended the Treaty, claiming that it was 'very advantageous and, on the whole, satisfactory', public opinion in England was firmly against it. The terms agreed were extremely favourable to France, who maintained her hold on most of the territories she had gained during the wars of the preceding ten years. Doyle, *The Oxford History of the French Revolution*, pp. 380–1; Emsley, *The Longman Companion to Napoleonic Europe*, p. 257; Markham, *Napoleon and the Awakening of Europe*, pp. 67–70. Since these lines are also included in 'Cerdd a wnaed i filitia Cymru', possibly printed in 1799, they may refer, rather, to the respite from war in the period between the American War of Independence and the French Revolutionary wars. The Denbighshire militia had also been embodied during the former conflict. See Bryn Owen, *History of the Welsh Militia and Volunteer Corps 1757–1908: Denbighshire & Flintshire (Part 1)* (Wrexham, 1997), pp. 18, 20.

line 33 Service in southern England was the norm for the Denbighshire regular militia both prior to the Peace of Amiens and as late as 1812. In that year they were sent northwards to Sheffield and Hull, before moving back south to Cheshire. See ibid., pp. 21–32.

line 42 There were exactly 420 members in the Denbigh regular militia corps during 1796–9. Although this was reduced to 344 private men in 1802, a supplementary militia ballot to augment numbers was held again in Denbighshire when peace broke down in 1803. Western, *The English Militia in the Eighteenth Century*, p. 450; Owen, *History of the Welsh Militia and Volunteer Corps 1757–1908: Denbighshire & Flintshire (Part 1)*, pp. 21, 27, 28.

lines 47–8 Sir Watkin Williams Wynn III (1772–1840) inherited the family's Wynnstay estate, at Ruabon in Denbighshire, upon his father's death in 1789. Although he held the parliamentary seat for Beaumaris and for Denbighshire (in 1794–6 and 1796–1840 respectively), was lord-lieutenant of Merioneth and Denbighshire, and president of the second Cymmrodorion Society (1820–40), his main interests were military. He raised 'The Ancient British Fencibles', a cavalry regiment, in 1794, and took part in suppressing the Irish rebellion of 1798. He was involved in the Denbighshire militia from 1797. Williams Wynn's passion for being involved at the scene of conflict was gratified further when he undertook command of the Third Provisional Battalion of Militia (established in February 1813), a battalion taken from the ranks of the Denbighshire Regular Militia to serve in France. The battalion arrived too late to take part in the battle of Toulouse on 10 April 1814, and only remained in France until June of that year; nonetheless,

Williams Wynn was given a hero's welcome back to Denbighshire, and presented with a cistern inscribed with two *englynion* composed by Robert Davies. He resumed command of the entire Denbighshire Regular Militia corps and was still in his post in 1825. *DWB*, s.n. Wynn family, of Wynnstay, Ruabon; Owen, *History of the Welsh Militia and Volunteer Corps 1757–1908: Denbighshire & Flintshire (Part 1)*, pp. 32–5, 81, 82, 83.

lines 49–50 John Lloyd was a descendant through his mother of the Thelwall family of Blaen Ial, Denbighshire, and inherited Gallt Faenan, Henllan, Denbighshire from a relative, on condition that he took the name Salusbury. See introduction to Denbighshire Record Office, Galltfaenan MSS on 'Archives Network Wales' at *http://www.archiveswales.org.uk*. He enlisted as captain with the Denbighshire militia in 1794, had been promoted major by 1798 and was still in his post in 1803. He is not included in the 1811 list of officers provided by Owen. Alongside the details regarding the other officers named in the ballad, this information may help suggest an original date prior to 1811 for the composition of the ballad included in this edition. Owen, *History of the Welsh Militia and Volunteer Corps 1757–1908: Denbighshire & Flintshire (Part 1)*, pp. 80, 81.

lines 51–2 John Powell Foulkes enlisted as captain with the Denbighshire militia in 1794, was promoted to the post of lieutenant colonel in 1810, and remained in his post as late as September 1825. Ibid., pp. 80, 81, 82, 83.

line 54 This line may refer either to John Spiler Hughes, surgeon with the Denbighshire militia from January 1794, or to his successor, James Hughes, who served from March 1797 until as late as September 1825. James Hughes was among the officers of the Third Provisional Battalion who embarked for France in February 1814. Ibid., pp. 34, 80, 81, 82, 83.

38.

Author:
For Robert Morris, see note to no. 27.

Tune:
'Belisle March', also given the Welsh title 'Mynediad i'r Tir Teg' here. See note to no. 4.

line 1 The regiment named as that of Gwynedd may in fact be the Denbighshire Regular Militia. The area known in medieval times as Gwynedd Is Conwy included the county of Denbigh. Note that no. 37, lines 1–2, refers to the Denbighshire militia as the militia of the 'fair land of Gwynedd'.

lines 15–16 Invasion fears are invoked here as in lines 45–8.

lines 75–6 This may refer to the same brief moment of peace as no. 37, lines 5–6.

Appendix: the Ballad Tunes

The following appendix contains settings to music of the words of the first stanza (or in one case, the first and second stanzas) of nine of the ballads contained in the anthology. The vast majority of these are named on the original printed ballad sheets, the exception being 'Mentra Gwen' (which can with confidence be linked to ballad nos. 31 and 34, on account of the pattern of the refrains). Other ballads which do not name tunes have not been represented in this appendix.

The musical sources used include a manuscript of the Welsh ethnomusicologist, J. Lloyd Williams, and of the early folk-song collector, John Jenkins (Ifor Ceri). The majority of the tunes, however, have been taken from work by Phyllis Kinney, published in two articles in the Welsh Folk Song Society's journal, *Canu Gwerin*. Occasional slight adjustments have been made to note lengths and barring in the source material in order to ensure that the natural stress of the words coincides with the flow of the melodies. No note lengths have been changed, however, without compensating for this with the use of pause marks. Repeat marks have also been added to suit the requirements of the ballads. Anyone who attempts to sing the words to the tunes will find that the elision of vowels is at times essential for their smooth delivery: although the edited texts in this anthology seek to elide vowel sounds to some degree, even greater elision is called upon in some cases when singing the tunes. Elisions have been marked with a slur sign in the words placed beneath the melodies. The singer will take upon him or herself the freedom to adapt the words of subsequent stanzas or other ballads to the melodies in this way.

Recordings of the stanzas set to music in this appendix can be found on *http://frenchrevolution.wales.ac.uk*.

(i) Belisle March

Edward Pugh, '[Cerdd] o ganmoliaeth i'r Duke o' York, a diolchgarwch i Dduw, am gael y ffafr o orchfygu ein gelynion, sef y Ffrancod' (no. 4)

Holl bry -dydd - ion de - thol doeth- ion, Yn
O, clod - fo - rwn a chan - mo- lwn A

fawr - ion ac yn fân, Sy ag
rho - ddwn yn un rhyw Y

a - wen ryw - iog, giw - rus gae- rog, O -
gw - rol d'wy - sog Yorc ar - dder- chog (Ca -

1. di - dog, g'lon- nog, glân;   2. lon- nog, en - wog yw). Yn

nheyr-nas Ffrainc yn ffri Ge - lyn - ion sydd heb ri';   Y
an - nwyl frawd a fu Rhwng ped - war ge - lyn cry'– Duw

duc a'i ar- mi sy'n eu gorch - fy- gu A'u
oedd yn myn- nu i - ddo'u gorch - fy- gu Er

na - du nhw i'n gwlad ni. O!
hyn - ny, gwn, yn hy. *Brave*

mol - iant, mol - iant a go-gon- iant I
Welsh and Eng - lish, Scots and I- rish, We'll

Dduw, yn ben - dant bur, Am
fi- nish them all of hand; We'll

ga - dw'r gwe - ddol dduc gra - su - sol A'i ra -
rise through Eng - land, Wales, Scots and Ire - land, To be

go - rol w - rol wŷr. A'i *un- der the duke's com- mand.*

Source: Kinney, 'The Tunes of the Welsh Christmas Carols (I)', 49.

(ii) Gwêl yr Adeilad

Richard Roberts, 'Ychydig o hanes brenhines Ffrainc;
y modd y cafodd ei difetha, sef torri ei phen
a rhwymo ei dwy fraich ar ei chefn, Hydref 17, 1793' (no. 7)

Pob un sy â theim-lad__ yn-ddo, Yn
bu mewn gwlad na__ theyr-nas Rai

gy-wrein-deg dowch i wran-do– Rwy'n cwy-no ar
mi-lain gwaeth eu ma-lais, Drwy ddi-ras

1. gan-iad; Ni
dor-iad.

2. Mae Ffrainc heb fre-nin ar ei
ddaw rhyw ddi-al o-ddi

mainc, Na chwaith fren-hi-nes. (On'd tost yw'r
draw– Mae Duw yn ddi-au yn ho-gi'i

ha-nes?– Wrth go-ffa ar gy-ffes mae'n
gle-ddau; Nhw ddôn' i'r ddal-fa o

a - bl___ cru - go   craig!)   Nhw   la - ddai'r ddau   yn
waith eu___ briw - iau   braw;   Gwaed gwir - ion sydd   yn

fa - rw,   Roedd hyn - ny'n so - rw   saig.   Fe
gwei-ddi   Am eu rho-ddi'n rhych y   rhaw.

Source: Kinney, 'The Tunes of the Welsh Christmas Carols (I)', 34

(iii) King George's Delight

Richard Robert[s], '[Cerdd newydd] yn gosod allan y moddion am y
rhyfeloedd presennol rhyngom a'r Ffrancod, a dull y grefydd babaidd' (no. 8)

Ow'r   hen   Fru-tan-ied,   bur eu bwr-iad, Gwael eu   syn-ied —
mawr be-cho-de   fel cy-my-le Yn ga-lw am ddi-a-

gwyl-iwch   sen! Os   y-dyw Duw yn   ddig,   Daw
le-dde a'i   lid; Mae'n   rhy-fedd iawn gan   rai   Fod

1.   **2.**

per-yg' am eich   pen. Mae'n   Ond   e-to mae'i fy-
Duw yn go-dde'   cyd.   bod ein pur e-

gyth-ion   Ar   droi-on drym-ion   draw;   Mae
lyn-ion   Yn   greu-lon ac   yn   groes   (Mae

barn wrth li-nyn   cyn   y-le-ni, A   hyn-ny'n pe-ri
bryd cyth-reu-lig   Ffran-cod ffyr-nig I'n rhoi dan le-wyg

braw.   Mae'r   cle-dde noeth a'r   pow-dwr poeth Yn
loes),   Bydd   Duw ar ran pob   Cris-tion gwan; Rhag

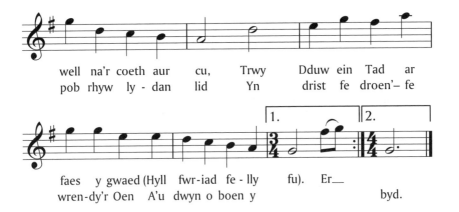

well na'r coeth aur   cu,   Trwy   Dduw ein Tad   ar
pob rhyw ly - dan   lid   Yn   drist fe droen'– fe

1.   2.

faes y gwaed (Hyll fwr-iad fe - lly   fu).   Er___
wren-dy'r Oen A'u dwyn o boen y   byd.

Source: Kinney, 'The Tunes of the Welsh Christmas Carols (II)', 18

(iv) Tempest of War

Jonathan Hughes, '[Cerdd] o galondid i'r milwyr gwladychaidd yr ydys yn godi
yn y deyrnas hon i gadw porthladdoedd, pa rai a elwir yn gyffredin milisia' (no. 11)

Source: a four-part setting in NLW, J. Lloyd Williams, AH 1 / 48, unpaginated

(v) Duw Gadwo'r Brenin

Hugh Jones, '[Cerdd] yn rhoi hanes brwydr a fu rhwng Lloegr a Hisbaen,
y 14 o Chwefror 1797, a'r modd y gorchfygwyd yr Ysbaeniaid
gan Syr John Jervis, admiral Lloegr' (no. 17)

Source: Kinney, 'The Tunes of the Welsh Christmas Carols (II)', 7

(vi) Y Dôn Fechan

John Thomas, 'Cerdd newydd ar ddull ymddiddan
rhwng rhieni a'u plant, pa rai sydd allan yn y rhyfel presennol' (no. 32)

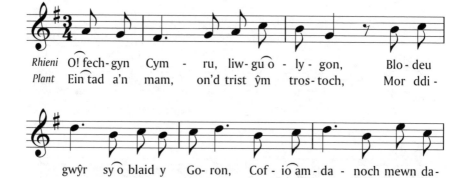

Rhieni O! fech- gyn Cym - ru, liw-gu o - ly- gon, Blo- deu
Plant Ein tad a'n mam, on'd trist ŷm tros- toch, Mor ddi -

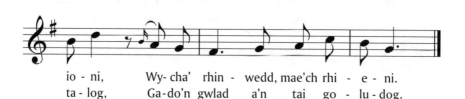

gwŷr sy o blaid y Go- ron, Cof - io am - da - noch mewn da-
gy - sur y'n ma - ga- soch; Ga - do Cym - ru a'n teu - lu

io - ni, Wy- cha' rhin - wedd, mae'ch rhi - e - ni.
ta - log, Ga- do'n gwlad a'n tai go - lu - dog.

Source: NLW 1940Aii, f. 95ʳ., no. 101

(vii) Mentra Gwen

Ioan Dafydd, 'Cân newydd am ailgymeriad Bonaparte,
ynghyd â'i anfoniad i St Helena' (no. 34)

Wel, wel, rhaid ca - nu e - to, gwir yw'r gair, gwir yw'r
gair, Fe gae - thi - wyd yr hen gad - no, gwir yw'r
gair; Sef___ Bo - na - parte y fi - len, Fe'i___
da - liwyd_ ef dra - che - fen; Mae___ lla - wer gŵr yn
lla - wen, gwir yw'r gair, gwir yw'r gair, Ar___
ddŵr ac ar y ddae' - ren, gwir yw'r gair.

Source: Kinney, 'The Tunes of the Welsh Christmas Carols (I)', 39

(viii) Ymadawiad y Brenin

Ioan Dafydd, 'Cân o anogaeth i bawb i olygu Duw
yn flaenor i'r cynghreirwyr yn Ffrainc' (no. 35)

Dewch yn fwy - naidd, fo - ne - ddig - ion,
Hen ac i - fanc, ca - nol oed - ran –

Gwŷr a gwra - gedd___ a gwy - ry - fon,
Rwyf yn eich ga - lw i gyd yn gy - fan,

Ac yn tei - ly - ngu ar-noch beu-nydd Ddy- mu-no llwydd yn

rhwydd i'r pry-dydd I ddweud y gwir___ trwy bob sir, Yn

gy - wir ar gan - iad, Fel y ga - llo

gael der - byn - iad Ym mhob rhyw ffair a___ phob rhyw farch- nad.

Source: Kinney, 'The Tunes of the Welsh Christmas Carols (I)', 36

(ix) Trymder

R[obert] Davies, 'Cân milisia Dinbych' (no. 37)

Mi - li - sia Din - bych, gwych eu gwedd, Gwlad

Wy - nedd wen, Bu gor - fod in - ni go - di o'n parth I

ga - dw'n pen. Ar ôl rhoi un - waith
A pha - ro - toi cyff -

ar - fau i lawr Mewn he - ddwch me - gis han - ner awr, Daeth
ro - ad hir, Ar - fau a thân ar fôr a thir, Yn

u - chel floedd i Bry - dain Fawr Ba - ro - dol fyw;
er - byn sain ge - lyn - ion clir Sydd yn ein clyw.

Source: Kinney, 'The Tunes of the Welsh Christmas Carols (I)', 38

Select Bibliography

Reference works, including web resources

Archives Network Wales at *http://www.archiveswales.org.uk*.

Y Beibl Cymraeg Newydd yn cynnwys yr Apocryffa (Swindon, 1988).

Bodleian Library Broadside Ballads: The *allegro* Catalogue of Ballads at *http://www.bodley.ox.ac.uk/ballads/ballads.htm*.

Cronfa Baledi at *http://www.e-gymraeg.org/cronfabaledi*.

Davies, J. H. (ed.), *A Bibliography of Welsh Ballads Printed in the Eighteenth Century* (Aberystwyth, 1911).

The Dictionary of Welsh Biography down to 1940 (London, 1959).

Geiriadur Prifysgol Cymru (4 vols., Caerdydd, 1950–2002).

The Holy Bible (King James Version).

Owens, B. G., Rhiannon Francis Roberts and R. W. McDonald, *A Catalogue of the Cwrtmawr Manuscripts Presented and Bequeathed by John Humphreys Davies*, II (Aberystwyth, 1993).

Oxford Classical Dictionary, edited by Simon Hornblower and Antony Spawforth (rev. 3rd edn., Oxford, 2003).

Oxford Dictionary of National Biography at *http://www.oxforddnb.com*.

Oxford English Dictionary at *http://www.oed.com*.

Parry, Charles, *Libri Walliae: A Catalogue of Welsh Books and Books Printed in Wales 1546–1820. Supplement* (Aberystwyth, 2001).

Rees, Eiluned, *Libri Walliae: A Catalogue of Welsh Books and Books Printed in Wales 1546–1820* (2 vols., Aberystwyth, 1987).

Rowlands, William, *Cambrian Bibliography Containing an Account of Books Printed in the Welsh Language, or Relating to Wales*, ed. D. Silvan Evans (Llanidloes, 1869; facsimile reprint, Amsterdam, 1970).

Stephens, Meic (ed.), *The New Companion to the Literature of Wales* (1986; Cardiff, 1998).

Welsh Ballads Online at *http://cat.llgc.org.uk/ballads*.

Manuscript material and printed ballad collections

Baledi a Cherddi (collection of printed ballads housed at the National Library
    of Wales).
Ballads and Fugitive Pieces, 4 vols. (collection of printed ballads housed at Cardiff
    City Library).
Casgliad o Gerddi Prydyddion Llŷn ac Eifionydd (collection of printed ballads
    housed at the National Library of Wales).
Cerddi Bangor (collection of printed ballads housed at Bangor University Library).
J. D. Lewis, Casgliad o Faledi (collection of printed ballads housed at the National
    Library of Wales).
NLW 1897E, I and II, Jenkins family letters.
NLW 1940Aii ('Per-seiniau Cymru').
NLW 7166D, autograph letters.
NLW 12350A, 'Diary . . . of John Davies, Ystrad, 1796–9'.
NLW, Bodwenni 246, *The Militia-Men's Garland, containing 4 new songs.*
NLW, Brogyntyn Estate Records, PQH1/5.
NLW, Broom Hall.
NLW, Chirk Castle: B Denbighshire Quarter Sessions Records 1. Manuscript
    volumes, no. 117.
NLW, D. Rhys Phillips.
NLW, Elizabeth Baker.
NLW, Garn Estate Records, FPB 1/5, Letters by Robert Griffith.
NLW, J. Lloyd Williams, AH 1/ 48.
NLW, Llanelwy 2379, 'The Chapter of Kings[:] A Favorite Historical Song Sung
    by Mr. Collins in the Evening's Brush', printed source, pp. 134–5.

Books, pamphlets, articles, journals and unpublished theses

Adkin, Mark, *The Waterloo Companion: The Complete Guide to History's Most Famous
    Land Battle* (London, 2001).
Anon., *A collection of constitutional songs. To which is prefixed, a collection of new toasts
    and sentiments written on purpose for this work,* I (Cork, 1799–1800).
Anon., 'Simon James 1770s–1820s', at *http://www.werelate.org/wiki/Simon_James_
    1770s-1820s.*
Anon., *The Antigallican Songster* (2 parts; London, 1793).
Anon., *The Anti-Levelling Songster* (2 parts; London, 1793).
Ashton, Glyn M., 'Arolwg ar Brydyddiaeth Gymraeg, 1801–25', *Llên Cymru*, 14,
    nos. 3 and 4 (1983–4), 224–52.
—— 'Arolwg ar Brydyddiaeth Gymraeg 1801–25 (Parhad)', *Llên Cymru*, 15,
    nos. 1 and 2 (1984–6), 106–32.
—— (ed.), *Hunangofiant a Llythyrau Twm o'r Nant* (Caerdydd, 1962).
Baker, Keith Michael, *Inventing the French Revolution* (Cambridge, 1990).

Baker-Jones, Leslie, *Princelings, Privilege and Power: The Tivyside Gentry in their Community* (Llandysul, 1999).

Barker, Hannah, *Newspapers, Politics and Public Opinion in Late Eighteenth-Century England* (Oxford, 1998).

Bowen, H.V., *The Business of Empire: The East India Company and Imperial Britain, 1756–1833* (Cambridge, 2005).

Broers, Michael, *Europe Under Napoleon 1799–1815* (London, 1996).

Bromwich, Rachel (ed.), *Trioedd Ynys Prydein* (3rd edn., Cardiff, 2006).

Brown, Michael, Catriona Kennedy, John Kirk and Andrew Noble (eds.), *United Islands? Multi-lingual Radical Poetry and Song in Britain and Ireland 1770–1820* (London, forthcoming).

Buchanan, Robert, *Poems on Several Occasions* (Edinburgh, 1797).

Burne, A. H., *The Noble Duke of York* (London, 1949).

Burrows, Simon, 'Britain and the Black Legend: The Genesis of the Anti-Napoleonic Myth', in Philp (ed.), *Resisting Napoleon*, pp. 141–57.

Cadbury, Deborah, *The Lost King of France: Revolution, Revenge and the Search for Louis XVII* (London, 2002).

Cannadine, David (ed.), *Trafalgar in History: A Battle and its Afterlife* (Basingstoke, 2006).

Carpenter, Stanley D. M., 'The British Army', in Dickinson (ed.), *A Companion to Eighteenth-Century Britain*, pp. 473–80.

Carradice, Phil, *The Last Invasion: The Story of the French Landing in Wales* (Pontypool, 1992).

Chandler, David G., and Ian Beckett (eds.), *The Oxford History of the British Army* (Oxford, 1994; paperback edn., 2003).

Charnell-White, Cathryn, *Bardic Circles: National, Regional and Personal Identity in the Bardic Vision of Iolo Morganwg* (Cardiff, 2007).

Christie, Ian R., 'Conservatism and Stability in British Society', in Philp (ed.), *The French Revolution and British Popular Politics*, pp. 169–87.

Colley, Linda, *Britons: Forging the Nation 1707–1837* (New Haven, 1992).

Constantine, Mary-Ann, '"The French are on the sea!": Welsh and Irish Songs of French Invasion in the 1790s', in Louis Grijp (ed.), *Proceedings of the International Ballad Conference, Terschelling, 2010* (Trier, forthcoming).

—— and Elizabeth Edwards, 'Bard of Liberty: Iolo Morganwg, Wales and Radical Song', in Brown, Kennedy, Kirk and Noble (eds.), *United Islands?*

Cookson, J. E., 'The English Volunteer Movement of the French Wars, 1793–1815: Some Contexts', *Historical Journal*, 32 (1989), 867–91.

Davies, Caryl, *Adfeilion Babel: Agweddau ar Syniadaeth Ieithyddol y Ddeunawfed Ganrif* (Caerdydd, 2000).

Davies, D. Elwyn J., *'They Thought for Themselves': A Brief Look at the History of Unitarianism in Wales and the Tradition of Liberal Religion* (Llandysul, 1982).

Davies, Hywel M., 'Loyalism in Wales, 1792–1793', *WHR*, 20, no. 4 (2001), 687–716.

—— '"Very different springs of uneasiness": Emigration from Wales to the United States of America during the 1790s', *WHR*, 15, no. 3 (1991), 368–98.

Davies, J. H., *The Letters of Goronwy Owen (1723–1769)* (Cardiff, 1924).

Davies, Luned, 'The Tregaer Manuscript: An Elegy for Charles I', *NLWJ*, XXXI, no. 3 (2000), 243–70.

Davies, Russell, 'Language and Community in South-West Wales *c.*1800–1914', in Geraint H. Jenkins (ed.), *Language and Community in the Nineteenth Century* (Cardiff, 1998), pp. 101–24.

Davies, W. Lloyd, 'The Riot at Denbigh, 1795', *BBCS*, IV, part I (1927), 61–73.

Davis, Michael T., '"An Evening of Pleasure Rather Than Business": Songs, Subversion and Radical Sub-Culture in the 1790s', *Journal for the Study of British Cultures*, 12, no. 2 (2005), 115–26.

Delon, Michel, and Paul-Édouard Levayer, *Chansonnier révolutionnaire* ([Paris], 1989).

Desan, Suzanne, 'The French Revolution and Religion, 1795–1815', in Stewart J. Brown and Timothy Tackett (eds.), *The Cambridge History of Christianity: Englightenment, Reawakening and Revolution 1660–1815* (Cambridge, 2006), pp. 556–74.

Dickinson, H. T., 'Popular Conservatism and Militant Loyalism', in *idem* (ed.), *Britain and the French Revolution*, pp. 103–25.

—— (ed.), *Britain and the French Revolution 1789–1815* (Basingstoke, 1989).

—— (ed.), *A Companion to Eighteenth-Century Britain* (Oxford, 2002).

Dinwiddy, John, 'England', in *idem* and Otto Dan (eds.), *Nationalism in the Age of the French Revolution* (London, 1988), pp. 53–70.

—— 'Interpretations of anti-Jacobinism', in Philp (ed.), *The French Revolution and British Popular Politics*, pp. 38–49.

Doyle, William, *Origins of the French Revolution* (3rd edn., Oxford, 1999).

—— *The Oxford History of the French Revolution* (2nd edn., Oxford, 2002).

Dunne, Tom, 'Popular Ballads, Revolutionary Rhetoric and Politicisation', in Gough and Dickson (eds.), *Ireland and the French Revolution*, pp. 139–55.

Dyck, Ian, *William Cobbett and Rural Popular Culture* (Cambridge, 1992).

Eastwood, David, 'Patriotism and the English State in the 1790s', in Philp (ed.), *The French Revolution and British Popular Politics*, pp. 146–68.

Edwards, Alaw Mai, and A. Cynfael Lake (eds.), *Detholiad o Faledi Huw Jones: 'Llymgi Penllwyd Llangwm'* (Aberystwyth, 2010).

Elliot, Marianne, 'The Role of Ireland in French War Stragegy, 1796–1798', in Gough and Dickson (eds.), *Ireland and the French Revolution*, pp. 202–19.

Emsley, Clive, *The Longman Companion to Napoleonic Europe* (London, 1993).

Evans, G. G., *Elis y Cowper* (Caernarfon, 1995).

—— 'Yr Anterliwt Gymraeg', *Llên Cymru*, I, no. 2 (1950), 83–96.

—— 'Henaint a Thranc yr Anterliwt', *Taliesin*, 54 (1985), 14–29.

Evans, John James, *Dylanwad y Chwyldro Ffrengig ar Lenyddiaeth Cymru* (Lerpwl, 1928).

Evans, R. Paul, 'The Flintshire Loyalist Association and the Loyal Holywell Volunteers', *Flintshire Historical Society Journal*, 33 (1992), 55–68.

Evans, Theophilus, *Drych y Prif Oesoedd* (1740 edn.), ed. by David Thomas (Caerdydd, 1960).

—— *Drych y Prif Oesoedd yn ôl yr argraffiad cyntaf: 1716*, ed. by Garfield H. Hughes (Caerdydd, 1961).

Forrest, Alan, Karen Hagemann and Jane Rendall (eds.), *Soldiers, Citizens and Civilians: Experiences and Perceptions of the Revolutionary and Napoleonic Wars, 1790–1820* (Basingstoke, 2009).

Franklin, Alexandra, and Mark Philp, *Napoleon and the Invasion of Britain* (Oxford, 2003).

Fraser, Antonia, *Marie Antoinette: The Journey* (2001; London, 2002).

Furet, François, and Mona Ozouf (eds.), *A Critical Dictionary of the French Revolution*, translated by Arthur Goldhammer (London, 1989).

Gammon, Vic, 'The Grand Conversation: Napoleon and British Popular Balladry' at *http://www.mustrad.org.uk/articles/boney.htm*.

Ganev, Robin, *Songs of Protest, Songs of Love: Popular Ballads in Eighteenth-Century Britain* (Manchester, 2010).

Gates, David, *The Spanish Ulcer: A History of the Peninsular War* (1986; London, 2002).

—— 'The Transformation of the Army 1783–1815', in Chandler and Beckett (eds.), *The Oxford History of the British Army*, pp. 132–60.

Gilmartin, Kevin, '"Study to be Quiet": Hannah More and the Invention of Conservative Culture in Britain', *ELH*, 70 (2003), 493–540.

Goodrich, Amanda, 'Surveying the Ebb and Flow of Pamphlet Warfare: 500 Rival Tracts from Radicals and Loyalists in Britain, 1790–1796', *British Journal for Eighteenth-Century Studies*, 30, no. 1 (2007), 1–12.

Gough, Hugh, 'The French Revolution and Europe 1789–1799', in *idem* and Dickson (eds.), *Ireland and the French Revolution*, pp. 1–13.

—— and David Dickson (eds.), *Ireland and the French Revolution* (Dublin, 1990).

Griffiths, Margaret Enid, *Early Vaticination in Welsh with English Parallels*, ed. by T. Gwynn Jones (Cardiff, 1937).

Hagemann, Karen, '"Unimaginable Horror and Misery": The Battle of Leipzig in October 1813 in Civilian Experience and Perception', in Forrest, Hagemann and Rendall (eds.), *Soldiers, Citizens and Civilians*, pp. 157–78.

Harris, Mary Corbett, 'Wandering at Waterloo', *Country Quest*, 10, no. 9 (1970), 5–6.

Harris, Michael, 'A Few Shillings for Small Books: The Experience of a Flying Stationer in the 18th Century', in Robin Myers and Michael Harris (eds.), *Spreading the Word: The Distribution Networks of Print 1550–1850* (New Castle, Delaware, 1998), pp. 83–108.

Havard, Robert, *Wellington's Welsh General: A Life of Sir Thomas Picton* (London, 1996).

Haydon, Colin, 'Religious Minorities in England', in Dickinson (ed.), *A Companion to Eighteenth-Century Britain*, pp. 241–51.

Hole, Robert, 'British Counter-revolutionary Popular Propaganda in the 1790s', in Jones (ed.), *Britain and Revolutionary France*, pp. 53–69.

Holloway, John, and Jean Black (eds.), *Later English Broadside Ballads, Volume 2* (London, 1979).

Horden, John, *John Freeth (1731–1808): Political Ballad-writer and Innkeeper* (Oxford, 1993).

Howard, Sharon, 'Riotous Community: Crowds, Politics and Society in Wales, *c*.1700–1840', *WHR*, 20, no. 4 (2001), 656–86.

Howell, David, *The Rural Poor in Eighteenth-Century Wales* (Cardiff, 2000).

Hughes, Jonathan, *Gemwaith Awen Beirdd Collen* (Croesoswallt, 1806).

Hutton, Ronald, *The Royalist War Effort, 1642–1646* (2nd edn., London, 2003).

Huws, Daniel, 'Melus-Seiniau Cymru', *Canu Gwerin*, 8 (1985), 32–50.

—— 'Melus-Seiniau Cymru: Atodiadau', *Canu Gwerin*, 9 (1986), 47–57.

James, E. Wyn, 'Rhai Methodistiaid a'r Anterliwt', *Taliesin*, 57 (1986), 8–19.

—— 'Welsh Ballads and American Slavery', *The Welsh Journal of Religious History*, 2 (2007), 59–86.

Jenkins, Geraint H., *Cadw Tŷ Mewn Cwmwl Tystion: Ysgrifau Hanesyddol ar Grefydd a Diwylliant* (Llandysul, 1990).

—— *The Foundations of Modern Wales* (Oxford, 1993).

—— *Thomas Jones yr Almanaciwr 1648–1713* (Caerdydd, 1980).

—— 'Almanaciau Thomas Jones 1680–1712', in *idem, Cadw Tŷ Mewn Cwmwl Tystion*, pp. 51–85.

—— 'Glaniad y Ffrancod yn Abergwaun ym 1797', in *idem, Cadw Tŷ Mewn Cwmwl Tystion*, pp. 256–72.

——, Ffion Mair Jones and David Ceri Jones (eds.), *The Correspondence of Iolo Morganwg* (3 vols., Cardiff, 2008).

Jenkins, R. T., *Hanes Cymru yn y Bedwaredd Ganrif ar Bymtheg: Y Gyfrol Gyntaf (1789–1843)* (Caerdydd, 1933).

—— *Hanes Cymru yn y Ddeunawfed Ganrif* (Caerdydd, 1928).

—— 'William Richards o Lynn', *TCHB* (1930), 17–68.

Jones, Colin, *The Longman Companion to the French Revolution* (Harlow, 1988).

—— (ed.), *Britain and Revolutionary France: Conflict, Subversion and Propaganda* (Exeter, 1983).

Jones, Dafydd Glyn, *Gwlad y Brutiau* (Abertawe, 1991).

—— 'Dragwniaid yn y Dref' (forthcoming).

—— '"Y Misoedd", gan William Williams, Llandygái', *Llên Cymru*, 22 (1999), 93–107.

—— (ed.), *Canu Twm o'r Nant* (Bangor, 2010).

Jones, David (ed.), *Blodeu-gerdd Cymry* (Mwythig, 1759).

Jones, David J. V., *Before Rebecca: Popular Protests in Wales 1793–1835* (London, 1973).

—— (= Jones, D. J. V.) 'The Corn Riots in Wales, 1793–1801', *WHR*, 2, no. 4 (1965), 323–50.

Jones, Ffion Mair, 'Pedair Anterliwt Hanes' (unpublished University of Wales PhD thesis, 2000).

—— '"A'r Ffeiffs a'r Drums yn roario": Y Baledwyr Cymraeg, y Milisia a'r Gwirfoddolwyr', *Canu Gwerin*, 34 (2011), 18–42.

—— '"Brave Republicans": Representing the Revolution in a Welsh Interlude', in Mary-Ann Constantine and Dafydd Johnston (eds.), *'Footsteps of Liberty and Revolt': Essays on Wales and the French Revolution* (Cardiff, forthcoming).

—— '"Gwŷr Lloeger aeth benben â'u brodyr eu hunen": Y Baledwyr Cymraeg a Rhyfel Annibyniaeth America', *Y Traethodydd*, CLXVI, no. 699 (2011), 197–225.

—— 'Huw Morys and the Civil Wars', *Studia Celtica*, XLIV (2010), 165–99.

Jones, Francis, *Historic Carmarthenshire Homes and their Families* (new edn., Newport, 1997).

—— *Historical Cardiganshire Homes and their Families*, ed. by Caroline Charles Jones (Newport, 2000).

[——] 'An echo of 1797', *The Pembrokeshire Historian*, 3 (1971), 81–2.

Jones, Hugh, *Gwedd o Chwareyddiaeth sef Hanes Bywyd a Marwolaeth, Brenhin, a Brenhines Ffraingc: Ac amryw eraill o'u Deiliaid. Hefyd Darluniad o Grefydd Babaidd: A'r modd y darostyngwyd y Pabyddion yn y Tymestl diweddar* (Trefriw, 1798).

Jones, J. D., *Caniadau Bethlehem; yn Cynnwys Carolau Nadolig, Gan Brif Feirdd Cymru; Gyda Thonau Priodol, Wedi eu Cynganeddu a'u Trefnu i Wahanol Leisiau* (Rhuthun, 1857).

Jones, James Ifano, *A History of Printing and Printers in Wales to 1810, and of Successive and Related Printers to 1923: Also, A History of Printing and Printers in Monmouthshire to 1923* (Cardiff, 1925).

Jones, Richard, 'Gwaith Argraffwyr Machynlleth o 1789 Ymlaen', *JWBS*, XI, no. 1 (1958), 25–8.

Jones, Tegwyn, 'Baledi a Baledwyr y Bedwaredd Ganrif ar Bymtheg', in Geraint H. Jenkins (ed.), *Cof Cenedl VI: Ysgrifau ar Hanes Cymru* (Llandysul, 1991), pp. 101–34.

—— 'Brasolwg ar y Faled Newyddiadurol yng Nghymru cyn y Cyfnod Argraffu', *Canu Gwerin*, 25 (2002), 3–25.

—— 'Hiwmor yn y Baledi', *Canu Gwerin*, 24 (2001), 3–16.

—— 'Welsh Ballads', in Philip Henry Jones and Eiluned Rees (eds.), *A Nation and its Books: A History of the Book in Wales* (Aberystwyth, 1998), pp. 245–51.

[Jones, William], *One Penny-worth of Truth from Thomas Bull to his Brother John*, in *Liberty and Property Preserved against Republicans and Levellers: A Collection of Tracts Number I* (London, 1793), pp. 1–5.

Keay, John, *The Honourable Company: A History of the English East India Company* (London, 1991).

Kendrick, T. D., *British Antiquity* (London, 1950).

Kennedy, Catriona, 'From the Ballroom to the Battlefield: British Women and Waterloo', in Forrest, Hagemann and Rendall (eds.), *Soldiers, Citizens and Civilians*, pp. 137–56.

Ketcham, Ralph (ed.), *The Anti-Federalist Papers and the Constitutional Convention Debates* (London, 1986).

Kinney, Phyllis, 'The Tunes of the Welsh Christmas Carols (I)', *Canu Gwerin*, 11 (1988), 28–57.

—— 'The Tunes of the Welsh Christmas Carols (II)', *Canu Gwerin*, 12 (1989), 5–29.

Kinross, John S., *Fishguard Fiasco: An Account of the Last Invasion of Britain* (Tenby, 1974).

Klingberg, Frank J., and Sigurd B. Hustvedt (eds.), *The Warning Drum: The British Home Front Faces Napoleon. Broadsides of 1803* (Berkeley, 1944).

Knapp, Oswald G. (ed.), *The Intimate Letters of Piozzi and Pennington* (London, 1914; 2nd edn., Stroud, 2005).

Knight, Roger, 'The Fleets at Trafalgar: The Margin of Superiority', in Cannadine (ed.), *Trafalgar in History*, pp. 61–77.

Lake, A. Cynfael, *Huw Jones o Langwm* (Caernarfon, 2009).

—— 'Evan Ellis, "Gwerthwr llyfrau a British Oil &c."', *Y Traethodydd*, CXLIV, no. 613 (1989), 204–14.

—— 'William Jones a'r "ddau leidir baledae"', *Llên Cymru*, 33 (2010), 124–42.

Lavery, Brian, *The Line of Battle: The Sailing Warship, 1650–1840* (London, 1992).

Le Fevre, Peter, and Richard Harding (eds.), *Precursors of Nelson: British Admirals of the Eighteenth Century* (Rochester, 2000).

Lever, Evelyne, *Marie Antoinette: The Last Queen of France*, translated by Catherine Temerson (New York, 2000).

Lewis, Aneirin, 'Llythyrau Evan Evans (Ieuan Fardd) at Ddafydd Jones o Drefriw', *Llên Cymru*, I, no. 4 (1951), 239–58.

Lewis, Mrs Herbert, *Folk Songs Collected in Flintshire and the Vale of Clwyd* (Wrexham, 1914).

Linch, Kevin B., '"A Citizen and Not a Soldier": The British Volunteer Movement and the War against Napoleon', in Forrest, Hagemann and Rendall (eds.), *Soldiers, Citizens and Civilians*, pp. 205–21.

Lloyd, Nesta (ed.), *Blodeugerdd Barddas o'r Ail Ganrif ar Bymtheg*, I (Barddas, 1993).

Löffler, Marion, *Welsh Responses to the French Revolution: Press and Public Discourse 1789–1802* (Cardiff, forthcoming).

—— 'Serial Literature and Radical Poetry in Wales at the End of the Eighteenth Century', in Brown, Kennedy, Kirk and Noble (eds.), *United Islands?*

McCalman, Iain (ed.), *An Oxford Companion to the Romantic Age: British Culture 1776–1832* (Oxford, 1999).

McDowell, R. B., 'The Age of the United Irishmen: Reform and Reaction, 1789–94', in Moody and Vaughan (eds.), *A New History of Ireland. IV*, pp. 289–338.

—— 'The Age of the United Irishmen: Revolution and the Union, 1794–1800', in Moody and Vaughan (eds.), *A New History of Ireland. IV*, pp. 339–73.

—— 'Parliamentary Independence, 1782–9', in Moody and Vaughan (eds.), *A New History of Ireland. IV*, pp. 265–373.

Mahoney, James, *Colonialism and Postcolonial Development: Spanish America in Comparative Perspective* (Cambridge, 2010).

Mansel, Philip, *Louis XVIII* (Stroud, 1999).

Markham, F. M. H., *Napoleon and the Awakening of Europe* (London, 1954).

Marsh, Christopher, 'The Sound of Print in Early Modern England: The Broadside Ballad as Song', in Julia Crick and Alexandra Walsham (eds.), *The Uses of Script and Print, 1300–1700* (Cambridge, 2004), pp. 171–90.

Marshall, P. J., 'The British Empire at the End of the Eighteenth Century', in *idem* (ed.), *Cambridge Illustrated History: British Empire* (Cambridge, 1996), pp. 16–23.

Maund, Kari, *The Welsh Kings: The Medieval Rulers of Wales* (Stroud, 2000).

Means, Philip Ainsworth, *Fall of the Inca Empire and the Spanish Rule in Peru: 1530–1780* (London, 1932).

Meurig, Cass, 'Canu i Gyfeiliant Ffidil yng Nghymru'r Ddeunawfed Ganrif', *Canu Gwerin*, 24 (2001), 20–41.

—— (ed.), *Alawon John Thomas: A Fiddler's Tune Book from Eighteenth-Century Wales* (Aberystwyth, 2004).

Miller, Peter (ed.), *Priestley: Political Writings* (Cambridge, 1993).

Millward, E. G. (ed.), *Cerddi Jac Glan-y-gors* (Barddas, 2003).

Miskell, Louise, *'Intelligent Town': An Urban History of Swansea, 1780–1855* (Cardiff, 2006).

Moody, T. W., and W. E. Vaughan (eds.), *A New History of Ireland. IV. Eighteenth-Century Ireland 1691–1800* (Oxford, 1986; paperback edn., 2009).

Morgan, Gerald, *Ceredigion: A Wealth of History* (Llandysul, 2005).

—— 'Baledi Dyffryn Conwy', *Canu Gwerin*, 20 (1997), 2–12.

Morys, Huw, *Y Rhyfel Cartrefol*, ed. by Ffion Mair Jones (Bangor, [2008]).

Moylan, Terry (ed.), *The Age of Revolution: 1776 to 1815 in the Irish Song Tradition* (Dublin, 2000).

Nagel, Susan, *Marie-Thérèse: The Fate of Marie Antoinette's Daughter* (London, 2009).

Navickas, Katrina, *Loyalism and Radicalism in Lancashire, 1798–1815* (Oxford, 2009).

Newman, Jon, '"An Insurrection of Loyalty": The London Volunteer Regiments' Response to the Invasion Threat', in Philp (ed.), *Resisting Napoleon*, pp. 75–89.

Owen, Bryn, *The History of the Welsh Militia and Volunteer Corps 1757–1908: 1. Anglesey and Caernarfonshire* (Caernarfon, 1989).

—— *History of the Welsh Militia and Volunteer Corps 1757–1908: Denbighshire & Flintshire (Part 1)* (Wrexham, 1997).

Owen, Hugh J., *Merioneth Volunteers and Local Militia During the Napoleonic Wars (1795–1816)* (Dolgelley, [1934]).

Palmer, Roy (ed.), *The Rambling Soldier: Life in the Lower Ranks, 1750–1900, through Soldiers' Songs and Writings* (Harmondsworth, 1977).

Parkinson, Roger, *The Hussar General: The Life of Blücher, Man of Waterloo* (London, 1975).

Parry, Thomas, *Baledi'r Ddeunawfed Ganrif* (1935; 2nd edn., Llandysul, 1986).

Parry-Jones, Lilian, 'Astudiaeth o Faledi Dafydd Jones, Llanybydder: Eu Cefndir a'u Cynnwys' (unpublished University of Wales MPhil dissertation, 1990).

Pedersen, Susan, 'Hannah More Meets Simple Simon: Tracts, Chapbooks, and Popular Culture in Late Eighteenth-Century England', *Journal of British Studies*, 25 (1986), 84–113.

Peele, Michael, *Shropshire in Poem and Legend* (Shrewsbury, 1923).

Pennant, Thomas, *Free Thoughts on the Militia Laws . . . addressed to the Poor Inhabitants of North Wales* (London, 1781).

Philp, Mark, 'Music and Politics, 1793–1815: Section 1', in *idem* (ed.), *Resisting Napoleon*, pp. 173–8.

—— 'Politics and Memory: Nelson and Trafalgar in Popular Song', in Cannadine (ed.), *Trafalgar in History*, pp. 93–120.

—— (ed.), *The French Revolution and British Popular Politics* (Cambridge, 1991).

—— (ed.), *Resisting Napoleon: The British Response to the Threat of Invasion, 1797–1815* (Aldershot, 2006).

Pincus, Steve, *1688: The First Modern Revolution* (London, 2009).

Pinn, William, *Poems, on various subjects: in which is a most beautiful and novel description of His Majetsy's review of the Kentish Volunteers* (Chatham, 1800).

Quinault, Roland, 'The French Invasion of Pembrokeshire in 1797: A Bicentennial Assessment', *WHR*, 19, no. 4 (1989), 618–41.

[Richards, William], *Cwyn y Cystuddiedig a griddfanau y carcharorion dieuog, neu, ychydig o hanes dyoddefiadau diweddar Thomas John a Samuel Griffiths, y rhai goddef gorthrymder tost a chaethiwed caled . . . yn ddi-achos, a gawsant eu rhyddhau . . . yn Hwlffordd . . .* (Caerfyrddin, 1798).

Rivers, Isabel, and David L. Wykes (eds.), *Joseph Priestley, Scientist, Philosopher and Theologian* (Oxford, 2008).

Robinson, Penny, 'Caneuon Ffarwél', *Canu Gwerin*, 24 (2001), 54–67.

Rodger, N. A. M., *The Wooden World: An Anatomy of the Georgian Navy* (London, 1986)

—— 'The Significance of Trafalgar: Sea Power and Land Power in the Anglo-French Wars', in Cannadine (ed.), *Trafalgar in History*, pp. 78–89.

Rogers, Nicholas, *The Press-gang: Naval Impressment and its Opponents in Georgian Britain* (London, 2007).

Rose, R. B., 'The Priestley Riots of 1791', *Past and Present*, 18 (1960), 68–88.

Rosser, Siwan M., *Y Ferch ym Myd y Faled: Delweddau o'r Ferch ym Maledi'r Ddeunawfed Ganrif* (Caerdydd, 2005).

—— 'Golwg ar Ganu Rhydd Jonathan Hughes, 1721–1805' (unpublished University of Wales MPhil thesis, 1998).

—— (ed.), *Bardd Pengwern: Detholiad o Gerddi Jonathan Hughes, Llangollen (1721–1805)* (Barddas, 2007).

Saer, D. Roy, 'Carol y Cymro ac Anthem y Sais', *Welsh Music*, VII, no. 9/10 (1985), 6–19.

St Clair, William, *The Reading Nation in the Romantic Period* (Cambridge, 2004).

Schama, Simon, *Citizens: A Chronicle of the French Revolution* (1989; London, 2004).

Scrivener, Michael, *Poetry and Reform: Periodical Verse from the English Democratic Press 1792–1824* (Detroit, 1992).

Semmel, Stuart, *Napoleon and the British* (New Haven, 2004).

Smacker, Isaac, 'Historical Sketch of the Welsh Hill, Licking County, O.' (in two parts), *The Cambrian*, I, no. 2 (March/April 1880), 46–53; no. 3 (May/June 1880), 81–6, at *http://ohio.llgc.org.uk/erth-lick-h.php*.

Spurr, John, 'The Church of England, Comprehension and the Toleration Act of 1689', *EHR*, CIV (1989), 927–46.

Southey, Roz, 'The Volunteer Band, Newcastle upon Tyne', in Philp (ed.), *Resisting Napoleon*, pp. 179–84.

Stott, Anne, *Hannah More: The First Victorian* (Oxford, 2003).

Thomas, Ben Bowen, *Drych y Baledwr* (Aberystwyth, 1958).

—— (ed.), *Baledi Morgannwg* (Caerdydd, 1951).

Thomas, David (ed.), *Corph y Gaingc* (Dolgellau, 1810).

Thomas, D. O. (ed.), *Price: Political Writings* (Cambridge, 1991).

Thomas, J. E., *Britain's Last Invasion: Fishguard 1797* (Stroud, 2007).

Thomas, John (Penffordd-wen), *Telyn Arian: sef Llyfr Barddoniaeth; yn cynnwys Carolau, Cerddi, Awdlau, ac Englynion, &c. Ar amryw Destynau, ac hefyd, Cerddi a phenillion, yn gymysgedig o Gymraeg a Saesonaeg, Ond y cwbl ar gynghayedd [sic] a mesurau a arferir yn Gymraeg* ([1806]; 3rd edn., Llanrwst, 1823).

Thomas, John (Pentrefoelas), *Eos Gwynedd, sef Casgliad o Ganiadau ar Destynau Crefyddol, Moesol, a Difyrol, gan y Diweddar Mr. John Thomas, Pentre'r Foelas*, ed. by William Williams (Gwilym Caledfryn) (Llanrwst, [1845]).

Uffindell, Andrew, 'Women at Waterloo', at *http://www.historynet.com/magazines/military_history/3031026.html*.

Walters, Huw, *A Bibliography of Welsh Periodicals 1735–1850* (Aberystwyth, 1993).

Western, J. R., *The English Militia in the Eighteenth Century: The Story of a Political Issue 1660–1802* (London, 1965).

—— 'The Volunteer Movement as an Anti Revolutionary Force, 1793–1801', *EHR*, LXXI (1956), 603–14.

Whelan, Kevin, 'Politicisation in County Wexford and the Origins of the 1798 Rebellion', in Gough and Dickson (eds.), *Ireland and the French Revolution*, pp. 156–78.

White, Colin, *The Nelson Encyclopædia* (London, 2002).

Whiting, John Roger Scott, *The Spanish Armada* (1988; new edn., Stroud, 2004).

Williams, Gwyn A., *The Search for Beulah Land: The Welsh and the Atlantic Revolution* (New York, 1980).

—— *When Was Wales? A History of the Welsh* (1985; paperback edn., London, 1991).

Williams, H. Cernyw, *William Carey, D.D, a chan'mlwyddiaeth cenadaeth y Bedyddwyr* (Llangollen, 1891).

[Williams, H. L.], *An Authentic Account of the Invasion by the French Troops, Under the Command of General Tate, On Cerrig Gwastad Point, Near Fishguard* (1842; 2nd edn., Haverfordwest, [1853]).

Williams, Ifor (ed.), *The Poems of Taliesin*, English version by J. E. Caerwyn Williams (Dublin, 1987).

Wynne, Ellis, *Gweledigaetheu y Bardd Cwsc*, ed. by Aneirin Lewis (Caerdydd, 1976).

Zimmerman, Georges-Denis (ed.), *Songs of Irish Rebellion: Political Street Ballads and Rebel Songs 1780–1900* (Dublin, 1967).

Note to the Indexes

Two indexes are presented below. The first is an index to the translations of the ballad texts, with entries referring the reader to the ballad number, followed by a line number (e.g. 20.3 refers to ballad no. 20, line 3). This index provides a brief reference to names of people and places, together with a few additional entries thought to be potentially useful to the reader of the volume. Most of these names are given in the simple forms in which they appear in the text. Occasionally, additional information is provided in brackets to help identify the person or place. Where more than one name is involved, the two names have been reversed to provide the surname or main element of a place name first (e.g. 'Haslam, Captain' for 'Captain Haslam', or 'Britain, Isle of' for the 'Isle of Britain'). An exception has been made to this rule where several different name-forms are found: e.g. George III is referred to by a host of names, some varying only slightly from others. In cases such as this, a heading, 'George III', has been placed as the main entry, with the variant names listed beneath it. Readers can refer brief entries in this index to the second, or general, index to the volume, which provides full details for each entry. The general index relates to the introduction and the notes to the texts, together with the apparatus of the texts and the musical settings in the appendix.

Index to the Ballads

General Index

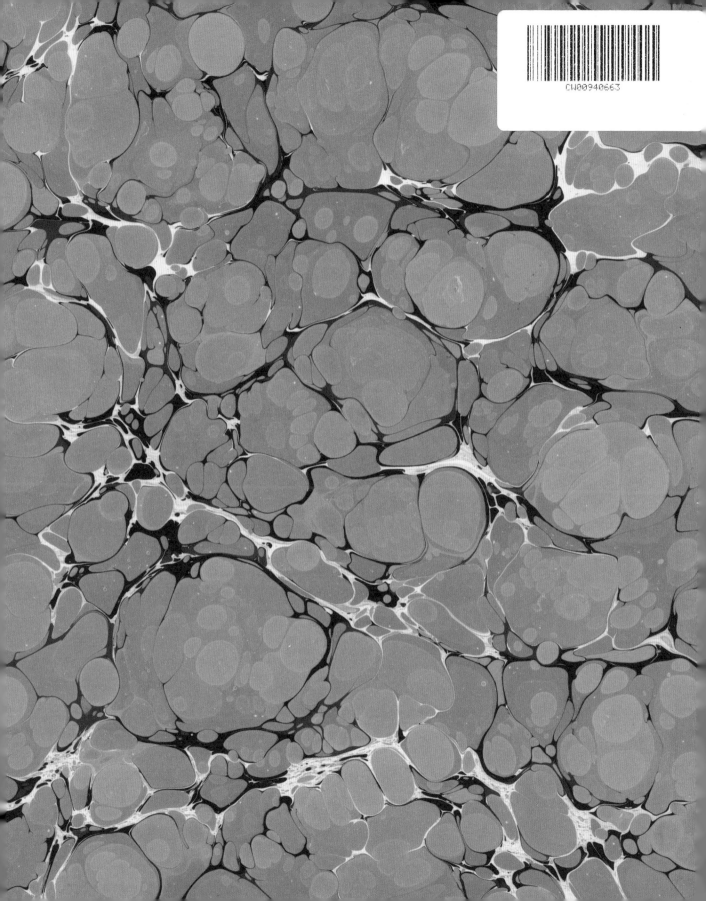

FOR CENTURIES, THE greatest explorers of their age were dispatched from the power-houses of Europe — London, Paris and Berlin — on a quest unlike any other: To be the first white Christian to visit, and then to sack, the fabled metropolis of Timbuctoo.

Most of them never returned alive.

At the height of the Timbuctoo mania, two hundred years ago, it was widely believed that the elusive Saharan city was fashioned in entirety from the purest gold — everything from the buildings to the cobblestones, from the buckets to the bedsteads was said to be made from it.

One winter night in 1815, a young illiterate American seaman named Robert Adams was discovered half-naked and starving on the snowbound streets of London. His skin seared from years in the African desert, he claimed to have been a guest of the King of Timbuctoo.

At a time when anything American was less than popular, the loss of the colony still fresh in British minds, the thought of an American claiming anything — let alone the greatest prize in exploration — was abhorrent in the extreme.

Closing ranks against their unwelcome American guest, the British Establishment lampooned his tale, and began a campaign of discrediting him, one that continues even today.

An astonishing tale based on true-life endurance, *Timbuctoo* vividly recreates the obsessions of the time, as a backdrop for one of the greatest love stories ever told.

TIMBUCTOO

TAHIR SHAH

TIMBUCTOO

BEING A SINGULAR
AND MOST ANIMATED ACCOUNT

OF AN ILLITERATE AMERICAN SAILOR,

TAKEN AS A SLAVE
IN THE GREAT ZAHARA AND,

AFTER TRIALS AND TRIBULATIONS APLENTY,

REACHING LONDON
WHERE HE NARRATED HIS TALE

TAHIR SHAH

SECRETUM MUNDI PUBLISHING

MMXII

Secretum Mundi Publishing
3rd Floor
36 Langham Street
London W1W 7AP
United Kingdom
info@secretum-mundi.com

First published 2012

© TAHIR SHAH

Tahir Shah asserts the moral right to be identified as the author of this work

A catalogue record for this book is available from the British Library

ISBN 978-0-9572429-0-6

Typeset in Bulmer, 14/20pt

For more information about this book please visit:
www.timbuctoo-book.com
www.secretum-mundi.com

Visit the author's web site at:
www.tahirshah.com

Design: www.rachanashah.com

Printed and bound in Hong Kong by Regal Printing Ltd.

This book is inspired by a true story.

For my mother,
whose love of the Regency is matched only by my own.

I

The Royal African Committee invites subscriptions — The ragged figure of a man collapses in the London snow — Mr. Cochran's letter to Beattie — The vagrant is almost run down by a carriage — Mr. Cochran informs Beattie of the Timbuctoo expedition — The vagrant is recognised by Viscount Fortescue — Mr. Cochran reports to Beattie on receiving a letter — Miss Fortescue takes breakfast with her father — Sir Geoffrey Caldecott interviews Major Peddie before the departure of the expedition — Beattie's letter to Mr. Cochran — At Camelford House the visitor is stirring — The visitor introduces himself to the Fortescues as Mr. Robert Adams, confirming that he has visited Timbuctoo — Viscount Fortescue takes Mr. Adams to the Royal African Committee — Sir Geoffrey Caldecott learns of Mr. Adams — Mr. Cochran advises Beattie of the arrival of the visitor — Mr. Adams moves into Mr. Cochran's Fleet Street chambers — Mr. Adams arrives to begin his narration at the Royal African Committee — The business of the Royal African Committee — Mr. Cochran receives a letter from Beattie — Mr. Adams commences his narration, describing how he was dispatched from America.

ONE

AN ORNATE QUEEN Anne brazier was crackling with coals at either end of the opulent meeting room.

The heat warmed the extremities, and left the fifty gentlemen seated at the central mahogany table wishing they had worn their woollen underwear instead.

Long portraits of the Committee's founders obscured the dim silk-covered walls, absorbing the light from a great Bohemian chandelier, suspended from the panelled ceiling above.

There was a tension in the room, as if each of the frock-coated gentlemen was well aware of his good fortune at being invited to attend.

The dark waxed table was strewn with papers, ledgers, and with maps of Africa, most of them little more than outlines — hinting at the vast unexplored regions and of the riches awaiting the foolhardy and the brave.

At the far end of it was seated Sir Geoffrey Caldecott.

A fleshy red-faced bulldog of a man of fifty-six, he lurched up from his chair, swept out the forked tails of his coat, and thumped the polished surface with his palm. His breathing was excitable and asthmatic, his manner aggressive.

'Gentlemen!' he boomed, raising his hand. 'Gentlemen, I call this session of the Royal African Committee to order!'

The hum of conversation subsided, and the prosperous-looking men seated turned their attentions to the chairman.

'Since the earliest glimpses of history,' Caldecott called out, 'chroniclers have documented its treasures. Ibn Battutah and Leo the African among them — all have recorded its astounding wealth. Never before has a land so abundant with bullion been known!'

William DeWitt, a meagre figure with small calculating eyes, seated to the left of the chairman, stood up. He coughed to gain the attention of the room. DeWitt was a merchant whose immense private fortune had been constructed on the misfortune of others.

He coughed again, more forcefully.

'Gentlemen,' he announced, 'I coax you to conjure your imagination. Picture an African El Dorado where the only known metal is gold! Storehouses overflow with it, and coffers are brimming with it. Roof tiles and cobblestones, cups and plates, buckets and bedsteads, all are fashioned from that most intoxicating yellow ore!'

'The purest gold,' Caldecott broke in, 'all of it awaiting any gentleman who subscribes to this sound project. Our own Major Peddie will be the first Christian, the first Caucasian gentleman, to journey to the golden land and back. And with him will come the entire bounty of that sacked metropolis! But we *must* hurry!'

'Just this morning a messenger has brought news of the French expeditionary force,' DeWitt added urgently, 'departed three nights ago from Marseilles. Their feet already tramp south across African sands.'

Caldecott nudged a finger at the wiry, hunched man to his right. Liveried in a flamboyant lilac frock coat with oversized cuffs, a froth of cream silk wound tight around his neck, Simon Cochran held the title of Committee secretary, although he spent most of his time carrying out duties well below his position.

He did not stand, but instead held up a crisp white sheet of laid paper and a goose-feather quill.

'Pledge your savings now, gentlemen,' Caldecott urged, 'and tomorrow you will be prosperous beyond all imagination!'

With the long-bearded founders peering down in witness from their gilded frames, the investors sprang to their feet. They huddled around the secretary, each one eager to sign the paper, headed with a single word in copperplate script — *TIMBUCTOO*.

TWO

SHOELESS AND FURLED up in a filthy blanket, shielding his face from the arctic wind, a lone figure staggered out into the street from the market stalls of Covent Garden.

Collapsing, his weight fell full force down onto the cobbles.

The last of the stallholders had gone home for the night as the bell of St. Paul's church struck six. The snow was coming down hard again, softening the sounds of carriage wheels running down to the Strand. The snowflakes gathered, settling on the blanket in silence.

The body beneath it did not move.

An hour passed. A pair of sailors burst out of the Red Swan Tavern, reeled across the square, laughing, boasting, spirits shored up by drink. A stream of bright yellow lamplight from the door illuminated the snow. It narrowed to a triangle and was gone.

Another hour ebbed away and the wind whipped up.

Then came the roar of steel-rimmed wheels, a carriage hurtling over cobbles. Charging from the blackness, its four mares cantered full tilt into the wind. Lashing at the reins, half-blinded by the blizzard, the coachman's face was wrapped in a makeshift calico hood.

The wheels thundered across the square towards the figure.

Fifty feet, thirty, fifteen…

A second before the rims struck flesh, the figure thrust an arm to the side. The coachman tore back on the reins. The horses whinnying, the wheels jammed, sparking, skidding against the snow.

THREE

Dearest Beattie,

Salutations, my little cousin, from a colder London day than I can recall. To think it is only October! I have stoked the fire since before dawn, but was frozen to the bone half the night. So cold was I, that I pulled on my breeches while under the covers. Imagine that! What suffering! This night I will sleep in three pairs of stockings and the maroon felt nightcap you so sweetly presented me with two Christmases ago.

The Committee's chairman, Sir Geoffrey, has been whipped into a maniacal state these past days. There is much talk of the French expedition. The very mention of it, and Sir G flies into a rage. Indeed, the mention of anything French drives him wild with rage. He refuses even the finest glass of claret — remarkable for a man with such an unquenchable thirst. But then, Waterloo is so recent in all our minds.

I have heard tell that the French contingent, under the command of General Dumas, has packed a hundred gallons of eau de cologne in which they intend to bathe the natives when they arrive. The chocolate shops of Mayfair resound to talk of how King Louis insists his monogram be nailed on the palace walls of far-off Timbuctoo.

Our only advantage is that Bonaparte is impotent at last, en route as I write this to his incarceration at St. Helena. Thank God for that, and for our victory last summer.

Major Peddie will set sail a week tomorrow from Plymouth, and plans to make landfall at Tangiers, leading the largest and best prepared expedition that has ever sought out that glorious desert emporium. The investors appear to have covered the costs for the mission many times over, much to the delight of Sir G.

There is no doubt that Major Peddie marches into history, holding high the colours of the Committee, of Britannia, and the King.

Yours affectionately, my dearest Beattie,
Simon

FOUR

THE WIND HOWLED up the Thames, tearing through Covent Garden, and buffeting the coach on its springs. Pulled to a halt so forcefully, the horses were champing furiously on their bits, their dark coats gleaming like Chinese lacquer in lamplight.

The coachman ran a palm down the back of the lead mare.

'Easy, me love, easy with ya.'

'What is it, Dunn?' shouted a voice from the carriage.

'A vagrant, sir. We almost struck 'im.'

The carriage door, which bore the monogram C.R.T.F., opened a crack and was flapped back on its hinges by the wind. The heel of a leather boot kicked down the folding step and a gentleman climbed out into the snow.

He was dressed in a cashmere coat with a fox stole tight around his neck, a beaver hat crowning his thin grey hair.

'Viscount, sir, please take your place inside the carriage. We'll move away as soon as the horses have calmed.'

'Is he dead?'

The coachman tugged the carriage lamp off its fastening, pushed forward, and held the flame to the man's face. The snow was bathed in syrupy yellow light. Stooping over, the driver pulled at the rag covering the vagrant's face.

'My gawd,' gasped the driver, lurching backwards.

'Tell me man, is he dead?'

'Alive, sir, barely so, but...'

'But what?'

'His face, sir. It's burned.'

'*Burned*?'

'Let us away, sir. This is no place for a gentleman.'

'Get back to the horses.'

The vagrant's eyes opened a fraction. Straining to focus, he was blinded by the lantern-light.

'Can you see me, man?'

The figure faded in and out of consciousness. The Viscount brought the lamp closer to chase away the shadows. He took a good look, examining the man's face with care. Its features were wind-chapped and weatherworn, the left eye bisected by a deep scar. It ran from the middle of the brow down as far as the cheek.

The raw lips parted and, in a whisper, he said:

'*Al Shahra Ahad*! The sun, the desert sun!'

The Viscount pulled a hipflask from his breast pocket and nudged its silver rim to the man's mouth. He struggled to sip.

'*Shukran*. Thank you,' he said, his words barely audible.

The Viscount leant closer, until his ear was half an inch from the man's lips.

'Your voice... It's...'

'American. I am an American.'

'*An American*? But where have you come from?'

'From an African Hell.'

FIVE

Dearest Beattie,

Snow has been falling here for five days now, and the coal merchants have raised their prices a shilling a sack, much to the exasperation of all decent Londoners. I would be protesting along with the others outside the Guildhall, but there is great commotion in the offices of the Committee!

I was this morn at my desk early, preparing for Major Peddie's departure to the Dark Continent. There are so many bills to be paid, details of every kind to attend to. Sir G is adamant that Peddie and his party must reach this desert El Dorado by Christmas if they are to trounce the French. He charges into the building shortly after breakfast, and stampedes about from his study to the library, to the meeting chambers and back to the library, tormenting all those he encounters. It may be freezing, but Sir Geoffrey's brow ever streams with perspiration.

So at my desk were I, adding numbers and squaring papers, when the sound of a stick running down the railings caught my attention. It caught Sir G's too. He pricked up his ears like an old hunting dog, barked a line of expletives, and ordered me to rebuke the rascal. Pulling on my coat, I stumbled out onto the icy steps, and found an urchin waiting there. He was shaking, grey with cold, clasping a note in his hand.

With a duck of his head, he presented it to me. I gave him a farthing for his trouble, sent him off, went back inside and regarded the envelope at the fireside. At once I recognised the impeccable script — that of my godfather, the Arabist Viscount Fortescue.

With affection, my dearest Beattie,
Simon

SIX

A BRIGHT-EYED young woman of twenty, with a delicate complexion and a mane of copper hair, was standing beside the marble-framed fireplace in the drawing room of Camelford House in Hanover Square.

The top of her head was reflected in the mirror above it, her face level with a blue jasperware vase resting upon the mantel. Her palms were pressed together in anticipation, the bow of her jade dress flopping unevenly to one side.

In the background, a long-cased clock chimed nine. From a distance came the sound of bone china rattling on a tray, as a maid ascended the stairs from the kitchen.

The Viscount entered.

Now in the warm, he seemed taller than he appeared the night before. He was fifty-five but looked a little younger, his skin anointed daily with almond oil, and the horseshoe of hair crowning the back of his head scented with *pomade de Nerole*. His movements were measured, his costume immaculate, and his back ramrod straight.

'Clara, dearest, shall we sit for breakfast?'

The girl smoothed a hand down over her copper locks, and bobbed towards her father.

'Tell me, Papa, tell me, who is he?'

'Who is who?'

'The man brought in last night. I heard the furore. The landing almost collapsed! I have tried the bedroom door but it's locked. I implore you, Father, whom do you keep as your prisoner?'

Viscount Fortescue glided past his daughter. He had small feet for a man of such height, and had enjoyed quite a reputation in his younger years for the quadrille.

Crossing the central medallion of a Persian carpet, laid over the beech parquet, he reached the mullion window.

Outside, the snow was falling once again, the light flat and ash-grey. Fortescue glanced out at a sheet of newspaper tossed up. He turned round to face the fire.

'An American,' he said, pronouncing the syllables slowly. 'My *prisoner* is an American.'

'But Father, our nations are at war!'

The Viscount touched a hand to his chin and smiled.

'I am well informed of the hostilities, my dear.'

'But surely it is not wise to allow the enemy into our home. Why, he could murder us in our beds! Or what if he is diseased?'

'Come now dear Clara, breakfast is ready.'

Fortescue ushered his daughter through to the adjoining parlour, where breakfast had been laid. The room was small, at least when compared to the grandeur of the reception rooms on the ground floor. It was warm, decorated with Japanese prints and a variety of other pictures. The largest was a treasured Hokusai wave in a thin gold frame, and the smallest, a silhouette of Clara's maternal grandfather made on the afternoon of his death.

Near the window an aspidistra stood on a turquoise china stand. Upon an octagonal walnut table beside it, sat an ironed copy of *The Times*. Clara took her usual seat, away from the window, her father across the table. She poured herself a cup of Darjeeling, added a drop of milk, and stared into the liquid for a moment.

'Please tell… what do you know of him?' she asked all of a sudden.

The Viscount looked up from the newspaper.

'Of whom, dearest?'

'The American.'

'Only that he has suffered greatly, and that he may be a key.'

'A key to what?'

'A key to a mystery that preoccupies us all.'

SEVEN

SIR GEOFFREY CALDECOTT was pacing in the library, a massive book-lined hall, at the rear of the Committee building.

The room had a domed ceiling, upon which was depicted an exotic interpretation of the African continent: the bulk of it ornamented with dense jungle and cannibal tribes. The library walls were laid with dark teak shelves, each one arranged neatly with books, thirty thousand of them, the spines in matching red morocco. The parquet floor was partly covered by a series of long Persian rugs, and a dozen large desks placed along one side of them, tooled map drawers arranged beneath each one.

A knuckle rapped softly at the door. Slowly, the great portal inched back, revealing Simon Cochran. He entered in silence. Close behind was another gentleman, in full cavalry dress. The two men made for a curious combination: one attired in dandy couture, the other in the livery of the Dragoon Guards.

As soon as the door opened, Caldecott dug his heels into the parquet, swivelled round, and hurried over boisterously to greet his guest.

The officer had the kind of face one would not pick out in a crowd — blue-grey eyes, a button nose and disappointing chin. But his marvellous red and gold uniform, replete with lanyards and a sprinkling of medals, compensated for any deficiency in facial features.

'Thank you for coming Major,' barked Caldecott when he was close up. 'I wanted to look you in the eye before you set off. After all, no communication can ever be so articulate as two men standing eye to eye.'

Major Peddie regarded Caldecott, taking in the broken capillaries on his cheeks, and the bloodshot whites of his eyes. As an army man, and one who had served under Wellington, he despised the rot that tended to fester among the civilian populace. The chairman may have had the highest hopes for the Major's ability, but he found himself angered by the aura of military arrogance.

They stood motionless, staring, until Cochran broke the silence.

'I have taken the liberty of presenting the Major with the latest and most up-to-date cartography of the African continent,' he said. 'Park's journey is featured, as well as Roentgen's.'

'You may leave us, Mr. Cochran,' said Caldecott, waving a hand at the door.

The secretary paced out, closed the door behind him, and pressed his ear to its reverse.

'Now I have you eye to eye,' said Caldecott, 'I will make myself very clear, Major. I don't care what sacrifice you have to make. It may cost dearly in human life, and in funds, but you must, I repeat — *must* — secure the golden city for our Committee and the Crown. The French will be defeated!'

Peddie, who had not yet spoken, pursed his lips, breathed in, and then frowned.

'We have planned the expedition as a military campaign,' he said, in a clipped tone. 'My men are veterans of Waterloo, all of them baptised in French blood. They have tasted victory against Bonaparte in Europe, and will scotch his comrades on *terra Africanus*. Rest assured, sir, we will hound them over the sands, hack them into mincemeat, burn their bones, and continue forward to claim our prize.'

EIGHT

Chavenage Hall
2nd November 1815

Dear Simon,

Forgive my delay in replying to your letters. Of late I have been compelled to attend my mother's strictest wishes. She insists on me playing the pianoforte through the long, dark afternoons. I regret having ever learned to play the accursed instrument.

Otherwise, I can report that all is quiet here at Chavenage, and am disappointed to remark that uproar of any kind is unknown to our simple lives.

This morning we had a call from a Mr. Thomas Wittershall, of Gloucester, who informed Mother that he has just become our neighbour, by purchasing the land to the west of Chavenage Hall. He is a hunter, it seems, par excellence, and is much admired if the reputation that precedes him is to be believed.

If my understanding is correct, Mr. Wittershall intends to build himself a large home on the hill the other side of the eleven-acre forest. He appears to have funds aplenty and owns a large property in London.

I hope that the business of the African Committee is not too taxing on your time, and that you will remember to write soon, my dear Simon,

Affectionately yours,
Beattie

NINE

UPSTAIRS, ON THE second floor, the visitor was stirring.

Through half-open eyes he scanned the room, and drowsily tried to make sense of his reverse in fortunes.

The bedroom was palatial. Its windows were hung with padded olive-silk curtains, its expansive walls adorned with lithographs and hand-coloured prints, most of them details of African scenes. The floor was oak parquet polished with beeswax, and the furniture all rosewood, except for the four-poster bed, which was carved teak.

A coal fire was clicking in the brazier. Beside it stood a leather camel saddle raised on a plinth, next to it a pair of bull elephant tusks. The visitor's eyes took them in, dilating sharply, as if sparked by memory.

At that moment the door opened without a sound, the brass hinges having been lubricated the week before with a feather dipped in linseed oil, on the Viscount's personal instructions.

A butler entered, his felt-soled slippers making no sound at all as they crossed the room, treading from parquet to carpet and back to parquet. He laid a tea tray on the table at the right side of the bed, pushed open the curtains one at a time, and cleared his throat.

'Good morning, sir.'

'Huh?'

'Good morning to you, sir. I am reluctant to say it, but the weather is rather inclement.'

The foreign visitor sat up.

'Can you tell me where I am?'

'You are, sir, at Camelford House, the London residence of Sir Richard Fortescue.'

'Where are my clothes?'

The butler pulled open the doors of a Chippendale wardrobe, revealing a row of fine gentleman's garments.

'I believe these are for your use, sir.'

The visitor drew a hand over his forehead, pushing back the mop of blond hair. He seemed anxious for a moment, confused.

'In the shirt I was wearing, there was in the pocket...'

'A lace handkerchief?'

'Yes.'

'The Viscount felt it might be of some importance. It is laid on the night-stand, sir.'

The man rolled himself forward. Spying the lace, soiled and worn, he touched it to his lips, and sunk back into the pillows.

'Thank God,' he said.

There was a pause. The butler moved over to a wooden damascene screen, inlaid with fragments of mother-of-pearl.

'Your bath is drawn, sir.'

'Drawn?'

'Yes, sir. The water is a good temperature. Would you like me to bath you?'

The visitor's face tightened.

'No, no, I can bath myself!'

'Very good, sir.'

TEN

AN HOUR LATER, Fortescue and Clara were still at the breakfast table.

They were about to adjourn, when the butler entered, sailed over to the Viscount, and whispered discreetly in his ear. Fortescue's eyes widened sharply.

'Well, show him in at once!'

Glancing up, Clara pushed back her shoulders in defence. Before she could utter a word, the visitor was standing before them. The Viscount found himself at a loss for words.

Unrecognisable now, the American was dressed in a white muslin shirt, riding breeches, and a pair of leather button-down boots. His tanned face, clean-shaven, was gentle but defiant, a mirror to the hardship he had endured. He had a square jaw, dark green eyes, and an aquiline nose. His hair was long, wetted from the bath, the colour of dark straw, and his shoulders broad, so much so as to be unnatural.

Viscount Fortescue tossed down *The Times*, leapt to his feet, and ushered his visitor into the parlour.

'Come in, please come in, sir!'

Clara placed the china cup in its saucer, looked up, and flinched at the sight of such a handsome figure.

'My dear Clara, I should like to present our distinguished guest — Mister...'

There was another pause. The American lowered his head a fraction, creasing his eyes engagingly in a smile.

'My name is Robert Adams,' he said.

'And how did you sleep, Mr. Adams?' asked Fortescue loudly.

Adams took a deep breath. His gaze scanned the array of foods, and moved naturally up to Clara's eyes.

'I slept more deeply than on any night I can remember,' he said in a soft, tender voice, 'and yet I swear that I am still dreaming.'

Blushing, Clara motioned to the chair beside her own.

'Will you not sit and have some breakfast, Mr. Adams?'

'Thank you, Miss…'

'Clara. My name is Clara.'

'And I am Fortescue.'

Adams lowered himself onto the chair slowly, mesmerised at being in the presence of so much food. There was oatmeal cooked with cream, smoked herrings, grilled trout in white butter sauce, a tureen of brazed kidneys, eggs, bacon, and an assortment of breads. As the visitor took in the feast laid out before him, Clara stole a glance. Blushing again, she felt her knees weaken, as she struggled to maintain her usual prim façade.

'Will you eat something, Mr. Adams?'

'I could swallow the table, legs and all!'

'There is no need to eat the furniture, sir, I assure you,' she said, her mouth easing into a smile, 'for plenty of food is at hand.'

Clara nodded to the manservant to offer the guest the silver platter of kedgeree. It was borne forward at chest height, supported between a pair of spotless white-gloved hands, held to Adams' left side. Piling his plate high with food, he set about devouring it as fast as he could using a soup spoon.

Clara looked on in fascination. As she did so, her father sprang to his feet energetically, and moved round the table to get a better look at his unusual guest. Filled with vigour, the Viscount remained silent. Only when he had feasted sufficiently on the sight, did he say anything at all.

'Mr. Adams, although we have not met, I believe I know who you are, and a little of the trials and tribulations to which you have been exposed. Divine providence threw us together last night.'

Adams did not look up. He was too busy eating.

Viscount Fortescue continued:

'A month ago I received a letter from an acquaintance of thirty years, a gentleman by the name of Joseph Dupuis.'

The American stopped mid-flow, the laden soup spoon poised by an open mouth.

'The Consul at Mogador,' he said, 'the man I owe my life… the one who was responsible for redeeming me. He is my truest friend.'

The Viscount smacked his palms together.

'Dupuis wrote of you,' he whispered after a studious pause, 'said you have supposedly achieved something, Mr. Adams, something that no other Christian has yet accomplished. And you have achieved it quite incidentally, and without the egoism that is the mainstay of our communal efforts.'

Adams let the spoon rest on his plate.

'I don't understand.'

Viscount Fortescue put a hand over his mouth and slid it down across his chin. It was a gesture that his peers might have regarded as beneath him. But the Viscount wasn't much concerned by the opinions of others.

'Almost daily, the bravest of men are dispatched from London, Paris and Berlin,' he said, 'set on that unconquered goal of goals, that prize of exploration, one that grips all society — all society but your own.'

Viscount Fortescue leant forward on the tips of his toes, his back even straighter than normal. Adams eyed the salver of fresh-baked breads lying just within reach; but his host's excited sense of urgency drew him away from the thought of food.

'You have so, have you not…?'

'Have so, what?'

'Have set foot at Timbuctoo?'

The butler crept into the room with the morning post. His name was Dalston and his face was expressionless, lids heavy over coal-black eyes. He had been in the Viscount's employment for thirty-six years, and his father before him had worked as an attendant at the family seat near Bath. He had never met an American before.

Adams scanned the room, taking in the butler, the doorman, the pair of maids standing to attention against the adjacent wall, Clara, and finally Fortescue himself. He reached for a large slice of toasted bread, took a bite, chewed hard, and washed it down with a gulp of tart pineapple juice.

'My feet have indeed tramped through that city,' he said distantly, 'I lived there six months, a guest of its king, until I was sold into slavery.'

'*Slavery*?' said Clara, her nose jerking back. 'But are you not a Christian?'

'That I am.'

'Then how could it be so?'

'Miss,' said Adams tenderly, 'these fine surroundings are a world apart from the inferno in which I have existed these past five years. My bondage at the hands of Moors led me through unimaginable torment. I walked a tightrope between survival and damnation.'

Fortescue pressed his fingertips together.

'Remarkable, truly remarkable. But how on earth did you keep going... endure what would have dispatched any ordinary man?'

'I was kept going by my faith and by a love so strong it replaced the blood in my veins and the breath in my lungs.'

Clara found herself gazing immodestly into the American's eyes as he spoke. She was attracted to his raw sensibility, and by the thought that he had been ravaged by a passionate wildness of nature, the kind unlikely ever to visit her life.

The Viscount returned to his seat, allowed Dalston to pour him a third cup of orange pekoe, and turned to look out at Hyde Park.

'There is a group of gentlemen,' he said, turning back towards

Adams, 'a Committee which I am sure would be most interested in hearing the details of your adventures, and your description of the golden metropolis.'

'But I must hurry back to Hudson. I hope to catch the first available voyage. I am anxious to be reunited with the life that was robbed from me, and with the woman who gives reason to my life.'

One of the maids swapped the dirty plate for a smaller one, from the same Wedgwood service.

'Even my best intentions to aid your situation would be thwarted,' said Fortescue. 'You cannot return home until there is a cessation of the conflict between our nations. As you must surely be aware, we are at war, sir, over trade.'

Adams pushed away the delicate patterned plate, and stared at the tablecloth, starched white like new sailcloth. It reminded him of a giant mainsail heaving in the Atlantic wind.

'I must get home,' he said, in a low strained voice. 'I must get back to Hudson. And I will. Five years with Death as my shadow, hanging in limbo, a common slave, has taught me to never give up. I will swim if I have to. But I *will* get home.'

Clara breathed in hard through her nose, stretching the corset tight on her chest, suffocating her.

'You must avail yourself of our gentle hospitality,' she said, without looking Adams in the eye.

'You are very kind, but why are you helping me?'

The Viscount nodded to Dalston, signalling that breakfast was at an end.

'Because I have the Devil in me,' he said.

ELEVEN

A DOORMAN WAS salting the steps of the Committee headquarters when the carriage pulled up. He saw a blur of monogram on the door, the letters C.R.T.F. and, although he was illiterate, he knew a monogram meant a gentleman, and a gentleman meant largesse.

Jumping down to the street, he readied himself to be useful. The horses drew to a halt, their breath billowing like gun-smoke, fusing with the sound of the brake levers pulled hard to the back wheels. The coachman climbed down, squared the footstep on the snow and signalled to his passengers.

The Viscount opened the door from the inside when he was ready, his lined leather glove taking the cold of the brass knob. He descended, and was followed by Robert Adams, now dressed in a heavy gabardine overcoat. The two men mounted the salted steps with care and, a moment later, they were inside, being ushered towards the library by Cochran.

Adams' eyes roamed the magnificent corridor, taking in the rows of marble busts, the exotic trophy heads, the chequerboard floor and, above it, the vaulted ceiling inset with coloured glass. He might have been fearful at finding himself in such a grand setting, but he wasn't in the least, just a little confused.

'What is this place?' he asked.

'The Royal African Committee, the bastion of His Majesty's exploration into the Dark Continent,' said Fortescue. 'Its governors intend to dispatch a great expedition to Timbuctoo.'

There was silence for a moment.

'Why the interest with that city?'

The Viscount smiled.

'Surely you are mocking the legend, are you not, Mr. Adams?'

Cochran opened the double doors to the library, and invited Adams to sit on a banquette lined in crimson velvet. He did so, and his eyes were soon locked on the fanciful mural of Africa painted across the dome.

'We shall leave you for a moment, Mr. Adams,' said Fortescue, 'for we must inform the chairman of your arrival.'

There was the sound of the doors opening again, and of the lock snapping shut, but Adams didn't hear it. He was transfixed on the ceiling.

As his eyes took in the jungle foliage and the cannibal tribes, his memory transposed over them five years of anguish.

TWELVE

IN A PRIVATE STUDY on the second floor, Sir Geoffrey was taking a pinch of ground tobacco from a tortoiseshell snuffbox. He enjoyed a blend of macouba prepared for him by William Hebb of Old Bond Street, priding himself on its expense.

There was a knock at the door.

Sir Geoffrey slipped the box away, called 'Enter!' and turned to receive his visitor.

Viscount Fortescue had no formal association with the Committee but, as a respected member of the gentry, a learned gentleman, and a linguist, he was always welcome, and was occasionally invited to advise. He shook hands with Caldecott, exchanged pleasantries, and moved over to warm himself beside the fire.

'I was much interested by your message this morning, Viscount,' Sir Geoffrey wheezed. 'But what new information could you have possibly received of the golden city?'

Fortescue declined an armchair and, instead, leant against the pink marble mantel, his leather cavalry boots reflecting the glow of the coals. He wanted to be standing when he delivered his punchline.

'You are aware that no Christian has ever reached it, and returned alive to tell their tale?'

'Quite so.'

'Well how would it sound to your ears if I were to inform you that a young man, a Christian, as pink as you or I, had reached Timbuctoo, and resided there as a guest of the king?'

'It would sound just as it is — *Preposterous*!'

Sir Geoffrey Caldecott had beads of perspiration on his forehead again. He felt his chest tighten with asthma, as it always did when he heard things he didn't appreciate. Crossing the room, he pushed up the window, letting in a blast of freezing air.

'Well,' said Fortescue, flexing his back, 'you may be intrigued to know that such a man claims to have been to the golden city, and has returned alive. But more to the point, he is not English.'

'A damned foreigner?'

'A foreigner, yes.'

'Where's he from then? From France?'

'No, not France.'

'Then Berlin. I knew it… He's a damned German!'

'No, Sir Geoffrey, not German either.'

'Italian?'

'No.'

'A Russian?'

The Viscount motioned the negative with his hand.

'Not from Europe at all.'

The chairman looked dumbfounded.

'Well who else is there?'

'In actual fact he is from across the ocean.'

'Excuse me?'

'He is an American.'

There was silence as Caldecott's overheated cranium processed the name of the unpopular republic. He was unable to respond at first. His face became dove-grey and, a moment after that, a surge of blood turned it cherry-red. Fortescue wondered whether he might pass out.

'Would you like a tonic, Sir Geoffrey?' he asked.

Caldecott held the back of his hand to his mouth and began to choke.

'Then if you have no objection, I shall fetch him,' said the Viscount easily.

'You brought him here?!' barked Caldecott, still choking.

Fortescue didn't hear the question. He had already stridden out, down to the library. Soon he was back at the door, Adams in his shadow.

'Sir Geoffrey, I have the distinct pleasure of introducing you to Mr. Robert Adams, from Hudson, in the state of New York.'

'Good afternoon,' said Adams, bending over Caldecott.

'He *is* American!'

'That I am, born and raised.'

'And, sir, I understand that you claim that you have been to Timbuctoo.'

'I claim nothing, but I've been there.'

'And what took you to Timbuctoo, Mr. Adams?'

'Slavery.'

'How many did you own?'

'No, no, I was not a merchant.'

'What?'

'You misunderstand. *I* was a slave.'

'A Christian… a Christian slave?'

'Yes.'

'I have never heard of such an outrageous thing!'

The conversation was almost too much for Caldecott to take. He began hyperventilating and staggered out of the room.

Cochran entered, his lilac tailcoat scented with rose water.

'I must advise you that Sir Geoffrey is prone to these attacks,' he said solemnly. 'They do not in general last very long. But I fear this one may last longer than most.'

Ten minutes later, Caldecott emerged. He was ashen-grey, and looked as if he had suffered a heart attack. He slouched in a chinoiserie chair beside the window, his stout form overflowing the sides.

'Tell me, Mr. Adams, why should I believe your assertion?'

Adams looked down at the chairman.

'I don't care if you believe me or not.'

Fortescue stepped forward until his shadow fell over Sir Geoffrey.

'Would it not be prudent for Mr. Adams to transcribe his recollections to paper? After all, the notes may be of assistance to your own Mr. Peddie.'

'Our *Major* Peddie can well do without the help of an American!' snapped Caldecott, rising to the bait.

'But surely any information that might reduce the hazards of the party has some value?'

'Very well, sir. We shall take your statement for the record.'

'I should like to help,' replied Adams, 'but I have to return to Hudson.'

'That is not possible as you are aware,' Fortescue broke in, 'not until the naval blockade is at an end.'

Adams dug a hand into his pocket, allowing his fingertips to caress the lace handkerchief.

'I have, sir, come to realise that *nothing* is impossible,' he said.

'Write us a full and detailed account of your reminiscences, Mr. Adams, and we shall afford you a passage back to America when the conflict is at an end. Cochran, fetch a quill and a ream of paper.'

'I am sorry,' Adams replied quickly, 'but writing my tale *will* be impossible.'

Fortescue looked at him with surprise.

'Are you sure?'

'Yes, very sure.'

'May I enquire why?'

'A difficulty prevents me. You see…'

'See what?'

'You see I can't read or write.'

Fortescue broke into a smile. Stuck in the chair, Caldecott waved a hand at his assistant.

'Mr. Cochran, as it seems as though inadequate American schooling has left Mr. Adams deficient in the art of literacy, you are to commit his narration to paper.'

'Very good, Sir Geoffrey.' It was a standard reply Cochran gave to any demand Caldecott made on him.

'Tell me, Mr. Adams, where are you lodging?'

'He is staying with me at Camelford House.'

'Under the circumstances,' said Sir Geoffrey, struggling to disengage himself from the seat, 'I think we ought to have Mr. Adams a little closer to us. Mr. Cochran, you have ample space in your chambers, Adams will be lodging with you.'

'Very good, Sir Geoffrey.'

THIRTEEN

16, Fleet Street
6th November 1815

My dearest cousin Beattie,

I hope that this little missive finds you in good spirits. I long to see you, and to take a walk with you in the open country. Here in London I am ensnared, unable to remove myself from duties of the Committee. From time to time, though, there are sparks of marvel, which illuminate the tediousness. One such wonder is currently sharing my chambers. His name is Robert Adams. He is an American. Imagine that! An American!

I have been charged with his responsibility, and with the transcription of his curious journey through the remotest reaches of Africa. For, apparently, Mr. Adams has set foot in the holy of holies — the golden metropolis of Timbuctoo.

He arrived here last evening, after reaching the Committee, and being presented by Viscount Fortescue. He is pleasing enough. Raw, but pleasing, and quite charming to the ladies, if his effect on my landlady Mrs. Pickeriff is anything to go by. She swooned at hearing his peculiar accent, and was stirred greatly by his rugged looks.

As you may imagine, Sir G was apoplectic at learning of the

existence of such a man, especially him being an American.
He maintained a brave visage in front of the Viscount, but in private
he is gravely alarmed. He dares not mention it, but he has sunk
the Committee's fortunes into a project which depends entirely on
Major Peddie's swift success.

I leave you, my little rose, with all my affection,
Simon

FOURTEEN

IT HAD RAINED all night, flooding Cochran's bedroom, and causing him much anxiety. He flitted about, mopping the wet with bundles of dirty clothes, desperately excusing the wretchedness of his lodgings.

The modest apartment on Fleet Street had never been free from damp. This was due largely to the fact that the lead seals had been stripped from the roof by thieves, who had sold the metal to buy one-penny gin. Afraid of even the most modest of heights, Cochran had never summoned the courage to investigate why the roof leaked like a sieve. His landlady, aged Mrs. Pickeriff, who believed a little damp was good for the bones, refused point blank to have any money spent on the building.

The apartment consisted of three rooms — a bedroom, a small sitting room, and a boxroom. Each one was filled with clutter acquired as the consequence of an untidy life.

Despite having a well-respected godfather, Cochran had been unable to muster the connections to find him a place at the Albany on Piccadilly, where his childhood friend George Byron had recently taken rooms. He dreamt of it all the same. After all, an address at the Albany marked one as a gentleman with prospects.

As a bachelor Cochran rarely admitted anyone into his lodgings, least of all strangers. He had never even invited his beloved cousin Beattie, to whom he hoped one day to propose, when his financial circumstances were improved. Even if it had been appropriate for her to visit, he feared she would shun him after setting eyes on such monumental disorder. But, as his friend George 'Beau' Brummell used to say, before he absconded to the Continent, hounded by his debtors, 'a gentleman's quarters are for a gentleman's eyes alone'.

The rain, which had subsided a little after eight o'clock, had warmed the air. The skies had cleared, and there was a balmy freshness, something London had not enjoyed for weeks.

As soon as he woke, Cochran pulled on his breeches, and coaxed Adams from his deep, childlike slumber.

'We will be late, Mr. Adams,' he said, 'and Sir Geoffrey's fragile disposition doesn't take kindly to tardiness.'

Adams pushed his face deeper into the pillow, a tangle of blond hair washing around it like waves on the shore. He never remembered his dreams except when woken suddenly from sleep and, when woken suddenly, the dream was always the same: A woman walking through a field of winter barley, dry and undulating, ready for the scythe.

She was moving towards him, smiling, not a full smile, but a smile that hinted at something very subtle, very warm. When they were within touching distance, she held out a hand, and pressed it into his. He felt something soft, a folded lace handkerchief. Touching it to his nose, he breathed in her scent.

FIFTEEN

TEN MINUTES AFTER waking, Adams was up, washed, dressed, and ready to begin the narration of his tale.

He had little interest in helping the Committee, and certainly had no interest at all in Timbuctoo, however, the promise of a passage home was too good to pass up. So he followed Cochran down the winding staircase, and out onto the street, persuading himself to believe that the last steps of his journey were about to begin.

The two men walked through light rain from the Fleet Street lodgings to the Committee's headquarters at Old Jewry. Cochran had traced the same route so many times over the previous five years, he hardly noticed his feet tramping the mile distance over the cobbles. But, having arrived in the capital a week before, starving and half-naked, Robert Adams was wide-eyed at it all, the showcase of empire.

By the time they reached the Committee headquarters, it was ten minutes past ten. Glancing up at the second floor, Cochran could tell whether his superior had arrived. If he had, the window above the portico would be open an inch, just enough for the flow of damp air to cool the chairman's ever-heated brow.

Fortunately, on the morning of Adams' first narration, Caldecott and the other directors were running late as well. They had been up until the early hours celebrating Major Peddie's impending departure to the Dark Continent, gorging themselves on broiled pheasant and plum pudding, washed down with a stream of warmed Madeira wine.

SIXTEEN

SIMON COCHRAN'S STUDY was cramped, cold, and overflowing with files. There were hundreds of them, each one recording a month in the Committee's history, a history dedicated to the creation of wealth at the expense of African lands.

Half the files were concerned with the ivory trade, with indigo, and salt — cut in slabs from the dry mineral lakes of the Niger delta. The other half was related to the only business that had ever brought the Committee any real prosperity — slavery.

For almost a century, the directors had run ships from Goré Island to the Caribbean. Tens of thousands of African souls had owed their suffering to the efficiency with which the company vessels could cross the Atlantic, disinfect their holds, and race back for another shipload of freshly captured natives.

Any other man might have resented such an uncomfortable and confined space to work, but Simon Cochran liked his room very much indeed. Most of all, he enjoyed the view out over Frederick's Place, even though much of it was obscured by a tall plane tree. When he was not stoking the fire, or staring out at the tree, he was daydreaming of escape, and of the life he hoped one day to share with his cousin Beattie.

As for actual work, there was very little of that. Cochran's chief daily activity was to stay out of Sir Geoffrey's way. On the rare occasions that their paths crossed, he did all he could to calm the chairman's inflamed temper.

Over the generations, the Committee's work had been finely tuned. Its ships would ply back and forth from Africa to the Americas according to a strict rota. Payments arising from the cargoes would be made through a series of intermediaries in Newfoundland and in the Caribbean. The arrangement had been devised in an effort to mask the source of the wealth, frowned upon since the Abolition Act was signed nine years before.

The funds gained from sale of healthy natives would be passed through the accounts of a cotton plantation on Hispaniola, which in turn paid the bulk to a company of fur traders in Labrador. They submitted the balance less their commission to the Committee's account at Hoare's Bank, at the sign of the golden bottle on Fleet Street.

Every Friday afternoon Caldecott would ride down to the bank in his barouche, take a glass of sweet sherry with the partners, and return to Old Jewry, a plump purse of guineas tucked under his cloak.

Each week the senior partner at Hoare's struggled a little harder than the week before to encourage Sir Geoffrey to accept bank notes rather than gold. After all, the Peninsular War had put bullion in short supply.

A stickler for what he knew and trusted, Caldecott scoffed at the thought of paper currency. The preoccupation with gold was the habit of a lifetime, one he was not yet willing to forgo.

SEVENTEEN

Chavenage Hall
12th November 1815

Dear Simon,

I do hope the cold is not too terrible down in London. Up here, the frost has been thicker than at any other year I can remember. The plants are frozen, brittle like glass. This morning I went for a long walk through the grounds of Chavenage, and felt myself in sorrow for the gentle creatures who make their homes in the gardens and down near the lake.

I found your information regarding the American quite alluring! Simon, you live such an exotic life, one filled with captivating people and circumstance. I have asked mother time and again to allow me to spend a little of the winter season in town. She says the journey is far too precarious for a young woman, and that I should be spoilt by the meanness of London society.

I bothered her all morning on the subject, and well into the afternoon. Then, an hour ago, at teatime, she expressed a reluctant agreement, that is, if a suitable chaperone could be found. I do believe her mind was changed by her wish to set eyes upon the London home of our new neighbour, Mr. Wittershall. An invitation there may be the excuse I have been waiting for so ardently these past months.

Affectionately yours,
Beattie

EIGHTEEN

RELIEVED TO HAVE some real work at last, Cochran was looking forward to taking down the narration of Adams' tale. Since childhood he had prided himself on the form and consistency of his script, a skill that had won him a class prize at Charterhouse when he was twelve.

He opened a slim drawer in the mahogany bureau, withdrew a new swan-feather quill, and inspected the nib.

'I shall be ready in a moment, Mr. Adams,' he said, angling the end to give a sharper writing edge.

Robert Adams took a seat beside the window and stared out at the grey. He was dreaming of the barley again.

'I do believe your thoughts are on the Dark Continent, Mr. Adams,' said Cochran, slipping away the knife.

'No, not Africa. My mind is a world away, on a little home across the fields.'

'Your family?'

'My wife…'

'You are married, sir?' said Cochran, flexing his rounded shoulders straight.

'Yes I am.'

Taking a seat at the desk, placing a sheet of foolscap squarely before him, Cochran dipped his quill.

'I am at your service, Mr. Adams.'

'Where should I begin?'

'Perhaps we ought to start at the moment your life deviated away from the course it had known.'

Adams looked hard at the plane tree, his eyes taking in the mottled detailing of the trunk.

'Hudson is a whaling port, up river from New York,' he began in a slow and deliberate voice. 'It was chartered thirty years ago, and is as idyllic as any place I have ever imagined. In the spring the meadows are ablaze with colour, the air scented with the perfume of peonies; and in the fall the trees are every shade of brown, the floor beneath them a patchwork of gold.

'It was there that I was born and raised. My father was a sail-maker, and my mother a seamstress, that is until she succumbed to consumption in the winter of 1801. We lived in a house my father built with his own hands, perched at the edge of the beech forest. To the east across a sea of barley lay Hudson and, to the west, a small but profitable ordnance factory where I found work.

'Its owner, Mr. Ferguson, was an arrogant man who treated his employees with contempt. In his view a young man without the knowledge to read or to write was a disgrace, unfit to call themselves a citizen, as low as a hog in a sty.

'During the three years I toiled making black powder for Mr. Ferguson, I became acquainted with his daughter, Christina, or rather, I became reacquainted. We had met as children at a Spring Fair. Something had drawn us together even then. In the long shadows of the Hudson afternoon we had held hands, and she had pressed her lips to my cheek. As her mother pulled us apart, I swore aloud that one day she would be my wife.

'Unlike her father, who was aggressive and pompous, Christina was mild-mannered, gentle, and possessed a kindness that touched everyone she met. Over the months I would do anything in my power to catch a glimpse of her, but I was uncomfortable for her to see me in such a wretched state.

'One evening in late spring she visited the factory, and found me covered in filth, filling cartridges. When I apologised for my appearance, she broke into laughter. I asked if she remembered me. Smiling, she said: "I am still waiting for your proposal, Robert Adams."'

Rising to his feet, the American stepped over to the fire, and stared at himself in the smoked sheet of glass hanging above the mantel. He took in the scar on his left eye and touched a fingertip to his mouth.

'My family may not have been blessed with wealth,' he said distantly, 'but I was raised to understand right from wrong, and was taught that, by perseverance, even the most far-fetched dream can and will come true.

'Over the weeks I found various opportunities to meet Christina again. She was shy, reserved at first, yet with a smile so warm it would have melted even the most frozen heart. I promised her again and again that I would do good, and we would have a life together. And, with time, we found that we had much in common — most of all a yearning to escape, to make something of our lives.

'By the end of the summer we had fallen in love, although we kept this from both our families. Christina greatly feared telling her father. She said he would slay me, and that he had killed before. Having worked for the man for three years, I believed her. He was a tyrant. I had once seen him whip a man to within a hair's breadth of life.

'Then one afternoon we met in secret as usual, under a beech tree at the edge of the barley fields. Christina's face seemed taut with worry. She held me close, whispered that her father had discovered our romance. He was hunting me even then, she said. I couldn't understand how such a swine had raised such a gentle young woman.

'So I fell to my knee and I proposed. "I may not be rich," I said, "but my hands are honest, and my heart God-fearing. If you accept I shall strive every moment to bring you the happiness you deserve." To my joy, she accepted. We went straight to the church on Union Street, where the pastor married us.

'We planned to quit Hudson in secret the next day, and head south to New York, where I hoped to get work at an ordnance factory near Wall Street. I begged Christina to leave with me that night. But she resisted, declaring it to be too dangerous. Instead, she returned home to pack clothes and her savings. She promised we'd flee together at dawn.

'We kissed, pledged our unfailing love for each other, and Christina turned to walk up the hill to her father's mansion. As she stepped away, I asked how I would endure the twelve hours without her. She smiled, leant forward and kissed my cheek, just as she had done at the Spring Fair all those years before. Then, pulling a lace handkerchief from the wrist of her dress, she passed it to me. "Let this be your memento of me," she said.

'I watched as the distance between us increased, the last throes of light catching the red velvet sash on her dress. Just before she was out of sight, she turned, and we glanced at each other. I touched the handkerchief to my nostrils, breathed in its scent, and wondered how I could ever withstand twelve hours without my beloved Christina.'

Again, Adams glanced at his reflection. He drew a fingertip down the scar, then gazed out at the rain.

'Fate is more cruel than any jailer,' he said.

Cochran reached for another sheet and dipped his quill.

'What was it, sir, that prevented your union?'

Robert Adams sat down beside the window again. His chest filling with the damp air, he breathed out in a sigh.

'The evening of our wedding,' he said, 'I went to a tavern on Cherry Alley to celebrate. It was a moment of solitude, but one tinged with extraordinary hope. I was sitting there sipping a mug of ale when the door was near thrust from its hinges.

'Mr. Ferguson was standing silhouetted in the frame. He scanned the room. A moment later he was towering over me, his henchmen huddled behind like spectres of death.

'"Touch my daughter and Oscar here will cleave off your hands," he yelled.

'I stood up, my courage buoyed by drink. I am never one to shirk from injustice, and I would never class myself a coward.

'"Christina and I were married this afternoon," I exclaimed. Before I could utter another word, a fist smashed my jaw and I was knocked out cold. My last memory of America is of Ferguson's face before me, flushed with rage.'

Cochran looked up from the sheet, dipped the goose-feather quill again and touched the nib to the rim of the crystal inkwell.

'I am not sure that I understand you, sir,' he said.

Adams turned to face him. He swallowed hard.

'The next thing I knew, I was locked in the hold of a ship, timbers creaking, rasping, groaning. I shouted out over the noise but no one heard me or, if they did, they took no notice of my cries.

'The darkness was illuminated by shafts of light streaming in from the deck. Over the first hours I struggled to get an accurate idea of the cargo. The hold was piled with Bibles and black powder, and was alive with a multitude of rats. I managed to find some hardtack and enough water to keep alive. I was in there four days before I smelled the salt.'

'Salt?'

'The ocean air. There's no smell like it in all the world. Mr. Ferguson had solved the problem of his unwanted son-in-law with an enforced voyage. The ship had sailed gently enough down the Hudson River, but the instant it pushed out into the Atlantic swell, it began to heave and shudder as if the end of the world were about to greet it.'

Adams ran the tip of his tongue over his upper lip.

'After five days the hatch was knocked back, and the rats and

I were blinded by the sunlight flooding in. A bucket of freezing Atlantic water was hurled down.'

'"Where am I?" I yelled.

'"On the high seas," called a voice.

'"Bound for where?"

'"For African shores."'

II

An encoded letter arrives for Sir Geoffrey Caldecott — Miss Clara Fortescue meets her friend Miss Caroline Lamb at Lackington's Temple of the Muses — Mr. Adams pauses in his narration — A large crate is delivered to Carlton House — Mr. Adams repairs to the Committee's library and continues with his tale, describing how the *Charles* was wrecked on African shores — Taxidermist to royalty, Mr. Bateman, unveils his latest work to the Prince Regent — Mr. Adams explains how the captain was slain by Moors — Mr. Cochran informs Beattie of the narration — Miss Fortescue has an interview with Caroline Lamb — Lord Alvanley takes luncheon at White's Club with Lord Byron and Mr. Bertie McCormack — The narration continues, with first public visitors attending — Mr. Bateman travels to London to take possession of a dead polar bear — Beattie advises Mr. Cochran of her imminent visit to London — Mr. Adams describes the first miserable days of slavery — Mr. Adams greets Miss Clara Fortescue — Mr. Adams receives a letter from Miss Fortescue — Mr. Bateman loads the polar bear onto his cart at the Tower of London — Mr. Albert Wicks, hangman to the famous and infamous, learns of an investment opportunity — Mr. Adams is traded to a second band of Moors and meets another Christian slave, Juan Sanchez — Mr. Cochran writes to Beattie in hope of an interview while she is in town — Messrs. Alvanley, Byron and McCormack meet at White's Club — The Moorish captors of Mr. Adams are themselves captured, and taken to Timbuctoo.

ONE

AT FOUR THAT afternoon, a polished silver salver was borne up the carved mahogany staircase by Falkirk, the porter of thirty years' service.

On the salver was a soiled envelope, addressed in smudged ink.

Caldecott was sitting in his study beside the open window, allowing the chill damp air to cool him. He had been counting piles of bullion in his head. As soon as Falkirk was close, the chairman snatched the letter. Breaking the seal, he found a series of numbers arranged across the page.

'Falkirk, fetch me the King James Bible!' he growled. 'You will find it in the library on the divinity shelves. And hurry with you, man!'

The porter nodded, and a few minutes later he was scaling the staircase again, the Bible square on his salver. The book was bound in red morocco, the spine lightly sunned, a little crisper than the covers. It had lain unopened for so many years that the top edge was black with a mixture of soot and dust.

Falkirk presented the salver to his master, and sneezed twice.

'Go down to Cochran's room and observe how that imbecile is advancing with the damned American.'

'Very good, sir.'

'And Falkirk…'

'Yes, sir?'

'Sneeze again in my presence and you will be out on your ear!'

The porter left the room, pulling the brass handle until the lock snapped shut. Caldecott leant over the lamp and turned up its wick until the room was bathed in creamy yellow light.

'Seven-fifteen-eight,' he mumbled to himself, flicking the pages until he came to the Book of Judges. '*And he smote them hip and thigh with a great slaughter.* Excellent. He's smitten the bloody French. Well done Peddie!' Caldecott glanced at the letter. 'Thirty-five-three-twelve...' he read. 'The thirty-fifth book... *Habakkuk.* And the verse...' his fingers flicked to the seven hundredth page. '*Thou didst march through the land in indignation, thou didst thresh the nations in anger.*'

Sir Geoffrey took a pinch of macouba and, wallowing in delight, he decoded the last passage: nineteen-ninety-eight-one, '*O sing unto the Lord a new song; for he hath done marvellous things: his right hand and his holy arm has wrought salvation for him.*'

The chairman placed the Bible on the desk, pushed the window open a little wider than usual, and poured himself a glass of tawny port. Peddie had been an obvious choice from the start, he thought to himself, the kind of soldier who that summer had bathed the fields of Flanders in French blood. Success was assured now that he had scotched the French expedition. With Peddie's success, the Royal African Committee would be celebrated once again, and the attention would be drawn away from the scent of scandal, a scent never far from its doors.

TWO

TWO MILES AWAY, Clara Fortescue was browsing the shelves of new novels at the Temple of the Muses, the vast bookshop on Finsbury Square owned by James Lackington Esq.

Hoping the American visitor would continue to reside with them, she had been disappointed when her father had returned alone. Before the chambermaid had changed the sheets in the guest room where Adams had slept, Clara had tiptoed in. Having made her way gingerly to the bedstead, she pressed her face to the pillow. The American's smell was faint, but it was there. Her heart beating a little faster, she imagined him holding her.

Unable to bear the house without its guest, Clara had taken the carriage to Lackington's in the hope of finding a copy of Miss Austen's *Emma*. But, alas, the novel had been late to arrive from the printers, and was not yet available.

'All of London is waiting for it, Madam,' a clerk informed her cheerlessly. He had used the line a dozen times that morning alone, followed by his favoured phrase — 'If we had a copy it would be the rarest jewel in all existence.'

Thanking him, Clara glanced out of the window. She had arranged to meet her best friend there. Lady Caroline Lamb and she tended to meet at the bookshop twice a week, except when the weather prevented it. The two had become close friends three years before in the weeks after Caroline's much-publicised affair with Lord Byron.

Since the previous morning Clara had been unable to think of anything but the American visitor. She dared not mention her infatuation with him to a single soul. But Caroline was different. Not only was she Clara's only trusted confidante, she was knowledgeable in matters concerning men.

The long-cased clock across from the rotunda chimed the half hour. There was still no sign of Caroline, which was not surprising, as she had never been known to arrive anywhere on time. Clara stepped over to the topographical section to enquire if Lackington kept any writings on the Dark Continent.

Although an avid reader, and a frequent visitor to the bookshop, she had never before had cause to venture to topography. As she was the daughter of a well-known scholar, it was not long before George Lackington himself was assisting.

He was a large man, fleshy on the face, with rough hands, a touch of gout, and a slow left eye.

'Africa, Miss,' he said caressing his fingers over the spines, 'it is a land best left to those of a raw and desperate temperament.'

'Do you have any writing on Timbuctoo, Mr. Lackington?'

The shopkeeper laughed imperiously, imagining that Clara was herself attempting to be droll. His left eye catching up with the right, he seemed anxious.

'Leo the African wrote a description of the city in his *Historie*,' he said.

'Do you have it?'

'Yes, Miss Fortescue. I believe we have an original edition bound in pigskin. It is in Latin of course.'

'Is it recent?'

Lackington glanced at the floor awkwardly.

'I believe it was written in 1556,' he said.

'Do you not have anything a little more recent?'

Mr. Lackington held out a callused hand and grinned.

'You may not be aware, Miss Fortescue, but you might as well be asking for a description of the moon.'

'But in all these volumes there must be something, surely.'

The proprietor spat an instruction to his army of staff. A dozen hands fumbled urgently up and down the shelves. A quarto-sized book was snatched from its place near the floor.

'We do have this,' said Lackington unctuously, wiping the dust from the exterior, 'Mr. Jackson's *Account of Marocco*. It *is* recent, printed by Bulmer's just seven years ago.'

'Did its author see Timbuctoo with his own eyes?'

James Lackington dabbed a handkerchief to his forehead.

'I believe, Miss, that the city is described from various authoritative sources.'

Through the shop's great window, Clara Fortescue spied her friend, Caroline, descending from a lacquered gig. She was not normally impolite, but was feeling a little mischievous, a reaction to having fallen in love.

'Mr. Lackington,' she said, standing as tall as she could, 'would you consider it satisfactory to read a description of London by someone who had never actually visited the city himself?'

Glowing with embarrassment, the shopkeeper shooed away his staff.

'Perhaps, Miss Fortescue, if you could wait a few months,' he said glancing at the floor, 'I dare say that the much discussed expedition pioneered by the Royal African Committee will furnish us all with an accurate description of the golden city.'

James Lackington looked up. But Clara was gone.

THREE

JUST BEFORE COCHRAN reconvened the narration, there was a muffled knock at his study door.

'Please come in!' he called out. The door opened, Falkirk standing in the frame.

'Excuse the disturbance, sir, but the Second Floor is asking for your attendance.'

Like almost everyone else in the building, the butler refrained from referring to Caldecott by name. It was a habit that had begun a decade before, when Sir Geoffrey had arrived from obscurity, to rule over the Committee.

'Thank you Mr. Falkirk,' said Cochran, adjusting his cravat, while peering into a miniature hand mirror he kept in the left pocket of his waistcoat.

Robert Adams was sitting at the window again, staring out at the plane tree. His mind was on Christina's smile. He could see it in perfect detail, the faint lines on her wine-coloured lips, a hint of white dividing them. He thought of how he had kissed them, and how he longed to be reunited with his wife again. The corners of Christina's mouth rose, and she smiled more broadly than he could ever remember.

A surge of energy nudged Adams from the memory.

The uncertainty of recent months was gone. He was now dressed as an English gentleman, and had been promised the passage home. Fate was steering him back towards Christina. Nothing could now keep them apart.

'I shall not be very long, Mr. Adams,' said Cochran softly. 'I ought to report upstairs for fear of setting off an attack.'

The secretary left the room and made his way to Caldecott's study. He knocked.

'Enter!'

Cochran strode in, stood to attention before Sir Geoffrey and his guest, one of the directors, Henry Jerome — a man with a grizzled appearance and a blotch of red below his nostrils, a result of a fondness for Hedges' snuff.

'Have you commenced transcribing that impostor's pack of lies?'

'Yes, Sir Geoffrey.'

'Tell me, Mr. Cochran,' said Jerome, inspecting his fingernails, 'how does the American strike you?'

'How do you mean, sir?'

'Would you say he is a charlatan?'

Caldecott pushed his rounded back deeper into the chair, and narrowed his eyes, and whispered, 'or a spy?'

'I would say that he is shocked, sir.'

'Shocked?'

'He stares blankly for hours on end, as if in a daze. Indeed, the only time I have seen him speak with fluidity is when he was recounting the events which resulted in his leaving America. Yet for all his illiteracy, his delivery is remarkably good.'

Henry Jerome poured himself a cup of tea, breathing the steam through his nose.

'I should like to see him,' he said in little more than a whisper. 'Please remove your transcription to the library.'

'Very good, sir.'

'Cochran…'

'Yes, Sir Geoffrey?'

'Get out!'

'Very good, Sir Geoffrey.'

FOUR

A BATTERED OAK crate of superlative size was being unloaded from the back of a cart at Carlton House, the private residence of the Prince Regent.

A team of labourers had fitted a pulley to a crude wooden scaffold, and were heaving on ropes in an attempt to raise the box by fractions, and lower it safely onto the pavement below.

One of the men had dusted the ground with sand. Another, taller than the rest, was giving orders.

'C'mon lads, muck this up and the Prince will have your guts for garters! *Heave*! *Heave*! *Heave*!'

Against the sound of the hemp rope stretching to near-breaking point, the crate was lifted just clear of the cart, and swung with fits and jerks in a wide arc towards the pavement.

Resting on his rifle in the shelter of the grand and elaborate portico behind, a Dragoon Guard filled his chest with the chilly air and yelled:

'Easy as you go, or you'll be left with matchwood!'

The crate was lowered an inch at a time until it touched the sand, and its great weight came to bear on the frozen flagstones beneath.

'Thank gawd for that,' said the foreman, motioning to his workmen to cluster round. 'Now get those 'andles and 'eave like the Devil's on yer backs!'

No more than twenty yards from the crate, the cart, and the winch, the coals were roaring in the Grecian fireplace of the crimson drawing room. The wind was wailing down the chimney flues, whipping up the flames as though the fire was a blacksmith's forge.

A low leather chair upholstered in coral pink had been pushed close to the coals. Lounging back into its cushion was a portly figure. A little over fifty, an overripe fruit of a man, he had an appearance far beyond his age. His eyes were glazed, cheeks red from drink, hands swollen, and his belly so grotesquely distended that he looked like a stuffed goose ready for a Christmas table.

On the left side of the chair a woman was perched on a scarlet velvet stool. She was of a similar age, plain-faced and was dressed in an ordinary outfit of cream silk, low cut at the front, her cleavage pushed up, for the obvious amusement of her companion.

'Georgie dearest,' she said in a whisper, nuzzling her lips up to his ear, 'I'm a little bored. You know how it is…'

'What do you crave my dear Issy?'

'Something lovely, something little and lovely.'

'A necklace?'

'Oh, I have necklaces galore, my dearest.'

'Then what…?'

'Something glittery and small.'

'Isabella darling you know how I cannot bear little things — if a thing has no size then it has no beauty, no value. Ask me for something enormous and I shall see what I can arrange.'

At that moment a footman appeared, approached cautiously and stood to attention to the right of the chair.

'I know! I'll have your portrait done,' said the Prince. 'A great towering study of your magnificence. I'll get Lawrence to do it. And I'll get a new one of myself too. His and hers.' He let out a chortle, kissed his fingers and brushed them against Isabella's cheek.

'But dearest, I can't bear to pose hour after hour. It's so boring.'

The Prince leant forward, jerked his mistress onto his lap, thrust his arm down her cleavage, and emitted a whooping sound.

'Georgie! Please! After all, we are not alone.'

'Are we not?'

Isabella nudged a finger at the footman.

'He's just a servant,' the prince replied, 'he's no one at all.'

'Don't you want to enquire what he wants?'

'No, not really.'

'But I think you ought. After all, it may be news from Windsor.'

'If only it would be that,' said the Prince Regent despondently, removing his swollen fingers from the Marchioness of Hertford's bosom. 'For god's sake, Clarkson, what do you want?'

'The exhibit, Your Highness, it has arrived.'

'Exhibit?' The prince thought for a moment, shifted in the chair, and sprang to his feet, allowing Isabella to slide onto the floor. 'Excellent!' he snapped, pulling the sides of his coat enthusiastically towards his stomach. 'I shall inspect it at once.'

FIVE

COCHRAN WAS DISPLEASED at being asked to continue the narration in the library. He found the room draughty, and disliked its easy accessibility. There was no way of preventing the Committee directors from blustering in and out, interjecting their comments and opinions. Nothing in the world was more exasperating for Cochran than being interrupted in mid-flow.

Leading Adams down into the library, he laid his quill and paper on the desk near to the long window. The room was dark and a little damp. Despite the books and the exotic mural of an African fantasy above, there was none of the cosiness of his own study.

'Would you mind if I stood?' Adams asked once they were inside. 'Walking to and fro helps me in reliving the memories.'

'Of course, Mr. Adams,' said Cochran, removing the silver lid to the inkwell. 'Let us begin where we adjourned. I believe you had explained how you had quitted the American coast.'

The American rose to his feet. Taking in the orderly shelves of red morocco, vertical spines adorned with gilt lettering, he began:

'As I have said, I was cast upon a ship against my will, bound for the African continent. She was the *Charles*, a brig of two hundred eighty tons, her owner a Mr. Charles Sitwell of Hudson, and her captain a Mr. John Horton. She was laden with flour, rice, salted provisions and two thousand missionary Bibles, and was bound first for Gibraltar, and then for the Canary Isles.

'I pleaded with the captain to allow me to disembark, so that I might return to my wife, and seek justice with her father. But he refused point blank. We were underway, he said, and nothing would prevent us from carrying out our duty, and delivering the precious cargo. He coaxed me to seize my unfortunate situation and make good of it, to take the meagre wage he was willing to pay and increase it through trade of my own. With no other choice, I relented, and began attending to the multitude of chores thrust upon me. Soon I found myself regarded as one of the ordinary crew.

'The others were, like me, from Hudson, all except for one, a Swede, called Nicholas. The ship's mate, Stephen Dolbie, showed me the ropes. He was a small man but one of enormous strength and an equal measure of good will. The two others who took most kindly to me were Unis Newsham and Martin Clarke.

'As my father was a sail-maker, I had been brought up with a knowledge of sails, so I made myself useful repairing tears, and strengthening the jib. We had fair winds, and the passage to Gibraltar took twenty-six days. Once there, we climbed the rock, and found ourselves gazing out at Africa.

'I could hardly believe it! *Africa*... a continent of which I knew nothing at all. A month before, I would have sworn on my mother's grave that it was a land I had no destiny ever to encounter.

'While docked at Gibraltar, we took on sand ballast, pipes of wine, blue nankeens, and a quantity of scrap iron. Captain Horton had orders to wait until the vessel's insurance papers were arranged. Days slipped into weeks and still we waited there. After a month of passing the time idly, the captain exclaimed he would not endure another moment of delay, and he gave the order to weigh anchor.

'We sailed out of the harbour, heading south south-west. The brig cut easily through those dark blue waters, the sails perfectly trimmed. Dolbie, Newsham, and the other crew, took great humour in the fact that I had been forced aboard. They confided that Christina's father had paid the brig's owner fifty dollars. The fee came with the order to remove me from American soil, and to ensure my feet never again walked upon it.'

At the sound of the library doors being pushed open, Adams paused. Cochran glanced up from the page. Resting the nib on the rim of the inkwell, he nodded his head in greeting to Henry Jerome and Sir Geoffrey who had stridden in.

With the good news from Peddie, the pair were delighting in their prospective success, amused by the idea of an American claiming to have achieved anything at all.

'Pray continue, Mr. Cochran,' said Jerome coldly. 'Pray allow us be a silent witness to our visitor's falsehoods.'

Cochran gestured for Adams to continue.

He did so without delay.

'Most of the time we were not within sight of the shore. But there was enough drinking water aboard, and provisions. And, in any case, were we to require water, it would have been far too perilous to venture ashore. The sailors we met at Gibraltar told of savage tribes lining the African shoreline. Step onto the sand, they said, and our heads would be hacked clean off our shoulders.

'Each night I said a prayer to God, beseeching Him to return me to my love, and reunite me with the life I had known until then. I swore that if I ever set eyes on Mr. Ferguson again, I would have retribution for the suffering he had caused me.

'During three weeks we followed the same course although, as the days continued, we began to fear increasingly. For it became quite obvious that Captain Horton's navigation was severely at fault. Being an ordinary deck-hand, I was never permitted into his cabin. But Dolbie ventured in there one night to offer the captain refreshment. He said the man was already drunk, and had torn his charts into pieces in a fit of rage. As he reported this to us, I felt a sickness in the pit of my stomach. The lives of us all were in the balance.

'For another eight days we sailed on, sometimes venturing hazardously close to shore. We spied rocky outcrops, and the line of a reef. At first the captain pretended we had reached the Canaries. None of us believed him for a moment. Newsham begged him to change course, or at least allow the crew to aid him in the navigation. But, refusing in the strongest terms, he declared it to be his responsibility, and his alone.

'On that eighth night, one of the crew, John Matthews, said he feared we were all about to meet death. We scolded him for daring to utter such a thing. But we all knew the odds of regaining course were fading with every hour. The captain had locked himself in his cabin, and became more intoxicated than he had been on any other night. We sat there on the deck, all of us, and we prayed. We prayed for our salvation, and we prayed that sense return to Captain Horton's mind.

'At three the next morning Matthews, who was at the helm, declared he had heard breakers through the pouring rain. He informed Dolbie, who questioned how it could be true. A heavy fog had rolled in. Against such a ghostly backdrop it was easy to imagine that we were about to descend into Hell.

'An hour later we were ripped from our dreams by a jolt of the most terrible force.

'The brig had struck the reef.

'The tender was lowered, and three seamen climbed aboard. But it sank immediately. Thanks to the grace of God, all hands made it to shore alive, even Nicholas who could not swim. I lay there on the beach with my hands clawing the sand, giving thanks to the Lord, reliving the shock of being wrecked. There were voices around me. It was the crew, gathering up what jetsam they could, as they set about making a fire.

'At dawn we got the first accurate idea of our position. The reef was less than a mile from shore, and the wreck was still clinging to it, a pathetic and disheartening sight if ever there was one.

'Captain Horton fell to his knees and wept uncontrollably. I felt pity for him, rather than anger. Never should he have been given command of such a voyage. He shouted a string of orders but none of us took any notice. As far as we were concerned his authority was at an end.

'I shall carry a memory of that morning to my grave. There was a silence, a serene peace, a sense that we had arrived at the most tranquil spot on all earth. It was almost as if we had reached Paradise. I made a joke of it, and told the others. They laughed, and we all congratulated each other for surviving the wreck. After that, we warmed ourselves by the fire, and set about planning how to bring ashore what we could salvage from the brig.

'Bending down, I took a handful of sand in my palm and let it fall through my fingers — each grain a reason to survive. I looked towards the reef and the wreck, and thought of my beloved Christina. "It's time to prove your love," I thought to myself.

"Survive this and get back to Hudson. She will be waiting… she loves you, and love will breach any distance and any amount of time."

'My eyes moved from the reef back to the shore, and onto Dolbie's face. His expression was suddenly contorted, a frenzy of terror. It seemed an eternity before I heard the sound, the scream. That sound… it was enough to turn blood ice-cold with fear.

'As he screamed, I heard the sound of horses' hooves tearing over sand.'

SIX

THERE WAS NOTHING the Prince Regent enjoyed more than an exhibit. Since childhood at Windsor he had developed a fascination for the exotic, and exhibiting the exotic was something that appealed to him very greatly indeed. His homes were filled with treasures of unparalleled rarity from Europe and the Orient. But it was African oddities that satisfied his interest most of all. He referred to them as 'The Collection'. And, as far as the Regent was concerned, Africa was a Promised Land, a realm where savage nature provided for immeasurable possibility.

The Collection was a symbol of the Prince's obsession with the Dark Continent. It was housed in a south-facing salon, the Corinthian Room, with tall windows giving onto Green Park, and to the small dairy farm there tended by a woman named Mrs. Searle. The walls were hung with olive-green silk, decorated by Crace three years before, from a shipment of fabric the decorator had acquired from the Isle of Formosa.

The same silk was draped from the centre of the ceiling from a brass hasp to give an alluring tented effect. As the Prince so often reminded his decorators, the purpose of a room was to strike surprise and delight into all who entered it.

The billowing silk tent was only part of the effect. For the room was furnished with the Collection — a zoological extravaganza, a showcase of the taxidermist's art.

In the middle stood a great bull elephant in charging stance, its head bearing low, tusks curled down as if attacking a foe. Beside it was an elephant calf. Across from them stood a pair of lions, male and female, arranged as if prowling through the long grass of the savannah. The room was dotted with painted trees, on which were displayed a flock of various birds — toucans, macaws and cockatoos. On the floor below them, away from the lions, stood a pair of zebra and, beside them, six pink flamingos were arranged around a pool.

The Prince had acquired most of the animals from the Tower menagerie. Its deplorable conditions ensured a continuous flow of creatures for his taxidermist's workbench. Whenever he was at a loose end, which was often, the Regent would wander around the room, and try to imagine for a moment that he was on the savannah himself.

Sometimes he liked to pretend he was a native, a Hottentot, all naked and dark, a spear in his hand, out hunting. But fearful of being mocked behind his back, the Prince never disclosed his African fantasy to anyone, not even to the Marchioness of Hertford.

The taxidermist was a shy retiring man named William Bateman. He had a cleft palate and a way of cocking his head up and to the left when he spoke. The high point of his life were the days on which he would travel down to London with his cart, aboard which would be laden the latest stuffed specimen.

On delivery days Bateman's wife would press his tattered old topcoat, and polish his shoes until they shone like coals. The taxidermist would spend an hour and longer scrubbing the fetid stink of animal flesh from his own skin. It was an aroma his nose had grown so accustomed to over time that he could no longer smell it. After much scrubbing he anointed his thinning hair with macassar oil, combing it back so as to hide his bald patch.

Bateman's team of apprentices would pack up the newest creation in an oak crate lined with newspaper, and would load it aboard the cart. The process would take hours, especially if the exhibit was large. With Bateman sitting up front, and his apprentice taxidermists crouching behind, the cart would move out from the workshop forecourt and trundle away towards the capital.

For William Bateman, the great fear was that the exhibit would be damaged en route. Most of his other clients sent him far smaller specimens — hunting trophies or their cherished pets. With them, there was always an opportunity to check the work before the curtain was pulled back on the final display.

But the Prince Regent was a different client altogether. He insisted on being present when the crate was opened, a point that led Bateman to endure great anxiety. The night before a delivery he would be unable to sleep at all, and would sit up beside the fire all evening consumed with worry. And there was reason to worry. On one occasion the year before, the master taxidermist had delivered one of the Prince's favourite Pomeranians, named Tiny, stuffed as requested in pointing position. Once at Carlton House, the sides of the wooden crate were prised off, while the Prince Regent stood watching. To his horror, the dog's tail was lying at its feet, snapped clean away during the journey.

Although he was not ever expecting to receive further work, Bateman's expertise was so great that Carlton House called him once again.

The tall crate had been heaved down to the lower level, and was in position by the time the Prince swaggered in.

Slapping his hands together, he yelled, 'Hurry up! Quick with it! I have been waiting for this!'

Bateman cocked his head to the side, an indication to his team to begin the unwrapping process. The apprentices got to work with their jemmies. It wasn't long before the side panels were off. The Prince covered his eyes with a row of bloated fingers.

'I cannot bear the suspense!' he squirmed to the Marchioness, who had been coerced to follow him into the Collection room. She dared not voice her aversion to the art, as it gave her beloved George so much pleasure.

When the final panel had been pulled away, Bateman nodded to the equerry, who coughed lightly into his fist.

'Are we ready?'

'Indeed, Your Highness,' said the equerry.

The Prince pulled away his hand. He gazed at the proud towering form of a male giraffe. A full minute went by as he inspected the pattern on the neck and on the rump, a full minute of fear for the taxidermist and his men.

The silence was so pronounced that Bateman could hear the sound of children playing out in the street, and the royal guards calling them to scatter.

Taking three steps back, the Prince Regent filled his chest with air, and clapped his hands again.

'Splendid!' he exclaimed. 'The taxidermist has surpassed himself. What do you think Issie?'

'It's… it's remarkable, Your Highness.'

'Quite so. Let's hope the female drops dead too. Then I'll have a pair!'

SEVEN

ROBERT ADAMS PAUSED mid-flow. He found himself staring at the tooled edge of the mahogany desk at which the Committee secretary was sitting. The memory of the shipwreck was so severe to his mind that he needed a moment to collect himself.

'What's the matter, boy?' shouted Caldecott from a chair positioned ten yards away. 'Forgotten the next falsehood?'

Cochran looked up. He could sense Adams' distress.

'Are you ready to continue, sir?' he said in a gentle voice.

'Yes, yes I am. Excuse me. Dolbie's face disappeared from my line of vision, and was replaced by the most terrible sight. Never in my life had I imagined such horror.

'Fifty Moors mounted on camels and horses were charging at us down the beach. They were cloaked in flowing black robes, matching turbans on their heads, their faces shrouded in jet black cloth, all of them wielding scimitars, like harbingers from Hell.

'We started running, every man frantic to preserve his life. Every one but the captain. Dolbie and Newsham ran towards the water. The rest of us fled down the beach. We scampered like rats before a pack of tigers. There was no chance of escape. In a movement of astonishing bravery, Nicholas, the Swede, tried to jump at his attacker's horse. The steel swept in an arc and sliced his arm clean off. He fell to the ground, as the rest of us sought to flee.

'As I ran, I turned to glance back, just in time to see Matthews severed in two. The lifeblood left him in an instant. It was the first time I had witnessed it, the moment of death. What struck me was how fast life vanished. The sight paralysed me.

'I stood there, the Moors charging forward, their blades glinting in the light. I couldn't move. An instant later, I had been kicked to the ground, my face thrust into the sand, my tongue pushed against it. I could not think. The speed with which we were attacked, and our lack of weaponry, had made any counter-attack impossible.

'Before we knew it, we had all been kicked down, our hands trussed up with twine like convicts, and our clothing stripped from us. And that is what we had become — prisoners, or rather slaves, as naked as the day of our birth.

'Dolbie shouted out that he wanted to bury Matthews, give him a Christian send-off, and he was smashed in the face for his trouble. The Moors wasted no time. They divided into three groups. The first guarded us, and the second set about plundering the ship, which was hanging on the reef like a crushed child's toy. As for the third group, they hurried down the beach to gather up all the debris that had been washed ashore.

'As the sun rose high above us, we watched them, impotent, shocked by the murder of our friend. Within an hour or two, Nicholas was dead, too. His skin turned pallid, the colour of slaked lime. The sand sucked in his blood as if it were nothing at all. As the day ebbed forward we were all consumed by thirst, or what we supposed thirst to be. I look back almost in humour at our raw condition. We were like sheets of white rag paper, clear of creases. There wasn't a blemish on us.

'The Moors managed to float bundles of cargo and supplies ashore. The skill with which they salvaged what there was to save, suggested they were no strangers at stripping wrecked vessels. By late afternoon, the beach was littered with equipment — pulleys and sail cloth, barrels, bedding, and bundles of tools.

'The Bibles had all been brought ashore with care, and were heaped up, as were the pipes of wine. The hardtack and other provisions were piled up, too, and then divided between the three groups. The crew and I sat motionless. Like me, each one must have been praying to the Lord, praying for an act of divine salvation.

'As the afternoon heat rose to its full intensity, and then began to wane, the bodies of our dead companions began to decompose. I was struck at how fast the flesh of men who had been healthy a few hours before, became infested with worms.

'That evening the ship's hulk was set alight. It burned furiously for a while, the flames fanned by the ripping Atlantic wind. Newsham began to weep and was flogged so badly for it he lost an eye. I felt consumed with fury, but bit my tongue. A single word of opposition, and the beach would have tasted my blood as well. So we crouched on our haunches, all of us, waiting for something to happen. And it did. One of our captors smashed the pipes of wine. After that he took his tinderbox, lit a touchpaper and tossed it onto the pile of Bibles. It went up like a bonfire, the flames reaching the stars.

'Responsible for the miserable situation in which we found ourselves, Captain Horton leapt up. He charged at another of the Moors, bawling obscenities for performing such an unthinkable act of sacrilege. A scimitar flashed in the firelight, and the captain's head was separated from its shoulders.'

EIGHT

16, Fleet Street
18th November 1815

My dearest Beattie,

Forgive me for not writing these last days. But I have been most preoccupied with attending to our American guest, and to discharging my duty of recording his narration for the benefit of the Committee.

He is a most singular man, whose history is only now becoming known to me. Although I find it quite fascinating in every way, Sir G can hardly conceal his revulsion. While listening for himself today with Mr. Jerome, he became quite agitated, and ordered the transcription to be halted until the morn.

I hope most sincerely, my sweet Beattie, that I shall have the pleasure of visiting your uncle's home for the purpose of gaining an interview with you, when you are here in London.

I wish you the most comfortable of journeys on the arduous drive south. I am enclosing a little reading material, a copy of George Byron's Hebrew Melodies. He was good enough to inscribe it to you when I dined with him last week. He said to declare how much he is looking forward to making your gentle acquaintance. I am certain you will enjoy his company as much as I, although these last weeks *he does not seem to be his usual ebullient self. I fear there is disquiet between him and Annabella. He spoke of travelling again, an eagerness to glimpse his reflection in the serene waters of Lake Geneva.*

Please write with details of your travel arrangements, my dearest.

Yours, most affectionately, as always,
Simon

NINE

VISCOUNT FORTESCUE LEFT the house as soon as breakfast was at an end. He did not reveal where he was going, only that he would be out all day on matters of an 'intriguing and confidential nature'. Devoted to her father, Clara was quite content when he was at home. But his absence allowed her to invite Lady Caroline home for an uninterrupted session of conversation, what Fortescue referred to as 'the banter of she-wolves'.

As soon as the Viscount's carriage had sped out from the portico, Clara dispatched the doorman with a message for her closest confidante. It read simply, '*Hasten here at once, C.*'

An hour later, a lacquered carriage drew up and Lady Caroline stepped nimbly down. She was ushered into the yellow parlour, where Clara was awaiting her.

'Whatever is the need for such haste, my dearest?' she exclaimed, sweeping into the room.

Clara didn't reply. She hardly knew where to begin.

'It's the visitor, is it not?' said Caroline, a tone of disapproval in her voice. 'The American you told me of at Lackington's. I warned you, I am sure this will lead to difficulties.'

'Sit down here beside me,' said Clara, pressing a hand to the cushion, and up over her red hair. 'I must confide in someone and you are my only trusted friend.'

'Pray tell.'

'You are right. It is Mr. Adams, the very same — the *American*. I can think of nothing but his smile, his shoulders, his brutal appeal.'

'I must get you into the country, my dearest. You need a change of air.'

'I would not quit London now for anything. I must see him again, and I am to impose myself on your benevolence.'

'What ever could *I* do?'

'This morning over breakfast father remarked that his godson, a Mr. Cochran, was taking the narration of Mr. Adams' story at the Royal African Committee. I thought we might drop by and have a listen.'

'Listen? I assume you mean, gawk... The eyes not the ears?'

Clara blushed and Caroline sighed.

'We shall need a chaperone. I shall ask my cousin Bertie. He's been bragging at the wealth he's sure to make from his investment in that daft expedition in search of Timbuctoo.'

'You have heard of the Committee's quest for the golden city?'

'My dear Clara, every drawing room in London resounds with talk of it.'

TEN

LUNCHEON HAD BEEN a feast of memorable proportions at White's as it was on any weekday. The club was eager that its cuisine might one day equal that of Boodle's.

The chef, Maximillian Fauch, an émigré from Alsace, had surpassed himself with a platter of roasted snipe. It was his grandmother's recipe, one that had been in the family six generations. Almost unknown in the depths of winter, the birds were served with all the trimmings, flambéed lightly in vintage cognac. As Fauch frequently reminded his staff, a spoon of flaming cognac is never noticed except when absent.

The meal had commenced with an *amuse bouche* of chilled calf's foot jelly dusted with cinnamon, and concluded with thin slices of pineapple dipped in dark chocolate. The dining room was filled to capacity, the club members in town for the pre-Christmas season, to see but, more importantly, to be seen. The main salon was shrill with conversation, with the boasts and bravado of a young generation who had survived or, more likely, successfully avoided, the Napoleonic campaigns.

At the far end of the room three gentlemen were seated on club chairs, allowing the game to digest, sipping port, and drawing gently on their pipes.

On the left was Lord Alvanley, a Regency Buck and trusted friend of the Prince Regent, a bulky flat-faced man not yet thirty, with large hands and an arrogance that exceeded even that of Lord Byron, seated on his right. George Byron's fame as a poet and author matched only his reputation for infamy. The drawing rooms of London were well stocked with ladies whose hearts had been broken by his charm and by the impressive consistency of his prose. Not least affected was Lady Caroline Lamb, whose brainless cousin, Bertie, was seated to Byron's right. Unlike his friend, he was not part of the royal circle, but was always impatient for news of it.

'Do tell, Alvanley, what's Prinny's latest pleasure?' he asked.

Lord Alvanley drew on his pipe, sniffed, and said, 'It's a female, twelve foot high and all covered in spots.'

'She sounds enchanting. Is she English?'

'Not quite. I believe she was born on African plains.'

'Golly,' said Bertie, frowning. 'An African mistress, and one so tall. I do believe it will be a challenging romance.'

'The snow will be back tonight,' said Alvanley all of a sudden, 'I feel it in my bones.'

Byron touched the rim of his glass to his lips.

'It won't snow again, not until the Near Year. I am certain of it, and I feel a wager coming on.'

'What shall it be?' said Alvanley, smacking his hands together. 'Smythe! Where are you, Smythe?!'

A butler crossed the room and stood to attention at the young lord's chair. His face was absent of any expression.

'Yes, M'lord?'

'Smythe, fetch the book.'

'Very good M'lord.'

The butler padded away, small steps across parquet, returning a moment later with a ledger bound in lizard-green cloth, tattered on the spine.

'What shall I put you down for? A hundred guineas, or two?'

'Let us make it three,' said Alvanley. 'Three hundred guineas says it won't snow before January first, Bertie our witness.'

He scratched the wager in the gaming book.

'You will regret it,' Byron replied.

Alvanley frowned.

'I pity you, sir, for requiring a profession. A life without a proper inheritance can be no life at all. You had better begin a new novel, for the debtors shall soon be at your doors.'

ELEVEN

IT WAS NINE in the morning, and the library clock had chimed the hour once, and then again. Cochran was thankful that Sir Geoffrey was late, for the chairman abhorred faulty equipment, and would have blamed the heat, as he did with mechanical malfunctions of any kind.

Standing in the same position as the day before, Adams was collecting his thoughts. Weaving his fingers together, he flexed them towards the parquet.

Cochran inspected the quill's nib.

'Sir Geoffrey cannot bear the climate,' he said. 'He believes we live in an inferno, that the damp London air is somehow diabolic, a searing desert heat.'

'I'd say he has the Devil perched on his shoulder,' said Adams.

Cochran smiled.

'I would gladly concur with that,' he replied in a whisper.

At a quarter past the hour he raised his nib in the air, dipped once, again, and said, 'I believe we have waited long enough. Pray let us continue, Mr. Adams and, if Sir Geoffrey graces us with his presence, we shall recapitulate.'

Robert Adams stared down at the floor, his eyes tracing the veins of the parquet.

'Our captain had been beheaded,' he said in a low voice, 'and the Word of the Lord had been set ablaze. Two of the crewmen were slaughtered. The rest of us were enslaved, our hands knotted up with thorny twine. Even if we could have escaped, where were we to have gone? Dolbie coaxed us to break free, to run into the waves and drown ourselves. At least then, he declared, we would meet our end with a measure of dignity.

'I urged him to seize every ounce of strength from the marrow of his bones. It was clear to me even then that survival depended on raw sinew, a vigour of the mind and, most of all, an ardent belief in the Almighty. As long as I was standing upright on the same earth as my beloved, I pledged to do everything in my power to beat a path to her. An ocean separated us, and I was stranded at the very margin of Hell. But I swore that I would not rest until I was holding her gentle hands in mine. Every moment that passed was a moment less to endure.

'At dawn the Moors began packing their spoils and loading them upon the beasts. The camels knelt down in the sand, groaning under the bulk of provisions and equipment. We were offered no food and nothing to drink. It had been a day and a night since our lips had tasted refreshment of any kind. My mouth was so dry that speaking became strenuous. It was probably for the best, for if I had uttered a word, my neck would have been touched by steel.

'The sun was high by the time we left the shore. First the horses, then the camels, and the crewmen trailing behind, wretched and whimpering. A pair of Moors followed in our haphazard footsteps, both with whips, ready to remind us to make haste lest we forget.

'Those first hours of trudging are scorched into my memory. I wept aloud, and sucked the tears down into my mouth. Each drop was an ocean of pleasure. The sun scalded my head and caused blisters to well up all over my scalp. I felt sure I might collapse. Then I did so. No sooner had my limp form crumpled onto the sand, than a leather tongue ripped open my back, once, twice. I struggled to my feet, my shipmates imploring me to stand.

'At dusk the Moors watered the animals, pitched a shelter against the wind, and lit a fire to keep away the wolves. Only as an after-thought did they throw a rotting carcass in our direction. The little meat on it stank and was riddled with worms. We all refused to eat, exclaiming it wasn't fit for a dog let alone one of us. So we went hungry, and thirsty too.

'By the next morning most of us were shaking with fever, except John Stephens. The youngest, not yet eighteen, he was dead.'

Robert Adams stopped speaking. He stood in silence, as

Cochran's quill scratched across the surface of the page. At the back of the room sat Caldecott and Jerome. Having entered boisterously while Adams was recounting his tale, they had been joined by a handful of others, all of them directors of the Committee.

Cochran was about to nod for Adams to continue, when the great teak library doors parted. Falkirk paced in as quietly as he could, making a beeline for Sir Geoffrey. He whispered something, and ducked his head.

'Whatever is *he* doing here?!' boomed Caldecott.

'What? Who?' said Jerome.

'It's that buffoon Bertie McCormack. He's come to listen to the narration. Says he has an interest as an investor.'

'The cheek of it.'

'Would you like to decline the request, sir?'

Caldecott pondered for a moment and looked up to where Adams was standing.

'No, on second thoughts, I think the pitiable Mr. Adams will aid us with a little publicity. Falkirk, inform Mr. McCormack that he and anyone else is quite free to join us. There are seats aplenty.'

TWELVE

WILLIAM BATEMAN RECEIVED a letter the next day notifying him that the menagerie had suffered another loss. A large male polar bear, gifted to George III by the late Norwegian King Christian VII, had succumbed in the night.

The letter, from the assistant to the assistant of the Prince Regent's private secretary, contained instructions for Bateman to hurry to the Tower of London and collect the remains of *Ursus maritimus* at once.

The master taxidermist had selected his profession for the usual lack of urgency in the work. He could not stand rushing, but knew very well that, even in winter, a large carcass decomposed very speedily indeed. Leave it more than a day or two and the fine preservation of the tissue for which he was fêted would be severely impaired. Bateman called his wife, Maud, to fetch his work clothes, a length of rope, and the knife with an ivory handle. He looked at her hard as he made or the door.

'And see that you get the benches ready this time, woman,' he said sternly, 'or I'll give you a hiding when I'm 'ome!'

A rowdy woman with a club-foot, Maud took pride in her husband's connection with royalty, advertising it with exaggeration to almost everyone who crossed her path. When she was younger she had longed to have a son who might continue the firm, which was established by Bateman's father, Jeremiah, fifty years before. But the only children she had given birth to were a pair of frail twin daughters.

Both had perished a week after birth, in the harsh winter of '89.

THIRTEEN

Chavenage Hall
9th December 1815

Dear Simon,

Thank you dear cousin for Lord Byron's Melodies, *which have brought warmth in these days of bleak winter rain. The inscription from the author was most touching, and your kindness in sending it, something I shall not forget.*

I hope you are seated reading this, because I have news. It is confirmed that I am to come to London! I shall make the journey with mother, in the carriage of the Baroness Palterpoint, and that we shall drive down this coming week, breaking the journey at the home of my maternal aunt, in Aylesbury.

We shall reside with my uncle, Sir Henry Montagu, at his home in Bloomsbury Square. I shall leave you now, for there is much packing to be done. I cannot express my excitement to be in the capital after an eternity in the wilderness.

With affection,
Beattie

FOURTEEN

EXCUSING HIMSELF, COCHRAN left the library to fetch a fresh swan-feather quill from his desk. The nib he had been using was wearing down, the stem becoming uncomfortable in his hand.

He climbed the stairs and was soon in his study, where he pulled out his pocket mirror and glanced at the state of his cravat. He took a moment to tidy it. When it was done, he removed the new quill, inspected it, and glanced out of the window.

It was snowing again.

Down in the library, he found Bertie McCormack, his cousin Caroline, and Clara Fortescue taking their seats. Acquainted with Caroline Lamb through his friendship with George Byron, he knew of her friendship with Miss Fortescue, albeit only by reputation.

Taking his seat, Cochran took care not to make eye contact with either of the ladies, for such a forward gesture would have been inappropriate for a gentleman.

Robert Adams scanned the room as he rose to his feet, and found himself staring at Clara. She was wearing a slender dress of fine yellow taffeta, the fabric ruched at the shoulders. As soon as she saw him looking in her direction, she glanced down at her lap modestly, and did not move until she heard the sound of his voice.

Sir Geoffrey Caldecott called for the narration to continue.

Adams waited for the quill to be dipped and to be relieved of its excess ink. He took a deep breath.

'Standing here in the grandeur of this chamber,' he said, leaning back on his heels, still staring out at Clara, 'we are a million miles from the Hellfire land I am attempting to describe. I encourage the audience to conjure the heat, the sand, the thirst, in their minds.'

He took another breath, even deeper than the last.

'As I have described, I was shipwrecked on the hostile African shore, stripped of my clothing, my hands trussed up behind my back. Our captain was butchered, the rest of us taken as slaves towards the interior.

'On the second morning one of our captors swaggered up with a skin of water. He had a dark complexion, was bearded, and had cold black eyes, with robes of matching black cloth. At his waist in a red scabbard was a dagger. Dripping a few drops of precious water into each mouth, he listened as our tongues pleaded for more. After I had been offered my ration, he turned to us and said in perfect English:

'"There is a way all of you can gain your freedom. I swear it. You can drink ten skins each, eat the finest meat, and regain your honour."

'"Are you the Devil?" whispered Newsham. The figure smiled.

'"I am your saviour," he said.

'"Untie us then, give us clothing and water," said another.

'"Renounce your god and I shall see to it that you are rewarded."

'"What?"

'"Look at me. I was one of you!"

'"Who are you?" said I.

'"My name is José Morales, and I was washed ashore just like you, fifty miles from here, at Capo Blanco."

'"What was your ship?"

'"The *Lucerne* bound from Cadiz. I am a Spaniard."

'"You *are* the Devil!" Dolbie yelled. "Away with you!"

'Morales put the skin to his lips and quenched his thirst.

'"Time will pass," he said, "and as it does you will either die, and your bones will lie here until they crumble into dust, or you will come to see your situation with wisdom. Renounce your Lord, convert, and these men will regard you as their equal."

'"Where are they taking us?" I asked.

'"Into the interior, into the Zahara. There is safety there. Laden like this we are a prize for bandits. Many others would have seen your ship broken up on the reef."

'"What will become of us?"

'The Spaniard poured a little of the liquid onto his hand and rinsed his face.

'"They will trade you," he said. "For you are nothing more than chattels to be bartered. You would do well to pray, for I assure you, no one else but Him is listening to your cries."

'Six days passed. Our bodies were roasted, and became covered in fetid sores. I would look at my shipmates in that state, feeling pity for them, fooling myself that I did not look as bad. Each night I would escape in my dreams and find myself standing in the winter barley, it swaying in the breeze. But then, before dawn, reality would strike like a hammer on iron.

'At the end of the first week of suffering, James Davison succumbed. He had been whipped so severely he choked blood until he coughed up part of a lung. On the last night, he begged the Moors to end his life. So they did, but not without a little sport. They chopped off his fingers one by one, taking it in turns, and then his toes, until half the world had heard his cries. Then they amputated his masculinity, while cackling like jackals. When he passed out, they revived him, and chopped out his tongue.

'At dawn he was still alive. It was a miracle. The camels were made ready and, before moving out, Davison's mangled body was branded with a scalding blade and propped up in the sand. I wondered why they would do such a thing, prop him up like that. Then I understood the reason — so that our poor shipmate could watch as the caravan moved on.'

FIFTEEN

COCHRAN HALTED THE narration, fearing for the sensitivities of the ladies present. He was about to recommend to Sir Geoffrey that the audience be restricted to gentlemen, when Bertie approached, presented himself, and introduced his companions.

Clara advanced and took a step sideways, so as to position herself beside Adams, who was on the right of Cochran.

'I had not been aware that your experiences were so terrible, Mr. Adams,' she said in a delicate voice, keeping her eyes trained on the floor. 'I do hope that the Committee is doing everything in its capacity to fortify your spirits.'

'Thank you. As you know I owe my change of fortune entirely to your father's kindness.'

Clara was eager to encourage the American to call upon her father, but could not construct a sentence in her mind that would appear suitably diffident. So she smiled, lowered her head, and touched a hand to cover her mouth. Excusing themselves, she and Lady Caroline exited the library and searched for a quiet corner in which to gossip.

As soon as they were out of earshot of the gentlemen, Caroline grasped Clara by the wrist.

'I do declare, my dear, he is a Greek god! Why did you not bring him to my attention earlier?'

'I did, I did! I tried to explain!'

'Well, my dear Clara, your description was faulty I am sure.'

Both women sighed in unison.

'We must tread with cautious footsteps,' said Lady Caroline. 'For your Mr. Adams does not enjoy the approval of society. Not yet, at any rate.'

'How could he…? He is an American.'

'A dilemma indeed.'

'Did you hear his voice?'

'My dear Clara, I did, but I must advise you that it was not my ears that were seduced, but my eyes.'

SIXTEEN

THAT EVENING, COCHRAN and Adams furled themselves up against the cold and took a walk. The snow had fallen evenly since tea, and was now freezing hard. Fleet Street was crowded with hawkers of Christmas wares — holly wreaths and mistletoe, long tallow candles in clusters of six, chestnuts, and geese, well hung and ready for plucking.

In a buoyant mood, Cochran felt of real use for once. His general satisfaction was boosted further by the fact that his new coat had arrived from his tailor, Mr. Henry Poole of Savile Row. It was a piece of couture well beyond his means but, as he was a member of the dandy set, debt was preferable to being in a state of under-dress.

As they walked, the hawkers stepped forward to offer their wares, and Cochran waved each one aside.

'Bachelorhood is not a life but a predicament,' he said.

'Why don't you find yourself a wife then?'

'Mr. Adams, it is not that easy.'

'Why not? You meet a girl, fall in love, and propose.'

Cochran let out a snigger.

'As I say, it is not that easy, sir. For a gentleman in London must have five thousand a year at least to survive, and that is certainly not a circumstance in which I find myself.'

'Why do you need so much?'

'Because of society, sir.'

'*Society?*'

'Indeed. A proposal not supported by an inheritance would make one a laughing stock.'

'But if you love someone, what does it matter if people laugh?'

'What does love have to do with it, Mr. Adams?' Cochran asked, pausing. 'Perhaps you misunderstand, for I am talking of marriage.'

As they arrived back at his chambers, the doorman held up a letter.

'Came by private carriage. A nice one, too. Had letters written on the door.'

Cochran removed his gloves, stuffed them in his pocket, and held the envelope into the lamplight. It was addressed to *Robert Adams Esq.*

'It's for you,' he said, passing the envelope to his guest.

'Who would have written to me?'

'Well open it and find out.'

Adams shook the fingers of his right hand warm, and tore back the top edge. Inside was a single sheet of writing paper, lilac in colour with a watermark of a single date palm, although in the dim light it was barely possible to make out.

'Bring it inside,' said Cochran, turning the key to his door.

They went in and, when the fire was stoked, and the lamp turned up, Adams passed the letter to Cochran.

'Would you read it to me?'

'Yes please.'

Cochran held the sheet in his left hand and raised it to his nostrils.

'*Bouquet Imperial*,' he said vaguely.

'What does it say?'

Cochran tilted the lilac sheet so that the neat copperplate script was highlighted by the oil lamp's flame.

Dear Mr. Adams,

You must forgive me for writing. I feel quite ashamed for daring to do so, as I have broken all rules of proper demeanour and etiquette, but I have to make contact with you in this way. I wish to advise you that I was most affected by the awful sequence of events you narrated today, and I find myself hoping with the greatest modesty that we may meet socially again before long.

Yours sincerely,
Clara Fortescue

P.S. I would be indebted if you would keep this correspondence in the strictest confidence.

SEVENTEEN

BATEMAN TOOK HIS cart to the great door of the menagerie and hammered with all his strength. He had spent the previous night at an inn on the outskirts of Colchester, where he had eaten a plate of roast beef, washed down with a mug of the local ale. The drink had been so pleasing he had asked for another. It was served by the publican's wife, a woman of considerable bulk with a wooden stump for a right leg. She had enquired if the taxidermist was travelling alone, to which he had answered that he was.

'I'll 'ave a little company sent to your room,' she said. 'Warm your bed up nice.'

Mr. Bateman considered his reputation as a man of principles and his expertise in taxidermy, a skill that was the talk of his trade. After all he was the taxidermist to the Prince of Wales no less. He downed the ale in one, picked a scrap of fat from his plate and gulped it down, too, then staggered to his room.

The night had reminded him that the female gender was capable of more than the services proffered by his wife of thirty years. He had been transported to the Elysian Fields and back. And, when the barmaid had asked for three shillings, he had given her a crown. His mind was so preoccupied with the bedstead in Essex that he had driven the cart all day with a glazed expression.

As the door to the menagerie inched open, Bateman waved the letter bearing the royal crest, and demanded to be taken to where the great white bear was lying frozen with rigor mortis. The keeper led the taxidermist through the central area, where cages of the rare and exotic were arranged closer than was wise.

'When d'he go?' Bateman asked in a distant voice.

'Three days past. Made a terrible racket. Kept up 'alf of London, I'd say. Now he's as stiff as a barn door.'

A grimy blanket had been draped over the creature, which

was stinking beyond belief. The master taxidermist approached, heaved away the shroud, and jabbed a finger into the flesh behind the front leg. After that, he examined the head, and poked his fingers into the mouth to have a look at the teeth.

'I think I'll do him growling,' he said. 'The Prince will like that. He likes growlers does the Prince.'

An hour later the arctic beast had been raised successfully up onto the cart, and the vehicle was trundling back towards Colchester. The polar bear, covered again in the putrid brown blanket, hardly moved as the cart jolted east in the direction of the nubile barmaid at the Essex inn.

Bateman usually spent the return journey pondering how best to preserve and exhibit the animal. But on this journey, the intricacies of taxidermy were the last thing on his mind.

EIGHTEEN

Down near the Thames at Wapping, Albert Wicks was drying out a length of handmade rope over the grate at his home. He twisted it slowly between his fingers making sure the heat penetrated the fibre evenly.

Wicks was haggard, grey-haired, and limped when he walked. He had no idea of his age, but when asked by someone he said he felt 'as old as the hills', and he would show them his gums. 'A set of gums,' he would say, 'can tell you more about a man than any amount of prattle.' His wife, a queen of prattle, had borne him six children, five boys and a girl. She had disappeared one night fifteen years before, last seen stumbling drunk towards the river. As for his children, they were all dead, or gone, the eldest son executed for theft, and the rest transported south to the penal colony at Van Diemen's Land.

Wicks rubbed his hands down the rope and pulled it tight until he heard the cracking sound his father had taught him was the sign.

'Dry as a bone,' he said to himself, as he sat down at his chair to tie the noose.

Albert Wicks' paternal grandfather was the first in the family to enter the profession, being appointed hangman to the Prince Regent's own grandfather, King George II. Albert had assisted in his first hanging at the age of eleven, just as his own father had done. It was a day of which he spoke often, recalling the sound of the neck snapping like a dry twig on a midsummer day. Now that he was advancing in years, his only regret was that his eldest son, John, had been hanged rather than becoming a hangman himself.

Wicks' father, who had manned the Tyburn gallows for thirty years, had disposed of a number of the most notorious highwayman of the time. Young Albert had been weaned on tales of execution, and had learned the tricks of the trade or, as his father liked to call them, 'the secrets of the craft'. He mastered how to dry the rope well, so that the knot slid tight in the blink of an eye, and how to position the noose high up the neck where the vertebrae were weak. 'Learn the craft, Bert,' his father would say, 'and you'll have a job for life.' And it had been true. For Albert Wicks had amassed a fortune over the years, one for which he had no heir.

For a respected hangman such as he was, the workload was relentless and the pay was good. Late the year before, his youngest son had been transported, and his own sister had passed away in the same week. Albert was left alone in the world. He grieved and then, a week later, he found himself in better spirits than he had been in years. He was free — free from a nagging wife and a family who spent their entire lives pilfering funds he had toiled hard to amass.

Then one afternoon the following March, he was called to hang a man accused of treason, at the Execution Dock. Since moving from the gallows at Tyburn down to the river, Albert had become acquainted with and then executed a roll of engaging criminals. They were all quite different from the coarse unworldly types he was used to executing. A number of them had been gentlemen, guilty of crimes against the Crown.

The one sentenced to death for treason was a gentleman himself, who went by the name of Cook. He was tall, well-mannered, and had plenty to say about life, business, and the state of the world. There had been trouble with the scaffold that day. While his apprentices worked away at firming up the gallows, Albert made small talk to Mr. Cook. He told him all about notable people he had hanged in his time, and even revealed some of the secrets of his craft. For, as he saw it, the secrets were unlikely to be passed on.

An hour before Cook climbed the wooden stairs, he asked Albert about the income he made.

'I keep it in a cavity in the wall by my bed,' Albert replied, once again, free with his information given the circumstances.

'If I were you,' Cook had said, 'I would remove it from the wall and invest it. By this time next summer you could be as rich as any man in London. And if you heed keenly I shall give you a tip.'

Albert Wicks had pricked up his ears and listened well. The next day, when Mr. Cook's neck had been snapped in two, he hastened to the address he had been given, the office of a Hugh Appleby Esquire on Wimpole Street. He had taken the liberty of borrowing the costume of a gentleman recently availed of his services. A coin to the undertaker had ensured the deceased's family were none the wiser.

In his pocket was a sackcloth purse, containing the proceeds from a career of forty years. The sight of the gold was enough to secure Mr. Appleby's full attention. He listened as Albert Wicks explained the brief yet close acquaintance he had enjoyed with the late Mr. Cook, and Albert paid attention as the broker outlined a scheme by which he could transform his nest egg into real wealth.

A balding man of thirty, Appleby had ice-blue eyes and the kind of face that instils genuine fear in small children. He rose to his feet, moved slowly to the window and peered out at the wind in the trees.

'You are a wise man, Mr. Wicks,' he said pushing out his chest like a cockerel strutting before the hens. 'I can see it in your eyes. With savings such as these, and a project such as this,' he paused to wave a thin dossier held up in his right hand, 'you will taste the kind of affluence that has fuelled your dreams.'

'How would I make the investment, sir?' Albert asked cautiously, a little ill at ease at sitting in an office for the first time.

'In the world of investment, Mr. Wicks, there are plenty of ways to lose a fortune and very few by which a sagacious gentleman such as yourself might seek to augment his pecuniary position. It seems though that fate is smiling on you, sir. For I have just this morning received a coded notification of a project of distinct possibility. I shall explain...

'A company of gentlemen with a record as distinguished as is possible, are embarking on a grand expedition. It shall take advantage of the wealth of a realm bedecked in treasure, the likes of which has never been known. The expeditionary force shall suppress the local militia and avail themselves of the kingdom's storehouses, each one filled with the purest gold bullion. Then they shall return with the booty to London, where the investors of this eminent project shall be rewarded for their shrewd and courageous speculation.'

Hugh Appleby fixed his ice-blue eyes hard on Albert Wicks. He held the gaze for so long as to be uncomfortable. Albert sat up and flexed his back. The coat was tailored for a man a little less broad than himself, and the seams were pressing hard, cramping his muscles.

Appleby pushed the dossier away from him, until it was sitting squarely in front of Albert Wicks. Brown manila, creased at one edge, it was labelled with the word TIMBUCTOO.

NINETEEN

AT THE AFRICAN Committee, Caldecott, Jerome and William DeWitt were sitting in the library waiting for the clock to strike nine. London society was not known for rising early or for punctuality of any kind. But the narration had attracted several ordinary members of the public. Unlike the gentry, for whom they tended to work, they kept good time. On Sir Geoffrey's orders, a footman had laid out a dozen chairs.

The chairman had nodded a greeting to Clara Fortescue, Lady Caroline and to her cousin, who had been joined by half a dozen of Bertie McCormack's friends.

Simon Cochran listened as the great clock chimed the hour. He stood up and motioned for Adams to do the same.

'Ladies and gentlemen,' he began, 'I am most honoured as a humble secretary to this esteemed Committee, to have the pleasure of introducing again Mr. Robert Adams, and in asking that he might grace us with the continuation of his fascinating narrative.'

Thanking Cochran, Adams took in the audience.

'As I have explained,' he said, 'the surviving shipmates and I were taken as slaves towards the interior of the great Zahara. As each day dawned, we had no idea if it were to be our last. But I for one had vowed an oath to survive, that I held sacred.

'Days and nights passed in a gruesome sequence of discomfort. Each night Morales, the Spanish traitor to our faith, would approach us, jesting at our derelict condition, tempting us with clothing and morsels from our captors' table. We cursed him, called him what he was — filth vented from the sewers of Hell.

'Then one morning the camels were gathered up and the spoils from our ship rearranged upon them. The Moors whipped my shipmates and me to our feet. I shouted out to Morales, imploring him to reveal what was going on.

'"The interior is a furnace where the horses will not survive," he said. "So they will stay with us near to the coast."

'As he spoke, one of the Moors climbed down from his camel, bound my hands with a strand of leather, and tied the other end to the saddle of the beast. He shouted something in Arabic.

'"You have been traded," Morales said calmly. "You will go with the others, into the interior, and there you shall die."

'That moment was one of the most fearful I have ever had the misfortune to experience. I stood there on the sand, naked but for a strand of leather covering my manhood, my friends hauled away from me. I shouted to them, tears in my eyes, and they called back. The last word to touch my ears was Dolbie's.

'"Survive!"

'The camels moved fast across the sand. If I did not keep up with their elongated stride, they would pull me, jerking me forward like a rag doll. By the afternoon, we had entered a new territory. The sand was much dryer, and the air stripped of its moisture. I struggled for breath. All I could think was to ask myself again and again where they were taking me.

'From one horizon to the next there was a sea of sand — flat, silent, baked hard by the sun. We crossed it walking fast, as if heading to a pressing engagement.

'As soon as we had traversed the emptiness, reaching the horizon, we were rewarded with another identical vista — an eternity of sand. From time to time there might be a low thorn bush. When the Moors set eyes on such a thing they became joyful. They would rush over to it and tug at it, until the roots were exposed. One at a time they would suck them, their laughter suggesting great pleasure.

'We marched for five days. Then, in the far distance, we set eyes on what I assumed was a group of trees. Yet as we drew closer, we saw it was moving. My captors seemed pleased. They increased the pace and, by dusk, we had reached their fellow group of Moors.

'That night, there was celebration. A fire was lit and an odd-looking animal was slaughtered, its carcass roasted. I did not recognise it or its smell. And, when one of the bones was hurled in my direction, I grew yet more curious. As I huddled gnawing at the bone, I heard a voice — an English voice.

'"Are you a Christian?"

'"Yes!" said I. "Who are you?"

'"Then I am your brother," said the man. "A seaman, from Cadiz. I was wrecked three years ago and taken into slavery, as you."

'"What's your name?"

'"Juan Sanchez. And you?"

'"Robert Adams."

'I told Sanchez that I felt much misery at being separated from my companions. To which he replied that the Moors saw Christians such as ourselves as objects to be bartered with one another, that there were hundreds just like us in the great desert. Then I asked him what animal had died so that I might suck at its bones.

'"It's a desert fox," said Sanchez.

'The next morning I asked my new friend how we might reverse our sordid condition. I expected him to hang his head low. But he didn't.

'"We can escape," he said quickly, "only if we can get to Mogador on the coast of Marocco, then the Consul there will redeem us. He will pay the ransom of any man who has not forsaken the Christian faith."

'I leapt to my feet and ran as fast as my legs could carry me to the place where my master was crouched.

'"Mogador! Mogador, take us there!" I pleaded to him at the height of my lungs in English. "Help us and the Consul will make you rich!"

'The Moor got up and struck my shoulder so firmly that the ball was expelled from the socket. Then, when I howled, he licked me with his whip. The following night, after a day of terrible anguish, Sanchez ordered me to bite on the leather strap that bound my hands. As I did so, he thrust the shoulder back into place.

'We marched on for another week, a procession of camels laden with an assortment of oddities gleaned from ours and other ships.

There were sails furled up in sacks, crates of hardtack, portholes threaded together on ropes, nails, hammers, and all sorts of other tools. And, on one camel — an unwieldy female — was bound the great carved figurehead of a ship, *Queen of the Waves*.

'From time to time our caravan happened upon another. The Moors would kiss each other's cheeks, praise their god, and trade ships' merchandise dug out of their packs.

'On one occasion we had been welcomed by a large gathering of Moors. My master presented his host with a pair of Bibles, the dry pages prized for tinder. The gift was well received and our host opened a chest filled to the brim with booty. Removing a spyglass and a Union flag, he offered them ceremoniously to his guest.

'As the days passed, Sanchez educated me in the art of survival upon the desert sands. He taught me to gather dew from the night air, and the skill of ruminating one's rations, like a camel, so as to gain maximum satisfaction from a meal. He taught me, too, how to drink from the flow of a camel's water without getting kicked in the face.'

Adams was interrupted by Cochran.

'I propose, sir, that we might rest for a moment, in order for another row of seating to be arranged.'

A pair of footmen began setting out the chairs, to accommodate a dozen members of society who had just arrived.

At the back of the room, Clara Fortescue stared uneasily at the floor. She felt embarrassed at having sent the letter the night before, and was nervous lest Lady Caroline find out. It would have been easier to have stayed at home, but her desire to hear every detail of the American's sufferings forced her to attend.

Before the narration recommenced, Sir Geoffrey strode from the library and charged up to his study on the second floor. He sent Falkirk down to fetch the Committee secretary, adding, 'If he is not here in fifteen seconds I shall dock your wages for the week!'

Well used to Sir Geoffrey's outbursts, Cochran had learned to weather their full force. Within a month of working at the Committee, he had acquired a sixth sense, enabling him to know precisely when the chairman's wrath would make landfall. He found that standing quite still, in absolute silence, eyes trained on the window ledge, worked well as a means of enduring even the most turbulent storm. If asked a question, he found it was best left unanswered.

Caldecott's brow was glistening with perspiration. He was so heated that he had removed the white gloves that frequently accessorised his costume, and was standing with his hands at his side. Cochran knocked, entered, and waited for the reprimand to strike.

Sir Geoffrey shifted his weight from his heels to his toes and back down to his heels.

'Simon,' he said in a voice so low that Cochran was uncertain he had heard the words at all, 'we have taken great pains to ensure the success of our expedition to the golden city. The very last inconvenience we wish is for a brawny and illiterate American to gain public attention for an association with Timbuctoo! You are to do everything in your power to lampoon Mr. Adams and his pitiable tale.'

Caldecott breathed in hard. He could feel his asthma coming on.

'Do you understand me clearly?'

Cochran blinked twice.

'Get out, and remember my warning!'

The study door opened a crack, and closed, the lock clicking shut. Sir Geoffrey fished out his macouba, took a pinch, and then another. After that, very slowly, he scanned the hand-drawn outline of Africa hung in an attractive gilt frame on his study's west wall.

'Peddie,' he said in a voice of fearful coldness, 'dare fail and I shall hunt you down and castrate you with these hands.'

TWENTY

16, Fleet Street
22nd December 1815

Dearest Beattie,

The narration is attracting a wide gambit of visitors, and is fast awarding Mr. Adams a level of celebrity that only augments the wonder of his remarkable tale.

I have hoped with the most earnest and genuine sincerity that I might have the opportunity of being granted a private interview with you over the Christmas season. I am uncertain whether you received my previous correspondence, or whether you left before the mail coach arrived.

In any case, I do hope most intensely that your journey has been comfortable, and expect with the greatest anticipation to hear from you at any moment.

You are ever in my thoughts, dearest Beattie,
Simon

P.S. I shall send this to Chavenage, although I realise that you have most likely already left.

TWENTY-ONE

THE SNOW WAS falling hard as Lord Alvanley crossed St. James's and entered the great oak doorway of White's. Kicking the slush from his boots, he passed his overcoat to the porter, and pretended not to hear when the servant wished him season's greetings.

Alvanley was in a bad mood.

On a whim, the Prince had decided to stay in town until the New Year, forcing his cronies to do the same. But, as he ascended the staircase to the drawing room, Alvanley comforted himself. At least, he thought, the wager with Byron had gone in his favour.

Thank God for the snow.

Upstairs, there was hardly space to sit. All the usual members were in position, lounging in their favourite chairs, sipping sweet sherry, hooting at jokes they imagined to be droll. As he surveyed the room, Alvanley noticed a number of unfamiliar faces, no doubt officers back from the war. He overheard a line about hand-to-hand fighting, and another on the subject of Napoleon's mount.

Then something curious caught his attention. A dandy named Greville, sitting in the centre of the salon, was speaking to another gentleman, Henry Carlisle, in his grating voice, about a rare and unusual opportunity. The line that caught his attention most, went: 'I swear on my mother's life that there will be an enormous and immediate return on my investment.'

Although this kind of matter might not normally have appealed to the young peer, he sat brooding quietly, fingertips pressed together and eyes half-closed. Just that morning he had received a letter from his father, the first Baron, advising him to learn to create wealth rather than specialising, as he had done, in the art of disposing of it. Alvanley had planned to write back with news of his successful wager against Byron, but the snippet of conversation gave him an idea. He would ask Greville for the details, withdraw a sum of money from his trust, and sink it into the sure investment.

Ten minutes later he was sitting with Byron and Bertie McCormack at the bow window, warmed with a sense of smugness. Greville had happily offered an introduction to Sir Geoffrey, and outlined what he knew of the Committee's expedition to far-flung Timbuctoo.

Ever a man of honour, Byron paid his debt immediately. And, always the gentleman, Alvanley did his best not to gloat.

Bertie changed the subject of conversation.

'I say,' he declared, 'did you hear that Brummell's effects are up for sale next week? A special seasonal extravaganza.'

'Poor old chap,' said Byron. 'London's not the same without him.'

'He was destined for ruin,' Bertie quipped. 'To think of it though, that a man so fêted could be so disgraced, hounded by his debtors all the way to France.'

'Are you in correspondence with him, Alvanley?' Byron asked.

'Indeed I am,' he replied, distantly.

'Does Prinny ever speak of him?'

Alvanley's index finger wagged a no. He wasn't really listening.

Outside, the snowflakes were falling with increasing force. It was not yet two o'clock but the daylight was almost lost.

A boy of about ten was stumbling through the snow. He was dressed in a torn cotton shirt and shoes riddled with holes. His father had sent him out to sell matches at dawn, and he was too frightened to go home, as no one had bought any of his stock. He spent some of the afternoon gazing into the window of Gunter's confectionery shop, until he was moved on. Then, as he neared St. James's Palace, he noticed the bowed window of White's. It was bathed in bright yellow lamplight, toasty and warm, the three gentlemen seated separated from him by glass.

Lord Alvanley peered down to the street and shuddered at the cold. He asked the butler to bring a bottle of chilled Veuve Clicquot so that he might drink to his new investment opportunity. Then he glanced back down at the street, his eyes holding on the frail wisp of childhood. They stared at each other, the boy looking up, and Alvanley looking down. There was the sound of a Champagne cork popping, and the fizz of bubbles touching glass.

'Let us drink to good fortune,' declared Alvanley cheerfully, holding his flute to the light. 'And at the very least,' he said, 'may none of us ever be touched by the discomfort of the cold.'

TWENTY-TWO

IN THE COMMITTEE'S library, fifty extra chairs had been laid out to accommodate the crowd. Word of Adams' narration had spread as far west as Bond Street, and as far east as Tower Hill. The audience from the day before had been enhanced by both ladies and gentlemen with an interest in a good tale, and an eagerness to set eyes on an American.

Sir Geoffrey Caldecott had insisted that the narration begin later than on previous days, in the hope that the public might find themselves engaged in activities of the season. The last thing he had expected was that the narration of the illiterate seaman would become an event in itself.

As the crowds amassed outside the building, William DeWitt had suggested bolting the doors. But then, as Caldecott reminded him time and again, if Adams could be discredited, the entire audience would become potential investors in the Committee's great expedition.

Robert Adams pushed a hand into his pocket, caressing the lace handkerchief that was always there. A direct connection to

Christina, it had in a way become the reason for his survival, and was her as much as it was itself. Merely by touching it, he was transported to Hudson.

The library was half-filled with people, resounding with chatter, the kind that has no purpose other than passing on hearsay. The audience paraded the latest fashions, embroidered bonnets and dresses of taffeta and silk, starched cravats, frock coats and canvas pantaloons.

Cochran called for the session to begin. He stood up, introduced the American, and wished the audience season's greetings.

Before he knew it, Adams was speaking again.

'One morning we awoke to find the sky black as night,' he said. 'As if a fierce storm were about to strike. There was a thundering sound, but no wind, a point that perplexed me greatly. I shielded my eyes, called out to Sanchez for an explanation. He seemed delighted, and cautioned me to stay calm.

'"It's manna from Heaven," he said.

'A moment after that, we found ourselves overrun by locusts, millions and millions of them. They covered the desert surface, each one desperate for sustenance. As with the flies that plagued our waking hours, they were searching for moisture.

'Wasting not a second, Sanchez showed me how the insects could be ripped apart and their abdomen devoured. In our famished state they were as delicious as the finest pork chops.

'Ten days passed. I would have sworn we were going round in circles, but the Moorish commander seemed to know the route as though it were a line on the palm of his hand. Never once did they regard us, their captives, with anything but utter loathing. With time, as I learned to comprehend their language, the depth of their revulsion for us became even more clear. They said that as Christians we had no souls, that we were as mean as the most wretched scourge of insect life.

'Then one morning, we spotted tents in the distance. They were low, black, and woven from coarse wool, set against a dune of tremendous height. I grew agitated and extremely satisfied, as did Sanchez. The sight of people signified hospitality, even for worthless slaves like us. But the Moors showed no pleasure in spying the encampment. They marched straight past, refusing to stop despite our pleas. As our caravan drew near it became apparent the camp was abandoned. Sanchez explained in a word:

'"Plague."

'We trudged on and on, one desert horizon giving way to the next. It seemed we had walked for an eternity but in reality we had only just begun. Then, suddenly, I observed low hills in the distance. The feature raised my spirits, although there was a danger of attack. Sanchez said we were near a place called Soudeny, a village peopled by Touareg, the natives of the Zahara.

'With care, the Moors led the caravan in a wide arc around the village, and concealed the camels in undergrowth at the foot of the hills. Sanchez, I, and most of the Moors followed our master to a position of vantage at the top of one hill. Once there, we waited.

'That evening, the women of the village left their stockade and climbed into the hills in order to bring in their goats. As soon as they were near us, the Moors descended upon them, seeking to enslave as many of the women as they could. In the midst of this conflict, the women screamed like lambs being led to slaughter. Several of them were taken, along with their offspring whom they carried swaddled on their backs. But then, before we had a chance to mount our escape, the menfolk charged out of the village, burning torches illuminating the night.

'They pounced on us in great number and with striking force. Several of the Moors were beheaded, and at least one was slit open from the neck to the groin. Sanchez and I showed the bindings on our wrists, indicating in the most strident manner that we were captives of the Touareg's defeated foe.

'We were taken into the village, where porridge was served to us, and a bed of parrot feathers was laid out. Our former captors were staked out on the sand and molested until their flesh was bleeding and raw.

'Sanchez cautioned me to take care in the amount of porridge I consumed. Eat too much, he said, and I would become much distressed. We slept in a tent that night and, in the morning, awoke to find ourselves the centre of attention. For the Touareg it seemed had not set eyes on Christians before.

'They stared at us, and leant forward to touch us with their fingers, and to stroke our long matted hair. The chief of the village strode up, a long jagged blade in his hand. He loomed over one of the Moors, pegged out in the sand. Then, without the slightest jot of emotion, he cleaved off his hand.

'A palaver followed between the elders of the village. The chief, who wore a beaver hat and a leopard's skin over his shoulders, spoke loudly. His people listened as he gave orders. Neither Sanchez nor I could understand any of the natives' language. Through a description acted out in mime, we came to understand that the Moors were to be taken to the chief of their chief, who resided in a metropolis fifteen days' march from where we stood.

'That city was known by the name of "Timbuctoo".'

III

Sir Joseph Banks introduces himself — Messrs. Adams and Cochran pass the shop of Rundell and Bridge as they make their way to Sir Joseph Banks's Christmas dinner — At the home of Sir Joseph Banks, Mr. Adams is introduced to several notable luminaries of society — Every woman in attendance is captivated with the American guest — During the dinner, Mr. Adams learns that the war between America and England is at an end — Mr. and Mrs. Bateman dine on roast polar bear — Messrs. Cochran and Adams awake to find the Thames frozen — Miss Emily Watts receives Sir Geoffrey Caldecott at Bedlam — Mr. Cochran is approached by a bailiff but succeeds in escaping — The Prince Regent hosts a Christmas luncheon — Mr. Cochran writes to Beattie, urgently hoping for an interview — Sir Geoffrey Caldecott advises Mr. Cochran to continue the narration on Boxing Day — Mr. Adams learns that he must continue with his narration — Lord Alvanley arrives at the Royal African Committee to be received by Sir Geoffrey Caldecott — Lord Alvanley invests in the Timbuctoo expedition — Mr. Adams recapitulates his journey thus far — Mr. Bateman delivers the polar bear to Carlton House — Mr. Adams dictates a letter to Mr. Cochran, for his beloved Beattie — Sir Geoffrey Caldecott reaches Messrs. C. Hoare and Co., at their bank on Cheapside — Attended by all society, Mr. Adams continues with his narration, describing Timbuctoo — Mr. Cochran receives a letter from Beattie, informing him of her proposed engagement.

ONE

AT THE END of the day's narration, Cochran was squaring his notes when a rotund gentleman in a wheelchair was pushed by a footman to where he and Adams were standing. Against a room rowdy with conversation, he exclaimed in an energetic voice:

'My dear sir, I have been most transfixed by the recitation of your turbulent journey!'

The gentleman halted, and stared into the middle distance. He was waiting to be introduced.

Cochran stepped forward half a pace.

'I have the great pleasure, Mr. Adams,' he said grandly, 'of introducing to you the most respected pillar of our society, Sir Joseph Banks.'

The gentleman struggled to dip his head modestly in a bow.

'I am pleased to meet you,' said Adams.

'I assure you, sir, that the pleasure is all mine.' Banks paused for a moment as if good etiquette required him to do so. 'I would be delighted if you gentlemen might consider dining with me tonight. It being Christmas Eve, I am having a little *soirée de la saison*.'

Cochran took a step backwards so that he might deliver a bow of sufficient depth.

'Sir Joseph, we would be most honoured,' he said.

TWO

AT SIX O'CLOCK the snow calmed a little and the temperature declined. It was bitterly cold and the streets were quite empty. From time to time a carriage would grumble past, the horses' shoes striking through the blanket of white to the cobbles beneath.

Despite his elaborate costume, Cochran had no means for private transportation. Years of London life had taught him the value of personal appearance. Giving an impression of wealth from one's costume was the first step towards gaining wealth, or so he thought. As Adams had been given nothing at all in the way of funds by the Committee, the two men walked from Old Jewry, past St. Paul's, towards the bachelor chambers on Fleet Street.

Adams dug his heels in the snow as they neared the top of Ludgate Hill. He sensed something was preying on Cochran's mind.

'What's troubling you?' he asked.

'Oh, nothing, nothing at all.'

'I am sure there is. I can feel it. You haven't said a word since we left the Committee.'

Cochran steadied his step with his cane.

'I had been hoping that my acquaintance would contact me,' he said. 'For I understand she was expected here in town three days ago, to stay as a guest of her uncle whose home is located in Bloomsbury Square. I have written to her repeatedly, but with no reply.'

'What's her name?'

'Beatrix. She is my second cousin. The familial connection has allowed me to communicate with her in a way that would have otherwise been unacceptable. We have never spoken of it directly, but I have long hoped to propose when my impecunious condition is alleviated.'

'Have you kissed her?'

Cochran choked at the question.

'Mr. Adams, I do declare!' he said, his eyes widening at the thought of actual physical contact. 'I have had the great pleasure of touching my lips to her hand, but anything more intimate would be quite unseemly.'

As they strolled uneasily down Ludgate Hill, the two men rested for a moment to gaze at the wonders in the mullioned window of Messrs. Rundell and Bridge. The master goldsmiths had been bestowed the royal warrant for the manufacturing of silver-gilt plate to the House of Hanover. Unlike all the other shops nearby, their flambeaux were ablaze, flames licking the freezing air.

Inside, a team of staff were working to pack up a series of six lustrous vases crafted from solid gold. The proprietor of the firm, John Bridge, was overseeing the work himself. A big-boned man of fifty, he had a mop of grey hair, flat feet, and small darting eyes. Mr. Bridge had never been lured by Christmas indulgence. He was far more motivated by the thought of accumulating wealth.

'Hurry with you!' he cried once, and then a second time, 'for his Highness is awaiting the delivery.'

The vases were polished a final time, and passed to the senior packer. With hands concealed in gloves of the softest Egyptian cotton, he examined each vessel for the faintest mark, before placing it in its own velvet-lined box.

When all the vases were packed up, the firm's finest carriage sped away, taking the delivery directly to Carlton House.

Mr. Rundell turned to his partner, John Bridge.

'Another fine season attended to, sir,' he said with satisfaction.

'Our coffers are brimming over once again. Thank God that the wealth of the nation is in the hands of a few foolish men!'

'Perhaps we ought to make use of the funds we have amassed,' said Rundell.

'Make use of them, sir?' Bridge replied in horror.

'Yes, sir, to allow wealth to beget wealth.'

The pair had been partners long enough for Bridge to know when Rundell had an idea. After all, he was a shrewd businessman, a man skilled in taking full advantage of a scheme.

'What have you heard, sir?'

'A certain project, one in which a stake will be rewarded with the most fabulous return.'

'How did you come of this information?'

'From a client.'

'Am I acquainted with him?'

'Perhaps.'

'What is his name?'

'Mr. Richard Carlisle.'

THREE

HAVING DESCENDED THE staircase from her dressing room, Lady Banks begged her husband to spend less time inspecting the household and a little more time inspecting himself. He smiled at the remark, pressed his lips to her hand, and waited for her to wheel him through into the drawing room to greet their guests.

At his modest chambers on Fleet Street, Cochran had outdone himself, dressing in his most elaborate evening costume, combing up his quiff to match the Grecian fashion pioneered by Brummell himself. Only a fop of Beau's supreme calibre could have drawn fashion away from the preoccupation of powdered wigs.

Cochran had spent an entire hour toiling at his cravat, a heap of rejected muslin on the floor beside the fire. As his exiled mentor had taught him, no amount of time or expense was excessive in obtaining the perfect cravat.

The contents of Cochran's wardrobe had been pulled out for the American's benefit. After forty minutes of trying on pantaloons, shirts, and frock coats, he had squeezed into a costume created by Henry Pool six years before. Adams felt a little ridiculous, quite awkward, and decidedly over-dressed. But Cochran insisted he looked as dashing as any man braving the elements of the West End.

The two men stepped out into the snow, and walked along the Strand in the direction of Soho Square.

Adams' thoughts were on his family, for it was Christmas Eve after all. He wondered if they ever expected him to return. Did they think he was dead? Or was there a candle burning beside the window, a flame of fading hope? For a few moments, he found himself back in Hudson. In his fantasies, he could delight in the detail of normality — doing chores for his father, or attending the Sunday service. Then, his mind wandering, Christina was on his arm. They were strolling near the brook, the one place they could be alone. He stopped her as she walked, gently pushed up the rim of her bonnet, and kissed her. She laughed, a glint of white teeth framed in pink, and she whispered that she loved him.

Cochran's voice pulled Adams back to the present.

'Everyone will be in attendance,' he said, as they marched briskly through the Aldwych. 'For Sir Joseph Banks is a gentleman treasured by all.'

'Who is he… this Mr. Banks?'

'*Sir* Joseph,' Cochran corrected. 'He is a scientist, a naturalist, who had the good fortune to accompany Captain Cook on his journey to the Antipodes.'

'*Antipod…*'

'Australia, sir, the farthest flung corner of the world.'

FOUR

THE LINE OF CARRIAGES snaked from the gates of Banks's mansion around Soho Square. As each vehicle drew up, a pair of footmen hastened forward, placed a step at the edge of the carpet, and aided the guests down and into the warmth of the house.

Cochran and Adams were the only guests to arrive on foot. They slipped inside and found themselves led directly to Sir Joseph.

'Dear gentlemen! Welcome!' their host announced in a thunderous voice. 'What a singular pleasure to have you in our circle on this auspicious night!'

Ever a master of appropriate decorum, Cochran mumbled pleasantries for them both, while Adams cast an eye around the drawing rooms. They were connected by central doors, their walls hung with blue velvet, their windows concealed by ruffled silk curtains, a deep shade of peach. Open fires raged at either end of the vast salon. A harpist was playing, her fingers gently caressing the strings, just fast enough to appear blurred to the eye.

Within an hour, eighty of the leading scientists and gentlemen of arts were circulating with their wives. Cochran motioned to an elderly figure sitting in a low plain Chippendale chair. He was leaning forward on his cane, speaking softly to a prim lady of about forty.

'The gentleman seated there is Mr. John Soane,' he said, 'the man who designed the Bank of England. He is in conversation with a novelist named Miss Austen. I shall present you.'

They stepped forward and Cochran made the introductions. Soane shook Adams' hand, looked him hard in the eye.

'From the honest surface of your palm, sir,' he said sternly, 'I would deduce you are the only gentleman in the room who has known the taste of privation. Are you a farmer, sir?'

Adams glanced uneasily at Cochran.

'Mr. Soane, sir, my companion is not a farmer but an American, recently returned from Timbuctoo.'

'Well, I do declare!'

Miss Austen looked up and found herself gazing into Adams' eyes.

'Your tale is the talk of the town, Mr. Adams,' she said softly. 'I understand that the Royal African Committee is most captivated by your journey. Would you grace us with a description of the golden city?'

'It's an ordinary place much like any other,' said Adams, stretching his shoulders back. 'That is, much like any other on the African continent. It is a low and wretched capital, ruled by a despot.'

Cochran broke in.

'I do believe that Mr. Adams shall be regaling us with a full and sensational description of the golden metropolis next week.'

He bowed and, excusing them both, swivelled Adams round, only to find Banks hurtling towards them in his wheelchair, dragging a fresh-faced man with him by the wrist.

'Mr. Adams, I should like to acquaint you with a young gentleman of luminous ingenuity,' he said. 'Mr. Stephenson has recently built an engine locomotive. He has grand plans for it. One day his "locomotives" will be found throughout the civilised world.'

'I am pleased to meet you, Mr. Stephenson,' said Adams.

'And I you. If you would forgive me for saying it, I hear an accent in your conversation.'

'I am American, from New York State.'

'Fascinating, sir. I have a vision that my locomotive engines will one day run from the Atlantic to the Pacific coast.'

Banks, who had begun to greet another guest, twisted round and boomed, 'I told you, he is a man of luminous ingenuity!'

A waiter served punch in crystal glasses. It was Banks's own recipe, flavoured with spices he had collected from the southern hemisphere.

'Will your engines run on roads, like carriages?' Adams asked.

Sipping his drink, Stephenson frowned at the taste.

'We are working on a system of rails, sir,' he said. 'Cast iron rails. They are the only contrivance I have found sufficiently robust to endure the great weight of the vehicle. One day such rails will connect all cities, villages and towns.'

'And will they cross America?' asked Adams.

'Indeed that is our intention, sir. A railway from sea to sea.'

FIVE

PERCHED ON A LOVE seat across the room, Lady Devonshire was watching Robert Adams. She was thirty, pale as alabaster with a taut smile and an air of superiority that never faded for a moment. Her husband, Sir Charles Devonshire, had been killed earlier in the year at Waterloo, a loss she had grieved in public, but celebrated in private.

For, as she had confided to her sister, Felicity, the man had been the bane of her life. Now that he was gone, she was ready to enjoy herself and the enormous fortune that he had bequeathed her.

As she sat there, undressing Adams with her gaze, another woman approached and kissed her lightly on the cheek. It was Lady Foxwain, in her younger years a society belle, whose complexion had remained good, the result of applying a salve made from green pineapple juice twice daily.

'I see you have spotted the butterfly among the grubs,' she said, fluttering an ivory fan delicately with her wrist.

'Who is he? I haven't seen him before.'

'An American.'

'*Really*?'

'A breed celebrated for their stamina.'

'What's his name?'

'I understand that it is Adams, Mr. Robert Adams.'

At that moment, a third woman joined them, Baroness Canning. Her scent was *eau de fleur d'oranges*, her hair, pinned up, and her neck garlanded in a string of pigeon-blood rubies, each one the size of a grape.

'Look at those shoulders,' she said.

'And that chest!'

'He is bursting from the coat.'

'Who will introduce us?'

'I will ask Sir Joseph,' said the Baroness, as she stepped away.

SIX

THE LAST CARRIAGE to arrive was just pulling up at number thirty-two Soho Square. Its passengers stepped down and hurried inside. Sir Joseph Banks excused himself from conversation and was wheeled over to greet the late-comers.

'Viscount Fortescue, allow me to extend the season's greetings to you and your charming daughter!'

'And to you Sir Joseph,' replied Fortescue, as Clara wasted no time in scouring the room.

That afternoon, Cochran had dispatched a message to the Viscount, in which he mentioned that Adams and he had been invited to attend the Bankses' Christmas dinner. One of the highlights of the season, the event was held according to continental convention, on the evening before the *fête*. Clara had come across the letter while spying on her father. He had been acting strangely since the discovery of the American, leaving the house early and returning very late. When questioned in a gentle manner, he would say nothing except that he was involved in research of an intriguing and delicate nature.

The Viscount's name was on a great many invitation lists. Yet he did not venture out very often, finding social engagements to be both superficial and dull. On this occasion though, Clara had urged him to accept.

Unable to spot Adams anywhere, she feigned a chill in order to steer her father towards the fireplace. It would have been unseemly for her to move through the drawing room without a chaperone, even in the company of such distinguished guests.

Fortescue paused to greet one or two acquaintances as they circulated. Having given up hope, Clara suddenly spied Cochran. He was trapped in conversation with a former guards officer, who had served under Nelson at Trafalgar a decade before.

Clara knew very well that if she found Cochran, Adams would be near. And she was right. He was sitting on a stool beside the fire, staring into the flames of a great yuletide log.

'The season forbids a cheerless disposition, Mr. Adams,' she said in a tender voice. He looked up, smiled, and she smiled back.

'I have found you in my thoughts,' she said forwardly, blushing, as her father stepped to one side to be greeted by an old acquaintance.

'I never thanked you for your note,' he said. 'I was very touched by it.'

Blushing again, Clara pressed a hand to her hair.

'Your narration has been most enthralling, sir,' she said, uncertain of quite what to say.

Just then, a gong sounded, and the butler announced that dinner was served. Lady Foxwain glided forward, the hem of her gown sweeping the parquet. In a single dexterous movement, that impressed all who caught it, she managed to position herself between Clara Fortescue and Adams, while extending her right arm at right angles to the side.

'I seem to have mislaid my husband,' she said dimly, 'perhaps you might be so kind as to escort me in to dinner.'

She nudged her arm. Adams looked down at Clara. The arm nudged again. Taking it gently in his, he followed the procession of guests towards the dining room.

Inside, a long table ran down the centre of a rectangular room. It was festooned with decorations, rococo candelabras, and monogrammed silverware. The walls were dark green, an Oriental scene laid over them in gold. Banks was positioned at the door, greeting his guests as they entered, twittering pleasantries. When he saw Lady Foxwain, he announced to Adams,

'It thrills me, sir, to find that your taste in the delicate gender is as ample as your taste for adventure!'

With deft sleight of hand, Lady Devonshire had managed to reposition the place cards to ensure herself proximity to the American. While at it, she placed Clara Fortescue, Baroness Canning and Lady Foxwain at the far end of the elongated table.

Sensible to his difficulty in literacy, Cochran searched for Adams' place name, motioning to a chair with a nod. He sat, and Lady Devonshire slipped in beside him.

'It seems as if good fortune has brought us together,' she said, gazing into Adams' eyes, oblivious of the commotion on the far side of the American. Baroness Canning had clawed her way into the seat, ejecting the wife of Admiral Smollet.

'News of your terrible sufferings is spreading across London,' the Baroness announced.

'I don't want to trouble others with my misfortune,' Adams replied. 'I am just trying to get home.'

Under the table, Lady Devonshire kicked off her shoe, and inched it towards her right.

'You are far too modest, sir,' she said. 'For we are all captivated by your bravery.'

The gloved hand of a waiter served the soup.

'Oh, how divine,' said the Baroness, 'my favourite.'

'What is it?'

'*Crème de tortue*, turtle soup.'

'Please do not be too hasty in your departure, Mr. Adams,' Lady Devonshire intoned, as she drew the rim of the spoon to her lips. 'For we value your company beyond measure.'

From the head of the table, Sir Joseph Banks called out,

'Mr. Adams, I do hope the soup is a little tastier than camel urine, what what?!'

The guests murmured at the comment. As they did so, Banks

struggled to rise from his wheelchair. With a footman assisting to hold him upright, he struck a fork to the crystal glass before him.

'My dear ladies and gentlemen,' he said in a deafening voice, 'I should like to offer a toast.'

The entire table fell silent.

'Season's greetings to you all, and our congratulations to Mr. Adams, our man from Timbuctoo!'

Across from Banks, a uniformed officer snarled in displeasure.

'Sir Joseph, I feel it foolhardy to salute the health of an American!' he said heatedly. 'After all we are at war.'

Just then, a butler slipped into the dining room, and presented Banks with a sealed envelope. Still standing, half a glass of claret in his hand, Sir Joseph broke the seal and examined the text. He grunted loudly.

'It seems, Major Odgers, as if your comment was spectacularly ill-timed. For I have just received word that hostilities of that asinine conflict are at an end. A treaty has been signed at Ghent!'

'Hoorah!' shouted the Baroness, raising her glass.

'Celebration!' added Lady Devonshire.

'Let us drink to Peace between our nations!' Banks declared.

'To Peace! To Peace!'

SEVEN

IN A WORKSHOP attached to his front parlour, William Bateman was fitting marbles as eyes to the polar bear's face. His staff had departed for the holiday, leaving him to complete the specimen alone.

Assisting when she could, his wife, Maud, enjoyed taking out the entrails and salvaging the edible off-cuts. In the years she had been married to Bateman, the household had borne witness to an astonishing variety of rare meats. They had dined on zebra twice, once stewed, and once as steak; had picked at roasted peacock on several occasions, had quite enjoyed flamingo pie, poached wildebeest, and a great tureen of boiled kangaroo. They had tried lion and lioness as well, but had both agreed the meat was a little tough, as was the elephant, the toucan, and the koala.

There was always the risk of disease, or that the meat had turned on the journey back from London, but the couple prided themselves on their cast-iron constitutions.

Popping the second eye into place, Mr. Bateman stepped back and applauded himself. The polar bear was standing on hind legs, front paws poised like a boxer ready to strike, with claws extended, the mouth scowling in frenzied rage.

'That'll do very nicely,' he said to himself. 'It will do very nicely indeed. I'll get it to town on Boxing Day.'

'There's no rest for the wicked,' said his wife. Mr. Bateman looked at her, half-wondering if she had discovered his affection for the barmaid near Colchester. But Mrs. Bateman, his consort of thirty years, looked back.

'Clean yourself up, my love,' she said warmly. 'It's almost time for Christmas luncheon. I've pressed your best coat and wiped your good shoes clean. By the time you are ready, the table will be laid.'

Mr. Bateman leant forward and kissed his wife on the cheek.

'You are a good woman,' he mumbled, going off to wash.

Fifteen minutes later, Mr. and Mrs. Bateman were sitting down in their front parlour, a pair of places laid at the worn dining table they had received from an uncle as a wedding gift. Outside, there was the faint sound of carol singers making their way down the street. It reminded Mr. Bateman that he had to stay tidy for evensong. Tying a kerchief around his neck, he poured two glasses of rum, and touched his glass to hers.

'I'll get the roast out of the fire,' said his wife.

'It smells very fine, my dear. Very fine indeed.'

'I hope it's cooked right through. Sometimes it's hard to tell.'

The pan touched the table, the fat bubbling all around.

'We have plenty to be thankful for,' said Bateman.

'Indeed we do, my love.'

'Let us raise our glasses to His Highness for gracing our table with such an exceptional feast.'

EIGHT

IN AN ERMINE dressing-gown with a matching nightcap, Cochran walked on tiptoes through the sitting room. He tugged the curtains back as gently as he could. It was almost one o'clock, although he had no way of telling the time, except by listening to the bells of St. Bride's, the mechanism of which tended to slow in the cold.

'A merry Christmas to you, Mr. Adams,' he said.

Outstretched on the chaise longue, the American guest opened an eye.

'Is the war really over?' he said urgently.

'Indeed it is, sir.'

'Then I can go home to Hudson!'

Cochran turned his back to the door and began rifling through a wicker basket, the letters 'F.M.' stencilled in black on the side. The gift had almost taken his mind off his beloved cousin.

Robert Adams sat upright.

'I can go home, can I not?' he repeated.

'That is the arrangement,' Cochran replied. 'I am sure the Committee will take the most eager delight in hastily acquiring your passage.'

'What do you have there?' said Adams, craning his neck.

'It appears, sir, that you have charmed all of London!'

'What is it?'

'A hamper of epicurean delights delivered by private messenger.'

'Who's it from?'

'From Lady Devonshire. It seems she is your most ardent admirer. And an influential one she is, enough so to have Fortnum and Mason open their doors on Christmas morning no less.'

Cochran looked out of the window. Fleet Street was covered in a mantle of white.

'Raise yourself Mr. Adams; we have time enough to take a perambulation,' said Cochran, jerking off his nightcap. 'Not five minutes ago Mrs. Pickeriff hurried upstairs with the news. The Thames has frozen solid from Blackfriars to London Bridge. Let's go and have a look.'

NINE

EMILY WATTS, A woman of fifty-three, was pulling a comb through her long greying hair, laughing as she did so. The window was fitted with bars, but she could see the rooftops all white, and nothing made her laugh like the snow. It reminded her of the daffodils she had seen as a child at her parents' home, frozen in mid-bloom by a freak blizzard from the north.

Seated on her bed, Emily waited for the nurse to arrive at her whitewashed cell. In her youth she had detested waiting for anything, but times had changed.

An hour passed, and the sound of the nurse's feet could be heard outside the door. Emily kissed her poodle, Moss, on the head, and told him sternly to sit still.

In the corridors there was laughter and tears, and the shrill tones of another patient singing off-tune. Emily was wearing her bedroom slippers and a robe made from Welsh lamb's wool. It was patched at the elbows, and darned at the hem.

She did not like to think of herself as mad, rather just a little contrary. Most of the time she refrained from consorting with Bedlam's other patients, whom she regarded as quite deranged.

All day she would sit on her bed, brushing her hair, or reading Psalm eighty-nine over and over, until her eyes stung. During the decade of confinement she had grown used to the solitude, and to the fact that no one ever came to visit, except on Christmas Day.

The hospital had moved a few weeks before from Moorfields to the grand new building at St. George's Fields, designed by Sir Sydney Smirke. It was a great improvement on the previous asylum, located at the edge of the City, and Emily for one was thankful for the superior lodgings. No longer had she to suffer the penny visits made by the public to the cells. The evenings had been awash with them, gentlemen and commoners armed with poking sticks. Worst of all had been the first Tuesday of the month, when entry was free, and half of London turned up to peer and jest.

Emily followed the nurse to the meeting room.

It was cold, a little damp, and painted a drab grey. A group of women were clustered in one corner near the window, an orderly coaxing them to sing the same carol in time, an exercise they found inordinately challenging.

In the middle of the meeting room there was a low table strewn with pewter mugs, and a dozen tattered copies of the King James Bible. Beside it stood a simple wooden chair facing away from the door.

'Sit there,' said the nurse.

Emily did as she was told, and ran the long nails of her right hand through her hair. She told Moss to sit on her lap and to be still. Five minutes later, a large red-faced figure stepped cautiously into the room. Pausing for a moment, he took a little snuff, then dabbed a handkerchief to his brow. He was well-dressed in an expensive navy frock coat, the silver fob of a Malacca cane in his palm, and a gold pocket-watch tucked away in the breast pocket of his waistcoat.

Emily glanced up as he approached.

She had not seen the visitor's face yet, but she knew he was there. She could smell him. The gentleman stepped forward, and touched her shoulder with his hand.

'Well this is a fine new institution,' he said awkwardly.

'Hello Geoffrey,' said Emily.

'Season's greetings to you, my dear.'

Caldecott pulled a chair from the table and squatted on it uneasily. He forced himself to smile.

Behind, near the window, the singers were doing their best to get through 'God Rest Ye Merry Gentlemen'.

'You do not have to stay,' said Emily, tilting her head to the side.

'I am pleased to be here, dearest,' he replied.

Emily ran a hand down the poodle's back.

'Do you remember my little dog?' she asked vacantly, looking at her lap. 'He's a good boy. Eats very little though. I am not certain why.'

Sir Geoffrey looked down at her imaginary pet.

'He's lovely, dear,' he said.

The nurse stepped forward.

'Would your cousin like to sing with the others?'

Caldecott looked towards the window, where one of the inmates was now climbing the curtains, and another was struggling to remove her dress.

'She is content in conversation,' he said firmly.

A tear welled in Emily's eye and slipped down her cheek.

'Why do you not tell them, Geoffrey?'

'Tell them what?'

'Who I am?'

TEN

THE GREAT BELLS of St. Paul's were pealing as Cochran and Adams walked down to the river and found themselves staring at a most unusual sight.

A frost fair had sprung up, the river's frozen surface covered in lines of tented booths, selling knickknacks and an assortment of foods. Skaters were gliding effortlessly across the ice, spiralling around the crowds. In the distance, against the sound of bells, there came the piercing squeal of bagpipes.

'I do declare, sir, this is a most incomparable feast for the eyes,' said Cochran, stepping clumsily onto the ice. 'Let us see what's on offer.'

With small footsteps the pair made their way uneasily to the middle of the river. Adams found himself thinking about the desert.

'I cannot believe the same feet that have trudged over the Zahara sands, are now presented with this,' he said.

Cochran was not listening. His thoughts were on the boiled oysters he had seen for sale at one of the stalls.

The American touched his wrist.

'At this very moment there are hundreds, perhaps thousands, of Christian seamen enslaved in the great desert,' he said. 'It's Christmas Day but they don't know it.'

Cochran was just about to reply, when he spotted a portly man wearing a flat cap and a tweed coat running in their direction. He had a cane stuck outwards like a sword, and a canvas satchel flapping at his waist.

'My God,' said Cochran sharply.

'What? Who's he?'

'Run for it!'

Cochran motioned to the row of tents that had been pitched downstream. Next to them a huddle of people were watching an acrobat dressed as a harlequin.

'Over there!' he yelled, struggling to get a grip on the slippery surface.

'Will you please tell me who we're running from?'

'I can't believe they'd come today, not on Christmas.'

'Who?'

'Do not trouble yourself with my dismal affairs, Mr. Adams,' said Cochran, shoving himself briskly into the crowd.

'If you don't tell me who that was, I'll strike you myself!'

Cochran covered his face with his hand.

'I am in debt, sir,' he said. 'And that is the bailiff. If he touches me with the tip of his cane, I'm bound to go to the debtors' prison or to the sponging-house.'

'*Sponging…?*'

'Sponging-house — it's where a debtor is squeezed until he pays up what he owes. I must avoid the cane at all costs.'

'Can't you just say he didn't touch you?'

'No no,' Cochran replied, pushing through the crowds. 'That would not be right.'

'Why not?'

'Well, you see it is a system built on honour. Failing to abide by the code would be unthinkable.'

Adams wiped the sweat from his brow, back onto his hair.

'You English,' he said, 'I'll never understand you.'

ELEVEN

AT CARLTON HOUSE the Prince Regent had enjoyed a long and lavish Christmas lunch, the feast held in the Gothic dining room on the lower level. Carême, the celebrated French chef, had been ordered to prepare a banquet of fourteen courses for His Highness' friends, the group known in the kitchen as the S.C., the Sycophantic Circle. There were twenty of them in all, twelve gentlemen and eight ladies, all requested to come in masquerade.

In addition to the menu, the great Parisian chef had been given instructions to construct a pagoda six feet high from raw asparagus, which was to be wheeled in at the sound a miniature hand-bell. It had taken all Carême's ingenuity to find the vegetable in such abundance, and out of season.

When it was finally complete, one of the sous chefs had spotted a large black spider crawling into the pagoda. There was no way to get it out. He hadn't dared tell the chef for fear of being asked to dismantle the entire structure and start again. Fortunately, the creation was not for eating, but it was the punchline of a joke the Prince was planning to tell.

It was wheeled into the larder and covered with a cloth.

At the end of the meal, the Prince Regent had announced that his guests were to accompany him to the Collection room, in order to admire his new giraffe. With the Marchioness of Hertford at his side, the group followed the Prince, all dressed obediently in their costumes.

Alvanley, made up as a minstrel, was the first to identify the latest arrival. He praised the animal's elongated neck and the size of its feet. The Duke of Norfolk stepped forward and slapped a hand on the creature's rump. He prided himself on never washing, and invariably disgraced himself by drinking far too much. Having coerced his tailor on Savile Row to dress him as Alfred the Great, he was now reeling about drunk.

The day before, the Prince had ordered the royal carpenters to place the larger animals on wheelable boards, so that he could imagine them moving, as if he were walking across an African plain.

He clapped his hands.

Two dozen liveried servants slipped into the room and took up their positions. Some of them manned the lions, others the elephants, the tigers, the bears, and the giraffe.

At the sound of the royal hands clapping, the animals began slowly to trundle around the room against the sound of a harpsichord playing a Handel sonata.

The Prince was delighted.

He insisted that his mistress and guests lavish praise on the sight. After fifteen minutes of random motion, he had someone fetch him a baton, in order that he might direct the movement.

All the while he roared with pleasure. Such was his delight that he quite forgot to tell the joke that required the giant asparagus pagoda, much to the fury of Antonin Carême.

TWELVE

My dearest Beattie,

Forgive me for taking the liberty of sending this missive by private messenger to the home of your paternal uncle, Sir Henry Montagu.

Even though we are related, I do understand that it might be construed as behaviour of an overly forward nature. And so I ask forgiveness once again, and hope most zealously that you will comprehend the extent of my eagerness to see you while you are here in London.

My fear is that you have caught the influenza, which tears through the city like a tempest. With every moment, I pray to hear the sound of your gentle voice, and to set eyes once again upon your delicate visage.

With devoted affection,
Simon

THIRTEEN

SIR GEOFFREY CALDECOTT had never planned to honour his promise of providing Adams with a passage home. Now that the dispute between the two nations was over, he wrote a message to Cochran, instructing him to cast the American back into the streets. But just before the Committee's messenger took possession of the letter, Caldecott had an idea.

If he could succeed in coaxing the public to discredit Adams, then the American would fall from grace, and the Committee's own expedition could only stand to gain. Sir Geoffrey returned to his desk and tore up the first message. He wrote another, instructing Cochran to advertise the narration as a public event, and to fling open the doors on Boxing Day.

As a postscript, he added a caveat — that to gain the passage home, Adams would be required to stay until the Committee was satisfied with his narration.

FOURTEEN

THE DAY AFTER Christmas, Robert Adams rose early and found himself filled with more energy than he had ever remembered. Running through into Cochran's bedroom, he shook his arm.

'Wake up! Wake up!'

'What? What is it Mr. Adams?'

'I must find a ship. I must get home! I'll take anything so long as it floats!'

Simon Cochran wiped the sleep from his eyes.

'It may take time to find a passage,' he said, 'after all, the Thames is frozen. I'll make enquiries nonetheless.'

Just then, Mrs. Pickeriff came charging up the stairs and slipped Caldecott's message through the gap under the door.

Cochran read it slowly.

'It seems as though Sir Geoffrey is more enthusiastic to keep you in London than you would imagine.'

'What do you mean?'

'He has added a caveat to his offer. In order for the Committee to bear the expense of your passage home, you are required to complete the narration of your journey in full.'

Adams scowled, his face flushed.

'To Hell with Sir Geoffrey and the Committee!'

'To Hell with them indeed,' echoed Cochran, 'but from where I am standing, it appears as if Sir Geoffrey and his inimitable Committee are providing an offer you would be unwise to refuse.'

FIFTEEN

AT THREE O'CLOCK a canary-yellow carriage drew up at the front of the Royal African Committee. Lord Alvanley stepped down and made his way up the salted steps.

In his right hand was a leather hunting bag made by Swaine and Adeney, monogrammed with his initials. Having come by special appointment, he was led up to a small meeting room on the second floor, in which Caldecott was awaiting him. The two men had never met before although, like everyone else, the chairman was conscious of Alvanley's unlimited connections, and his friendship with the Regent.

On seeing the carriage draw up, Sir Geoffrey had taken a pinch of snuff from its tortoiseshell caddy. He had then dabbed his forehead, and rubbed his thumbs in his eyes. One step removed from royalty, Alvanley was an acquaintance to be treated with the utmost discretion.

Falkirk led the visitor directly in without waiting for instructions. The peer greeted the Committee chairman and thanked him for his time.

'It has come to my attention,' he said, straining to sound grave, 'that your Association is leading an expedition to the golden city.'

'To Timbuctoo, sir,' Caldecott broke in.

'Indeed.'

'Not since the murder of Mungo Park has there been genuine expectation of attaining it.'

Caldecott motioned for his visitor to sit.

'Our man, Major Peddie, is at this very moment marching across the barbarian landscape of Africa.'

'What are his instructions?'

'To take control of the metropolis at all costs, to secure for the Committee and the Crown the prosperity of its monarch, a wealth that will in due course be distributed in full to our investors.'

'How can you be so certain this Peddie chap will crush a native force?'

Caldecott smiled, drawing his fingers slowly back over the arm of the chair.

'Major Peddie is in the company of two hundred fighting men,' he said sombrely. 'Each man has at his disposal a Baker rifle, with sufficient ammunition to suppress a rebellion on the grandest scale.'

'And what of the king of Timbuctoo?'

'He will be executed of course, replaced by a provisional leader from our own expeditionary force, until word is received here at our headquarters.'

Alvanley rose, then crossed the room until he was less than a pace from Sir Geoffrey. He took in the perspiration, the reddened eyes.

'Your Major Peddie,' he said, 'is he a man who can be depended upon?'

'Indeed, sir, he is the finest of leaders, as are his men, all of them veterans of Waterloo.'

'When do you predict he shall reach Timbuctoo?'

'Towards the end of January. By the spring the first treasure caravan will reach the shore, where our flotilla of ships will be ready to transport it to Portsmouth.'

'And what of your investors?'

'The backbone, sir, are members of the gentry, such as yourself,' said Caldecott obsequiously, 'as well as many more from the public at large.'

'A gentleman named Greville informed me of the venture,' said Alvanley, stepping back. 'It seems as if your project enjoys the benefit of strong leadership. For such an investment opportunity I am willing to commit a portion of my personal funds.'

Turning to the window, Sir Geoffrey mopped his brow furtively. He was aware how some regarded abundant perspiration, especially in winter, as a sign of deceit.

'My Lord Alvanley,' he replied cautiously. 'We should be honoured to welcome you into the folds of the Committee, and are at the ready to invite you to share in the fortunes, a treasure that shall soon be unloaded on the south coast.'

Sir Geoffrey pinched the end of his nose and sniffed.

'Might I enquire, sir, what level of investment you are considering?'

Alvanley bent down and touched a hand to the side of the monogrammed bag. He didn't like Caldecott and barely trusted him, but the scheme seemed charged with distinct possibility.

'I will pledge this,' he said.

Sir Geoffrey cocked his head. 'A sum of...?'

'Of fifty thousand pounds.'

Downstairs in the library, news of Adams' continuing narration had drawn an audience of remarkable size. Three hundred ladies and gentlemen from the upper ranks of society had arrived, their carriages backed up all the way to St. Paul's.

On the second floor, Lord Alvanley had signed the registration sheet, and handed over the contents of his hunting bag. Sir Geoffrey would have preferred the money in gold, but he dared not make a fuss. Thanking Alvanley for his faith, he blessed Peddie once and then again, so as to show his own commitment to the cause.

Falkirk appeared on cue to escort the peer out. As he did so, he whispered to Caldecott that another investor was waiting in the room adjacent.

'Who is it?'

'Mr. Philip Rundell of Ludgate Hill, sir, the jeweller to the King.'

SIXTEEN

Adams' hope of leaving for America at once was thwarted not only by the chairman's scheming, but by the schedules of passenger ships. There was not a single vessel set to traverse the Atlantic again until early spring.

On receiving the news from Cochran, Adams felt his back warm with rage. He was in the most modern city on earth and yet there was no possibility of finding a ship bound for home, even if he had the funds.

With no other alternative, he took his familiar position in the centre of the library, and was soon gazing up at the whimsical interpretation of the Dark Continent above.

Cochran stood up, called out greetings to the audience, and said,

'Ladies and gentlemen, the singular interest with which we hold the tale of Mr. Adams, a humble and illiterate seaman from distant America, is reflected in the numbers who have so graciously arrived to witness the events in his own words. Without further ado, I present to you Mr. Robert Adams.'

A handful of the audience clapped softly, their hands shrouded in white cotton gloves. At the back, a few of the gentry chattered noisily at seeing Adams for the first time. Cochran gave a nod, signalling that he was ready, quill in hand.

Then Robert Adams began:

'The Touareg warriors, in whose company we now found ourselves,' he said in a commanding voice, 'were willing to take a man's life with hardly a thought. Now bound in chains, the Moors expected to be executed. From time to time they would cry out to their god, known to them as "Allah". As far as they were concerned their lives had come to an end.

'After days of marching at a fast pace, a pair of the Moors managed to relieve themselves of the fetters and break free. They ran across the sand and were pursued at full speed by six Touareg. Sanchez and I shielded our eyes with our hands and watched. It was like witnessing wild dogs pursuing the chickens escaped from their coop. The Moors must have known there was no chance of escape. They were caught within a few hundred yards. The Touareg took great delight in devising their punishment. Once weeping and on their knees, they had their sight removed with the bluntest of knives.

'As they howled, their captors forced them to swallow each other's eyes. The savage act put an end to their pitiful clamour. The Touareg were in high spirits, laughing and bristling with impatience to execute the men. But their leader, a long-limbed warrior named Matuto, was not yet ready to dispatch them into the next world.

'Once he had sawed out their tongues, he carved open their bellies. The intestines of each were pulled out and fondled. I watched, retching at the sight, as did the Moors' brethren. They became very agitated, and called out prayers until threatened with their lives.

'The two men who had tried to escape, blind and almost dead, were then kicked onto the sand. An axe was brought out, and they were beheaded. The weapon was so blunt that the memory of those sordid executions will stay with me until my own dying day. As for the heads, they were threaded onto a cord, and hung from the lead camel, as a caution to the others.

'Over the next week those putrid trophies swelled with maggots, and stank so greatly, the Touareg leader was obliged to cut them free. The surviving Moors had lost all will to live. Each one would have taken his own life, but they had no means by which to do it.

'We marched on and on into a wasteland of unimaginable desolation — dunes towering like mountains and no sign of life. I felt sure the Touareg were lost, but they weren't. Every so often they would reach a stick poking up out of the sand, would dig down, and find a well of brackish water.

'First the camels would quench their thirst, then the skins would be recharged. After that we would take it in turns to drink a little of the foul liquid. Yet, no banquet could ever match the pleasure of the refreshment we found there.

'Gradually, the dunes subsided and gave way to a harder surface. From time to time we found low shrubs, whose leaves we chewed for moisture. Despite our communal exhaustion, the Touareg hurried

on at considerable speed, as if we were nearing the destination.
    'And we were.

    'As dusk fell, I saw something on the horizon. It looked like a
high mud wall, a boundary wall of the city… the city of Timbuctoo.'

SEVENTEEN

LATE ON CHRISTMAS afternoon, William Bateman had loaded the
polar bear onto his cart and set off for London. Working alone,
he packed the creature up himself, asking his neighbours to assist
him in winching the crate up onto the cart. The thought of making
the journey unaccompanied was appealing, for it enabled him to
continue his liaison with the barmaid he had met on the previous
journey.

    Before leaving home, he had waited until Maud was clearing
the plates, and had fished two crowns from the jar she kept
under their bed. From the day of their marriage his wife had held
the purse strings in her claw-like grip. As she had reminded her
husband almost each day since they took their vows, 'A man may
have strong hands, but his wits are as dim as a block of rusted tin.'

At Carlton House, the Prince Regent was so delighted by his African
panorama, he had commanded for the animals to be wheeled

through into the library where Sir Thomas Lawrence had set up his easel. As self-declared Field Marshal, the Prince had decided to commission a grand new portrait of himself, in celebration of victory at Waterloo.

The artist, who had been knighted in the most recent honours list, had painted His Highness on several occasions, and enjoyed full royal patronage. A master of embellishing his subject's shortcomings, he could strip away decades of accumulated corpulence with the deftness of his brush.

An army of mannequins had been dressed with thirty of the Prince's favourite military costumes, most of them unique, designed to his own fanciful specifications. Few pleasures in life gave the Regent more satisfaction than having a new uniform created, except for having his portrait painted by Lawrence.

The Prince's equerry, Francis Hastings, enquired in a low voice which costume His Highness would prefer to wear for the sitting. It was a question to which he already knew the answer, but presumption tended to ignite the royal temper.

'I think it shall be this one,' said the Prince, stroking a hand over the shoulder of his new Field Marshal's uniform, an aberration of his own design, encrusted with trimmings and with gold. 'I do have a fondness for it. Smarten it up with some of my decorations. I shall return in half an hour.'

'Yes, Your Highness.'

Hastings had been in service long enough to know that the Prince disliked questions on quantity. If there was a choice, as there generally was, His Highness favoured combining all possibilities together. His was a life dedicated to creating maximum effect through abundance, a life in which prudence had no place at all.

The equerry called for the keeper of the jewels to fetch all the royal decorations from the strong room. Ten minutes passed, and a team of subordinates hurried in, velvet jewellery cases stacked up their arms.

'Open them up,' instructed Hastings.

'Which ones, sir?'

'All of them.'

The boxes were laid out on a long table at the far end of the room. There were eighty-five of them. The clasps were clicked open, revealing a blinding array of orders, medals and insignia, crafted from gold, platinum, and precious gems.

A subordinate wiped each decoration with a strand of lint, and another passed them one at a time to the keeper of the uniforms. With appropriate care, he began pinning the honours onto the jacket's breast.

Half an hour later it was almost impossible to make out the ribbing or any of the blue fabric beneath.

The Prince Regent entered once again, a selection of the more manageable animals trundling behind him. The sound of servants' shuffling mixed with that of wheels grating. Striding slowly over to the mannequin on which the Field Marshal's jacket was displayed, the Prince took a good look at the metalwork, and snapped:

'Peacock plumage, get me a helmet with plenty of peacock plumage. And be quick about it! Oh, and put some damn epaulettes on it. The big gold ones.'

A fray of subordinates scurried around, Hastings directing them. A helmet was ushered forward. It resembled an upturned Champagne bucket, burnished silver, damascened in gold. A pair of long peacock feathers were stuffed into the plumage slits.

The Prince grunted, told Hastings to remind him which order was which. It wasn't that he had forgotten, rather that he liked to hear the roll of honour.

'This one, Your Highness, is the Order of the Tower and the Sword, and this is the Order of the Holy Spirit, a gift of His Majesty Louis XVIII. I believe that one is the Order of the Thistle, and this the Danish Order of the Elephant.'

'What's that one?' said the Prince, testing his equerry's knowledge.

There was silence.

'I believe, Your Highness, that distinguished decoration is the

Most Illustrious Order of St. Patrick.'

'What about these?' his index finger jabbed at a line of smaller decorations.

'Ancestral honours, sire.'

By four o'clock, the Prince Regent had been fitted into the uniform. His bulk was so immense that he required a troop of six attendants to dress him. Once the jacket had been fastened, the helmet was lowered onto the royal head, the peacock plumage fanning out above.

Hastings positioned the Regent's sword on the left, and attached a crimson sash across his chest, on which was pinned an enormous diamond star, crafted by Messrs. Rundell and Bridge of Ludgate Hill.

The weight and tightness of the apparel was so great that the Prince Regent could hardly move. Staggering over to where Lawrence had hung a backdrop, a sketch of the battlefield of Waterloo, he struck an appropriate pose.

'Come on, man, get on with it!'

For two hours, Lawrence worked away, taking breaks every ten minutes for his subject to sit down and rest his legs. As he worked, the team manning the animals were ordered to wheel them around in silence to alleviate the Prince's boredom.

At seven o'clock, a footman entered and whispered into Hastings' ear. The equerry nodded, and stepped forward.

'Your Highness,' he said softly. 'The white bear has arrived.
It awaits in the blue velvet room.'

'What's it doing up there? Bring it down here to the library, man!'

'Very good sir.'

Forty minutes passed, punctuated with cursing and with
groans, as a team of subordinates heaved the crate down the grand
staircase. Once it was positioned, William Bateman entered, bowing
and stooping appropriately. A pair of jemmies worked at the panels,
as Bateman held his breath. He didn't feel his usual self, a little
worn out after a night of frolicking at the Colchester Inn.

The last panel was levered off, and the polar bear was turned to
face the Prince, who called for the other animals to be halted so that
he might observe the new creature without distraction.

'Splendid,' he said, removing the helmet and sweeping back his
hair. 'Have wheels fitted right away. It will do very nicely for my
African arrangement.'

EIGHTEEN

SIMON COCHRAN HAD only been acquainted with the American
visitor for a short time, but felt as though he could trust him on the
intimate matter of his personal affections. In any case, there was no

one else to advise him. His dandy friends regarded any conversation of an amorous nature as quite inappropriate. They preferred to discuss the fashions of the moment, or the refined etiquette expected of a gentleman.

The American's notable appeal to the fairer gender proved his expertise in matters concerning women. Cochran felt sure that Beattie must have returned from London to Chavenage Hall. Next morning, as he and Adams took a cup of chocolate together, Cochran brought up the subject of his beloved cousin.

'Is she ready to marry you?' asked Adams.

'Only the Devil moves with haste,' Cochran replied.

'Move too slowly and she'll be poached by someone else.'

'Do you really think so?'

'Well why should she wait for you when you move at the speed of a tortoise? A hare will be along at any minute, and she'll be swept off her feet.'

Cochran emitted a high-pitched gasp.

'My goodness,' he said, 'perhaps you are right.' Reaching for a sheet of foolscap, he dipped his quill. 'I should write to her at once.'

'Yes you should.'

Cochran paused.

'Would you help me?' he asked.

'But I can't read or write.'

'I am aware of your illiteracy, sir, but you have a way with words, a way that appeals to gentle ladies…' Cochran paused again. 'It has to do with your forthright American attitude,' he said.

Adams looked into the middle distance.

'*My dearest Beattie,*' he began, putting on a stiff English voice, '*I feel at a loss for words for having economised with the truth all this time…*' He held short. 'Well, are you going to write it down or not?'

Flustered, Cochran dipped his quill again, touching the nib quickly to the inkwell's rim.

'Oh yes, yes!'

Again, Adams let his mind float away, and he began to dictate in an English accent:

'*My reserved actions until now had, I thought, been in the best interest of us both, yet I now write to you to reveal that in reality my sentiments run far deeper than one might have ever imagined.*

'*As I sleep, my dreams are filled with an image of your tenderness, your utter perfection. And in my waking moments you are always there. I need only close my eyes and I can see the chestnut curls falling at the sides of your face, and I can smell the scent of your lovely skin. The thought of being with you, of pressing my lips to yours, causes my heart to race, for I know that nothing is more true than the love I feel for you.*

'*It was as a child, my dearest, that I first understood my dire and immovable adoration for you, and was then, as we played together, that I knew my life would be nothing if not intertwined with yours. I have never been bold enough to make these feelings known to you. But I believe that the time has now come for us both to embrace the moment. I beg you, my darling Beattie, to feel the emotion with which I hold you in my heart, succumb to it, embrace it, and allow our souls to unite as one, your loving cousin, Simon.'*

Cochran scratched away, committing the dictation to the page. When he had finished, he was short-breathed.

'My dear sir! Do you really believe it appropriate to be so forward?'

Adams slapped his hands together.

'My friend, it's time for you to live,' he said.

NINETEEN

AT ELEVEN O'CLOCK Sir Geoffrey hurried down to Hoare's Bank on Fleet Street. He took sherry with the partners in their private salon, commenting on its aged oak flavour. Then, before sipping a second glass, he deposited the fifty thousand pounds from Lord Alvanley.

The Committee's chairman could hardly contain his pleasure.

'Even as we stand here, crystal in hand,' he declared to the bank's own chairman, Sir Richard Hoare, 'Our Major Peddie will be nearing the great gilded metropolis of Timbuctoo. I venture to say that by the spring I shall no doubt be requesting space in your most fortified strongroom.'

'Pray tell, sir, what is the nature of the wealth?' asked the banker.

It was the question Caldecott had been hoping for. He gulped down the contents of his glass, and announced:

'Gold! Sir! In an abundance as never before known. Everything is fashioned from it, from the bedsteads to the cobblestones. It is said that its people walk on shoes fashioned from the yellow metal, that the horses are bridled in it, and the roofs tiled with it!'

Sir Geoffrey's glass was filled a third time. Sipping the sherry, his weight shifted onto his back foot.

'If you would permit me to enquire, Sir Geoffrey, why has this wealth not been exploited until now?'

Caldecott took a pinch of macouba.

'My dear Sir Richard,' he said, 'the reason is unmistakable. Between the African coast and the golden city there lies a desert wilderness peopled by natives of the most savage and diabolical nature. They must be exterminated in their entirety before our force can gain entry to Timbuctoo!'

Sir Richard Hoare held out his glass so that the servant could replenish it. He was about to say something supportive, when Sir Geoffrey, his face flushed, declared:

'I can assure you in the strongest terms, Sir Richard, that our expedition has been mounted as a grand military campaign. It is founded on intelligence of the most intricate and artful variety. Our agents on the coast of Marocco have been informed by numerous traders and even by sympathetic natives who have themselves actually set foot in Timbuctoo!'

Sir Richard Hoare touched his palms together, sensing the moisture inspired by the thought of great wealth.

'We shall oblige you in every way we can, Sir Geoffrey, and would be prepared to open accounts for any investor whose fortunes are augmented by your Major Peddie's success.'

TWENTY

NEWS OF THE American's imminent description of the golden city continued to spread across London. By the early afternoon, it was the gossip of the moment as far afield as Knightsbridge and even in the village of Hampstead.

All of society was talking of Mr. Adams and his African explorations. In St. James's club-land, Brooks, White's and Boodle's were emptied of members, who had repaired to the Royal African Committee to hear the narration for themselves.

Inside the library almost four hundred people were already in attendance. Some had brought their own chairs, many more were milling about, resting on their canes.

At three o'clock, Cochran entered with Adams. A wave of susurration eased through the book-lined hall.

'That's him,' snapped Lady Devonshire to her friend, the Duchess of Beaufort.

'He is a fine figure indeed.'

'Who was it that said the Americans were a dreary race?'

'My husband for one,' replied the Duchess.

'Well he ought to swallow his tongue.'

Cochran welcomed the witnesses to 'Mr. Adams' most interesting and extraordinary journey' and, without a word more, invited Robert Adams to begin.

The American stepped forward, his eyes trained on the sea of heads.

'Under the cover of darkness our small caravan crossed the grand plateau,' he said, 'and made its way to the great mud walls of Timbuctoo.

'There was a full moon, and its light threw long shadows across the baked dirt. As we approached, the Touareg warriors became greatly spirited by the sight of the civilisation. They cried out, whooping, and struck crude metal cymbals which they had carried in their packs.

'Long before we had reached the wall, we spied the flames of burning torches. One or two at first, positioned high on the battlements, but after a little while there were many hundreds, as if the official guard had been summoned. The burning torches illuminated the walls, and drew to our attention countless human heads, festering on spikes, running the length of the battlements.

'I feared then that the people of the city might mistake us for an enemy. But the clashing of the cymbals identified us as friends.

'The doors to the city had been locked for the night. They were crafted from wood with great iron spikes protruding from them, each one crowned with a skull, a symbol for the uninvited to keep away.

'As we neared the great portal, the doors swung inwards and we found ourselves being welcomed into the city of Timbuctoo.

'A dignitary came out and kissed the hands of each Touareg in our party. After a word of explanation in their native tongue, he greeted my companion Sanchez, and me, and led us through the labyrinth of streets and alleys, to a large mud building, which I realised was the palace.

'The streets were lined with people, all of them black-faced and curious. The moonlight provided welcome illumination, and I found myself able to make out details on the buildings we passed.

'As we moved forward with the camels ahead of us, some of the local people leapt forward and struck the Moors with sticks. There was great hatred towards them, from the smallest of children to the most elderly of men. At seeing Sanchez and me, the people marvelled greatly. It appeared they had not before set eyes on Christians.

'We arrived at the palace, where another great portal was pulled open. A guard escorted us into a courtyard of considerable size, lit by hundreds of burning torches. Its walls were adorned with human heads, shaved of their hair, their faces contorted, their flesh putrid and decaying. Although it was still night, the square was occupied by a variety of mutants — dwarfs, hunched giants, men with grotesque deformities, and others walking on all fours.

'We waited as the monarch was roused from his sleep. The camels were relieved of their burdens and watered, as the Moorish captives were kicked to the ground in one corner of the yard.

'A retainer came forward and offered Sanchez and me refreshment, served from a wooden cup. An acidic juice of some kind, it was quite delicious. When we had finished it, the servant filled the cups again and, with a hand gesture, implied that there was an abundant supply of the beverage, which made us very content.

'Then the king arrived.

'He strode across the courtyard, preceded by a pair of young women, their breasts naked. With each stride they threw white feathers down, to soften the ground touched by the monarch's feet.

He was a portly man, enormous at the waist, advanced in years, and dressed from head to toe in blue nankeen. When he drew close I saw his small despotic eyes for the first time, and noticed that his right ear was entirely missing.

'Greeting the Touareg party, he presented each man with a carved piece of wood, an honour of some kind. Then, Sanchez and I were brought forward for his inspection. He seemed very inquisitive of us. Having asked many questions, he instructed me to come near so that he could observe my skin closely.

'When he saw my fairness, he laughed, and his minions laughed as well. Bowls of fruit were brought out, and more of the delicious juice. We indulged until the sun slipped up over the horizon. The king stayed with us. He liked to watch us eat. Every so often he would say something and all around him the minions would laugh.

'After dawn, when we had been in attendance for some time, the queen arrived. Far younger than her husband, her skin seemed to shine in the early morning light. Like her husband, she was dressed in clean blue nankeen, her hair braided with cowry shells. She sat beside the monarch on a dais, and would whisper to her servants, a throng of bare-breasted girls, wearing coarse fibrous skirts.

'One of the Touareg warriors motioned to the Moorish prisoners. The king gave an order, and three of them had their heads shaved and were then made to kneel. A minute after that their heads were severed from their shoulders by an executioner who, I was to realise, rarely left the king's side. The heads of the Moors were strung up with the others on the wall, and their surviving brethren were taken away.

'Once the beheading had taken place, the king clapped his hands in delight. As if having been summoned by the sound, four servants dressed in blood-red tunics stepped forward, each one holding a relic — a sculptured warrior's head apparently fashioned from gold. Wasting not a moment, the monarch leant forward and kissed each of the heads. I believed it to signify that the beheadings had been made in honour of the relics.

'Sanchez and I were then ushered to our own private quarters in the palace. The rooms were simple, but more splendid than I might ever have hoped after weeks of suffering. There was a mattress filled with straw, and a bowl in which a small blue flower was floating in water. I bent forward and smelled its scent, moved beyond words at such beauty. For I hadn't seen such a gentle expression of nature since leaving Hudson.

'Setting eyes on the petals transported me home, to the meadows I had so loved as a boy. I would stalk through the high grass with my brothers, all of us imagining we were hunters on the vast African plains. Never did I dream for a moment that my feet would one day roam the plains in reality.

'When I awoke, a pair of young women were standing over me. Like all the others, their breasts were uncovered, and they wore feathers in their hair. They smiled a great deal, their teeth as white as pearls. Beside them was a bucket filled with water. They washed me with it, taking great interest in touching my body with their hands.

'After they were done washing me, one of the girls left, and the other one stayed. She shut the door from the inside, fastened it, and pulled me towards the mattress. The thought of taking comfort was at that moment most appealing. But when she begged me in her native tongue, pulling me to her, it only strengthened my resolve to return to Hudson and to be in the arms of my beloved wife.'

Cochran raised a hand to draw the session to a close.

A voice called out something from the crowded back of the room.

'What about the bounty, the wealth of Timbuctoo?'

'Yes, what about the gold, sir?' cried another.

'The precious jewels! Where are the jewels?'

The Committee secretary stood up and held out his hands to calm the audience, who were becoming agitated.

'Mr. Adams shall continue in the next session,' he said, faltering. 'We shall reconvene on Monday afternoon at four o'clock.'

The library erupted in chatter, as the crème de la crème of society dissected the American's narration. The same word was on everyone's lips — gold.

Lady Devonshire pushed her way through the crowds and offered her hand for the American to kiss. Following Cochran's example, he thanked her for the hamper.

'It was a trifling gesture,' she said, 'yet I hope it brought a little happiness to a gentleman far from home.' Lady Devonshire advanced half a step and, when Cochran turned to greet the Earl of Buckingham, she ran her fingers along Adams' forearm.

'I know that society devours your time, sir, but I would be obliged for a private interview with you to discuss a matter of singular importance. May I send my carriage for you, next week perhaps?'

Adams smiled limply and, before he could reply, he noticed Clara Fortescue across the room. Excusing himself, he went over. Seeing him moving towards her, Clara's face lit up.

'All of London is in attendance, Mr. Adams,' she said, touching a hand nervously to her cheek.

'The more who stumble in here in their finery, the more I long for solitude,' he replied.

'You miss your wife,' said Clara in a whisper.

Adams' expression dropped.

'You read my thoughts.'

'And you shall be with her again. I am certain of it,' she paused, glancing at the floor. 'Yet it always seems that fate conspires to separate us from the ones we love.'

TWENTY-ONE

THAT EVENING, A special messenger from the household of Sir Henry Montagu arrived at the Fleet Street chambers of Simon Cochran. He knocked twice, then a third time, and was finally received by Mrs. Pickeriff, the landlady, who was drunk.

She staggered to the door wearing a tattered dressing-gown, which had belonged to her husband Oberon, before he had succumbed to a dependence on Cantonese opium.

The messenger asked if he had the correct address.

'Who are you looking for, darling?' asked Mrs. Pickeriff.

'Simon Cochran Esquire.'

The landlady snatched the envelope, slammed the door, and reeled up the stairs. A minute later, the letter was in Cochran's hand. Recognising the script at once, he broke the seal, turned up the wick, and read:

TWENTY-TWO

My dearest Cousin,

First of all I must exclaim my true delight and considerable surprise at the letter I have so recently received, written in your hand. I am not worthy of such devoted affections. Rather than reply in the spirit of your own correspondence, I think it prudent to provide you with a clear and succinct explanation.

But, before I continue with an attempt to elucidate the circumstances that have prevailed, I should like to ask your forgiveness. You have always treated me with the most noble and dignified attention and, rather than matching your sincerity, I find myself to be treacherous beyond reproach.

I believe that in one correspondence, I made remark of our recent acquaintance with a Mr. Thomas Wittershall, who had acquired lands adjacent to ours at Chavenage Hall. I believe that I mentioned too that Mr. Wittershall has a home in London.

Upon our arrival in town, Mother and I found ourselves invited for tea at the residence of Mr. Wittershall's mother, Mrs. Felicia Wittershall. She is a delightful lady, with a fondness for chatelaines, of which she has a magnificent collection.

The day after the invitation, we were surprised when Mr. Wittershall arrived unexpected at Bloomsbury Square. He appeared to be in the most anxious state, his brow running with perspiration, and his clothing ruffled as if he had not slept the previous night.

He was shown into the drawing room, where Mother received him and enquired, as delicately as she was able, as to the nature of his visit. After a long pause, and a considerable amount of stuttering, Mr. Wittershall clarified why he had come.

Firstly, he explained that his late father, Viscount Lucian Wittershall, had passed away in September last year. The terms of the will had indicated that, as oldest son, Mr. Thomas Wittershall would be entitled to inherit the fortune of the family in its entirety, but on one condition. To do so, he is expected to have a bride from a good family, born and brought up in the county of Gloucestershire.

As you can imagine, I was at first reluctant to regard favourably what amounted to a proposal from a man I hardly know. When Mother broke the news to me, urging me to accept, I felt quite unwell. But then she revealed two pieces of intelligence that I must allow to aid me in my decision.

The first is that, despite living in the comfort of Chavenage Hall, we are quite penniless, the loss of our investments in the Americas is solely to blame. The second piece of information — which Mother stressed most passionately — is that Mr. Wittershall is a man of significant affluence. His inheritance stands at £75,000, with a further annuity of £15,000 per annum.

My dear Simon, although I comprehend that your grief will be deep, I coax you in the most spirited terms to forget any affection you hold for me, other than that which is derived from blood.

I am,

Your devoted cousin,

Beattie

WHEN I SAW IT FIRST, I was lost in the bowels of the London Library, searching for an obscure volume on shrunken heads...

A leather-bound book, an inch thick, jammed up against a water pipe. Without thinking, I reached up and yanked it out. Cupping the book gently in my hands, I pulled it open at the title page and began to read. That was the moment my obsession with *The Narrative of Robert Adams* began.

Twenty years have passed since then. And, through that time, my fascination for the tale of an illiterate American sailor has gripped me like nothing else.

The book you hold is my own fictional version of what is surely one of the greatest stories of survival ever told. I can only offer gratitude to the reader for turning a blind eye to any historical inaccuracies, and for tolerating a novelist's liberties. I am no historian, and have massaged facts and fictions into place, re-conjuring history.

With that, let the tale begin...

TAHIR SHAH

IV

The Crane Boys exhume their latest cadaver in Hampstead — Sir Joseph Banks invites Messrs. Adams and Cochran to breakfast — Walking to the rendez-vous in Soho Square, Mr. Adams asks about His Majesty King George III — Sir Joseph Banks shows Mr. Adams his collection of tattooed human heads — At White's Club, Lord Alvanley informs Lord Byron of the investment he has made — Sir Geoffrey Caldecott is uneasy at receiving no news from Major Peddie — Sir Joseph Banks invites Mr. Adams to an execution — The Committee chairman advises his directors of the imminent success in reaching Timbuctoo — At the Execution Dock, Mr. Wicks has a short but revealing parley with Captain 'Lost Cross' Williams — Mr. Adams' narrative describes life in Timbuctoo and the brutality of King Woolo — Viscount Fortescue seems distant to Miss Clara Fortescue — Beattie discusses the marriage proposal with her mother — King Woolo takes a new bride after which Mr. Adams demonstrates to him the secret of making black powder — Dr. Philps takes possession of a cadaver — Mr. Thomas Wittershall and Beattie are wed.

ONE

It was midnight in Hampstead, a small village on the hill north of Regent's Park. The quarter moon, the fog, and the cold, had cleared the streets, and all honest folk were at home in their beds.

Four men were walking down Church Row, their footsteps muffled by the fresh dusting of snow. Two of them were cousins, the other pair, friends they had met at Marshalsea.

As they walked, the smell of roasting coal heavy in the freezing air, they bragged about recent success in their current line of work.

'I got one the other night,' said the first. 'Huge he was, more than six foot three. I dragged him out by myself down into the woods where I left him till I could get me some help.'

'I saw him,' said another. 'His legs were broken, smashed at the knees.'

'They had to do that to get him in the box,' said the first.

'Quiet lads!' snapped the fourth man. 'Think I 'eard someone.'

'It was just the wind, comin' over the wall!'

The group, who liked to be known as the Crane Boys, after the family name of the two brothers, heaved themselves over the granite wall and scurried down the side of the church. Assured that the sexton would be away on Christmas leave, they had been lured by the story of a local woman who had perished in childbirth the week before.

It took them no more than a minute to find her grave.

The faint scent of lilies hung over it. The flowers had been left that morning by the grieving husband, along with a card which read simply — *My beloved Heather, my world is pain without end.* His name was Frank Delouth, and he had spent Christmas alone, most of it staring into the embers at his home, lost in grief.

Kicking away the flowers, the Crane Boys got to work with the shovels, which they had stashed in bushes nearby on a previous night. It took a little muscle to get through the frozen topsoil. Once through it, the newly turned earth was easy to move. Billy Crane, the leader of the group, kept watch while the others took turns to dig.

After forty minutes' shovelling, his brother, Harry, reached the casket.

'That's a nice bit of wood,' he said, jabbing his spade. 'Sounds like oak.'

'Yeah, well look at the houses round 'ere. It's all toffs,' said John, the youngest, not yet seventeen.

'All right, let's get it out,' Billy replied, stepping forward with the pick.

He chopped away at the centre of the coffin and soon had opened it up. His father, an undertaker in his earlier days before he turned to thievery, had passed on to his sons the tricks of the trade. The first thing to learn was that even the most well-meaning undertaker scrimped on expensive wood. There was no need to use a full inch of oak when you could use half as much and back it with beech. The tendency to economise meant that the chest area was far less sturdy than it appeared.

Harry Crane jumped down into the grave, and used his oversized hands to pull away the timber. He bent down a little more, his calf muscles aching as he stooped. The fingers of his right hand fished about for a moment. They touched cloth, loose and silky, and then a leg. His hand travelled upwards to the point where the legs joined, and up a little more. Cackling, he brushed his fingers to his lips.

Then, in a single movement, using all his strength to lift the corpse, he passed it up and out.

'Got 'er lads?'

'Yeah, got 'er.'

Harry climbed out, and wiped his hands over the sides of his coat. His eyes had adjusted to the low light, but he couldn't quite make out the features of the cadaver's face. He ran a hand over it and down the chest.

'A nice little missus,' he said. 'If it weren't so bloody freezing, I'd give 'er a going over.'

'Let's get down to the stone door,' said Harry.

'Will the doc be there yet?'

'Course he will. He's always there.'

John pulled out a rank-smelling blanket they had used twenty times before. The Crane Boys walked back down Church Row, the corpse bent double over Billy's back.

Outside number forty-one, Harry paused to tie his shoelace. From the corner of his eye he noticed a single tallow candle burning in the window of a ground floor room. Sitting inside on a leather armchair facing the fire was a lone figure.

Harry had no way of knowing it, but the man was Mr. Frank Delouth, the husband of the woman Billy had bent across his back.

TWO

ON HIS TRAVELS to the dark side of the world, Sir Joseph Banks learned the importance of diversification. He was fêted as a botanist, but was equally attracted to an array of other fields, including geology, musicology and phrenology — the study of the contours of the skull. His journey with Captain Cook on the *Endeavour* had begun in 1768, and had taken three years. The experience had honed Banks's mind, given him time to think, and had introduced him to hardship on a rare and daunting scale.

Banks's fascination with Robert Adams went beyond the narration that he had attended at the Royal African Committee. He was interested greatly in the way the American's view of the world had been altered through adversity. It was for this reason alone that, the next day, he invited Adams and Cochran to his home to take breakfast.

A morning invitation to the Bankses' was not uncommon. Over the years, the eminent scholar had entertained most of the finest minds of the day, elevated conversation over buttered crumpets and toast.

Sir Joseph liked his guests to arrive by nine, and not to stay a moment longer than the noon chimes of his long-cased clock. As far as he was concerned, the mind was at its freshest the moment it rose from the bedstead, fatiguing a little more with each waking hour.

Simon Cochran had not slept a wink. He had sat upright all night, staring at the teetering wick of a long tallow candle poised on a table beside the window. Beattie's letter was lying open between the candle and an empty bottle of tawny port.

At first he had been consumed with anger. He swore aloud that he would hunt this Mr. Wittershall down and challenge him to a duel. Then he remembered his revulsion for combat of any kind. And, gradually, as the evening slipped into night, and the night into morning, he reflected on his foolishness at ever falling for Beattie at all.

Shortly after eight, Robert Adams woke, to find his friend crouching in a ball on the floor weeping, a bundle of his dear cousin's letters clutched to his chest.

'I think I shall kill myself,' said Cochran all of a sudden.

'What good would that do?'

'It would make me feel a little better,' he said.

THREE

AN HOUR LATER the pair were walking down Fleet Street. Neither of them had much interest in venturing out for breakfast. But, when Adams proposed that they go back to bed, Cochran rallied to Banks's defence.

'How could you suggest such a thing?' he said forcefully. 'Perhaps you are unaware that Sir Joseph has the ears of the most powerful men in England.'

'Even Sir Geoffrey's?'

Cochran let out a delicate laugh.

'Caldecott's weak as a kitten,' he said. 'But he's a kitten crouching under a magnifying lens. Don't be taken in by what you consider to be his size. No, no, it's Banks who has the ear of all, including the Prince Regent.'

A full minute of silence passed. Then Adams asked:

'Is this Prince like a king?'

'Indeed that's just what he is,' said Cochran, leading the way across Leicester Square, 'king in all but name.'

'But then why don't they call him king?'

Cochran's expression soured a little around the mouth.

'Because His Majesty King George III, our monarch for half a century, is still alive.'

'Where is he then?'

'At Windsor Castle. He resides there in seclusion.'

'Why?'

Pausing, Cochran turned to face Adams.

'He is there because he is deranged,' he said.

FOUR

SIR JOSEPH BANKS was sitting in his wheelchair at the foot of the staircase, watching the mechanism of his long-cased clock through a crude periscope he had designed himself.

He had had the clock's movement encased in glass, so that he could watch the cogs go round. As he would say very often to Lady Banks, cogs were like the human mind, reliable when balanced and serviced, yet doomed when out of kilter. Nothing fascinated Banks quite so much as a mind gone awry. It was for that reason that he visited each week the Bedlam asylum, a practice of forty years.

Before Cochran had pulled the bell chain, a servant appeared, wished the gentlemen good morning, and hurried them inside.

They removed their overcoats, and found Banks waiting beside the clock. He was not a tall man and all the shorter in his wheelchair. But his irrepressible liveliness made him appear far more imposing in stature.

'Gentlemen, my dear gentlemen!' he boomed. 'You have done me an honour far beyond my worth!'

Waving his arms frantically, he herded the men through to the salon, where they waited until the other breakfast guest had arrived. The walls were hung in fuchsia silk, woven in a paisley pattern, and covered in Audebon's birds, each one set in a delicate gilt frame. Under the windows was a marquetry card table and, on the other side of the room, flanked by a pair of porcelain negro servants, stood a stuffed tiger.

Sir Joseph looked at the clock on the mantel, an astronomical model from Basel. He squinted, then frowned.

'I do hope our dear Mr. Stephenson has not forgotten the appointment,' he said.

There was a sound of nimble feet stepping over the parquet. Lady Banks entered, greeted the guests, and announced that breakfast was served.

'My dear Madam,' said Banks, signalling to the footman to push him, 'whatever are you thinking? It would not be correct for us to begin until our distinguished friend has arrived, not right at all.'

Inspecting his fingernails, he coughed gently, and said, 'I know!' I shall show my dear Mr. Adams the blue room, for I am sure he shall delight in it.'

Lady Banks grimaced. She did not approve of the blue room or its *objéts*, most of which her husband had acquired during the second voyage with Captain Cook.

The blue room lay across the hall from the salon in which they had been sitting. It was cold inside, the curtains drawn shut.

Banks's wheelchair trundled in, the footman heaving the curtains apart.

'Forgive Lady Banks's sensitivity,' said Sir Joseph. 'You see, she has never tasted real discomfort, indeed, alas, never has she known uproar of any kind.'

Adams, who was standing in the middle of the room, took a sharp breath, as he set eyes on the collection.

The place was filled with specimens, some in glass cabinets, others propped up on the floor, or piled in the corners packed in crates.

Adjacent to the curtains there stood a tall display case. Inside were the remains of a mummified man. Next to it on the floor was a glass dome in which a preserved dodo was standing on a branch. On the east wall, against a background of indigo silk, was hung an assortment of human heads.

Made remarkable by their tattoos, their faces were covered in curved blue-black lines chiselled into the flesh. Adams couldn't take his eyes off them. They were dreadful but, at the same time, there was something alluring about them.

Sir Joseph Banks observed the American's interest in the heads. He pointed to one and asked Adams to take it down.

'Examine the way the work has been achieved,' he said, running a finger along one of the curves. They are known as *Ta Moko*. I was presented with them in Polynesia by a chief who had taken a great fascination in my hunting rifle. It was a most favourable exchange. Lady Banks abhors them of course,' he added as an afterthought. 'But then, her appreciation of beauty is limited to what our society regards as art.'

Sir Joseph wheeled himself over to a Chinese lacquer dresser on the right side of the entrance. His thick fingers pulled the miniature doors apart, and delved inside. With care, he removed a human head no larger than a grapefruit. The features were perfectly reduced in size, the skin as soft as a kid glove, the neck was hollow, and the hair as long as the length of a man's hand.

Banks passed the head to Adams, who crouched down so as to be on the same level as his host.

'What is it?' he whispered.

Sir Joseph moistened his lips with his tongue.

'A *tsansta*,' he said gently. 'Crafted in the deepest jungles of the Amazonas. It was the head of a warrior slain in battle, reduced with heat for the purposes of obstructing an avenging soul.'

Banks leant forward, his face no more three inches from Adams' cheek.

'Tell me, sir,' he said, also in a whisper. 'Did you ever see heads treated like these?'

Adams scanned back through his memories.

'I saw a great many severed heads,' he replied, 'some of friends, and some of foe. In the African heat the flesh would rot quickly, and turn black, festering with pus and worms. My captors showed no interest in the leftovers of execution. But once, while walking in the streets of Timbuctoo, the king, a despot named Woolo, had a man beheaded before him, as was his pleasure to have done. Rather than walking on, as he tended to do, he stopped, and gave an order. Accordingly, the head was picked from the ground and placed with care into a basket made from damp reeds.

'On the arrival at the palace, King Woolo gave another command. A servant brought the basket to him. The king seemed pleased. He picked up the head, smashed it over and over against a jagged stone until the brains were exposed. The king then took a wooden spoon and tasted the meat. When he had eaten his fill, he invited his courtiers to do the same.'

A woman's voice called out from across the hallway.

'Mr. Stephenson must have arrived,' said Sir Joseph.

Lady Banks had led Cochran and Robert Stephenson into the breakfast parlour, a spacious room with lavender walls. She slipped her husband a sour glance, even though she was quite devoted to him. As far as she was concerned there was nothing more repellent than the trophy heads he so dearly prized. Her threats to have them disposed of were so frequent that Sir Joseph had fitted a pair of detector locks to the door, crafted in the workshops of Jeremiah Chubb of Portsmouth.

The breakfast table was laid with a fine linen cloth, the border edged in lace, and embroidered in the centre with a paisley medallion. Lady Banks had spent a lifetime creating order from the turmoil in which her husband thrived. She saw to it that the entire house was dusted and cleaned each day by a multitude of staff, whom she brought from a village in Wales, where she insisted there wasn't a soul born without good manners.

Robert Adams was seated beside Stephenson, and across from Cochran, with Sir Joseph and Lady Banks at either end of the table. No sooner had they sat down, than the serving dishes began to arrive. In most privileged homes breakfast dishes were laid out on a sideboard, with guests helping themselves. But, as with almost everything else in his life, Sir Joseph Banks broke the accepted convention. Regarding the first meal of the day to be the most important for the mind, he liked to be served.

There were potted anchovies and partridge pie, ragout of wild duck, apple fritters, boiled currant pudding, braised herrings, sausages, diced pineapple, and slices of honey-roasted ham. Ten servants bore the platters into the room.

Raising a hand, Lady Banks apologised for the orange juice being a little tart. Her husband snarled.

'It is a delight my dear,' he said, 'but one we ought not to enjoy when there's snow on the ground. Heavens! One day all of London will treat themselves to delicacies out of season, a custom I abhor!'

'I congratulate you Madam,' said Cochran, 'in finding fruit at all on a winter morn like this.'

'Thank you Mr. Cochran,' Lady Banks replied.

There was a pause. Stephenson said something about using locomotives to transport perishables, but no one heard, or no one cared.

Then, Lady Banks took a sip of her tea, and asked,

'Mr. Adams, would you please enlighten me how you managed to survive the torment that took you across the face of the Zahara?'

He thought before answering, only speaking after a pause of long reflection.

'I survived the torment because the prize was so exceptionally great.'

'And what was the prize, sir?'

Robert Adams sipped his tea, and slid the porcelain cup into the groove on its saucer.

'The prize?' he said, still staring at the cup. 'The prize is named Christina.'

FIVE

Lord Alvanley was sitting with Byron in the bow window of White's. Both men were drinking hot chocolate, with a dash of apple brandy, a touch they had learned from Brummell the day before he absconded to Calais.

Byron was wearing a white cotton shirt, ruched down the front, and a linen cravat so tight it impaired his breathing. Between fervent gasps, he had described a poem he was about to write, an ode to love between a master and his maid. Bored by the conversation, Alvanley tried not to gloat, having won the wager the week before.

Leaning back, he dusted an imaginary hair off the lapel of his coat.

'If you pull your ear close, you might hear of a way by which to redeem your fortunes.'

Byron looked out of the window at the cold. He sniffed, and raised an eyebrow.

'You are too proud to ask, so I'll tell you,' said Alvanley. 'There is a company of gentlemen known as the Royal African Committee.'

'I know of them,' snapped Byron.

'Well, listen and I shall inform you. This distinguished Committee has dispatched an officer in their employ with a considerable fighting force, all of them veterans of Waterloo.'

'Dispatched them where?'

'To Timbuctoo of course.' Alvanley sniffed again, then laughed.

'I cannot entertain the fact you have not heard of the expedition.'

'I spend my hours working, not prattling gossip with fishmongers' wives.'

'Well it may be of interest for you to know that the Committee has attracted investors — gentlemen of judgement — who will benefit admirably once the golden city has been reached, and sacked.'

Byron touched a hand to his chin.

'Why do you think the Committee's latest sacrifice will succeed where Mr. Park failed, a disaster so recent in the memories of us all?'

'Good planning, sir, and God's speed!'

'I will believe it when the riches have arrived, hauled down Piccadilly in a triumphant cavalcade. Please do not tell me you have invested in such a senseless scheme, Alvanley!'

'What if I have?'

'How much did you throw into the African hat?'

Lord Alvanley sipped his chocolate. He felt a little awkward, but then his spirits were bolstered by a surge of resilience.

'Fifty,' he said.

'*Fifty thousand pounds*?' replied Lord Byron incredulously.

'I think I shall build myself a nice little folly with the proceeds,' said Alvanley, stretching back again. 'Something Grecian, with a touch of Gothic on one side. I'll do a tower in Portland stone, with a moat all round.'

Byron called for the porter to bring the gaming book.

'A hundred guineas says the African Committee's man will disappear without a trace,' he said.

'It's a wager,' Lord Alvanley replied.

SIX

SIR GEOFFREY SAT in his study, nice and close to the open window, cooling his scalp, yearning for news of the expedition to reach him.

Before Major Peddie set out from the Committee's headquarters on Old Jewry, he had made a solemn promise to the chairman that he would send an encoded message each week. But, since his departure from the south coast, the veteran of Waterloo had dispatched just two messages, coded as arranged using the King James Bible. The first had advised of his arrival on African soil, and the second had delivered the welcome news that his party had slaughtered the

French unit, also bound for Timbuctoo.

Although he had never ventured to Africa, Sir Geoffrey had once, in his youth, taken a passage to Barbados, in the capacity of a registrar for a wealthy trader. He had been responsible for checking the number of slaves coming ashore from a British vessel, sent out by the partner of a slave dealer, who had lost all trust in his associate.

The memory of inspecting the human cargo after the choppy Atlantic crossing still haunted him. He had counted seven hundred and eighty-one men and twenty women, in varying stages of wretchedness. But it was the corpses that had affected him most. They had not been thrown over, but had been left to rot as some kind of depraved caution to the living, all of them still in their chains. Caldecott had spent four months on the island of Barbados, most of it waiting to be relieved. Vessels would arrive frequently from Goré, packed to the gunnels with slaves. But there was no passage to Europe, and no way of sending a message home. On that journey, Caldecott had learned that weeks could pass without the slightest possibility of communication.

Assuming that Major Peddie was experiencing the same difficulty, Sir Geoffrey took a pinch of snuff and followed it with a few grains of laudanum. Then he sat back in his club chair, allowed the effect of the opium to calm his nerves, and mused on how best to use Robert Adams' narration to his advantage.

SEVEN

THE BANKSES HAD taken great pleasure in hosting the American at their home. When their guests had left, as the long-cased clock struck noon, Sir Joseph had commented on Adams' singular gentleness. Overjoyed at finding someone who appreciated the Maori heads as much as he, the eminent botanist had invited Adams on a little outing later that very afternoon.

Shortly before four, just as the winter light faded into dark, Sir Joseph's carriage rolled briskly down Fleet Street and paused outside Cochran's chambers. The horses had not been out in three days, and were relishing the exercise, their shanks damp with perspiration.

Adams came down and, a moment later, found himself seated across from Sir Joseph. He had left Cochran to attend the fortnightly meeting of the Committee directors, an event that had prevented the narration from taking place that day.

Rubbing his hands together, Banks gave the order to drive on. The coachman jerked the reins and they were away, speeding east towards St. Paul's.

'It is a splendid day for justice,' said Sir Joseph easily. 'I do hope I shall have the opportunity of making a phrenological examination of the candidate.'

Removing a gold pocket watch from his waistcoat, he checked

the time and, without thinking, twisted the bezel three turns to the left. 'You see I have mounted my inspection almost every week for thirty years,' he said. 'The criminal mind being what it is, there is never a shortage of candidates.'

'Candidates?' said Adams, a little unsure of what Sir Joseph was talking about.

'Candidates,' he repeated. 'You know… criminals… offenders whose day of judgement has arrived.' Glancing at his pocket watch a second time, he held it to his ear. 'It doesn't do to be late,' he said.

'Late to what, Sir Joseph?'

'To the execution, of course.'

EIGHT

THE DIRECTORS HAD assembled in the Committee's great meeting room. All of them were present, except for Lord Woodruff, who had been thrown from his horse two days before, and was lying in bed at his country estate with a pair of broken legs. The remaining twenty directors were anxious for information on Major Peddie's progress. As soon as Sir Geoffrey entered, they fell silent, greeted their chairman, and waited for news.

Caldecott nodded to Cochran, seated on his left.

The signal indicated it was time to lock the doors. Cochran

motioned to the footman. The ornate brass key was turned twice clockwise. Then the chairman slapped a hand on the mahogany table and announced that the meeting was in session.

Rising to his feet, he stepped forward, rested his hands squarely on the table, his weight forcing down on the wood.

'Gentlemen,' he said in a grave voice, 'there may be snow on the streets of London, but all of us, I am sure, have our thoughts with the courageous Major Peddie and his party, enduring the fiery desert heat. I have received word from Peddie. And there is tremendous news!'

Caldecott held short for a moment, piquing the directors' anticipation. Across from him, Viscount Wakeham called out energetically:

'Has Peddie reached the golden city?'

'He is near it, sir. He is near!'

'Then what is your intelligence?'

'That the Major and his men have encountered the French contingent and have dispatched them. The desert has drunk well of the Gallic blood.' Sir Geoffrey paused again, relishing the fresh triumph over an ancient enemy. 'So I have the great honour of advising you, gentlemen, that the route before our expedition is clear, open all the way to Timbuctoo!'

'Sir Geoffrey,' said Viscount Wakeham, sitting straight in his chair. 'Can you please advise us when you estimate Peddie will reach the gates of the city?'

Caldecott wiped the beads of perspiration from his brow.

'With the greatest accuracy at our disposal,' he said, 'we anticipate that Peddie shall arrive there in less than a week.'

NINE

ALBERT WICKS HAD not slept well the previous night, on account of eating a plate of goose livers that he feared had turned. He never missed his wife except at Christmas, and only because she had cooked a very fine goose, just the way he liked it, the meat a little raw under the wings. Since her disappearance fifteen years before, he had been invited each year to the home of his sister, Flo. She lived in Rotherhithe with her husband and a son crippled from birth. Albert had never been close to his sister, but had an affection for her all the same. He liked the way she showed kindness to strangers, and appreciated her taciturn nature. His only significant irritation was that she had no idea of how to prepare a goose.

The gallows were ready at Execution Dock.

It was a bleak afternoon, with a grey sky and the threat of blizzard. The air was so cold that only the foolish were out, the foolish and the voyeurs who frequented public hangings.

Despite his aching stomach, Albert had been up early, testing the equipment, and working on the noose. Unlike Tyburn, the Execution Dock was not about quantity but quality. Only the most notorious outlaws were disposed of there and, as their executioner, Albert Wicks took a certain pride in attending to their departure.

A few days before, he had withdrawn his life savings from the cavity in the wall, and taken them down to Wimpole Street, to the office of the broker, Hugh Appleby Esq. Once there, he had pledged it all on the victorious outcome of the Royal African Committee's expedition to Timbuctoo.

Handing over the purse, dressed in the costume of a recent client, Albert had felt valued, as if he was part of something historic, something bigger than just himself.

Across from the gallows, in an armoured cell, sat a slim grizzled man. He was calm, reflective, and was polite to his guards. For half his years he had sailed the waters of the Mediterranean, searching for ships, and relieving their crew of their valuables and their lives. The British navy had first given him the nickname he stood by now, Captain 'Lost Cross' Williams. The name was derived from a story that a cross, tattooed on his back as a young sailor, had been removed by Moors near Tripoli, when he was taken prisoner by the Sultan's army fifteen years before.

Shortly after breakfast Albert Wicks had gone to introduce

himself to Captain Lost Cross. Before they mounted the scaffold he liked to meet the men due to avail themselves of his services. As he saw it, making the effort to shake the hand of a man about to quit the mortal world was only good manners.

During the hour they had spent together, Albert and the Captain had engaged in an animated conversation, which both of them had enjoyed. They had spoken of the little pleasures in life that people tended to forget — the smell of rain on dust, the sound of a woodpecker in the willows, and the taste of cool water after a night of debauchery at a country inn.

After they had chatted for fifty minutes, Albert Wicks leaned forward to the Captain and, in a voice of such softness that it was barely audible, he said:

'I assure you, Captain, that the responsibility charged to me shall be undertaken with the greatest attention, and shall be the cause of minimum distress.'

The two men shook hands.

'You seem like a good man,' said Captain Lost Cross Williams, 'and I am thankful for your sensibility.'

'Do not fear,' Albert replied, his callused hands now pressed together, 'I am certain the next world will be better than this.'

The Captain managed a smile.

'Look in my eyes,' he said, 'and tell me with sincerity you believe

I am bound for Elysian Fields!'

Outside, a large crowd had arrived at the dock in the earnest anticipation of witnessing the former pirate swinging by his neck. Most of the spectators lived locally, and were regular visitors, eager for any free entertainment they could get. Some of them remembered Captain Wooster swinging in the breeze, and one spectator, named Josiah Mott, could even remember the hanging of the pirate James Lowry, back in 1762.

In the middle of the mob a hawker was selling baked potatoes. Over the years he had learned that people bought his wares as pocket warmers in winter, and ate them on the way home. He was advertising his wares when Sir Joseph's carriage pulled up at the far end of the dock. Reining the horses to a halt, the coachman jumped down to square the step and unload the wheelchair.

Banks clambered into the chair, which he had designed himself. He cursed the gout that had robbed him of his legs, and asked Adams if he might push him to the front.

'A fine turnout,' he said gently, before repeating himself a little louder. 'I do like a good hanging. Don't you, Mr. Adams?'

The American did not reply, but tugged the lapels of his coat a little tighter to his neck. Banks glanced at his pocket watch.

'Just in time, sir,' he said. 'I see the Lord of the Admiralty already in attendance. It seems as if we are here not a moment too soon.'

The crowd pressed forward, some jeering, others holding their silence. Adams eased the wheelchair up to the base of the scaffold. The First Sea Lord climbed down to greet Sir Joseph. In his left hand was a silver oar, the symbol of his authority.

A drum began to sound, slow and funereal, as the condemned prisoner was brought from his cell.

Captain Lost Cross paused in the doorway on seeing the audience. His hands were bound in irons, his coat torn at the back where it had caught on a carriage door while he was being transported from the naval headquarters across the river at Greenwich.

Against the steady drumbeat, the captain was marched in a straight line from the cell block to the shore. As he walked towards the scaffold, he looked out at the Thames, its cold black water rippling at the sheets of ice.

As the drumbeat quickened, the prisoner mounted the steps one at a time, until he reached the platform. Standing there, a noose in his hand, was Albert Wicks.

The executioner waited for the First Sea Lord to administer the formalities. Then he stepped forward, nodded to the condemned man, and drew a black bag over his head. Moving with expert dexterity, Albert's fingers positioned the noose he had made that morning for Captain Lost Cross Williams' neck. He raised it under the ears as his father had shown him.

The drumbeat grew faster, and faster still.

Then the floor fell away, and Captain Lost Cross Williams was swinging in the breeze.

TEN

THE NEXT MORNING, as the Committee library bustled with London's privileged set, Robert Adams rose to his feet, ready to provide his long-awaited description of Timbuctoo.

The room was so full that, despite the cold, a pair of windows on the north side had to be opened for ventilation. Sir Geoffrey Caldecott had moved from his usual position near the doors, and taken a seat in the front row.

Nearby, Cochran flexed his fingers, took up the quill, and nodded to Adams.

'Ladies and gentlemen,' Adams started in a calm, measured voice, 'as I have described to you, I arrived in the city of Timbuctoo where I was taken before the cruel monarch, King Woolo.

'Along with the other Christian slave in our party, I was spared from execution or from the cells in which my former captors were readily imprisoned. Sanchez and I were afforded every comfort, and considered ourselves free men.

'During our first days in the city, I spent much of the time regaining my strength which had been so depleted during months of slavery. Twice a day a servant would bring millet porridge to my room, as well as meat and, from time to time, boiled root tubers that I found most satisfying.

'I was very grateful for the hospitality, although I had no idea how long it might continue. As I took time to explore the city, I was regarded with fascination by all who lived there. It appeared that most of the residents of Timbuctoo had never before set eyes on a Christian. The children were especially curious. They would follow me wherever I went. Yet if I was ever to turn to regard them, they would run to their mothers as if the Devil were about to seize their souls.

'The palace was a large mud-built structure on the north side of the city. The king's chambers were on one side, and the queen's on the other. I grew to understand that the two led largely separate lives, both of them taking concubines. About sixty servants resided in the palace, the majority living in cramped quarters. Only Sanchez and I were provided better accommodation, and soon realised that our living arrangements were reserved for honoured guests.

'And, as guests of the king, we lived like royalty ourselves, certainly when compared with the primitive existence we had endured over the previous months.

'Each evening, when the sun had disappeared below the

horizon, we were expected to attend the royal court, where King Woolo enjoyed what he considered to be entertainment. Usually he would hear the disputes of ordinary folk who dared bring their grievances to his attention. Only the unhinged could have thought it sensible to protest to their king.

'On most occasions Woolo's decision was made even before the petitioners had finished speaking. With a whimsical flutter of his blue kerchief, he would signal which plaintiff was to be executed. More often than not, a pair of kerchiefs was waved, and both claimants were dispatched right there and then by the resident executioner. The heads would be hung on hooks in the courtyard, to the great delight of King Woolo.

'As time passed, I learnt more of the geography of the city. It covers a considerable expanse, with the Niger River half a day's walk to the south. From the outset, Sanchez was uninterested in exploring. He spent most of his time lying on his mattress being indulged by the servant girls, or having his skin anointed with a preparation of goat-milk butter.

'I, on the other hand, became fascinated how such a metropolis could exist in the middle of the Great Desert.

'Contrary to popular belief, the roofs are not tiled in gold, nor is there a wealth of any kind, that is, what we might comprehend to be wealth. Most of the jewellery is made from shells, taken from the river, or made from camel bone. The houses are crafted from blocks of mud, and the majority of the townsfolk live a most squalid existence.

'King Woolo reigns with absolute authority, and controls all wealth. There is no gold except four warrior heads kept as sacred relics. And, as I was to discover, even they are iron adornd with gold. But, there is wealth of a far greater nature, a *real* wealth, and one in plentiful abundance."

Adams stopped speaking.

He took a moment to take in the audience, dressed in their finery, revelling in their self-importance. The statement on the lack of bullion in Timbuctoo had been unpopular. As soon as it had slipped from the American's lips, the audience murmured with displeasure. The only thing that prevented a universal outburst was the prospect of something even greater in value than gold.

Robert Adams waited until there was silence once again.

'Spend months and years enslaved on the sands of Africa,' he went on, 'and you begin to regard what is important, and what is not. I do not pretend to you that I am wise, but I have learned to discern true worth.' He paused again, staring at Caldecott. 'I say it once again: there is no gold in Timbuctoo. Not an ounce of it. But there is something which its people regard as far more precious, and more useful. It is so valued by them that they are ready to die for it, and so cherished that the king hoards it in storerooms beneath the ground.'

On the left side of the room, Clara Fortescue touched a hand to her friend Caroline Lamb's arm.

'I wonder what it might be,' she whispered.

'What could be more valued than gold?!' roared Bertie McCormack, seated to Caroline's right.

Adams again waited for the clamour to die away.

'I shall inform you about this treasure,' he said, 'the fortune that fills the king's magazines, and the notion that fills the dreams of every man, woman and child in Timbuctoo. It is a white powder, so common to us all that we regard it without a thought.'

'What ever could it be?!' exclaimed Bertie.

'It is salt.'

The din erupted again, as each member of the audience gave voice to their opinions.

A tall gentleman at the back of the room shot to his feet.

'This is a travesty! A lie! An *American* lie!' he yelled.

'Quite so, sir,' cried another. 'How could such a gentle audience give credence to such claptrap?!'

Across from Adams, Sir Geoffrey shifted in his chair, his white gloves damp with sweat. Rarely a man of hesitation, he was unsure whether to call the narration to an end, or keep silent so that Adams would make even a greater mockery of himself. Weighing up the situation, he dabbed his brow, and kept his lips sealed.

The American gave Cochran a nod, then continued:

'Beneath the palace there were nine vast storage magazines,' he said, 'each one filled with blocks of salt carved from a dry lake. The king ensured his wealth by controlling the commodity. Every week a caravan would arrive at the city, offering all manner of wares in return for a little of the precious salt. The city is an emporium of goods, most of them traded for the prized mineral.

'Down on the western margin of Timbuctoo is the great market where all manner of merchandise is bartered. There is dried fish and ostrich feathers, ivory, fruits, and stall after stall of objects, most of them washed up on the faraway African shores.

'One morning, while roving through the market, I came upon a selection of odds and ends that had just arrived. Among them were a sextant and callipers, a ship's medical box, six Bibles, and a large marble model of the *Mayflower*. The boat caught my attention, for I had seen it aboard our ship the *Charles*.

'At another stall nearby, I spied an old man crouched in the shade. He was smoking a long clay pipe, and appeared very eager to speak with me. But he knew no English, and I knew little Touareg. He told me to wait, which I did. A few minutes later he returned holding something in his hand. It was wrapped in a strand of calico.

'He passed it to me. I unfurled the cloth and found inside the flag of my nation, its fifteen white stars on a background of blue. The man made clear that the flag was a gift. I thanked him, shook his hand and, pressing that delicate fabric to my face, I wept.'

ELEVEN

VISCOUNT FORTESCUE WAS holding his newspaper at a distance from his face, reading at the same time as nibbling a slice of rye toast. Seated opposite as always was Clara, waiting for her father to finish with the news.

The Viscount took a sip of orange pekoe, followed by another bite of toast. He mumbled something to himself.

'Excuse me, Father? I didn't hear.'

'It's terrible, truly terrible.'

'What is?'

The way in which the medical profession supports the trade in cadavers. London's cemeteries are being picked clean.'

Clara Fortescue frowned at the thought of it. Even she had heard of the dons who, nightly, helped themselves to the remains of the newly interred in graveyards across the capital.

After the death of his own wife, Laetitia, the Viscount had ordered a special iron cage to be constructed and to be set over the grave.

On more than one occasion he and Clara had visited the burial ground to lay flowers, only to find evidence that the dons had tried to break the locks.

Folding the newspaper, Fortescue placed it on the table. Over the previous week he had seemed uncharacteristically distant. His daughter had noticed it, as had the butler, Dalston, and a number of the other staff.

'Father,' said Clara in a tender voice. 'Is everything all right?'

The Viscount looked across at her, hardly focussing.

'Quite so,' he said vaguely. 'Quite so.'

'You do not seem yourself.'

'My mind is puzzling something. I dare say that it will, given time, reach a conclusion.'

'I attended the narration yesterday,' said Clara.

'*Narration?*'

'Mr. Adams' narration, Father. The Committee's library was about to burst, and I can report that very few gentlemen there found amusement in Mr. Adams' description of Timbuctoo.'

Viscount Fortescue's attention was sharpened by the name.

'Tell me, how did our young American friend describe it?'

'As the most sordid destination, a place of no wealth or treasure of any kind, none that is except for salt.'

'And how was this news received, my dear?'

Clara smiled, the side of her nose creasing.

'With horror!' she said.

TWELVE

AT NUMBER FIFTEEN Bloomsbury Square, a pallid young woman of twenty-two was poised at a low dressing table, brushing back her hair with long sweeping strokes. Her expression was a little taut at the mouth, her eyes glazed, and her skin cold to the touch. Standing behind was her mother, an austere woman twice her age, whose chief objective in life was to marry her daughter well.

'I have told you time and again, dearest Beattie,' she said in an abrasive tone, 'Mr. Wittershall is a godsend for whom we all must be eternally thankful. But there is need for haste. I have told you that before.'

'But why, Mother? Why does the wedding have to be so swift? There is something a little distasteful about rushing with one's vows.'

'Nonsense, my dear. And you know the reason, I have explained to you the terms of the will.'

'But I am sure Mr. Wittershall would wait, at least until the spring. For I dream of a country wedding.'

'He cannot. He has made it quite clear — the marriage must take place by Twelfth Night.'

THIRTEEN

As NEWS OF Adams' description of Timbuctoo spread far and wide, it was received with considerable displeasure by the investors in Major Peddie's expedition.

A handful of them had turned out to extract answers from the Committee's directors. One elderly man who ran an eel stall at Clerkenwell had gone so far as to chain himself to the railings outside the Committee's building. He was making as much noise as he could, and had taken to slamming the railings with his wife's old frying pan.

Inside, the American was continuing with his tale.

'From the moment I arrived in Timbuctoo,' he said, 'I sought a way to quit it, a free man. To do so, and to survive on the journey back to civilisation, I knew very well that I would require equipment, maps and information. And so, over the next weeks, I set about gathering together whatever I could. Visiting the city's main caravanserai, I came across traders from across North Africa.

'Over time, I learned the Moorish language, and set about attending anyone who could assist me in creating an accurate map. Gathering my information a little at a time, I made a chart on a square of sail cloth. For ink, I used the boiled sap of baobab roots.

'My intention was to learn enough of the language and customs of the Moors so that I could go undetected amongst them. Of course, my skin was not sufficiently dark. But I found that by steeping a particular cactus in water, and then bathing in it, I could considerably darken the shade of my skin.

'Over the months, I learned to write the Arabic language, even though I have never learned my own, and I memorised certain passages of their Holy Book as well. For, as I had seen so often, the test between an infidel and one of Musalman belief is the ability to recite a few well-chosen words from the scriptures.

'As time passed, life at the palace became ever more restrictive. The queen took a great liking to me, and fed me choice pieces of meat and fruit from her own plate. She made the most open overtures, virtually imploring me to join her in her private apartment. Her husband did not seem in the least bit disturbed by this, although it may have been because I refused all her advances.

'My friend Sanchez fell in love with one of the courtiers, a girl of about sixteen, named Marat. They were inseparable. Sanchez would tell me how he planned to marry her, and raise a family in Timbuctoo. Whenever I described my plans for escape, he would remonstrate, and beg me to stay, to find a local wife of my own. I would repeat to him the reason I could and would not — that I was already married, and to the most beautiful woman on earth.

'With each day King Woolo appeared ever more merciless. He took to being carried through the streets on a litter, his executioner at his side. From time to time he would close his eyes. Then, when he opened them, the first person he saw would be beheaded. Each time that an execution took place, the four servants, dressed in blood-red tunics, appeared as if from nowhere, and presented the golden warrior's heads for the king to kiss.

'One night with a full moon, I climbed up onto the roof of the palace to watch the stars. I hoped that far away my beloved Christina would be gazing at them too. They were a celestial bridge between us. As I looked out of the city, I heard jackals fighting at the base of a low hill near Timbuctoo. Staring in the direction of the sound, I saw something glowing yellow on the hill. Unsure of what it was, I planned to investigate the next day.

'At that moment, Sanchez came up and informed me of the news. The monarch was going to take another wife, despite having five consorts already. Again, Sanchez begged me to stay in Timbuctoo, declaring that we were in a Paradise, albeit a Paradise in Hell.

'"Is this really Paradise?" I answered him fiercely. "A despot is holding the strings above us, playing with us as though we were puppets. Look at us!" I shouted, "we are just creatures in his menagerie. What will happen when he tires of us?"

'The next day I crept out of the city and made my way to the hillside where the jackals had been fighting. To my surprise, I found that the yellow rock I had seen was actually sulphur. Breaking off as much as I could carry, I hurried back to the palace. There, in my quarters, I set to work.

'The next evening, a stream of warriors issued forth through the dirt streets of Timbuctoo. Their faces were hidden by the most fearful masks, rising up fifteen feet above their heads, their long forms carved with grotesque images of death. In their hands were knives and, bound to their ankles, skulls of victims they had slain.

'The king reclined on a dais in the palace courtyard, his queen and concubines attending him. All around, acrobats leapt and danced, as the masked "dogon" warriors streamed in, their bodies gyrating like harbingers from Hell.

'Sanchez and I were afforded a prominent position, overlooking the dais. We watched as five young women from the court were brought before him in a line. One of them was Marat, the girl Sanchez had chosen as his own. King Woolo motioned a hand at one of the girls, the one he had selected as his bride. Taking a sharp breath, Sanchez was relieved beyond words that his dear Marat was not selected.

'But then, to our horror, the executioner stepped forward with his axe. The four women rejected by Woolo were ordered to kneel. Without delay, their heads were swiped off.

'We stood there unable to move, both of us lost in shock. Allowing his disbelief to turn to rage, Sanchez lurched toward the king.

I managed to catch him, to hold him down with all my force, and to calm him.

'As had happened at the previous decapitations, the four servants stepped from the shadows bearing the golden heads. The king pressed his lips to each one in turn.

'When the blood had soaked into the sand, I took a lamp and moved around the courtyard, quickly lighting the touchpapers of fifty fireworks I had made using the sulphur from the hill. The black African night was illuminated with platinum fire.

'King Woolo leapt up. Thrusting his new bride to one side, he ordered me to reveal the secret of making black powder. I made clear that I would give him the formula if he would grant me absolute freedom, and furnish me with supplies so that I might quit his kingdom.

'The old king agreed readily and swore an oath upon his own life. Taking him at his word, I showed him how the powder is mixed, and from where to acquire the component parts.

'The next day, he called me to where he was sitting. I almost expected to be executed, so fickle was his nature. But instead, he presented me with a "mapara" locket attached to a leather cord. The size of a chestnut, it was fashioned from a seed as hard as stone.

'"Wear it always," said King Woolo, "and only give it up to a man who saves your life."'

FOURTEEN

DR. HORACE PHILPS was standing in the low stone doorway of
St. James's Infirmary. A little over five foot two, he was broad on the
shoulders, had large scarred hands, and an intense expression that
made it seem as if he was frowning even when he was not. Philps
had been at the door for thirty minutes and was about to leave, when
the signal came. Returning it, he whistled twice, shrill as a lapwing.

The sound of feet followed, heavy and fast over the frozen gravel,
followed by a dull thump.

'’Ere she is,' said the voice.

'Where did you get her?' replied Philps in a hushed voice.

'Up at ’ampstead.'

The doctor counted out the fee.

'She's worth more than that. Double I'd say. We've brought ’er
across London we ’ave.'

'Here's your money. Take it or leave it. Now go, and next time
find me a younger specimen.'

'A child?'

'Yes, nice and young. Below puberty. Look at the dates on the
headstones.'

'But you know as well as me that the fresh ones don't ’ave no
’eadstones. And you like ’em fresh, don't you?'

Crane hurried away into the night, while the doctor carried

the body inside. He disliked associating with the dons, but it was the only way of acquiring enough cadavers for his dissections. With far fewer hangings than in previous years, physicians were thankful for whatever they could get.

Inside his workroom, Dr. Philps laid the body out on the bench and sprinkled it with ammonium carbonate to quell the stench. Warming his hands over a burner on a small side table, the doctor turned up the gas lamp and took a good look at the cadaver.

It was a female. Good teeth. Well-kept nails. She must have been twenty, he thought to himself. First he removed her clothing and inspected her womb. There was no sign of pregnancy. Nor any indication she had died giving birth. He examined her body, pressing his fingers gently into the flesh. No obvious breaks, fractures, wounds, or swelling of the chest. The only abnormality was a blotch the shape and size of a pear just above the sternum. Excellent, he pondered. Just what he liked.

A little mystery for his students to solve.

FIFTEEN

As BOTH SECOND cousin and a cherished friend of the family, Simon Cochran received an invitation to the wedding, to be held the morning before Twelfth Night.

He had no intention of attending, but instead sent a simple card expressing his good wishes for the couple's future. The more he tried to cast all thoughts of the marriage from his head, the more preoccupied he became with it.

On the morning of the wedding itself, Cochran left his chambers at Fleet Street, and walked the long distance west to Hyde Park. There, lost almost in a stupor, he walked slowly around the Serpentine in a clockwise direction. As his feet trudged forward, his mind was on social propriety, on Beattie, and on the chill expanse of water. He considered jumping in and drowning himself, and might have, were he not so fearful of death.

The wedding guests had been limited to close relations and a handful of old family friends. The best man was Horatio Rickman-Watts, a boyhood chum of Thomas Wittershall. Beattie's uncle Henry stood in for her late father, in giving her away.

The service was held at the Mayfair Chapel, with a small reception afterwards at number fifteen Bloomsbury Square. The atmosphere was on the sombre side, despite the abundance of pink roses and chilled Moët Champagne. Beattie wore a dress of ivory taffeta that her grandmother, mother, and sisters had worn before her. The cuffs were stained from generations of bridal tears.

Thomas Wittershall stepped forward. Having commended his good fortune at finding so lovely a bride, he made a toast to his wife and to the King. Then, as the guests sipped at their fluted glasses, he made another announcement.

'Dear friends and distinguished guests,' he said, with a touch of stammering on the consonants, 'I have the pleasure to inform you that my wife and I shall depart without delay on the Grand Tour. Florence awaits us!'

V

Mortified by losing his beloved to another, Mr. Cochran continues taking down the narration — Deceived by King Woolo, Mr. Adams enters slavery once again — The Prince Regent hosts a luncheon of the season to show off his Collection — Napoleon's field carriage is made ready for exhibition at Mr. Bullock's Egyptian Hall — Mr. Cochran describes the duel in which his father perished — Napoleon's field carriage is unveiled to the public — Mr. Adams describes his return to slavery in the most cruel of circumstances and is witness to a vast caravan of death — At Bedlam, Lilly Small is tied to a post having gone blind — Viscount Fortescue has an interview with Emily Watts — Lady Devonshire and her closest confidantes discuss Mr. Adams — Sir Geoffrey Caldecott reprimands Mr. Adams for his outburst — A stranger arrives at number 10 Duke Street — The Prince Regent sits for his portrait — Miss Fortescue declares her undying affection for Mr. Adams — The chairman comes to know that Major Peddie and the Timbuctoo expedition have been slaughtered — Continuing with his tale, Mr. Adams describes a series of tribulations in the desert, as the Prince Regent arrives to witness the narration.

ONE

AT THE LIBRARY the next day, Cochran could think of nothing but the loss of his true love. In an effort to keep his mind off the misery of it all, he kept a tally of who was in attendance and who was not. He had counted a duke, six earls, three viscounts, and a marquis. Taking out his pocket-knife, he trimmed the edge of his nib. Just then he felt a hand on his shoulder. It was Caldecott.

'Simon,' he said in a bitter tone.

'Yes, Sir Geoffrey?'

'You do remember our little chat, do you not?'

'Yes, of course, Sir Geoffrey.'

'There is no news from Peddie, and the directors are growing anxious. The last thing we need is for the halfwit American to be taken credulously. We have him in our sights. You saw how displeased our audience became at hearing the preposterous report that the golden city is not,' he paused, 'not… *golden.*'

Cochran placed the quill on his desk.

'I understand you, Sir Geoffrey.'

Adams stepped forward as the chairman pushed out into the flood of dignitaries. Then, once Cochran had called the session to order, Adams was in the desert again.

'The day after King Woolo presented me with the locket,' he said, 'I spent many hours consoling my dear friend Juan Sanchez.

He was deeply disheartened at losing the girl to whom he had become so attached. I tried to coax him into joining me in my break for real freedom and, eventually, he agreed.

'We made a pact that we would set out on the following full moon. That night, I went up onto the roof of the palace, as was my habit. I liked to look at the stars, and felt in a way as if I was in conversation with Christina. There was no sound, nothing at all, except the occasional howl of the jackals far away. Surveying the vast unending emptiness, I made out a small caravan nearing the city from the west.

'The next day I went down to the emporium, taking with me some of the extra black powder I had made. I bought a sextant, a fine ship's compass, as well as a quantity of other equipment — blankets, cord, water skins, knives, and such like. Stowing the materials in the shop of a trusted Touareg, I hurried back to the palace.

'King Woolo was in high spirits. He had received the small group of Moors who had arrived the previous night. They had brought him a gift of black tobacco, three great bales of it. Beside himself with joy, the king ordered that his two-headed sheep be slaughtered. The meat was roasted in honour of the guests. Then he called his harem to come out from seclusion, and he offered the Moors their pick of the womenfolk.

'There was much laughter. King Woolo had his executioner set fire to a cask of black powder, a product he had valued above all else only a day or two before. I was about to go up to my chambers, when one of the Moors pointed at me. The monarch replied, although I did not understand what he said.

'At dawn, the door to my sleeping room was broken open by the king's guards. Until then I had regarded them as friends. Together with Sanchez, I was hauled out into the early morning light. The executioner was standing in front of us. He was sharpening his axe. I said farewell to Sanchez, that I would look for him on the other side. We were fearful, of course, but restrained, as there was no possibility of escape.

'An hour or two passed, and the sun rose up until it was equal to the lower palace walls. Then the king arrived. He was still grinning from the night before. He clapped his hands, and my former captors were dragged out from the dungeons. Half-dead, their bodies were wasted from hunger and disease. In all my travels I had never seen men so emaciated or forlorn. They assumed they were about to be executed too. And I swear they were relieved. One of them looked at me, as if asking whether I had any idea of their fate. Like him, I was uncertain. But then, a moment later, the situation was revealed to us.

'The tyrannical King Woolo had exchanged Sanchez, me, and the incarcerated Moors, for the tobacco. Stripped of my clothing, I was manacled and kicked to the ground. All I could do was to voice my disgust.

'"You promised to give me my freedom!" I yelled. "You promised! You swine!"

'But the king was not listening.

'Climbing up onto his dais where his young wife awaited him, he lit a pipe of the tobacco. As he and his courtiers looked on, Sanchez and I were dragged away from the palace courtyard, through the mud streets, and out of Timbuctoo.'

TWO

THE ANIMALS WERE on the move again at Carlton House. The Prince, who had taken delivery of an Indian mongoose from Bateman, had insisted that the entire collection, including the elephants, lions and giraffe, be pulled outside into the garden. That morning while taking a bath, he had come up with the idea of throwing a winter picnic.

It had snowed heavily in the night, and the gardens of Carlton House were prettier than on any winter day the Prince Regent could remember. He had ordered Hastings to instruct Carême to concoct something festive for lunch, and to send out a handful of invitations to his closest friends. The messages were headed, '*Un hiver dans la neige rassemblement d'émerveillement*'.

All morning the footmen struggled to heave the creatures from the Collection room, down the long corridor, and into the garden.

The great bull elephant went first. Hastings entrusted the Prince's *jouet du jour* to his second in command, a man with naval training named Henry Locke.

With little experience of manoeuvres on land, it had escaped Locke, a veteran of Trafalgar, that wheels and snow made for an uneasy combination. Ten footmen dragging at the bull elephant's ropes, the creature inched through the house and out through the verandah doors.

Just then the Prince passed.

The sight of the proud pachyderm rolling into the grounds was almost too much excitement. He called for the footmen to keep going, across the stone slabs and onto the snow-covered grass. The wheels sank immediately and intractably into the blanket of white, Locke standing behind, his face beetroot with rage.

'Oh dear,' said the Prince, going back inside. 'I do wonder what you will do now.'

Locke may not have had much experience on land, but he had a knowledge of moving cannons about deck under fire. He sent for a carpenter, some wood, sand, buckets, and for six hundred feet of rope. Within an hour, a figure eight had been arranged around the garden using sturdy wooden planks. Before the boards were laid down, the snow beneath them had been carefully scooped up in the buckets, the frozen ground sprinkled with sand, and the snow laid back on top, concealing the path from view. All around the circuit, braziers had been positioned, each one with an attendant of its own.

By two o'clock, when the Prince's circle arrived, the animals were all in position on the boards. The picnic had been laid out on a pair of low platforms in the circular loops of the figure eight. Unfazed by the request, the great Carême had taken the order in his stride. It consisted of a culinary extravaganza. There was *potage de pigeons à la marinière* and *turbot avec sauce aux crevettes*, *darne de saumon au beurre de Montpellier*, *oeufs brouillés aux truffes* and even a galleon impeccably fashioned from ice, in which was placed fresh fruit.

As soon as the guests were heard making their way through the pink salon, Locke blew a whistle and the footmen began pushing the creatures, great and small, over the boards.

By the time the Prince stepped out into the verandah, his mistress, the Marchioness of Hertford, was moaning about the cold. The Regent surveyed the scene manufactured from his imagination. He sniffed, and touched one nostril with a lace handkerchief.

'Hastings,' he said deliberately, 'What *are* you thinking?! It's far too cold outside. We shall dine indoors, upstairs in the circular dining room.'

Stiffening his neck, the equerry took a deep breath of freezing air, and replied,

'Very Good, Your Highness.'

THREE

AT SIX THAT evening, Frederick Johnson descended from the small second floor office at number one hundred and seventy Piccadilly, the so-called Egyptian Hall. He had been in the employ of its owner, William Bullock, for eleven years and nine months, and had spent most of that time searching for curiosities suitable for exhibition.

An employer with a sharp eye for sensation, Bullock was a man who had risen from the gutters of the East End, and now enjoyed a position of some social prominence. From the first moment he had met Frederick Johnson, Bullock knew he would serve him well. Mild-mannered, with a hint of a Welsh inflection in his voice, Johnson had a reserve that some found disconcerting. But the master showman appreciated it greatly. For nothing caught his ire more than a man with too much to say.

The Egyptian Hall had gained a reputation across England and beyond. Its façade was adorned with hieroglyphic friezes, pharaonic columns, and a pair of exquisite statues fashioned in Coade stone — one of Isis, and the other of Osiris.

Lined with cabinets and displays, the interior contained more than fifteen thousand items of curiosity, from a 'living' skeleton to a splinter from the true Cross, and a scaled-down model of the Egyptian Sphinx. Yet there was no object that had ever attracted as much attention as the one now standing in the entrance of the hall.

Fred Johnson came down the stairs one at a time. An injury in childhood had left him with an impediment in walking. Although his father had hired the best surgeon he could afford, nothing could correct the limp which had caused Johnson to be known as Limpet by his friends.

For weeks, Mr. Bullock had bragged at how the entire civilised world would venture to his Egyptian Hall to set eyes on the most celebrated trophy of the Peninsular Campaigns. And now it stood right before them in the central hall, ready to be unveiled — Napoleon's bullet-proof field carriage.

As he limped over to the dark-blue carriage, Johnson found his eyes welling with tears again, as they had done so many times in the previous week. The Thursday before, his beloved daughter, Catherine, had been found dead upstairs in her room. A doctor had been called but nothing could be done to revive her. A full examination of the body had been made, which found nothing, but an odd blotch in the middle of her chest, the shape of a pear.

Wiping away the tears, Johnson blew his nose, and checked the carriage was ready for the public. They would be arriving any moment. His wife had begged him to take a few days off, but he knew that Mr. Bullock needed him more than ever, now that the carriage was finally in situ at the Egyptian Hall.

And, in any case, working took his mind off the loss.

FOUR

SIMON COCHRAN WAS not much interested in the Peninsular War. His flat feet had kept him out of the services, his flat feet that is and his contempt for weaponry.

For as long as he could remember, he had detested the idea of armed combat. While other children were playing with bows, arrows, and home-made swords, Cochran had been down at the river-bank drawing patterns in the mud.

So when his childhood friend, George Byron, had invited him to Bullock's Hall for the unveiling of the trophy, Cochran had been indifferent. He had paced up and down his bedroom for an hour, tutt-tutting while brushing his hair.

In the cramped sitting room Adams was still sleeping on the hard sofa. He was woken by footsteps.

'Are you all right, Simon?'

'He's a caricature of pomposity,' snapped Cochran. 'An egotistical blight on the face of decent society!'

'Who is?'

'George Byron of course.'

'But I thought you were close friends.'

'We were, as children at least. It wasn't friendship though, so much as a pretence — a great ludicrous pretence.'

Cochran strode over to the salon window and, using all his

strength, he whipped it open wide.

'What are you doing? It's freezing out there!' said Adams, furling himself in his blanket.

'Feel it, Mr. Adams! Feel it in your bones!'

'What?'

'The cold… the damned cold.'

'Believe me, I do feel it!'

'Breathe in that stinking city air! Fill your lungs with it, Mr. Adams, and you shall grasp the depraved wretchedness of Byron!'

Cochran hurled the hairbrush at the door. The ivory handle snapped in two, but he didn't care. He sat down and put his head in his hands.

'They taunted me,' he said, the tone of his voice calmed. 'They all did. Byron led them. They used to say that I was a coward because I would not take up the sword, because I would not duel with them. But they never knew why.'

Adams crossed the salon and touched a hand to his friend's shoulder.

'Why wouldn't you fight with them?'

Cochran pulled his hands away from his face. His fingers were wet with tears.

'I wouldn't fight them,' he said, 'I wouldn't fight them because…

because of my father.'

'Did he forbid it?'

'No, no. He was a champion of conflict. He loved war, he adored everything about it.'

Simon Cochran raised his head and stared into the American's eyes.

'My father lost his life in a duel with a gentleman,' he said, 'a futile and pointless combat.'

'When?'

'On Christmas morning when I was eight years old. It was on the hill outside our family home at Rye. My father left the house at dawn, his servant attending him. I knew what was happening because they had taken the box of flintlock duelling pistols from the library cabinet. I watched them from a distance, my stomach filled with bile. The silhouettes of two adult men standing back-to-back, marching ten paces, and firing. The man on the right fell onto the grass, his servant huddled over. I ran towards the hill, screaming. I knew it was my father.'

'How did you know?'

'Because I saw his soul leave his body. I swear it. A spray of vapour and it was gone.'

Adams stepped over to the window, and eased it shut.

'What were they fighting for?' he asked.

'Lord Fallock, the man with whom my father was duelling, had apparently disputed my familial right to hunt on the Beaufort Estate.'

'That's ridiculous.'

Cochran's eyes seemed to glaze over.

'It is honour,' he said slowly.

FIVE

AT EIGHT O'CLOCK the doors to the Egyptian Hall were swung open wide. Frederick Johnson stood to attention to the right of the entrance, inspecting tickets and drawing the visitors' attention to the steps that led up to the galleries.

A red carpet had been laid out from Piccadilly, through the doors, up the steps, and in to where the carriage of the former emperor was standing beneath a voluminous red sheet. At the far end of the carpet, beside the veiled carriage, stood William Bullock like a prize-fighter before a successful championship bout.

His back was straight, his smile that of a showman about to perform. He was wearing a costume that had been specially tailored on the south side of Savile Row. It consisted of a charcoal-grey frock coat, with an ermine waistcoat beneath, and cavalry trousers, so starched that they looked more like board than cloth. On his head was a hat of his own design, flat at the sides, and rounded on top.

As the guests charged in, Bullock did the arithmetic. For every visitor, he was a shilling richer. Congratulating himself, he watched as the public lapped around Napoleon's field carriage. And congratulations were in order, for he had pulled off the coup of the century.

Byron was one of the first visitors to arrive. Mr. Bullock's gallery of curiosities was just across from his rooms at the Albany. A frequent visitor even before the arrival of the carriage, Byron found inspiration in the objects collected by William Bullock. His favourite was the splinter from the Cross. The relic had been acquired from a bishop up north who had fallen on hard times, and had cost Bullock the grand sum of six guineas. Rumour had it the wood had been hacked from the pews in Durham Cathedral, but Byron didn't care. To him it was a symbol, a fragment of sheer romance.

By nine o'clock, more than four hundred and fifty members of the public had parted with a shilling each, and were milling about, waiting for the blood-red sheet to be drawn back. Cochran led Adams up the stairs a moment after nine. They were the last men in, before Fred Johnson heaved the pharaonic doors shut.

The great hall fell silent.

Bullock announced that Lord Byron was going to unveil the trophy, quite fitting, as his *Ode to Napoleon Buonaparte* had been published the year before. The poet's immense popularity ensured a mob even if the carriage itself failed to draw in the crowds. Pushing forward through the hordes, Adams and Cochran made their way to the front.

After a short preamble, Bullock introduced Byron, the one man who needed no introduction at all. Thanking the audience, Byron congratulated Wellington on his victory, condemned Napoleon, and gave a word of publicity about his new publication.

Then, stepping back, he clapped his hands so softly that they made no sound at all. Fortunately, Bullock's porters had caught the signal. They lugged back the shroud and the carriage, polished like a shiny new button, was revealed.

Surging forward, the crowd inspected the modern conveniences of which they had all read. For weeks, the papers had told of how the carriage could be converted into a bedroom, a bathroom, or even a dining room, and how the panels were bullet-proofed in steel.

With no interest in the carriage, Cochran stepped up to greet his childhood friend.

'Simon, you really must attend to your neck-cloth,' said Byron, 'for the fashion has changed, don't you know?'

Cochran didn't rise to the bait. Instead, he motioned a hand to his left.

'Would you permit me to introduce you to Mr. Adams?'

Byron dipped his head in a bow.

'A pleasure, sir.'

'Mr. Adams is the gentleman who suffered greatly on the African plains, and visited the metropolis of Timbuctoo.'

'Timbuctoo? Ah, the American, yes I have heard tell of your claims.'

'My claims?'

'That those eyes of yours have witnessed the jewel of jewels.'

Robert Adams almost bristled at the English deprecation.

'Believe me, Timbuctoo is anything but a jewel,' he said.

An elderly woman stepped up, applauded Byron on his latest work, and was washed away into the crowd.

'But you are enjoying the attention nonetheless, I am sure.'

Adams might have felt irritated by the poet, but he wasn't. Rather, he pitied him.

'I enjoy the attention as much as a caged bird enjoys singing to a fool,' he said.

'Pray tell me little bird,' replied Byron, stiffening his neck, 'where would you fly if your cage were opened?'

'To my home,' said Adams, 'another world away.'

SIX

NEXT DAY, WITH the library more crowded than ever before, Cochran gave the signal for the narration to continue.

Rising once again, Robert Adams began without delay:

'Our dismal caravan departed Timbuctoo, and pushed north into the vast desert of the Zahara. We were like a parade of ants marching with purpose over a field of sand. As I trudged forward in chains, I made an oath that if I were ever able, I would return to the desert city and serve King Woolo with his due. But then, as I pondered it, my flayed bare feet tramping over sand, the Lord is the ultimate scale of justice. He sees every deed and misdeed, and it is He who metes out judgement when the right time has come.

'So we walked, and we walked, and we walked — the first horizon followed by fifty more. The manacles on my wrists and ankles cut deep into the flesh, and the lacerations turned to sores. When I shouted out in pain, the Moorish commander howled with laughter, and offered to remove my hands and feet to relieve my discomfort.

'Leaving the agreeable lodgings of Timbuctoo took a toll on both Sanchez and me. We had grown used to sleeping on smooth mattresses, and to eating as much as our stomachs could take. In a way I was content though, however severe the curse of crossing that emptiness. For I knew that the only way of returning to Christina was by placing one foot squarely in front of the last. Sitting in the court of that despot there was but one assurance — of never setting eyes again on my wife.

'Sanchez did not share my contentment. From the moment we embarked from the mud city, his spirits became forlorn. He wept for three horizons, and was flogged for his trouble by the Moors. One night, as we lay there, watching the stars and waiting for sleep, he whispered that he would escape, and retrace his steps to Timbuctoo.

'"You will be hunted," I said. "And they will catch you. After all, how can you run with those shackles?"

'"One minute of freedom is equal to a lifetime of custody," he replied.

'"We must stay with the caravan until the desert sands subside a little," I said. "Flee now, and death is the only certainty. We must take our time and choose the moment well."

'I fell asleep gazing up at the stars. Then, suddenly, I awoke. It was the middle of the night and a great commotion had ensued. The Moors leapt to their feet, greatly enraged.

'A group of them lit fiery torches, mounted their camels, and charged into the night. I sat up to ask Sanchez what was happening.

'But he was gone.

'At dawn, the Moors returned. They climbed down from their camels and, in turn, strode over to where I was crouching. In his hand the commander clutched the grimmest trophy — Sanchez's bloodied head.

'He threw it at me.

'I held it, weeping. As I did so, the other soldiers tossed down trophies of their own — two feet and a pair of hands. I wondered how long Sanchez had lived as the Moors hacked him to pieces. But it did not matter now, for he had succeeded in escaping.

'Before the caravan moved on, I struggled to bury Sanchez's remains in the sand. As I dug ferociously with my hands, I could feel my departed friend gazing down at me. Dressed in white, unblemished by scars and blood, he was at peace. I admit it, that I contemplated running like he had done, in a bid for freedom. But something inside me stirred, and I chastised myself at contemplating what amounted to suicide.

'So we marched on, the Moors riding their camels, and I lumbering over the desert. In some places the sand was baked hard like terracotta, and in others it was rolling loose, interspersed with immense dunes.

'The Moors who had been kept prisoner in Timbuctoo were severely weakened. Their ribs were poking through their chests, their faces gaunt and their stomachs distended from starvation. The night after Sanchez had left us, one of them fell down dead. He didn't make a sound, for his body was almost weightless.

'The day after that, another two succumbed. The commander

looked back, but did not give the order to stop. He was a vindictive man, who regarded Christians as vermin. Yet as a leader he was skilled. If the caravan had paused for a single moment, we would not have reached the dank waterhole that night, and the lives of the camels would have been put in danger.

'As it was, the largest of the she-camels fell to her knees in the afternoon heat. I looked round at the other beasts and, when I turned back, she was dead. I suppose her heart had simply given in. Without wasting any time at all, the Moors drained her paunch, skinned her, and cut out the meat.

'The commander fed the choicest morsels to the men who had been starved. Some of the bones were wrapped up, along with the flesh, and packed on other camels.

'We marched for another week or more. The camel meat was rationed, although I was given only the bones. I cracked them open, sucked at the marrow, and felt much the better for it.

'Another day or two passed and the meat ran out.

'Then two of the Moors became deranged. They ran off into the desert, howling like dogs. Although agitated, the commander chose not to save them. It seemed as if we were in the driest expanse of the great Zahara, and that survival depended on the disciplined march. I considered breaking free, doing as the Moors had done. But alone there would have been no chance of survival at all.

'Each day the commander forced more from the group. There were twenty of us now. He would start a little earlier, breaking only for Musalman prayers, and for half a mouthful of precious water every few hours.

'Then, one evening, we lay down to sleep. I was dreaming of my childhood, splashing in the river, bathing in its waterfalls. Suddenly, I was woken by a wind of astonishing force.

'It ripped over the surface of the desert, howling like Death itself. Fumbling frantically, the Moors tethered their animals and piled their bundles together. The night was moonless, but I didn't need light to sense the terrible fear.

'It was as if the world were about to end.

'An hour after first hearing the wind, it arrived — blinding, choking, suffocating man and beast. With no clothing to protect me, the skin was chafed from my back, and the hair ripped from my head. Three of the camels were buried alive, as were the men who were holding them down. The wind raged the entire night, grinding away. Pushing my face into the belly of a male camel, I prayed he would not be buried.

'By noon the following day the wind had dropped and the commander took stock of the situation. Four camels had been lost together with five men. A pair of valuable water skins had vanished, too, and a second pair were torn. Without sparing a moment, our leader gave the order to march.

'After a mile or so of walking we reached dunes again. There was no alternative but to surmount them. With the camels groaning, we ascended, and found ourselves at a vantage point, gazing down at a sight from the infernos of Hell.

'On the plain below lay the remains of an immense caravan, a caravan of death — a thousand camel skeletons, and at least twice as many men. They had been buried alive long ago, suffocated, unearthed by the sandstorm. It seemed they were destined for the Musalman city of Mecca, many months to the east.

'We tiptoed past the contorted faces and the torn, twisted skeletons. I tried not to look but, gripped by lewd fascination, I could not help myself from scanning the desiccated, tortured expressions, skin dried taut over bones.

'As I gazed at them, each one a story of grim submission, I could only wonder whether we were destined for the same horrible fate.'

SEVEN

THE SOUND OF Lilly Small's screams had kept the whole of Bedlam awake. A week before, the young mother had lost her infant son, Joshua, to tuberculosis. The little boy had choked for much of the night then, to her satisfaction, had fallen into a deep sleep as she sang to him. The next morning she pushed the curtains open, leant over the crib, and touched her fingers tenderly to his cheek. She had known instantly. It was a mother's intuition.

The shock was so great she had fainted, and that was where her sister, Caroline, found her a little later. When Lilly was roused, she felt a great pain in the back of her head. Her eyes were open, but she could not see a thing.

She had gone blind.

So she screamed and she screamed, in grief and in rage, and nothing could quell her screams, not even a night and a day spent kneeling in church. Joshua was baptised and buried, and still Lilly screamed.

Her sister took her to Bedlam in the hope that the doctors might calm the anguish. Still in her nightdress, she was brought in tied to an oak post. For, in her sightless state, she had taken to tearing out her hair, and gnawing at her arms.

The cell beside Emily had been empty for three weeks, since its inmate had hanged herself with a strip of cloth torn from the mattress. A pair of orderlies bustled Lilly in, still tied to the post, still screaming.

When night came, she was trussed to the bed on the orders of the director, a dark overbearing man named Leach.

'Cease your ululations, Madam!' he cried, 'or feel the lick of my displeasure!'

At first, Lilly had taken no notice of the director. Then, when he came within striking range, she spat at him, hitting his right eye, screaming all the while. Mr. Leach called for his preferred cane, a supple strand of willow, one he reserved for special sessions of discipline. Flexing its shaft in his hand, he struck Lilly Small across the back and buttocks until her nightdress was drenched in blood.

EIGHT

THE MORNING AFTER the unveiling of the emperor's carriage, Viscount Fortescue climbed into his own carriage and ordered Dunn to drive him east, through the city and across London Bridge.

The air was cold but a little clearer than on previous days, the coal fog lifted, with no wind at all. At breakfast, Fortescue had told Clara that he was going to read at Brooks's, but he had different intentions.

It was eleven o'clock by the time his carriage rolled up outside the gates of Bethlem Royal Hospital. The wheels came to a halt, and the Viscount climbed down even before the coachman was ready for him.

He was met at the door by Mr. Leach.

'As I said in my message, Viscount, we would be agreeable in assisting you in any way we can,' the director said unctuously.

'Thank you, sir. I am sensible of your attention.'

'I believe the woman you are concerned with is residing in the east wing. I shall have her brought out at once.'

Fortescue thanked Mr. Leach again, followed him into the sanatorium, and waited in the meeting room. He went over to the long windows and stared out at the courtyard, where a group of female patients were being exercised in the cold.

Leach reappeared.

'She will be ready in a moment,' he said.

'Very good.'

The director noticed Fortescue's interest in the women outside.

'I am a believer in the physical,' he said. 'A little frigid air does wonders in purging.'

'Are the patients not frozen to the bone?'

'We like to refer to them as misfortunates, Viscount,' he said sternly. 'They may be cold, but the purging warms them, brings colour to their cheeks. I assure you that we give those in our tender care only the most compassionate attention.'

Just then Emily Watts was brought in.

'Here is the misfortunate you asked to see,' said Leach.

An orderly led her over to a chair, positioned in the shadows away from the window. Her expression was distant, her long grey hair combed straight back.

Leach introduced her to Fortescue.

'I will leave you now,' he said.

The Viscount sat down opposite Emily, perching uneasily on the bare wooden chair. His backside was more used to upholstery.

'Madam,' he said, in a gentle voice, 'I have come here because your situation has been brought to my attention.'

Emily looked up, but she did not speak.

'I believe that you are acquainted intimately with a certain respected gentleman. His name is Sir Geoffrey Caldecott.'

At the name, Emily's eyes lit up a little.

'Geoffrey,' she said.

'You know him?'

'Yes, yes. Of course. We are…'

Emily paused, turned to look round at the orderly who was helping another misfortunate to her cell.

'He is my…'

'*Your*?'

'My husband,' she said.

Viscount Fortescue held up a hand at right angles.

'Excuse me,' he said once, before repeating it a second time. 'Can you tell me why you are here?'

'Because of my attacks,' she said. 'Geoffrey said I was taken with them in the night, especially when the moon was a quarter full. He insisted I could not reside in decent society, that I would have to live here.'

'Does he ever visit you?'

'Once each year, on Christmas morning.'

Thanking Emily warmly, Fortescue rose to his feet, and left the meeting room. His carriage was soon racing through the streets of London for a rendez-vous with Sir Joseph Banks. In the back, the Viscount pulled on his gloves and stared out at the snow. His mind was on Emily Watts, and on the barred windows that kept her from the life she had once known.

NINE

LADY PENELOPE DEVONSHIRE had invited her sister and three close friends to luncheon at her residence in Bedford Square. The house had been designed by Nicholas Hawksmoor as a home for his mistress, Matilda, and was made all the more appealing by the floral motif incised into the façade.

Officially, Lady Penelope was still in mourning after the loss of her husband, Sir Charles Devonshire, whom she had met as a debutante twelve years before. He had been shot in the abdomen at Waterloo, and had died from blood loss while a surgeon was doing his level best to extricate the musket ball from his stomach. Even when wounded, Sir Charles was strong as an ox. With no opium available to dull the pain, it had taken six men to hold him down.

A decade married to Sir Charles, a man interested in nothing but hunting, butchery, and war, was a life of terrible boredom, a life from which Lady Penelope had been instantly freed on the morning of Waterloo. The couple had spent much of their married lives apart, Sir Charles up in the Highlands bagging trophies for the walls, and Lady Penelope at home in London or at their country estate in Gloucestershire, playing whist with her lady friends.

At luncheon, the conversation had soon turned to Robert Adams and the narration, which each of the ladies present made certain they attended. Lady Penelope breathed in with force, while straining to appear modest, a quality that had never come easily.

'If I were not in mourning,' she said all of a sudden, 'I would lure him here, pack the servants off to their rooms, and would shower him with my every attention.'

'Pennie dearest, really, how can you speak so?' demanded Lady Dartford, blushing.

'I give voice to your own fantasy,' Penelope replied.

'It's a fantasy common to half of London,' added Harriet Bowes. 'After all, Mr. Adams' rugged appeal has attracted not only us ladies.'

'My goodness, are you sure?'

'Just see how those foppish boys parade in and out, quizzing him with their *lorgnettes*.'

Lady Dartford touched her napkin to the corner of her mouth and waited for the right moment.

'Perhaps,' she said quietly, 'it is Mr. Adams who prefers the company of his own.'

The other women paused and broke out in a fit of giggling.

'How can *you* speak so?' said Lady Penelope, gasping.

'Well regard him. He's always with that Mr. Cochran, the Committee's secretary. They are joined at the hip it seems. And whenever one of us even looks at him, he runs for his life, babbling about the love he left in America.'

'Her name is Christina,' said Harriet.

'I declare she is a *he*, a young man by the name of Christian!'

TEN

IN HIS CHAMBERS on Fleet Street, Cochran was worrying about his debts. A letter had come from the law courts ordering him to pay up at once or be cast into the squalid depths of the debtors' prison at Marshalsea.

'Surely your family could lend you the money to pay,' said Adams.

'I could never tell them of it,' Cochran replied. 'It would be dishonourable. My mother has struggled terribly since the death of my father. She received so many proposals of marriage but turned them all down.'

'Then what about Fortescue, can he not help you?'

'Indeed, he is wealthy, extremely so, but I could never let him know of this predicament.'

'What if *I* told him?'

'No, no!' said Cochran, standing up, 'that would not do, it would not do at all. I shall find a solution.'

There was silence for a moment. Then Adams stood.

'Do you really think the Committee will get their man to Timbuctoo,' he asked, 'bring back a fabulous treasure, and hand it out to anyone who ever had faith in them?'

'There is a hope.'

Adams looked at Cochran in disbelief.

'What are you saying? Your own hand has written my description of that worthless city. Are you suggesting you don't believe me?'

'I no longer know whom to believe.'

An hour later, both men were sitting in the library in awkward silence. Neither had said a word on the way from Fleet Street to Old Jewry. Sir Geoffrey came down from his study, greeted a handful of the gentry, who were pushing in through the open doors.

He peered over at Adams caustically.

Clara Fortescue entered with Lady Caroline Lamb and her cousin, Bertie. They took their usual seats beside Lady Devonshire and her circle, and waited for Adams to stand. For each of them, half the attraction was staring at the American, watching as he relived the emotion of his turbulent journey. They had all fantasised about it, dreaming of him gazing up at the African mural, and then down onto the rows of women who hung on his every word.

When the library had reached capacity, Cochran gave the signal, dipped his quill, and waited.

The American got to his feet and looked out at the sea of gentry.

'Ladies and gentlemen,' he said in a low, dominant tone, 'before I continue with my narration, I should like to make an announcement.'

The women at the back moved restlessly on their seats, and Sir Geoffrey glanced at the row of Committee directors and then at Robert Adams.

'I stand before you a humble sailor, an American sailor, who is consumed with a single ambition. It is to return home as soon as possible to the life which became separated from me. I do not ask that you believe anything I say, nor do I ask that you regard me or my story with pity. But I do have one request. I request that you strip off your fancy costumes, if only in your minds, and put yourselves in my place. To judge me you must feel as my senses have done, and taste the desert on your tongues.'

Sir Geoffrey shot to his feet.

'Mr. Adams, the Committee would appreciate it if you would curb your theatrical presentation,' he barked, 'and continue at once with the narration.'

'Very well,' Adams replied, holding short until Cochran had dipped his quill a second time.

'As I have recounted, a sandstorm raged, exposing an immense caravan of death. We skirted around it for much of the next day. It became clear to me that when they perished, all supplies of water had run dry. Every man in that dismal procession had been searching for the same thing — a waterhole that all believed to be near.

'And it was.

'We came to it about a mile to the north of the last skeleton. It had been covered with stones, brought there for the purpose, but the sands and the wind had hidden it from view. It was our camels who sensed it. As we neared it, they went down on their haunches and refused to rise. The commander jumped onto the sand and ordered his men to search for a sign. To me it seemed like lunacy. For there were dunes all around, and not a drop of moisture.

'We inched forward, the camels groaning like I had never heard them groan. Then, all of a sudden, one of the beasts pressed its nose in the sand. He could smell water. The Moors dug, and they dug, and they found stones. Whooping in delight, they pulled away the cover and fought each other to be the first to drink.

'But the exhilaration quickly turned to despair.

'The Moors began to weep. They fell on the sand, ripped off their turbans and pulled out their hair.

'The waterhole was dry.'

ELEVEN

HARRY THORNLY HAD worked for fifteen years as the porter of number ten Duke Street, an elegant building in St. James's. He prided himself on his ability in remembering the names and faces of every gentleman who stepped across the threshold. If he were ever offered a tip, as he occasionally was, he would politely decline. For Harry nothing was so important as a man's principles.

Every so often he was asked while out drinking where he was employed. He would reply that he worked for a group of gentlemen engaged in the shipping business.

Sometimes Harry helped the gentlemen up the stairs with heavy suitcases. The luggage was always the same size and shape, crafted from well-tanned ox-hide, the seams double-stitched. The instruction never altered: 'Take it to the third floor, and leave it at the door.'

On the morning he had arrived for the position in January 1801, it had been explained to Harry in a severe manner that the business chamber itself was absolutely private. No visitor, however well dressed or important, was permitted to enter, and that went for Harry himself.

Most of the time the building was empty. The partners explained this by saying their work took them to government offices, and for meetings at the coffee houses down on the Strand.

But each Friday afternoon, at precisely five-fifteen, four of the business partners would arrive. Always impeccably dressed in jet-black frock coats and well-starched cravats, they would wish Harry a good day and hurry upstairs.

Sometimes they brought the heavy cases with them, and sometimes they did not. But as soon as they crossed the threshold, they always removed their boots. Harry often wondered why they would do such a thing, but he was too well-mannered to ask.

Ten minutes after the first partners had arrived, another six came in and, after them, another five. They would stay until about ten o'clock, and would leave separately, almost as if they did not want to be seen in the same company. It was unknown for any of the gentlemen to miss a meeting, even when the weather was stormy as it had been of late.

On Friday mornings Harry would spend a little extra time

polishing his shoes, and shining the brass buttons on the coat he had worn since the day he had begun work at number ten. The partners appeared to appreciate his cleanliness. They rarely commented on it, yet he had a sense that it was noticed all the same.

At five forty-five p.m., a gentleman arrived at the front door. Harry had not seen him before. He was taller than average and his coat was cut at odds with the fashion, a little loose on the shoulders, and a little tight at the hip. On his feet he was wearing a pair of slim lacquered shoes.

'Can I assist you, sir?' he asked.

'I should like to know if this is Alta Templis,' the gentleman replied.

'*Alta Templis?*'

'Yes, Alta Templis.'

Harry shook his head.

'No, sir,' he said. 'It is a company of gentlemen engaged in the shipping business.'

'Are you certain of this?'

'Yes, sir, I am most certain.'

Giving thanks, the gentleman stepped out into the street. When he was gone, Harry stood inside the door and found himself a little worried. No one had ever arrived unannounced before, nor ever asked about the activity that went on inside number ten.

He wondered whether he ought to inform the gentlemen who employed him, but eventually dismissed the thought, assuming the visitor had mistaken the building innocently for another.

TWELVE

THE PRINCE REGENT was sitting for Lawrence in the rose satin room. Filled with the scent of pink lilies, grown under glass in Barnes, the flowers were brought each morning by special delivery. After the first three sessions, the Prince had sent the artist away to fetch another, much larger, canvas so that a selection of his animal Collection could be featured in the background.

He had changed his uniform twice as well, and had finally ordered a new one to be created overnight by Gieves and Hawkes of Savile Row, a firm until then warranted only as velvet cap makers to royalty. The new costume was similar to the previous Field Marshal's uniform, but had grander epaulettes, and was cut a little tighter at the waist.

Lawrence, who was quite accustomed to the Regent's indecisive nature, had returned unfazed, his assistants struggling under the weight of an enormous canvas. It measured eight feet by nine, and was quite large enough to accommodate the entire flock of creatures assembled behind the sitter.

The artist was mixing a dab of cream-coloured paint, when

Alvanley entered.

'There you are,' said the Prince. 'Tell me, how do you think Lawrence is capturing his subject? I am his subject and he is mine!' The Regent let out a giggle, and covered his mouth with a row of distended fingers.

Experience had taught Lord Alvanley that the worst thing one could do was to give any opinion whatsoever. Any critique whether good or bad was always held to account at a later date. So, he crossed the room, stood behind Lawrence for a minute, nodding energetically.

'Yes, oh, yes,' he said.

'How does it look?'

'Very, um, oh, yes, really quite…'

The Regent furrowed his brow.

'It's not good, is it?' he snapped.

'No, no, Your Highness, it's good.'

'Very good?'

'Yes, oh yes, it's considerably pleasing to the eye.'

The Prince was tiring of Alvanley's obsequiousness. He clapped his hands, abandoned his pose, and turned to examine the animals.

'This will not do!' he said loudly. 'It won't do at all.'

Lawrence leaned forward, waiting to hear the reason for royal displeasure.

'We need something big behind, Lawrence.'

'A palace, Sir?'

'No!'

'A mountain, perhaps?'

'Not a mountain, nor a palace. No, I think something with life about it.'

'Well, Your Highness, I had the pleasure of capturing the giraffe and the great elephant.'

'Good, good. They fill the background well. But we require another creature, large but different.'

Lawrence put down his brush.

'*Different*, Your Highness?'

'Indeed, different.' The Prince Regent clapped his hands again. 'Hastings!' he yelled. 'Where is that damn fool of a man?'

The equerry's name echoed down the long corridors of Carlton House, and was followed by the sound of leather soles running fast over marble.

Hastings was suddenly at the door. He was sweating from the sprint. Straightening his back, he snapped his heels together and dipped his head.

'Your Highness?'

'There you are, at last,' said the Prince. 'Now, Hastings, go down to the Tower and get me an animal for the portrait. Something large and not gloomy like the damned elephant. Something with stripes. Go on, man. What are you waiting for? Jump to it!'

THIRTEEN

EACH EVENING JUST before climbing into bed, Clara knelt before the cross on her wall, and she prayed. She prayed that her father would live a long and happy life, and that her mother's soul would watch over them both. Through years, the nightly ritual had remained unaltered. But now, as Clara knelt, she had a third request.

Her eyes tightly closed, hands clasped together at her chin, she prayed the raw American might fall in love with her as she had done with him.

As ever, her dreams were filled with scenes from the romantic novels she so adored. But the leading man was no longer a conceited aristocrat from the Shires, but a burly straight-speaking American, named Robert Adams. She would imagine him recounting adventures in distant lands, making little of the dangers he had faced.

Sometimes, he would hold her hand in his, feeling the warmth of his fingers on hers. She would glance down, touch her left hand to his heart, and whisper that she loved him.

As dawn melted the fantasies, Clara lay in bed thinking of him. She could imagine him perfectly, lying beside her, his blond hair tangled, his face nuzzled into the goose-down pillows. She would watch him, plan out their lives together, laugh with him, kiss him.

Then she would get out of bed and, like a burst soap bubble, the dream would be gone. Clara would wash and dress, prepare for breakfast with her father, and find herself back in the prison of convention that was her life. It was as though in the waking moments she was dead, the lifeblood sucked from her veins. The only freedom came when she met her friend and confidante, Lady Caroline.

On most occasions it was not deemed proper for the two women to be seen out alone, even though Lady Caroline was well known in society. The only place they could meet discreetly was at Lackington's in Finsbury Square and, even then, Clara required an excuse. Caroline Lamb's tempestuous affair with the younger Lord Byron had been so ill-reported that the majority of London regarded her as a disgrace.

A man of liberal views, even Viscount Fortescue had raised an eyebrow at the thought of his daughter fraternising with Lady Caroline.

Slipping into his thickest winter coat, he announced that a matter of a detective nature was taking him to St. James's. As soon as he was out of the house, Clara hurried upstairs, changed a dress, and asked Dalston to fetch her favourite winter coat.

'I am going to Lackington's to find a particular book,' she said.

The book was Walpole's *Castle of Otranto*, widely regarded as the forerunner of the Gothic novel. Clara was quite certain that her father's collection was lacking the volume, and equally sure that the great bookseller would be unable to locate a copy on account of its tiresome prose. Lackington's Temple of the Muses was after all famed for stocking only volumes of a readable nature.

An extensive search would give Clara time to chat to Lady Caroline on the uppermost level, where members of the gentry rarely ventured.

On receiving her message, Caroline had rushed to the bookshop. She lived nearby, and both women arrived at the same time.

'Whatever is the matter, my dearest?' said Caroline as they entered.

Clara looked at the ground and, as she did so, a tear rolled down her cheek.

'I love him,' she whispered.

A few minutes later, the two women were sitting on a bench on the third level, where the penny-books were sold in barrels. No one valuing their reputation would have been seen there, making it the perfect spot for privacy from the upper classes.

Pressing a hand to her bonnet, Clara made sure it had not slipped on the steep ascent. Her expression was wan, her eyes dull.

'Have you been weeping much?' asked Lady Caroline in a

concerned tone.

Clara nodded.

'Never before have I given in to temptation,' she said very slowly. 'You know how I am, for you are my dearest friend. My fantasies remain locked away, hidden from all view. But now I find them spilling over into this, the real world.'

'Dearest Clara,' Caroline whispered, 'you know as well as I that Mr. Adams is spoken for, that the prospect of his wife enabled him to endure the most diabolic torment.'

'I know, I know,' Clara replied, nudging a lace handkerchief to her nostril. 'But for the first time in my life I am yearning for this...'

'For what?'

'For passion... raw, wild, unbridled, unspoken passion — the variety which *you* have known.'

Lady Caroline lifted her hand and smoothed a crease from her dress.

'The uproar of lust and the frenzy of passion,' she said pensively, 'are emotions ruled by the heart and not by the mind.'

'*Yes*! And it's my heart that is bleeding. Can you not sense it? Can you not see it in my eyes?'

Caroline dipped her head in a nod.

'It is clear as day, for all to see,' she said.

FOURTEEN

SIR GEOFFREY CALDECOTT took a pinch of macouba and followed it with a glass of Madeira. He had chilled the bottle out on the window ledge overnight, and took great satisfaction in the fact that there was a touch of frost on the sides. Sipping the drink, he leaned back in his favourite chair. It had just been returned by the upholsterer in cloisonné-blue silk.

William DeWitt knocked, then entered.

'The narration will recommence in thirty minutes,' he said.

'Bloody Cochran,' grunted Sir Geoffrey quickly. 'Go and tell Falkirk to fetch Jenkins. We have no choice but to avail ourselves of his services. No choice at all.'

DeWitt went back to the door. As his fingers touched the brass knob he remembered that Falkirk had given him a letter on the way up, declaring that it had just arrived by private messenger. He pulled the letter from his inside pocket. It was small, smudged with dirt.

'I believe this came for you, Sir Geoffrey,' he said.

Caldecott took the letter and stared at the front of the envelope. It was addressed to him. He broke the seal and scanned the short text. DeWitt said something, but he didn't hear.

'Is it from the expedition, Sir Geoffrey?' said DeWitt a second time. 'Major Peddie...'

'Has he reached the golden city?'

'Major Peddie…'

'Yes?'

'Major Peddie and his entire party have been slaughtered by savages.'

FIFTEEN

HALF AN HOUR later, Adams was standing before the audience in the library once again. He didn't enjoy narrating his tale, or having to endure the inane comments of London society. But then, as he continually reminded himself, every word spoken brought him a little closer to Hudson.

He waited for Cochran's signal.

When it came, he stood up, thanked the audience for their attendance, and began.

'We had reached a dry waterhole,' he said. 'The Moorish Commander wept like a child. Until that moment he had been a man of considerable ability, a tower of strength to his party. But the dry hole destroyed his will to continue. He fell onto the baked ground and tore out his hair, jerking his body back and forth like a madman.

'"We will die now," he said despondently in his tongue. "Our death is certain."

'I spoke up, declaring that we could kill one of the camels, drain its paunch and drink it. The leader abhorred being advised by anyone, especially a Christian.

'"You did not hear me, slave!" he shouted. "Death! He rides with us, his shape forms the shadow of every man."

'There may have been no hope, and I may have been a Christian, but the Commander did as I had suggested. A male camel was slaughtered and its paunch was drained. The foul liquid was poured into the skins, the blood drunk, and the meat packed up. A little time later we moved on, our footsteps far slower than before, as if each man could sense the spectre of Death beside him.

'After three days of marching we spied an encampment.

'The Moors were greatly excited by the sight. Their step quickened and we were soon being welcomed by the leader of the place. He was an old man called Touliq, whose face had been severely burned at one time. The right side of his face was missing its ear, its eye, and part of the nose. When he saw me though, his good eye seemed to light up. Pointing in my direction, he said something to the Commander.

'The two men shook hands, and I found myself the possession of Touliq.

'A week after our arrival, the Moors who had taken me from Timbuctoo departed. None of them, not even the Commander, looked at me or said farewell. As far as they were concerned, I was a chattel, an object without value, especially as we were so far from anyone prepared to pay for my redemption.

'My new master, Touliq, eked out an existence with his family on the margin of the desert. His sheep spent their lives searching the baked earth, hunting for roots or whatever they could find. He had three wives. The older two were haggard and both blind. They had no respect for their husband and regarded each other with contempt. Yet, the person they loathed more than any other on earth was their husband's third wife. She was a girl of about twenty years named Aisha.

'Unlike them, she was agile, soft-skinned and was extremely gentle in the face. When she saw me, she sent her servant to feed me porridge. It was mouth-watering. Each night a bowl would be brought to me, and I lapped it up like a dog that had been starved.

'Two weeks after my arrival there, Aisha asked if I would attend to her small flock of goats, as she feared they might be eaten by wolves. She promised to pay me, and pointed to an empty bowl, indicating that more of the porridge would be served. I watched over the animals willingly, but she did not pay me. I may have been a slave in their eyes, but I felt that I ought to be paid as promised. So, that afternoon, I remonstrated, to which she promised again, declaring that payment would come that very night.

'When my master and his other wives were asleep, Aisha sent her servant to me. I asked her for my bowl of porridge. She said that her mistress would give it to me herself. So I went to her tent. She fed me a large bowl of the food and, when I had finished, she gave me even more.

'I was very content and I thanked her greatly. She smiled, approached me, and pushed the garment off her shoulders. It fell to the floor, leaving her entirely naked. Then she forced herself upon me, declaring that her husband did not satisfy her. I pushed her away, exclaiming stridently that I was spoken for and that, in any case, such a liaison would be a death knell.

'Aisha stood to her feet and she screamed.

'"We will both be killed!" I shouted.

'"Only you will die," she replied.

'An instant passed, then my master, Touliq, arrived at the door of the tent. As soon as his good eye spied me there, he called his sons to catch me. They held me down on the ground and their father came over to execute me. The blade was about to strike my neck, when a voice told him to stop. It was another old man who had been staying with Touliq as a guest.

'Raising his hands in the air, he declared that execution by the blade was too good for me, that it would be death for a man with honour. He promised his friend that, the next day, he would take me into the desert and leave me for the wolves. The sword was thrown to the ground and I was guarded for the remainder of the night, lest I run into the desert alone.'

Hearing a commotion at the back of the library, Adams stopped mid-flow. The audience began mumbling and, as the mumbling grew louder, they stood up, and looked to the door.

Suddenly Cochran gasped, stood up too, and bowed his head.

Adams was unsure what was happening. He looked around and spotted an immensely fat figure looking at him. It was the Prince Regent, who had come from the portrait sitting, and was still wearing his new Field Marshal's uniform. Standing on his right was Lord Alvanley.

'That is the American, Your Highness, the one who claims to have set eyes on Timbuctoo.'

The Prince held up a hand, commanding the audience to be seated.

'Carry on!' he cried out in Cochran's direction. 'You may pretend that I am not here!'

Caldecott charged over and attended to his royal guest, who had taken a seat on a low chair at the back of the room. The doyens of high society were buzzing around the Prince like bees before a hive.

Cochran signalled to Adams to continue.

'At dawn, I was tied to the back of a camel and taken into the desert once again,' he said. 'That beast walked until the sun was high above us. It was so hot that I could smell my naked back roasting.

Touliq had sent his oldest son to make certain his friend kept his promise to execute me.

'I passed out and, when I regained consciousness, the camel had stopped. Its master ordered me to climb down. Touliq's son watched as I was pegged out on the sand. My wrists and ankles were bound so tightly that the blood ceased from flowing. I passed out again. Touliq's son must have then left, because when I came to once more he was not there. But his father's friend was still standing over me.

'He had waited for the boy to leave, then he unfastened the bindings and forced me to follow him. He had never intended to dispatch me, for as I was a Christian slave he knew that, somewhere, there would be a consul ready to pay a ransom for my life.'

Adams finished speaking, and waited for Cochran to catch up with the transcription. At the back of the room, the Prince Regent was struggling to avoid Caldecott's fawning advances.

'Your Highness, it is a pleasure beyond our most distant expectations to have you within our humble company,' said Sir Geoffrey, wincing.

The Prince had only just met the chairman, but was bored to death by him.

'How could I remain isolated from this distinguished gathering?' he asked. 'After all, it is the talk of London.'

'How very kind, Highness.'

'To think of it…' said the Regent, lumbering to his feet, 'that an American has beaten you all to Timbuctoo. How perfectly delicious!'

Caldecott's face turned lilac with ire.

'It is a trifling achievement,' he replied, 'but America is after all a land of scant success.'

'If it be so trifling an achievement, sir, then why have our most celebrated pioneers been eluded by the feat?'

Sir Geoffrey felt his scalp overheating. With gritted teeth, he said:

'Your Highness, it appears that the brawny American constitution is well-suited to the rigours of the African continent.'

'I should like to make the acquaintance of the American,' replied the Prince, walking in the direction of the lectern where Adams was still standing.

'At once, your pre-eminence, at once.'

Caldecott waved a hand to Cochran, scowled, and waved again. A moment later, Adams was face to face with the Regent.

'If Your Royal Highness would permit me to introduce to you the individual in question.'

'Charmed, sir, I am quite charmed,' said the Prince.

'I am pleased to meet you,' replied Adams.

The Regent raised his quizzing glass and inspected the American.

'How were you amused by Africa, Mr. Adams?'

'*Amused*?'

'Indeed, how were you touched by its raw appeal?'

Uncertain how to reply, Adams just smiled.

'Did you see any fauna?'

'Fauna?'

'Any animals?'

'Yes, plenty.'

'Excellent! How did you like them?'

Again, Adams remained silent, unsure of what to say. He cocked his head in a nod.

'Excellent,' said the Prince Regent again, 'then you must come and see my Collection. For I would value your opinion on the new acquisition prowling my African savannah.'

'What creature is it?'

'A polar bear!'

VI

Sir Joseph Banks undergoes a dental operation —The fraternity of Alta Templis convenes at Duke Street — The Prince Regent receives Messrs. Adams and Cochran at Carlton House — Much dental discomfort continues at the Banks residence — Mr. Adams examines the Regent's Collection — Messrs. Adams and Cochran reflect on being invited to Brighton — The corpse of a hanged man is prepared for public dissection — Dr. Philps begins the dissection — The brotherhood of Alta Templis convenes once again — Messrs. Adams and Cochran are attacked — The chairman of the Royal African Committee announces that Mr. Adams is dead — A kangaroo is prepared for taxidermy — An emaciated young man takes to begging outside the pie shop of Mrs. Potts — In the Committee library, Messrs. Adams and Cochran appear, bloodied but alive — Mrs. Potts invites the young man inside; he introduces himself as Mr. Florence — A royal carriage arrives to take Messrs. Adams and Cochran to Brighton — A private messenger presents a letter from Amsterdam at the Royal African Committee — Sir Geoffrey Caldecott reads the letter — Breaking their journey at Tunbridge Wells, Messrs. Adams and Cochran sample the waters of the spa — The arrival at the Brighton Pavilion.

ONE

Sir Joseph Banks had not attended the most recent sessions of the narration on account of a terrible toothache. Over six days and nights the pain had grown increasingly worse until he could stand it no longer. His wife, Lady Felicity, was charged with calling for Mr. Harrowby, a Yorkshireman with a dental practice in Camden Town. Lauded by polite society, Mr. Harrowby was a recognised expert in the art of removing teeth without distress.

He had manufactured a set of levers which he used for this purpose. Their effectiveness was so celebrated, that he used them on all his patients. For, as far as he was concerned, teeth were an impediment best done away with as speedily as possible, and replaced with whalebone dentures.

During his time with Captain Cook, Sir Joseph Banks had developed an understanding for psychotropic flora, and had brought back with him a range of plants used by primitive peoples through the Polynesian archipelago.

Over many years he had managed to cultivate a number of the specimens, and grew them under glass for his own personal use. When exposed to pain of an unbearable nature, he resorted to *Brugmansia arbori*, an hallucinogenic member of the potato family native to the Americas. The plant was identified by its long trumpet-like flowers, which tended to be white, and gave off an eerie perfume after dusk.

Banks had learned to concoct a balm from the flowers, which he applied to the skin on his forehead using a strand of lint. Reclining on his chaise longue, he would find himself slipping into delirium within ten minutes.

After a chorus of angelic voices and rainbow-like colours, he would be entertained with a sensation of growing wings and flying like a bird over the rooftops of London. It was in this state, half-conscious and reeling, that the dentist found the respected botanist.

Francis Harrowby had taken his apprenticeship with his uncle, Samuel Darkin, who was famed in his younger years as a bleeder. Harrowby was a stout man, with a long pointed nose and hands that quivered when he walked.

He asked Banks to open his mouth. There was a delay as the patient's clouded mind processed the request. The lower jaw slowly descended, and Harrowby peered inside.

'Oh, my goodness,' he said, smoothing down his cravat. 'Disposal is required, sir, much disposal.'

Banks faded into unconsciousness for a moment.

'Disposal?' he said dreamily.

'Those wicked teeth,' Harrowby said scathingly, 'we will have to extricate them at once. For they are a clear and palpable encumbrance, the certain cause of your discomfort, sir.'

He asked a servant to fetch a bowl of boiling water, a sponge, a saucer, and a low table. When they had been gathered, he laid out his levers, dipped the sponge in the water, and plunged it into the back of the patient's throat.

As Banks struggled to breathe, the physician set to work with the levers.

A moment later, the entire staff at the mansion were cringing at the sound of pain. Lady Banks, who had not wished to be present for the treatment, believing that a patient had the right to privacy, hurried into the drawing room where the extractions were taking place.

'Doctor!' she cried. 'Is my husband's condition so grave that he need weep like a babe in arms?'

Mr. Harrowby did not reply. He was too preoccupied toiling with his levers, twisting and rotating, as the patient howled. An hour after he had begun his work, the entire bottom set of Banks's teeth were lying in the saucer.

Banks was staring at the ceiling, in shock. His wife was fussing around behind the chair in which he was laid out. She had called a footman who ran down to the kitchens for a pound of lard. The congealed fat was used to soothe her husband's bloodied gums.

The dentist took a breather after the lower extractions. He asked for port and was served it in a crystal glass. The vintage was so pleasing that he asked for another, and then a third.

'I shall now commence with the upper impediments,' he said, slurring his words.

Banks clenched his mouth shut and refused to open it.

'I fear that my husband is fatigued,' said Lady Banks. 'Shall we not reconvene the surgery at a later date?'

Harrowby motioned for the bottle of port to be brought to him.

'It is best, is it not, to strive for completion of such matters?'

The dentist downed a fourth glass of port and clapped his hands.

'Call a pair of footmen to hold the patient down,' he said, grasping a lever in each hand.

TWO

ON THE THIRD floor of number ten Duke Street, the gentlemen had assembled for their meeting. The doorman, Harry Thornly, had welcomed each one, assisted them in removing their boots, and had heaved a pair of bulky ox-hide cases up the stairs. As usual, he had positioned them at the threshold of the first door on the right, and retired to his post downstairs.

Inside the meeting room the assembly had begun.

The fifteen gentlemen were standing in a circle, their hands at their sides, and their faces covered in black hoods. On the floor before them stood an octagonal figure sculpted from beeswax and scented with lavender.

Fifty-one candles were burning in the room, each one inscribed with a Greek letter, and dipped in pig's blood. The walls were shrouded with crimson cloth, as were the windows.

The figures had stood in silent meditation, some rocking gently back and forward on their heels, others quite still. Sensing the moment to be appropriate, the largest of the men greeted his fellow members.

'Disciples,' he said in a hushed tone, 'we are gathered by the sacrament of Alta Templis, as is the custom of our flock. Peace on you.'

'And peace on you Master,' said the other gentlemen in unison.

'What is our cause?'

'The green pastures.'

'And what is our support?'

'The crook of Alta Templis.'

'I call upon this flock of Alta Templis to abide by our instruction. Do you abide?'

The fourteen gentlemen stood to attention.

'We abide!' they said in unison.

'Be still my brethren,' said the leader of the group. 'I have news. There is pain to bear, but the pain will amplify our strength.

The expedition that has been dispatched. It is no more. Peddie and his men are slaughtered, their blood has seeped into the African sand.'

The chief disciple paused to allow the news to be received. Allowing his hands to fall to his sides, he raised them again. 'But no matter,' he said. 'Peddie's death is our eventual gain. The public sale of stock has exceeded all expectation. The Committee's coffers are charged and the funds are at hand. We can proceed.'

'Master,' said the tallest of the hooded figures, 'what of the sailor, the American?'

'Is he not a thorn in our side?' asked another.

'Nay, my disciples, nay. I have attended to Mr. Adams. His preposterous tale will be the mockery of London as sure as night follows day.'

THREE

THE PRINCE REGENT was sitting for Lawrence in the old throne room. He had gone against the artist's wishes and elected to stand in the spot with the least natural light. Not daring to protest, Lawrence had instructed his servants to convey the canvas and easel through Carlton House and position it wherever the Prince desired. From time to time, Isabella would flit in, moan at the weather, or at the lack of fresh flowers, and disappear again.

The Collection had been arranged next door in the throne room, by an expert newly hired for the purpose. During his interview the man, a German named Herman Frosch, had claimed to have an understanding of the way the fauna of the savannah tracked their prey. The fact that he had never been to Africa himself seemed of little importance. The Prince had approved of him as he was undaunted by the range of creatures in the Collection, and because he had insisted that the animals be displayed in order of size.

At two o'clock the following afternoon, Cochran brought Adams to Carlton House and, as directed, requested the footman to call the Prince's private secretary, Francis Hastings. Cochran's spirits had been bolstered a little after days of melancholy. That morning he had received a letter from Beattie. Sent from Paris, it explained that she was about to depart for Geneva, and then across the Alps to Italy on a tour of the classical world. She asked for Cochran to forget her but, in a postscript, confessed that she would always love him very deeply.

The Committee secretary tucked the letter under his shirt, pressing it to his heart. He had decided not to mention it to the American. Keeping it secret somehow made him feel a little warmer inside.

'To think of it,' he said all of a sudden, 'that His Highness himself has become interested with the narration of your tale!'

'He's a clown like the rest of them in that damned Committee,' Adams replied frostily.

'Hush hush, sir, the Prince is a man of exquisite taste and sensitivity.'

'But he's a clown all the same.'

At that moment the footman returned, and asked the gentlemen to follow him. They entered the great hallway, and proceeded through to the grand staircase. Descending it, they reached the bow room below. It was there that Lawrence was now dabbling away at the Regent's corpulent outline. Poised before him like a Roman emperor, in his newly tailored uniform, was the Prince.

To his right stood a liveried guard, in whose hand was one end of a substantial leather leash. The other end was attached to a studded collar, tied around the neck of a live full-grown male tiger.

'Bait it, man!' snapped the Regent. 'I want it snarling.'

The animal was prodded with a cane, but didn't move. Its lack of natural enthusiasm irritated the future monarch, who had planned to entitle the portrait 'A Pair of Tigers'.

'Imagine that it's growling, Lawrence,' said the Regent, straining to stand straight. 'And you can forget the other animals. It's the tiger that must have pride of place. He's a symbol after all — a symbol of the House of Hanover.'

Hastings stepped forward.

'Excuse me, Your Highness.'

'What? Hastings, you know how I dislike being disturbed!'

'Your Highness, it is the American, the American from Timbuctoo. He has arrived.'

'Has he? And what does he want?'

'The Collection, Your Highness, I do believe you invited him to view the Collection.'

'Ah, yes, very well. Bring him in.'

Robert Adams was ushered into the throne room, where he found himself standing between the giant canvas and the Regent.

'Hello,' he said.

'Ah, the American. Please do come in and join our happy party.'

Cochran followed Adams into the room. Greeting the Prince, he jumped at seeing the tiger.

'Is it alive, Your Highness?'

'Of course it is, man!'

The Regent allowed the cape he was holding to slip to the floor. He was tiring of the posture and hoped that Lawrence could execute the rest of the painting from imagination as he usually managed to do.

'We are finished, Mr. Lawrence,' he said coldly. 'It is up to you now. Get it done by next Tuesday and I shall pay you double. Hastings, make a note of that. If Lawrence hastens, he shall be rewarded.'

'Thank you, Your Highness,' said the artist.

'Now, follow me, Mr.... What is your name, it eludes me?'

'It is Adams, Robert Adams.'

'Then follow me, Mr. Adams, and I think you will be pleasantly surprised.'

FOUR

AFTER DISPOSING OF Sir Joseph's natural teeth, Mr. Harrowby set off to fashion a crude set of dentures from teeth gathered from the battlefield at Waterloo. An enterprising survivor in the Dragoons had spent the morning after the battle knocking out French teeth with a hammer he had taken specially for the purpose. The stock of six hundred and twenty-three teeth of all shapes and sizes, had been sold to Harrowby for the grand sum of five pounds.

Sir Joseph Banks took another dose of *Brugmansia*, and after it he swallowed a drachm of laudanum. He didn't approve of the remedy, but the pain was so severe that he was willing to surpass his usual self-administered dosage.

Lady Banks pressed a cool sponge to his jaw and whispered sympathy.

'Damned bloody quack!' barked Banks, after an hour of silence.

'Artificial teeth are all the fashion, my dear,' said Lady Banks.
'They may be fashion, Madam, but I do not care to have some
young buck's smile in *my* mouth!'

FIVE

IN THE COLLECTION room the animals were being dusted by Herman
Frosch, who had been kept on a retainer to ensure the fauna were
in satisfactory condition at all times. It was his responsibility to
ensure the animals were herded back to the Collection room once
the Prince was finished with them. He was also charged with raking
the thick layer of sand that had been imported from Norfolk, and
sieving it of shells.

Frosch had been born in Hamburg, and was the son of a
bookkeeper who had wedded a former mistress to royalty. The
noble association was a source of considerable pride, and allowed
him to let his delusions wander a little further than they might have.

He was brushing the hind leg of the great giraffe when a footman
burst in.

'Look to it!' he cried, 'he's on his way.'

Frosch stowed the duster and brush, and stood to attention.

The Regent stormed in, with Adams behind him, and Cochran
behind him. After them came Hastings, a pair of servants and the

tiger, its leash held tightly by an attendant.

'This, Mr. Adams, is my savannah,' exclaimed the Prince. 'Not bad, eh? Not bad if I say so myself.'

'Did you get them from Africa?' asked Adams.

'Good heavens, no! They come from the menagerie at Tower Hill.'

The Regent said something to Hastings, who motioned to Frosch. The German took three steps backwards and blew a miniature silver whistle he had fixed to a silk lanyard. For a moment or two, nothing happened then, slowly, the animals began to move over the sand.

'Tell me, Mr. Adams, are you reminded by such a scene of your own adventures?'

The American thought carefully before replying. He could see the Collection meant a great deal to the Prince Regent, and did not want to disappoint him.

'It is as if I had not left the rugged African landscape,' he said.

The Prince turned to him, his eyes glazed with tears. He dabbed them with a fragment of lace kept for the purpose.

'Your commendation has pleased me,' he said. 'I should like you to be my guest at Brighton. I have built a modest pavilion there, which brings me joy in great measure.' The Prince went silent. He touched a set of fingertips to his cheek. 'I know,' he said, as if startled, 'we shall take the animals along!'

SIX

'Brighton! To think of it!' said Cochran at breakfast down at Mrs. Potts'. 'The Prince has engaged the finest architects to complete his fantasy on the south coast. All of society marvels at its elegant décor. They say that it is the epitome of the fantastic. Gaze at it and your feet float up from the ground!'

'Does anyone in "society" have their feet *on* the ground?' Adams replied. 'The rich have all the wealth, while the poor scrape along with the bones. Think how the Prince lives! He's coddled in miles of silk and gold. There's shame in it.'

'And America, is that much different?'

Adams swallowed a last mouthful of porridge and laid the spoon back on the table.

'Equality,' he said pensively, 'it's our ambition. We may not achieve it in everything we set out to do, but it's there, always there, an ideal for us all.'

'One day, when my debts are cleared, perhaps I shall repair myself to America. What do you think of that?'

'A fine idea!'

'My uncle fought in your Civil War. Did I tell you?'

'You did not.'

'He was wounded,' said Cochran, 'at the Battle of White Plains. Had his foot amputated. The surgeon who cut it off preserved it in wine vinegar. My uncle kept it on his mantel in a glass jar. Most proud of it he was.'

'Simon, I tell you with all my heart that America is a land of possibility in all things.'

'But what would I do there?'

'Follow your dream. Build a house, marry a God-fearing girl, raise children.'

Cochran sipped his chocolate. The smile disappeared from his lips.

'I will tell you something,' he said all of a sudden.

'What?'

'We lampoon America's state of infancy. Yet one day, years from now, it will reach adulthood, and our own empire will crumble.'

'But how many more lands like ours will be ravaged by your fleet before then?'

'If the Earl of Liverpool would have his way, the entire world would fall under the Union flag.'

'And Timbuctoo? Will it really be a trophy for the English?'

'It is the Committee's hope.'

'So that it can sack the fabulous treasure vaults that don't exist.'

'Robert, don't you understand? Timbuctoo represents far more than the treasure that may or may not be there. It's about a fantasy, a legend, a myth of the golden city.'

'But with no treasure there will be no wealth.'

Cochran asked Mrs. Potts for more hot chocolate.

'The treasure is not so important as the legend,' he said. 'It's like the aroma given off by a delicious apple pie. The smell has no value except to heighten one's desire. It's the same as Timbuctoo. The Committee has raised a far greater fortune through public subscription than it could ever hope to acquire through the expedition. The coffers are full to bursting. I've seen the balance sheets myself. All of it given in good faith, pledged for the benefit of the Committee. Sir Geoffrey and the directors have their fortune already, and there's no need to haul it back from darkest Africa.'

'But Caldecott believes in Major Peddie and his campaign.'

'You are right, he does, at least in part,' said Cochran. 'So complete are his powers of persuasion that he has begun to believe in it himself.'

SEVEN

THE CORPSE OF a hanged man was brought in to the public viewing theatre on the east side of Albemarle Street. A pair of porters who carried it in groaned at the stench. The criminal, a Russian named Leo Polkovich, had been hanged a fortnight before. His crime had not been made public, although a rumour circulating the crowd suggested he had attempted to commandeer a Royal Navy frigate as it took on supplies at Greenwich.

Surgeon Horace Philps instructed the porters to hold back from placing the corpse up on the examination table. Before the public arrived to observe his dissection, he liked to look a cadaver over on the floor. It gave him a chance to knead his fingers into the groin and the small of the back. For, as Philps always said, a little kneading of a fetid corpse did a great deal in achieving a clear medical understanding.

EIGHT

As far as Cochran was concerned, grey January days were gruelling on the health and tedious on a man's faculties. Since childhood he had found the winter months especially harrowing, largely because his father had forced him to sleep outdoors to harden him up. His great fear was that his only son would be called to war or, worse still, to fight in a duel. So every spare moment of Cochran's infancy had been occupied with endeavours that might add to his general durability.

Until his sudden departure, Cochran senior had insisted his son walk barefoot across the Pennines on miles of sharp flint track. He had employed a boxing instructor, too, and forced his son to

learn the art of fencing at Angelo's academy. But the result was a
character with a deep-seated loathing for hostility of any kind.

The last event in London that Cochran would have taken an
active interest in attending was one of Dr. Philps' public dissections.
He found the idea of a rank-smelling, rotting criminal being chopped
up for societal amusement, too much for his sensitive disposition
to bear.

When Sir Geoffrey ordered him to view the dissection that
morning at eleven, he had to steady himself by holding the back
of a chair.

'The doctor has been good enough to dispatch us an invitation,'
said Caldecott. 'You will attend on behalf of the directors.'

'Very good, Sir Geoffrey,' said Cochran, sensing the blood drain
from his face.

'And take that damned American with you. It may do him some
good!'

To Cochran's relief, the row of seats nearest the examination
table were taken. He and Adams filed in, as Dr. Philps' assistant
begged the public to ready themselves for the dissection at hand.
About two hundred and fifty gentlemen were in attendance.

Lit by a central cupola, the theatre echoed to the rapturous
excitement that tended to accompany public dissections, especially
those conducted by a surgeon so celebrated as Dr. Philps.

At five minutes to eleven, Sir Joseph Banks wheeled himself into the theatre and halted at the front of the room, a yard and a half from the table itself. He was out of breath from the exertion, his cheeks the colour of ripe plums.

'Upon my word!' he said in a slurred voice at spying Cochran in the row behind. 'Upon my word! My dear friends, you must join me in a more privileged position! Come forward! Gentlemen, please come forward!'

Cochran and Adams moved to seats beside Banks's chair.

At that moment, the surgeon entered.

He had changed in a back room into a pair of navy blue pantaloons and a waistcoat of starched beige cotton. Beneath it he wore a white shirt and a blood-red cravat. As soon as the audience set eyes upon him, they cheered.

'It is an honour above my humble station,' said the doctor in a well-rehearsed stage voice, 'to stand before you this morning for the dissection of a criminal of Russian persuasion named Polkovich. I have the singular pleasure in reducing the mortal remains to their constituent parts, and to exhibiting for public attention the various and intriguing aspects of the human form.'

Dr. Philps motioned a hand to the porters who lifted the cadaver up onto the table. It went down with a thump, and was fully clothed, the skin graphite-grey, and the feet bluish-black. The surgeon stroked a hand through the cadaver's oily ginger hair and down across the face. Then he nodded to his assistant, a man with a limp called Charlie Flounder who, until the year before, had worked as a sexton at St. Martin's church, Oxfordshire.

'Mr. Flounder shall oblige us by removing the criminal's abdominal clothing,' said Philps, as he selected a scalpel. Holding the blade up, he allowed it to catch the light from the cupola above. A brass hand-bell sounded in the background, and the dissection began.

'And now to work,' said the surgeon, drawing the edge of the blade down along the chest. The audience leered forward as the contents of the Russian's thoracic cavity were exposed to the light.

The dissection progressed for an entire hour, by which time Philps had reached various conclusions. The main one being that the criminal would have soon succumbed to malady even if the hangman had not snapped his neck. Philps found a cyst of considerable size on the left kidney, a pathological feature that brought a smirk of curiosity to his lips.

There was nothing like a good cyst to occupy the mind.

NINE

LESS THAN A mile from the public dissection on Albemarle Street, the fifteen members of Alta Templis were standing to attention, hooded, in their blacked-out meeting room at number ten Duke Street. They had caught Harry Thornly by surprise, arriving unexpectedly, something they had never done before.

The candles were burning, their flames fanned lightly by the draught creeping in from between the window frames.

The Master stood before the others.

'Disciples,' he said in a hushed voice, 'we are gathered by the sacrament of Alta Templis, as is the custom of our flock. Peace on you.'

'And peace on you, Master.'

'What is our cause?'

'The green pastures.'

'And what is our support?'

'The crook of Alta Templis.'

'I call upon this flock of Alta Templis to abide by our instruction. Do you abide?'

As before, the disciples stood to attention.

'We abide!' they said as one.

'I have news my brethren,' the master replied. 'So urgent that it dare not wait until the next reconvention of our hallowed fraternity. We have crossed a mark in the sand, a mark behind which we cannot now recede. Our plan is in motion. Long live the true King!'

'Long live the true King!' cried the disciples.

TEN

AFTER REMOVING THE Russian's lungs, heart and spleen, Dr. Philps had instructed Flounder to undress the corpse. When the pantaloons had been cut away, he took up a second scalpel, held it to the light, and proceeded to slice through Polkovich's belly from left to right. The intestines and bloated stomach spilled out onto the table. The doctor, who had acquired an appreciation for the stench of rotting flesh, enjoyed few pleasures more than rooting through a mammalian digestive tract.

Having spent much of his youth carving open sheep at his father's farm, and making careful inspections of their intestines, he prided himself on his ability for meticulous intestinal observation.

Sir Joseph Banks wheeled himself forward to get a better look.

'My word!' he exclaimed, 'that's a fine one. Look at it, Mr. Cochran! Regard the abundant quantity of gut!'

The intestines were removed by the doctor, and laid in a spiral around the corpse. The stench of putrefied flesh filled the theatre. Having doused his handkerchief in *4711 eau de Cologne*, Cochran pressed it tightly over his nose and mouth. He felt as if he were about to collapse.

Adams touched his shoulder.

'Shall we leave?' he said.

'Yes. Yes. A superlative idea.'

Cochran stood up and led Adams towards the door, where the surgeon's assistant was standing.

'We need a little air,' said Cochran, pushing his way past.

'Make haste, sir, or you shall miss the division of the cranial cavity!'

Outside, Cochran paused to regain his composure. He rested his back on the wall of the building.

'Is this how fine English society amuses itself?' said Adams, 'it's reminiscent of things I have seen in Africa.'

'It is indeed a descent into barbarism!'

'But see how the room was full.'

'Just as they jostle themselves into the Committee to hear your narration.'

Adams froze.

'Is that what I have become, Simon?'

'What is that?'

'An amusement, an entertainment?'

'Well in a way, I do suppose it is.'

Cochran took a last sniff of his handkerchief and pushed it down his sleeve.

'But then again, like Dr. Philps you are fulfilling a need for information.'

'Hah!'

'Shall we return to the Committee by way of the Jamaica Wine

House? I think a fortifying beverage is in order.'

The two men strolled down Piccadilly, past Bullock's Egyptian Hall, and on towards Leicester Square, where they availed themselves of a sedan chair each.

Forty minutes later they were sitting in the comfort of London's foremost coffee house, a purveyor of tonics, hot and cold. A man who normally abstained from hard drink, Cochran took a double brandy and followed it with another. Adams ordered the same.

An hour slipped quickly by, and they blustered back out onto the street. In the background was the sound of carriage wheels running over cobbles. A pall of smoke hung in the air from a soap boiler's factory that was ablaze, the flames fanned by the breeze ripping up over the Thames. Cochran took no notice of the smell. After all, fires in London were almost too common to mention.

He was describing to the American the sound of the church bells in the Cotswold village where he had spent the summers as a boy, when a figure jumped out from behind a cart.

Six feet two, unshaven, he had watery blue eyes and matted brown hair. His coat was made from heavy cotton twill, torn on the left side, and frayed at the seams. In his right hand was a cane.

He thrust it towards Cochran.

'Run for it!' cried Adams.

They fled towards Cheapside. The bailiff followed, his stride dwarfing theirs. Charging over the flower-beds, they sprinted down King Street in the direction of the Guildhall.

'Hurry, this way, Robert!' Cochran yelled, steering the American down a narrow passage at the back of the Guildhall. The echo of the bailiff's boots were growing louder.

'He's gaining on us.'

'Damn them, damn them all!' shouted Cochran.

'Down here.'

'No, not that one. It's a dead end.'

'Then this.'

'Yes. Down there.'

Cochran turned into an alley frequented by harlots after a night of carousing at the Saracen's Head.

'We have lost him! Celebration!'

'You speak too soon,' said Adams quickly. 'There! He's seen us!'

The bailiff's shadow swept down the alley, his cane held out at arm's length. Turning, Cochran realised they were trapped.

'Oh, what catastrophe! It's a dead end after all!'

A moment later the bailiff was on them. Adams lurched forward to knock the cane from his hand. But their assailant jerked the end, revealing a triple-edged blade. He jabbed it at Adams, stabbing him in the shoulder.

'You're no bailiff!' yelled Cochran.

Adams ripped a length of copper guttering from one of the walls and, with all his strength, thrust it at the assailant, knocking him to the ground. Bearing over the man, Adams grabbed the weapon, and pushed its blade to his neck.

'Who sent you?! Tell me! Tell me before I sever your windpipe!'

Twisting to the side, the assailant threw Adams onto his back. Then, raising up the sword, he lunged towards his throat, exclaiming:

'On the chairman's orders!'

ELEVEN

BY FOUR O'CLOCK the library of the Royal Committee was packed to bursting. Three days had elapsed since Adams had last narrated his tale, and society had grown impatient for the next instalment.

Sitting in the front row was Clara Fortescue, her cousin Henry Fitzwilliam chaperoning her. By chance, he had travelled from Paris, arriving in London the evening before.

Sir Geoffrey Caldecott withdrew the gold Breguet chronometer from his waistcoat and inspected the dial. It never lost a moment thanks to the tourbillon movement. In a bullish mood, his cheeks flush with expectation, he stood, made his way to the front of the room, and signalled to William DeWitt. In turn, he clapped three times in an effort to hush the audience.

When silence prevailed, Caldecott raised his hands.

'Ladies and gentlemen!' he called once and then again a little louder. 'As ever I have the distinct pleasure in welcoming you to the esteemed chambers of the Royal African Committee. I know that many have found fascination in the singular tale of Mr. Adams, but I must advise you most gently that our American acquaintance shall not be continuing with the narration.'

A surge of anticipation swept through the library.

'Where is he?' called a voice.

'Run back to America!' cried another.

'He's been unmasked as the charlatan he is, of course,' shouted a third.

In the front row, Clara felt a pang of fear in the pit of her stomach. She clutched her cousin's arm.

Caldecott held up his hands again.

'Ladies and gentlemen,' he said in a sombre voice. 'It is my cheerless duty to inform you that some most unpleasant news has only just reached my ears. I regret to inform this tender assembly that Mr. Adams is dead.'

TWELVE

The Prince Regent had given explicit instructions that the entire Collection be transported to Brighton, and arranged there by Frosch in the Pavilion's grand ballroom.

Tired of waiting for natural causes to relieve the menagerie's only kangaroo of its life, the Prince had sent Hastings to Tower Hill with five pounds, in the hope that the creature's end might be reached a little more swiftly. The next day a special messenger rushed to Carlton House with the news that the marsupial had dropped dead in the night, after a short and mysterious illness. Its keeper, a gaunt-faced man called Massey, had encouraged the kangaroo to swallow two handfuls of laudanum, stirred in with its feed.

Bateman was called to the Tower for yet another taxidermy. The next night he and his wife, Maud, dined on kangaroo steak. Both of them commented on the subtle flavour of the meat and expressed hope that they might with time taste it again.

Three days later, the master taxidermist hurried to London with the animal on the back of his cart in a crate. Making his usual stop outside Colchester, he arrived at Carlton House the next afternoon at five with a broad grin on his face.

Hastings was called to take delivery.

There was no time for unpacking, as the Prince was already on his way to Brighton. So the kangaroo was placed in the hallway with the other animals, which had already been packed up.

Herman Frosch was pacing up and down uneasily, fearful that the Collection might be damaged on the less than adequate English roads. When Bateman entered the vestibule with the kangaroo, the two men looked at each other disapprovingly.

'What is it?' asked Frosch icily.

'A Can Gaa Roo,' the taxidermist replied.

'From Africa?'

'Indeed, I believe so.'

'Very well, place it beside the white African bear.'

The crate was lumbered over, dropped down beside the giraffe, and daubed with a red cross by Frosch. An hour later it was en route to Brighton with the other animals.

THIRTEEN

AT NUMBER THIRTY-SIX Fleet Street Mrs. Amelia Potts was cooking steak and kidney pie. A silver-haired woman of hardy constitution she had, as a child, been weaned on goat's milk straight from the teat at her uncle's farm in Hertfordshire. For forty years she had baked six pies a day, and made curd cheese by night. And for the same amount of time she had fed almost every bachelor living within a mile of her chop house.

Twice daily Cochran dined under Mrs. Potts' roof. As soon as he walked through the door each evening, a plate of pie was slapped down in front of him. While, at breakfast, he ate kippers with bread dipped in melted lard. Mrs. Potts regarded him as one of her regulars, and used to joke that she would have married him if she were thirty years younger, and he half as posh.

On the morning that Jenkins was sent off to do away with Adams, an emaciated, stone-faced man took to begging outside Mrs. Potts' chop house. Dressed in little more than rags, his vision was lost in a dreamy gaze.

Mrs. Potts sent one of the lads who worked in the back out with some leftovers. She assumed he was one of the multitude of impoverished seamen who were to be found begging on London's streets now that the Peninsular campaigns were at an end.

FOURTEEN

On hearing of Adams' death, the library erupted into a frenzy of commotion, the kind of which rarely touched the lives of the upper classes. Clara Fortescue fainted, her frail body slumping onto the floor. Her cousin fanned her with his hand.

At the front of the room, Caldecott was doing his best to regain order. With desperation, he attempted to counter the fusillade of questions.

William DeWitt smacked his hands together.

'Dear friends,' he exclaimed in the loudest voice he could muster, 'as our chairman has brought to our attention, the American sailor has been attacked and killed on the streets of London, along with our faithful secretary, Mr. Cochran. What irony there is in it — that Adams, a man who had survived such expansive adventures on the Dark Continent, should succumb to the streets of our own capital.'

Another surge of uproar swelled, the wave reaching its height. Again, DeWitt pleaded for silence.

'I should like to temper this distressing information,' he said, 'with the news that our Major Peddie has reached the Niger, and is now within sight of the golden city. I would like…'

DeWitt broke off suddenly.

'I, um, er, well, er…'

Standing beside William DeWitt, Sir Geoffrey followed his gaze to the great doors, which had opened a crack and closed with a click. A pair of men were standing beside them, unnoticed, in silence.

They were both covered in blood.

'Dear God,' said DeWitt, his small eyes swollen.

'Mr. Adams, Mr. Cochran,' he cried out. 'What jubilation!'

'They are alive!' cried a voice in the audience.

'Alive?'

'Indeed, sir! See, there!'

Clara Fortescue opened her eyes a fraction, and pushed herself up in her chair.

'Robert, oh dear Robert!' she exclaimed.

Adams led Cochran slowly through the audience, to the front of the library. He had purposely not washed or changed, so that the audience might understand that the threat of danger had not been confined to the African shores.

Cochran made his way to the podium. He held up a hand to calm the commotion.

'Please forgive our tardy arrival,' he said. 'We were met with a little inconvenience while strolling down here. Mr. Adams should like to continue with his narration instantly. Again, please accept our apologies.'

With Caldecott and DeWitt staring at him, both incandescent with rage, Robert Adams took his place, and began to speak.

'As I have informed you previously,' he said, removing his coat to reveal a blood-drenched shirt, 'I was pegged out on the desert by the guest of my former master, tarred, and left for dead. But salvation came to me by way of the man's greed.' Adams broke off. Very slowly, he turned to the left to stare full face at Caldecott.

'Greed,' he went on. 'The lowest and most depraved vice known to humanity. Yet I am thankful for it, for it has saved my life just as it has conspired to end it.

'Once alone with me, my supposed assassin untied the bindings, manacled my hands, and dragged me behind his camel.

'We walked for days. I have no idea quite how many. The sun was more fierce above us than at any other time I can remember. My back, still tarred, erupted in sores that led to great discomfort.

'As we trudged northwards, the dunes increased in height. Some were like mountains, towering above us. The camel struggled to surmount them, as did I. Each night I would wrestle with the manacles. They were bolted at the sides, but I had no device with which to overcome them.

'After more than a week, the dunes melted away, and were replaced by harder ground. My new master seemed pleased. We gathered speed, walking twenty miles or more each day. Then, finally one morning we spied something on the horizon.

'To my half-blinded sight it looked like a castle. My master shouted "Water! There is water!" and hurried forward at a tremendous pace.

'By the afternoon we were nearing the structure, a vast stone fortress. I gazed on it in wonder that anyone could have transported so many blocks of stone to such a deserted location. My master informed me that the structure had been built by spirits. He called them *Jinni*.

'On the rear side lay a pair of colossal battering rams, which seemed to have breached one corner of the structure. The castle was all but ruined. We neared it, stepping into the cooling shade of the great walls. There was absolute silence, a divine serenity. The camel knelt down and refused to move. Knowing this to be a sign that it had smelled water, our master took a crude spade from his pack and started to dig.

'As he jabbed at the hard red sand with the spade, I crouched beside the camel, relieved at the respite. Nearby I noticed a scrap of sun-bleached cloth poking out from the sand. I went over and tugged at it. To my horror, the cloth exposed the dead leathery face of a corpse.

'I fell backwards and, as I did so, I heard my master screaming.

'A pair of Touareg warriors were rushing towards us from the fortress. Behind them were another two and, after them, five more. They made a beeline for my master.

'Seizing the moment, I ran to the camel, pulled hard on her reins until she was standing. Then, in one movement, my hands still shackled together, I leapt onto her back and rode like the wind away from the ruined castle. As I ran, I glanced back in time to see my master's head roll onto the sand.

'Filled with both fear and exhilaration, I rode without stopping.

'At dusk, I halted for enough time to dismount, cut away all but the most necessary luggage and, after much anguish, to free my hands from the manacles. I only achieved this by dislocating my thumbs. Thankfully there was a full moon to light my way, and I rode through the first night and on through the next morning.

'By noon on the second day, the ground had become much harder. I expected the camel to be content, as it made her stride easier. But I had pushed her so severely that she fell to her knees, unable to go on. Rather than beating her, as my master might have done, I rubbed a hand over her jaw, and comforted her. I could see that she was about to expire.

'A little time later she was dead.

'I ought to have taken a knife, drained her paunch and sliced away the choicest morsels of flesh. But my heart was so heavy at losing a friend, that I left her unharmed.

'Taking the last water skin and a knife, I prayed to God, thanking him for my freedom, and I set off on foot.

'Each day, the sun rose, roasted me, waned, and gave way to night. I had no means to make a fire, and felt terrible sorrow in my loneliness. I would pray each night, weep, and struggle to stay warm. I had no food, and resorted to chewing at roots gleaned from the scrub that now littered the desert. As for water, I rationed the little in my possession, as if it were the most precious treasure which, of course, it was.

'For six days I marched, always northwards, for that was the course my master had followed. Every memory, every thought in my mind, rose to prominence and vanished, as I strained to stay upright, to place one foot before the next.

'At the end of seven days and nights, I had no more than a cup of water left. I was so thirsty that I lanced a vein in my arm and drank the blood, but it only added to my thirst. Then, just as I was about to fall upon the ground, I spied a nest of enormous eggs.

'Experience had taught me that they were laid by a bird known as the "ostariche". It stands ten feet tall, has an elongated neck, runs fast, and is flightless. I hurled myself at the eggs. Their shells were so thick that the only way to get to the liquid inside was by throwing one onto the next. As I smashed the second egg, and sucked the delicious contents into my open mouth, I heard a terrific sound, and was knocked back by the female bird.

'She came at me again and again. I pulled out a knife and held it out against my opponent. When the bird dived at me a second time, I severed her belly, the blood flooding down over me. All afternoon I devoured the raw eggs.

'The next day I continued my march, and walked for another week. Again, depleted of vigour, and ravaged with thirst, I felt as if I would now at last succumb.

'The pain I had endured for days gradually departed, and I became overcome with gentle delirium. At dusk I saw a bright light on the horizon, a platinum white. Somehow I knew it was not the setting sun, but the hands of our Lord stretching out to welcome me. I staggered towards it, my body broken and feeble.

'As I jolted clumsily forward, weeping without tears, the light softened and gave way to a sight which I had dreamt of each night. It was not the gates of Heaven, or Hell, but a cluster of huts ahead, and beside them a flock of sheep.

'I fell to my knees and thanked God for my salvation.'

FIFTEEN

MRS. POTTS REMOVED an oyster pie from her oven and left it on the counter to cool. She looked over at the pendulum clock hanging on the wall. It was a quarter after six. There was plenty of time, she thought to herself, before the first of the regulars trooped in.

In the winter they tended to arrive at about seven o'clock, and would stay for much of the evening, sipping their ale, pressed around the fire.

Outside, the ragged seaman was sitting on a sheet of sackcloth. He had been there all day and was frozen to the bone. His right leg was badly bruised as if he had been beaten. Taking pity, Mrs. Potts went to the door and invited him in for a plate of her pie. It took him more than a minute to stand. He staggered inside, limping across the threshold and along the wall to the fire.

An hour later Cochran and Adams arrived. They had left the library as soon as the day's narration was at an end, and retired to Cochran's chambers to change their clothing. Clara had called out as they had departed the library, but Adams hadn't stopped. He feared for his safety, that Sir Geoffrey would send his henchman to finish the job.

Mrs. Potts welcomed the gentlemen and showed them to the table beside the fire. Adams was still fuming, and the Committee secretary still in shock.

'I shall write to Viscount Fortescue,' said Cochran, 'and explain the circumstances. I know you are perceived as a threat, Robert, but I cannot understand why you should be selected for execution, and I at the same time.'

'I'm going to get even with Caldecott,' said Adams blankly.

'That is unwise. It will enrage the authorities.'

'What do I care? I'm not from this godforsaken island.'

'Put a foot out of line and the Committee will have you swinging from the end of a rope before the week is out. Don't you see it? They are just waiting for you to react.'

'So what do we do?'

'We act as if nothing untoward has occurred. We continue with the narration, finish it, and you go on your merry way back to Hudson.'

There was silence for a moment, as the two men sipped their mugs of ale. Then a frail voice said:

'You from Hudson?'

'Yes, I am. What about it?'

'Well so am I,' said the ragged seaman.

'You're American?' asked Adams.

'Yes. And you?'

Adams nodded.

'What's you name?'

'Richard Florence. And you?'

'Robert Adams.'

Mrs. Potts came over and filled the mugs from a jug of warmed ale. She asked if the seaman was more comfortable. He thanked her. Adams enquired what he was doing in London.

'I was shipwrecked on the coast of Africa,' said Florence. 'Taken slave by the Moors and redeemed after many adventures.'

Cochran and Adams stared at him in disbelief.

'I managed to make my way to London in the hope of finding the American Ambassador,' he said. 'For I am hoping to get back to Hudson as soon as I can.'

Adams smiled broadly.

'I am you, and you are me,' he said.

'What do you mean?'

'Our stories, they are two halves of the same.'

'Tell me, Mr. Florence,' said Cochran. 'Were you taken as a prisoner to Timbuctoo?'

Sipping his ale, the seaman ran a hand down his chin.

'Not I,' he said. 'But I heard of it. Heard it is a mud city ruled by a tyrant in the most impenetrable expanse of the Zahara.'

'His name is Woolo, the king's name is Woolo,' said Adams.

'You have been there, to Timbuctoo?'

'Yes I have. But to think of it, another man from Hudson wrecked and enslaved like myself. What are the chances?'

'Far greater than you know. There are hundreds of Christian seamen enslaved in the desert,' Forence replied, 'tormented at the hands of the Moors. I was taken to a slave market at Algiers. There were three hundred Christians there, half of them lame and the other half no more than skin and bones. We were kept like dogs, or worse than dogs. Each night a dozen men perished. And, each day, another dozen arrived, brought to the market by the caravans that ply the Zahara sands.'

'But why were the Christian slaves not redeemed straight away?' asked Cochran.

'Because the Consul had been put to death, or that's what we were told. The Moors believed that by bringing their slaves to Algiers they were certain of a fine bounty. But it was not the case, or not so when I was prisoner there. When they realised their journeys had been in vain, most of them took their anguish out on the Christians in their possession. Some were beheaded right there at the gates to the city, others were whipped or tortured, expiring from their wounds.'

'How did you get redemption then?' Adams asked.

'One night I was blessed with a stroke of extraordinary fortune. The guard of the pen in which I was kept was smoking a narcotic tobacco they call "hash-eesh". He was delirious. My wrists had become so wasted that I managed to disjoint my thumbs and slip off the manacles. Then I stowed away on a barque bound for Valetta.

'After a month in Malta I caught another ship bound for Plymouth, and made my way here to London. I have been here a month now, and am reduced to begging. The American Ambassador would not see me. The doorman at his residence called the Bow Street Runners and they beat me.'

Robert Adams leant over and touched his hand to Florence's withered arm. He looked him in the eye and raised his mug.

'You must stay with us,' he said. 'Is that all right, Simon?'

Cochran raised his eyebrows.

'Excellent, that is settled. Now let's drink to quenching the unquenchable thirst, and to the dear companions we were forced to leave on the desert sands.'

SIXTEEN

A CARRIAGE BEARING the royal crest pulled up at Cochran's chambers shortly after dawn. Lacquered in canary-yellow, a colour favoured by the Prince Regent, it had been waxed and then polished until the bodywork shone like a bronzed mirror. While the coachman calmed the horses, the footman jumped down to knock at the door.

Mrs. Pickeriff appeared in the doorway, and screwed up her face in a snarl.

'In the name of dear God, what time d'you call this?'

The footman stepped into view.

'His Royal Highness' carriage awaits to carry Mr. Robert Adams to Brighton.'

'Mr. Adams? His Royal Highness? Brighton? Oh my good Lord!'

Pulling the front of her night dress tight, Mrs. Pickeriff smoothed down her greasy grey hair and hurried inside. She clambered up the stairs as fast as she could.

'*Mr. Adams*!' she bellowed. 'A royal carriage is here! I may be dreaming it. I do declare!'

The door opened and Cochran stepped out.

'Thank you, Madam,' he said. 'We shall be down in a trice.'

He closed the door firmly and returned to finish his toilette. Fifteen minutes later, he and Adams descended the stairs, with Mrs. Pickeriff scurrying ahead of them like an apron of foam before a wave. The sense of rush turned into panic.

Between them they carried a metal trunk in which was packed an array of clothing and accessories. Uncertain of quite how to prepare, Cochran had packed the entire contents of his wardrobe, in the hope it would be sufficient to dress the American and himself.

London society reverberated with tales of the Prince's Brighton home. Some said that it had been brought brick by brick from the Orient, others that it was staffed by a race of pygmies purchased by the Regent at auction in Paris. The rumours were inflated a little more each month and, most of the time, contradicted each other. But all agreed that the Prince's home on the south coast was a pleasure dome devoted to indulgence, uproar, and to conspicuous consumption.

SEVENTEEN

SIR GEOFFREY CALDECOTT crossed his study, went over to the bookcase and removed his tortoiseshell box of macouba snuff. He took a pinch, nipped the end of his nose, and took another pinch. He had arrived at the committee early in the hope of receiving news from his henchman, Jenkins. But none had come. *I'll kill that imbecile*, he thought, *can he do nothing without making a pig's ear of it?*

There was a knock.

'Enter!'

Falkirk pushed the door open a crack and slipped in, a polished salver on his hand.

'A letter, sir. Arrived by private messenger.'

'Bring it over, then. Be quick about it!'

The butler strode up to Caldecott's chair, and was met with a blast of cold air from the open window. He presented the salver with both hands, as he had been taught to do by his father, a butler in service to Lord Rothermere fifty years before.

Caldecott snatched the envelope and broke the seal.

'Get out!' he hissed, settling back into the chair.

Retreating, Falkirk slipped out of the study, closing the door behind him. When he was alone, Caldecott read the text:

Leidseplein, Amsterdam
10th February 1816

My dear Sir Geoffrey,

I have been privileged to be present in certain circles on the Continent, and have become acquainted with information that may be of interest to you.

Six months ago in Lisbon I was introduced to an English gentleman recently returned from Africa, where he had been eking a living as best he could for the previous seven years. He was in poor health and, so he advised me, he had survived an arduous journey from across the mighty desert to Timbuctoo, which he reached in the month of January 1810.

At our initial interview, the gentleman described for me the very wondrous features of that golden metropolis — its gilded towers, and lake glinting with precious jewels. I became fascinated in the story he told, made enquiries, and found that every detail — as far as I could ascertain — was correct in every way. Please forgive me for not at this time revealing his identity, but I believe that doing so may impede the delivery of this message.

With sufficient funds to my name, I advanced enough capital to restore his fortunes. He is currently residing with me here in Amsterdam, and is quite prepared, if it is in accordance with your wishes, to put his name to your Committee's endeavour.

If indeed this information excites your curiosity, I would ask that you advance the small sum of £400 as a token gesture of assuring your genuine interest.

I am, sir, your obedient servant,
Hans Winkel

EIGHTEEN

AT TUNBRIDGE WELLS, the carriage changed horses and its occupants passed the night at the Walks. Before retiring, Cochran and Adams strolled down to the source that had made the small spa town a fashionable retreat during the reign of Queen Anne. Once there, they sampled the medicinal waters.

Cochran downed two glasses, and found himself aroused in a way he could not explain. He began ranting on about his unrequited love for Beattie, his heart overflowing with his most intimate emotions. Adams spared no time in making light of his friend's passion.

'Love!' exclaimed Cochran defensively, 'is a quality that we English possess in good measure, but one we regard expressing verbally as foolhardy.'

The American finished his own glass of the mineral water.

'My travels have been limited to barbarian regions of Africa, to England, and to the land of my birth,' he said, 'but I declare that in my journeys I have never come across — nor imagined — a less passionate race.'

Cochran's face fell.

'Steady on,' he said.

'Well look at you all,' Adams retorted. 'You are incapable of letting down your guard, of telling the one you love of your true feelings. Simon, I have watched you writing limp-wristed letters to your beloved Beattie. You talk about the weather, and she about her dogs, when you are both gripped with a ferocious need to seduce each other.'

'Robert!' snapped Cochran. 'It is not seemly to speak so!'

'Seemly?!' shouted Adams. '*Who* gives a damn whether we are being seemly or not?!'

Cochran did not reply, not at first. When he had regained his composure, he said,

'Society does.'

NINETEEN

NEXT MORNING THE carriage set off a little after sunrise.

Adams leant forward and watched as the fields and forests of Kent moved gently past to the sound of horses' hooves on McAdam's new road. Seated across from him, Cochran's face jolted an inch from the glass, his mind on Beattie's face.

By luncheon, the yellow carriage had passed the village of Lewes and, by late afternoon, it was almost at Brighton.

'I can smell the sea air!' said Cochran. 'Can you not smell it?'

'Yes I can,' Adams replied, filling his lungs. 'It reminds me of the ocean.'

'The English Channel is but a pool compared to the mighty

Atlantic. To think of it, that our sceptred isle is separated from our monstrous neighbour by only twenty miles of sea.'

Perched on the rear running board, the footman swung forward and tapped twice at the door.

'Brighton approaches, sir. We shall reach the Pavilion within the hour.'

'Almost there. I can hardly wait. Imagine, we guests of the Regent!' said Cochran, his excitement spilling over.

'Simon, are you really impressed by the Prince?'

'It can certainly be said he is not the man his father was nor will be again,' said Cochran, 'but he is the head of the family royal and, as such, I declare myself his humble and most obedient servant.'

'But you've seen him and that ridiculous Collection!'

'And a most eloquent study of fauna it is.'

'Eloquent? It's nonsense!'

'Well,' Cochran replied, while struggling to retie his cravat, 'it is eloquent nonsense then.'

Thirty minutes later the carriage approached the Pavilion from the East. Adams wiped his sleeve over the window to clear the condensation. In his wildest dreams he had not imagined such a building.

Conjured from the Prince Regent's fantasy, it was a blend of Indian and of Gothic, funded in entirety by the privy purse.

A vast and eclectic oriental aberration, a folly, it boasted abundant domes, towers and minarets. Against the grey winter sky it appeared somehow lost, as if transported from the distant Orient to the English seaside town by supernatural means.

Adams stared out, unable to move away. The footman jumped down, opened the door, and still he stared.

'Would you like to descend, sir?'

'Huh?'

'To get down?'

'Oh, er, yes, yes.'

He stepped onto the foot block and then down onto the gravel. A pair of footmen, liveried in crimson and gold, hastened from the portico. They led the way inside into an olive-green reception hall, where the equerry, Francis Hastings, was awaiting them.

'I trust your journey was comfortable, gentlemen,' he said courteously.

'Indeed, most pleasant,' Cochran replied.

'And you, Mr. Adams, were you comfortable?'

'Very much so, thank you.'

'I am pleased to hear it, after all we could not bear for you to endure any more distress,' said Hastings, looking Adams in the eye. 'You shall be taken to your apartments. Please repair yourselves to the yellow drawing room when you are sufficiently rested.'

A footman appeared as if from nowhere and led the guests down a long passageway, the walls of which were hung with radiant pink silk, embroidered with staves of bamboo and bordered in gold tapestry. Matching bamboo chairs ran down either side of the corridor, above them Chinese lanterns festooned with scarlet tassels.

The footman turned left and continued down another galleried hallway, longer than the first. It seemed to run to eternity, and was lined with prints of the Chinese emperors.

At the far end of the passage, a pair of doors opened from within. Adams stepped forward and found himself in a suite of rooms. He was welcomed by a valet, who assisted in removing his overcoat. The bedroom was decorated in lilac silk, the ceiling highlighted with palm foliage, the ruched curtains a pale lavender, tied back with rope crafted from yards of Chinese silk.

Robert Adams waited until the manservant had left him. Then he sat on the corner of the bed, and washed his hands over his face. He opened his eyes wide, taking in the ornate details.

But all he could see was Sanchez's mutilated head lying before him on the sand.

VII

Sir Geoffrey Caldecott opens a secret cupboard in his study — The Prince Regent goes riding in the Pavilion — Mr. Adams meets the Prince — Dinner is served, at which Mr. Adams castigates the other guests, to the delight of the Prince Regent — The brotherhood of Alta Templis discuss their plan to depose the Regent — Mr. Adams describes America to the Prince — Mr. Cochran disappears — Sir Joseph Banks attends the narration with Dr. Pfaffmann — The narration continues, Mr. Adams explaining how he was reunited with his former crew mates — Mr. Cochran is still missing — Mr. Adams is taken to Marshalsea Prison to search for Mr. Cochran — The chairman arrives at Messrs. C. Hoare and Co., to withdraw the Committee's entire wealth — Viscount Fortescue locates Mr. Cochran on a prison hulk — The Royal African Committee's wealth is transported from the bank — The Prince Regent becomes an aeronaut — Mr. Cochran recovers at Camelford House — The Regent's balloon flight is the talk of London — Farmer Hazelmere and his wife arrive at Carlton House — The chairman learns that Mr. Cochran has been saved from the prison hulk — Having described being redeemed by the British Consul, Monsieur Dupuis, Mr. Adams is arrested for lying to the Royal African Committee.

ONE

SIR GEOFFREY LURCHED out of his chair and wrote a pair of letters. He preferred to write standing up at a lectern that once stood in a small chapel outside Bath.

The first letter was to William DeWitt, ordering him to hurry to Hoare's and to have a note of credit made out for the sum of four hundred pounds. The second letter, addressed to Hans Winkel Esq., expressed considerable interest in the gentleman who claimed to have visited Timbuctoo the year before Robert Adams.

A few minutes later Falkirk had passed the letters to the Committee's private messenger and, shortly after that, Caldecott was standing at his study bookshelf. He ran the thumb of his left hand over the spines of Shakespeare's collected works, pausing at *King Lear*. Like the others, it was bound in turquoise morocco, the corners tooled elegantly in gold.

With care, Sir Geoffrey pulled the book out and opened it. The interior had been cut away, leaving a cavity three inches square. Inside was a steel and brass key, which fitted the lock on the walnut cupboard behind the door. Caldecott opened it and pulled out a box that he kept on the second shelf. Smiling to himself, he removed a silver figurine of Aphrodite.

'Damn fools,' he said. 'A little hocus pocus and they obey without a thought.'

TWO

THE PRINCE HAD consumed an enormous luncheon and was sleeping it off in the library. In the background, an exquisite Apollo clock with an ormolu base, a gift from Paris, chimed five times. The polar bear and the zebras had been wheeled in by Frosch, and placed beside the Regent's chair while he dozed. The German had come to understand that his master thought very much as he did, a point he put down to common Teutonic blood-lines.

Forty guests had been invited for the weekend, and there were more than three hundred staff to wait upon them. All the visitors were in their apartments, reclining, except for Lord Alvanley. He was reading William Beckford's Gothic novel, *Vathek*, in the north drawing room.

The Prince's favoured architect of the moment, John Nash, had halted work on the Pavilion's exterior. He knew very well that the Regent detested setting eyes on workmen of any kind. He found them repulsive, largely because he liked to pretend that Chinese labourers from Malacca were doing all the work.

At five-thirty, the Regent woke from his slumber, sneezed, and called for Hastings. The equerry, who was standing outside the library, stepped inside and bowed.

'I think I'll go riding,' said the Regent.

'But the weather, Your Highness, it has just begun to rain.'

'What of it?'

'Well, the wet, Your Highness. It is a disagreeable element.'

'No matter. Have my mount saddled up.'

'May I repeat in the gentlest terms… the rain, Your Highness.'

The Prince pushed himself up on the chaise longue.

'Hastings, are you deliberately trying to provoke me?'

'No, Your Highness.'

'Then have her brought in here. I'll go for a little wander through the house. And open the windows … let in some fresh air.'

'Very good, Highness.'

THREE

ADAMS WASHED, CHANGED into clean clothes and climbed out throught the open window into the garden. He found the bedroom's overwhelming Chinoiserie too much to bear. Outside, he walked along the West Front where a gardener was pruning miniature fir trees. He tried to strike up a conversation, but the gardener ducked his head, eyes trained on the grass at his feet.

'What's the matter?' said Adams gently.

'Nothing, sir.'

'Then why will you not talk to me?'

'Because sir, because…'

'Because what?'

'Because you are a gentleman, sir, and I just a lowly gardener.'

Adams walked around the Pavilion, taking in the extraordinary surfeit of detail. He was bewildered by the size and by the fact that a single man could be the centre of such communal attention. Circumventing the Pavilion, he arrived at the main hallway through which he had entered earlier in the afternoon. Having asked directions from a footman, he was escorted through a maze of long corridors.

Inside the yellow drawing room a fire was crackling, and a tall aristocratic figure was taking snuff at the window. He was long-limbed and muscular, his ancestors having been well-fed over many generations. Observing Adams as he entered, he waited to be introduced. Unhindered by the limitations of English etiquette, the American stepped forward and introduced himself.

The gentleman, Lord Salisbury, was about to respond, when the doors to the room were flung open and a horse galloped in, its fore legs rearing upward.

It was the Regent on his favourite filly.

'Tally-ho!' cried the Prince. 'Hastings! Where are you man?!'

There was the sound of feet running fast over parquet and Chinese rugs, and the equerry hurried into the drawing room, his face blotchy red.

'Yes, Your Highness?' he said gasping.

'Get that damned box in here, so that I can climb down.'

'At once, Highness.'

Before Hastings could turn, six footmen burst in carrying a solid wooden structure with steps down one side. They placed it beside the horse, and grappled with the Regent's immense bulk, gently lowering him to the ground.

'Nothing like a little exercise to reduce gastric swelling. Don't you agree, Salisbury?'

'Quite so, Your Highness.'

The equerry stepped forward, and introduced Robert Adams.

'Adams? Adams? Who in damnation is Adams?'

'The American, Highness.'

'Ah, yes. The American, indeed. I am longing to hear all about Timbuctoo. I would rather like to have it recreated for me at Windsor. Mr. Adams, what do you think about that?'

Bowing his head to the Prince, the American winked at Cochran who had just entered.

'I think it is the most stupid idea I've ever heard,' he said.

The Regent jerked round and narrowed his eyes.

Hastings and Salisbury froze.

'What did you say?'

'You heard me.'

The Prince gaped at Adams, his eyes unflinching. Then, all of a sudden, he began howling with laughter.

FOUR

THE GREAT CHEF Antonin Carême had been at work in the kitchens since five that morning, overseeing the legions of staff. The subjugation of Napoleon had been a triumph in every way. But it was the Regent who had celebrated most of all, for it had enabled him to poach Carême from the emperor's foreign minister, Charles Maurice de Talleyrand.

An architect as much as he was a gourmet, the chef was celebrated for adorning banquet tables with *pièces montées*, elaborate sculptures crafted from spun sugar, pastry and marzipan. As for his cuisine, he blended delicate flavours and colours, concocting menus the likes of which even the gastronome Regent had never imagined, let alone ever seen.

Before quitting London for the coast, Carême was advised by Hastings of Adams' invitation, and instructed to create a special dessert. The budget was set at £100, for a pudding that was to be more elaborate than anything he had created before.

When it came to his guests, the Regent liked to feign forgetfulness, but in reality there was not a detail that slipped his shrewd attention. And few things gave him as much joy as to fashion a spectacle that would be admired by all.

The Pavilion kitchens were cavernous, as large as the banqueting hall itself, and were regarded as the most advanced of their kind ever constructed. There were mechanically operated roasting-spits, huge tent-like copper awnings to waft away the heat, special sash vents in the roof and, in the middle of the room, a thirteen-foot steam-heated preparation table.

Bronze pots and pans covered the walls, hung by their handles, the burnished undersides reflecting the lamplight. An army of sous chefs was darting about, obeying their orders. As for Antonin Carême, he himself was huddled over a sheet of paper in a back room, sketching out a design with which to surprise the Prince.

Dinner was normally served at seven, but having overindulged at luncheon, the Regent instructed for it to be delayed until eight. Waving a hand in the direction of the filly, he ordered her back to the stables, and excused himself to dress for dinner.

Adams found himself alone with Cochran and Lord Salisbury.

'You would do well to be sensible to our host,' said the peer curtly.

'Indeed, Robert,' added Cochran, 'it is not prudent to condemn the notions of the Prince.'

Adams took a step backwards.

'Are you telling me to bite my lip?'

'Indeed we are,' said Salisbury. 'He is the Regent, after all.'

'Well maybe it's time for you English to get rid of your royal family,' said Adams, rising to the bait. 'You'd be better off without them. The French seem quite improved, and I can tell you that across the Atlantic we certainly haven't missed the royal touch. Look around! Look at the fortune that's been lavished on this place! A child of ten would have had more sense than to waste so much.'

Cochran patted a hand to the air in front of him.

'I would caution you, Mr. Adams,' said Salisbury, stiffening his neck. 'For such a seditious attack on the ruler of the realm is a foolhardy pursuit.'

'If speaking out is going to get me locked up in the Tower, that's fine. You have all forgotten how the people you're suppressing live. Sometime, when you're not parading around like peacocks, I suggest you take a look out there.'

Hastings hurried in.

He was followed by Frosch and by a team of porters. They had been instructed to remove the entire Collection to the music room, where the orchestra was preparing something a little unusual for the Prince's American guest.

Frosch pointed his baton at the bull elephant.

'Start with that,' he said, 'and then the others. Move them in order of size. And take care of the wheels.'

The sound of the great pachyderm rolling forward mingled with the grunts of the porters. When the beast was gone, Hastings invited the three gentlemen to join the other guests in the south drawing room.

Entering, Adams prepared himself for war.

Thirty of the most self-infatuated members of English society glanced to the doorway making sure it was not the Prince himself, who was expected at any moment. A string quartet was playing Handel's oratorio *La Resurrezione* near to the window, the lichen-green curtains forming a pleasing backdrop. Most of the gentlemen were standing, the ladies seated primly on chairs made specially by Hervé, and upholstered in striped yellow silk.

Cochran and Adams were introduced by Hastings to an elderly gentleman poised ponderously beside the fire. He was staring into the flames, reminiscing of a time when his bones did not ache and his eyes were not misted by cataracts.

'Sir Frederick, I should like to present to you Mr. Adams and Mr. Cochran, both of whom are associated with the Royal African Committee.'

The old soldier drew his gaze from the flames and moved it up and over to Adams.

'I have heard of your narration, sir,' he said. 'I should not say it but my granddaughter seems quite smitten with you. Your name is the only word on her lips.'

'Has she attended the narration herself?' asked Cochran.

'Indeed. She has hardly missed a moment. And quite a trouble it is, for she is chaperoned by my cousin, the former Ambassador to Berlin. It appears that your journey has excited much animation.'

'I don't know why so much attention is being devoted to me,' Adams replied.

Sir Frederick stared back at the fire.

'The reason seems very obvious,' he said. 'Your intentions are well-meaning of course, but you have stumbled into a contest and seem remarkably naïve as to its rules.'

'To which contest do you refer, Sir Frederick?'

'The contest of Timbuctoo, of course. It is after all far more than the name of a distant destination. It's a symbol of the unreachable, a legend, the reality of which can never be attained. And of course, my dear Mr. Adams, our faulty society has no conception of it. For it is only when a man nears blindness that he can see with clarity.'

'Are you saying that you have not sunk all your money in the Committee's expedition?' said the American with a grin.

'Hah, no!' replied Sir Frederick. 'I would be more likely to place every penny I have at my disposal on whether a lame dog could juggle apples.'

The room fell silent and all eyes moved quickly to the doorway, where the Regent was standing, his equerry at one side.

'Salutations, my dear friends!' exclaimed the Prince, who had bathed in rose water and was wearing a red dress top, adorned with medals, his chest bisected diagonally with a sash. 'I am most honoured that you should have ventured here to my little retreat, most honoured indeed.'

The Prince stepped into the drawing room and mingled with his guests.

'He is not the man his father is,' mumbled Sir Frederick.

'You mean that his father *was*?' corrected Cochran.

'His Majesty may be of unsound mind, trussed up like a common convict at Windsor but, believe me, he stands tall over *that*.'

Sir Frederick cocked his head towards the Regent, who was lumbering across to them.

'Gentlemen, a good evening to one and all,' said the Prince. 'What a pity the weather is a little dismal, for a perambulation of the grounds makes for a pleasurable diversion.'

Hastings stepped forward and whispered in the direction of the Regent's ear.

'Ah, excellent!' said the Prince. 'Gentlemen, shall we lead the way to dinner?'

The banquet hall was panelled in silk friezes depicting successive generations of Chinese court life, illuminated by free-standing lamps. The ceiling was domed, edged in gilt, painted with banana leaves, and hung with a chandelier of colossal proportions, a fire-spitting dragon leering from its base.

Beneath the fixture, a long oval dining table was arranged down the centre of the room. It was laid for forty-one, with a silver service completed by Rundell and Bridge only seven days before.

As the guests entered, they were shown to their seats and attended to by a bevy of waiting staff.

The Prince Regent took his place at the head of the table, seating himself on a chair upholstered in crimson calfskin. Before changing for dinner, he had given the seating plan to Hastings, who had been required to commit it to memory.

On the Prince's right was his mistress, the Marchioness of Hertford and, on his left, Robert Adams. A connoisseur of the unusual, the Regent regarded his American guest as by far the most interesting guest of all. Cochran had been placed at the other end of the table, opposite Sir Frederick Ponsonby, and across from Lady Poole.

The tablecloth, starched Egyptian cotton, was blindingly white, and laid with a vast array of silverware. Each setting had a dozen forks and spoons of varying sizes — ranging from diminutive to very large, and as many knives, some sharp, others blunt or curiously shaped. There were a dozen glasses for each guest, again in a range of sizes, all of them lead crystal from Tutbury. As for the service, it was royal blue, rimmed in gold, crafted by Spode at their factory in Stoke-on-Trent.

No sooner had the guests been seated than the stewards poured the first wine, a Muscadet, chilled to the point of crispness. The Regent took a gulp and called for the sommelier. The man appeared within the blink of an eye, a tastevin hanging like a pendant around his neck.

'What do you call that filthy liquid?'

The sommelier stooped, then stepped backwards so that he could stoop all the more.

'The Muscadet de Sèvre, from La Chapelle-Basse-Mer, Your Highness.'

'Is it now? Well I wouldn't feed it to pigs. Get it out of here at once!'

'Of course, Your Highness.'

Fresh glasses were laid and the offending Muscadet was hurried away and poured into the drains.

The Prince jabbed a hand at the menu card, which was covered in an ornate black script.

'I do hope you find the menu satisfactory, Mr. Adams,' he said.

'Thank you, I am sure I do. But I cannot read, sir.'

'Have trouble with your eyes, do you?'

'No, Your Highness. I have never learned to read.'

The Regent held up the card.

'We shall begin with a selection of twenty entrées — *Les profitralles de volaille à la moderne, Le sante de poulardes à la d'Artois* and *Les côtelettes de lapereaux en lorgnette*. After that there will be *Les bécasses bardées Les sarcelles au citron, Les gelinottes, Le dindonneau,* and after that, some pudding!'

Wide-eyed, Adams leant forward and reached for the glass of Château Lafite a steward had just poured.

He picked it up.

The room went silent, all eyes pinned on his fingers fastened around the crystal stem. To his left, Lord Alvanley coughed, grunted, and nodded his head at the glass.

'You do not drink before the Prince has done so!' he hissed.

The Regent applauded.

'Excellent, excellent! Mr. Adams is the first man I have encountered in twenty years who's ready to show a little gall.'

The guests sat in silence, quite uncertain of whether the Regent was fuming or amused.

'I should like to make a toast!' he cried. 'A toast to my American friend, Mr. Adams of Timbuctoo!'

Reluctantly the guests picked up their glasses and took a sip of the Médoc.

'Now,' said the Regent, leaning back in his chair. 'Please inform me, sir, what are the fashions in Timbuctoo?'

'The fashions?'

'Indeed, sir, pray tell, how is the hair being worn? Are they still in powdered wigs?'

'Wigs?'

'Yes, sir,' said the Regent attentively. 'For I am sure that all of us are united in our desire for such valuable information.'

Adams took a sip of wine. He glanced to his right where the Regent was lounging back, glass in hand, and then to his left down the table of assembled aristocracy.

He wiped his mouth with his hand.

'Observing the fashion was not my priority, Your Highness.'

'Oh dear,' said the Prince. 'I had so hoped for a little information.'

The Marchioness of Hertford stroked her hand over the cream-coloured terrier on her lap.

'Do tell us, Mr. Adams, what *was* your priority while at Timbuctoo?'

'Escape, Madam. It was escape.'

Alvanley cleared his throat.

'Would you be so good as to inform us, sir,' he said slowly, 'how you prevailed when our renowned Mr. Park fell short in reaching Timbuctoo? What was your method, sir?'

'My method?'

'Yes, sir, your method.'

Again, Adams thought before replying. Then, looking Alvanley in the eye, he replied:

'My method was slavery.'

'Slavery?' echoed Lady Asquith, seated to Alvanley's right. 'How very quaint!'

'*Quaint?*'

Lord Exeter raised his glass.

'To slavery!'

'The abolition of the practice was a veritable crime!' said Lord Greville, at Exeter's right, a man whose family prided itself on not working for six generations.

'A crime indeed!' echoed Alvanley rowdily.

'Good honest work,' added Lady Asquith with a grin.

Adams stared down the table in disbelief.

'Slavery is an unspeakable trade!' he said coldly, rising to his feet. 'Your ignorance is surely a comedy!'

The guests looked at the American, then at the Regent, waiting for him to say something. But he remained silent, and so the table turned their attention back to Adams. There was a clatter of bowls as the stewards moved nimbly around the table serving soup, *potage de mouton à l'Anglaise*, garnished with fresh chives.

Still standing, Adams ran a hand back through his hair.

'Only a man whose wrists have felt the shackles of bondage, who has been starved, beaten and bartered like a common runt, can understand the meaning of the word "slave".'

Lord Alvanley began to say something, a tight grin on his face, but Adams cut him off:

'Seated here in grandeur, dining on fine food, and pampered like lapdogs, *you* cannot begin to understand… to understand the fear, the torment of real suffering. To watch as your friends are beheaded for no crime at all, to sever the veins on your arm to quench the kind of thirst none of you will ever know!

'You mock the notion of Christian slavery — the "white" variety, and certainly it is a misdemeanour that we universally decry. But the other form — heathen natives dragged from their African huts, shackled and shipped to a distant land… taming the savage as you see it. Black, white, yellow — the colour of the skin is irrelevant.'

Unable to resist, Lord Exeter poked a hand at Adams.

'What is the negro for, sir, if not for a source of labour?'

Adams sniffed as if disgusted by the company.

'The senses, the sinew, the mind,' he said, his vocal cords straining, 'they have no colour. A man is a man. It doesn't matter what his clothes are like, how he holds himself, the tone of his speech, his ambition. What matters is the essence inside.

'I may be an American, and an illiterate one at that, uncertain which fork is which, ignorant of your etiquette and your customs. You can ridicule me and despise my country, but don't demean yourselves by speaking with sincerity in support of slavery!'

'I say,' quipped Lord Rothermere from across the table. 'Steady on, sir! I caution you to keep in mind the company in which you find yourself.'

'That is exactly what I am doing!'

The Regent took a sip of his wine, put down the glass and began to clap.

'Bravo!' he called once and then a second time. 'Bravo to Mr. Adams! Now please sir, seat yourself and take advantage of the epicurean delights that await us.'

FIVE

THE BRETHREN OF Alta Templis had convened for another extraordinary session at number ten. It was a little after nine when the first gentleman arrived. He was greeted by Harry Thornly, who had only been advised of the meeting that afternoon. Harry had planned to dine with his elderly aunt that night down at Rotherhithe. He put on his usual façade of courtesy, but inside he was brooding.

By nine-twenty-five the candles were lit and the members of the fraternity were all in attendance, standing in their circle, their heads shrouded in hoods.

Bowing to the disciples, the Master began with the customary words of greeting. When he was finished, he stepped forward to a low altar that had been placed in the middle of the circle. Upon it stood the figurine of Alta Templis, a long-handled knife and a bowl of pig's blood. Snatching the knife, he removed his hood. Then, dipping the fingers of his right hand in the blood, he daubed them across his cheeks and perspiring brow.

'My brethren, the hour has come to lift the veil,' he said. 'Come forward and be anointed.'

One by one the disciples stepped up to the altar, pulled off their hoods, and had their faces smeared with pig's blood by Sir Geoffrey Caldecott, their Master. When the last disciple had been anointed, he picked up the bowl with both hands and sipped the remaining blood.

'Our quarry is today at Brighton,' he said in a sour tone. 'Encircled by a coterie of imbeciles. But his hours are numbered. The sand streams down through the glass. And, when the final grain has tumbled, this absurd Regency will be dispatched to oblivion and our work shall begin.'

Caldecott moved over to a candle bearing the letter omega.

Snuffing out the flame with his fingers, he touched them to his pursed lips. Since infiltrating the brotherhood of Alta Templis three years before, Sir Geoffrey had introduced a new ritual to the order. In secret, he prided himself on his ingenuity. A little time and effort had allowed him to turn the brethren, each an influential pillar of society, to his own ends.

'With the Regent fallen,' he said, the Duke of York will rise, and the Act that scorns our union shall be repealed. Within a month, the vast fortune we have gleaned from subscriptions will be harnessed, and our scheme set in motion. We are near now, brothers, be patient for we are near.'

'Master,' said one of the disciples. 'What of the fleet?'

'The plans are ready, brother, and the funds accrued, forty slave ships to ply the Atlantic, hastening the soulless from the jungles of Africa to our plantations in the west.'

'And what of the slave station, Master?'

'That too is designed, the funds accounted for, the plantation land already purchased at Tobago, and the plans for our immense new slave docks on either side of the ocean complete.'

Sir Geoffrey stepped up to the altar once again, picked up the knife, and ran his fingers down its long tooled shaft.

'My brothers,' he cried. 'The day of Alta Templis is near!'

SIX

At the end of the meal, the ladies retired to play whist, and the gentlemen filed through into the music room. None but Adams and Cochran gave a second thought to the lavish banquet. As far as most of them they were concerned, an abundance of gastronomic delight was the norm, just as hunger was a sensation they were unlikely ever to know.

Frosch had left the music room moments before the guests arrived. He had arranged the Collection in a new formation based on concentric circles. The Prince's resident orchestra were seated at the east end of the room, with the handsome organ pipes rising up behind them like a forest of golden bamboo.

The scent of orange blossom was heavy in the air. The Regent, who had been finding it a little hard to breathe, had loosened his cravat and his whale-bone corset. Hastings escorted him to a low leather chair, in which he could lie back and rest his bad foot on a goose-feather cushion. The gout had grown increasingly worse, and by the evening tended to cause him considerable pain.

Cochran had marshalled Adams away from the other guests, for fear he might erupt again. Lords Exeter and Alvanley stepped forward to make conversation with the Prince. Each of them was hoping to steer the Regent into condemning the American. Exeter brought up the subject of the colonies, eager that it would prove to be a spark.

'A great pity, Your Highness,' he said in an unguent tone, 'that the Americas were lost, for His Majesty had so enjoyed the notion of such an extended landscape.'

Pushing himself up on a crimson cushion, the Prince frowned.

'The father favoured restraint over liberty,' he said. 'Were he to have had his way, reform would be a word unknown to the English ear, and every African would be in chains.'

'Not a bad thing, as we have already discussed,' whispered Alvanley with a smile.

'Mr. Adams,' exclaimed the Prince, 'would you not join me here? Hastings, fetch a chair!'

Robert Adams turned and strode over to the Prince, circumnavigating the great bull elephant.

'Tell me of America, sir,' said the Regent. 'I should like to have an account from a man who knows it.'

A cabriole chair was placed adjacent to the Regent, its iron frame overlaid with bamboo. Adams sat down, his back forced straight as a ramrod.

'What would you like to know of America?'

'How does it look?'

Adams gazed down at his lap in silence.

'America is a land touched by the hand of God,' he said, the lids lowering over his eyes. 'Its meadows stretch from the ocean to the end of the world and are the thing of dreams. The late summer fields of corn roll on mile after mile, their golden sheaves brought in by every man, woman and child. And they, the people,' said Adams slowly, 'are inspired by a sense of freedom and duty, and by the knowledge that hard work will reap them rewards. Every man is an equal to the next, and every child is raised with the belief that boundless opportunity awaits anyone willing to strive for it in an honest way.'

The Regent moved his foot to reduce the pain.

'And what shall you do, Mr. Adams, when you return to America?'

'I will set up home with my wife, find employment, and raise a family.'

'Will you return to Africa, sir?'

Adams froze, then swallowed hard.

'My dream is to disappear into the obscurity from which I came, Your Highness,' he said.

SEVEN

Two DAYS AFTER leaving Brighton, Adams and Cochran reached Fleet Street, where Richard Florence was settled comfortably in the chambers. He had spent the weekend drinking his way through a case of vintage port, which had been bequeathed to Cochran by his uncle Henry who was slain at Waterloo.

It was a damp evening, the rain chilled by a north wind. Too drunk to stand, Florence remained in bed while the other two men took dinner at Mrs. Potts' — roasted veal with baked potatoes, washed down with a bottle of plum wine. They had hardly spoken on the return journey from Brighton. Cochran was worrying about his debts, and the fact that someone was trying to kill him. Beyond that, he was irked that his guest had invited a fellow countryman to stay.

After dinner he set off to deliver a letter to Viscount Fortescue at Camelford House. It explained how the Committee chairman had hired an assassin to do away with Adams and himself.

The two Americans waited up, but Cochran did not return.

Next morning Adams knocked at the bedroom door, but there was no reply. He pushed his head inside but, to his surprise, found Cochran's bed empty and unused. In the small salon, Richard Florence was asleep on the floor, a bottle of port beside his head filled to the brim with cold urine.

Adams waited all morning and into the afternoon, but still Cochran didn't appear. Aware of Sir Geoffrey's proviso, that missing a scheduled session of the narration would forfeit his passage home, he got dressed, put on his coat, and paced up Ludgate Hill in the direction of the Committee.

The peal of bells at St. Paul's got Adams thinking about the English. They were obsessed with the wealth of Timbuctoo, he thought, when it was they who had unmatched prosperity without realising it.

On the steps of the Committee, Adams found Falkirk.

'Has Mr. Cochran arrived?' he asked quickly.

'No, sir, he's not 'ere.'

'Are you certain?'

'Quite certain, Mr. Adams.'

'What about the chairman?'

'He was inside at six this morning, sir, and in a foul mood he is.'

Stepping across the threshold, Adams removed his coat and made his way up to Cochran's study. The room was warm, the fire prepared by the scullery maid who lodged upstairs in an attic room.

On the desk lay a sheaf of letters tied up with a length of lilac ribbon. Adams picked them up and breathed the scent, *eau de floris*.

'Beattie,' he said aloud, 'how could you have crushed him like that?'

There was a knock at the door.

It was Falkirk.

'Sir Geoffrey is asking for you, sir. He is awaiting you in his study.'

Adams dropped the letters on the desk and a moment later was standing before the chairman.

'I trust Brighton was amusing, Mr. Adams.'

'Very much so.'

'And Mr. Cochran? Where is he today?'

'I have not seen him. He didn't return last night after dinner.'

Caldecott took a pinch of snuff.

'Without Mr. Cochran,' he said, 'you cannot complete your narration, and alas you will not be eligible for your passage home. A crying shame, sir, a crying shame.'

EIGHT

AT HIS HOME in Soho Square, Sir Joseph Banks was soothing his gums with tincture of cantharides. The medicament was prepared from an odourless liquid, secreted onto the back of the male blister beetle while mating. The pain elicited by the remedy was considerable, but its effectiveness was championed by Banks's house guest, a Bavarian apothecary and physician named Dr. Ludwig von Pfaffmann.

The doctor, whose work had been drawn to Sir Joseph's attention only the year before, had developed a widespread following for his work on curing syphilis using live frogs and quicksilver.

Banks had accompanied his guest to the public dissections held on Albemarle Street the previous week. Both men had a thirst for medicinal knowledge, and were concerned with medicinal and scientific research.

In the mornings Dr. von Pfaffmann would excuse himself after breakfast and retire to his room, where he would engage in an amateur study of the human eye. He was developing a new method of blowing glass into balls in such a way that they might be inserted into the ocular cavities of the blind, with a simulated iris painted onto the front.

After lunch, he and Sir Joseph would ride the streets in an open barouche, even in the rain. Von Pfaffmann believed that forward motion aided the brain, and that precipitation assisted in cooling the heat derived from what he called 'the cranial proclivities'. The doctor insisted that genuine thought could only be achieved while moving faster than walking pace.

Sir Joseph, who had become quickly used to the ways of his distinguished house guest, found his level of conversation unequalled. Mention a random subject, and he could be certain that Dr. von Pfaffmann had done all the background reading on the matter in English, German, Latin and Greek. Quite often, the doctor had himself published the leading theory of the day.

On the afternoon that followed Cochran's disappearance, Banks and Ludwig von Pfaffmann were touring the streets near St. Paul's, when Sir Joseph remembered the Royal African Committee and its singular narration. He called to the driver to repair at once to Old Jewry, in the hope of finding the narration in progress.

As luck would have it, Banks's barouche drew to a halt outside the Committee just as society was arriving. Lowered down into his chair by a footman, Sir Joseph was wheeled by the Bavarian scholar down the long corridor.

At its far end, the magnificent library was already half full.

Robert Adams had spotted Clara Fortescue in the audience. He hastened over to ask if Cochran had visited Camelford House the previous night.

'No, Mr. Adams, I regret to say that he did not,' she replied, touching her hand nervously to her hair. 'My father was at home all evening, and did not receive any visitors at all.'

'Then where could he be?'

Clara shook her head.

'I shall mention it to my father,' she said, 'perhaps Mr. Cochran has written to him as you say.'

Adams turned to look around the room.

'Well I don't know what to do,' he said. 'Without Simon I cannot narrate. Caldecott is looking for any excuse to question my story.'

Clara's anxious expression dissolved.

'I have an idea,' she said with a grin.

She hurried over to Sir Joseph Banks and whispered in his ear.

A moment later she rushed back to where Adams was standing.

'Salvation is at hand,' she said, her face lighting up. 'And I can assure you that Sir Geoffrey Caldecott would not dare refuse Sir Joseph the honour of transcribing your tale.'

NINE

SIR JOSEPH BANKS was wheeled to the desk at which Cochran had transcribed the previous narrations. A goose-feather quill, ink, and a ream of handwritten sheets, were placed before him. Fitting a pair of pince-nez to his nose, he scanned the last page of text.

As a hush fell over the audience, Robert Adams took his place.

'I believe you were describing the taste of freedom, Mr. Adams,' said Banks, the new French teeth causing him to lisp.

'Thank you Sir Joseph, I had described the feast of enormous eggs, and my arrival at the outskirts of a village known as Wadi Noon.

'I approached from the south, the afternoon sun throwing long shadows over the landscape. As I drew nearer I saw ever more huts, and realised that I had succeeded in crossing the great expanse of desert. Overcome with emotion, I thanked the Lord for my salvation. It was then that I noticed smoke rising from one of the rude huts. Without wasting a moment, I advanced towards it.

'A little girl of about five years ran out and set eyes on me. She stopped quite still. It seemed as if we stared at each other for an eternity — the girl terrified at the sight of an unclothed Christian, and I elated at seeing anyone at all.

'After a long while, she filled her lungs and screamed in the most feral and strident manner. An instant later, a man was in the doorway of the hut with a knife in his hand. A moment after that he was running towards me. I held out my hands, ready to embrace another man, a friend. But he was not interested in friendship. Forcing my arms behind my back, he tied them up with a strand of leather.

'He took me over to the doorway of his hut and kicked me to the ground. His wife called all her neighbours to look at the family's new and unexpected prize.

'And that was how I became enslaved once again.

'Late that afternoon, the man dragged me to the middle of Wadi Noon where a slave market was in full swing. Slave owners had come from all over the region, all of them fuelled with greed and high hopes for a good sale.

'My new master stopped to speak to his friends, boasting at how he had come by me so unexpectedly. I took advantage of his palaver and rested beneath an acacia tree. I was sitting there, bemoaning my new situation, when I heard a frail voice.

'In my weakened state I thought it said in a whisper, "Robert? Robert? Is that really you?"

'I looked around.

'There was no one except a haggard-looking slave. I closed my eyes, slipped back to my memories. But the voice came again. "It's me, Robert, do you not recognise me?"

'I turned a second time.

'The slave was closer now, his blue eyes a few inches from mine. I was about to say something, when the man said: "I am Simon Dolbie, ship's mate from the *Charles*."

'Like a pair of frail old men we staggered towards one another and hugged and wept. After a while, Dolbie said: "We thought you were dead."

'"*We?*"

'"Newsham and Clarke, they are alive. Come with me and I shall take you to them."

'As my master was still parleying with another slave owner, I followed my former shipmate to the far side of the broad acacia tree, where our companions were crouching. For a few minutes we forgot our wretched state, rejoicing at the reunion. Each one of us was touched by a sense of absolute delight, the kind we had almost forgotten existed in our cruel world.

'Before I stumbled back to my master, fearing his retribution for going astray, Dolbie spoke out.

'"Our master is here buying slaves," he said. "He's the one

with a single eye. Look strong and he may buy you. He knows that Christian slaves are redeemed by the Consul at Mogador, and his longing for easy wealth has led him to acquire as many of us as he can."

'At dusk, my master led me to the patch of dirt where the slave auctions took place. Were I stronger, I would have struck him down and fled, so enraged was I at being forced into servitude once again. Yet I was so feeble that I struggled to stand upright, unable to display any strength at all.

'Dolbie called out to me, urging me to pretend some kind of worth, while he and the other two coaxed their master to take note of me. I must have made for a pathetic sight. But, thanks to Dolbie and my other friends, the one-eyed master clapped twice, the sign he would purchase me. I fell to the ground, weeping in joy at being reunited with my companions.'

Adams paused to allow Sir Joseph's arthritic hand to catch up. The library was silent, except for the sound of the quill scratching inelegantly across the page.

'Pray continue, sir,' said Banks, once he had dipped the nib again. 'My hand is not as sprightly as Mr. Cochran's but I assure you, I have stamina like no other man alive.'

Thanking Sir Joseph, Adams continued:

'During the first weeks of my new captivity,' he said, 'I took advantage of the kindness proffered by my friends. They saw to it that I was fattened up after the hardship of the great Zahara. Each night, Dolbie and the others would share their porridge with me, insisting that I take it, and reminding me that I would do the same for them. As the days passed I grew stronger and, with my strength, came the one overriding desire — to escape.

'Our master was a sullen man, fortunate to enjoy a high standing at Wadi Noon. The other owners of Christian slaves there appeared to look up to him. I discovered that the high esteem in which they held him arose from the fact that he had once torn out a Christian's heart with his bare hands, and fed it to the jackals that encircled the village each night.

'There must have been twenty shipwrecked seamen living there. Some of them were withered beyond belief, their eyes sunken, their ribs sharp across their chests. Most of them had resigned themselves to death. Some even looked forward to the event, as if it would release them from appalling servitude.

'Of all the slaves I encountered there, the most pitiful was a woman, named Francesca. A Venetian by birth, she was twenty years of age, although three summers of slavery had given her the appearance of one far older in years. The vessel in which she had been crossing the Mediterranean had been swept onto the African shore in a ferocious gale. The male survivors had all been beheaded on the beach, as soon as the Moors discovered them. But, as a woman, Francesca was spared death, and a life of indescribable torment began.

'Her master forced himself upon her in the most vicious and wicked way. He encouraged his brethren to do the same and, with time, she gave birth to a son. Uncertain who had fathered the child and, sensible to the fact Francesca had not renounced her faith, the master took the infant out into the desert and snuffed out its fragile life.

'The following week a trader arrived at Wadi Noon. He was tall, big-boned, and wore blue robes and a turban of unusual quality. I was sitting with Dolbie and the other slaves, pausing from our chores, when he came over and greeted us. To our universal surprise, he spoke English fluently. He said his name was Abdul-Malik, the "Servant of God", but that he had been born a Frenchman and was called Maurice Trouin. He had been wrecked twelve years before, on the *Montezuma*, a brigantine bound from Liverpool.

'"Surrender your faith," he said whispering, "and the Moors will regard you as their brother. They will give you a wife and a gun and will grant your freedom."

'"I will *never* renounce my faith," I replied, "even if it were the only way I might escape this Hell."

'"Then you are a fool," said the Frenchman, "and so you will die.

The sand will drink your blood and the dogs will eat your flesh."

'When he had left, I rallied the others.

'"If only we could get word of our captivity to the Consul in Mogador," I said, "we have a chance at redemption."

'Never an optimist, Newsham reminded us we had neither paper nor ink.

'"I have a scrap of paper," said Clarke. "It is small, but we must make do with what we have."

'"But we have no ink," Newsham repeated.

'There was a bent ship's nail on the ground. I picked it up and lanced my forearm.

'"Here is your ink," I said, "and there's no shortage of it!"

'Dolbie took up a stick, and snapped it in two to make a nib.

'"What shall I write?" he asked.

'I cleared my throat.

'"Your Excellency," I began, "we are Christians held in servitude at Wadi Noon, desperate in our state. Our ship, the brig *Charles*, was wrecked upon these savage African shores. We ask you by all the ties that bind man to man, by those of kindred blood, and everything you hold dear, to advance the money for our redemption."

'By chance, another trader visited the village at the next full moon. He was overheard to declare he was travelling to the coast. I tended his camel for a week and, in return, he promised to deliver the message to the Consul at Mogador.

'A few days passed. Then, one morning, my master's son ordered me to tend his goats. It was Friday, the day we were permitted to rest. I informed him that as it was the Musalman Sabbath, I was not obliged to work.

'"You are a Christian dog!" he cried, and you will toil every day or I shall take your life!"

'I bared my neck.

'"Then kill me now and be quick about it!"

'The man fetched his scimitar and brandished it. The spectre of Death had hung over me for so long that the end would have been a merciful release. So I knelt and waited for the blow, my hands clasped tightly at my chest.

'I closed my eyes.

'Then I heard the blade as it arced through the air and became embedded in my face. The pain was not apparent at first. As fortune would have it, my head was cocked downwards, and so the blade did not sever my eye, but only the meat above and below it. I fell to the ground, and was immediately kicked from all sides by a group of Moors who had heard the commotion.

'Once they had beaten me, shattered my ribs and disjointed my shoulder, I was pegged out on the sand and left to die. I soon slipped into delirium, but Newsham, Clarke and Dolbie took it in turns to offer me water, holding a skin to my lips.

'My mind blurred with fever, I asked the ship's mate to take a message to my beloved when I was dead, to say that her name was the last word to pass my lips. He agreed to perform the favour as if he could complete it effortlessly, travel from that forsaken purgatory back to Hudson.

'Three more suns rose, baked me, and cooled to dusk. When it was clear I was about to succumb, my master cut the bindings. He was not without mercy. Newsham and Clarke hurried me into the shade. They fed me water and bowl after bowl of porridge. I told them to keep their own rations for themselves, and for Dolbie. Then it struck me, I hadn't seen Dolbie. I asked most urgently after him. Newsham's face turned pale. A single tear welled in his eye and tumbled down his cheek.

'"Dolbie is dead," he said.

'The next day I woke to find the desert sky had turned scarlet. The Moors were much vexed. My master said it was a sign from the Musalman god, the one they called Allah. He slaughtered a sheep in his name. Clarke and Newsham would not look at me. I wondered if the sky had affected them.

'In the afternoon of the following day, they walked up to our master's black wool tent. I watched them followed by their shsdows. Then I understood why they would not look me in the eye. They had decided to relinquish their faith.

'In the evening a fire was kindled and the Moors clustered around. A sharp knife was brought out. My fellow shipmates bared their manhood to the blade, and repeated the vow that professed them as Musalmans.

'The sight of Christians forgoing all they held sacred brought great sorrow to my heart. When they came to me asking for my blessing, I could not look upon them. They held up blankets and other gifts they had been presented by the Moors. Their spirits were high.

'"Robert, join us as Musalmans," said Clarke, "and you shall be rewarded like us."

'My stomach was filled with bile, for I had never witnessed such a loathsome loss of dignity.

'The next morning the Italian woman, Francesca, fell ill. One of the other female slaves attended her. She told me that a torrent of blood flowed from her body. By nightfall, life departed her. I dug a grave for her under an acacia tree. Standing there alone, I recited the twenty-third Psalm.

'Two days after Francesca expired, a Moorish trader arrived at Wadi Noon. My master presented the new converts to him with much relish. They all ate together, while I went to tend the sheep at the edge of the village. Late in the afternoon, the visitor came to where I was sitting, watching over the flock. He asked me in the Moorish tongue if I was still a Christian. I replied that I was.

'It was then that he revealed his true identity. He was the agent of Mr. Joseph Dupuis, British Consul at Mogador. Pulling out a letter from his boot, he passed it to me. I explained that I was unable to read.

'"Then I shall read it to you," he said in English.

'"Wait," I said, "for I must fetch my shipmates." The agent looked down at the ground. He seemed displeased. Although I was enraged at their conversion, it was my duty as a member of the *Charles*' crew to include them.

'Newsham and Clarke were greatly pleased by the prospect of redemption. They laughed as we walked back to where the agent was waiting. Newsham had received the most schooling and so he asked if he might read the letter.

'Breaking the seal, he ran his eyes over the lines of precise black script.

'"My esteemed friends," he began. "I was most moved and gratified to receive your message this morning. I have frequently heard of the miserable fate of your ship, *Charles*, and have these past months and years endeavoured to obtain information of its crew. I am at once dispatching my most trusted agent, Omar bin Assad, with merchandise and currency with which to effect your immediate release. Yours most sincerely, Joseph Dupuis."

'Clarke fell to his knees and thanked the Lord. Standing close beside him, Newsham let out a shrill wail and began to weep.

'"What is it? What is it Unis?" asked Clarke.

'"There is a postscript," he said, trembling.

'"What does it say?"

'"I am permitted to redeem only those who are still Christian, and have not forsaken their souls."'

TEN

THAT EVENING, Mrs. Potts prepared a large dish of toad-in-the-hole and chopped it up, ready for her regulars. She had been feeling a little feverish, a touch of influenza, and sat to warm herself beside the fire. As she stared at the flames licking a great log of beech, she thought back to her childhood, to the long walks she had taken with her brothers up in the Highlands fifty years before.

The door opened, and Mrs. Potts looked up quickly from the fire. She smiled.

'Good evening, Mr. Adams,' she said, 'and to you Mr. Florence. Is there still no word of Mr. Cochran?'

Robert Adams shook his head.

'It's a mystery,' he replied. 'No one has seen him for more than a day. I am worried for him.'

'Sit yourselves down, gentlemen,' said Mrs. Potts, 'and I'll fetch you a warm rum punch.'

She clattered away into the side room which doubled as a rudimentary kitchen, and shuffled back with a pair of mugs.

'Poor Mr. Cochran,' she said, returning to the fire. 'Toad-in-the-hole is his favourite.'

'*Toad-in-the*?' said Florence.

'In the hole, sir. Pork sausages in batter.'

Adams smiled.

'I cannot wait to taste it.'

A moment of silence passed. Mrs. Potts seemed anxious.

'Excuse me, Mr. Adams,' she said slowly. 'I do not like to be thought of as the kind of woman who pries or is given to gossip. But Mr. Cochran is my most esteemed and highly regarded regular. I value his custom very greatly and it is for that reason I am prompted to speak out.'

'About what?'

'Well, a few days ago I had occasion to overhear Mr. Cochran discussing his financial predicament.'

'His debts?'

'Yes, Mr. Adams, precisely, his debts. It seems that the bailiffs were searching for him.'

'What if they caught him?'

'Then, sir, the most prudent place to search would be Marshalsea.'

ELEVEN

A FOG DESCENDED over London during the night, so dense that the sedan chairs were lined up in rows at the St. Paul's end of Cheapside. Their porters clumped together playing cards, waiting for the vapour to ease.

Fearful of what might have happened to her preferred regular, Mrs. Potts sent her nephew, Figgis Potts, to lead Adams down to the debtors' jail at Marshalsea. A mild-manned young man with a hint of the Highlands in his voice, he had small dark eyes that seemed trained most of the time on his feet.

They crossed the river at London Bridge and, despite the atrocious visibility, were soon nearing the prison. Figgis had spent five years locked up at Marshalsea for smuggling bootleg whisky south. He was hardened by the ordeal.

Adams asked him how he endured the custody.

'I prayed to the Lord,' he said softly as they walked, 'begging Him for redemption. And I kept up my spirits. Lose faith and you fell ill. Fall ill and they'd carry you out and on the knacker's cart.'

'How did you keep your spirits up?'

Figgis thought before he answered.

'I made every day a new adventure,' he said.

Ten minutes more and they were at the wooden gate, the smell of coal tar heavy on its planks. The guard asked their business.

'We are searching for our acquaintance.'

'Male or female?'

'Male.'

'When d'he come in?' The voice was gruff, East End from Bow.

'We're not certain he's 'ere,' Figgis called out. 'Just want to 'ave a look.'

There was the sound of a key twisting in a lock, an iron bolt being drawn back through tight-fitting rings, and hinges pressing back on themselves.

The guard led the way in through a second wall of fortification. He was cheerless, fat on the thighs, a cloth cap pulled down over his ears.

The prison was packed to capacity.

Hundreds of men, women and children, entire families, locked up for debt and misdemeanour. A few were well-dressed, from the upper classes, but almost all were in little more than rags.

The smell caught Adams' attention. It was the stench of squalor.

'England may be proud of her navy and her empire,' he said to Figgis Potts, 'but she forgets to inform the world of this.'

'There's no pride 'ere Mr. Adams,' Figgis replied under his breath, 'no pride at all.'

Marshalsea Prison comprised more than twenty buildings, set back to back, dank halls made from dark shale bricks. Despite the fog and the cold, there were children scurrying about barefoot, running with the rats. Their parents lay about, some drunk, others weakened by illness and disease.

The guard opened the door to a windowless wooden building, seventy feet square. It was like a barn with a pitched roof, empty of furnishings, but filled with people. There must have been two hundred of them, most young, others younger, and a few very old.

In the darkness at the back was the sound of a child weeping, and an old man choking as if about to expire.

'All these came in since Tuesday,' said the guard. 'I'll give ya ten minutes. Poke yer 'eads around.'

Adams put his hands to his mouth and began calling out Cochran's name. He moved fast through the crowd, scanning the faces, glancing at the clothes.

Suddenly a woman began screaming.

She fell onto the floor, her knees plunging into muck, her body writhing in grief. A child lay beside her on a mound of damp hay. It was grey-skinned and cold. The guard blew his whistle twice, the shrill tones echoing off the black plank walls.

A moment later, two more guards appeared.

They moved swiftly over to the child. One of them touched the face and made a sign with his hand. He carried the infant off, as the other held the distraught mother back.

TWELVE

SIR GEOFFREY CALDECOTT ordered the porters to bear him up to Hoare's shortly before noon. In the fog he preferred not to use the carriage as the horses became alarmed, and a ride with distressed animals guaranteed discomfort.

After a glass of sherry in the partners' salon, Sir Geoffrey was ready to broach the matter for which he had come. The bank's chairman rubbed his hands together as if warming them, but his mind was not on the cold.

'I shall send for the clerk to take the deposit, Sir Geoffrey,' he said.

Caldecott raised a finger, then smiled.

'Sir Richard, I am not here to deposit.'

'Oh?'

The chairman's eyebrows rose quizzically, his forehead creasing in lines.

'No, sir, not a deposit.'

'Then how may I assist you, sir?'

'I am here to make a withdrawal, Sir Richard.'

The chairman of the bank took great pleasure in his work. There was nothing that he did not enjoy about banking, nothing, that is, except withdrawals.

'Might I enquire, sir, the amount you have in mind?'

Sir Geoffrey Caldecott took a pinch of snuff. He had never liked bankers, despite his impressive ability to feign friendship with them.

'Of course you may enquire,' he replied, inspecting the well-rounded fingernails of his left hand. 'I should like to make a complete withdrawal.'

Sir Richard Hoare began to choke. A clerk rushed over and tapped him lightly on the back.

'Complete?' he said, still choking.

'Indeed. Complete.'

A glass of water was brought in. Sir Richard took a sip, and coughed hard. He called for a ledger. It came at once.

'The Royal African Committee's account stands at six hundred thousand, two hundred and fifty pounds, three shillings and sixpence,' he said.

'Very good. Please have it ready by tomorrow afternoon. I shall send transport to collect it.'

'If it is indeed your wish sir, I shall have the bank notes awaiting.'

Caldecott took another pinch of macouba, working the tobacco high into the nostril.

'No bank notes if you please,' he said. 'We shall require the entire amount in gold.'

THIRTEEN

ROBERT ADAMS WAS about to venture down for dinner across the street, when there was a loud knock at the door. It was Viscount Fortescue, his face flushed from charging up the stairs.

'I have found him! I have found Cochran!' he exclaimed. 'Quickly, come with me!'

'Come where?'

'To Hell on earth.'

As soon as they were safely aboard the carriage, the Viscount opened the window and called out,

'Dunn, drive as fast as you can, to Woolwich! To the hulk *Warrior* moored at the docks!'

The wheels thundered over the cobbles, the horses champing ferociously at their bits. Thankfully, the fog had lifted, swept away by an Essex breeze.

'There's not a moment to lose, Mr. Adams,' said the Viscount, lurching from side to side as they gathered speed. 'I have received information that our dear Mr. Cochran has been incarcerated in HMS *Warrior*, a prison hulk.'

'What's that?'

'A decommissioned ship of the line, a veteran of the battle of Copenhagen, no longer fit for sea. I hear her conditions are deplorable beyond even the most depraved imagination.'

Fortescue slapped a hand to his thigh.

'I wish I had known of his debts!' he said.

'He was too proud to tell you of them.'

'Pride is a valiant attribute, Mr. Adams, but a perilous quality that can impede survival.'

'Where is the prison ship?'

'At Woolwich. South of the river. We can thank the loss of the American colonies for it. Were America still British soil, our dear Mr. Cochran might at this moment be on his way to a transportation settlement.'

An hour later, the carriage drew to a halt at the dock. The prison hulk sat a few feet from the quay wall, low in the water, its timbers creaking against the tide. There was not a light aboard, except for a single lantern at the stern. Adams was not unused to wretched circumstance, but the sight filled him with dread.

The darkness, the dim outline of what seemed like a death ship, and the swirls of mist ebbing around it on the black water, conjured a sense of terror. He thanked God he was not alone.

The Viscount's cavalry boots marched briskly over the gangplank bridging the ship with the dock. In his hand was a swordstick, the blade unsheathed. Robert Adams followed close behind and behind him was the coachman, Dunn, a carriage lantern in either hand.

'Open the hold!' yelled Fortescue, climbing onto the deck.

'In whose name have you authority?' snapped a guard.

'In the name of the King!'

The Viscount pulled a folded sheet of paper bearing the royal seal from his breast pocket.

Without delay, the hatch was unfastened and wrenched open, the lead-lined cover swinging back with a thud.

A gust of warm rank-smelling air rose from the opening.

'My God,' said Fortescue in a whisper, removing his tall beaver hat.

'Pray wait until first light, sir,' said the guard. 'Down there is no place for a gentleman, not in darkness at any rate.'

'We cannot wait until dawn. We cannot delay a single moment.'

'Very well, sir,' the guard said grudgingly, 'I will take you in.'

He turned round and, clutching the lantern in his right hand, eased himself down the ladder.

'How many souls do you keep here?'

'About seven hundred, sir. Although consumption has reduced

the number of late.'

They descended: the guard, Fortescue, Adams and Dunn. With each step down the ladder, the temperature and the stench doubled. It was almost impossible to imagine that there could be so many trapped in such a place.

Adams took one of the lanterns from Dunn and held it high, illuminating the space around him in an arc. There were bodies everywhere laid out on the deck, dozens of them, all men in varying degrees of distress. The only movement was that of the rats, darting for the darkness as the light dispersed them.

'This is the first deck, sir,' said the guard. He paused for a moment, and added. 'When did your acquaintance get here?'

'About two days ago.'

'Then he won't be up 'ere. You see, when you first get in, you're sent right down bottom and, as the years pass, you rise up.'

The Viscount touched the blade of his swordstick to his boot.

'How many levels are there?'

'There are seven, sir.'

'Waste not a moment then. Down into the abyss we must descend.'

'Right you are, sir.'

The guard led the way, down one ladder after the next, his lantern giving flashes of illumination to the gloom. As before, the stink and the heat increased immeasurably until the air was thin.

They picked their way along the seventh deck towards the bows, stepping over the dying and the dead.

'We are well below the waterline,' said Adams.

'To think that man could do this to his fellow man!' exclaimed Dunn, excusing his outburst.

'Mr. Cochran!' shouted Fortescue, 'can you hear me, Mr. Cochran?' There was silence.

Then, suddenly, a figure stripped of his clothing ran towards the light. He was screaming, his arms flailing about, his mouth foaming.

'Is it Cochran?'

The guard punched the man squarely in the jaw. He fell to the floor, knocked out cold.

'A madman, sir.'

'How could any man keep his sanity down here?' said the Viscount.

Adams led the way, calling Cochran's name.

There was no answer.

'My informer was insistent, that he was brought here.'

'Maybe he's over in *Discovery*, sir. She's moored at Deptford.'

'Alas, we have come in vain.'

Fortescue turned to lead the way back to the stairs. Adams followed him, with Dunn taking up the rear. As they passed through the mid section of the ship, a frail voice filtered through the darkness. It was little more than a sigh.

'Robert. Robert.'

Adams tugged the lantern high and moved smartly towards the voice. A man was crouching in the corner where the deck reached the hull. He was bent over, shaking. As the light fell upon him he began to weep.

Adams leant down and touched his hand.

'Simon, dear Simon, thank God we have found you.'

FOURTEEN

AT NOON THE next day six landau carriages arrived at Hoare's Bank. Each one was identical, lacquered in black with gold trim, the drivers liveried in uniforms of moss-green and blue. The windows were blacked out with waxed cloth, their frames reinforced with steel struts. The leaf springs, by which the wheels were suspended from the bodywork, were strengthened specially, so as to allow for a greater load. Each coachman carried a knife in his boot, ready to defend himself and his cargo if attacked.

Sir Geoffrey Caldecott descended from the first vehicle.

His cheeks were even ruddier than usual, his step buoyant, as if all his worries had vanished. A lifetime of misdemeanour had taught him long before that a small gratuity could go a long way.

Five guineas to the debtors' judge had secured Cochran a place on HMS *Warrior*, the grimmest prison hulk in existence. A little more had been sufficient to borrow the armoured carriages from an acquaintance down at the docks. As for Robert Adams, Caldecott smiled at the thought of his plan for the man who had so nearly thrown the grand scheme of Alta Templis into disarray.

Mounting the stone steps, he entered the bank.

Sir Richard Hoare was waiting in the foyer, pacing anxiously. It was a black day for the partners, and one that their director hoped to avert by pleading with the Committee's chairman.

As soon as Caldecott crossed the threshold, Sir Richard swept forward, squirming as he had never squirmed before.

Sir Geoffrey grinned and, as he did so, he dabbed his brow with a square of ivory silk.

'The carriages are waiting outside,' he said hastily. 'I would be grateful if they might be loaded as soon as possible.'

The banker wiped his mouth hard with his hand. There were tears in his eyes.

'My dear Sir Geoffrey,' he intoned, his knees weakening, 'I am quite certain we can come to an arrangement. The bank would be in agreement to augment the remuneration of interest paid on your holdings.'

Caldecott said nothing. Smirking, he shook his head.

'Very well, sir,' said Sir Richard, 'so be it.'

He nodded to the chief porter. Within a moment, the ten-pound bags of gold sovereigns were being carried up from the vaults, out of the door and into the carriages.

Sir Geoffrey was led into the partners' salon to wait in the warm, while Sir Richard Hoare went to his private chamber to gulp down a tumbler of Delamain cognac.

The youngest partner, Henry Blythe, slipped in and poured the Committee's chairman a glass of sherry. He was an awkwardly large young man with an affliction of oily warts on his hands. A promising record at Eton had been marred by his being sent down from Oxford for setting fire to his college during a prank. Family connections had, fortunately, ensured him a career at Hoare's.

He placed the decanter on its silver tray.

'If you would permit me to say how very chuffed I am, Sir Geoffrey,' he said, 'at the Committee's appreciation for Timbuctoo!'

'Quite so,' Caldecott replied, staring into the middle distance.

'I have invested my entire inheritance in the project, sir, and have encouraged my father to do the same. If it is not impertinent, may I ask when you anticipate the expeditionary force might reach the golden city?'

Sir Geoffrey tapped the gold pocket watch attached to his waistcoat by a chain.

'At any moment,' he replied.

FIFTEEN

As the fortunes of the Royal African Committee were shuttled down to Old Jewry, a crowd had gathered in Green Park. Three hundred members of the gentry, and at least twice as many commoners, had ventured out into the cold to watch the elderly Mr. Sadler ascend into the atmosphere in his latest and most celebrated creation.

The aeronaut, as he styled himself, had spent much of the morning filling his flying apparatus, an immense balloon, with hot air. The guy ropes were now stretched tight, almost to breaking point, as the spectators pushed forward in urgent anticipation.

A child called out, asking when the contraption would rise up into the heavens. Mr. Sadler held up a hand,

'All in good time!' he shouted. 'All in good time!'

Just then, there came the sound of horses and a carriage moving swiftly over the grass. The audience turned in surprise, for riding over the parkland was prohibited by law. Another voice exclaimed something. Then another. There was a great deal of murmuring followed by a hush.

Some of the spectators lowered their heads in a bow.

The carriage pulled to a halt a few feet from the balloon. The door, bearing the royal fleur-de-lis in gold, was pulled back and an over-sized mounting block was positioned squarely in place by a pair of footmen.

A minute passed.

Then, slowly, the corpulent bulk of the Prince Regent was eased out from the carriage by an army of liveried staff. A handful of the spectators from the lower classes managed a cheer, their applause lost on the breeze.

The Prince lumbered over to the basket and was greeted by Mr. Sadler. The mounting block was hastened from the carriage and up to the balloon. Realising what was about to occur, the crowd applauded loudly.

'He's going up into the sky!' screeched a little girl.

'Yeah, but 'e'll come down on his 'ead!' roared a man selling mince pies.

Mr. Sadler's assistant climbed into the basket with a low mahogany chair, upholstered in red velvet, bearing the Prince of Wales's crest embroidered in gold thread. When the seat was in position the Prince, again assisted by his footmen, was ushered over the edge of the basket and into the balloon.

The crowd cheered.

At that moment the Marchioness of Hertford arrived, accompanied by her lady-in-waiting, Elizabeth. It appeared that they had both walked from Carlton House without a chaperone. The Marchioness's face was oyster-grey with worry. She moved as fast as she could, the heels of her slender court shoes pressing into the grass, her hair flowing from the sides of her bonnet as if she had tied it in haste.

She hurried to the balloon.

'George dearest!' she called in as soft a voice as she could muster. 'What in heavens are you thinking, dearest?'

The Prince had just got comfortable on the chair. He turned.

'Madam,' he said forcefully, 'one is about to become an aeronaut. Is that not right, Mr. Sadler?'

'Indeed, Your Highness.'

'Well let us proceed at once. There isn't much time before dinner!'

'Very good, Your Highness.'

James Sadler signalled to his assistant, who had clambered out of the balloon. The guy ropes tethering the craft were loosened and, without delay, the balloon and the basket beneath it began to rise rapidly into the air.

SIXTEEN

AT CAMELFORD HOUSE, Simon Cochran spent the afternoon with Viscount Fortescue's retinue of servants fussing over him. His filthy frock coat was taken away and burned on the Viscount's orders, and a tailor sent for from Savile Row.

Down in the drawing room, Cochran was holding court. Dressed in borrowed clothes, he was telling tales of days and nights in the nether regions of HMS *Warrior*.

'I can never repay your thoughtfulness, Viscount, or yours Mr. Adams,' he said. 'Were it not for you both, I would surely have perished, another carcass tossed over into the Thames.'

Clara Fortescue had planned to go out to Lackington's and was putting on her coat when her father burst in with his guests. The sight of the American in her own home again was a wish fulfilled. Unbuttoning her coat, she tossed it over the banisters along with her bonnet.

'How did you survive such a wretched experience, Mr. Cochran?' she asked, leaning over to where he sat bundled in blankets beside the fire.

'My dear Miss Fortescue,' he replied, 'it was terrible, and yet I know that I am free. I appreciate all the more the fortune which smiles so favourably upon me, good fortune I have taken for granted all my life.'

'What I do not understand,' said Fortescue, stiffening his back, 'is how a common debtor would be incarcerated on a hulk, and not at Marshalsea. There were foul forces at work, that is for sure.'

'I wager that Sir Geoffrey and his cronies are behind it,' said Clara harshly, her gentle face turning crimson in a blush.

'Dearest Clara, I am sure you are correct in your evaluation,' the Viscount replied. 'Yet I fear that sooner rather than later Sir Geoffrey's wrongdoings will catch up with him.'

Although Fortescue and his guests were unaware of it, at that very moment a wicker basket was hurtling over the building in which they stood. Inside it, clinging to guy ropes, were Mr. Sadler and the Prince Regent. Had the windows not been so firmly shut, or the silk curtains drawn across them, they may have spied it, arcing across the sky on the sharp winter breeze.

The Prince had used every expletive in his vocabulary. His bloated fingers were wound up in the ropes, his immense weight acting as ballast, preventing the craft from reaching the upper echelons of the capital's atmosphere.

One hour and nine minutes after ascending, the basket touched down with a thud on a patch of farmland west of Hammersmith village. The Regent thanked his creator for delivering him safely back on *terra firma*. He kissed the signet ring on his left hand, bid Mr. Sadler a good day, and struggled with great difficulty to transfer himself from the basket to the grass.

The Prince's entourage had attempted to follow the aircraft from its ascent at Green Park, but had soon lost it. Taking control of the situation in the hope of saving the Regent's life, Hastings dispatched the royal guard to comb London and its environs for the Prince of Wales.

It was ten o'clock by the time the Regent was recovered from
a farmyard in Stamford Brook. He was sitting at a kitchen table,
attended by a bewildered farmer and his wife, eating his way
through a brace of well-cooked mallard ducks.

'There you are, Hastings,' he said distantly. 'I don't know what
kept you, really I don't. Were it not for Mr. and Mrs. Hazelmere,
I would have gone wanton.

'I have invited them to call upon us tomorrow afternoon.
Mr. Hazelmere is of a curious disposition and shares my fondness
for animals. I think he shall enjoy the royal Collection.'

SEVENTEEN

NEWS OF THE Prince's flight over London was reported on page
three of *The Times*. As the story passed from ear to mouth it was
embroidered with the kind of detail that only gossip can provide.
A fishmonger's wife in Knightsbridge claimed that the Regent had
tossed down a golden sovereign as he passed above her. And a
woman in Kensington said that the sight of the balloon had caused
her chickens to lay eggs with double yolks.

At Carlton House, the Prince had been so fatigued by the
adventure that he slept all morning and into the afternoon. When

finally he awoke, he found himself to have an abundance of energy, the like of which he had not enjoyed for years. As soon as he was dressed, he scoffed eleven kippers and half a dozen hardboiled eggs, washed down with half a bottle of fruity young Riesling.

Isabella, the Marchioness of Hertford, scooped up a bowl of strawberries and fed the fruit to the Prince one by one.

'You might have been killed, you silly sausage,' she said, doting.

'Let my detractors be informed that courage still flows in the blood royal!' the Prince exclaimed, before calling for Carême to prepare him a trifle layered with fresh cream and fortified with his favourite maraschino liqueur.

At the same moment he was giving orders to the chef, the farmer's wife, Winifred Hazelmere, was pressing the Sunday best using an iron filled with coals. Never in her wildest dreams had she imagined that royalty would grace their modest home. Her neighbours, some of whom had seen the balloon descend, lavished her with attention as word of the unlikely encounter spread.

More modest than his wife, Mr. Hazelmere refrained from speaking of their invitation to Carlton House. At ten o'clock they set off in their battered old cart to make the journey from Stamford Brook. Neither of them had ever been to London before. They had never had reason to make the journey. As the cart trundled east towards the village of Chelsea, the farmer wondered aloud if it was such a good idea to call upon the Prince.

His wife snapped a hand to the side of his head.

'You heard him as clear as day, inviting us to tea,' she said.

'Well what if he doesn't remember?'

'Of course he will! I am certain the finest silver will be laid out, with crumpets, tea, cakes and strawberry jam. Imagine it, us received by royalty!'

EIGHTEEN

PHILIP RUNDELL, OF Messrs. Rundell and Bridge, had arrived five minutes early for his appointment with Uriah McIntyre, keeper of the Prince's accounts. The master craftsman had visited Carlton House on numerous occasions, almost always to solicit funds owing to his firm. Unfortunately, the Regent's extravagance in commissioning luxury, was not matched by his ability to pay for it. His spending habits had passed into legend, and were frequently lampooned by Lord Liverpool's government.

The accountant's waiting room at Carlton House was stark, plain grey walls devoid of cornicing or wainscot. The floor was stained dark to conceal the low quality of the grain, and there was no carpeting at all. Opulence was not a requirement, as the Prince himself never set foot in the accountant's chamber. Indeed, he didn't even know where it was.

Mr. Rundell expected the senior accountant to question the recent invoices for six large gold vases and a silver service made for Brighton. Priding himself on his attention to the smallest pecuniary sum, Mr. McIntyre could not help himself when it came to economising.

The church clock of St. Martin-in-the Fields struck four. As it did so, the accountant's assistant emerged briskly from the front office to lead Mr. Rundell through to his appointment.

Out on the street, a horse-drawn cart was pulling up. Frederick and Winifred Hazelmere climbed down, brushed the dust and horsehair off their coats and made their way timidly up to the magnificent portico of Carlton House.

The Dragoon Guard, standing to attention to the right of the door, swung round, thumping the butt of his musket onto the pavement.

'Where do you think you are going?!'

'Excuse me, excuse us both,' said the farmer. 'But His Highness the Prince has invited us to call upon him for tea.'

Were he not in uniform, the guard would have fallen down laughing. 'And who might you be?'

'I am farmer Hazelmere, come all the way from Stamford Brook. And this is my wife, Mrs. Hazelmere.'

The guard snatched up the musket and held it taut across

his chest, the base of the bayonet in line with his eyes.

'Move another inch and I'll carve you in two,' he said.

'But we have an appointment,' said the farmer's wife.

'Of course you do,' said the Dragoon. 'And I'm the Earl of Chester!'

NINETEEN

At the Royal African Committee, Falkirk broke the news to the chairman that Simon Cochran had been redeemed from HMS *Warrior*. Sir Geoffrey slapped his hands together, cursed, slipped out his pocket watch and weighed it in his hand.

It was just after ten.

'Falkirk, you are to inform Mr. Jerome that I require all the Committee's directors to be present this afternoon at the narration.' He paused, stuffed the watch back into his waistcoat. 'That is if Mr. Adams graces us with his presence.'

'Very good, sir.'

Once the butler had left his study, Sir Geoffrey Caldecott touched the tips of his fingertips together pensively, removed a keychain from the drawer of his desk, and strode down the stairs to the basement.

In a storeroom hidden behind a pair of steel gates, lay the entire wealth of the Royal African Committee, all of it in gold.

Unlocking the gates, Caldecott bent down. Opening one of the bags, he tapped a few sovereigns into his hand.

There was a lump in his throat.

TWENTY

THAT AFTERNOON, COCHRAN and Adams reached the Committee, delivered there by hackney carriage. They had spent the morning down at the docks, where Adams had enquired which vessel would be next to set sail across the Atlantic.

A rumour had spread through the clubs on St. James's Street that the American was dead, murdered the evening before by a thief in Whitechapel. The gossip reached the ears of Clara Fortescue as she entered the library once again with her cousin Henry Fitzwilliam.

Robert Adams was impatient to complete the narration of his tale. He had learned that a trading vessel, the *Francis Rose*, was taking on cargo down at the Tobacco Dock, preparing to set sail for New York on the dawn tide.

By the time he was in position at the front of the room, an audience of five hundred had packed themselves inside, with more arriving every minute.

Sir Geoffrey Caldecott was conspicuously absent. He was up in his study writing an encoded message to the Duke of York:

The means are ready with which to furnish the change, he wrote.
I shall send word when we are ready to act. Please remember, sire,
that we must proceed with the most grave and circumspect attention.

Down in the library, Cochran read through the passage inscribed
in longhand by Sir Joseph Banks. He unfastened the lid of the
inkwell, dipped his quill, and nodded.

The audience's shrill conversation grew muffled and died away.

The American stepped forward.

'As I remember,' he said, 'I had described how the agent of
Mr. Joseph Dupuis, the British Consul at Mogador, revealed himself
to me, and how he had been given instructions to redeem only
those who had not renounced their faith. I could never absolve my
colleagues of forsaking the Lord. But, despite my disappointment,
I was much saddened at leaving them.

'They had hoped to follow our little caravan. After all as
Musalmans, they were both free men. But our former master
declared they were forbidden ever to quit Wadi Noon. Attempt to
do so, and he would hunt them and end their lives.

'And so it was that, two days later, the consul's agent, his servants
and I, set off towards Mogador. As we left Wadi Noon, Martin Clarke
and Unis Newsham ran after us, their bare feet digging into the sand.
They had not gone more than a few yards when our former master
ran out and struck them down with his whip.

'Omar bin Assad and I continued walking for thirteen days. On the fourteenth morning we reached the brow of a low hill and, in ascending it, we set eyes upon the most attractive sight: a harbour, in which there were sailing ships bobbing about like toys, sailors attending to the rigging, and stevedores hurrying the cargoes ashore. It was a magical moment. I felt as if I had been rewarded with a new life. The agent took me to the home of his master, Mr. Dupuis, who welcomed me like a lost son.

'I spent several weeks making a full description of the desert as I had seen it, and of my trials and tribulations in captivity. Before I could leave Marocco, I was obliged to venture into the interior of the country, to the walled city of Fez, in order to obtain permission from the Sultan himself.

'Mr. Dupuis was courteous enough to make the journey with me. We travelled first to the city of Marrakech and then over the towering Mountains of Atlas. And, after many adventures, we arrived at the palace gates.

'An executioner was standing guard at the most colossal of doors, a scimitar in his hand. He demanded to know why we had come. Mr. Dupuis presented his credentials. At once the doors opened inwards and, before we knew it, we were admitted to the throne room.

'The Sultan was a large man with cultivated manners and a

great fondness for stuffed dates. He took an interest in the fact that I had been enslaved in the great desert, and graciously signed the documents for me to leave his kingdom.

'It was with a heavy heart that I prepared to leave Mr. Dupuis, with whom I had formed a close friendship. Before we parted, I presented him with the locket fashioned from a seed, which the king of Timbuctoo had given to me. It was a fitting gift. For the tyrannical King Woolo had instructed me to present it to whoever saved my life.

'By chance, I found passage on a ship bound for New York. But, unhappily, it was wrecked in a gale off the coast of Wales. I managed to get ashore near Holyhead. Destitute, I made my way to London, where I hoped to gain an interview with the American ambassador.

'It was then that, having been robbed on the streets of London, and left in a wretched state, I was discovered by Viscount Fortescue, who brought my attention to this Committee.'

Adams took a step backwards, and thanked the audience for listening to his narration. 'Now that you and this Committee have heard my tale,' he said, 'my life can begin again. Without delay I shall return to my wife, a love for whom has enabled me to endure the most terrible of hardships.'

Robert Adams fell silent.

Suddenly, the library's doors swung open and Sir Geoffrey

Caldecott stormed in. Behind him, moving fast over the waxed parquet, were the directors of the Committee. After them, marched two pairs of Grenadier Guards.

'Seize this imposter!' Caldecott shouted at the top of his lungs. 'For he has lied not only to this august gathering, but to a Royal Committee!'

Pushing the desk forward, Simon Cochran leapt to his feet and stood in front of Adams. One of the guards thrust him aside. The directors, who had fanned out around the library, began hurling insults at the American. Some members of the audience had joined them, railing against the tale.

The chairman waved a long document, sealed at the bottom with scarlet wax.

'I have the legal authority to have this American criminal locked up in the Tower for perjury against the Crown!'

Struggling against the iron manacles that had been fastened around his wrists, Robert Adams was led away.

VIII

Sir Geoffrey Caldecott receives a second letter from Amsterdam — On honeymoon in the Alps, Beattie discovers her husband in union with another man — Mr. Adams finds himself locked up in the Tower of London — Viscount Fortescue sends a secret letter through the Foreign Office — In the crypt of St. Paul's, Sir Geoffrey Caldecott has an interview with the Duke of York — Mr. Horace Evett arrives for work as an orderly at St. Bartholomew's — Mr. Florence arrives at the cell in which Mr. Adams is incarcerated — Mr. Evett contracts variola — Mr. Adams foils a plan against him — The American Ambassador, John Quincy Adams, discusses the situation at Camelford House — Lord Alvanley comes to learn that Major Peddie and his team are dead — Sir Geoffrey Caldecott plots with Mr. Jerome — A message arrives at The Tower for Mr. Adams — The golden wealth of the Royal African Committee is transported down river — The Prince Regent summons Mr. Sadler — A visitor arrives in some urgency at Camelford House — The Royal African Committee is mobbed by investors — Beattie's letter to Mr. Cochran, explaining her discovery and subsequent misery.

ONE

A PRIVATE MESSENGER arrived on foot at the Committee an hour after the audience had dispersed. His face chapped and his clothing ragged, he went by the name of Kees van Beers.

He had ridden from Amsterdam, taking passage across the Channel on a merchant's sloop. The journey up from Dover had taken two weeks, twice the normal time. Highwaymen had struck near Sevenoaks, relieving him of almost everything but his clothing. The robbery had forced him to borrow funds from one of his master's associates, who lived at the nearby village of Paddock Wood.

The only thing van Beers had managed to save was a letter from his master, a Dutch businessman, to the chairman of the Royal African Committee.

What the messenger did not know was that the same evening he had been robbed, the highwayman and his troop were apprehended by a posse of villagers. They had struck so many locals in recent weeks that mob justice took over. At dawn, the posse slung nooses over the branches of a sycamore tree and meted out justice of their own.

At Old Jewry, the doorman received the letter and looked the messenger up and down. Too well-mannered to ask how the man had got into such a bad state, he thanked him, and said to go round to the back door and ask cook for a plate of hot food.

The letter was passed to Falkirk, who placed it on his salver and ascended the stairs.

Breaking the seal, Sir Geoffrey held the text to the light.

It was a second correspondence from Mr. Winkel of Amsterdam.

Thanking the chairman for the sum of £400, he revealed a fresh piece of valuable information. His English acquaintance had, he asserted, been presented with sixteen ingots of gold by the king of Timbuctoo. Each ingot weighed in excess of twenty pounds. However, the gentleman, who wished to remain anonymous for the time being, found himself in a quandary. He had no way of transporting the bullion from the African shore in safety.

So he had secreted it away in caves outside Algiers.

For the trifling sum of £2000, to be paid in advance, he was prepared to allow the Committee to take advantage of the difficult situation. Were they to assist in the transport of the bullion across to Europe, they could count on receiving a third of the entire hoard as payment.

Sir Geoffrey read the letter once, and then a second time a little more slowly. Suspicious by nature, he might have taken the claim with a pinch of salt. But, at the bottom of the letter, as a postscript, Mr. Winkel had written: *I have had a sample of the metal tested by jewellers to the royal court here in Holland, and it has been found to be exceedingly pure, with a trace of platinum.*

The detail dispelled any doubt that Caldecott might have held. For he had read in Mungo Park's reports that gold mined in the Timbuctoo region was high in platinum, a fact of which Robert Adams had appeared to be unaware.

The proposal seemed like a chance to further discredit the American sailor, as well as making a tidy profit in the bargain.

Sir Geoffrey stepped over to his writing desk, took out a sheet of watermarked paper, a quill, and twisted off the stopper of his crystal inkwell half full with walnut ink. Pausing to think for a moment, he smiled to himself, and began:

My dear Mr. Winkel, I was so pleased to hear from you once again…

TWO

TRAVERSING THE ALPS in the middle of winter had been an optimistic plan. Thomas Wittershall and his frail bride were carried over the highest passes in specially designed palanquins, their attendants forced to stumble after them through the ever-deepening snow.

Beattie had suffered from the altitude since leaving Geneva, and found herself in the most miserable state. Her husband did his best to seem compassionate, yet was of little support.

By the time the couple reached Turin, they were both battered, bruised, and feeling despondent. Fortunately, Wittershall's connections had secured them use of the baroque Palazzo Carignano, commissioned almost two hundred years before by Prince Philibert Amadeus of the House of Savoy. The private apartments were lavish, adorned with medieval tapestries, rare brocades and acres of silk.

On the first night they shared a magnificent gilt bedstead of considerable size, veneered in walnut and ivory. Through England, France and Switzerland, Beattie had prepared herself nightly for the inevitable ritual of deflowerment. But, each evening, when the lamp was dimmed, her husband had drifted straight to sleep, as if forgetting he was not alone. Beattie did not particularly like the man she had wed, but felt a duty to concede to consummation. Towards this end, she bathed in water scented lightly with orange bergamot, before dressing herself in the most graceful nightgown she possessed.

Wittershall came late to bed, a little after twelve. He found his wife propped up in bed reading Defoe's *Robinson Crusoe*. She yawned, laid the book on the nightstand, and tenderly stroked a hand down the pillow beside her own.

'I have an early start,' said Wittershall sharply, as if answering her solicitation.

'Thomas, my dear, ought we not to…'

Beattie blushed.

'To what?'

'To do what is right in the eyes of the Lord,' she replied, touching a finger to the collar of her nightdress.

Wittershall turned down the wick and, almost at once, began to snore.

Next morning, Beattie awoke to find her husband already departed. The maidservant informed her that he had risen at dawn and ridden out for hunting with the Prince of Piedmont. Writing to her younger sister, Phoebe, Beattie confided that the marriage was not yet consummated.

Late the same afternoon, she took a stroll through the Palazzo Carignano, her maidservant, Emily, accompanying her. They walked for miles, marvelling at the artwork and the grandeur, still thankful beyond words for surviving the Alpine crossing. Beattie joked that she would be willing to spend the remaining years of her life in Turin, so long as her husband would rise to his duty.

The maidservant was about to reply, when they were both startled by a sound coming from a nearby room.

'What could that be?' said Beattie, alarmed.

'One of the servants, I am sure,' Emily replied.

Then came the noise of glass shattering, of shouts, and what was apparently a male voice reaching ecstasy.

Beattie stepped forward, her small feet moving nimbly over the floor. She thrust open the door to a study of some kind.

Inside was a single piece of furniture, a low desk with ormolu fittings. Upon it, on his back was a naked man, and upon him — also naked — was her husband, Thomas Wittershall.

THREE

SIX JET BLACK ravens were tearing at a sheep's carcass with their beaks, on a lawn, a stone's throw from the White Tower. The birds had been kept at the royal fortress on the Thames for centuries, perhaps even as far back as Richard the Lionheart. They owed their endurance to a remark uttered by King Charles II, who had declared that if the ravens left the Tower, the British monarchy would fall.

One of the Yeomen of the Guard, Basil Talefrot, was charged with the responsibility of maintaining a good number of the birds. He had never liked them much, but took advantage of the duty. Each week, when sent to buy meat from Smithfield, he would obtain the cheapest, most foul lump of animal flesh he could lay his hands upon, and keep the balance, paid for by the Privy Purse.

Over the eight centuries since its construction, the fortress had boasted a roll of eminent prisoners. They included King Henry IV and Elizabeth I, Sir Walter Raleigh, the Duke of Orleans, and the conspirator Guy Fawkes. Some had spent decades there, while others were executed on the day of their arrival, or once their usefulness had reached its end.

Robert Adams was taken to a small cell in the Lanthorn Tower. Its walls were grey stone, blackened where previous captives had set fire to anything they could find in order to chase away the cold. The window was barred, with a view out over the south side of the menagerie. From time to time a giraffe, elephant, ostrich or lioness would stride into view in the courtyard below.

The American might have been surprised at the sudden turn in events but he was not in the least. With Caldecott at its helm, the African Committee was, in Adams' mind, little better than King Woolo's regime. Both men were repressive in their own way, champions of avarice and perversion.

As soon as Adams had been led to the cell, and his manacles removed, he had sat on the bare floor and prayed. As ever, his thoughts turned to Christina. Over the previous handful of days he had found himself wondering if she had given up on him, perhaps forced into a marriage to one of her father's business associates. His disappearance would surely have given way to a dissolution, after all he had been gone five years.

He pulled out the frail lace handkerchief, soiled with dirt, the embroidered border long torn away. Kissing it, pressing it to his face, he thanked the Lord for sparing him through endless tribulations.

Once the sun had gone down, the jailer opened the door, keys jangling on their ring. In his left hand there was a bowl of gruel and a chicken bone. He had worked at the Tower for forty years and was known by all as Raffan, although his name was in actual fact Josiah Digby.

''Ere's ya grub,' he said, slipping the bowl into the darkness. 'And what are you in 'ere for?'

The American gave thanks.

'I am here for speaking the truth,' he said.

'Well you're not the first,' came the reply fast. 'And I dare say there will be others once your neck's been snapped out there at Traitors' Gate.'

Adams asked about the animals.

'That's the menagerie,' Raffan said, slurring. 'Royal animals they are.'

'When were they brought here?'

'God bleeding knows,' said Raffan. 'I'd say they were left 'ere after the flood.'

FOUR

Across London, Viscount Fortescue was seated at his writing desk scratching a message swiftly, dipping only once the quill was quite dry. The letter was addressed to his old friend Joseph Dupuis, British Consul at Mogador. If there were to be a solution for Robert Adams, the Viscount was convinced the French-born diplomat would be part of it. Having been the one who introduced Adams to the African Committee, he felt a responsibility for alleviating his state of imprisonment.

Once he had finished writing, Fortescue sealed the letter, imprinting the wax with his monogram. Then he called Dalston. The manservant was already positioned outside the study door, ready for the instruction to enter.

In the years he had attended the Viscount, he had learned to take note of the clues. The bitter aroma of sealing wax, which seemed to seep through the entire house, hinted at an urgent letter needing delivery.

'Have a messenger take this to Sir Robert Montgomery at the Foreign Office,' he said.

'Very good, sir.'

'Oh, and Dalston?'

'Sir?'

'Please speak to no one of this instruction.'

The butler did not reply, but nodded instead. He was the one man in the Viscount's employ who could be depended on for absolute discretion.

As he left the study, Clara knocked and, in the same movement, burst in.

'Father,' she said, her usual composure lost in fluster, 'there must be something we can do to resolve this horrid affair.'

'We would all do well to be patient, my dear. The moves are delicate. Make a false one and Mr. Adams could lose his life.'

'Do you really believe that?'

'Believe what?'

'That the blithering Mr. Caldecott is capable of it?'

'Indeed, I do. *Sir* Geoffrey Caldecott has his back up against the wall. There's no telling what he will do to secure his loathsome position.'

'But what can we do?'

'Very little at the moment, my dear. We can do very little indeed.'

FIVE

A FIGURE WAS standing alone at the tomb of Horatio Nelson in the crypt of St. Paul's. He was dressed in a long coat of fine charcoal worsted that, in the dim light, appeared almost invisible. His face was rounded and pink, clean shaven that morning by a valet, his eyes swollen from the cold.

Despite his faith in the cryptic communications from the Master of Alta Templis, the back of his neck bristled with anticipation. Until that moment the notion of ousting his brother was just that — a notion, a fantasy. But his attendance at the designated meeting place heralded a point of no return.

Five minutes past four o'clock, there was the sound of leather soles moving quickly over stone. Sir Geoffrey Caldecott hastened from the shadow of the tomb's far side. He was wheezing, his left hand pressed hard against his chest.

'Forgive me, Your Highness,' he said, bowing low, his breath straining all the more. 'I wanted to be quite certain I was not followed here.'

The Duke of York said nothing at first. He looked at the Master's face, scanning it, as its features inched forward into the light.

Only after a full minute of silence did he speak.

'As leader of your assembly,' he said, 'I presume you comprehend the hazard that accompanies this conspiracy.'

'Indeed, I do, Your Highness, as do the brethren of Alta Templis.'

The Duke removed a gold pocket watch from his waistcoat.

'Each second we stand in conversation poises us closer to the hangman's noose. Speak swiftly and omit no detail.'

Sir Geoffrey touched a handkerchief to his brow, wrapping its length around his hand.

'The Royal African Committee has raised a significant sum with which to alter the succession, Your Highness, the succession as planned by His Majesty before the veil of malady descended.

'On the first of February a servant at Carlton House shall be found to be infected with variola. Fearing an outbreak of the disease, and the infection of the Regent, the physician royal shall insist on replacing those staff most intimate to His Highness. The replacement will be made without delay.'

'And the substitute staff?'

'Loyal to us, all of them ready to die to place Your Highness where you rightfully belong.'

'The army are behind me,' said the Duke reflectively, touching a hand to the granite memorial beside him. 'It is the navy that gives cause for concern.'

'Fear not, Your Highness, we shall use our accumulated funds to win new friends on the seas.'

'And what of my brother?'

Sir Geoffrey pressed down his cravat, the dampness on his fingertips soaked up by the cloth.

'I suggest that he be disposed of, Your Highness.'

'In the Tower?'

'I think not. Cast him into a cell and, though his life hang by a thread, there would still be a threat. Forgive me for speaking so candidly, Highness, but there are plenty who will take delight in viewing the bloated corpse of a buffoon swinging at Execution Dock.'

The Duke of York glanced back into the shadows of the crypt.

'I heard something!' he said, alarmed.

Both men ceased speaking. They listened. A bat flapped fast towards them out from the darkness.

'There is no one,' said Caldecott, breathing deep. 'I assure you.'

The Duke swallowed. He moved a little to the left in order to get a better view of the Master's face.

'If you fail me,' he said after an extended pause, 'I shall kill you and your family, and those of all brethren. I'll boil down the bones and make pig's swill from the blood. Do you understand me?'

Sir Geoffrey Caldecott, chairman of the Committee and Master of Alta Templis, allowed the weight of his portly frame to fall onto his right knee. Leaning forward, he lifted the Duke's right hand in his, and kissed the knuckles.

'I shall never fail you, Your Majesty,' he said.

SIX

AT A HANDSOME new building in Smithfield, a fresh-faced young man named Horace Evett arrived for his first day of employment. He had been the only candidate for the job and, as such, was welcomed with open arms by the officious director of

St. Bartholomew's Hospital, Dr. Ebenezer Spruce.

The boy, who was seventeen years of age, explained he had worked as a member of the Regent's household until leaving the post for private reasons. He had shown no loss of cheer when it was made plain to him that all the patients confined within the sanatorium's wall were suffering from variola, the fearful smallpox virus. Indeed, young Horace's spirits seemed curiously buoyed by the news. And, when the matter of his wage was brought up, there was none of the usual muttering at the pittance on offer. Instead of voicing dissatisfaction, Horace had asked enthusiastically when he might begin.

Dr. Spruce took time to show off the wards and introduce the infected, their skin festooned with terrible pustules. While in the third room, where the most distressed patients were contained, he demonstrated how to restrain a victim using a cudgel, buckles and leather thongs.

On the hour, each hour of the day and night, an orderly would roam the corridors with a special ventilating machine, a scarf wound tight over his nose and mouth. The billowing grey-green vapour was so pungent that it stupefied the patients and staff alike. Having devoted his career to the treatment of variola, Dr. Ebenezer Spruce was adamant that the best way to treat a pustulating body was from the inside out.

SEVEN

SINCE HIS RELEASE from the prison hulk, Simon Cochran had been beleaguered by insomnia. He had taken to drinking a tincture of valerian root an hour before bed, as a way of coaxing himself to sleep. The remedy had been prescribed by Sir Joseph Banks, who had called in the week before to enquire about Robert Adams.

Greeting the distinguished botanist warmly, Cochran had explained that there was no way of gaining admittance to a prisoner confined in the Tower.

The American's custody had filled the Committee secretary with anger, a kind he had never quite known before. Unable to look Sir Geoffrey in the eye, he was ready to relinquish his post, and would have resigned immediately had he not been advised otherwise by Viscount Fortescue.

In the Fleet Street chambers, Adams' spot on the sofa was now taken by Richard Florence, the fellow American sailor they had taken in. Cochran had been brought up to give help to those in need, but, even so, he found Florence's company to be quite contrary. The sailor had pleaded poverty and had resorted to begging. Yet, on the morning after Adams' incarceration, Cochran found him with a £5 note. When asked how he could have come upon such an enormous sum, Florence exclaimed that it had been presented to him by the American Ambassador, John Quincy Adams.

Twenty days after Adams was marched out from the Committee's library, Florence thanked Cochran for his hospitality, and announced his intention of leaving the next morning on a brigantine, *Jezebel*, bound for New York. By dawn the following day he had disappeared.

Relieved that Florence had gone, Cochran enquired about the vessel, and was informed that no craft of any such name had set sail from the London docks for a year or more.

At noon on the same day, Robert Adams scratched the outline of a face on the floor of his cell. Then came the sound of keys jangling. It meant that Raffan, the jailer, was coming with a bowl of gruel. Listening to the sound of feet moving over stone, he looked up. Something was wrong. The footsteps were uneven, as if the jailer were walking with a limp. The hatch in the door opened and an American accent called Adams' name.

'It's me,' said the voice.

'Who?'

'Richard Florence!'

EIGHT

AT SMITHFIELD, HORACE Evett found that restraining the patients with the straps enabled him to fondle their pustules without them shying away in pain.

When Dr. Spruce and the other orderlies left him alone, Evett rubbed his hands over their faces, before touching the fingers to his own face and down across his chest. Unlike the others who came into contact with the patients, Dr. Spruce included, Evett was not repulsed by them. Rather, he found himself strangely drawn to their condition, as if there was beauty in the illness's dramatic symptoms.

For as long as he could remember, Horace Evett had harboured masochistic tendencies. They had begun a few years before when he had contracted cholera, and had almost died. Instead of being despondent at being so weakened, he found himself rather cheered and sexually aroused.

On the second week of his employment, Evett was assigned to night duty. He found it all the easier to maintain contact with the infected during the hours of darkness. The first two nights passed quietly enough. Then, on the third evening, a young woman began screaming, tearing at her sores. She was so wildly distressed that Horace led her into an adjoining room. At first she struggled to resist him, but in her anguish she was no match for his strength. Slamming the door shut, he bound her wrists and ankles to a low chair, forced a restraint into her mouth and tied it into place. Then, as she struggled frantically to free herself, Horace Evett thrust himself upon her.

The next afternoon he awoke at his lodgings in Clerkenwell.

His head was pounding, his face pouring with perspiration. Without thinking, he ran a hand up his undershirt over his chest. The skin was riddled with bumps the size of peppercorns. Scribbling a line of words in capitals on a scrap of paper, he opened the window, and called out to a pair of porters who were resting their sedan chair across the street.

'Sixpence if you take this to Old Jewry, fast as you can!'

NINE

RICHARD FLORENCE TRIED every key until he had opened the door. He limped over to Adams, and the two men hugged.

'How did you get in here?'

'I slipped the guard a little something to turn a blind eye for an hour.'

'How's Simon?'

'He's worrying about you.'

'What news is there?'

'So much. But I can't tell you. There's not the time.'

Removing his coat, Florence gave it to Adams.

'Quickly, put this on,' he said. 'I will leave the doors behind me unlocked. In five minutes make your way to the yard. One of the zebras has died. It's been loaded aboard a cart, ready to be taken away. Get under the canvas that's drawn over the back. I'll meet you on the other side of the gate.'

Adams ran to the window and glanced down. There was a cart and some commotion, a group of figures struggling with ropes.

'Thank you, Richard,' he said, his tone sincere.

Florence hurried out, leaving the cell door ajar.

Robert Adams went back to the window. The men had vanished now and an eerie silence had fallen over the Tower. The only sound was the macaques screeching down in the menagerie.

As he waited for five minutes to pass, he remembered a conversation with Raffan, in which he had learned that a prisoner caught attempting to escape would forfeit his right to a trial. Raffan had described how a well-known traitor had been tricked in such a way, and led out to the gallows the next morning.

Adams looked out of the window again.

The familiar sound of guards' boots striking the flagstones was gone. Then it struck him — there were no soldiers on duty. It was as if the Tower had been left unguarded on purpose.

He thought back to the first meeting with Florence, and how Cochran and he had taken him in. What a coincidence that the only other American he had met in London had come from the same town as he. *Coincidence... that was it*. It wasn't a coincidence at all.

Adams rubbed a hand over his face. He wasn't going to surrender his life so easily to Caldecott.

Pacing over to the iron door, he pulled it shut.

TEN

JOHN QUINCY ADAMS arrived at Camelford House precisely at eight. He and Viscount Fortescue had only met twice before — once at the home of Sir Joseph Banks, and once at a lecture at the Royal Academy. After reading a monograph by the Viscount on Indo-European linguistics, he was eager that they might become better acquainted.

The American Ambassador was a lean man with a lengthy nose, piercing black eyes, and a mouth that seemed more satisfied closed than open. He lived nearby in a mansion on Grosvenor Square and had walked across to the Viscount's residence in Hanover Square, against the advice of his private secretary.

Having been escorted into the grand drawing room by a footman, he made a beeline for the fireplace. He was standing there warming his hands, when the Viscount strode in.

'Your Excellency,' Fortescue said, slowing as he approached, 'what an honour to have you here at Camelford.'

'Believe me, sir, the honour is all mine,' Quincy Adams replied.

A butler approached, bearing a tray upon which sat a decanter of bohemian crystal, filled to the neck with oak-aged port. Two glasses were poured and served by a second servant.

The Viscount placed his glass on the mantelpiece and twisted it so that the cut glass edge caught the light. He cleared his throat, and smiled as if he were about to say something of importance.

'I am not certain if you are aware, Ambassador, but a young American has been narrating the tale of his captivity in the great African desert to the Royal African Committee.'

'Yes, yes, of course I have heard of him,' Quincy Adams responded at once. 'All of London knows of him, do they not? And what a tale it is!'

Fortescue lifted his glass from the marble mantel and took a sip.

'Might I enquire, sir, if you have made the acquaintance of the young man?'

'No, Viscount, no I have not. I regret that my mind has been on ameliorating the discord between our nations. But I understand he has been incarcerated. My staff have requested an interview with him, although I believe that permission has been refused.'

Viscount Fortescue cleared his throat again.

'Yes, of course, there is a protocol to follow with regard to prisoners charged with perjury before a Royal Committee.'

'Poor fellow,' said the Ambassador reflectively. 'I have decried slavery of any kind my entire life. And, as if the hardship he endured in Africa was not deplorable enough, his incarceration is preposterous. Perhaps I ought to write to His Majesty at Windsor.'

'Alas,' said Fortescue, 'it appears as if the King has been gripped by another of his bouts. His faculties are otherwise engaged.'

'Then what is there to do?'

The Viscount smiled wryly.

'I have devised a little scheme,' he said in little more than a whisper. 'I anticipate that with time it will provide us with some dramatic results.'

ELEVEN

BYRON AND ALVANLEY were seated in the bow window at White's. Neither had said a word for fifteen minutes. Both were brooding on Timbuctoo — Lord Alvanley on his investment, and Lord Byron on a poem he was writing on lust for the golden city.

The distant destination conjured a sense of anticipation, the like of which the two men could only dream of. Born into wealth, Alvanley had never known a day without luxury or pampering, but even so he yearned for more. For him, Timbuctoo was an opportunity to instantly augment the already vast family fortune.

As for Byron, he may have been born a baronet, but it was the hope of celebrity gained from his pen that fuelled his ambition.

He knew little of the African Committee's quest but, from what he had heard, he guessed it was based on deception.

The silence was broken by the arrival of Byron's publisher, John Murray. A mild-mannered Scot, he scurried rather than walked, his left hand clenched at his waist, eyes alert, his nose pricked upwards like a shrew's.

Murray was anxious to inform his most notable author of recent sales, but was sensible of the fact that affairs of business were deemed inappropriate for a gentlemen's club. Exploiting Byron's meteoric rise to fame, had made him wealthy, and had transformed his rooms on nearby Albemarle Street into the heart of London's literary scene.

'Gentlemen!' he said, filling the word with warmth, 'my greetings to you both on this crisp winter day!'

Byron motioned to the butler and, a moment later, a cup of steaming chocolate was placed before his guest. The three engaged in pleasantries, discussing the weather, until Alvanley could stand it no more.

'Tell us the news, sir,' he said to Murray. 'What gossip seeps through the walls of Albemarle Street?'

When in public, the publisher disapproved of gossip, as spreading it tended to backfire. But in private he liked nothing more than to pass on the latest chitchat. Lulled by the distinguished company, and by the chocolate, he lowered his head.

'There is something that appears most curious,' he said.

'Oh?'

Lord Alvanley pushed himself up in the low chair.

'News from the far-off shores of Africa.'

'*Africa*?' echoed Byron.

'Indeed.'

'Pray, tell, sir.'

'Well it concerns the fêted expedition to the metropolis of gold, to…'

'To Timbuctoo?'

'Yes, sir, to Timbuctoo.'

Byron jerked forward, stuffing another cushion under his misshapen right foot.

'To which expedition do you allude, Mr. Murray?'

'That of the Royal African Committee.'

Alvanley's large body jolted to attention. He leant forward, struggling to retain his composure.

'Tell me, sir, tell me without delay, have Major Peddie and his force captured the city of Timbuctoo?'

John Murray took a neatly folded handkerchief and dabbed it to his right nostril. He sniffed.

'Alas,' he said. 'I must reply in the negative. I understand from my sources that the lives of Major Peddie and his entire unit have been extinguished, snuffed out by savages upon the wide African plains.'

'My God,' said Byron in a low voice.

Seated beside him, his face mirrored in the bow window, Alvanley sat motionless, as if he had been informed that his entire family had been hanged. With a vacant expression he rose slowly, and excused himself.

'There is an urgent matter I must attend to,' he said.

TWELVE

THE MESSAGE FROM Horace Evett was carried in to Caldecott by Cochran, as Falkirk was away on sick leave. It read simply:

THIS IS THE FIRST DAY. H.E.

Cochran glanced at the note as he ascended the mahogany staircase. He might not have understood its meaning, but he knew that a ruse of some kind was underway. Snatching the message, Sir Geoffrey squinted at it, and barked an order for his overcoat.

An hour before, Cochran had heard the news about Peddie, the very same that had reached Mr. Murray's ears. If it were true, he assumed that Caldecott had received the information well in advance. The silence from Africa suggested that the expedition had met a violent end some time before.

Sweeping from the Committee building, Caldecott ordered his coachman to take him to an address in Covent Garden. The rims of the carriage wheels were soon moving swiftly over the cobbles, as Sir Geoffrey bounced about on the padded bench. On the way out, he had overheard the doorman at Old Jewry informing the footman about the slaughtered expedition. It was only a matter of time before the whole of London would be discussing Major Peddie's ignominious end.

The carriage trundled to the right of St. Mary-le-Strand, and turned away from the river up into Covent Garden. The fruit-sellers were packing up their wares, fending off the beggars hoping for handouts. A woman was lying on the ground at the foot of a stall heaped with muddy cabbages. Her ragged clothing was infested with lice, her face scarred from burns. In her hands was an empty bottle of gin.

Caldecott's carriage sliced passed the woman, missing her by an inch. It came to a halt outside a fine Palladian mansion on the southern side of King Street. Sir Geoffrey descended and rapped at the building's door. When it was opened by a butler, the chairman burst in.

'Tell Mr. Jerome to come down at once!' he said urgently.

'Very good, sir. If you would await him in the drawing room.'

No sooner had Sir Geoffrey seated himself beside the roaring fire, than Henry Jerome appeared. He was about to say something, but Caldecott cut him off.

'We are ready to move forward,' he said. 'The boy from Prinny's household has contracted the disease. I will send word for him to return to his duties at Carlton House, while you send a message to the Duke of York advising him that we are ready to assist in his elevation to the throne.'

Jerome took a pinch of snuff from a walnut box, and sniffed.

'And what of His Majesty?' he asked darkly.

'It is regrettable, I know, but we have no other recourse.'

Henry Jerome raised an eyebrow quizzically.

'Laudanum,' said Caldecott slowly, 'administered by the surgeon royal.'

'But could you arrange such a thing?'

'I already have.' He smiled. 'Everyone has a price,' he said.

'The timing is just as well. News of Major Peddie's death has broken and is sweeping London.'

Sir Geoffrey checked the mantel clock against his Breguet.

'We will have to move the funds from the strong room,' he said, 'I shall have it done tonight.'

'And what of the American?'

'Adams?'

'Yes, Mr. Adams.'

'He failed to take the bait to escape. A pity,' said Caldecott. 'But no matter. Our future will cleanse us of our past. And it shall put an end to this absurd Regency. Mark my words — Mr. Adams will swing from a rope before the month is out.'

Jerome took another pinch of snuff and sneezed.

'There's another matter to attend to.'

'What?'

'Alta Templis.'

Sir Geoffrey Caldecott stared into the flames.

'The brethren,' he said, smirking. 'Why cut an apple in pieces when you could enjoy the entire fruit?'

'Would you sacrifice those you hold so dear?'

Caldecott rose to his feet. His face was suddenly flushed with rage.

'Indeed I would,' he said.

THIRTEEN

RAFFAN HAD BLOWN the guinea given him by Florence, whoring the night before. He prided himself on the ability to satisfy numerous women even in the most inebriated condition. All morning and for much of the afternoon, he had dozed on a straw mattress positioned outside the row of cells. He was fast asleep when a messenger arrived and hammered on the guard gate.

'Who's there?' yelled Raffan, lurching up with a start.

'A message for one of the prisoners!'

'Away with you!'

The sound of silver on the messenger's palm silenced the jailer. He got up, and moved briskly to the gate. The coins were passed over.

'Who's the message for?'

'For the American.'

'Give it to me.'

'It's not in writing. I've been ordered to recite it.'

The jailer signalled to the guards. The gate was unlocked and, soon after, the messenger was standing at the hatch to Adams' cell.

'Mr. Adams?'

'Yes, I am he.'

'Greetings to you. Viscount Fortescue has instructed me to hasten here. I bear a message of the most urgent and important nature.'

Adams jumped up from the corner in which he was sitting.

'Thank you! Please tell it to me.'

Pushing his face against the bars of the inspection hatch, the messenger cleared his throat.

'You must listen very carefully,' he said.

FOURTEEN

AT MIDNIGHT, WITH a dark grey mist seeping up the Thames, thirty Dragoons loyal to the Duke of York arrived at the rear entrance of the Royal African Committee. Sir Geoffrey Caldecott was alone in the building. He led the soldiers down into the basement and unlocked the gates into the strong room.

'These sacks must be moved as quickly as possible,' he said to the sergeant.

'We'll need dozens of carriages to move all this, sir.'

Caldecott held up the lantern and jabbed a finger towards the door.

'Not by road,' he said. 'We'll move it down the river. Come with me. I will show you.'

A slim passage ran under the street from Old Jewry, south to the river. It had been created in secrecy decades before by a previous chairman of the Committee, for the purposes of smuggling slave wealth into the building to evade the prying eyes of the city's tax inspectors.

The Dragoons removed their jackets and began ferrying the gold down the passage. They formed a chain, working together in relay, and were soon all drenched in sweat. Sir Geoffrey Caldecott made his way down the line. He unlocked the door that gave on to the river. A steam-powered barge was waiting, bobbing on the high tide, the paddle-wheel at the stern gleaming in the lantern-light. Before being carried aboard, the bags were packed into square elm crates, numbered in red paint, and nailed shut.

By one-thirty, the barge was weighed down.

Caldecott clambered aboard with the Dragoons and ordered its captain to make haste to a secure warehouse at St. Saviour's Dock.

FIFTEEN

A MALE ZEBRA of average height was delivered at Carlton House the next morning by Bateman. The Prince Regent was informed of its arrival over a late breakfast served in the circular dining room. He gave instructions for Frosch to open the crate and to place the creature in the Collection room. His equerry, Hastings, asked if His Highness would not prefer to see the animal being unveiled for himself, as had become the custom. The Prince of Wales shook his head. He was tiring of the Collection altogether. A new and far more appealing hobby had captured his interest — flight.

'I am thinking of having the whole lot packed up and sent to Windsor,' he said, chewing a mouthful of kedgeree. 'The animals would I am sure bolster the spirits of His Majesty, eh what?'

Bowing, Hastings walked backwards towards the door.

'Fetch Mr. Sadler. Have him brought here at teatime today.'

'I believe, Highness,' said the equerry tensely, 'that Mr. Sadler the aeronaut is currently soaring over the south coast in his balloon. I understand he is hoping to traverse the Solent, to fly from the mainland to the Isle of Wight.'

The Regent wiped his mouth.

'Then you had better hurry in getting word to him!' he said.

SIXTEEN

AT THREE O'CLOCK the gates of Camelford House were pulled open, and a blue lacquered carriage sped inside. The team of six stallions had ridden full tilt since dawn. The coachman eased them to a halt, their muzzles foaming, eyes swollen from the run.

The doors to the mansion were thrown open. Viscount Fortescue ran out and accompanied his guest inside.

An hour later, the Viscount's private messenger left in the monogrammed carriage with a message for Sir Geoffrey Caldecott. It read:

I suggest, sir, you avail yourself of tomorrow morning's Times *at your earliest convenience.*

Yours truly,

Richard Fortescue

SEVENTEEN

ON OLD JEWRY, a group was gathering at the doors of the Royal African Committee. Most of them were shopkeepers and the like, concerned at the reports circulating of Major Peddie's demise. One person who stood out from the rest was Lord Alvanley. He stormed into the building and ordered Falkirk to inform the chairman of his arrival.

'Forgive me, sir, but Sir Geoffrey is currently out of town.'

'Is it true that Peddie is dead?'

Falkirk stared into the air between himself and Alvanley.

'It would be inappropriate for one to comment, sir.'

'Come on, man, I am sure nothing in this building escapes your attention! Tell me, is it true?!'

Falkirk looked at Lord Alvanley squarely, his eyes unflinching. Then, slowly, he blinked.

EIGHTEEN

Palazzo Carignano, Turin
7th March 1816

My dearest Simon,

I have dipped the quill six times and sat here staring into space, wondering quite how to begin. I do not know who else to turn to, or indeed what to say. You have known me since childhood, since the carefree days of summer at Chavenage. And you know me well enough to grasp that my marriage was one constructed upon obligation rather than affection.

Mr. Wittershall and I reached Turin a day or so ago. We travelled by way of Paris and Geneva, before making the arduous Alpine crossing. The horror of the journey was erased at being welcomed here at the splendid Palazzo Carignano.

My dearest Simon, my tears smudge the ink as I write this. I am at a loss for words, and forlorn in my awareness of your gentle sensitivity. Yet I feel I have no choice but to speak directly.

During the journey thus far my husband declined to complete the duty expected of him before the eyes of the Lord.

This afternoon, while strolling through the Palazzo with my servant, I heard a raucous clamour from a nearby room. Without *a moment's thought, I turned the handle and thrust open the door. Inside, in the most depraved and abominable state imaginable, was my husband in carnal union with another gentleman.*

He, Mr. Thomas Wittershall, was much alarmed by my intrusion. After pretending that the act was a customary tradition in the region, he came to his senses and admitted that the fairer gender is of no interest to his eyes.

Expecting me to be enamoured by the prospect of a spouse so inclined, he insisted that it would permit me to take certain liberties. But I am not enamoured, not in the least. I have wept for half a day, and feel myself desiccated from the tears.

At dawn tomorrow I shall leave here and return by ship to London and, if the grace of God has respect for my wishes, I shall never set eyes on Mr. Wittershall again.

I am,

Your affectionate cousin and dearest friend,

Beattie

IX

An invitation is advertised for an addendum to Mr. Adams' narrative — The plan is initiated to dispose of His Majesty King George III — Protestations continue outside the Royal African Committee — The Regent is advised of variola in his household — Monsieur Dupuis addresses the public in the Committee's library, after which Sir Geoffrey Caldecott is unmasked as a bigamist — New servants arrive at Carlton House — The brotherhood of Alta Templis are fed poison — Mr. Adams is released — The Prince Regent is taken prisoner — While strolling down by the river, Mr. Adams is attacked and wounded — Viscount Fortescue has a flash of inspiration — Mr. Adams and Emily Caldecott are buried at Hampstead cemetery — Viscount Fortescue arrives at Duke Street to find the members of Alta Templis dead — At Hampstead, the sexton exhumes the second grave, to discover Mr. Adams alive — The Royal African Committee continues to be mobbed — The Prince Regent is incarcerated in a stable block — Mr. Adams arrives at Camelford House — The Regent's equerry escapes to sound the alarm — King George fails to drink the poison.

ONE

CLARA FORTESCUE WAS the first to be seated for breakfast. She was dressed in a plain black cotton dress, her copper hair tied up tight in a bun. A servant moved nimbly between the table and the aspidistra, leant forward and poured a cup of Darjeeling. Clara added a drop of milk and, poised motionless like a porcelain doll, breathed in the steam.

The imprisonment of Robert Adams and the threat of his execution had filled her with a terrible sadness. She spent her days resting in her room, eating almost nothing, and refusing all invitations, even those of her friend and confidante, Lady Caroline Lamb.

At ten minutes past nine, Viscount Fortescue charged into the room. He moved round the table, kissed Clara on the crown of her head, and asked the servant if *The Times* had arrived. The newspaper was ushered in on a salver by Dalston.

It had been ironed down in the scullery and was still warm.

The Viscount took it and unfolded the front page.

'Excellent!'

'What is it, Father?'

Fortescue placed the newspaper on the linen tablecloth. The front page, filled as a rule with small advertisements, was empty but for a single, bold announcement. It declared:

THE ROYAL AFRICAN COMMITTEE
INVITES DISCERNING MEMBERS OF THE PUBLIC
TO ATTEND AN EXTRAORDINARY ADDENDUM
TO THE NARRATION OF THE AMERICAN,
MR. ROBERT ADAMS.
THE SESSION SHALL BEGIN TODAY
AT THREE O'CLOCK PRECISELY
IN THE LIBRARY OF
THE ROYAL AFRICAN COMMITTEE,
OLD JEWRY

TWO

SIXTEEN DRACHMS OF laudanum were prepared in a draughty anteroom at Windsor Castle by Sir Anthony Smythe, the physician royal. The opiate's astonishing calming properties were employed for almost every conceivable ailment, from menstrual cramps to the discomfort of the heart. A drachm or two never failed to dull even the most severe pain. Ten drachms were sufficient to kill the strongest man, and twice that ample to bring down an elephant.

Recent progress made by His Majesty in the battle for lucidity had waned, and he was confined to his bedchamber. At times he was trussed to the bedstead, guarded by orderlies specially selected for their discretion. The curtains had been sewn shut so that no one could look in at the monarch who had reigned England and her dominions for as long as almost anyone could remember. The room had been purged of all sharp objects and glass, or anything by which the distressed patient might bring harm to himself.

Sir Anthony held the laudanum to the light and turned the crystal dish towards the lamp. He had served the royal household in one capacity or another since the Prince Regent was a boy. Through the long years of incarceration at Windsor, he had watched his sovereign descend ever further into the abyss of mania.

There were times at which the King appeared to regain his faculties at least in part, before slipping back into the void, his eyes clouded by blindness, his mind robbed of all clarity.

The physician thanked God that the public at large had no way of seeing their beloved ruler in such a wasted and pitiable state. Although disapproving of the eldest son and his infantile Regency, he recognised that the Hanoverian bloodline would be best served by a king rather than a regent. As the years had come and gone, Sir Anthony had, like everyone else, faced the truth that King George was unlikely ever to resume his throne.

There it was then — a glimmer of hope for the House of Hanover, a new future ready and waiting, a future that would begin with a handful of grains.

Smythe had considered carefully the events that would take place.

Once given the signal, he would administer the opiate in His Majesty's evening milk and, once he had succumbed, the sad but inevitable announcement would be made. The public would grieve, and the new king would in time be crowned at Westminster.

THREE

THE DOORS TO the Royal African Committee were bolted shut on the inside, and locked twice. Sir Geoffrey stuffed the brass-tipped key in the left pocket of his waistcoat.

'To Hell with them all!' he shouted out at the protestors.

The morning newspapers had each carried news of Major Peddie's death and at least one claimed to have a first-hand account from an Arab merchant who witnessed the slaughter with his own eyes.

The loss of the expedition had been regrettable, but it was the last thing on the chairman's mind. Cochran had slunk upstairs fifteen minutes before, presenting him with a fresh copy of *The Times*.

'Draw the shutters over the windows!' Sir Geoffrey ordered Falkirk, 'and send word to Sergeant Harris that we require two dozen Dragoons.'

Sir Geoffrey glanced at his pocket chronometer. It was nine thirty-five. Horace Evett would have returned to his post at Carlton

House, he thought to himself. By now his infectious condition would have been disclosed, and pandemonium would have ensued as the household staff were changed.

At ten o'clock two messengers arrived simultaneously.

The first bore a letter addressed to Caldecott. It was from Hans Winkel, the Dutch charlatan who, until then, had done well for himself from the chairman's greed. The messenger gave the letter to a man standing on the Committee's top step. With his back to the door, it had appeared as if he were attempting to calm the rowdy investors. In the circumstances it was an understandable blunder. As soon as the messenger had sloped away to get some rest, his duty discharged, the man tore the letter into pieces, to the delight of the crowd.

The second messenger was carrying a note for Simon Cochran. It was from Fortescue, and gave an instruction for the doors to the Committee to be opened at a quarter to three. As luck would have it, the messenger went round to the back of the building and gave it to the scullery maid, with whom he happened to be having an affair.

FOUR

THE PRINCE REGENT heard the commotion while he was being shaved. In the next room there was a scuffle, a loud piercing shriek and the sound of feet running fast down a long corridor. Having been shaved on one side, the Prince waved the blade away from his cheek and sat up.

'What was that?!'

The servant put down the razor and the cup of warm water, lather floating like whipped cream on the top.

He hurried into the anteroom.

A muffled conversation followed. It ended in a line of exclamations and the sound of more feet running. The Prince strained out of the chair, his face half covered in lather.

'What the devil is going on?!'

The chamberlain burst into the room, then jerked still like a statue.

'It is Horace, Your Highness,' he said.

'Horace? Horace who?'

'Evett, Horace Evett, Highness, a factotum in the household.'

'What about him?'

'Um, er, Highness,' said the chamberlain, clearing his throat and wincing at the same time, 'he has an acute pustulic infection.'

'An infection?!'

'Precisely, Your Highness.'

'Does it have a name?'

'I believe, Highness, it is known in medical circles as…'

'As what?'

'As variola, Highness.'

'As what?!'

'As smallpox, Your Highness.'

FIVE

TWENTY MINUTES BEFORE the hour, Cochran crept past Sir Geoffrey's study and descended the mahogany staircase. In one hand he had the narrative of Robert Adams and a quill and, in the other, a brass-tipped key. A year previously, on the chairman's orders, he had had a second key cut to the great oak doors of the Committee headquarters. While at it, he had taken the liberty of requesting that the locksmith cut a third key, which he kept in a vase on the wall of his study.

First, he retracted the bolts at the top and bottom of the door. Then, with due care, he inserted the key into the lock and turned it to the left.

The Viscount was standing outside with Clara and a tall gentleman with a Gallic face. Behind them there was a mass of people pressing forward, some investors eager for news of their savings, others members of the gentry lured by the advertisement in *The Times*.

'Where is Sir Geoffrey?' said the peer quickly, as soon as he saw Cochran's face in the doorframe.

'Upstairs, in his study with Lady Caldecott.'

'Good. It's time for the glorious Royal Committee to come crashing to the ground. Tell me, what do you know of Alta Templis?'

'Nothing,' replied Cochran. 'I have never heard mention of it. What is it?'

'It is the common link. But I am still ignorant of its exact nature. Time will unravel the mystery. Make haste, open the doors as wide as you can, and lead these people into the library.'

Viscount Fortescue stepped to the side and the crowd surged forward, flooding through the oak doors into the Committee headquarters.

Within fifteen minutes, the library was filled to capacity, with hundreds more spilling down the corridor and out onto the street.

As soon as he understood what was going on, Sir Geoffrey charged down the stairs. Bellowing obscenities, he leapt into the sea of people and was carried along with them into the library.

'What is the meaning of this?!' he roared, at spotting the Viscount poised near the lectern.

'Merely a completion of the tale, Sir Geoffrey.'

The chairman clapped his hands forcefully. The noise subsided.

'Ladies and gentlemen,' he said in a loud, strident tone. 'I apologise, but you have been attracted here under false pretences. We ask most respectfully that you now disperse.'

The Viscount took a step to the right and blocked Caldecott's line of view.

'Sit down Sir Geoffrey!' he snapped. 'Your contribution to these proceedings is *not* required! I have the pleasure of informing this distinguished assembly that fresh information has come to light in the case of Mr. Robert Adams, the American who so eloquently described his captivity and residence at Timbuctoo. If you would please take your seats, these extraordinary proceedings will commence.'

As a wave of rowdy chatter swept through the book-lined chamber, Simon Cochran stepped forward and conversed with the Viscount.

His face flushed like never before, Sir Geoffrey had no choice but to take his seat. As soon as his backside had touched the red velvet upholstery, Cochran addressed the room. He seemed a little anxious yet roused at defying his superior.

'The purpose of this gathering,' he said in a slow, even voice, 'is to bring to the public attention certain outstanding points of communal interest. If you will remember, Mr. Adams, the American seaman, was sent from this chamber directly to the Tower of London where he remains imprisoned even now.'

'The reason is simple — he was unable to provide suitable proof that he had indeed ever set foot in Timbuctoo.

'If you would afford me a little of your precious time, I should like to clarify various points of curious information which will, one hopes, alter our understanding of Mr. Adams and his tale.'

Cochran looked down at the parquet beneath his feet.

'Without further ado,' he said, 'I should like to acquaint you with a gentleman who was himself introduced to you in Mr. Adams' narration. Having travelled from the distant shores of Marocco, he stands here today in defence of Mr. Adams. His name is Monsieur Joseph Dupuis, the British Consul at Mogador.'

The slim dark man seated beside Viscount Fortescue shifted his weight forward and rose to his feet. Almost sixty years of age, his grey hair was streaked with white, his clothing creased from days and nights on the road. His eyes were fanned by lashes of unusual length, and his voice was soft, melodious, with a light French inflection. He had never visited England before, but he spoke the language faultlessly, the result of his appreciation for its literature.

Monsieur Dupuis moved to the lectern and whispered thanks to Cochran.

'Ladies and gentleman,' he said, scanning the sea of heads, 'I am honoured to stand before you, and even more so to come to the humble assistance of a friend in need. When I received a letter from

Viscount Fortescue, I knew instantly that it was my duty to hurry from the kingdom of Marocco, to this fine capital, to help cleanse the name of a man who ought to be fêted, rather than chastised.'

Dupuis's address was broken by the sound of hobnailed boots pacing quick-march down the corridor, growing louder as they approached. The consul turned, as did Caldecott, Cochran, the Viscount, and the entire audience.

A pair of Dragoon Guards clattered into the library, muskets slung over shoulders, bandoleers tight on their chests. Between them, unshaven, filthy and confused, was Robert Adams.

Viscount Fortescue motioned for the soldiers to place their prisoner to the left of the lectern. On seeing Dupuis, Adams seemed overcome by emotion, and reached forward to greet his old friend.

Another wave of discourse undulated through the audience.

'If you would permit me to continue,' said the consul, pinching the ends of his moustache.

He took a step backwards, regained his concentration, and said:

'Ladies and gentlemen, I would ask you to look at Mr. Adams, the so-called "prisoner" who stands before you, his wrists and ankles chained. Is he one of you? *No*, surely not. His face hasn't been powdered, his fingernails are not manicured... his manners, his accent, they seem uncouth to your gentle sensibilities, do they not?

'Yet I would surmise that your shared disapproval runs far deeper than Mr. Adams' appearance or his inadequacies in English etiquette. For this young man has accomplished what your greatest explorers have been incompetent in achieving. Indeed, Mr. Adams has attained quite by chance your dream of dreams. For he has walked upon the dusty streets of Timbuctoo, and lived to tell the tale!

'And yet, rather than salute him as a champion, you scoff, loath to accept that you have been beaten to your fantasy by an illiterate American and, at that, one who appears indifferent to the achievement.

'You have denounced him as a liar and locked him up like a common criminal, until he can prove his story. Well, ladies and gentlemen, I have hastened from the Afric' shores to bring you the incontestable proof you desire.'

The consul paused, raised his hands to his neck and carefully untied his starched white cravat. The audience broke into whispers at such an outrageous breach of decorum. With the tie on the floor at his feet, Monsieur Dupuis unbuttoned his shirt. There were cries of hostility from the back of the room, and at least one lady fainted.

Hanging around the consul's neck, suspended from a string, was a large black seed.

Removing it, the Frenchman held it high for all to see.

'This is the mapara seed locket presented to Mr. Adams by King Woolo of Timbuctoo!' he said in a voice of firm authority.

Dupuis was about to continue when a portly figure seated in a wheelchair at the centre began applauding. He appeared overwhelmed with pleasure. It was Sir Joseph Banks.

'*Deserta mirabilis!*' he cried. 'It is *Deserta mirabilis*, the sacred seed of Timbuctoo! Our Mr. Park sent one back from the Niger. We have it at Kew. The seed is incontestable evidence that Mr. Adams has indeed journeyed to the golden city!'

The guards restraining the American relaxed their grip. Adams fell forward as Sir Geoffrey Caldecott sprang to his feet and strode up to the lectern.

'This is preposterous, laughable at best!' he exclaimed. 'Guards, take Mr. Adams back to his cell!'

The Dragoons looked to the Viscount for an instruction. He held up a finger.

'One moment,' he said. 'For I believe that this gathering would be interested in a second revelation.'

'Viscount, what are you to claim now about Mr. Adams? That his veins run with the blood royal?!'

Fortescue touched his fingertips together.

'The second revelation does not concern Mr. Adams,' he said.

'Then who does it concern?'

'It concerns you, Sir Geoffrey.'

The chairman lowered his head, face poised squarely forward, like a bulldog ready to attack. His brow was running with perspiration, his cheeks glowing with rage. He smiled obsequiously.

'I am certain, sir, there are no revelations regarding myself that would be of interest to this distinguished assembly.'

'You are, Sir Geoffrey, are you not, a married man?'

'Indeed I am, sir. My wife, Lady Caldecott, is sitting there, having graced us this afternoon with her presence.'

Fortescue raised a finger once again. He nodded to Cochran, who strode to the door, returning a moment later with a frail, grey-haired woman.

'If that is your wife seated in the front row, Sir Geoffrey, would you elucidate for us as to who exactly this is standing here before us all?'

'It is…'

'Yes, sir?'

'It is… Emily.'

'And who, sir, is Emily?'

'She is… she is… she is my wife.'

The library resounded with uproar as it had never done in the long and illustrious history of the Royal African Committee.

'But bigamy,' said Fortescue, holding out a hand to calm the room, 'is only one of many felonies to which you have applied your name. The funds of the Royal African Committee, amassed through slavery, were part of a grand deception. I have it on good authority that the income acquired from honest subscribers has been procured with the intention of rewarding the most deceitful in the land. I put it to you, Sir Geoffrey, that it was never your intention for Peddie's expedition to reach the desert metropolis of Timbuctoo!'

The audience heckled, barracked and jeered and, as they did so, Caldecott staggered forward wielding an unsheathed malacca swordstick.

In one tidy motion, he snatched Emily by the neck. And, the blade against her throat, he moved backwards to the door.

SIX

THE CHAMBERLAIN ORDERED Horace Evett to be taken out and flogged, and a dozen household staff to be sent away for a period of enforced quarantine. The private apartments were cleansed with a dense, pungent haze of burning camphor.

At five o'clock a troop of substitute household servants arrived, twelve of them. They were dressed in the appropriate attire and, when asked by the chamberlain where they had sprung from, their superior replied that they had rushed from Windsor as soon as word of the outbreak had reached them.

The Prince announced that, from that moment, all staff and

members of the under classes would be inspected for symptoms of the disease. Anyone found with pimples, pustules or blemishes of any kind would be taken away and thrashed by the royal guard.

SEVEN

HARRY THORNLY FOUND himself missing the old days when the directors of the firm came and went according to a precise and unchanging routine. During the past few weeks, the gentlemen would come and go to Duke Street, hurrying up the stairs and back down with a speed and intensity that hardly befitted their status.

At six o'clock Sir Geoffrey Caldecott entered the building alone and rushed up the staircase. As Harry greeted him, he noticed that his gloves were speckled with fresh blood. But he said nothing.

On the third floor, the brethren of Alta Templis were waiting for their Master, hoods drawn down, candles flaring in the draught.

Sir Geoffrey strode in, his face veiled. The brethren stood in a circle, anxious for news of the usurpation. Caldecott took his place.

'Disciples,' he said quickly, 'we are gathered by the sacrament of Alta Templis, as is the custom of our flock. Peace upon you.'

'And peace upon you, Master.'

'What is our cause?'

'The green pastures.'

'And what is our support?'

'The crook of Alta Templis.'

'It is time to laud the new beginning,' said Caldecott. 'The Regent's household staff have been replaced by soldiers loyal to the Duke of York. At the signal the Prince and his father shall make the journey to Paradise.'

The hooded figures cheered.

'Oh disciples of Alta Templis, let us seal this triumph with a communion,' said the Master.

One of the figures, Henry Jerome, stepped forward.

In his hands was a chalice filled with wine tinged with aconite. He moved round the circle, offering it. One by one, each of the disciples drank, all except for the Master and the bearer of the cup.

EIGHT

THE DRAGOONS UNFASTENED the manacles, and Adams stepped forward a free man.

'Words cannot express the depth of my thanks,' he said to Viscount Fortescue. 'I am grateful to the very bottom of my heart. And, Monsieur Dupuis, once again I owe you my life.' He shook the consul's hand. 'But what of Sir Geoffrey?'

'He may not comprehend it,' said Cochran boldly, 'but his

lifeblood streams like sand through an hourglass, and there are precious few grains left to fall.'

The Viscount cleared his throat.

'I see the riddle laid out before me,' he said, 'but something continues to elude. The Committee's coffers were brimming over with wealth from the trade of humanity to Tobago, and yet the vast subscription was apparently also required.'

'The expedition to Timbuctoo?' asked Adams.

'Precisely.'

Fortescue fell silent.

'There is, I feel, a layer of intelligence that remains concealed from us.'

'Caldecott has escaped along with the explanation,' said Adams.

'Fear not,' the Viscount added, 'given time, a maggot always rises to the surface.'

Just then, Mr. Murray scurried up to where the three men were standing in conversation.

'Forgive me, gentlemen!' he said, 'but I must intrude. Mr. Adams, I have been transfixed by your narrative and should be most disposed to publish an account it. If you would permit me, I would be willing to offer an immediate advance of five hundred pounds.'

NINE

RECLINING ON A low chair in his dressing room, the Regent called out angrily for a servant to shave his right cheek. But there was silence. For the first time in his life, the Prince of Wales was utterly alone. The chamberlain and staff under his authority had vanished, sent into forced quarantine. Half an hour passed, and the Regent still lay there, his jaw bared for the blade.

'Damn the lot of them!' he yelled. 'What impudence!'

All of a sudden, Hastings swept in.

'Apologies, Your Highness,' he said, crossing the threshold, 'the new stewards have arrived.'

'Well send them in at once, man! There's a cheek to shave!'

'Very good, Your Highness.'

The equerry turned to summon the servants, who had been instructed to wait in the corridor. To his horror, he found they were already in the dressing room. But instead of bearing towels, tonics, and soap, they were armed with knives.

'What treachery is this?!' called the Prince.

'Hush, or this dagger will drink your blood!' exclaimed the substitute chamberlain.

Calling out to his men, he ordered them to tie up the equerry and the Prince Regent, and lead the prisoners away down the servants' stairs.

TEN

THE NEXT MORNING, Cochran and Adams went down for a celebratory breakfast.

'I had been so worried about you, sir,' said Mrs. Potts as soon as she saw the American. 'Sit down and eat your fill.'

She shovelled a pair of kippers onto plates.

'Thank God for freedom,' said Adams, grinning. He thought for a moment. 'You know, this morning I think I shall take a walk. I have longed to see trees these past weeks.'

'An excellent idea,' Cochran replied. 'And I shall enquire when the next vessel will leave for America.'

'What of the Committee?' asked Adams.

'To Hell with it!' snapped Cochran.

After breakfast Robert Adams walked through the Temple gardens down to the Thames. The air was cool, the sunlight sharp, and the river packed with barges laden with goods now that the winter freeze was gone.

As he watched the water, its shiny surface shrouding the currents beneath, Adams found himself thinking of his friend Stephen Dolbie. However hard he tried, he could not erase the image of his grave at the edge of Wadi Noon.

Standing on the riverbank, he put his head in his hands. There was a sense that his long journey was coming to an end.

He caught the cry of gulls swooping and pitching in the background. Adams looked up.

A figure was standing near. He was dressed in a pea-green frock coat, made from simple cloth, the deep turned cuffs black with grime. In one hand he carried a short pointed sword, its blade scored with a recurring arabesque motif.

It was Caldecott's henchman.

The assailant, Herbert Jenkins, lunged at the American's face. Instinctively, Adams raised his wrist to deflect the blow. The tip of the blade scored his forearm. His blood fortified by adrenalin, he took flight. He sprinted down the riverbank faster than he had ever run before. Yet, to his surprise, his attacker did not take chase. Glancing back, he saw him following at walking pace.

Adams hurried towards the Inns of Court. As he ran, he felt his face streaming with sweat, his vision clouding. His muscles were straining with acid, his heart burning. The assailant's blade had been dipped in a decoction of henbane and digitalis.

Fighting for breath, reeling forward, Robert Adams collapsed.

ELEVEN

OVER HIS THIRD cup of orange pekoe, Viscount Fortescue had a flash of inspiration. Clara had asked him something, but he didn't hear.

'What is it, my dear Viscount?' said Monsieur Dupuis, who was eating a slice of toasted rye bread.

'Alta Templis,' Fortescue said distantly. 'I do believe…'

'Believe what, Father?'

'That I have understood the mystery.'

There was a pause. Dupuis sipped a cup of thin milky tea.

'What is Alta Templis?'

'A sect dedicated to uproar.'

'Sir Geoffrey Caldecott?'

'Indeed. He and the directors of the Royal African Committee.'

The Viscount stood up, pushing his chair back.

'You must excuse me,' he said absently, walking briskly from the room.

TWELVE

AT HAMPSTEAD CEMETERY, the sexton had dug a pair of graves by the time the church clock had struck the noon chimes. In the first, Emily Caldecott, *née* Watts, was laid to rest, her jugular cleanly severed. A mound of fresh upturned soil marked the grave. The sexton, whose name was Percy Waitley, wiped a rag to his face and asked the pair of gentlemen present if they were ready for the second casket to be interred.

'Get on with it, and be smart about it!' said the red-faced man in a naval coat. 'There'll be three crowns in it if you have him buried before the hour's out.'

Single-handed, Percy struggled to lower the casket down into the grave.

'The mist is descending, Sir Geoffrey, I suggest we leave,' said the second man, Henry Jerome. Unlike Caldecott, he was unsettled at the idea of being hunted by the Committee's plentiful investors. 'There is still the message to be sent to Smythe,' he said, hoping it would provide enough of a reason to quit the cemetery.

'I am not leaving this spot,' Caldecott replied, 'until the damned Mr. Adams is buried and gone.'

Ten minutes before the church clock struck one, Percy's shovel tossed the final scoop of earth up onto the mound.

'I'll need their names,' he said, wiping his face again. 'For the register.'

Sir Geoffrey took the coins from his pocket and dropped them onto the sexton's palm.

'Conjure something appropriate,' he said, as he turned on his heel and left.

THIRTEEN

VISCOUNT FORTESCUE REACHED number ten Duke Street as Sir Geoffrey Caldecott was leaving the churchyard. The doorman, Harry Thornly, remembered him at once as the gentleman who had mistakenly arrived several weeks previously.

'Can I help you again, sir?'

'I have come for Alta Templis.'

'Excuse me, sir, but as I informed you before, there is no firm by that name in the building.'

Fortescue charged past Thornly and up the staircase. The doorman raced after him.

'I have orders to allow no one to enter!' he cried out, taking the stairs two at a time.

'This is a matter of extraordinary importance,' Fortescue called back. 'Impede my investigation and you shall answer to a royal committee. In which room do the gentlemen congregate?'

Thornly caught the flash of danger in the Viscount's eyes. He had pledged loyalty to his employers, but of late had become increasingly concerned at the strange sounds on the third floor, not to mention the comings and goings at all times of day and night.

'They meet up there,' he said in a low voice, 'the second door on the third floor landing.'

Fortescue ran up the stairs. He tried the handle. It was locked.

Putting his shoulder at right angles to the door, he burst it open, Thornly a pace behind.

Inside, there was a scent of vanilla.

The windows had been blacked out. As their eyes adjusted to the lack of light, the Viscount and the doorman grasped the full scope of the horror that had taken place.

Dressed in matching black robes, the hooded brethren of Alta Templis were lying on the wooden floor, dead. Thornly, who had military training, checked the corpses for signs of life.

'I can see no loss of blood, sir,' he said in a gentle tone. 'It seems as if they have been...'

'Poisoned.'

'Yes. I would say so.'

Fortescue went to the window and ripped away the black shroud. The room was filled with light. On the makeshift altar he found the chalice. There was still a liquid in it. He sniffed.

'I would say hemlock of some variety,' he said. 'Tell me, Mr...'

'Thornly, sir, Harry Thornly.'

'Tell me Mr. Thornly, when exactly did these gentlemen enter the building?'

'Yesterday, sir.'

'How many of them did you see leave?'

'Two, sir. Mr. Caldecott and Mr. Jerome. They descended a little before a quarter to eight.'

'Did it not strike you as peculiar that the other gentlemen did not leave?'

'No sir,' said Thornly, 'each member has a key, in case they have cause to enter or exit when I am absent.'

One at a time the doorman removed the hoods from the dead.

'Excuse me for asking, sir,' he said, 'but what is the reason for all of this?'

Viscount Fortescue shook his head.

'I am not certain yet,' he said, 'but I fear diabolical forces are at work.'

FOURTEEN

Shortly after Caldecott left Hampstead, a fog descended over the village. It seeped down from the Heath, along Church Row and through the cemetery at the end of the lane. Percy Waitley would have headed home, but the coins had triggered his greed, which had been compounded by two points of detail.

The first was that the caskets were of the lowest quality, damp pine, the sides uneven and the lids hardly fitting at all. The second, more important, point was that the mourners had provided no names for the deceased.

Working fast, Percy exhumed the second casket, the thickening mist concealing his work. The soil came away easily. Within a few minutes he had reached the coffin.

While drinking in a tavern at Chalk Farm the week before, he had found himself in conversation with Billy Crane. Over many jars of ale, he was coaxed into an arrangement on which he was eager to capitalise.

As any sexton knew, removing a casket from a grave was far more cumbersome than placing it there. In the twenty years he had been digging plots at St. John's, he had never had cause to make an exhumation. Pulling the coffin out alone was not an option. The answer was to prise off the lid and remove the cadaver first.

Jabbing the side of the shovel into a gap where the box's sides fell short of the lid, Percy jemmied it hard. To his surprise the nails popped up with no effort at all. Hurling the shovel out of the hole, he wiped his face again. As he did so, the lid of the casket was flung backwards.

Gasping for air, his body twisted from shock, Robert Adams leered forward from the box.

FIFTEEN

On Old Jewry three hundred enraged members of the public were attacking the front elevation of the Royal African Committee. The building's great oak doors had been pulled shut, double locked, the windows shuttered from inside. By dusk, every pane of glass had been shattered and the building was ablaze.

Heading the assault was Albert Wicks, hangman to the King. He had identified a weakness, a wooden staircase leading from the street down into the front basement. Setting it alight helped to ease his fury at losing a lifetime's savings on a questionable expedition to Timbuctoo.

Shortly after dark, the mob gained entry to the rear of the building. Caldecott and the other directors were long gone. The only man they found was Falkirk. He was on guard, a last wretched stand, armed with a fire poker, a silver salver as a shield.

Albert Wicks raced forward into the library where he found the butler.

'Where's our money?!' he yelled.

'Gone, every farthing, along with the directors.'

'Where?'

'How should I know?'

'They'll rot in Hell!' shouted a voice from behind. It was Philip Rundell, purveyor of silverware to the Regent and the King, a man more usually noted for his composed disposition. 'We shall get our retribution,' he shouted back to the mob, 'if we must hound them to the infernos of Hades. I swear it upon all that is holy, the Lord my witness!'

SIXTEEN

HASTINGS REMOVED HIS frock coat and laid it on a stool in the icy stable at Buckingham House, in which he and the Regent had been interned.

'Seat yourself, Your Highness,' he said. 'I shall do all I can to alleviate your discomfort.'

'The pustular outbreak was a ruse,' said the Prince pensively. 'But who could be behind it?'

The equerry coughed, and touched a knuckle to his lip.

'Any number of malevolent forces,' he said, 'Highness.'

'No, no, this is the work of someone with a taste for dominance, a man with a grievance, and a knowledge of the royal household.'

'But who could that be?'

'Freddie,' said the Prince Regent frigidly, 'my brother Frederick.'

SEVENTEEN

THE FIRE WAS blazing in the drawing room of Camelford House, providing a little comfort from the torrential rain. Clara Fortescue was sitting before it rereading *Sense and Sensibility* for the third time. The novel helped to take her mind off the worry. Robert Adams had not been seen for more than a day. The last sighting was from a merchant who reported spying a man of his description being attacked down at the Thames.

Viscount Fortescue had spent the morning sending messages to his network of informants. He had devoted a lifetime to cultivating contacts in the underbelly of society.

Meanwhile, wasting not a minute, John Murray's staff had edited the narrative, which had been typeset by the master printer William Bulmer Esq. of Cleveland Row. The first draft had been sent over to Monsieur Dupuis for his annotations.

The diplomat sat in the library at Camelford House, wrapped in a blanket, his feet resting on a brass bed-warmer, the manuscript on his knees.

The morning's *Times* had recounted in detail the Royal African Committee's demise, and had asked in its leader how such a prestigious institution could have betrayed so many investors. The editor was calling the affair a second South Sea Bubble. He had posed in black and white the question that so preoccupied Viscount

Fortescue and half of London — Where was Sir Geoffrey Caldecott and the accumulated wealth of the Committee?

At six o'clock Clara looked up from her book.

'What was that?'

'What, dearest?' her father replied, the nib of his quill scratching over a sheet of fine laid writing paper.

'I thought I heard something.'

'Where?'

'Outside.'

Clara stood up. Placing the novel on the mantel, she went to a window that gave onto the gardens at the front of the house.

'I am sure it is just the wind, my dear,' said the Viscount, his eyes rereading his last line.

Clara craned forward, leaning right up to the window pane. She froze.

'Oh my!' she called loudly. 'Father, come quickly!'

The Viscount hurried from his chair and caught a glimpse of a drenched forlorn figure staggering towards the house.

'Do you think…?'

'Yes, Father, yes!'

Running into the hallway, Clara thrust open the door. A moment later she was out in the rain, clinging to the figure.

Roused by the commotion, Monsieur Dupuis rushed in from the

library, his face flushed.

'What has happened, Viscount?' he asked urgently.

'It's Adams!' he said. 'He's alive!'

EIGHTEEN

THE RAIN CLATTERED onto the roof of the stable block, fuelling the Prince Regent's anger, and causing his equerry to wish he could find a way for them to escape.

As the hours passed, Hastings found himself thinking about his childhood, and his early apprenticeship as a roofer's lad in Sterne Minster, Dorset. His father, a thatcher by trade, had foreseen an end of the old ways, and a rise in terracotta tiles. At fourteen, Hastings had learned the art of roofing and, throughout his adult life, had always found his eye drawn to baked clay tiles.

The stable was guarded by a pair of soldiers loyal to the Duke of York. A square building of dressed Portland stone, it had a central drain and diagonal grooves carved at even intervals across the floor. The roof was pitched, supported by a pair of beams, laid with bisque tiles of superior quality.

Evening ebbed into night and the Regent's stomach began to growl. He was cold and damp, but it was the sense of hunger that alarmed him most. In his fifty-four years he had never been hungry, not once. The sensation was not only new, but distressing.

'I'd give a hundred guineas for a leg of lamb,' he said, 'or for a great tureen of blancmange!'

Hastings' thoughts were not on food but on freedom. Having studied the tiles, he had worked out a route through them and onto the roof.

The Prince began moaning again.

'I have a terrible pain in my stomach, Hastings!' he said. 'I fear I shall faint if a doctor is not called.'

The equerry mumbled sympathy.

'Your Highness,' he said, 'I am going to escape and raise the alarm. It is our only hope.'

'You cannot leave me captive here alone!'

'My apologies, Highness,' said the equerry, as he climbed up using the tackle hooks on the far wall, 'but I have no other choice.'

NINETEEN

SIR ANTHONY FAULKS received a coded message at sunset from a messenger posing as a stable lad. He was instructed to proceed according to the plan, and administer the laudanum without delay.

It was a quiet evening at Windsor, light spring rain gushing down the guttering, the grooms shutting up the stables for the night.

King George was in his bedchamber sitting on a milkmaid's stool. A few yards away a footman was standing to attention, reading aloud from *Twelfth Night*, a copy bound in speckled calf.

The physician royal entered without a sound. In his hand was a glass of milk, warmed to blood heat and fortified with sixteen drachms of the opiate.

The King, who knew every line by heart, was acting it out at whim.

'Put some life into it, man! It's Viola's line. She says:

I am all the daughters of my father's house,

And all the brothers too: and yet I know not.

Sir, shall I to this lady?'

The physician stepped forward, glass in hand, hand outstretched.

'Your Majesty, I should be most obliged if you might drink this beverage.'

'Drink it yourself!'

'*Please*, Your Highness.'

'Leave it on the table!'

'I beg you, Highness.'

'I shall do my best to accommodate your wishes at the end of the act. Now get out! Interrupting Shakespeare is a crime worthy of execution!'

'Very well, Majesty. I shall leave the glass here beside you.'

Sir Anthony left the room.

The King waved a finger at the milk and then at the footman.

'A guinea for you if you drink that in one!' he boomed.

The servant's eyes glinted in the lamplight. He reached over, scoffed the warm milk, and was rewarded with a gold coin.

'That's enough,' said the King. 'I am fatigued. We shall continue tomorrow. Leave me in peace. I am retiring for the night.'

With the sovereign's lamp extinguished, Windsor Castle came alive. Down in the kitchens, the chefs, stewards and butlers were carousing as they did on most nights, helping themselves to one of the finest cellars in England.

The footman, a Richard Winkman, had bade the King a good night, and hurried to join the festivities downstairs. It was not long before the laudanum began to take hold.

Winkman had found himself perspiring as he had never perspired before. Tearing off the coat of his tight-fitting uniform, he doused his face in a basin of freezing water. The sweat kept pouring and his vision began to darken. He staggered down to the kitchens, reeling left and right. A group of other footmen slapped him on the back, impressed he had got drunk before them.

Five minutes later Richard Winkman was dead.

Sir Anthony Smythe went to bed at nine. He locked himself in his room, prayed, and coaxed himself to believe he had done the right thing in ending the suffering of an old man. He longed to hurry over to the royal apartment and check the King's pulse, but forced himself to stay in his room. After all, it would seem far less suspicious if His Majesty were discovered by the servants in the morning.

At midnight, the festivities in the kitchen eased, and the staff began to turn in for the night. The first to slope away was the head chef. He took a bottle of vintage Armagnac and a scullery maid to his quarters.

An hour later, a horse approached the castle galloping at full tilt. The rider tore down the drive, lashing the reins, jabbing the stirrups into the animal's girth. It was Francis Hastings.

He called out to the guards at the gatehouse.

'Open up! Open up at once!'

'Who goes there?'

'Equerry to the Prince Regent!'

Within a few minutes the sound of boots charging through the castle woke up Smythe, who had already fallen into a slumber. Assuming the laudanum had taken effect, and that the King's body had been discovered, the physician stayed locked in his room for fear of being implicated.

The royal chamberlain was woken and the situation described.

'You *must* wake His Majesty!' shouted Hastings. 'He is the only man alive who can save the kingdom!'

'His Majesty's mind is clouded,' said the chamberlain, his voice straining.

Hastings slapped his hands together.

'Take me to the King!'

The chamberlain tapped lightly on the mahogany door. There was no reply. He tapped again, a little harder. Still nothing. Hastings stepped forward and pounded with his fist.

'Who's there?' said a frail voice.

'The equerry to the Prince Regent, Majesty.'

'What is it?'

'A matter of life and death!'

X

At Windsor Castle, soldiers are roused to ride to the Regent's aid — The Prince Regent is rescued — Miss Clara Fortescue has an interview with Mr. Adams — The Committee's wealth is prepared to be loaded aboard a clipper — Accompanied by Messrs. Adams and Cochran, Viscount Fortescue hastens over London Bridge where they capture Sir Geoffrey Caldecott — The chairman is locked up in the Tower of London — Beattie arrives at Mr. Cochran's home — The Prince Regent decorates Messrs. Adams and Cochran and Lord Fortescue — Mr. Wicks, the hangman, prepares the noose for Sir Geoffrey Caldecott's neck — Mr. Adams reflects on his imminent return to America — The chairman is hanged at the Execution Dock — Mr. Cochran and Beattie are married at St. Bride's church, and Mr. Adams boards a brig to America — At long last, Mr. Adams reaches home, and is reunited with his true love.

ONE

A HUNDRED HORSES thundered east towards London, arriving at Buckingham House just before dawn. On each was a mounted soldier, dressed for battle, weapons at the ready. A black lacquered carriage drawn by six stallions took up the rear.

The first stop was the stable block, in which the Regent was still imprisoned. The guards were soon overpowered and the Prince of Wales released. His Highness struggled to get up from the floor where he was lying on his equerry's coat. Sobbing, he exited the stable, dabbing his eyes with a square of Welsh lace. He found himself surrounded by horsemen, their burning torches illuminating the last throes of night.

Hastings dismounted and ran over to the Prince.

'I have sent for another contingent of cavalry from the King's Mews at Charing Cross, Your Highness. They shall join us at Carlton House.'

'Where have you been all night? I have been frozen to the bone!'

'At Windsor, Highness.'

'You saw His Majesty?'

Before the equerry could answer, there was a roar from behind. The door to the black carriage had been flapped back and, despite poor sight, a figure dressed in a woollen dressing-gown and matching slippers jumped out.

'What uproar!' shouted the King. 'Where is the son?'

The Prince Regent scurried forward.

'Your Majesty, what a pleasure!'

'Hush you buffoon! Can you not be trusted with anything?!'

'It is Freddie, Father, he has run awry. He tried to do away with his own kith and kin.'

The monarch climbed back into his carriage and was followed by the Regent, who needed the help of three grooms to get him inside. The iron-rimmed wheels began to turn, and the vehicle trundled the short distance towards Carlton House.

By the time the carriage arrived, the Prince's London home was surrounded front and back by soldiers loyal to the King. The Duke of York, who had severely miscalculated his coup d'état, was brought down under armed guard.

'Your Majesty,' he gushed, at seeing his father alive, his night-clothes buffeted by the morning breeze. 'What a charming surprise.'

'Freddie!' yelled the Regent. 'You scoundrel!'

An hour after the arrival of the King's carriage, the rebellion had been quashed and the soldiers dispersed. The Duke of York was stripped of his authority, and banished to his estate in Gloucestershire. King George was helped into his carriage and returned to Windsor. A decision was arrived at not to make the uprising public, for fear of eroding confidence in the House of Hanover.

With the monarch departed, the Prince Regent strode into Carlton House and ordered Carême to prepare a breakfast fit for a king.

TWO

ON DOCTOR'S ORDERS, Robert Adams spent four days in bed at Camelford House. During the afternoon of the second day, Joseph Dupuis left for Paris, before beginning the long journey back to Mogador. As the two men said their farewells, they both knew it was likely they would never meet again.

The lesion on Adams' arm was badly infected, suppurating with pus. The Fortescue family doctor lanced the wound twice each day. Other than for the visits of the physician there might have been silence. But every few minutes Clara burst in with a glass of water, a damp compress, or yet another blanket. In the afternoons she would read aloud to the patient, and they would laugh together.

On the fourth morning she sat on the edge of the bed, dabbing the perspiration from his face.

'Your tenderness will stay with me always,' he said.

Clara blushed.

'Dear Robert, you have brought excitement to our lives with the description of your adventures. How will we ever bear it when you are gone?'

'There will be other excitement.'

'I think not.'

Adams leant forward and touched his lips to Clara's cheek.

'Thank you,' he said.

Clara picked up the book she had brought in to read, but her mind was not on entertainment. Aware that she might not be alone with the American again, she put the book down.

'Soon you will be away from here,' she said, 'and my life will be empty, stripped of joy and of hope.'

'Clara, my dear friend,' said Adams warmly, propping himself up in bed, 'it is fate that rules our fortunes. You know as well as I, that even if we were to fall in love, the rigid rules of your family would forbid a union of any kind with a lowly American such as me. And, although it has never been in my nature to care for what others think about me, I am well aware that you must care what they think of you.'

'You are right,' Clara replied, her cheeks streaming with tears. 'Please forgive me. I have crossed every boundary of propriety and am surely damned.'

Adams smiled.

'You have no idea how fond of you I am, Clara,' he said. 'But my future belongs across the Atlantic. It's my love for another that causes me to be here at all.'

At that moment, Dalston knocked at the open door. He cleared his throat, surprised at seeing patient and would-be nurse in such close proximity to one another.

'Mr. Cochran has arrived downstairs and asks if you might grant him an interview, sir.'

'Of course. Please tell him to come up.'

The sound of feet ascending the stairs was followed by the sight of Cochran in the door frame.

'Robert! Robert!' he said jubilantly. 'What hullabaloo!'

'How glad I am to see you. Now please tell my little nurse here that I'm fit enough to be released from this confinement.'

Cochran stepped forward, a package in his hands.

'I have a surprise,' he said.

'What is it?'

'Open it!'

Adams tore away the sheets of brown paper, revealing a handsome quarto-sized book.

'It's time for you to learn the art of reading,' said Cochran.

Clara resumed her place on the edge of the bed. She opened the book to the title page and read:

'*The Narrative of Robert Adams, a Sailor, Who Was Wrecked on the Western Coast of Africa, in the Year 1810, Was Detained in Slavery By the Arabs of the Great Desert, and Resided Several Months in the city of Timbuctoo.*'

'I have just hurried here from Murray's. He is gleeful at the book's triumphant success. Lackington has sold five hundred copies this morning alone, and Hatchard's twice as many. You may be unable to read your book, Robert, but you are outselling Lord Byron five copies to one!'

There was another knock at the door. It was Viscount Fortescue. He gave congratulations but appeared a little sombre.

'Why the solemn air, Father?' asked Clara.

'It is Caldecott,' he replied. 'For days my informants have endeavoured to trace his whereabouts, but he has eluded them. It seems that he may have escaped on a brig bound for Trinidad.'

'Daily, investors pick over the ruins of the Royal African Committee,' said Cochran. 'But without Sir Geoffrey there is no hope of ever recovering the funds.'

'He's a crafty old fox,' mumbled Fortescue.

'That he is,' added Cochran.

Adams pushed himself up in the bed.

'And what does a fox do when he's surrounded?' he asked.

'He goes to ground,' said Clara.

'That's right. I am certain he would not have left, not without the gold.'

The Viscount crossed the room and glanced out at the gardens. He seemed lost in thought.

'But where would he have gone?' he said distantly.

'Find the gold and we shall find him,' said Cochran.

'How did he move it, the gold?'

'From Hoare's in a convoy of carriages, then through a tunnel which runs from Old Jewry down to the Thames.'

Fortescue turned from the window, his eyes suddenly brighter.

'A steam barge down the river,' he said. 'But where would it dock?'

'Oh my,' said Cochran all of a sudden. 'I think I have the answer to that question.'

'What is it?'

'When I was engaged in preparing the Committee's accounts, there was a small yet regular amount due each month for the rental of a stone warehouse at St. Saviour's Dock. I believe it was owned by a man named Saunderson, and boasted a quay of its own on the river.'

The Viscount called Dalston to bring his coat and boots.

'We shall go at once,' he said. 'There is not a moment to lose!'

Adams swept away the blankets.

'I am coming with you!'

'Absolutely not!' snapped the Viscount.

'You must rest, regain your strength,' said Clara.

'I am coming,' Adams replied forcefully. 'For no one could ever wish to catch Caldecott more than I.'

THREE

A CLIPPER, *ESMERELDA*, was taking on provisions at the rear of a dour granite magazine at Hagan's Wharf, the twilight behind it fading to night. Aboard, a single hurricane lamp hung high on the mast, its flame doing little to illuminate the approaching dark.

Down below the captain was consulting his charts, a pair of callipers in his right hand, a bottle of Barbados rum in the left. The vessel, owned by a Mr. Farlands of Liverpool, was due for repairs at Portsmouth, but had been chartered on the sly to carry goods to the Caribbean.

On deck, the mainsail and jib were readied for the voyage, the boatswain supervising the work, barking orders to his men. From time to time the captain would call out from his cabin, demanding to know the state of the rigging, or whether the stevedores had arrived.

Fifty yards from the quay, the warehouse was silent.

A drunk sailor had stumbled out of the nearby King's Head and was relieving himself on the rear wall. Finishing his business, he ambled back into the tavern. Just then another man approached.

A beaver hat crowning his head, he was well dressed in a heavy black frock coat, an immaculate cravat at his neck. Suddenly, an assailant slipped from the shadows. He stabbed the gentleman cleanly through the heart. Death was instant.

A moment later the gentleman's body was floating face down in the Thames.

Sheathing the blade, the assailant stuffed it in his boot. He glanced to the left, then right, opened a small door set in the far corner of the side wall, and hurried inside.

The warehouse interior was spacious, damp, and floored in stone. Its windows had been backed with dark cloth to prevent any of the dim lamplight inside from seeping out. A system of battered pulleys were attached to the rafters for swinging goods from one area to the next.

On the left side of the magazine, two hundred and fifty crates had been arranged in rows of ten. Across from them there stood a desk of surprising quality, aged walnut veneer, the legs cabriole, ending in ball and claw feet.

Behind the desk sat Sir Geoffrey Caldecott.

He had heard of the failure of the coup, and that the Duke of York had been taken away. His only hope now was to escape while he could, taking the accumulated wealth of the Royal African Committee along with him.

'What was that noise out there, Jenkins?' he hissed.

'A sailor, sir, worse for wear. Fell into the river, he did.'

'Keep your knife sheathed you fool! If we are to take flight, our priorities ought to be focussed on moving this cargo into that vessel out there,' said Sir Geoffrey urgently, pointing to the door.

'Mr. Jerome should return in a moment with the stevedores,' said Jenkins. 'I shall go out and see if he has come.'

FOUR

VISCOUNT FORTESCUE'S LACQUERED carriage hastened down Tooley Street, having crossed London Bridge. Inside the cabin sat the Viscount, Cochran and Robert Adams, each one armed with a Parker duelling pistol.

The streets were for the most part empty, surprising for the time of day and Cochran made remark of it.

'Perhaps they can sense the evil,' said Fortescue under his breath.

'I do believe that we have almost reached the warehouse,' said Cochran suddenly.

The Viscount struck the ivory knob of his cane on the padded ceiling above his head.

'Stop here, Dunn. We shall continue on foot!'

'Right you are, sir.'

The coachman slowed the horses, jumped onto the cobbles and kicked down the folding step. A light mist was seeping south across the surface of the river, muffling the sound of boisterous laughter at the King's Head.

Before leaving the cabin, the three men loaded their weapons and checked the flints. The Viscount led the way, north up Mill Street, moving fast with the pistol at his side. Cochran followed in his footsteps and Adams in his, no more than a yard or two between them.

They traversed the distance to the warehouse quickly, hastening down the building's left flank.

'Look!' said Cochran, 'down there at the quay.'

'They're arranging the rigging,' added Fortescue. 'They'll be away on the tide.'

'But the boat's not laden yet,' said Adams.

'How can you tell?'

'The hatches are open. The boatswain would batten them as soon as the cargo's aboard.'

Just then, there came the sound of the door to the tavern slamming shut. Another sailor staggered out and peed in the gutter.

'What do we do?' asked Cochran.

'I will investigate the magazine,' said Fortescue. 'Be ready to come to my aid if I call.'

The Viscount crept through the shadows to the door. As he approached, he heard Caldecott's voice inside.

'Where the Devil are Jerome and those damned stevedores?'

'I saw no sign of them, sir,' Jenkins said, crossing the room. 'Shall I get some sailors from the King's Head?'

'You fool!' said Sir Geoffrey irately, 'and have every brigand in London upon us?'

Jenkins approached the desk. He was calm, his mouth closed, his eyes a little narrowed as if he were about to act out a premeditated plan. Leaning down, he removed the dagger from his boot and drew it back, preparing to lunge. In a single moment, Sir Geoffrey understood what was about to occur.

Inhaling hard, he watched as Jenkins fell onto the flagstones. The henchman lay there, dead, as the sound of the shot echoed between the walls, the stench of gunsmoke heavy in the air.

Fortescue stepped across the threshold.

'Thank God you have come!' exclaimed Caldecott in a strident voice. 'This man has appropriated the funds of the Committee and held me prisoner through days and nights!'

The Viscount called for Adams and Cochran.

'As one who has followed your sordid trail,' he said, 'I cannot admit surprise that a person who would stoop to such ignominy would lie to the man who has just saved his life.'

'I am grateful beyond measure,' Caldecott implored.

The Viscount nodded to Adams and Cochran as they entered the warehouse.

'We fished Mr. Jerome's corpse from the water,' said Cochran.

'Again, let me salute you, sir,' Sir Geoffrey said, wiping his face.

'You are my saviour indeed.'

Viscount Fortescue strode over to the crates. He prised the lid off the first, removed one of the bags, and knocked a few gold sovereigns onto his palm. Then, turning slowly to face Caldecott, he said, 'Please do not be misled. I saved your life for one reason — in order that those you have defrauded might have the pleasure of witnessing you losing it at the Execution Dock.'

FIVE

TEN DAYS FOLLOWED the capture of Sir Geoffrey Caldecott, who was by chance held in the same cell that had housed Robert Adams. On the night of his arrival he made the mistake of talking down to the jailer, Raffan, and was put on half rations as a result.

In the same week and a half, the Prince Regent attempted to fly in a hot air balloon for the second time, on this occasion the craft decorated with the royal crest. The flight took place amid much pomp and ceremony, but ended with the basket plummeting to earth and the Prince spraining his left ankle.

Decreeing that aeronautics of any kind were a danger to one's health, he pledged to his mistress that he would never again set foot in another flying craft. Instead, he promised, he would reawaken his interest in his animal Collection.

The next day, an adult hippopotamus passed away at the menagerie. The reason was simple starvation. The keeper, a former criminal from Bath, had fed the creature rotten pig's meat instead of grain. Had Sir Geoffrey the inclination, he could have seen it by leaning through the bars, and craning his head to the right. But his thoughts were not on the fauna kept at the Tower.

They were on saving his neck.

Word was sent swiftly to William Bateman to preserve the hippo as soon as possible and hasten the specimen to Carlton House.

Toiling over the carcass for four days and nights, the taxidermist to royalty embalmed the animal. Exhausted by the feat, he called his assistants to man the ropes and haul the great river horse onto his cart.

As they heaved away, the hemp rasping their hands, Maud butchered the edible quarters. There was so much meat that the taxidermist's wife shared it out between the five assistants and their families, while keeping the best cuts for her own table. She even went so far as to salt some of the meat in the hope of preserving it.

Eager to reach the inn at Colchester, and renew his liaison with the barmaid, Bateman put on his Sunday best and was quickly on the road. He had no time or interest in eating hippopotamus.

Little did he realise he would never see his wife, his assistants, or their families again.

For, during the embalming process, a bottle of copper arsenite solution had accidentally been poured over the hippopotamus's cadaver. Mrs. Bateman, the five assistants, and eighteen of their relatives, found themselves light-headed minutes after sitting down to eat. They became dazed, fell into a stupor and collapsed.

None of them ever revived.

SIX

As the bells of St. Bride's sounded the evening mass, a carriage drew up at Cochran's chambers on Fleet Street. A footman climbed down and rapped at the door. Mrs. Pickeriff stumbled out, a half-empty bottle of gin in her hand.

'What's all this noise?'

'A visitor for Mr. Cochran. Is he at home?'

The landlady thrust her hand back in a bid to conceal the drink.

'I shall enquire if he is,' she said, in as posh a voice as she could muster.

A moment later, Cochran emerged. Making his way to the carriage, he found Beattie, her sister Phoebe acting as chaperone.

'Dearest cousin,' he said in surprise, as soon as he set eyes on the ashen complexion of his true love. 'Take me to him and I shall dispatch him from this mortal world. Oh, how he has wounded you!'

Beattie leant forward, relieving her face of the shadows.

'It is I who have wounded you,' she said in little more than a whisper.

'Where is your husband, for I shall kill him with these hands,' Cochran exclaimed.

'Mr. Wittershall...' said Beattie, '*he* and I are no longer attached. Our marriage has been annulled.'

'Then?'

Beattie smiled, her lower lip caught between her teeth.

She blinked very slowly.

Phoebe blushed.

'My dearest cousin,' said Cochran anxiously, 'I should be most obliged to have the honour of an interview with your mother.'

SEVEN

THE NEXT MORNING, an envelope was delivered by private messenger at Camelford House. The cream-coloured card inside was gilt-edged, embossed with the fleur-de-lis of the Prince Regent. Below, in perfect copperplate script, was a handwritten invitation for Robert Adams, Mr. Cochran and the Viscount, to attend Carlton House at five o'clock.

They travelled together, the carriage bouncing over the cobbles of St. James's Street.

'Thank God the entire fortune was recovered,' said the Viscount all of a sudden. 'I hear that the investors are to be reimbursed in full and without delay.'

'And what of Caldecott?' asked Adams.

Fortescue smoothed down his cravat.

'The Admiralty has appointed Sir Joshua Faulkes to adjudicate,' he said. 'I would be surprised if Sir Geoffrey were to survive the next week.'

The carriage drew up to Carlton House, sweeping in beneath the grand portico. The door was opened by a towering Dragoon, who did his best to bow while squaring the step.

Across the street stood Bateman's cart, a large crate poised upon it, an old roan shire horse feeding from its nosebag at the front. The taxidermist had enjoyed his evening at the Colchester inn, but since that morning had found his nether regions burning as if a red-hot poker had been thrust upon them.

Endeavouring to keep his mind on the delivery at hand, Bateman went round to the kitchens to ask the serving staff to assist him in getting the crate down off the cart.

The Prince Regent was seated in front of the fire in the blue-velvet salon. He was nursing his ankle and feeling down on his luck. The pain of the injury was exacerbated by gout, and had caused him to overeat even more than was usual.

For breakfast he had consumed a pot of braised kidneys and, for lunch, he had devoured an enormous tureen of jugged hare, washed down with a bottle of Médoc from his favourite Chateau Lafite.

The curtains were drawn, the lamplight a little sombre, and the salon's floor sprinkled with sprigs of lavender. A harpist was seated in the far right corner of the room, playing a piece by Nicolas-Charles Bochsa.

Hastings appeared at the door, and announced that the visitors had arrived.

'What do they want?' asked the Prince vaguely.

'To be praised for their accomplishment.'

'Accomplishment?'

'In capturing Sir Geoffrey Caldecott, Your Highness. Perhaps you remember, Highness, we spoke of it this morning.'

'Did we?'

'Indeed, I believe we did. Your Highness made the decision to award them the Order of the Bath.'

'Whatever for?'

'For the capture of Sir Geoffrey Caldecott, Highness.'

'*Who*?'

'A bigamist accused of defrauding the honest investors of the Royal African Committee, Your Highness, the directors of which, it appears, had underwritten the Duke of York's attempt at unseating the Regency.'

The Prince sat up in his chair.

'They must be decorated at once!' he said.

The guests were shown in and presented.

'Ah, yes, the American from Timbuctoo!' said the Regent at seeing Adams again. 'And where will your next journey take you… to the moon?'

The Regent guffawed at his own joke. The laughter was echoed by everyone else in the room, except for Adams. Smiling politely, he said,

'With God's help, it will be across the ocean, back to America.'

'When do you hope to leave?'

'In a day or so.'

The Prince clapped his hands, a theatrical affectation he had acquired from Tsar Alexander, during his recent visit.

'Hastings, bring the boxes!'

'At once, Your Highness.'

'In light of your communal apprehension of…'

'Of Sir Geoffrey Caldecott, Highness,' prompted the equerry.

'Quite so,' said the Regent. 'In light of your apprehension, I have great pleasure in awarding each of you the Knights Grand Cross of the Order of the Bath.'

The first presentation box was opened by Hastings and the medal passed to the Prince.

The Viscount was the first to step up.

'You will have to kneel,' said the Prince Regent, 'for I have injured my ankle. Ballooning, don't you know? A hazardous sport with little future.'

'I am most honoured, Your Highness,' said Fortescue as the medal was pinned to his chest.

Cochran was the next to step forward and kneel, and was followed by Adams. As the Prince's bloated fingers struggled to pin the award to his chest, a footman arrived at the doorway. He signalled to Hastings with the faintest of nods. Waiting until the Prince had finished with the ceremony, he cocked his head gently towards the door.

'What is it?'

'The taxidermist, Highness.'

'What about it?'

'The specimen has arrived.'

'Why did you not inform me sooner?' he cried excitedly. 'Don't dilly-dally! Bring it in here at once!'

Hastings nodded to the liveried footman, who walked backwards to the door, bowing acutely. There was the sound of feet running, a gruff voice calling an order, and the groans of the entire kitchen staff as they staggered forward under the great weight.

The crate was hauled into the salon.

'Put it there, in the middle of the room!' shouted the Prince. 'Ballooning may have no future but there is one pursuit that I am sure will become remarkably popular!'

'And what, Your Highness, would that be?' asked the Viscount courteously.

'Taxidermy, sir!' bellowed the Regent. 'Taxidermy!'

William Bateman stepped forward meekly, still quite unaware that his wife, staff, and their families had been dispatched by the infected meat.

'Hurry up!' shouted the Prince. 'I do loathe dawdling. Get to it man!'

A pair of footmen assisted the taxidermist in prising off the side panels. The wood was removed, revealing the cumbersome outline of a creature covered in a beige sheet.

Bateman scratched his crotch furtively. He nodded to the footman, who nodded to Hastings, and he to the Prince.

'Very well, let's be having it!' snapped the Regent.

Hastings signalled to the footman, who nodded back to Bateman. The taxidermist's hand jerked back the sheet.

'Glorious!' said the Regent, 'what, what?!'

'What is it?' asked Cochran in a whisper.

'*Hippos-ho-potamios*!' cried the Prince, 'the River Horse!'

EIGHT

ALBERT WICKS THREW a handful of coal on the fire and wiped his palm down the front of his shirt. Leaning back into his chair, he stared into the flames and cursed the cold. Then he cursed his back for aching and, after that, he cursed the Royal African Committee for almost swindling him out of his life savings.

Outside, the wind howled over the river, the capital gripped by yet another cold snap. The ground was swathed in a crust of thick frost, smoke rising from every chimney, as Londoners huddled for warmth indoors. It seemed as though spring had not quite come.

Had he the choice, Wicks would have drifted off to sleep, lulled by the fantasy of a life he might have lived had his paternal grandfather decided not to enter the profession. But there was no time for sleeping. There was work to be done.

On the table beside his chair was a sheet of paper bearing an announcement. It read:

AT FIVE O'CLOCK ON

SATURDAY 30TH MARCH 1816,

THE DISGRACED PEER SIR GEOFFREY CALDECOTT

FORMER CHAIRMAN OF

THE ROYAL AFRICAN COMMITTEE

SHALL BE HANGED BY THE NECK

UNTIL HE IS DEAD

Wrapping a blanket around his shoulders, Wicks took up the end of a rope. He hunched forward to the brazier to dry it out. The drier the better, and the speedier the moment of death.

But then he paused.

This was no ordinary execution. It was a matter of revenge. Albert pulled the rope away from the heat, spat on it, his mouth snarling.

'There'll be no speed for you, you bastard!' he crowed, his fingers weaving the rope into a noose.

NINE

THE DINING ROOM at Boodle's was widely regarded as the finest in club-land. The entrée of the day was veal brains served *glacée à la Macédoine*, and the main course partridge *à la maréchal*, presented with a sauce *financière*, and with artichokes *à la Lyonnaise*. At the far end of the room, the Marquess of Bute was boring half a dozen guests with his reminiscences of Trafalgar.

Beside the window, with a view down onto St. James's Street, sat Viscount Fortescue, Robert Adams and Cochran. They had finished with the game. Their stomachs full, the conversation eased gently from the trials and tribulations of past days, to the future.

'Tell me, Mr. Adams,' said Fortescue, stiffening in his seat, 'what are your plans?'

'To return across the ocean, sir,' he said. 'I have booked a passage on *Cassandra*, a brig bound for New York.'

'When does she away?'

'In three days' time.'

'And what of you then?'

Adams pushed the plate away from him a little.

'For these past years I have prayed for my survival,' he said. 'And my prayers have been selfish — so that I might once again gaze into the eyes of the woman I love so dearly, and to hold her hands in my own.'

'You are returning with prospects a great deal improved,' Fortescue replied. 'As you know, wisdom comes through experience.'

Cochran raised his glass.

'To experience!' he said softly.

The three men touched the crystal to their lips and rinsed their mouths with claret.

In the background a long-cased clock struck the hour.

'Oh my Lord!' said Cochran, waving his hands in a fluster.

'What is it, Simon?'

'Sir Geoffrey… at five o'clock… he…' Cochran pinched a thumb and forefinger to his neck and winced.

The Viscount sent word for his carriage to be brought round.

'How could we disappoint Sir Geoffrey by not attending?' he said.

TEN

DESPITE THE CHILLY conditions, seven hundred and thirty members of the public had turned out to witness the entertainment at Execution Dock. Half of them had no idea at all who Sir Geoffrey Caldecott was, but they liked a good hanging all the same. The other half were investors in the ruined African Committee, all of them eager for a share in the retribution.

The gallows were never washed with water, but were brushed down with sand. It had been found that the congealed blood, the vomit and the filth, which accompanied a hanging, were most easily removed in this way.

A scaffold had stood there, at the Thames in Wapping, for four centuries, since the reign of Henry IV. In that time, some of the kingdom's most notorious conspirators had met their end at the dock — men, women, and the occasional child.

At fifteen minutes before the hour, Sir Joseph Banks arrived, his carriage drawing right up to the gallows. He was lowered into an awaiting chair by a pair of footmen, just in time to greet the First Lord of the Admiralty. Five minutes later, Viscount Fortescue's carriage swept up.

Cocking his head over the crowd, Cochran checked whether the First Sea Lord was present.

'I see the silver oar, Viscount,' he said, leading the way to the front. 'I believe we are just in time.'

They greeted Sir Joseph and, as they did so, the condemned man was brought out. Attired in a dark blue frock coat, his eyes were low, his fingers woven together on his chest.

As soon as he was in clear view, a woman began screaming from the middle of the crowd — the second Lady Caldecott.

Her husband mounted the steps of the scaffold, taking them one at a time. He seemed lost in his own world.

A chaplain recited a prayer from the Book of Romans. The First Sea Lord raised the oar, signalling for the execution to commence. Albert Wicks stepped up with the damp noose in hand. As he arranged it low on the neck, he leaned forward to Caldecott's ear.

'To Hell with you, sir!' he said in a whisper.

The crowd jeered and cheered. There was a hush. Half the thrill of a hanging was to hear the neck snapping. A snare drum began to strike a slow rhythmic beat, increasing in speed.

Faster and faster.

Albert Wicks stepped back, away from the trap door.

The drum roll was racing now.

The woman suddenly screamed all the louder.

The floor fell away, followed by the sound of neck vertebrae being separated.

Sir Geoffrey Caldecott was dead.

ELEVEN

THE PEAL OF church bells rang out across the city from St. Bride's. There was blazing sunshine once again. Simon Cochran stood in the door of the church chewing at his knuckle. He was dressed in a flamboyant fusion of naval uniform and cutting edge dandyism. Beside him was his American friend, in a newly tailored costume, his hair slightly damp. Cochran had asked him to be best man.

At two o'clock the guests began to arrive, more than a hundred of them. First came Cochran's elderly mother, then Viscount Fortescue and Clara. After them, in twos and threes, more relatives and friends, until the pews inside were filled.

An hour later, the organist began to play Pachelbel's Canon in D-major. And, as the church interior resounded with harmony, the bride entered, once again on the arm of her uncle, Sir Henry Montagu.

The congregation rose and turned in anticipation.

Ignoring her mother's unease, Beattie had worn the ancestral wedding dress a second time. Her hair tied up at the back with a lilac ribbon, she clasped a posy of purple hyacinths in her hand. As she glided forward, even steps across the flagstones, she caught the first glimpse of her husband-to-be. And, smiling demurely, she thanked God for a second chance.

TWELVE

Next morning, Robert Adams stood in the shadow of the brig *Cassandra*, watching as she took on her last supplies. It was a bright day, the light filtered through haze. Beside him stood Cochran.

'I have been so rapt in my own thoughts,' said Adams, 'that I have not asked what work you will do now.'

Cochran swallowed hard.

'As you have surmised,' he said with a grin, 'my work at the Committee is at an end. But it seems that when one door closes, another opens. I have the honour to say that the Viscount has asked if I might consider acting as a private assistant.'

'What of your debts?'

'I shall pay them off slowly and, with Viscount Fortescue's generous employment, there will, I hope, be an end to my misfortune.'

The American cleared his throat.

'The sales of my narrative have been considerable,' he replied. 'Murray has promised to send further payments to me, and has paid handsomely for the first sales.' He fumbled to remove a thick envelope from his inside pocket. 'Take this,' he said.

'How could I ever even think of it?'

'Well don't, just take it with my thanks.'

There was the sound of footsteps behind Adams. He turned. It was Clara, her hair pushed up in a bonnet, her slender form in a dark maroon coat, trimmed at the collar and wrists in fur. She held quite still, staring into Adams' eyes, then hurried forward, small steps making fast across the quay.

'Mr. Adams…' she said, the tone of her voice fluctuating with emotion. 'I can only tell you that my life shall never be the same. When this vessel sails away, a piece of me shall be excised. I fear that I shall never be quite whole again.'

The American stepped forward, lifted Clara's hands, holding them gently in his. 'Your kindness will stay with me,' he said. 'And in the days and years that follow, the memory of it shall remain in my heart. I will never forget you.'

THIRTEEN

THE SUN SLIPPED down behind a screen of poplars, its outline broken by the naked branches. Two women were sitting alone in the house they had inherited when their father died suddenly four years before.

One of the women was reading *The Vicar of Wakefield*. She had never married, although she hoped one day a man would arrive and ask for her hand. The other, a little younger, had once been wed down at the church on Union Street. But on the night of her marriage, her husband had disappeared.

Two summers had passed before she had discovered the truth, that her father had disposed of him. She vowed to wait, until the end of her life if need be, for her love, a man named Robert, to return. Unsure where he had been sent, or what had become of him, she felt in the bottom of her heart that he loved her more deeply than any other thing — that he was alive and was desperately working to cover the distance that separated them.

Lighting a candle, she placed it on the window ledge, as she did each evening at about the same time. Then, she put on her coat, tied back her hair, and stepped outside to listen to the birds as they roosted in the chestnut trees.

Choosing her route over the damp ground, she walked to the field of ripe winter barley and stared at the sun as it inched down through the branches. She closed her eyes, felt the last touch of warmth on her face, and she prayed.

A cart had pulled up at the farm, halting just long enough to allow a traveller to jump down. A moment later it was gone, the wheels leaving no mark at all on the baked mud ruts.

The traveller placed his cases on the ground. As if lost in a dream, he walked very slowly out into the field. There, he saw the woman's figure standing tall, the fingers of her right hand extended, stroking the stems of barley.

Without a sound, he walked towards her.

In his hand was a fragment of lace, so black with dirt that it was hardly recognisable as cloth.

He touched it to his lips one last time.

The woman turned.

She frowned, stretched out her arms, and held him tight.

FINIS

AN ADVERTISEMENT TO THE MAPS

RICHARD HORWOOD'S LATE-EIGHTEENTH century map of London was a labour of love the likes of which had not been known to cartography before, and have probably not been seen since.

Having decided to chart the entire capital, down to each individual building, Horwood set about canvassing subscriptions in 1790. He intended to publish the complete map within two years, at a scale of 26 inches to a mile. But the scope of the project was so daunting, and the cost so exceptionally high, that the map's thirty-two sheets took almost a decade to release.

Despite acquiring royal patronage from King George III, the project was dogged by financial woes. Yet true to his word, Horwood never cut corners and, eventually, published the entire map. The last sheet was made available in 1799.

As for Richard Horwood, master cartographer of his age, he died in Liverpool shortly after the great map was completed, impoverished and forgotten.

BIBLIOGRAPHY

The Narrative of Robert Adams
Narrated by Robert Adams
John Murray, London, 1816

The Narrative of Robert Adams, A Barbary Captive: A Critical Edition
Edited by Charles Adams
Cambridge University Press, Cambridge, 2005

Geographical Historie of Africa
Johannes Leo Africanus
G. Bishop, London, 1600

Travels In North and Central Africa
Heinrich, Barth
Longman, London, 1857

Travels Through Central Africa to Timbuctoo
René Caillé
Colburn, London, 1830

Journal of a Second Expedition into Africa
Hugh Clapperton
John Murray, London, 1829

The Quest for Timbuctoo
Brian Gardener
Cassell, 1968

An Account of the Empire of Marocco,
to Which is Added an Accurate and Interesting Account of Timbuctoo
James Grey Jackson
W. Bulmer, London, 1809

Travels in Western Africa
Alexander Gordon Laing
John Murray, London, 1825

A Narrative of Travels in Northern Africa
Captain George F. Lyon
John Murray, London, 1821

Travels in the Interior Districts of Africa
Mungo Park
John Murray, London, 1799

Historical Account of Discoveries and Travels in Africa
Hugh Murray
Archibald Constable, Edinburgh, 1817

A Narrative of the Shipwreck of the Ship Oswego
Judah Paddock
J. Seymour, New York, 1818

The Loss of the American Brig Commerce, With An Account of Timbuctoo
Captain James Riley
John Murray, London, 1817

The Gates of Africa: Death, Discovery and the Search for Timbuktu
Anthony Sattin
Harper Perennial, London, 2010

COLOPHON

Timbuctoo is set in Bulmer, a serif typeface created by master typographer William Bulmer (1757-1830), in association with expert type-founder William Martin, and recreated by Linotype. William Bulmer was responsible for setting and printing not only *The Narrative of Robert Adams* in the font that bears his name, but many other books for John Murray Ltd. He was regarded as one of the very finest printers of his age, regularly printing for the East India Company, the British Museum, and the Royal Society. The extraordinary quality of his work can be found today in the books he printed two centuries ago, their cost and longevity a testament to his craft.

N34567865437.W36754761
Y6456544321.786543267E
PPAAACPS.RRRIDOPPAWW
AHGRDSCOULTTALAAAIQ
IXTCUBMITSPCUSTCLFM
OOITUDELKAUHOPEIXO
N4373894536382900.187
274469.S3665282516199